AQA
A-level

Philosophy

For A-level Year 1 and AS

Epistemology and Moral Philosophy

1

Jeremy Hayward
Gerald Jones
Daniel Cardinal

HODDER
EDUCATION
AN HACHETTE UK COMPANY

Acknowledgements

The Publishers would like to thank the following for permission to reproduce copyright material.

Text credits: pp.21 436 (Anth 1.1) E. Gettier, 'Is Justified, True Belief Knowledge?' in A. Philips Griffiths, (ed.) *Knowledge and Belief* (1967) © Oxford University Press; **pp.99, 100, 104, 106, 438 (Anth 1.4), 440 (Anth 1.9), 445 (Anth 1.19 and Anth 1.18)** Gottfried Leibniz, *New Essays on Human Understanding* (1765) in the version presented at www.earlymoderntexts.com; **p.240,** Peter Singer, 'Animal Liberation', New York Review (1975) © NYREV; **pp.241, 242, 243, 451 (Anth 2.4)** Peter Singer (ed. H. Kuhse), *Unsanctifying Human Life* (2002), © John Wiley & Sons; **p.401** William Golding, *Lord of the Flies* (1958) © Faber and Faber ; **p.410,** R.M. Hare, *The Language of Morals* (1952) © Oxford University Press; **pp.442 (Anth 1.13), 443 (Anth 1.14), 443 (Anth 1.15), 443 (Anth 1.15), 444 (Anth 1.16), 457 (Anth 2.21),** George Berkeley, *Three Dialogues between Hylas and Philonous in Opposition to Sceptics and Atheists: The First Dialogue* (1713), in the version presented at www.earlymoderntexts.com; **p.450 (Anth 2.2 and 2.3),** J.S. Mill, *Utilitarianism* (1863) in the version presented at www.earlymoderntexts.com

Photo credits: p.116 Library of Congress Prints & Photographs/LC-DIG-ds-00175

Every effort has been made to trace all copyright holders, but if any have been inadvertently overlooked, the Publishers will be pleased to make the necessary arrangements at the first opportunity.

Although every effort has been made to ensure that website addresses are correct at time of going to press, Hodder Education cannot be held responsible for the content of any website mentioned in this book. It is sometimes possible to find a relocated web page by typing in the address of the home page for a website in the URL window of your browser.

Hachette UK's policy is to use papers that are natural, renewable and recyclable products and made from wood grown in sustainable forests. The logging and manufacturing processes are expected to conform to the environmental regulations of the country of origin.

Orders: please contact Bookpoint Ltd, 130 Milton Park, Abingdon, Oxon OX14 4SE. Telephone: +44 (0)1235 827720. Fax: +44 (0)1235 400454. Email: education@bookpoint. co.uk. Lines are open from 9 a.m. to 5 p.m., Monday to Saturday, with a 24-hour message answering service. You can also order through our website: www.hoddereducation.co.uk

ISBN: 978 1 5104 0025 2

© Jeremy Hayward, Gerald Jones and Daniel Cardinal 2017

First published in 2017 by Hodder Education,
an Hachette UK Company
Carmelite House
50 Victoria Embankment
London EC4Y 0DZ

www.hoddereducation.co.uk

Impression number   10 9 8 7 6 5 4

Year   2021 2020 2019

Cover image by Barking Dog Art

Illustrations by Tony Randell, Barking Dog Art and Peter Lubach

Typeset in Chaparral Pro Light 11/13pt by Aptara, Inc.

Printed and bound by CPI Group (UK) Ltd, Croydon, CR0 4YY

A catalogue record for this title is available from the British Library.

Contents

Key to features

Activity

A practical task to help you to understand the arguments or concepts under investigation.

Essential
Terminology | Aa

Essential Terminology

These are key terms, appearing in CAPITAL LETTERS, that are highlighted in the AQA specification as ones you should be able to understand and use correctly.

Experimenting with ideas

Plays around with some of the concepts discussed; looks at them from different angles.

Quotation

A direct quotation from a key thinker.

Learn More

Learn more

Introduces related ideas or arguments that aren't required by the AS-level specification, but which provides useful additional material.

anthology
0.00

Anthology extracts

When you see the Anthology icon in the margin of the book then you should refer to the relevant extract in the Anthology extracts section at the end of the book.

Glossary

Words or phrases that appear in CAPITAL LETTERS are key terms and ideas that are explained in the Glossary at the end of the book.

Introduction

What is philosophy? An introduction

This A-level may represent the first time you have formally studied philosophy, although you might have debated numerous philosophical issues with friends, family or even with yourself. Unlike some other A-levels, the nature of the subject is not immediately clear from the name alone. This is because 'philosophy' is used to cover a great many things and is used differently by different people. To see this, you only have to wander into the philosophy section of your local bookshop or library, where the chances are you will find books like this one alongside books on UFOs, tarot cards and personal therapy.

Even amongst philosophers themselves, there is no clear consensus as to what the subject involves. Indeed, the photographer Steve Pyke photographed over 50 philosophers and asked them each to describe the subject. Perhaps not surprisingly, over 50 different answers were given. Here is one of them by John Campbell, a Professor of Philosophy:

> *Philosophy is thinking in slow motion. It breaks down, describes and assesses moves we ordinarily make at great speed – to do with our natural motivations and beliefs. It then becomes evident that alternatives are possible.*[1]

Philosophers like to make things complicated, but perhaps this is because they are careful: they want to get things exactly right. So rather than taking one approach to answer the question 'What is philosophy?', we think it would be helpful to look at four approaches:

- the stuff philosophy talks about (its subject matter)
- the way it has developed (its history)
- how it works (its method)
- and most importantly, what it is like to actually *do* philosophy (its activity).

In this introduction, we outline all four approaches to introduce some key philosophical ideas, and to help you to come to your own understanding of what philosophy is.

1 What is philosophy? Understanding its subject matter

Philosophy can be divided up into separate disciplines (or branches), each of which has its own area of interest, and in many respects its own language. Three of the most important branches of philosophy are: METAPHYSICS – the study of the ultimate nature of reality; EPISTEMOLOGY – the study of what we can know; and MORAL PHILOSOPHY – the study of how we should live and act (moral philosophy is also referred to as ethics). Underpinning all of these branches is a fourth discipline, reasoning, which encompasses the skills of critical thinking, of analysis and of logic (**Figure 0.1**). In this book, you will be studying Epistemology and Moral philosophy, and if you go on to the second year of the A-level, then you will be studying Metaphysics in the form of the philosophy of mind and religion. But throughout your studies you will be building up your reasoning, critical thinking and logical skills.

Within these key areas there are further subdivisions: in metaphysics we will find questions grouped around the philosophy of mind (Do I have a soul? How does my mind work? What is consciousness?) and the philosophy of religion (Is there any PROOF of God's existence? If God exists, why is there so much pain and suffering in the world?). Other subdivisions of philosophy include: the philosophy of language, political philosophy and aesthetics (which can be grouped together with moral philosophy, under the heading 'axiology', meaning the study of value). However, some of this categorisation is artificial; for example, issues within the philosophy of language (what makes statements TRUE or FALSE, and whether certain terms refer to anything 'real') emerge in nearly all branches of philosophy.

Essential
Terminology Aa

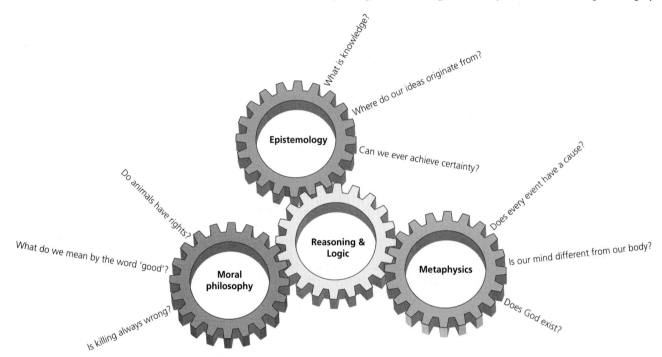

Figure 0.1 The different branches of philosophy

A further difficulty with defining the boundaries of philosophy is that it has a tendency to stick its nose in and tread on the toes of other subjects – it deals with the cutting-edge and abstract questions at the forefront of most other fields of KNOWLEDGE. So there is a philosophy of history, critical theory (in English literature and the arts), philosophy of science, philosophy of maths, and so on. Indeed, if you ask enough difficult questions about any aspect of the world, you will end up with a philosophical question:

Essential
Terminology Aa

Why did the car start?	*Because I turned the key.*
But why?	*Because it links the battery to the spark plugs which ignited the fuel.*
Why does this happen?	*Because fuel ignites at a certain temperature.*
Yes, but why?	*Well, that's a law of physics. Everything that happens follows a physical law.*
But why are there physical laws?	*That's just the way the universe works. Nothing can happen without a reason or cause.*

But why?
Could the universe not follow different laws?
Why is there even a universe at all – does it have a cause?

Eventually, this discussion leaves science proper and drifts into the metaphysical and epistemological questions that make up the philosophy of science. Seen in this way, philosophy is all around us; it is just a matter of asking the right questions. Most of the time though, we are happy to get on with our lives and so we do not ask these difficult questions. As soon as we do, we start to realise that our explanations about life and the world come up a little short and we find ourselves philosophising.

But why should we bother with these questions? In one sense, we cannot avoid them. The unreflective life takes for granted common-sense assumptions which enable us to get on with the business of living. But these common-sense assumptions themselves represent answers to philosophical questions, and so relying on these assumptions is still to rely on a particular philosophy. However, the common-sense approach is just one possible view of things and one which is often beset with inconsistencies that we ignore. But if you scratch beneath the surface, problems can arise.

Consider someone who just wants to live their life and get on with things. Perhaps they want to get a job, earn some money, get a set of wheels and buy a house, and so on. But why does this person want to do these things? Is it because they think it will make them happy? Do they think happiness is a goal worth pursuing? Is it achievable? Is the term even meaningful? If the person has not asked themselves these questions, then it would seem they are just going about their life with no clear idea of what it is they are ultimately pursuing. We might want to ask: although such an unquestioning life is possible, is it a GOOD life? The Greek philosopher Socrates would say it was not:

> *The unexamined life is not worth living.*[2]

In avoiding these philosophical questions that challenge the way we think and live, most people are choosing to live the unexamined life. But you have taken a different route – so congratulations for not hiding away from these issues and choosing to confront them head-on. Congratulations for choosing to live the examined life.

2 What is philosophy? Understanding its history

Like many academic subjects, philosophy has its origins in ancient Greece; even the word 'academic' has its roots in an Athenian term, Ακαδεμια, the 'Akademeia', which was the name of the garden where Plato founded his famous school of maths and philosophy. In ancient Greece, 'philosophy' had a meaning very different from the one it has today. *Philia*, meaning 'love of ', and *sophia*, meaning 'wisdom' gave rise to the word philosophy, meaning 'love of wisdom'. But this love of wisdom encompassed nearly all fields of knowledge. If you were studying philosophy at Plato's Academy or Aristotle's Lyceum, then you might find on your timetable maths, physics, chemistry, biology, geography, psychology, law, politics (although most of them would be grouped under the heading 'philosophy'). In ancient Greece, philosophy was the study of everything that humankind wanted to gain knowledge about.

Over the centuries, from 400 BCE to the present day, many areas of thought have peeled away from philosophy and developed into separate disciplines:

for example, chemistry, physics, biology (once termed 'natural philosophy'), and recently psychology, all became subjects in their own right, not merely subsidiaries of philosophy. Why was this so? Well, many subjects developed their own methodologies, their own tools and techniques enabling their own specific ways of answering the questions they were interested in.

How does this help us to understand philosophy? We could say that philosophy has always been the subject that asks the questions that humans cannot yet answer. In Greek times, these included questions like 'What is light?' and 'Do other planets have moons?' as well as questions like 'What is existence?' and 'Can we know anything for certain?' As thinkers discovered and agreed upon techniques and tools that could address questions about the planets and light, then these questions became scientific rather than philosophical. So nowadays we think we have an answer for the first two questions, but philosophers continue asking questions like the last two.

The history of philosophy is also the history of the people who studied philosophy, their thoughts, arguments and influences. We can trace the discussions in this book back hundreds of years, to the medieval and ancient philosophers, and their writings are treated as 'live' (which means you will often find philosophy books using the present tense to talk about the ideas of dead philosophers, because the ideas themselves are still alive and relevant). You will see throughout this book, quotes and drawings from philosophers past and present. **Figure 0.2** shows some of the most important philosophers who talked about ethics and epistemology – people who have influenced the direction and parameters of these disciplines.

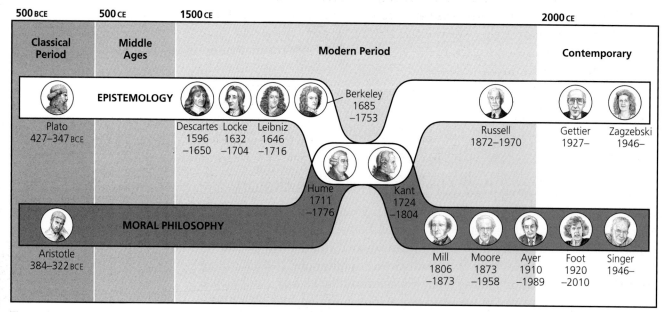

Figure 0.2 Key figures in the history of philosophy you will be studying in Epistemology and Moral philosophy

In order to help you remember what period these figures came from, we have followed the common practice of dividing up Western thought into three ages: the classical period (up to the fall of the Roman Empire); the Middle Ages (up to the Renaissance) and the modern period. Added to these three ages, we have included a large slice of contemporary philosophers, that is, those working in the last 50 years or so, as philosophy is not an archaic subject, but is very much alive and kicking today. You will notice that two philosophers, Kant and Hume, are central to the development of both epistemology and moral philosophy. You may also have noticed a lack of figures from the Middle Ages. This is not because this was a 'dark' age, but because the concerns of medieval philosophers were primarily religious concerns, which we look at in the second year of the A-level.

3 What is philosophy? Understanding its method

Every subject has its own distinct method and tools: in art, you use materials; in science, you use experiments; in music, you use instruments; in geography, you use … er … felt-tip pens. What is the medium or method that philosophy uses? The answer is REASON. Philosophers reason, argue and persuade. Earlier, we saw philosophy characterised as thinking in slow motion. 'It [philosophy] breaks down, describes and assesses moves we ordinarily make at great speed'.[3] For the remainder of this introduction, we will attempt to 'think in slow motion' and highlight some of the different methods of reasoning that you will meet in the book and that you will hone as you develop as a philosopher.

But what is reasoning? In general, reasoning is the process of thinking by which we move from certain initial facts or ASSERTIONS and attempt to establish further CLAIMS. By 'claim', here, we mean the same as a PROPOSITION or what is asserted by a declarative sentence, as opposed to a question or a command. A simple example might be, 'The cat is on the table'. A claim tells us that things are a certain way, and if we understand it, then we know what it is saying. One test of whether something is a claim is whether it can come after 'that' as a clause, as in 'I believe that the cat is on the table'. Normally, what someone claims is what they believe to be true. Of course, they are not always right in their BELIEFS, so claims may be true or false. We will use the terms 'claim', 'assertion' and 'proposition' interchangeably to refer to these basic building blocks of arguments. Now, the initial claims in an argument are termed reasons or PREMISES, and those which follow from or are supported by the premises are termed CONCLUSIONS. Reasoning may sound like a peculiar activity from this outline, but it is actually something you do every time you plan a route, argue with a friend, calculate the correct change and so on. When thinking in this way, you are working out what conclusions can be drawn from your initial beliefs or evidence (that is, your premises), and in the process you are constructing arguments. In studying philosophy, you will be introduced to range of arguments, and your job is to evaluate how effective they are. These are not arguments in the sense of shouting matches or quarrels, but in the sense of 'reasoned persuasion' – that is, an attempt to defend a claim by offering evidence or reasons in support of it.

Essential Terminology Aa

Identifying arguments

You will notice, particularly in philosophy, that arguments are buried in paragraphs of dense texts. So how can you tell whether what you are reading or hearing is an argument? The answer is that you can recognise an argument because of its structure, for every argument must have premises which support a conclusion, and this structure is revealed by the language employed. This 'language of reasoning' involves the use of certain indicator words. The most obvious clue that something is an argument is the appearance of the conclusion-indicating term 'therefore'. But this is not the only such indicator, and while some of these indicators signal that a STATEMENT represents the conclusion of a piece of reasoning, others, like 'because', signal a premise. **Figure 0.3** gives us a list of such indicators. Note that this list is not comprehensive, and you may find it useful to add to it as you encounter further argument indicators.

Conclusion indicators	Reason indicators
• So	• As
• Thus	• For
• Hence	• Since
• Shows	• Because
• Supports	• Given that
• Establishes	• Inasmuch as
• Therefore	• Granted that
• Proves that	• Follows from
• Which implies	• As is shown by
• Consequently	• As indicated by
• We may infer	• The reason is that
• It follows that	• For the reason that
• Which means that	• May be derived from
• Which entails that	• May be inferred from
• Justifies the belief that	• May be deduced from
• Which demonstrates that	• In view of the fact that
• Points to the conclusion that	• The reasons are, firstly... secondly...etc.

Figure 0.3 Some argument indicators

When we move from the premises to a conclusion, we are said to 'infer' the conclusion. So the progression from a premise (or collection of premises) to a conclusion is called an 'INFERENCE'. An inference is the move we make in reasoning when we reckon that one claim or belief provides evidence for us to assert some further claim. Inferences are like the cement which binds together the various building blocks of an argument (that is, the premises and conclusions), and which give it its structure, so all arguments ultimately have this same basic form: at least one premise and conclusion, and the inference which binds them together:

However, arguments may have more than one of each of these elements. As they work towards their main conclusion, there may be staging posts, called intermediate conclusions or sub-conclusions, which provide a platform for the next stage in the argument. And there may be several premises being offered to support a conclusion or sub-conclusion. But ultimately, every argument can be reduced to these three elements, and this means that they can be represented in a diagram or map which reveals the structure. As an example, take this argument:

My senses have deceived me in the past and I will not trust completely what has deceived me. Therefore I will not trust my senses. And so I cannot be certain of the nature of what I now perceive around me.

We can label each element (Premises, Intermediate Conclusions and Main Conclusion) and then represent its structure diagrammatically, thus:

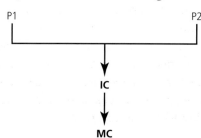

As well as representing the argument as a diagram, we can also express the argument in a formal, standard, way:

Premise 1	My senses have deceived me in the past
Premise 2	I will not trust completely what has deceived me
Intermediate conclusion 1	I will not trust my senses
Main conclusion	I cannot be certain of the nature of what I now perceive around me

There are three main types of inference used in arguments: deductive, inductive and abductive inferences, giving us three forms of argument or reasoning – deduction, induction and abduction. We will introduce each of these types of reasoning in turn before you get a chance to practise identifying each type on page xvii.

Deduction

We have seen that all arguments involve progressing from premises to a conclusion. But what is distinctive about a DEDUCTIVE ARGUMENT is that if the premises are true, then the conclusion *must* also be true. In other words, in a deductive argument, if we accept the premises, then we are forced into accepting the conclusion as well; it is impossible for the reasons to be true and the conclusion to be false. Such arguments are also called 'deductively valid', or simply 'valid'.

Here is an example of a deductive argument. Notice that the argument is presented formally as a set of numbered premises and conclusion, rather than as an ordinary piece of prose. This is in order to reveal the structure and is a standard way of presenting arguments; you will find examples of arguments presented in standard form like this throughout the book.

Premise (P) 1	All birds have feathers
Premise 2	My Parrot, Kenny, is a bird
Conclusion (C)	Therefore Kenny has feathers

This is a typical three-line argument, known technically as a *syllogism*. There are many different variations, but typically they have a general claim, a more specific claim and a conclusion. A little reflection on this simple syllogism should enable you to see that if both premises are true, than the conclusion would also have to be true. And this is the great strength of deductive arguments. For if we can be certain of the premises, then we can be equally certain of the conclusion. Deductive arguments, in other words, preserve truth.

Here is another example:

P1 If a mushroom has brown gills, then it is safe to eat
P2 This mushroom has brown gills
C Therefore, it is safe to eat

In this deductive argument, the first premise is a known as a *HYPOTHETICAL* claim. Hypothetical claims have two parts: the 'if' part, known as the *ANTECEDENT* – in this case, 'a mushroom has brown gills' – and the 'then' part – in this case, 'this mushroom is safe to eat'. Hypothetical claims do not so much tell us what is the case, but only what would be the case *if* the antecedent is true. In this argument, because Premise 2 tells us that the antecedent is true, we can conclude that the CONSEQUENT is also true.

Essential Terminology

Despite the strength of deductive arguments that they preserve truth, a criticism often made of this type of reasoning is that it does not provide us with any new information. All the information that we get in the conclusion is already contained in the premises; at best, the reasoning just draws out what might not be obvious at first sight. For this reason, it is often said that deductive arguments are not much use when it comes to discovering new truths.

We can now summarise the key features of a *valid* deduction as follows:

- The conclusion *must* follow from the premises.
- If the premises are true, then it is certain that the conclusion is also *true*.
- All of the necessary information is in the premises and no new information is gained in the conclusion.

Valid and sound arguments

Two key terms that you need to understand in relation to deductions and other forms of argument are 'validity' and 'soundness'. Validity relates to the form of the argument. Soundness relates to an argument's premises and its form (to remember this, you could think of premises as a building – for example, 'Keep off the premises' – and hopefully the premises will have a *sound* foundation and a solid *form*, or else the building/argument will fall down). Let us take the example:

P1 All bunnies can speak French
P2 Tiggles is a bunny
C Tiggles can speak French

Here, the form of the argument is the same as the one above about my parrot Kenny, so it is a deductive argument. Deductive arguments have a form which is valid, which just means that if the premises are true, the conclusion must also be true. However, in this argument at least one of the premises is not true (in case you did not spot it, it is Premise 1 – bunnies cannot speak French), and this has meant that the conclusion has turned out to be false. Arguments with false premises like this one are said to be unsound. So although the form of the argument is valid, it is not a sound one. It's worth noting here that we commonly refer to SOUND ARGUMENTS as proofs. A sound argument is also said to PROVE its conclusion.

Here is another example:

P1 All bunnies are mammals
P2 Speedy the lizard is not a bunny
C Therefore Speedy is not a mammal

Is this a valid argument? Well, the premises and the conclusion appear to be true. However, this is not enough to make it valid. For, although true, the conclusion does not actually follow from the premises, so, as far as this argument can show, it might have been false. To see this, we can replace some of the terms while keeping the same structure:

P1 All bunnies are mammals
P2 Wilbur the cat is not a bunny
C Therefore Wilbur is not a mammal

As we know that cats are mammals, we can see that the conclusion is false, even though the premises are true, and this shows that this form of argument is invalid.

Essential Terminology | Aa

Why does deduction work?

Learn More

Philosophers such as Leibniz argue that deduction works because of a few fundamental principles or laws of thought. Here are three of those laws:

■ *Law of non-contradiction* – an object cannot be both B and not B at the same time. So a ball cannot be blue all over and not blue all over.
■ *Law of identity* – an object is the same as itself.
■ *Law of the excluded middle* – an object is either A or not A. A ball is either round or it is not round.

Consider this deductive argument:

P1 All living birds have a heart
P2 My parrot, Kenny, is a living bird
C Therefore Kenny has a heart

This seems sound enough, but why does it work? How is the conclusion 'drawn' from the premises? Well, Kenny either has a heart or not (this follows from the law of the excluded middle). Consider the possibility (X) that Kenny does **not** have a heart. We know that Kenny is a *living* bird and that living birds have hearts, so we are now in the awkward position of asserting both that *All living birds have hearts* and that *Some living birds do not have hearts* (that is, Kenny). But this is a contradiction ('Living birds have hearts' and 'Living birds do not have hearts'). The law of non-contradiction says that this cannot be the case, so we must reject possibility (X). So it must be the case (by the law of the excluded middle) that Kenny has a heart.

You can see that deductive arguments, though intuitively obvious, rely on some very fundamental laws of thought and are often based around avoiding a contradiction.

Induction

A second kind of reasoning, and one you use every day, is known as induction. This type of reasoning involves generalising about how the world is and/or will be. The two key types of induction are:

A Generalising from the **past** to the **future** – for example, observing that the number 343 bus has been late every day this week, so believing it will be late again today.
B Generalising from a **restricted** number of cases to an **unrestricted** number (all cases) – for example, observing that all life forms on earth are carbon-based so claiming that all life forms in the universe are carbon-based.

The belief about the bus in A) above is based on only a few examples, so might be termed weak induction. In contrast, believing that a stone will fall to the ground when dropped is based on a large number of experiences, so would be a stronger claim.

Induction is a type of reasoning that can occur quite formally – often in science – where experiments are repeated many times to see if the same results follow. But induction is also something that our minds do automatically for us. We all, often subconsciously, look for patterns in the world and expect to see them in the future. Do you believe that your friend will answer your next message? That your teacher will turn up on time? That the pavement will support your weight when you walk? That rain makes things wet? That fire burns? Where do you get these beliefs from? From observing the world and then believing that the future will be similar. This is the process of induction. It is a process of reason, because, like all reasoning, you are moving from initial claims to new judgements.

INDUCTIVE ARGUMENTS are based on observations of how the world is, and the truth of the conclusion is never guaranteed, even if the premises are true. Take this inductive argument as an example:

P1 All humans have died before the age of 140
C Therefore I will die before the age of 140

Now, while it is no doubt very likely that I will die before I reach 140, it is not guaranteed. Maybe, if I eat my muesli every morning, I will live to be 141. This possibility is perfectly conceivable, even if we accept the truth of the premise, and this is because how the world has behaved in the past does not determine how it must behave in the future. Bertrand Russell provides a comical example of the perils of induction by imagining a turkey which, having been fed every morning of its life, wakes up confident of being fed again. Unfortunately, the turkey is in for an unpleasant surprise, as this morning is Christmas Day.

The conclusion of an inductive argument goes beyond the evidence presented in its premises, and this is why it is not guaranteed to be true, even if the premises are true. But while we risk going wrong in inductive arguments, the pay-off is that we can extend our knowledge beyond what we already know. So induction promises to extend our knowledge in a way in which deduction cannot.

The key features of an induction are:

- Even if the premises are true, the conclusion is never guaranteed to be true.
- Inductions can come with different degrees of probability, depending on the strength of evidence.
- Inductions attempt to go beyond the premises to make claims about how the world is, or will be.
- Inductions move from cases/examples/effects in the past or present to conclusions about the present or future.

Abduction

A third type of reasoning is ABDUCTION, which is often described as *inference to the best explanation* (and, unfortunately for those of you looking for an injection of excitement and mystery into this introduction, it has nothing to do with being taken away by aliens in the middle of the night). Abductive reasoning usually draws on an inductive understanding of the world, but is distinguished from induction, in part, because of the direction that your reasoning takes you (that is, the direction of the inference).

For example, a deduction might have the form of *If A, then B*. A is true, so B must be true too: If it rains on my house, my roof gets wet. It is raining on my house, therefore my roof is wet. (We encountered this form of deductive argument above, on page xi.)

Let's consider another example. Inductions too might move from A to B: In the past, when it has been sunny after rain, I have seen a rainbow. Today it has been sunny after rain, so I can expect to see a rainbow.

In contrast, abductions generally move in the opposite direction from an effect (B) to a possible cause (A): Sherlock Holmes notices the pavements outside 221B Baker Street are wet, and after much pondering, chin-stroking and consideration of all the alternatives, he concludes that this is because it has been raining.

These three different directions are illustrated in **Figure 0.4**.

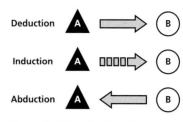

Figure 0.4 The direction of inference in three types of reasoning

Let's consider another example. Imagine you let yourself into your home. You go straight to the kitchen. No one is there, but you notice that:

B The kettle is boiling.

Your mind immediately wonders what the best explanation for this might be. Did the kettle turn on by itself? Did the cat turn it on by accident? Was it a ghost? However, after brief consideration, you conclude that the best explanation is:

A Someone has recently turned the kettle on.

Here your mind moves from an effect (the kettle being on) to a possible cause. Again, this method is used in science. In trying to understand the natural world, scientists come up with theories which account for or explain what we observe. Why does the sun rise every morning? There are various possible explanations that have been put forward over time. The ancient Egyptians thought the sun was a god reborn each morning who sailed his chariot across the sky. The ancient Greek astronomer, Ptolomy, thought the sun was a fiery disc set in an invisible sphere which rotated around a stationary earth. These days, most of us accept that the best explanation involves the claim that the earth turns on its axis every 24 hours.

The key features of abductions are:

- The conclusion is never guaranteed, and an even better explanation is always a possibility.
- Abductions attempt to go from an effect or observation to a possible reason or cause.
- Abductions rely on our current beliefs concerning the way the world normally works.

Because it cannot guarantee the truth of its conclusion, abduction, like induction, is not deductively valid. But it can on occasions masquerade as deduction (Sherlock Holmes mistakenly calls his abductive inferences 'deduction'), so we need to be careful to recognise abduction when it occurs, and not be fooled into thinking that it gives full support to its conclusion. The abductive inference is, in other words, a logical FALLACY, just meaning that from a deductive point of view, it is a piece of flawed reasoning. To see this, consider the example given above, of rain making my roof wet. This can be expressed as an A-to-B deduction.

Premise (A)   If it is raining above my house, my roof will be wet
Premise (A1)   It is raining above my house
Conclusion (B)   My roof will be wet

The first premise is a hypothetical, if ... then ... statement. The second affirms that the antecedent is true, so the consequent necessarily follows. However, it would be wrong to work this reasoning backwards like this:

P1 If it is raining above my house then my roof will be wet
P2 My roof is wet
C It is raining above my house

After all, something else might have caused my roof to be wet. My neighbour could have sprayed it with a hose. A flock of seagulls may have urinated over it. Just because A implies B, this does not mean that B implies A. To think that B does imply A is a logical error known as *affirming the consequent* or the *post hoc ergo propter hoc* fallacy. This is not to say your reasoning is entirely worthless. My roof may well be wet because it was raining; however, as a deductive argument it fails, as it does not show that it *must* have been raining.

However, this fallacy of reasoning is exactly what abduction consists of. Abduction involves going from the consequent to the antecedent or cause. But in the case of abduction it is not a fallacy, as the reasoner is not claiming that a particular cause must be the case, only that it is the best explanation – and it is important that they are clear that this is abductive rather than deductive reasoning. In a deductive argument, the conclusion *must* follow. However, in good inductive arguments, the conclusion is only probable. And in a good abductive argument, the conclusion is only the best explanation given the available evidence – it is not guaranteed to be the case.

4 What is philosophy? Understanding its activity

Philosophy is not a theory [a body of doctrine] but an activity[4]
Wittgenstein

One of the many important philosophers that you will not find in the timeline (**Figure 0.2**) is Ludwig Wittgenstein, who created not one, but two, distinct approaches to doing philosophy which influenced much of twentieth-century thinking. Wittgenstein's writings are full of pithy, intriguing insights, and in the quote above he is drawing our attention to the mistake we make if we think that it is possible to 'learn' philosophy by learning a whole load of ideas and theories.

We do not think you can learn philosophy by reading a textbook like this, and then writing an essay that summarises our summaries of other people's philosophical arguments and concepts. Perhaps you can do that with other subjects, but we do not think that when you study A-level Philosophy you should just memorise some theories, learn about what some historical figure has said and practise your exam techniques. It is true that you do need to understand, and learn about, what the great philosophers have written, thought and argued. But in the process of doing this with your teacher and classmates – in evaluating and assessing, in tearing apart and reconstructing, and in arguing and clarifying the arguments of those key figures – together you are engaging in the activity of philosophy. So to learn philosophy you must *do* philosophy.

Throughout this book, we have tried to create ways that help you engage in the activity of philosophy: to bring the concepts and arguments to life, with diagrams, thought experiments and some ridiculous examples which will hopefully also make the ideas easier to remember. The point of these activities is to test your understanding, to allow you to practise being philosophical, and to try to connect the concerns of the philosophers with the concerns of everyday life.

The activities in the book are best done with other philosophy students: sharing the tasks rather than just doing them individually, and to get you started, here is an activity related to the three types of argument and inference that you have just read about: deduction, induction and abduction.

Using deduction, induction and abduction in everyday life

We use all of these three types of reasoning (and others) all the time, often without realising. Read through Robin's day at school and identify what type of reasoning is being used at each stage.

Experimenting with ideas: Robin's day at school

1 For each of the **bold capital** letters, decide whether it is a deduction, induction or abduction.
2 Give each belief a certainty rating of 1–10, where 1 is extremely uncertain and 10 is extremely certain.
3 Overall, would you feel more certain about the beliefs formed by deduction, induction or abduction?

Robin walked down the road. She waited for the number 3 bus. **A)** She did not expect to wait long, as number 3s generally came every few minutes. **B)** She heard a rumbling noise behind her and reckoned this was the bus. The ticket cost £1. **C)** She gave the driver £2 and worked out that she should get £1 back in change. **D)** She got off at the corner of the park – the school was at the opposite corner. The park was square in shape and 1 km wide. Robin reckoned that by walking diagonally through rather than round the perimeter she would only walk approximately 1.4 km, as opposed to 2 km. **E)** In the park she came across a section that contained lots of wild flowers and grasses; she looked at the pattern and concluded that a gardener must have planted them. **F)** The grass was a little wet underfoot, however she knew that the ground would support her weight and she would not sink into the mud. **G)** At school, her first lesson was due to be with a new science teacher. There were some rumours spreading round that the teacher was a bachelor. If true, she reckoned this meant that the teacher was both a male and unmarried. **H)** During the lesson they lit the Bunsen burners. Robin knew that her hand would start to feel pain were she to touch the flame. Wisely, she decided not to. She carried her test tubes carefully to the bench, knowing that if she dropped them they would **I)** fall down and **J)** break. **K)** For the second half of the lesson the class was split into two, based on ages. Robin's friend Tamsin was put in the younger group. Robin was younger than Tamsin, so she worked out that she should be in that group too. **L)** During the period she heard a loud crash from the other side of the classroom. A beaker had fallen to the floor. No one owned up to it. Robin thought that something must have caused it to fall though, as every event is caused by something.

Structure of the book

This book covers sections 1 and 2 of the A-level Philosophy specification published by the AQA. Together, these comprise paper one of the examination. Paper one can be sat alone as an AS-level qualification or with paper two as an A-level. The book has two main sections: Epistemology and Moral Philosophy, and within these two sections there are chapters that correspond to the AQA specification.

Towards the end of the book, Section 3 gives you guidance and tips on passing the AS exam, and includes an important subsection on 'How to read philosophy'. Here we have provided some ideas, or 'lenses', which will help you to read and understand these texts and so improve your philosophical analysis. You might want to read this when you first come across an 'anthology icon'. The anthology icon appears when we are summarising a philosopher's ideas. It prompts you to flick to Section 4, where we have provided *extracts* of most texts found in the AQA online Anthology, so you can read the philosopher's original words and identify for yourself the arguments and types of reasoning that they use.

A final note on philosophical terminology

As you can see just from this introduction, philosophy, along with other A-level subjects, has its fair share of fancy terminology. This can be a bit daunting at first, and as we have mentioned, we have included various diagrams, charts, activities and thought experiments throughout the book to help you to unpack some of the philosophical terms (these activities are indicated by the symbols on page iv). Look out for the 'essential terminology' symbols too: we have placed these when we first use one of the key terms that you should be able to understand and use, and the meaning of these terms is outlined in the 'Essential Terminology' section of the glossary. We have already encountered some of these, and here is a complete list:

Essential Terminology Aa

assertion/claim/proposition	*tautology*
antecedent/consequent	*dilemma*
analytic/synthetic	*paradox*
a priori/a posteriori	*prove/proof*
necessary/contingent	*true/false*
consistent/inconsistent	*justification*
objective/subjective	*sound argument/proof*

One good thing about learning terminology in the all-encompassing subject of philosophy is that the terms also apply across a range of other areas too. The best way get to grips with the technical terms within philosophy is to take ownership of them. Say the words aloud, use them in discussions and also try using them in your writing. This means you will be practising writing as if you are a philosopher, until eventually these terms become a part of your language and the way you think. As Aristotle would say, you become a philosopher by first of all doing philosophy – so just by reading this introduction, and trying to answer the question 'What is philosophy?' you have started your own journey towards becoming a philosopher. Good luck!

1.1 What is knowledge?

When a friend says to you, 'This chocolate is delicious', it is clear what they mean. It is a fairly straightforward sentence conveying the FACT that the chocolate your friend is eating (but for some reason not sharing with you) tastes very, very nice. Imagine that, later, the same friend says to you, 'I *know* that I will get a grade B in my exam'; do you understand what they mean? Are they guessing? Do they have a strong hunch? Are they making a fair prediction based on their past grades and the work they have put in? Do they have 'inside' information about the contents of the exam? Are they being modest, or overconfident to try to impress you, or even belittle you slightly?

The difference we want to highlight between the first and the second sentences, is that in the second sentence your friend is using the word 'know'. We use this word all the time, but it is not always clear what someone means when they say they *know* something. For this reason, philosophers have often felt that before they could produce a proper theory of KNOWLEDGE, they would need to get clear what they were theorising about. Without a good idea of what something is, one cannot say much of interest about it. Accordingly, EPISTEMOLOGY often begins with the question of what precisely knowledge is. This question is made harder by how the term 'knowledge' does not have just one meaning.

Experimenting with ideas

Consider the following uses of the word *knowledge*, or *know*, in sentences A–J, then answer the questions that follow.

A Bees know how to make honey.
B I know kung-fu.
C Do you know the way to San José?
D Ravi knows the smell of petrol.
E I know the difference between right and wrong.
F Jaspal knows the capital of Peru.
G A baby knows how to suckle.
H I know that it rained yesterday.
I Maya knows what Vegemite tastes like.
J I know that 2 + 2 = 4.

1 Do you think the word is being used in the same way each time?
2 Which examples describe an ability of some kind?
3 Which examples describe a familiarity with a person or sensation?
4 Which examples describe a fact or facts about the world that a person has learnt?

Ability, acquaintance and propositional knowledge

Because there are different ways the word 'know' is used, philosophers have traditionally divided knowledge into three main types:

1 Practical knowledge or ability knowledge (knowing 'how').
2 Knowledge by acquaintance (knowing 'of')
3 Factual or propositional knowledge (knowing 'that').

Practical knowledge or ability knowledge (knowing 'how')

This is knowing how to do something, or 'know-how'. For example, we talk of knowing how to swim, how to speak Russian or how to bake a soufflé. Such knowledge involves a skill or capability to perform a certain kind of task, but need not involve having any explicit understanding of what such a performance entails. In other words, I may know how to swim without being able to explain how. I may know how to tie my shoelaces, but would find it extremely hard to give verbal instructions. So it is possible to know how to do things, without being able to articulate our knowledge. This suggests that practical knowledge is independent of any ability to communicate it in language or of having any conscious knowledge of precisely what one knows. After all, swallows seem to know when and how to fly south in winter, without having read a single book or even so much as glanced at a map.

However, some forms of know-how do seem to depend on other forms of knowledge. For example, knowing how to get to the British Museum or how to use the offside trap (in football) seem to require other forms of knowledge and BELIEF, rather than just exercising a simple skill, such as walking or breathing. In this sense, it can be argued, some forms of know-*how* are dependent on the ability to know x, y and z. In contrast, some philosophers, notably behaviourists, claim that practical knowledge is the key category which all the other categories can be *reduced* to. Their claim is that all forms of knowledge are really forms of know-how. For example, being able to answer quiz questions using language is just a form of knowing *how* to succeed in a particular task. In other words, all types of knowing *that* are just a fancy form of knowing *how*.

Knowledge by acquaintance (knowing 'of')

This is 'knowing' in the sense of knowing a person, place, thing, SENSATION or feeling. For example, we often speak of knowing somebody because we have met them, or knowing Paris by virtue of having visited it, or knowing the taste of pineapple having tried it. As with practical knowledge, knowledge by acquaintance need not involve any capacity to give a verbal report of what it entails. I may know the taste of pineapple without being able to describe it and without knowing any facts about it. Some philosophers regard knowledge by acquaintance, particularly with our own sense data, as the foundation of all our knowledge about the world. Their claim is that all of our knowledge is built up from our acquaintance with shapes, colours, sounds and tastes, and without these elements there would be no knowledge at all. Without the input of the senses, our minds would be a blank slate, or a *tabula rasa* (see page 106 for more on this).

Factual or propositional knowledge (knowing 'that')

This is knowing *that* something is the case. For example, we speak of knowing *that* 2 + 2 = 4, or *that* the earth orbits the sun, or *that* Shakespeare wrote *Hamlet*. Unlike the other two types of knowledge, when we know some fact, what we know can, in principle, be expressed in language. Thus if someone to know that Shakespeare wrote *Hamlet*, he or she claims that the sentence 'Shakespeare wrote *Hamlet*' is true, that is, claims that the sentence accurately reflects what happened in reality.

A proposition is a sentence that makes a claim about the world. Not all sentences make claims. For example, sentences such as *Shut that door* or *Where is my glove?* do not assert anything about the world. In contrast, other sentences make specific claims: *I am hungry. There are four fish in the bowl. China is well big.*

What is asserted by such sentences (that is to say, what they claim about the world) is called a proposition, and for this reason, factual knowledge is often called propositional knowledge. A good way to remember the meaning of this term is to think of this kind of knowledge as *proposing* that the world is one way, rather than another. So saying that you know that Paul McCartney wrote 'Let It Be' is to *propose* that a certain version of the world is true (as opposed to a version where John Lennon, or someone else, wrote the song). Hence the term *propositional* knowledge.

The other two forms of knowledge, by acquaintance or ability, do not have to involve any propositions about the world. A bee can know how to make honey without resorting to any claims about how the world is or is not. Likewise, knowing what vanilla tastes like does not involve understanding any propositions (indeed it is very hard to describe your experience of tasting vanilla using meaningful sentences). Any claim to propositional knowledge is usually preceded by the word 'that'. For example, I know *that* it is snowing in Scotland, or Taz knows *that* Arsenal were unbeaten during the 2002–03 season. The word 'that' sets up the proposition that the person claims to know.

It is interesting to note that these three different forms of knowledge are distinguished in many languages. French, for example, has *connaître* (for acquaintance) and *savoir* (for propositional knowledge) and *savoir-faire* (for practical knowledge). German has both *kennen* and *wissen*, whereas English just has *to know*.

Have a go at the activity on page 3. There is no easy answer to the last question! However, there are interesting differences between the kinds of knowledge in

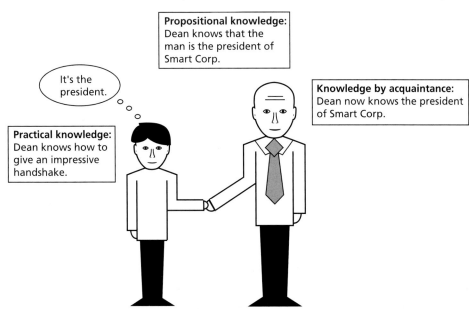

Figure 1.1 Three different kinds of knowledge. Dean is meeting the president of Smart Corp. The three forms of knowledge all come into play.

▶ **ACTIVITY**

Revisit the list of knowledge claims on page 1.

1   Do all of the examples fit neatly into one of the three categories of knowledge (practical, acquaintance and factual)?
2   How do you usually come to gain each kind of knowledge?
3   Which type of knowledge do you think you have the most of?

terms of how they are acquired/transmitted. I can be taught 'know-*how*' by others, for example, by them helping me to tie my laces. Also, other people can introduce me to new forms of knowledge by acquaintance, for example, by giving me liquorice for the first time – although I actually have to experience this myself to have the knowledge of the taste. I cannot learn this by reading about the taste or by talking to others.

Because propositional knowledge involves language, this means it can be passed swiftly and rapidly through books, the internet, lectures, and so on. This form of knowledge seems more or less exclusive to humans and is the cause of the rapid spread and growth of technology in the last few thousand years. With a simple swipe or click of a mouse, we are now able to access much of the propositional knowledge that has been gained in the current and preceding lives of billions of people. Our 'know-how' and 'know of', however, are not so easily transmitted.

This chapter is primarily concerned with factual, propositional knowledge. We will examine the conditions under which it can be properly said that a person knows a fact. Before we begin, we need to explore some related key words.

Because factual knowledge is expressed in language, it seems to involve holding *beliefs*. A swallow does not need to have any specific beliefs to fly south (know-how) or to know its chicks (by acquaintance), but propositional knowledge is different. If I have knowledge of certain facts, I *believe* certain propositions to be true; in other words, I *assent* to these propositions. Because factual knowledge deals with knowing facts, and so with having beliefs, these beliefs can be either *true* or *false*. These key terms, namely 'belief', 'proposition', 'fact' and 'truth', have somewhat ambiguous meanings in ordinary English, so if we are to make headway in our analysis of knowledge, it is important that we give working definitions of these terms (see **Figure 1.2**).

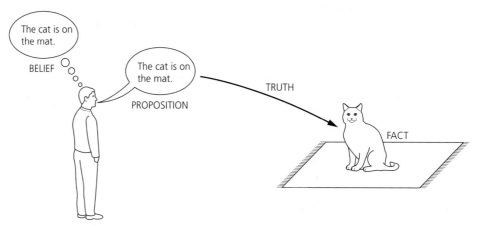

Figure 1.2 Beliefs, propositions and facts

- A *belief* is a thought which is about the world. It is a mental representation which claims that something is the case. Beliefs can be true or false. In the figure, Sam has the belief that the cat is on the mat.
- A *proposition* is what a STATEMENT says or asserts about the world. Like beliefs, propositions can be true or false. When Sam utters the sentence, 'The cat is on the mat', he is expressing the proposition that the cat is on the mat.
- A fact is something that is the case in the world. Here the fact is the cat's being on the mat. Facts cannot be true or false, they just are.

Truth is a tricky CONCEPT, but one account of truth is that it involves a correspondence between a belief or a proposition and the world. If Sam's belief that the cat is on the mat corresponds with the world – that is, with the facts – then it is true. So his belief will be true if the cat is indeed on the mat.

Knowledge, certainty and ordinary language

Having given brief definitions of some key terms (*belief, fact, proposition* and *truth*), it is worth quickly reminding ourselves of what the undertaking of this chapter is. The chapter aims to explore the concept of knowledge and to see whether a definition can be reached. However, giving a definition of knowledge could involve one of at least two different things. We could be trying to give a definition of what the concept of knowledge *should* be (this would be a PRESCRIPTIVE account of knowledge) or we could be trying to give a definition of what the concept of knowledge *is*, in its ordinary usage (this would be a DESCRIPTIVE account of knowledge). We are aiming for the second kind of definition, although it is often very tempting to slip into the first kind of definition. To see how easily this slippage can occur, consider the following activity.

▶ **ACTIVITY**

For sentences A–G:

1 How many of these things would you agree to knowing? All of them?
2 But how many do you *really* know?
3 Can you think of ways in which you could be mistaken about each one?

A You know what you will do tomorrow.
B You know there is no life on the moon.
C You know that you are looking at a book right now.
D You know who you have spoken to today.
E You know if you are currently in pain or not.
F You know that you are experiencing black ink-coloured lettering sensations that seem to spell out words and sentences.
G You know that you exist.

It seems there is very little we can be certain about; after all …

A … your plans for tomorrow could suddenly change with the weather/world events.
B … there may be living organisms living in lakes deep beneath the surface of the moon.
C … you could be dreaming and not looking at a real book.
D … some of the people you think you have spoken to today might have been other people in disguise or even clones.

If such doubt is possible, then can you really be said to *know* any of these things? What about sentences E–G? Is it possible to doubt these statements too? Perhaps these are harder to doubt and might be the only statements you would count as *proper* knowledge?

What these considerations are designed to show is that we intuitively link the concept of knowledge with the concept of certainty. However, we also intuitively believe that we are capable of knowing a lot of things. These two INTUITIONS can be contradictory:

a) We can only know things if we are certain about them.
b) We know lots of things.

The more we emphasise certainty a), the less we are likely to actually know b). The more we emphasise b), it seems that knowledge is less about certainty a). This conflict relates to two different purposes we may have in seeking to define knowledge: prescriptive or descriptive. We might intuitively be inclined to say that we *should* only count things we know for certain as knowledge (prescriptive), whereas in ordinary language we *are* inclined to count lots of things as knowledge, and not require certainty (descriptive). The danger in giving in to our intuition about certainty is that we will no longer be analysing/describing the concept of knowledge as it is used in ordinary language. Instead, we would be trying to explore how we might want to use the concept of knowledge, or even simply exploring the concept of certainty itself. Either way, we will not be analysing the concept of knowledge as it is used in ordinary language.

For the time being, we will leave the concept of certainty behind. But if knowledge does not need to involve certainty, what *does* it need to involve? To answer this, we need to give some sort of definition for the concept of knowledge.

Propositional knowledge – the nature of definition

But what *kind* of definition do we need? You may think that all definitions are alike, but philosophy is rarely so straightforward. Definitions differ subtly in approach, and it is useful to be aware of these differences so we can be clear about exactly the kind of definition we are seeking. The philosopher Linda Zagzebski (1947–) has articulated some of the key ways in which definitions differ, often summarising the philosopher John Locke (1632–1704).[1]

The status of the thing defined

Humans divide and classify the world in all sorts of ways. Some of these ways are artificial and some reflect genuine underlying differences in the nature of objects/events. For example, compare the concepts of *water* and *weeds*. There are lots of liquids in the world and we classify some as water. Likewise, there are lots of plants in the world and we classify some as weeds. However, the two classifications do not have the same status. There is a genuine difference between liquids on a molecular level, such that some liquid is called water (H_2O) and some is not. In contrast, there is no underlying genetic difference between weeds and non-weeds; the classification is culturally specific – a question of which plants humans like in their gardens. Locke suggested that water has a *real essence*, whereas weeds do not.

The term 'natural kind' is also used in philosophy for the same distinction. The category of water forms a natural kind, whereas the category of weeds does not. We could put water under a microscope and investigate the real difference between water and other liquids, in a way that we cannot put weeds under a microscope to the find the difference between weeds and other plants. In the case of water, there is a real essence we could discover; in the case of weeds, there is no real essence waiting to be found.

For those objects that have a real essence, we can seek what Locke termed a *real definition*. A real definition picks out the real essence of an object. For example, the real definition of water is H_2O. (Locke suggested that one of the key roles of science is to make our real definitions match the real essences.) However, for

'Water' has a real essence and can be defined: $\boxed{H_2O}$

'Weed' has no real essence and no one definition – what is classed as a weed is culturally dependent.

a real ← definition.

those objects that do not have a real essence, we cannot seek a real definition. The definition will always be <u>artificial</u> to some extent – although it might be something that we can agree on, or that <u>accurately reflects our use of language</u>.

Definition   **Essence**

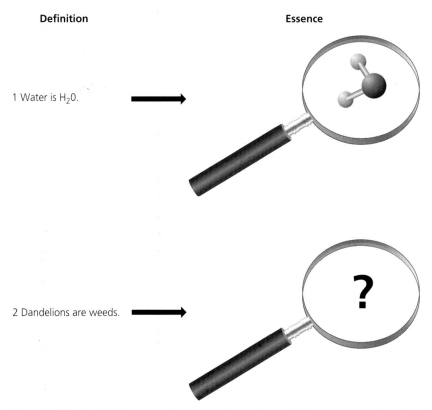

1 Water is H_2O.

2 Dandelions are weeds.

Figure 1.3 Real definitions, real essences. Some of our definitions correspond to the real essence of objects. In these cases, a *real definition* is possible. In the second set of cases, the definition does not relate to any real essence, so a *real definition* is not possible.

The example of planets is an interesting one, in as much as there has been considerable controversy over whether Pluto is a planet or not. This is decided in part by investigating Pluto (it is clearly not a sun), but beyond this, what we class as planet or just a large rock orbiting the sun, is a matter for humans to decide. There is no real essence of a 'planet', so a real definition is not possible. However, just because a real definition is not possible, this does not mean it is pointless seeking a definition. Many concepts we use may not correspond to real essences, but <u>still are important classifications</u> – important to our understanding of ourselves and the world.

Zagzebski thinks it is ambiguous whether concepts such as *intelligence* and *knowledge* can have real definitions. She is fairly sceptical about whether knowledge has a real essence, in part because the term has varied so much in its use historically. For example, only recently has <u>immediate perceptual awareness</u> of the world counted as knowledge – previously the word *knowledge* was only used in relation to our conceptual understanding. This suggests that the concept is a cultural one, not a natural kind. However, she suggests that we should treat knowledge as if it does have a real essence, and so should seek a real definition. We should only give up if we are defeated in the project.

Zagzebski: 'knowledge' might not have a real essence, but we should still seek a real definition. We should only give up if we are defeated in so doing.

▶ **ACTIVITY**

Which of the following do you think has a real essence, such that a real definition is possible? Another way of posing the same question is to think of which of these constitutes a 'natural kind' and which an artificial kind:

1 Gold
2 Suns
3 Planets
4 Puddings
5 Monsters
6 Death
7 Intelligence
8 Knowledge
9 Plants

7

Different ways of getting a definition

The traditional philosophical approach to defining concepts like *knowledge* has been to look for the conditions/factors that must be true for an example of the concept to occur. In other words, what is it that happens when someone *knows* something, which does not happen when they only *believe* something? This approach to defining concepts is called philosophical or conceptual analysis, and generally involves breaking down a concept into its various parts by exploring what conditions are NECESSARY for a true example of the concept (for example, knowledge/love/happiness/justice) to occur. Although this approach to philosophy has sometimes been questioned, it is the approach that Zagzebski recommends and the one we take in the rest of the section.

Even within this approach there are different types of conditions that might be emphasised over others. In particular, some definitions emphasise the cause of the thing being defined, whereas others do not. For example, a definition of sunburn would not just outline the symptoms, but also what caused the sunburn (UV light). In contrast, other definitions do not include the cause: in defining a triangle, for example, there would be no mention of how triangles come to be.

As we will see below, some definitions of knowledge (RELIABILISM and VIRTUE EPISTEMOLOGY) emphasise the cause of knowledge, whereas others do not. Zagzebski thinks that both approaches can be valid and they are not mutually exclusive – it might be possible to correctly define knowledge in terms of cause, and also to correctly define it in another way.

Pitfalls to avoid

Lastly, Zagzebski outlines some key pitfalls to avoid in giving any sort of definition. Definitions should not be:

- *Circular*. This means they should not include the term being defined – for example, saying that *justice* is what happens when *just* acts occur.
- *Obscure*. The terms in any definition should not be more obscure than the original term, as the definition would not further our understanding.
- *Negative*. Defining a term by what it is not does not help either. For example, defining a good act as 'one that is not wrong'.
- *Ad hoc*. This means coming up with a definition that is specific to meeting a particular problem. For example, defining knowledge as a justified true belief that is not a Gettier counterexample (this will only make sense once you have read pages 20–23).

Truth-conditional analysis as a way to define knowledge

So our quest in this chapter is to come up with a definition of propositional knowledge using conceptual analysis. To do this, we have to find the conditions under which knowledge occurs. If we can list these conditions and so say exactly when someone does and does not know something, then we will have a pretty good idea of what propositional knowledge is. This may seem a fancy approach, but it was one first adopted by Plato nearly 2,500 years ago.

Essential Terminology Aa

To makes our quest for a definition easier, it will be useful to abbreviate the expression, 'Someone knows a proposition' to 'S knows that p'. Here 'S' stands for the subject (the person doing the knowing – for example, Sharon), and 'p' for the proposition that she knows (for example, that Paris is the capital of France). So we need to determine what conditions must be satisfied in order for us to assert 'S knows that p' (Sharon knows that Paris is the capital of France).

▶ **ACTIVITY**

1   To get started on our search for a definition of 'knowledge', let us try to distinguish it from belief. Begin by writing a short list of things you would normally claim to *know*, and another list of things you merely *believe*. These may be things that you know or believe have happened or exist. Try not to be too influenced by sceptical arguments and simply use the terms 'know' and 'believe' as they would be used in everyday life.
2   Having done this, consider what has to be the case for you to claim that you know something, as opposed to simply believing it. What makes the knowledge claims different from the belief claims?
3   Now read on to see how your answer compares with Plato's.

Socrates and Plato

Socrates was a famous ancient Greek philosopher. He was renowned for engaging others in dialogue and examining interesting ideas and concepts such as love, justice and knowledge. Socrates liked to challenge conventional thinking, which led to some clashes with the authorities. Socrates was eventually accused of impiety (not believing in the gods) and corrupting the youth of Athens. He was tried and sentenced to death by drinking hemlock. It is likely that had he wished, he could have escaped to live in exile. However, he chose to remain in Athens, his city of birth, and willingly drank the hemlock that ended his life.

Socrates attracted many disciples, usually young men, who were interested in philosophical discussion. One of these disciples was Plato – who would have been about 29 when Socrates died. Plato was born in Athens in around 430 BCE, into a relatively wealthy aristocratic family. After the death of Socrates, Plato travelled widely before returning to Athens at the age of 40 and founding perhaps the first proper college in Western society, known as the Academy. The school went on to last for nearly a thousand years. The great philosopher Aristotle was one of its first students.

To aid the teaching in his school, Plato wrote many dialogues, all concerned with philosophy. In many of the dialogues, Socrates is the main character and he usually engages in a debate about a philosophical issue. Indeed, it is primarily through the writings of Plato that we know of the life and teachings of Socrates.

Plato on true belief and knowledge

Having begun to think about the differences between knowledge and belief, we can now examine how Plato approached the problem. In his dialogue, the Meno, he tries to work out the difference between someone having a true belief and someone having knowledge. He begins by pointing out that true belief has much in common with knowledge. Indeed, it would seem that the two are equally valuable as guides to action. Socrates, the character expounding Plato's views, explains his reasoning to his fellow debater Meno, as follows:

Socrates *Let me explain. If someone knows the way to Larissa, or anywhere else you like, then when he goes there and takes others with him he will be a good and capable guide, you would agree?*

Meno *Of course.*

Socrates *But if a man judges correctly which is the road, though he has never been there and doesn't know it, will he not also guide others aright?*

Meno *Yes, he will.*

Socrates *And as long as he has a correct belief on the points about which the other has knowledge, he will be just as good a guide, believing the truth but not knowing it.*

Meno *Just as good.*

Socrates *Therefore true belief is as good a guide as knowledge for the purpose of acting rightly.*[2]

Here Plato is arguing that so long as my beliefs are true, then they are as useful to me and to others as if I had knowledge. So why, the question arises, should we prefer knowledge to true belief? Are they in fact the same thing and, if so, why is knowledge so highly prized? Socrates' answer has many facets, but we will focus on just one aspect, which contrasts the stability of knowledge with the flightiness of belief.

Socrates *True beliefs are a fine thing and do all sorts of good so long as they stay in their place; but they will not stay long. They run away from a man's mind, so they are not worth much until you tether them by working out the reason … Once they are tied down, they become knowledge, and are stable. That is why knowledge is something more valuable than right belief. What distinguishes one from the other is the tether.*[3]

This all sounds rather cryptic. What can he mean by beliefs failing to 'stay in their place'? What is to 'tether them by working out the reason'? Plato seems to be saying that part of the reason we value knowledge is that it is more steadfast than mere belief, since it is backed up by REASONS or EVIDENCE. The evidence acts as a kind of glue, which retains the belief in the mind by giving us good reason to continue believing it. By contrast, a belief for which we have no evidence – even if it happens to be true – has nothing to make it stick in the mind. If I have no good reason for believing a proposition, it will not take much for someone to dissuade me from it. But if I know it, I will not readily withdraw my assent. So Plato is suggesting that it is a kind of tethering that converts belief into knowledge. To have knowledge is to have a true belief secured by reasons. In another dialogue, the *Theaetetus*, Plato offers other considerations in support of the idea that knowledge is more than mere true belief.

> **Socrates**   *Now, when a jury has been persuaded, fairly, of things which no one but an eyewitness could possibly know, then, in reaching a decision based on hearsay, they do so without knowledge, but get hold of true belief, given that their verdict is fair because what they have been made to believe is correct.*
>
> **Theaetetus** *Absolutely.*
>
> **Socrates**   *But if true belief and knowledge were identical, my friend, then even the best juryman in the world would never form a correct belief, but fail to have knowledge; so it looks as though they are different.*[4]

Plato's point here is that we can hold true beliefs that we would be reluctant to call knowledge because of the nature of the evidence supporting them. A juror can come to a correct decision on the balance of evidence presented in court. But if the evidence available to him were circumstantial and less than absolutely conclusive, we would be reluctant to call this knowledge. By contrast, an eyewitness to the events in question could indeed be said to know. Consider also the example of a gambler who believes that the next number on the roulette wheel will be red. Even if he happens to be right, we would be reluctant to say that he truly knew. These examples show that the manner by which one acquires a true belief, or by which one *justifies* it, is important to its counting as a piece of knowledge. Because of basic considerations such as this, Plato is led in the *Theaetetus* to consider the view that 'true belief accompanied by a rational account is knowledge',[5] or, as we might say, knowledge is a *justified, true belief* – that is, a true belief for which the believer has adequate reasons or evidence.

So it seems we have an early candidate for a definition of factual knowledge. A person knows something if they have a belief that is *true* and that has a good JUSTIFICATION.

Essential Terminology

Experimenting with ideas

1 Think up your own examples, like those above, to illustrate the difference between having a true belief and having knowledge.

2 The last activity (on page 9) involved writing down some things you claimed to believe and other things that you claimed to know. Go back to these statements and see if the missing ingredient in the two cases is indeed the degree of justification for the belief.

To test whether the *justified, true belief* account of knowledge seems plausible, consider the following example. Innocence and Pete the Cheat are playing cards (see **Figure 1.4**). Innocence has a strong feeling that the card on the top of the deck, about to be turned over, is the Queen of Spades. She has no particular reason for this feeling though. In the game she needs it to be a Queen and just has a strong hunch that it is the Queen of Spades. Lo and behold, the card is indeed the Queen of Spades! Innocence had a true belief; however, as this was just a guess/hunch, would we say that she *knew* it? Probably not. This would seem to imply, as Plato suggested, that a true belief is not enough to grant knowledge. Now, Pete the Cheat also had a very strong belief that the card on the top of the deck was the Queen of Spades. It was his deck and some of the cards had tiny markings on the back which the casual observer would not notice. It was a marked deck! Pete could see that the card on the top of the deck had a mark on it that indicated it was the Queen of Spades. When turned over, it was indeed the Queen of Spades! Pete had a true belief; however, in this case, his belief was justified. Would we say that Pete *knew* it? Probably yes. So, on the basis of this example, it seems that defining knowledge as a *justified, true belief* has some merit. However, as we will discover in the remainder of this chapter, philosophy is rarely this straightforward!

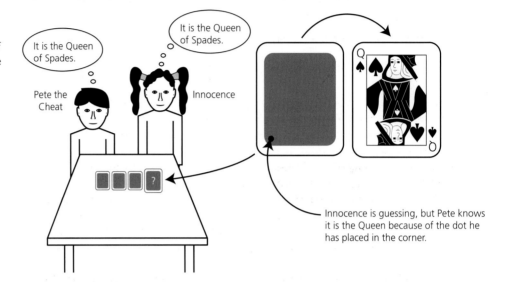

Figure 1.4 Innocence and Pete the Cheat are playing cards. Innocence has a belief that the card on the top of the deck is the Queen of Spades. Pete also has the same belief; however, his is justified as they are playing with his marked deck of cards.

Innocence is guessing, but Pete knows it is the Queen because of the dot he has placed in the corner.

1.1.1 The tripartite view: knowledge as justified, true belief

The definition of knowledge as justified, true belief is the traditional one. If it is correct, it means that if someone knows a proposition, then three conditions must be satisfied. The person must *believe* the proposition, it must be *true* and it must be *justified*. These conditions can be set out as follows.

S knows that p if and only if (for example, Sharon knows that Paris is the capital of France if and only if …):

1 S believes that p (the belief condition: for example … Sharon believes Paris is the capital of France)
2 p is true (the truth condition: for example … Paris is indeed the capital of France)
3 S has adequate or sufficient evidence for p, or is justified in believing p (the evidence condition: for example … Sharon has read that Paris is the capital of France in a trustworthy encyclopaedia).

Experimenting with ideas
1 Read the scenarios A–G. Using your common-sense intuition, decide in each case whether the person in bold knows the fact in question.
2 Then check to see whether:
   a) the person believes the fact (the belief condition)
   b) the fact is true (the truth condition)
   c) the person would be justified in believing it (the evidence condition).

3 If all three conditions are met, then according to the JTB (justified, true belief) definition, this should be a case of knowledge. If one or more of the conditions is not met, then this is not a case of knowledge. Did using the three conditions match your own intuitions in each of the cases?

4 Consider whether justified, true belief is a good analysis of the concept of knowledge. What problems could the definition run into? How good must the justification be? (Remember: we are looking to establish the criteria for the everyday concept of knowledge, and justification need not be perfect for knowledge to be claimed in everyday parlance. So avoid ruling out examples just because absolute certainty is not established.)

A **Davina** thinks that monkeys are more intelligent than humans because her mate told her so.

B **Ravi** reckons the sun will set at 19:02 on Sunday, having read as much in the paper. And it does.

C Having been told by his parents and having read books and watched DVDs on the subject, young **Victor** is convinced that Santa Claus exists.

D **Tamsin** learns from a textbook that *Hamlet* is Shakespeare's longest play (which it is).

E **Wanda** watches five DVDs of Shakespeare plays and concludes by their length that Hamlet must be Shakespeare's longest play.

F Colin is going out with Simone. However, at a party, he drunkenly, yet inexcusably, kisses Fiona. No one sees a thing. Back at college, Nigel is secretly in love with Simone. To try to get Simone and Colin to split up, he makes up a rumour, telling Brian that Colin and Fiona got off at the party. Later on **Chanise** hears this rumour and believes it.

G **Samma** has been dating Joel for five years now. She knows that he is faithful to her. She just knows it in her heart.

In the activity, you have been testing the justified, true belief (JTB) analysis of knowledge. In other words, you have been considering whether each condition is necessary by asking whether we can do without *belief*, *truth* or *justification*. You may also have considered a slightly different question when you got to scenario F), namely whether or not together the conditions are sufficient. In other words, you may have been wondering whether someone who has all three conditions definitely has knowledge. It is important to recognise that these two questions are distinct.

In the following discussion of the traditional analysis of knowledge, we will treat each question separately. First, we will ask whether the three conditions are *individually necessary*. This means seeing whether we need each one by seeing if we can do without any. Second, we will examine whether they are *jointly sufficient*. This means seeing whether having all three definitely guarantees knowledge, or whether there are some cases where you can have all three (a justified, true belief) and still not have knowledge.

Necessary and sufficient conditions

NECESSARY AND SUFFICIENT CONDITIONS can seem like complex ideas, but the principle behind them is fairly commonplace. If an element is necessary, then without that element you could not have the thing in question. Being a man is a necessary condition of being a father. If you are not a man, then you cannot be a father. The definition of a necessary condition can be summed up as: *X is a necessary condition of Y if without X you cannot have Y.*

Having a necessary condition is not always enough to have the thing in question though. For example, being a man is a necessary condition of being a father, but it alone is not enough. Not all men are fathers. Other conditions need to be met in order to be a father. If having certain necessary elements/conditions always guarantees having the thing in question, then these elements are called sufficient. For example, having never been married and being a man are sufficient conditions for being a bachelor. Every time you have a man who has never married, you have a bachelor. There is nothing more you need; the two elements are sufficient. (They are also necessary – you cannot be a bachelor without being a man or without being unmarried.) The definition of sufficient conditions can be summed up as: *X and Y are sufficient conditions of Z if the occurrence of X and Y guarantees the occurrence of Z.*

Experimenting with ideas

Often it can be hard to articulate all of the sufficient conditions of a concept. Think about all of the elements that, if present, would guarantee you were looking at a square. Having four sides is not enough, as not all four-sided objects are squares. Having four sides of equal length is not enough either (consider a four-sided object drawn on a ball, with equal sides, but not with angles of 90 degrees).

1   Look at points A–C below. Which of the elements are necessary for the concept in question? In other words, could you have the concept in question without the particular element?
2   Are the elements jointly sufficient for the concept? In other words, do the elements together always yield the concept?

A Elements are – *three angles, three lines* and *red*. The concept is **triangle**.
B Elements are – *water, drops* and *falling*. The concept is **raining**.
C Elements are – owning a valid ticket, the six numbers on the ticket are the same as the lottery draw, the ticket is for the right draw. The concept is **a person having a winning ticket for the lottery jackpot**.

In example A, having three angles and three lines are necessary conditions for a triangle, but red is not. Three angles and three lines are not jointly sufficient though, as there are many combinations of three angles and three lines that are not triangles. The lines have to at least join together and enclose a space to be a triangle.

In example B, the three elements seem to be necessary. If there is no water, there can be no rain. (Although can it not rain frogs? Or blood?) The water would need be falling (otherwise it is mist or just a cloud) and there would need to be drops rather than a big sheet of water. However, they are not jointly sufficient, as someone holding up a watering can meet the three conditions of *water, drops* and *falling*, without it raining. So the three elements being present do not guarantee rain; other elements are needed.

In the last case, the three elements would each seem to be necessary. Together they also seem to be sufficient. If all these three elements are together, then surely the person *has* won the lottery? However, maybe you can come up with a counterexample? Either an example of someone who has won the lottery jackpot without one of these elements being present, or an example of all three elements being present and yet the person not having a winning ticket for the jackpot.

Issue: are the conditions individually necessary?

Returning to the concept of knowledge and the conditions of truth, justification and belief (JTB), we will now explore whether each of the elements is necessary for propositional knowledge, and whether together they are jointly sufficient to guarantee knowledge.

The belief condition (B)

Do you need to believe something to know it? The belief condition says that a necessary condition for your knowing that p is that you *believe* that p. In other words, you must believe that the proposition is true, or hold that what it says really is the case. This is certainly plausible. After all, it appears that you cannot *claim* to know something to be true if you do not even believe it. So, for example, it is incoherent to say, 'I know that it is raining, but I do not believe it is'. Nonetheless, philosophers have disputed the belief condition by arguing that knowledge and belief are *separable*, so that each can exist either with or without the other.

Some philosophers have even claimed that belief and knowledge are mutually *incompatible* – in other words, that if you have one you cannot have the other. While Plato in the *Meno* adheres to the view that knowledge entails belief, in a later work, *The Republic*, he develops an incompatibilist view known as INFALLIBILISM (see page 25). There he reasons that since knowledge is infallible (cannot be wrong) and belief is fallible, they must be fundamentally different ways of apprehending the world.[6] To believe is to be less than certain, whereas knowledge involves no such hesitation. So to know something does not entail also believing it, but rather involves going *beyond* mere belief. There is no need to discuss Plato's argument in detail here, but one might defend such a position by pointing out that people often speak as if knowledge and belief were distinct, as when tennis players say, 'I do not believe I will win, I *know* I will'. Does this not imply that to come to know something is to cease to believe it? In fact it is doubtful that it does, for surely this is just a more emphatic way of saying, 'I do not *just* believe that I will win, I know I will'?

The view that one can have knowledge without belief has also been defended by philosophers who claim that knowledge is more about how one acts than about what beliefs one might entertain. So it is argued, for example, that knowledge is more about responding correctly to questions than it is about any state of mind. If I forget that I have learned the history of the Civil War and am quizzed on it, it might be that I am able to give correct answers, but believe them to be mere guesses. Since I am guessing, I seem not to have belief, and yet my getting the answers right suggests I do have knowledge. Despite this, it would seem that some tendency to assent to a proposition is required of knowledge. Perhaps just choosing an answer, however unsure I may be, is sufficient to count as belief. So long as I am disposed to assent to a proposition, then I can be said to believe it, and, in this minimal sense, belief certainly seems necessary for knowledge.

However, in cases of action and abilities, some people have knowledge without any form of assent. Consider the following example.

Clara cannot drive. Her friend Jared has just got his full licence and is going to take them both on a trip to San José. Jared drives over to pick up Clara. He reveals that his satnav is broken and that he has never been to San José. Clara goes every Saturday with her dad to a rock climbing venue; however, Clara does not pay much attention to the route and she also claims not to know the way to San José. Her dad laughs and says that of course she knows it. They set off and as Jared starts driving Clara realises, one by one, that she recognises the roads and that she does know the route after all and directs them safely to Route 101 which leads to San José.

Before setting out, Clara did not believe that she knew the way to San José. But did she know it?

She was certainly able to get them there. Is it possible that she did know the way, without believing she did? Her father certainly would claim that she knew the way, having driven her there over 30 times.

Perhaps she was being modest; she did really believe, but pretended not to, much like someone might say, 'I do not believe it!' when they clearly know (and believe) that they have just won the Oscar for best director. Maybe Clara did really believe she could find the way and so did know.

Also, this example might be considered a case of know-how rather than propositional knowledge which we are currently examining. Swallows can know the way south, without having specific propositional beliefs, so the example is unfair as the two sorts of knowledge are very different. However, as this case involves road directions, it can fairly easily be turned into a sequence of propositional beliefs rather than just a specific ability to get from A to B.

Consider this. Clara herself may have individually believed that:

- Kings Road leads to Humboldt Road
- Humboldt Road turns into Glenpark Way
- Glenpark Way turns into San Bruno Avenue
- San Bruno Avenue leads into Bayshore Boulevard
- Bayshore Boulevard leads to Route 101
- Route 101 leads to San José.

If asked, she may have been able to give any one of these road changes; however, she may not have ever put this information together in her mind and so did not believe that she knew the way to San José, or even believe a specific fact that the shortest way from her house to San José involved six road changes. Is this possible? If so, then maybe belief is not a necessary condition for knowledge.

Belief, though, is certainly a necessary condition for someone to *claim* they have knowledge. It makes no sense to say, 'I know that Paris is the capital of France, but I do not believe it.' Someone claiming knowledge of a fact will always believe the fact too. However, other people might be more inclined to attribute knowledge on behalf of a person without that person themselves claiming a belief. My history teacher may claim that I did know the facts about the Civil War, even though I felt I was guessing. Clara's dad may claim that she did know the way to San José, despite her not believing it.

Despite the odd, vaguely plausible counterexample, the philosophical consensus certainly claims that belief is a necessary condition of knowledge. If a person does not believe a fact, then they cannot know it.

The truth condition (T)

Does a fact need to be true for you to know it? The truth condition is fairly uncontroversial. It says that if you know something, it must be true. To test this condition, try to think of a case where you knew something that was in fact false. Is this possible? Often we *claim* to know something that turns out to be false, but this does not mean that we actually do know it. Thinking you know something is not the same as actually knowing it.

Consider Raquel, a cavewoman living thousands of years ago. She believes that the earth is flat. She has compelling evidence for this belief. First, it looks flat. Second, if the ground were curved, then things would roll off towards the edges and eventually fall off, and so on. Does she know that it is flat? Surely not. If she knows that the earth is flat, then the earth must be flat.

Correspondence theory of truth

We are likely to reject Raquel's claim for knowledge as it is not *true* that the world is flat. So it cannot be a justified, *true* belief. However, this rejection relies on an implicit understanding of what truth is – and there are different, competing theories on this matter. One of the most popular and intuitively plausible ones says that truth consists in a correspondence between a belief and the relevant fact. According to the correspondence theory, a belief (or a proposition) is true just if what it claims is the case actually is the case. And if there is no fact corresponding with what the belief says, then it is false.

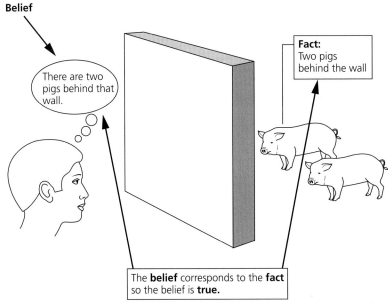

Figure 1.5 The correspondence theory of truth

Here the belief corresponds exactly to the fact, so the belief is true. If there were one or three or no pigs, then the belief would not correspond to the fact and so would be false. According to this theory, truth consists in this correspondence between belief and fact.

On this theory, Raquel cannot know the world is flat, as her belief does not correspond to the fact. It is false belief, and knowledge requires true belief.

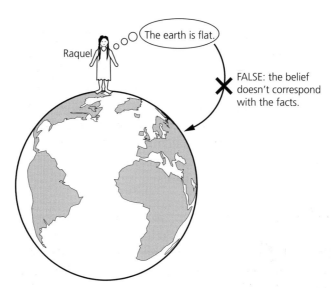

Figure 1.6 Knowledge is impossible without truth. Raquel the cavewoman believes the earth is flat, but in fact it is round. Since her belief does not correspond with the facts, it is not true. And if it is not true, it cannot count as knowledge. The truth condition is 'external' since, unlike the belief and evidence conditions, it is not 'in her mind'.

Coherence theory of truth

However, other theories of truth may be more generous with Raquel's knowledge claim. The coherence theory of truth has different varieties, but one kind proposes that a belief is true if it is one of the web of beliefs held by a society to be true. This web of beliefs is internally coherent, with the beliefs supporting one another. So back in Raquel's day, the web of true beliefs would have included the claim that the world was flat. Indeed, imagine Raquel appearing on a prehistoric *University Challenge* and being asked what shape the world is; her answer of 'flat' would be taken as the true answer. The belief in the flatness of the world fitted in with lots of other beliefs about the world, some based on evidence, which were also held as true. On the coherence theory, this would make the belief true – in which case, Raquel did have a justified, true belief and did know the world was flat.

You may be inclined to think this is wrong. The world simply is not flat, so Raquel could not have *known* it was. The world is round and that is the plain truth. In contrast, the coherentist would point out that over time our web of beliefs has changed, such that the world being round is now held as the true belief. Back in Raquel's day, it was true that the world was flat, and now it is true that the world is round. However, like Raquel, we cannot escape our web of beliefs and claim to own the 'real' truth. Just like Raquel, we are humans, caught in a period of history, with a web of beliefs that we hold as true. The shape of the world may not be the most convincing example, but other concepts, such as the concepts of mass and matter, have changed significantly as science changes its theories, and may well change again in the future. What we term 'true' now, might be considered false in the future. And the same will apply to that future too. We can never transcend time and see some ultimate 'truth'. We have to accept that what makes a belief true is whether it is one of the web of coherent beliefs generally held to be true. This is what it means for anything to be true.

Although these theories of truth differ, on either account you can still argue that truth is one of the conditions of knowledge. It is just that using the coherence theory of truth, we are more inclined to allow people to have 'known' things in the past – things that we no longer would count as knowledge now. And this is because the concept of truth was bound to the belief system of that time, not of our time. In contrast, the correspondence theory claims that the facts do not change over time. So it was never true that the world was flat and Raquel never knew it was. However, both theories require knowledge to be true.

Truth as an external criterion

One important point to draw from either theory is that whether or not a person knows something cannot be established by *internal* criteria alone (meaning internal to their mind). Raquel cannot simply inspect her belief to determine whether it counts as knowledge. By examining her mind, she can establish that she fulfils two of the conditions for knowledge: she has a belief for which she has good justification. She knows this because these two criteria are internal, they are directly accessible to her, since they are 'in her mind', as it were. But for it to count as knowledge, it must also be true. Her belief must actually correspond with reality (or cohere with a general set of beliefs), and this is an *external* criterion. So a justified, false belief is not knowledge, and truth is considered to be a NECESSARY condition of knowledge.

Essential Terminology

The evidence/justification condition (J)

As we have seen, Plato argued that we are reluctant to grant someone knowledge if they have acquired a true belief by inadequate evidence, or by sheer luck; and a third condition is needed. So if S claims to know that p, then she must be able to justify it by appeal to evidence, since otherwise she is simply making an unsubstantiated assertion. A good way of illustrating this point is to consider the example of a racist juror. Suppose the juror comes to believe that a defendant is guilty purely on the basis of the colour of his skin. Let us also suppose that, as a matter of fact, the defendant is guilty. In this case, the juror has a true belief. But is it knowledge? It is generally thought that the answer here must be no, since the juror has no good justification for her belief. Her belief is based on irrational prejudice, not on the evidence presented to her in court.

So an *unjustified*, true belief is not knowledge. We need the justification criteria to distinguish knowledge from lucky guesses, though quite how 'justified' a belief needs to be to count as knowledge is not clear. As we will see below, the issue of what counts as proper justification becomes quite complex. However, for the time being, it may be useful to think of a belief being sufficiently justified, if the type of justification given is one that is usually good enough to attribute knowledge (although this is a circular definition – as we are defining knowledge in terms of being of justified and then defining justification in terms of giving knowledge).

Is the justification condition really necessary? Do you always need some form of justification to truly know something? In the activity on page 13, is it not possible that Samma just knows in her heart that her partner is faithful? Maybe her claim to knowledge is based on the evidence of her partner's behaviour and so is justified; but could it just be based on the feeling in her heart? Many people would claim to know that God exists or to know that they will go to heaven, and they may have no rational justification for this, just a very strong feeling and belief. However, most people would doubt whether this would count as knowledge at all – specifically *because* there is no rational justification. But consider this case:

John has a rare gift. If you give him any date in the future, say 15 March 2123, he is able to tell you what day of the week this will be (for example, a Monday). He is unable to say how he does this, though he is incredibly accurate: 15 March 2123 will indeed be a Monday.

Would you say that John knows this? This is a case of true belief, but with no rational justification. As we discuss later, some philosophers claim a reliable process that produces the true beliefs is what counts as knowledge (see reliabilism on page 31). How John gets the answers right is a mystery, but he *is* very reliable. Justification, though nice, may not always be *necessary* for knowledge.

This possible counterexample aside, for the moment we will assume that knowledge does require justification. We will also assume that it requires belief and truth. Assuming all three are necessary, the next question is: are they jointly sufficient?

Issue: are the JTB conditions jointly sufficient?

We have seen why philosophers have felt that each condition is individually necessary; and hence that you cannot do without any one if you want to have knowledge. But if the traditional account of knowledge is right, we must also show that the conditions are jointly sufficient – in other words, that if you have all three, then you are guaranteed to have knowledge. So is justified, true belief sufficient for knowledge? Does J + T + B = K? As you may have seen in the activity on page 12, the J + T + B definition seems to match many everyday uses of the word 'knowledge', but maybe there are examples of J + T + B that do not equate to knowledge.

Cases of lucky true belief: Gettier-type counterexamples

The best way of showing that the JTB conditions are *not* sufficient would be to give examples of JTBs that do not count as examples of knowledge. In 1963, one philosopher, Edmund Gettier (1927–) did just this. Gettier published a short paper entitled 'Is justified, true belief knowledge?' The paper was only three sides long, but has had a large impact and led to many other philosophers writing papers, chapters and books exploring its consequences. Gettier himself never published any philosophy again.

His paper gives examples of *beliefs* which are both *true* and apparently *justified*, but which we are inclined not to count as examples of *knowledge*. In other words, while accepting that the three conditions are individually necessary, he questioned whether they were jointly sufficient. The examples he and others have subsequently used have become known as Gettier counterexamples.

Gettier's first example – Smith and Jones

The first example involves two men, Smith and Jones, both going for a job interview. Gettier writes:

> *Suppose that Smith and Jones have applied for a certain job. And suppose that Smith has strong evidence for the following conjunctive proposition:*
>
> *d) Jones is the man who will get the job, and Jones has ten coins in his pocket.*
>
> *Smith's evidence for d) might be that the president of the company assured him that Jones would in the end be selected, and that he, Smith, had counted the coins in Jones' pocket ten minutes ago. Proposition d) entails:*
>
> *e) The man who will get the job has ten coins in his pocket.*
>
> *Let us suppose that Smith sees the entailment from d) to e), and accepts e) on the grounds of d), for which he has strong evidence. In this case, Smith is clearly justified in believing that e) is true.*[7]

anthology 1.1

Gettier's language is a bit formal (he specialises in logic!), but what he is claiming is this: Smith has good evidence for believing that Jones will get the job and good evidence that Jones has ten coins in his pocket. From this, he then goes on to believe the proposition, 'The man who will get the job has ten coins in his pocket'. Now, as it turns out, there is an unexpected change of events and Jones does not get the job. Smith does. Also, by coincidence, Smith has exactly ten coins in his pocket (he did not know this earlier). This leads to a possible counterexample in the JTB account of knowledge. Did Smith know proposition e) 'The man who will get the job has ten coins in his pocket'?

a) Smith certainly was *justified* (to some extent) for his belief (he had counted Jones' coins and been told by the president of the company that Jones would get the job).
b) Smith's belief was *true*.
c) Smith had a *belief* that the man who would get the job had ten coins in his pocket.

Smith had a *justified, true belief* that 'The man who will get the job has ten coins in his pocket', but would you be willing to say that Smith knew it? If we are not willing to say that Smith knew it, then it seems that having a justified, true belief is not the same thing as having knowledge. The three elements are not sufficient conditions. Either the account is the wrong approach or some extra element is missing.

Most people would claim that Smith did *not* have knowledge. This is because there is luck involved. He was unlucky that his belief about Jones getting the job was wrong (although he lucked in with the job!), and was lucky that he also happened to have ten coins in his pocket. As suggested earlier, we have a strong intuition that knowledge should not involve luck.

Gettier's second example – Brown in Barcelona

Gettier gives a second example in his short paper. This one involves Mr Smith having plenty of evidence that his friend Mr Jones owns a Ford car. (Gettier does not say what this evidence is, but let us imagine that Mr Jones has talked about owning his lovely Ford just last week and Mr Smith saw him driving it that very day.) On the basis of this, he believes that a) *Jones owns a Ford*. Smith has another friend Mr Brown. He has no evidence of Mr Brown's whereabouts at the moment, but on the strength of his first belief is able to form a new disjunctive belief that c) *Jones owns a Ford or Brown is in Barcelona*. (Barcelona is chosen at random.) This belief is justified as Smith had no reason to doubt the first part. However, it turns out that Jones no longer owns a car (let us imagine he wrote it off in an accident and has been driving a hire car for the week, which was also a Ford), but by a weird coincidence, Brown, unbeknownst to Smith, was in Barcelona. So his belief that *Jones owns a Ford or Brown is in Barcelona* was true and was justified – but did he know it? Most of us would say not. As with the previous example, there seems to be a case of double luck. Smith was unlucky in his belief about Jones and the Ford and very lucky in his belief about Brown being in Spain. We have a strong intuition that knowledge does not involve luck, so would not want to count this case of an apparent justified, true belief as a case of knowledge.

Gettier's two examples convinced most philosophers that the account of knowledge as a justified, true belief needed some form of modification or patching up. The rest of this chapter consists of looking at these attempts to amend the definition.

Before we move to look at these, it is worth exploring some more Gettier-style counterexamples, where a justified, true belief seems to fall short of being knowledge.

Experimenting with ideas

Consider the Gettier-style counterexamples below. Then answer the questions that follow.

Example 1: killer whales

Imagine that one evening you watch a nature programme and you hear David Attenborough say that the killer whale is the fastest-swimming sea mammal. As a consequence, you acquire the belief that the killer whale is the fastest sea mammal. As a matter of fact, this belief is true: killer whales are indeed the fastest of all sea mammals. Moreover, it is justified since David Attenborough is a reliable source of information about wildlife. So here is a clear-cut case of a justified, true belief. However, unremarked by you, the evening in question was that of the first of April, and the nature programme was a spoof littered with amusing falsehoods about the natural world. Given this extra fact, could you still be said to know that the killer whale is the fastest sea mammal?

Example 2: hop, skip and jump

Jonathan comes home from work early in order to watch the world triple-jump championships. He does not know it, but the BBC is having technical difficulties with their broadcast, so to keep the viewers happy, they show a replay of the triple jump final from four years ago, and in the mayhem forget to put on the symbol that shows it to be a repeat. Jonathan switches on the TV and is excited to see Richard Long win the event with a jump of 18.27 metres. Naturally, he does not realise this was a replay. As it happens, while the replay was being shown, Richard Long did actually win this year's triple jump, remarkably with a jump of 18.27 metres. Does Jonathan know that Richard Long won the triple jump?

Example 3: the fake barn

A man, Barney, is driving, unknowingly, through a place called fake-barn county, where, by the side of the road they have built lots of fake barns consisting just of a barn front with nothing behind (like on a movie set). The driver does not pay much attention, but then looks to the side and sees a big red barn. On the basis of this, he believes there is a big red barn by the road. However, it just so happens that this is the only real barn in the whole area! Does Barney know there was a big red barn there?

Example 4: Taz and Boris Johnson

Today London is hosting a Boris Johnson lookalike day for charity. Thousands of Londoners are roaming the streets dressed up as the dishevelled politician, sporting appropriate wigs, and so on. Many of them are very convincing. Taz has just landed at Heathrow airport and knows nothing of the charity day. She takes a taxi to her hotel in Park Lane. While the taxi is driving into the centre of London, she passes many Boris Johnson lookalikes, but does not really notice them. As she gets out of the taxi to pay, she glances up and for a few seconds sees a man riding past on a pink bike looking just like Boris Johnson. It is, in fact, the real Boris Johnson. She stares in surprise for a moment. She goes into the hotel and texts her friend all about it. Does Taz know that Boris Johnson was riding a pink bike that morning?

Example 5: Luke and Boris Johnson

On the very same day, Luke was travelling to his office. (Unlike Taz, he knew about the Boris lookalike charity event.) Outside his office, Luke saw a 'Boris' cycle past on a pink bike. He was completely convinced it was the real Boris. It was not; it was a very good impersonator. Luke, seeing the fake and believing it to be real, then formed a belief that Boris Johnson was riding a pink bike that day, which of course he was. Does Luke know that Boris Johnson was riding a pink bike that day?

1. Do you think the person in each of the examples has knowledge?
2. Do you think the person has a justified, true belief?
3. Do you think these examples mean that having a justified, true belief is not the same thing as having knowledge?
4. Do these examples have anything in common?
5. Can you come up with your own Gettier-style counterexample showing a case of a justified, true belief that we are unlikely to accept as a case of knowing?

In each of the cases, the people have a *true belief* that seems to be reasonably *justified*, and so all three conditions of the JTB have been met, yet many would argue that they do not have *knowledge*. There seems to be a strong element of luck involved in each of these cases and we are not inclined to award knowledge on the basis of luck. However, there are some important similarities and differences between the cases.

In example 2, Jonathan was watching the wrong event, which just (luckily) happened to match the real event in some ways. In this case, the belief that he was watching this year's final was (unluckily) false, but the result on the replay (luckily) turned out to be true of this year's final event too. Jonathan did not watch the real event, but saw something false that was coincidentally true. This example matches Gettier's own example quite closely.

Fake barns

In examples 1, 3 and 4 something subtly different is going on. In example 1, you heard a true fact about a mammal in a programme that contained lots of other falsehoods. However, the fact you heard was true and your belief was not coincidentally true; it is just that in the context of the April Fool's programme it was lucky that the thing you remembered was one of the few true facts.

Example 3 is luckily true in the same way that example 1 is. It is the more famous example, such that examples 1, 3 and 4 can be termed fake barn-style cases (as opposed to Gettier-style).

In the fake barn case, Barney saw a real barn with his eyes, believed there was a real barn and there was a real barn. The luck involved is that it happened to be the only real barn for miles and he had no idea that the others were fakes. Like example 1, this relies on the wider context making the belief seem luckily true. In the other, Gettier-style counterexamples, a false belief/assumption turns out to be coincidentally true. So, we can define the two types as:

- Gettier counterexamples. These involve a belief about something/someone luckily being true about something/someone else.
- Fake barn cases. The belief is about the correct subject, but the believer does not know that she is in an unusual context which makes her belief seem luckily true.

Examples 4 and 5 show these two different types together. In example 5, Luke saw a fake Boris, but his belief was luckily true because of the coincidence that the real Boris was on a pink bike too. This is a standard Gettier example. Contrastingly, in case 4, Taz actually saw the real Boris and formed her belief based on seeing the man himself. There is no coincidence or error here. The only element of luck was that she did not know it was a lookalike day, so it could easily have been a fake that she saw. In other words, the context meant that there was a bit of luck involved. This is a fake barn-style Gettier counterexample.

Luke saw the wrong person and his belief was luckily true, whereas Taz saw the right person, but the context makes it seem a bit lucky. Who are you more inclined to say knew that Boris was on a pink bike – Taz, Luke or neither?

Some people are inclined to say that Taz *did* know that Boris was on a pink bike, and Barney *did* know there was a barn, and the viewer *did* know the fact about the killer whale. As we will see below, the fake barn-style cases come into the discussion quite a bit, and in some cases, philosophers have argued that these do count as knowledge and are not counterexamples at all. However, all of these examples seem to throw doubt on the idea that knowledge is simply justified, true belief. How are we to react to such problem cases?

Responses to the issues with the tripartite view

Initially, perhaps the most attractive response is to defend the traditional account by arguing that the reason that we are reluctant to say that the people above have knowledge is simply that their beliefs are not justified in the proper way. The idea would be that we need to define our notion of justification more strictly, so as to rule out these counterexamples. This is more or less the approach taken by all subsequent attempts to account for knowledge. We explore four key responses.

1 Justification should be so strong the belief *must* be true (infallibilism).
2 Justification should not be based on false beliefs (no false lemmas).
3 Justification should be based on reliable processes (reliabilism).
4 Beliefs should be true because they are based on skilful justification (epistemic virtue).

Although each theory is different, they all attempt to overcome the Gettier examples in a similar way. They seek to show that, according to *their* definitions, the Gettier examples would not be classed as knowledge in the first place.

Infallibilism

Gettier-style counterexamples rely on cases where the believer seems to have reasonable justification for their belief, but where there is a large element of luck involved in their belief being a true belief. And, as we saw with Plato previously (page 11), we are not inclined to award 'knowledge' to anyone on the basis of luck. One way to remove this element of luck from the process is to require the justification to be so strong that the truth is guaranteed – in other words, to claim that knowledge can only be allowed if the belief is infallible (meaning impossible to be wrong).

Infallibilism (sometimes called the guarantee condition) is the theory that we should only count as knowledge those things which we cannot rationally doubt. Note that infallibilism is *not* the claim that we must *feel* certain in our beliefs to have knowledge. Certainty is a SUBJECTIVE feeling, one that can fluctuate with moods and might vary between people who have exactly the same evidence for a belief.

Essential Terminology

Even within one person, the feeling of certainty may vary with mood or stress, but we would not want to say that knowledge fluctuates accordingly. Infallibilism is not the claim that knowledge is true belief that you feel certain about, but the much stronger claim that we should only count as knowledge those things which we cannot rationally doubt.

Consider the activity in the margin; most infallibilists would claim that only B, C, D and F would count as knowledge because they cannot be rationally doubted. This is because they all concern knowledge of our own minds. To see why, let us consider the example of pain C. You may be mistaken about what is causing you pain, say because you feel pain in a limb which has been amputated, or because you are a brain in a vat and have no body at all. But even if you are a brain in a vat (see page 174), you cannot be mistaken about the fact that you are feeling the pain. In other words, if you are feeling pain, then it is not possible for you not *really* to be in pain. And if no alternatives are possible, then your belief that you are in pain is infallible. Beliefs about our own mental states contrast in this respect with beliefs about the external world. For beliefs about the world outside the mind need to correspond with external reality in order to be true, and yet it may always be doubted that they do. But beliefs about my own mind, precisely because they do not go beyond what I am directly aware of, leave no room for doubt. Without a gap between the belief and an external reality, there is no space for the sceptic to exploit, and so such knowledge appears to be infallible.

The philosopher René Descartes (1596–1650) assumed an infallibilist approach to knowledge in the *Meditations* when trying to find a belief that could not be doubted, where no HYPOTHETICAL alternatives were possible. His plan was to doubt all of his beliefs, so that only those that cannot be rationally doubted would remain. He could then build up a system of knowledge where every belief was infallible.

Some years ago I was struck by how many false things I had believed, and by how doubtful was the structure of beliefs that I had based on them. I realized that if I wanted to establish anything in the sciences that was stable and likely to last, I needed – just once in my life – to demolish everything completely and start again from the foundation.[8]

▶ **ACTIVITY**

I Which of the following beliefs A–H cannot be rationally doubted?

2 Which of these have alternative possibilities to the belief being true?

3 Are points I and 2 above asking the same thing?

A You believe that it will rain tomorrow.

B You believe that 2 + 2 = 4.

C You believe you currently are in pain or not.

D You believe that you are experiencing black ink-coloured lettering sensations that seem to spell out words and sentences.

E You believe that you are reading a book.

F You believe you know that you exist.

G You believe you ate breakfast this morning.

H You believe the sun will rise tomorrow.

Descartes – a quick biography

Descartes was born into a relatively wealthy family living in La Haye, in northwestern France. At around the age of nine, the young Descartes was sent to study at a nearby Jesuit college. Because of ill health, Descartes was allowed the unusual privilege of lying in bed until 11 a.m. each morning – a habit that stayed with him for the rest of his life.

After completing his studies at university, Descartes joined the army. During this period, when shut away in a small, stove-heated room in Germany, Descartes claimed to have a series of visions, which he interpreted as bestowing on him a divine mission to seek the truth through the use of reason. He pursued this mission throughout his life.

In his later years, Descartes was persuaded to move to Sweden to teach Queen Christina. The Queen required her philosophy lessons to begin at five in the morning. Descartes, being accustomed to much later starts, died after about six months of this tough new regime.

After a slow start, Descartes' fame had grown steadily throughout his lifetime, particular in his later years. After his death, he became increasingly renowned. A measure of his fame is that during the transportation of his body from Sweden back to France, several pieces of his corpse were removed by relic collectors!

As we will see on page 120, Descartes concluded that he could *know* that he existed as this was impossible to rationally doubt (as someone must be doing the doubting!). Descartes called these infallible beliefs *clear and distinct ideas*, and these would be the building blocks of his new system of knowledge. Descartes also would have counted B, C, D and F as examples of CLEAR AND DISTINCT IDEAS that cannot be doubted.

Infallibilism: knowledge and belief

Although we are using examples of *beliefs* here, some holders of the theory of infallibilism claim that we should distinguish belief from knowledge. They claim that knowledge is not a kind of belief; it is a separate thing. Imagine that you are in your bedroom and you hear an engine-style noise coming from outside your house. According to this version of the infallibilism, you would know that you are experiencing a certain kind of revving noise at that moment. You cannot be wrong about this, even if you are dreaming or hallucinating. No alternatives are possible whereby you think you are experiencing a noise but you are not. This is infallible, so you know that you are experiencing a noise. You might *believe* that the noise is caused by a car outside, but you cannot *know* this, as there are other possible alternatives. In claiming there is a car outside, you are making an INFERENCE and you may be wrong. In this way, some infallibilists claim that belief and knowledge are different things.

Beliefs only occur when doubt *is* possible and knowledge occurs when it is impossible. To show this difference, the philosopher Price cites the example of pain. When you are in pain, you *know* you are; you cannot be wrong. He claims that it makes no sense to say you *also* believe you are in pain, as you know you are.[9] It is just not an issue of belief. Someone else may observe you and infer that you are in pain. In this case, the person would hold a *belief* about your pain. They would not know you were in pain – as there is the possibility of an alternative explanation/error (you could be faking it!). But there is no possibility of your being wrong about your pain, so you *know* that you are in pain. Knowledge involves no other possibilities, but beliefs involve other possibilities and therefore may involve erroneous inferences.

The standard theory of knowledge suggests that it is a form of justified belief. However, some infallibilists suggest that belief and knowledge are different beasts. The next activity in the margin might make you lean one way or the other. Question 3 is the important one. If you feel that the cases of knowledge involve belief, then you side with the standard theory. If you feel that none of the cases of knowledge involve belief then you may agree, along with some infallibilists, that knowledge is not a form of belief, but a different type of thing. This means that you would not agree with the claim earlier (page 15) that belief is a necessary condition for knowledge.

Summary of infallibilism

Should we adopt infallibilism? On the positive side, infallibilism is not open to Gettier counterexamples. None of the examples given would count as knowledge in the first place, as all are open to some doubt/alternative explanations. Once knowledge is restricted to those things that cannot be doubted, there is no room for Gettier counterexamples to thrive. This is because Gettier examples necessarily involve beliefs which might have been false, but turn out by luck to be true. Another positive feature of this theory is that it accords with our intuition that knowledge involves a level of certainty – although in this case it is absolute certainty!

The main criticism of the theory (and it is a big one) is that it goes against our intuition that we can know lots of things. Infallibilism would imply that we have very little knowledge. For example, we cannot acquire knowledge from television documentaries, since it is always possible that the programme makers are pulling our legs. We cannot gain knowledge of what time it is, as it always possible that any/every clock might be wrong. Those apples in my fruit bowl might be wax ones; they might not be apples at all.

According to the infallibilist, what we can know is rather limited. We can know some logical truths (things that are true by definition), such as a triangle has three sides. This cannot be doubted, as there are no alternatives. We can also know facts about our minds, such as the sensations we experience. We may also be able to know one or two other things through careful, undoubtable reasoning, such as 'I exist'. In the *Meditations*, this is about all that Descartes establishes with certainty. (He establishes more if you accept his proof of God!) Under the theory of infallibilism, this would be the extent of our knowledge. All other things we ordinarily claim to know are susceptible to alternative accounts.

Now, this may not be a problem. It may be that our common definition of knowledge needs such radical revision. This is certainly the approach that many philosophers (such as Descartes) have taken in the past. However, most contemporary philosophers are reluctant to pursue such a radical redefinition of our ordinary view of what counts as knowledge. To diverge too radically from common usage, they argue, involves our leaving behind the very concept we are setting out to define. Only by holding some sort of connection with ordinary usage and our ordinary intuitions can we be said to be analysing the concept of knowledge at all. We should

▶ **ACTIVITY: BELIEF OR KNOWLEDGE?**

Are some infallibilists right to distinguish belief and knowledge? For A–H, decide:

1 Is this a case of knowledge?
2 Is this a case of belief?
3 Which of the cases of knowledge are also cases of belief?

A Shaffique knows that God exists.
B John knows he is in pain.
C Alison knows that Arsenal will win the Champions League next year.
D Billie knows she is awake.
E Reuben knows he ate cornflakes for breakfast.
F Casper knows that Shakespeare wrote *Hamlet*.
G David knows that dinosaurs once roamed the planet.
H You know you are reading a book.

be asking how we know what we know, and so getting clear about what our concept of knowledge actually is. We should not seriously be wondering whether we really know what we commonly suppose we do. Infallibilism seems to be prescribing what our concept of knowledge *should* be, rather than analysing/describing what it *is*. We do have an intuition that knowledge should involve a level of certainty, but infallibilism seems to be defining certainty, rather than knowledge.

J + T + B + N (no false lemmas)

So far we have seen the traditional account of knowledge as JTB (justified, true belief) called into question, as some cases of JTB seem to be luckily true (Gettier counterexamples). We would not want to count these as knowledge, so need to amend the account of JTB.

Our first solution was to strengthen our account of justification. This way we can argue that Smith was never properly justified in his belief about the person getting the job having ten coins in pockets (and so on), so this was never a case of knowledge to begin with. However, if we take an infallibilist position and define 'proper justification' in such a strict way as to eliminate the possibility of error, this creates another problem. It restricts knowledge too much. It involves us in saying that we do not really know the things we ordinarily think we know and so entails a radical redefinition of our concept of knowledge.

A less drastic approach is to tighten the account of proper justification just a little – enough to restrict Gettier-style counterexamples, but still allow most cases of JTB to hold as knowledge. The easiest way to do this would be to say that knowledge consists of true, justified beliefs which are not Gettier counterexamples nor lucky beliefs. Though tempting, this approach would fall foul to Zagzebski's requirement that the definition of knowledge should not be *ad hoc*. That is, it should not be a definition that is specific to meeting a particular problem – which this would be.

No false lemmas

Another approach is to look for the reason *why* some JTBs can be luckily true and try to exclude this reason from our account of knowledge. This is exactly the approach taken by the *no false lemma* account of knowledge. Note that a LEMMA is not some kind of suicidal, furry animal, but a term used in logic and mathematics, formally meaning a subsidiary proposition that is assumed to be true and is used to demonstrate another proposition. For our purposes, a lemma can be taken to mean a belief or assumption that is held to be true and is used to justify a piece of knowledge.

The no false lemma account of knowledge tries to pinpoint why it is that some seemingly 'justified' beliefs can be 'luckily' true. The suggestion is that in Gettier's two examples (see page 21), the 'justification' for the beliefs should not be considered valid because they both involve, or rely upon, a false belief. In the first case, Smith's belief that *the man who will get the job has ten coins in his pocket* was based on the *false* belief that *Jones would get the job*.

Smith's reasoning might have proceeded like this:

a) I believe that Jones has ten coins in his pocket (having seen them).
b) I believe that Jones will get the job (having been told as much).
c) I believe that the person who gets the job will have ten coins in his pocket.

However, b) is a false belief/assumption. It is a *false lemma*. Gettier's second example also involves the use of a false assumption in the believer's reasoning (*that Jones owns a Ford*). So, to eliminate these counterexamples, the no false lemma theory claims that knowledge is a justified, true belief, where the justification is not based on a false assumption. To put it more formally, it claims that:

Knowledge = J + T + B + N (where N = no false lemmas)

This theory adds an extra 'external' element to the account of the knowledge. A believer may have strong justification for a given belief, but if her belief was based on a false lemma and is 'luckily' true, then even though it may feel to her like a case of knowledge, it is not one. This seems a reasonable addition to the account of knowledge. In most cases, when we justify a belief using a false lemma, the belief itself will turn out to be false, and so would not count as knowledge.

For example, imagine you were checking the football results in the back of a Sunday newspaper, but without realising it was a paper that was a year old. In doing this, you have made a false assumption/lemma. As a result, most of the beliefs you form as to Saturday's football scores will simply be false in the real world. However, if one of them happens to be true by coincidence, then we would not want to count this as knowledge either, as we do not want knowledge to be based on false beliefs that luckily turn out to be true.

How does the no false lemmas theory cope with Gettier?

The no false lemmas theory copes well with some standard Gettier cases. We should expect this, as it was one of the first attempted 'solutions' to the Gettier problem, and the two cases presented by Gettier both rely on false lemmas to justify the belief. However, in other cases it is not so clear that a false belief was involved. Consider this example:

You are driving through a small village at around noon and look up at the clock tower to check the time. The clock says 12 o'clock and so you come to believe that it is 12 o'clock. In fact, it is 12 o'clock. Checking a clock is an excellent justification for your belief and so we have here an example of justified, true belief. However, unbeknown to you, the clock has in fact stopped. And the fact that it was telling the correct time at precisely the moment when you chanced to look up at it is a remarkable coincidence. Can you be said to know at that moment that it is 12 o'clock?

Few would want to claim this as knowledge, as your belief that it is *12 o'clock* seems luckily true. But does this rely on a false belief? You see the time on a clock and believe it to be 12 o'clock, and even though the clock is broken, the time is coincidentally right. In this example, your thought processes might go something like this:

a) You believe it is roughly the middle of the day.
b) You see a clock that says 12 o'clock.
c) You believe it is now 12 o'clock.

In this case, your belief that it is 12 o'clock is not based on any obvious false lemma. You had a rough belief about the right time, which was true. You saw a clock, which did indeed say 12 o'clock. No PREMISE/belief was false,

► **ACTIVITY**
1 Revisit Gettier's two examples on page 21 and the counter-examples on page 22.
2 Do all these cases rely on a belief?
3 If so, what is the false belief?

yet you would not have knowledge. As such, the theory of K = J + T + B + N must, on the face of it, not work, as this looks like a case of J + T + B + N *not* equalling K.

Learn More

From no false lemmas to no essential false assumptions

It may be possible, however, to resurrect a different version of this theory if we also include tacit or hidden assumptions when we consider what might count as a false lemma. Revisiting the case of the clock, if we included hidden assumptions as well as consciously held beliefs, we could outline the reasoning process as follows:

a) You believe it is roughly the middle of the day.
b) You see a clock that says 12 o'clock.
c) You (tacitly) believe that the clock is working (hidden assumption).
d) You believe it is 12 o'clock.

This version of the reasoning process includes the new assumption c). It is unlikely that you actually stop and think about this every time you look at a clock: in other words, it is not a consciously held belief. However, you could argue that it is an essential assumption that you make in concluding that it is 12 o'clock. As this is a false assumption, then you do not know it is 12 o'clock and this particular Gettier problem no longer exists.

As we saw above, the no false lemmas theory can cope with some of the standard Gettier examples by claiming they would not count as knowledge in the first place. And by modifying this theory to include hidden assumptions, the no essential false assumptions theory can cope with an even wider range of standard Gettier cases. However, both theories run into trouble with some standard Gettier-style cases based on perceptual evidence, and also with some fake barn-style cases.

Gettier cases based on perception

You walk into the kitchen and see two apples in the fruit bowl. From this, you then believe that there are two apples in the kitchen. Now, it turns out the items in the fruit bowl were fake, wax apples that your mum/friend/flat mate has purchased for an art project. But in the cupboard, out of sight, there are, indeed, two apples. So your belief that there are two apples in the kitchen is correct. But did you know it?

In this standard Gettier-style case it is not clear what false lemma, or hidden assumption, is being made. When we form beliefs based on perception of the world, there is no reasoning process involved, such that we might go wrong with a false assumption. You see two 'apples'. That is all there is to it. You *could* try to argue that your belief is based on a hidden assumption that the apples were real, or that you are not asleep or being deceived. However, it is not obvious that any reasoning process is present in such cases, such that an assumption, hidden or otherwise, could take place. You simply see two 'apples'.

Hidden assumptions and fake barns

You might be persuaded that, in fact, there is a hidden assumption in the example above. But in the case of the fake barns, this becomes even less plausible. Barney is driving, unknowingly, through Fake Barn County. He looks up and sees the one real barn. His thought process (if there is one at all) is something like this.

A Barney seeks a big barn.
B Barney believes there is a big barn.

In this case, there are no false lemmas and there do not seem to be any essential false assumptions either. We cannot reasonably claim that Barney is assuming he is *not* in Fake Barn County as he may never have heard of such a place. Although it is hard to define what might reasonably count as a hidden assumption when arriving at a belief, it would be hard to come up with a definition that would include this as an assumption!

Interestingly, the philosopher William Lycan (1945–), who devised the no essential false assumptions theory, actually agrees with this CONCLUSION.[10] He agrees that in some fake barn-style cases, the belief does not involve any essential false assumptions, but instead claims that these are *actual* cases of knowledge. Barney does know there is a big barn sitting there. This counter-example is not a counterexample at all. It is simply a case of knowledge.

These cases all seem to involve an element of luck, although the luck is derived more from having a true belief in a rather haphazard context, rather than simply having a belief (based on a false belief) that is coincidentally true. Our intuitions seem to suggest that knowledge should not involve luck, so should we rule out the case or not? Luck can of course be involved in acquiring knowledge without ruling it out. We may discover many things about the world by chance; however, this is different from holding a belief that is luckily/coincidentally true. The fake barn cases seem to raise something of a problem with our luck intuition. Yes, there is luck involved, but there is no false belief/coincidence involved either. Perhaps it is up to you, the reader, to decide whether these cases count as knowledge or not …

Summary of no false lemmas

Gettier's initial counterexamples rely on someone holding a false belief, then making another belief based on this that is luckily true. The no false lemmas theory was devised to overcome these counterexamples by showing that they were based on a false premise, and so were not true. The no essential false assumptions theory expands on this by ruling out knowledge in cases not just involving false premises, but also false hidden assumptions. This overcomes a wider range of possible counterexamples. However, the fake barn case involves neither false premises nor assumptions. According to both these theories, these cases should then count as knowledge, but our intuition about luck suggests that they do not. Lycan, in defending his theory, suggests that, yes, they do count as knowledge. The fake barn counterexamples are not counterexamples at all, as they count as knowledge.

Reliabilism (R + T + B)

So far, we have explored the idea that knowledge is justified, true belief. Through Gettier, we have seen that there are examples of JTBs that we would not count as knowledge and have explored different ways of amending the standard account to try to overcome these counterexamples. So far, the approaches we have looked at have tried to shore up the idea of what counts as knowledge-worthy

▶ **ACTIVITY**

Let us reconsider those fake barn cases. Do you agree with Lycan that they count as knowledge?

1 Example 1 on page 22: you hear a true fact in an otherwise fallacious spoof documentary (you do not realise it is a spoof). Do you now know that the killer whale is the fastest sea mammal? There are no false lemmas. There are no essential false assumptions. (Well, you could reasonably claim that there is an assumption the programme is not a spoof documentary, but we will overlook this.) Do you know the whale-related fact?

2 Example 4 on page 22: does Taz *know* that Boris is on a pink bike?

3 The fake barn case itself on page 22: does Barney know he is looking at a big red barn?

31

justification: first, the idea that adequate justification must rule out *all* other possibilities and so guarantee the truth (infallibility); and second, that adequate justification must not be based on any false premises or assumptions. Below we will explore two very different approaches. The first approach (reliabilism) argues that rather than seeking the right sort of justification for knowledge, we should seek the reliable processes that tend to yield truth. The second approach (virtue epistemology) explores the sorts of qualities a good 'knower' might have.

A reliable process

The theory of reliabilism, or rather the theory of *process reliabilism* that we will be exploring here, can get quite complicated, and there are many different varieties of the theory. However, at its heart is a fairly simple idea. Consider these two cases:

1 You read in *Viz*/the *National Enquirer* that a man in China has 15 fingers.
2 You read in *The Guardian*/*The Times* that porcupines are mostly nocturnal.

In the first case, even if it were true, could you be said to *know* that the Chinese man has 15 fingers? Probably not. Can you be said to know that porcupines are mostly nocturnal? Probably yes.

One key difference between the two is that the information in the second case is from a reliable newspaper. There may be other factors at play as to why we might attribute knowledge in the second case but not the first, but the reliability of the source is likely to be a key factor. The more reliable the source, the more likely we are to say that the discerning reader *knows* the fact.

But what do we mean by a reliable newspaper? In this case, we mean that a reliable newspaper is one that tells the truth with a high level of regularity. The more often a source or process produces the truth, the more reliable it is. Reliability, in this sense, is defined in terms of truth giving.

Reliabilism is a theory of knowledge that claims the reliability of the cognitive process involved in generating a belief is the key factor in whether we should call it knowledge or not. Formally, the theory claims that knowledge is a true belief that is produced by a reliable process (K = T + B + R).

Experimenting with ideas

1 What cognitive process is in play in each of the cases A–H?
2 On a scale of 1–10, rank how reliable you think each cognitive process is for arriving at true beliefs (1 is not reliable and 10 is reliable).
3 In all of the cases the belief is true, but which of the cases would you class as examples of *knowing*?
4 Do your answers to question 2 correlate with your answers to question 3?
5 If you enjoyed this activity, then repeat it with the examples on page 13.

A Adding six and four in your head to make ten.
B Eating hallucinogenic mushrooms and believing your friend is about to call you. (She does.)
C Reading (and believing) on www.conspiracies4ever.com that the Prime Minister worked for the Bank of England. (Theresa May did.)
D Believing that you will have children because of the pattern of lines in your hand. (In fact, you do go on to have children.)
E Seeing your friend up close and believing he is back from his holiday. (He is.)

F Seeing a hazy black and white shape in a field far away and believing there is a cow in the field. (There is a cow, but this is out of sight. What you can see is a horse.)

G Multiplying 246 by 327 in your head to give 80,442.

H Reading on Wikipedia (and believing) that Nelson died at the Battle of Trafalgar.

Although these beliefs were all true, you might not count all of them as examples of knowledge. What this activity may show is that there is a strong correlation between how generally reliable a cognitive process is for producing/arriving at the truth and whether we would attribute knowledge. Some of the cognitive processes above are not very reliable, and even though truth was achieved, for some processes this would be a rarity. A reliabilist claims that this link between reliability and knowledge is precisely because knowledge is a true belief that is produced by a reliable cognitive process (K = T + B + R).

How reliable a process needs to be for knowledge to be attributed is a matter of debate; some might count tricky mental arithmetic as reliable and others not. But this elasticity precisely matches our ordinary concept of knowledge, where some are more willing to attribute knowledge than others. In general, processes such as wishfully believing, seeing when hallucinating, glimpsing from a distance, complex mental arithmetic, remembering things from a long time ago and guessing do not often regularly produce a true belief. As a result, they are not reliable cognitive process and the beliefs they generate should not be classed as knowledge. On the other hand, processes such as seeing things up close, simple arithmetic and reading from a trustworthy source tend to produce true beliefs and so are reliable and should be classed as knowledge.

To see how the theory works, consider this example:

a) An experienced vet picks up a guinea pig, examines it and concludes it is a male.

b) A ten-year-old boy notices a guinea pig twitch its ear when he calls it 'Hector', so concludes it is a male as 'Hector' is a boy's name.

In both cases they are right – the guinea pig *is* a male. Do they both *know* the sex? The vet has studied animals to the extent that she has reliable cognitive processes (recognising features and comparing these to memories, and so on), which enable her to reliably identify the sex of guinea pigs. She has knowledge. The ten-year-old boy's process does not reliably produce true belief, so is not knowledge.

A reliable process as a definition of justification

Notice that the account of reliabilism suggests that K = T + B + R, not that K = J + T + B + R. The J is missing in the definition. Reliabilism is *not* saying that knowledge is a *justified*, true belief that has been formed by a reliable process, it *is* saying that knowledge is a true belief that has been formed by a reliable process. In other words, the idea of a reliable process is not in addition to the justification condition, it *replaces* the justified condition. It is more or less claiming that what we mean by a justified belief (for the purposes of knowledge) is a belief which is produced by a reliable process. Below we explore further whether it is acceptable to explain justification in this way. But first we turn to Gettier.

Figure 1.7a A reliable process. The farmer sees the sheep and clicks the counter as each one enters the field. This is a reliable process as her counter works perfectly; she gets it right nearly all the time. The farmer **knows** she has 19 sheep in the field.

Figure 1.7b This farmer just looks in the field and makes an estimate. She believes there are 20 sheep. This process is not reliable. Even if it is true, she does not know this.

Reliabilism and Gettier: the problem

How does reliabilism fare with Gettier counterexamples? Can the theory claim that these are not cases of knowledge and so are not valid counterexamples? There is no straightforward answer to this. Reliabilism grew out of philosopher Alvin Goldman's (1938–) causal theory of knowledge, which was developed as a reaction to Gettier.[11] However, since then, reliabilism has grown into a whole area of philosophy itself, much of it connected with the relationship between justification and reliable processes, and this has somewhat overshadowed the Gettier debate. We have seen that the standard JTB definition of knowledge needs some patching up to cope with Gettier. Reliabilism replaces the justification condition to create a new theory where knowledge is reliably produced true belief (RTB). Just in the way that the JTB account needed patching up to cope with Gettier, so does the RTB account.

Consider Gettier's second example (page 21). In this case, Smith uses verbal and visual evidence to believe that *Jones owns a Ford*. These are pretty reliable processes, meaning they are processes that very frequently yield truth. We can rely on them. Smith then joins this belief to another arbitrary one about Mr Brown being in Barcelona, to form the new disjunctive belief, *either Jones owns a Ford or Mr Brown is in Barcelona*. Although this belief is a bit weird, inferring disjunctives (propositions with the word 'or' in) is a standard logical procedure. If you believe A is true, then it is fine to believe that either A or B (or both) is true. So, in this example, we seem to have a case of a reliably formed, true belief. So, according to reliabilism, it should be a case of knowledge. Yet it was luckily true (Brown being in Barcelona was a coincidence) and we are not inclined to count it as a case of knowledge. How can the reliabilist respond? There are many different responses out there. We briefly explore three of them.

Solving Gettier using reliabilism: redefining the process

In the case above, we described the cognitive process in terms of forming an initial belief from visual and verbal evidence (*Jones owns a Ford*) and then inferring a new disjunctive belief from the initial one (*Jones owns a Ford or Mr Brown is in Barcelona*). And we suggested that this is a reliable process (or *processes*, as there are two of them in play). Notice that these processes were described using very general terms: *visual evidence* and *inferring*. We could easily describe the second stage of Smith's cognitive process differently. Instead of saying it was a case of inferring (from A, to A or B), we could describe it as a case of inferring from a *false belief* (that *Jones owns a Ford*) to a new belief (*Jones owns a Ford or Mr Brown is in Barcelona*). Put this way, it is not a reliable process. Making inferences from any false belief is not likely to reliably produce truth, so it is not a reliable process. By reclassifying the process, the reliabilist can show that the process at play was not a reliable one. In both of Gettier's examples, the final belief is inferred from a false belief (or lemma), so the reliabilist can say that the process was not reliable and this was not a case of knowledge.

Criticism

Although this approach solves the two Gettier cases, it does raise a general concern with reliabilism as a whole, which is, how general or specific should we be when describing a belief-forming process?

Consider the case of seeing a friend on the other side of the road on a slightly foggy day. This single example could be described in lots of different ways. As an example of *seeing* (which is fairly reliable). As *identifying someone across the street walking fairly fast* (less reliable). As *identifying someone across the street, walking fast, on a foggy day* (even less reliable). Or perhaps as *identifying someone who is wearing highly distinguishing clothing* (she was wearing her crazy customised yellow jacket) (much more reliable). The event was exactly the same in each case, it is just being described in different ways – each of which might affect how reliable we think of the underlying process as being.

Every example of gaining knowledge from a reliable process is unique. Each individual case can be termed a *token* case of knowledge. However, for reliabilism to work, it has to be a more general theory that describes the *types* of processes that are generally truth-bearing. But deciding how general these types should be has proved to be a challenge for the theory of reliabilism. If we define a process narrowly enough (for example, 'Amy looking at a peach from 10 metres away on an overcast day'), then each case becomes unique and we are unable to say whether the process, in general, is reliable. It will either be 100 per cent reliable or 0 per cent reliable, as there is only one such case! If we make a case too general (for example, 'seeing things') and claim it as reliable, then the theory cannot cope with legitimate exceptions such as 'seeing things from a distance in poor light' or (as in the case of fake barns) 'seeing things in highly deceptive circumstances', which are not reliable processes. Accurately classifying a token example into a general type of reliable process has proved a problem for the theory, though one that philosophers are actively working on.

Solving Gettier using reliabilism: no relevant alternatives

Goldman (the father of reliabilism) suggested that we should only count a process as reliable if that process is able to distinguish between the truth and other relevant possibilities. Goldman gave the example of identical twins, Trudy and Judy.[12] Imagine you have met them once, very briefly. A few weeks later, you see one twin up close and believe that it is Judy. It is. But did you know it? Goldman suggests that a relevant alternative is that it could have been Trudy. Would you have spotted that? If not, then your process of identifying the twin is not reliable enough, as it could not distinguish between the truth (Judy) and a relevant alternative (Trudy). As such, you would not *know* it was Judy. However, if you *can* reliably tell them apart, then you would know it was Judy (even if you did not know *how* you were able to reliably tell them apart). Goldman developed this approach, in part, to deal with the fake barn case. Recall that Barney sees the only real barn in Fake Barn County, so his belief that there is a barn is lucky and should not count as knowledge. Now, in general, seeing objects from fairly close is a reliable process. However, in this unusual context, would Barney be able to distinguish between seeing the real barn and seeing a relevant alternative (in this case, a fake barn)? Probably not. In which case, his belief was not formed from a reliable process and Barney did not know there was a barn there. This is an intuitively plausible solution to the fake barn case. Consider this example. You, presumably, have a reliable way of identifying your favourite trainers. But imagine they were stolen and placed in a room of identical used trainers, all the same size. Would you 'know' which are yours? Is your normal process of identification able to distinguish between all of these relevant alternatives?

Note that on this version of reliabilism, the successful knower only has to be able to distinguish between *relevant* alternatives and not between *all* alternative possibilities – for example, the possibility that you are a brain in vat or being deceived by a demon (see page 173). To require you to be able to reliably distinguish between *all* possible alternatives would be to give an infallibilist account of knowledge. The challenge for this variation of reliabilism is to decide what counts as a relevant alternative for the purposes of classing a process as reliable.

Solving Gettier using reliabilism: add a sensitivity condition

Another (very similar) Gettier-busting way of patching up reliabilism is the philosopher Robert Nozick's (1938–2002) *sensitivity condition*.[13] Here, a process is a reliable way of generating a belief as long as:

If *p* were false, *S* would not believe that *p*.

For example, imagine you are holding a furry creature in your hand and believe it to be a hamster. It is a hamster. But do you know it? This depends on whether your belief is sensitive to the truth. If it were not a hamster (say, a guinea pig), would you still believe it was a hamster? If you would no longer believe it was, then your original belief that it is a hamster is sensitive to the truth, and you know it is a hamster. If you would still believe it is a hamster even when it is not, then your original belief is not sensitive to it being false and is not a case of knowledge.

This approach works well with most Gettier examples (although it is possible to construct ones where it does not work). Recall Gettier's first example (page 21) and Smith's belief that:

P   The person getting the job has ten coins in his pocket.

This was luckily true, as Smith, not realising *he* would get the job, had no idea that he also had ten coins in his pocket. Now if P had been false (for example, if Smith had 12 coins in his pocket), would Smith still believe P? Yes, he would – he had no idea how many coins were in his own pocket. Smith's belief is *not* sensitive to P being false. Because of this, Smith does not know P and it is not an example of knowledge. Likewise Smith's weird belief that *Jones owns a Ford or Brown is in Barcelona*: if this was false – if Brown had been, say, in Paris – would Smith still have held his belief? Yes, he would. He had no idea where Brown was. Again, Smith's belief is not sensitive to it being false, so Smith did not have knowledge, even though it was a true belief.

By *reclassifying the process* or by adding either the *sensitivity* or the no *relevant alternatives* conditions, reliabilism is able to cope with most Gettier counter-examples.

Reliable process or justification: are they the same?

We have seen that reliabilism replaces the 'justified' condition for knowledge (J) with the idea of a reliable process (R). Some people have criticised this switch, arguing that knowledge needs justification and this is a different sort of thing from a reliable process. The two cannot be equated; JTB is not the same thing as RTB. One difference, they claim, is that justifications are *internal* to the believer. This means they involve conscious thoughts that the thinker is aware of, and as such, the believer can tell you why and how their beliefs are justified – for example, 'I saw it with my own eyes', or 'John told me'. However, being a part of a reliable process does not necessarily involve conscious thought processes. The reliable processee (person involved in the reliable process) cannot necessarily tell you that the process is reliable, or necessarily explain the process. In this sense, reliable processes can be *external* to the believer, in as much as they cannot always tell you if the process was reliable or not. The criticism concludes that as justifications are internal and reliable processes are external, they cannot be the same thing.

Reliable process or justification: which is best?

Consider the example on page 20 again, with the gifted John who can tell what day of the week any calendar date in the future will be. Would you say that John knows which day of the week a particular date will be? He certainly has a belief that it is true. You would not say his belief is lucky, as he seems to have an ability to predict the day. However, he does not seem to have any sort of justification that a person who typically knows what day a future date might be would have,

▶ **ACTIVITY**

Revisit the Gettier counter-examples (page 22).

1 For each case, decide if the process leading to the belief was a reliable one or not.
2 Can you reclassify the process (for example, not a case of *seeing*, but of *seeing in deceptive circumstances*) to show that the process was not a reliable one, so is not a case of knowledge?
3 Would the believer in each case be able to distinguish between relevant alternatives?
4 Is the belief in each case sensitive to the truth/falsity of what is being believed?

such as 'I have a spreadsheet that works out the days', or 'I looked it up on a calendar website', or 'My phone can tell me'. According to the JTB definition, John would not know what day of the week it would be as he lacks this sort of justification. According to the RTB, John does know what the date will be. His accuracy means that the process is reliable. John has a true belief that is reliably formed, so he has knowledge, even though John could not describe the process. This example could be a strength or weakness of the theory, depending on your intuitions about whether John has knowledge or not.

In favour of replacing J with R

Some see moving away from internal justification to external processes as a strength of reliabilism. One possible advantage is that it provides an account of how animals have knowledge. According to the JTB account of knowledge, animals are unlikely to have knowledge as they could not justify their beliefs. Reliabilism, however, would disagree. Animals have evolved to have reliable processes of vision, hearing, memory and so on that enable them to eat the right food and avoid the right dangers. Although animals may not have propositional knowledge in quite the same way (for example, 'I know that ...'), they certainly have reliable processes that move from sensory input to the ability to accurately interact with the world, such that we can call it knowledge of some kind. The RTB account of knowledge can account for this in a way that the JTB account cannot. Again, this could be a strength or weakness, depending on your view of animal knowledge.

Another strength of the RTB account is that the term 'justification' is quite open and vague. It is not easy to articulate what might count as suitable justification for the purposes of knowledge. Reliabilism, on the other hand, gives a simple answer: a belief is sufficiently 'justified' if it is caused by a reliable process. This means a process that regularly produces true belief. The old way of explaining knowledge in terms of justification is to explain one epistemic term (knowledge) in terms of another (justification). This, it can be argued, will never produce a satisfactory answer. Defining knowledge in terms of the process that leads to true belief is a much better approach. This could potentially move the question of knowledge from philosophy into that of cognitive science. Instead of philosophers giving 'internal' accounts of which justifications are good ones, cognitive scientists can give 'external' accounts of the neurological processes that lead to true belief – for example, exploring how sight and memory combine to form recognition and reliable identification.

Against replacing J with R

One argument against replacing J with R is that the two concepts are not the same thing. This can be shown by considering how the two accounts respond to radical SCEPTICISM, specifically the idea that we might be a brain in a vat (BIV) (see page 174).

Consider the activity in the margin. A typical justification might go along the lines of, 'I recognise it as a pen, it feels like a pen, I can write with it', and so on. These justifications are reasonable enough, to the extent that we can say you are *justified* in believing there is a pen. Well done!

Now let us imagine that you are really just a brain in a vat (BIV), but do not know this. Imagine in this BIV world that you have been asked to hold up a pen and justify you know it is a pen. Would the justification be different? Presumably not. Blissfully unaware you are in BIV world, you would say it looks like a pen,

Learn More

▶ **ACTIVITY**
1 Hold up a pen.
2 Do you know there is a pen there?
3 Using the normal conception of justification, justify your belief.

feels like a pen and so on. Your justification in BIV world would be *exactly* the same as in Norm(al) world. As you are justified in Norm world in believing there is a pen, then you must also be justified in BIV world in believing so. It is just that in BIV world, the belief is not true. (Remember that not all justified beliefs are true ones. Only infallibilism claims this.) So a good justification in Norm world is a good justification in BIV world.

In contrast, reliabilism produces a different result. In Norm world, holding up a pen, seeing it, feeling it and so on, is a reliable process. This means it regularly produces true belief. So according to reliabilism, in Norm world your belief is 'justified' (meaning it was caused by a reliable process). However, in BIV world it is a different case. Seeing things and holding them up in BIV world does not produce true beliefs, as there are no pens or other objects that you might genuinely hold up. In BIV world, this is not a reliable process and so you are not justified.

Using a traditional account of justification, your pen belief is justified in both Norm *and* BIV world. Using the reliabilist approach account of justification (as a truth-yielding process), your pen belief is justified in Norm world, but not in BIV world. Because the two accounts differ, the argument goes, the reliabilist account of justification is not the same as our ordinary account.

(Also the reliabilist position can be seen as being contradictory. On the one hand, it claims that your pen belief in Norm world is justified, as the process is reliable. But in BIV world, the belief is not justified. However, given that we do not know if we are in BIV world or not, reliabilism seems to be claiming that the belief is simultaneously justified and not justified. This is a problem.)

A second criticism suggests that the reliabilist account of justification is circular. According to the reliabilist, the reason we know something is true is because the belief was produced by a reliable process, and, in turn, we know it is a reliable process because it is one that produces true belief. Consider this possible conversation with a reliabilist:

Q   How do you *know* it is true that you are seeing cheese?
A   Because seeing is reliable.
Q   How do you know seeing is reliable?
A   Because when I see cheese, the cheese is there.
Q   But how do you know it is true that you are seeing cheese? (... and so we are back to the first question!)

The problem is that we can only know that a process (sight) is reliable if we first know that some beliefs formed by the process are true. However, in turn, we can only know a belief based on a process (sight) is true if we know that the process is reliable. Our knowledge of truth is defined in terms of reliability, and reliability is defined in terms of our knowledge of truth. This is circular.

There are possible reliabilist defences for both these criticisms; however, to explore these would take us way beyond the level of knowledge needed for your exam!

Summary of reliabilism

Reliabilism sought to replace the idea that beliefs should be justified with the idea that beliefs should be formed by a reliable process. Reliabilism can cope well with many Gettier-style counterexamples, including fake barns, by either redefining what process is at play or by adding the conditions of sensitivity to truth or relevant alternatives. The theory would seem to imply that any suitably reliable cognitive process would count as knowledge without the need for 'internal' justification. So animals, or even very accurate fortune-tellers, could be seen as having knowledge This may be a strength or a weakness of the theory, depending on your intuitions. Some have questioned the idea of replacing 'justification' with 'truth-yielding processes', claiming the two are not equivalent and can lead to circularity.

Virtue epistemology (V + T + B)

Virtue epistemology is a new approach to thinking about questions of knowledge and justification. It follows an approach in ethics (called VIRTUE ETHICS; see page 293) that puts the character traits of the individual at the heart of morality. In virtue ethics, the question shifts from 'Is this a good act?' to 'Is this a good person?' Similarly, virtue epistemology seeks to justify knowledge in terms of intellectual VIRTUES and VICES of the knower.

In virtue ethics, an act of kindness would be one that achieves its goal (say, giving a thank you card to a friend) and would be an act that sprang from the virtue of kindness. Two key elements in characterising an act of kindness are that the act is successful and that its success stems from virtue.

Likewise, with intellectual acts, such as knowledge. An act of knowledge occurs when the belief is successful (it is true) and where its success *stems* from intellectual virtue (so is not, for example, just luckily true).

Intellectual virtues

In the previous section, we saw how reliabilism replaced the idea of justification with the concept of a belief being formed by a reliable process. In doing this, reliabilists started to discuss not just specific instances of how a belief was formed, but also considered processes in general and how reliable they might be. Processes such as *wishful thinking, guessing, reading tarot cards, believing dreams* and *recalling events from drunken evenings*, and so on, tend not to be reliable, as they are not accurate. Whereas processes such as *seeing objects nearby on a close day, remembering recent events, reasoning well* and *reading about events in quality newspapers* tend to yield a much higher rate of true beliefs.

The tendency (often called the DISPOSITION) to use reliable processes, and so more frequently gain true belief, can be termed an intellectual virtue. The tendency to use unreliable processes can be termed an intellectual vice. This is fairly intuitive. We all have well-developed ideas about what are good intellectual processes and what are bad. If a friend is intellectually virtuous, then we tend to believe what they say. If a friend often uses unreliable processes (vices), then we tend to believe they are not justified and might not fully believe them. This process of evaluation is a part of everyday life and in doing so we are making assessments of the epistemic virtues of a person.

For example, if a friend, Sammy, says he had a dream that there was a turtle in the village pond and claims, on the basis of how vivid it was, that he knows this must be true, then you might nod your head to humour him, but would probably secretly doubt this knowledge claim. However, if another friend, Tessa, had seen a turtle close up in the pond, then you would be more likely believe her.

The differences here can also be explained by reliabilism. But whereas reliabilism would claim that Tessa has knowledge because her (true) belief is generated by a reliable process, virtue epistemology claims that Tessa has knowledge because her true belief was formed as the result of her intellectual virtues operating in a suitable way.

Formally speaking, virtue epistemology might state that knowledge is a true belief brought about by a virtuous intellectual disposition – in other words, a virtuous true belief. So K = V + T + B.

Triple A rating ('AAA')

The philosopher Ernest Sosa (1940–) is one of the pioneers of virtue epistemology.[14] He often compares cases of knowing with cases of athletes performing a particular task. In the same way that an athlete's skilled performance results from their athletic virtues, so an individual's accurate knowing (or epistemic skill) stems from their intellectual virtues.

His most famous example is that of an archer shooting an arrow. In accurately shooting an arrow, Sosa identifies three key elements:

1 **Accuracy** – whether it hits the target. A shot is accurate if it hits the target. Accuracy is only a measure of whether the arrow hits the target, so an accurate shot can come about through luck or even with low levels of skill, as even an unskilled archer will sometimes hit the target!
2 **Adroitness** – how skilfully it was shot. An adroit shot is a skilful one. It is important to note that not all adroit shots will hit the target – for example, a sudden gust of wind or the target moving might make the shot miss. However, adroit shots will hit the target more often than non-adroit ones.
3 **Aptness** – the shot hits the target *because* it was adroit. An apt shot is one that is accurate, and is accurate because it was adroit. Note that not every accurate, adroit shot is apt! It is possible to hit the target with a skilful shot, but for it not to be apt. A footballer may take a skilful free kick that a gust of wind pushes away from the target, only for the ball to hit a defender and deflect into the back of the net. *Goal!* The strike was skilful (adroit), the free kick was accurate, but it was *not* apt. It did not go in the goal *because* it was skilful – luck was involved. So not every accurate, adroit performance is apt.

Knowledge is apt belief

Sosa suggests that this AAA model for analysing skilful performance can also be applied to intellectual performance and knowledge. An *accurate* belief is one that is true. An *adroit* belief is one that is formed by an intellectual virtue (a reliable cognitive process such as seeing up close, simple mental arithmetic, deduction and so on). An APT BELIEF is one that is true *because* of the intellectual virtue. The performance of our intellectual skills works in similar ways to the physical skills of the archer outlined above.

1 **Accuracy** – An accurate belief is a true one. Just as not all accurate shots are skilful ones, not all true beliefs are skilfully formed (adroit). A believer may have a lucky belief that turns out to be true (for example, guessing correctly that she will roll double six), but as this belief did not stem from intellectual virtue, it is not apt and would not count as knowledge.

> **ACTIVITY**
> 1 Write down the names of five people you know. This could include celebrities.
> 2 Rank the five in order of their intellectual virtues.
> 3 Rank the five in order of who is likely to be a source of knowledge.
> 4 What does this activity tell you?

Figure 1.8a An apt shot. This shot was apt. It was accurate, and it was accurate because it was adroit (skilful).

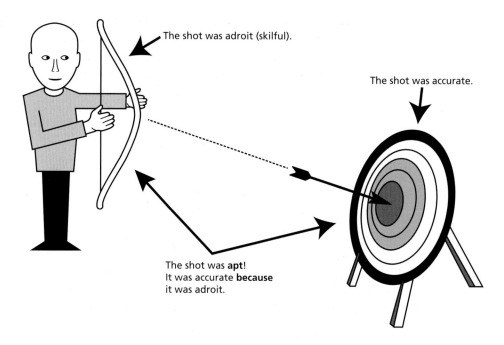

The shot was adroit (skilful).

The shot was accurate.

The shot was **apt**! It was accurate **because** it was adroit.

Figure 1.8b An apt belief. Casper believes there are eight apples in the bag. He knew there were ten before. He has taken two out to eat and works out that there are eight apples left. His belief is accurate, as it is true. His belief is adroit as his eyes are working well and he is good at simple mental arithmetic (he has good intellectual virtues). His belief is apt as it was accurate *because* it was adroit. Because his belief is apt, Casper has knowledge.

Casper's belief is adroit – it is formed by intellectual virtue.

There are now eight apples in the bag.

Casper's belief is accurate. There are eight apples in the bag.

Casper's belief is **apt**. It is accurate **because** it is adroit.

2 **Adroitness** – An adroit belief is one that was formed on the basis of intellectual virtue (using a reliable intellectual process). Not every skilful shot is accurate, and likewise not every adroit belief is a true one. For example, Eve might form a very well-justified belief that her best friend, Bess, is in Spain. Bess told Eve she was going and even updated her online profile with photos from Spain. However, it was all a trick to conceal the surprise birthday party Bess was planning for Eve – she was in the UK the whole time. In this case, Eve's belief that Bess was in Spain was adroit (skilful), but not accurate. As the belief was not true, it cannot be a case of knowledge.

3 **Aptness** – An apt belief is a true, adroit belief that is true because it is adroit. For example, imagine that you form a belief, on the basis of careful calculation, that you will need a hundred 10 × 10 cm tiles to cover an area

of 1 m². Here the belief was skilful and true, and true because it was skilful (it was no lucky guess). This is an example of an apt belief, so it is a case knowledge. However, it is important to remember that just as not every accurate, adroit shot is apt, likewise not every virtuously formed true belief is an apt belief (and so a case of knowledge). This is an important distinction, as it covers the Gettier cases of luckily true belief. For example, imagine that you see a chicken on the other side of the road. On the basis of this clear perceptual experience, you believe there is a chicken on the other side of the road. There is indeed a chicken on the other side of the road, but the chicken *you* saw was in fact an incredibly lifelike robot chicken. However, hiding in fear behind a nearby bin was a real chicken, so:

1 You hold an accurate belief (it was true).
2 Your belief was formed on the basis of a clear perception (an intellectual virtue), so it was adroit.
3 But your belief was not a true one *because* it stemmed from your intellectual virtue. It was luckily true. As such, it was not an apt belief, so was not a case of knowledge. It was a Gettier-style, luckily true belief.

By linking the truth of beliefs to the intellectual virtue that forms them, Sosa is able to separate those cases of skilful, but luckily true beliefs (Gettiers) from those beliefs that are true *because* they were skilfully formed, which are cases of knowledge (apt belief).

▶ **ACTIVITY**

1 Which of the following *beliefs* in A–I are:
   • accurate (true)?
   • adroit (believed due to an intellectual virtue)?
   • apt (accurate *because* of the use of intellectual virtue)?
2 Which of the following beliefs would you classify as examples of knowledge?
3 Do the cases of apt beliefs match the cases of knowledge?
4 Which are cases of accurate, adroit beliefs that are **not** apt (not accurate *because* they were adroit). Are these all Gettier-style counterexamples?

A Carrie believes that the moon is made of cheese because she dreamt that it was.
B David buys four apples and six pears. He puts them in his empty bag and believes there are now ten individual fruits in his bag.
C On safari, John sees a vague black and white shape in the hazy distance. He believes it is a zebra. It is.
D On safari, Ali sees a black and white shape in the distance beyond the river. Ali believes there is a zebra in the area beyond the river. There *is* a zebra just beyond the river, but it is lurking unseen behind a bush. What Ali saw was a bongo antelope.
E Having rolled two sixes in a row, Austin believes the next roll will be a six. It is.
F Tabby believes that Father Christmas exists. She has been told this is true by every adult she has met and her belief is also confirmed by books and films. Further, she has the evidence of receiving a stocking at Christmas.
G Joel, as a trained vet, is very good at distinguishing the sex of guinea pigs. He sees Olga the guinea pig and, after a quick inspection, believes it to be male. However, Olga is a hermaphrodite, born with both sex organs.
H Amir is an astronomer. Having studied the matter for years, he believes that there will be a partial eclipse of the sun on Thursday, visible from England. He is right.
I Reuben is in the hallway and hears the sound of a cat meowing coming from the lounge. Because of this, Reuben believes that a cat is in the lounge. This is true. There is a cat in the lounge, but the meowing noise was coming from an audio track of animal noises, mainly featuring a cat meowing (see **Figure 1.9**).

Virtue epistemology and Gettier

How does virtue epistemology fare with Gettier-style counterexamples? In general, it fares well. Gettier examples involve cases where the believer has a justification, but somehow the belief is 'luckily' true. In most cases, a belief that is true because of luck is not going to be an apt belief. Lucky beliefs are true because of luck, and this implies that they are not true because of intellectual virtue. In Gettier's own example, Smith was right that the successful candidate had ten coins in his pocket. However, the trueness of the belief was not as a result of any intellectual virtue; it was just a coincidence. It was an accurate and skilful belief, but it was not accurate because of intellectual virtue, so it was not apt. Under Sosa's version of virtue epistemology, Smith's belief would not count as knowledge in the first place, so the counterexample is not a problem.

The same is true of examples D) and I) above, which are also standard Gettier-style cases. In each of these cases, there is an accurate belief – the belief may even have been skilfully formed – but crucially, the belief was not true as a result of the skill, so was not apt and would not count as knowledge (see **Figure 1.9**).

Figure 1.9 The belief is not apt. Reuben believes a cat is in the lounge. His belief is accurate, as it is true. His belief is also adroit, as he generally has good hearing and is good at recognising cat sounds (he has good intellectual virtues). However, his belief is not apt as it was not accurate because it was adroit; it was accurate because of luck. So Reuben does not have knowledge. In this way, virtue epistemology can overcome the standard Gettier examples by showing that they are not cases of knowledge.

Virtue epistemology and fake barns

On first impressions, fake barn-style cases prove to be a little tricky for virtue epistemology. In the case of Barney, he has a clear visual impression of a barn, and on the basis of this, believes there is a barn – which there is. Barney's belief is accurate, adroit and apt (accurate because it was adroit), so it should be a case of knowledge. Yet many would not count this as a case of knowledge. So how would a proponent of virtue epistemology respond? Sosa suggests that Barney *does* have a form of knowledge, which he terms *animal* knowledge.

Sosa acknowledges that Barney's belief does have a AAA rating (it was accurate, adroit and apt) and so would count as knowledge, but he classifies this kind of knowledge as animal knowledge – the sort that (non-human) animals can have too. So for Sosa, apt belief is equated with animal knowledge. To have *human* knowledge requires the believer to have an additional belief or awareness about how apt, or otherwise, their initial belief is. Human knowledge requires the ability to reflect on your belief, so it is also termed *reflective* knowledge.

To explore this, let us revisit the case of the archer. Imagine that on an incredibly windy day, the archer attempts a very long-distance shot. He makes a rough estimate of the effect of the wind and takes aim. The arrow curves wildly in the air, but still hits the target. The shot was apt – it hit the target and the hitting was based on the skill of the archer. However, in this case, the archer knows that hitting the target on such a windy day would take normally about 20 shots or so, and there was a strong element of luck involved. The shot was apt, but in this case the archer can reflect and form a belief about how lucky, or not, the shot was. The archer has a reflective belief about the nature of the shot.

Contrast this case of physical skill to the intellectual skill (or otherwise) of the fake barn case. Here, Barney is unaware of his unusual context. He does not know he is in Fake Barn County. So Barney has animal knowledge (his belief is apt), but he does *not* have reflective knowledge. He cannot tell if his belief is apt or not, or make a judgement about whether it was lucky or not. If Barney was aware of his unusual context, he would then be able to form a reflective belief about the likely accuracy of his initial belief. Indeed, Barney may not even claim to know there was a barn.

To recap, Sosa claims that, beyond animal knowledge, humans can also have *reflective* knowledge – that is, they are able to reflect on their own claims to know. This involves the believer having a meta-belief about their initial belief (most beliefs are about things in the world; meta-beliefs are about beliefs themselves). The shot of the archer on the windy day was apt, but in this case he had a very good belief about exactly how apt it was and how much luck was involved. Barney lacked this reflective belief; he has no understanding of how it was luckily apt, so did not have reflective knowledge.

Criticism

Critics have taken issue with this approach of Sosa, claiming he has moved the goalposts in trying to describe knowledge. The whole analysis of knowledge starts out by asking under what conditions a person knows x or y. However, Sosa, in introducing the idea of reflective knowledge, seems to be exploring under what conditions a person is able to assert that they have knowledge – which is a different project altogether. Someone might have knowledge, but not be in a suitable position to claim it, and likewise someone might be in a suitable position to claim knowledge, but not have it. Describing the conditions for knowledge is a different project from describing the conditions for warranted assertion of knowledge – and Sosa, it is argued, is mixing up the two.

Summary of virtue epistemology

Virtue epistemology is a new area of philosophy, of which we have only explored a part. It tries to analyse knowledge by exploring the relationship between beliefs and the intellectual virtues that bring them about. Beliefs that are true because of the exercise of intellectual virtue count as knowledge. This theory can cope well with standard Gettier counterexamples. However, the analysis of the fake barn case becomes more complex, and Sosa introduces the distinction between animal and reflective knowledge to account for such scenarios.

Chapter summary

In this chapter, we have explored how philosophers have attempted to analyse the concept of knowledge. Focusing on propositional knowledge, we saw how the standard definition of knowledge as justified, true belief can be traced back to the writings of Plato. However, Gettier's famous paper in 1963 put a spanner in the works. It gave two examples of justified beliefs that are true, but luckily so, and that we would not class as cases of knowledge. The standard definition needed reworking.

The rest of the chapter examined several different theories that attempted to analyse knowledge in a way that avoids the Gettier-style cases. See Table 1.1 for a brief analysis of the main theories (there are a lot of other theories besides these). Gettier's short paper has given birth to a mini-industry in the philosophical world, with hundreds of articles and books devoted to trying to solve the problem. At times, the writing becomes very technical and detailed, with increasingly complex theories and counterexamples. Gettier's name is even used as a verb sometimes! If a theory of knowledge has some counter-examples that it cannot explain away, then it has been 'Gettiered'.

Other philosophers have stood back from the endless debates and wondered if the whole approach might be flawed. Earlier we saw that it can be very difficult to give the necessary and sufficient conditions for a simple concept such as rain. If this is a difficult enterprise, then attempting to give some simple conditions that explain every instance of knowledge might seem like a foolish enterprise. Human knowledge is a vast and complex domain, covering anatomy to apple varieties to astrophysics. And that is just the 'A's! Maybe the use of the word 'know' is very vague, context-dependent and even subjective, and there is no simple definition that will cover all cases. Perhaps the concept of knowledge is not analysable after all.

Table 1.1 Theories of knowledge

Theory	In a nutshell	Does it describe knowledge well?	How does it cope with Gettier?
Standard theory $K = J + T + B$	Knowledge is a justified, true belief.	Yes. We tend to want beliefs to be justified to count as knowledge. How justified they need to be is a bit slippery, but in exactly the same way that the concept of knowledge is slippery.	It copes badly. Gettier came up with his counterexamples precisely to show the flaws in this theory. It seems that we can have a justified belief that is luckily true! Our instincts tell us this cannot be knowledge, so the theory has a big problem.
Infallibilism	Your justification needs to be so strong that it is impossible to be wrong. (It is tempting to say that your *belief* must be infallible; however, many holders of this theory claim that *beliefs* describe claims that are not certain, claims you only *believe* to be true.)	No. We do intuitively link knowledge with a degree of certainty, but this seems to go too far. It implies that we know very little, which goes against our intuitions. The theory seems to be saying how we *should* use the term 'knowledge' rather than describe how we in fact do use it.	It copes very well. Under this theory, none of the Gettier-style cases, including the fake barn cases, would count as knowledge, so there is no problem that needs explaining.
No false lemmas $K = J + T + B + N$	Knowledge is justified, true belief, where the justification does not involve any false premises.	Yes. It matches our everyday use fairly well. It allows us to know lots of things, but rules out knowledge if the belief was based on a false premise. This matches our intuitions well.	It copes with Gettier's own cases very well, as these are based on false premises. It copes with other Gettier-style cases less well, as the belief may be based on false hidden assumptions rather than premises. (As a variation on this theory, the no essential false assumptions theory copes with a wider range of Gettier-style cases.) The theory does not rule out fake barn cases, as there are no false premises in these cases.
Reliabilism $K = T + B + R$	Knowledge is a true belief that has been caused by a reliable process.	It matches our use fairly well. We are good at gauging how reliable a process is. The theory allows animals to have knowledge and also grants knowledge to any reliable process (for example, an incredibly successful fortune-teller). Some think this is a weakness of the theory, some think it a strength. How reliable a process needs to be to have knowledge is a bit slippery, as is how we describe what the process is before assessing its reliability.	With some modifications (sensitivity condition or the no relevant alternative conditions), it can cope well with nearly all Gettier cases, including fake barns.
Virtue ethics $K = V + T + B$	Knowledge is a belief that has been formed as the result of an intellectual virtue being employed. According to Sosa's version, knowledge is an apt belief – that is, a belief that is formed by an intellectual virtue and is held as true because of the use of this virtue.	It matches up fairly well to our ordinary use. We intuitively rate other people's knowledge claims on the basis of their intellectual virtues.	It can cope well with many Gettier cases as beliefs must be accurate because of the intellectual virtue, not because of luck. The fake barn cases are a problem again, as intellectual virtue seems to be well-applied and the true belief arises as a result. Sosa claims the believer lacks an understanding of their context and so lacks the ability to judge how apt, or not, their belief is. Because of this, he claims that in fake barn cases, the believer has animal knowledge, but lacks reflective knowledge.

1.2 Perception as a source of knowledge

Introduction

How do we acquire knowledge of the world? An obvious answer is that we learn about it through our senses. We know that the cat is on the mat because we can see it there. We know that it is a hot day because we can feel the warmth of the sun on our backs. However, it is undoubtedly true that our senses can deceive us from time to time. Optical illusions are a case in point; take the examples in **Figure 1.10**.

In the Müller-Lyer illusion, the horizontal line in a) appears to be longer than in b). However, if you measure the two, they turn out to be the same length. Our eyes appear to have deceived us. Another case of our eyes deceiving us is when an oar appears to bend when half-immersed in water (see **Figure 1.11**). It looks bent, but we know it is really straight. Such observations raise doubts about the reliability of our sense organs in telling us about the world. So just how accurate are they as indicators of the way the world really is?

It is interesting to observe in this connection that other animals have senses that are far more sensitive than our own. Dogs, for example, can hear sounds that are too high for us to hear, and they can smell all kinds of things that we cannot. Does this mean they are perceiving the world more accurately than us? Other creatures have senses completely different from ours. The ability of sharks to sense the electric field created by living things, or of bats to use sound to navigate, raises the question of what the world must seem like to these animals. How do their senses represent the world in their minds? In colours and shapes? In textures and sounds? Or in some way we simply cannot imagine? Perhaps these animals have a truer PERCEPTION of the world than we do. Or perhaps no animal sees the world as it truly is.

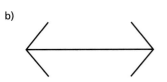

Figure 1.10 The Müller-Lyer illusion. The two horizontal lines appear to be of different lengths, but are, in reality, the same length.

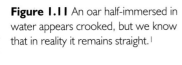

Figure 1.11 An oar half-immersed in water appears crooked, but we know that in reality it remains straight.[1]

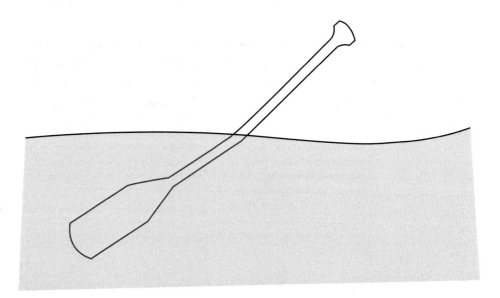

Experimenting with ideas

1 a) Do you think your favourite food tastes the same to a dog as it does to you?
   b) Do you think dog food tastes the same to you as to a dog?
   c) Who has a truer perception of the world: dogs or humans?
2 Some creatures lack the senses we have. They may be blind or deaf. Others have senses that we do not have. They may detect electricity or magnetic fields. How many senses must a creature have for it to get a true picture of the world? Make a list of the necessary senses.
3 Dogs can hear high-frequency sound waves that we do not register. Likewise, elephants hear frequencies lower than we can register. Does it follow that all humans are partially deaf? Are some sounds so low and others so high that no creature can hear them?
4 As with sound waves, we only perceive light waves within a particular bandwidth. Imagine meeting an alien who does not perceive the frequencies of light that we do, but perceives a whole set of higher ones, such as ultraviolet and beyond. The alien represents these waves in a range of colours much as we do. Who sees the true colours of the world: humans or aliens? If neither of us does, does that mean that no colours are the real colours?
5 Can you be sure that, when you and your friend share a piece of chicken, the flavour you are experiencing is actually the same for both of you? Similarly, is there any way of telling that you are seeing exactly the same colours as someone else?
6 Sound is caused by compression waves of air hitting your ear drum. If a tree fell down in a forest and there were no ears around (human or otherwise), would it:
   a) make a sound?
   b) just produce airwaves?
7 Where are rainbows? Are they in the sky, in rain droplets, in people's minds or nowhere?

The questions above raise deep puzzles about how what we perceive connects up with the world around us. Are we perceiving reality directly or is there some indirect relationship between what we perceive and what is really there? In other words, is there something which *mediates* or gets between us and the world and which might mean that our perception may not always reveal things as they truly are?

What should be evident from your reflections on the activity questions is that we need to be clear about what is going on in perception before we can be completely confident about our answers. In other words, we need to develop some kind of theory of perception. In this chapter, we will consider some of the main philosophical theories of perception, each of which offers different accounts of how we acquire knowledge of the world around us.

Realism

He thought he saw an Elephant,
That practised on a fife:
He looked again, and found it was
A letter from his wife.
'At length I realise,' he said,
'The bitterness of Life!'

'The Mad Gardener's Song', Lewis Carroll

Much of the philosophical debate over perception hinges on the question of how much of what we perceive is really a feature of the world and how much is a feature of our minds. In other words, how much of what we are perceiving is really out there? This question of what is real or not is also central to many other areas of philosophy. If you are a REALIST about something, then you believe it exists independently of our minds. If you are an ANTI-REALIST about something, you think it is mind-dependent. The following activity should draw out whether you are a realist or an anti-realist about a range of entities.

▶ **ACTIVITY**

For each of the following, consider whether the object or topic in question is real or not. For this exercise, take 'real' to mean 'has an existence independent of minds – human or otherwise'. If something is 'not real', then it exists only in the mind. Copy and complete the table.

	Real	Not real	Don't know
1 Numbers (for example, the number 7)			
2 Your reflection in the mirror			
3 Colours (for example, red)			
4 Smells (for example, of coffee)			
5 Morality (for example, the wrongness of murder)			
6 Electrons			
7 Scientific laws (for example, $E = mc^2$)			
8 Ghosts			
9 Matter (that is, physical stuff)			
10 Aesthetic features (that is, beauty)			
11 Relations between things (for example, being similar to, or north of)			
12 The past and the future			

Real or not?

1 **Numbers** (for example, the number 7). Whether numbers are real or not has vexed many a philosopher and is still a current debate. Plato famously thought that numbers exist independently of the mind, not in the physical world that we see and touch, but in a world we can only perceive with our minds; a world of ideas or 'forms'. One reason for thinking this is that it would seem that mathematical truths remain true whether or not there is anyone around to recognise them: 7 + 5 has always equalled 12, even before human beings first appeared on earth. The times tables you learnt at school will reflect truths about numbers which will remain true long after you leave school, and long after any children or grandchildren you may have leave school. Indeed, it seems they have always and will always be true. Plato was greatly influenced in this view by another ancient Greek philosopher, Pythagoras, who thought that to understand the world truly, one must look for the mathematical structures that lie

behind appearances. Pythagoras sought to uncover these structures and, among other things, revealed how music and harmony have a mathematical basis.

2 **Your reflection in the mirror**. Is your reflection behind the mirror, in the mirror, in your mind or nowhere? The mirror seems to be a window into another world, but one that does not exist in real physical space. So is your reflection a part of the physical world? Or is the mirror world just an illusion in the mind? What mirrors seem to show is that the way we locate objects in the world around us is a result of the direction that rays of light enter our eyes. So sometimes these rays can enter our eyes at angles that suggest to our minds the presence of an object that is really somewhere else.

3 **Colours** (for example, red). Some will argue that the word 'red' refers to the way humans see a particular wavelength of light when it hits their retinas. Others see it as the name for the particular wavelength itself. It could also be the name for a physical object's propensity to bounce back visible light at a particular frequency. So red could be in the head, in the air or on the tomato. The same, of course, is true of colours generally, such as the colour green and trees (see **Figure 1.12**).

4 **Smells** (for example, coffee). This is discussed on page 62.

5 **Morality** (for example, the wrongness of murder). Are good and evil OBJECTIVELY real? This is a key question in Moral Philosophy and is discussed in detail in Section 2. Those who think that morality exists independently of human minds and that there is a fact of the matter about whether or not murder is wrong, are ethical realists. Those who think that morality is in some sense a product of human minds are ethical anti-realists.

Essential Terminology

6 **Electrons**. Some take the view that electrons and other theoretical entities that cannot be directly observed are just a useful story we invent to make sense of experimental data. On this view, they are part of a model which helps to explain what we can observe, but beyond this, they have no independent existence. Some taking this view will argue that it is conceivable that if science had taken a different direction, electrons would not have figured in our scientific theories; that we could have developed different models, equally capable of explaining and predicting the behaviour of the world. Others – scientific realists – believe that terms such as 'electron' pick out real features of reality and that they possess the properties we attribute to them.

7 **Scientific laws** (for example, $E = mc^2$). These are formulated in the minds of humans, but to be successful they must be able to explain and predict aspects of the world. This raises the question of how real they are and whether there is something out there to which the law could correspond. Some anti-realists take the view that the laws do not correspond to anything and cannot really be said to be true or false – they are merely instrumental in helping humans manipulate the world. A realist may take the view that scientific laws, as they slowly evolve, edge ever closer to the truth – that is, to matching the laws of the universe.

8 **Ghosts**. We leave this for you to decide.

9 **Matter** (that is, physical stuff). Some philosophers argue that the only things of which we are ever aware are ideas or sensations in our minds and

that matter is just a convenient way of talking about these sensations. Most people, however, believe that there really is a MATERIAL universe that we perceive all around us and that it exists independently of our minds. This is a realist view about physical objects and is the subject we explore below (page 53).

10 **Aesthetic features** (that is, beauty). Some may argue that the concept of beauty – whether in the setting of the sun or the song of the nightingale – is so universal that there must be an external standard of beauty to which these things refer. Others think that beauty is subjective – or at most culturally ingrained – and is thus solely in the eye of the beholder.

This second view is probably more common these days. However, consider that it does seem odd to suppose that *anything* could be beautiful. We might think a person did not really understand the meaning of the word, if they claimed that their chewed pen lid was a thing of beauty.

11 **Relations between things** (for example, being similar to, or north of). It may be thought that what exist are ultimately just individual things, such as oak trees, rabbits, cities and planets. To exist, such things would seem to have to be in a particular place at a particular time. Because they exist in space and time, we are able to identify them by our senses. And yet, we also normally think that particular things can be related to each other in various ways. For example, if we say that Edinburgh is north of London, we seem to be making a claim about a relation between these two cities which exists independently of the mind. Edinburgh would be north of London, even if no one recognised this fact. We also talk of two things being similar. Oak trees are like beech trees in various ways. But if relations like 'north of' or 'similar to' are real, then they must be rather peculiar kinds of thing. For such relations are not things that can exist in a specific place at a particular time. They are not something that we can detect with our senses. This has led some philosophers to deny they are real and to claim that they exist only in the mind. That is to say, we bring our ideas of two things into a relation by thinking of them as related and so they do not have any mind-independent existence.[2]

12 **The past and the future**. It seems obvious that everything that happens and all that exists has to be in time. But while we are able, more or less accurately, to remember events that happened in the past, and predict what will happen in the future, both the past and the future are not actually with us now. So while dinosaurs existed once and their fossils are here now, the beasts themselves no longer are; and while our great-great-grandchildren may be a twinkle in the eye, they similarly do not – as of yet – actually exist. This suggests that only things existing now and only the present are truly real. And if things and events from the past and the future do not exist, then perhaps we should conclude that they are not independently real, but depend for their existence on our capacity to remember or predict them.

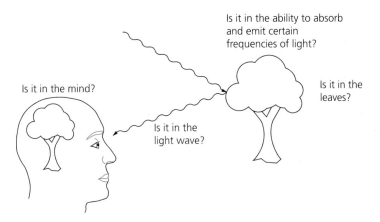

Figure 1.12 Where is the green of the tree? The word 'green' appears to have various meanings. It can refer to something in the leaves themselves: the objective property that the naïve realist says they have. It can refer to the power the leaves have to absorb and emit various wavelengths of light. It can refer to the specific wavelength itself that leaves typically emit. Or it can refer to the experience of the colour as it appears to us in our minds.

Realist theories of perception

If you examine your ordinary assumptions about the way perception works, then you will probably find you hold a realist view. Common sense, in other words, is committed to REALISM about the world around us; it believes that physical objects exist independently of our minds. Another way of making the point is to say that physical things and their properties are objective, meaning that they exist out there in the world and have a specific nature regardless of how they are perceived. In other words, these properties are not merely "subjective", a term used to denote the mind dependent nature of certain experiences or beliefs. Common sense also tends to support DIRECT REALISM: the idea that we perceive things immediately – that is, without anything getting between us and the objects we perceive. So let us sketch out an initial version of this common-sense view, a view sometimes called naïve direct realism, since it is what people tend to adhere to before really engaging in philosophical reflection on the matter.

1.2.1 Direct realism

Direct realism claims that objects are composed of matter; they occupy space, and have properties such as size, shape, texture, smell, taste and colour. These properties are perceived directly. In other words, when we look at, listen to and touch things, we see, hear and feel those things themselves with no intermediary. The naïve view tends to suppose this means that we must perceive objects as they truly are. So, when you look at your red door, the reason you see it as red is that it really is red. And when others come to visit, they also see the same objects with the same properties. Importantly, objects also retain their properties whether or not there is anyone present to observe them; when you turn out the light to go to bed, the objects you can no longer see remain where they are and with the same shapes and colours as before. You may not be able to see it, but your door is still red.

53

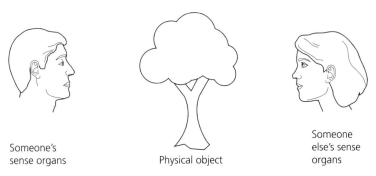

Figure 1.13 Direct realism. Direct realism identifies two elements in perception: the perceiver and the thing perceived. We perceive mind-independent objects and their properties and our senses put us in immediate contact with them. Our sense organs detect properties of objects which exist out there in the world, and all of us perceive the same objects with the same properties.

Someone's sense organs

Physical object

Someone else's sense organs

If a tree falls in a forest and no animal or person is there to hear it, then does it make a noise?

a) What do you personally think?

b) What would a direct realist say?

The direct realist would say that the tree does make a noise. The world is how is appears to be, and whenever someone is present as a tree falls, they are immediately aware of the noise it creates. If we can observe falling trees making noises, we can be confident that this is what they do, regardless of whether anyone happens to be present. In sum, the direct realist is saying that we perceive objects with certain properties because they are there and have those properties, and we know they are there and have the properties they do because we can perceive them.

Issues with direct realism

Most philosophers have felt that direct realism, at least in its naïve version as we have so far characterised it, cannot be maintained. The philosopher David Hume (1711–76), for example, claimed that once one had engaged in 'the slightest philosophy',[3] one would be forced to give it up.

Issue 1: perceptual variation

Many of the difficulties that direct realism faces were highlighted by the great British empiricist philosopher, George Berkeley (1685–1753) in his *Three Dialogues between Hylas and Philonous* (1713). The character of Philonous, Berkeley's spokesman, asks Hylas to consider what the colour of some distant clouds is (see **Figure 1.14**).

Since the clouds may appear red from a distance, and any number of colours from different perspectives, according to Berkeley it makes no sense to suppose that they have any real colour. This goes just as well for any objects. If we look closely at a flower through a microscope, its colour will be different from how it looks to the naked eye. The conclusion that may be drawn is that the colour is merely an effect made upon us by physical things, and not something in the objects themselves. In other words, colour is an appearance to us, not something objectively real.[4]

Figure 1.14 Berkeley's example of observing clouds. The clouds appear different colours to different observers. But who is right? No one has any privileged perspective, so no one can observe the true colour. Therefore colour is an appearance to observers, and not something real.

Someone far off

Someone close

anthology
1.2

Bertrand Russell makes this same point in *The Problems of Philosophy* when discussing the appearance of his table, which, because of the way light reflects off its surface, appears to be different colours from different points of view. He concludes that the colour cannot be something which is really in the table itself. Rather it is an appearance which depends upon how the light falls upon it and the position of the spectator. Russell then considers a possible objection. You might be tempted to claim that the real colour is the colour as seen by a person standing near the object under normal lighting conditions. This certainly seems to be what we ordinarily mean when we talk about *the* colour of the table (see **Figure 1.15**).

Figure 1.15 Russell contemplates his table. 'When, in ordinary life, we speak of *the* colour of the table, we only mean the sort of colour which it will seem to have to a normal spectator from an ordinary point of view under usual conditions of light. But the other colours which appear under other conditions have just as good a right to be considered real; and therefore, to avoid favouritism, we are compelled to deny that, in itself, the table has any one particular colour.'[5]

However, the difficulty for this defence is to determine which distance and lighting conditions should be given the privileged status of revealing reality. The apparent colour of an object will change throughout the day, from the bright light of noon to the soft light of the evening, so that it would be impossible to determine which time of day reveals the 'true' colours. The French impressionist painter Claude Monet painted a series of haystacks at different times of day in order to explore the effects different light had on their appearance. But it makes no sense to ask which painting reveals the true colour, since we have no way of choosing. And even if certain colours appear more commonly than others, this is still no basis for favouring them over the less common.

Locke discusses our perception of heat in the same vein. He asks us to imagine putting a hot hand and a cold hand into the same bucket of lukewarm water. The water then feels cold to one hand and hot to the other. But clearly the same small area of water cannot really be both hot and cold at the same time. This would be a contradiction. So the conclusion follows that it must merely appear to be hot and cold. Heat and cold, therefore, are not real properties of objects, but appearances; they are effects such objects have on observers like us. (Leibniz provides a telling objection to this ARGUMENT when commenting on it in *The New Essays*. You can read his comment in the Anthology.)

Hume and Russell extend this line of reasoning to the size and shape of objects.[6] Russell points out that his table appears to take on different geometric forms when observed from different angles. If we attend carefully to the appearance in the way we might if trying to draw the table, we will note that the sides, which in reality we

anthology
1.3

anthology
1.4

suppose are parallel, converge slightly, the further away from the spectator they go. And the angles at the corners of the table hardly ever appear as right angles. The apparent shape also changes as we move around the table (see **Figure 1.16**).

Figure 1.16 How a rectangular table appears in perspective.
The way the table actually appears to us may be accurately represented by an artist, and the appearance has a different shape from what we take the real shape to be. The angles are either obtuse or acute, and the sides are not parallel. And yet the real table is rectangular.

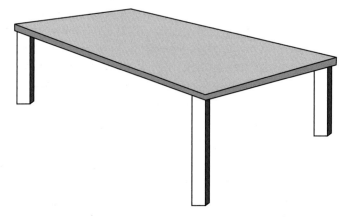

Since the table cannot really be changing its colour and shape continually, and neither can different observers be accurately perceiving it to be different colours and shapes at the same time, it seems that the direct realist must concede that objects cannot be exactly as we perceive them to be. What Russell, following Locke and Hume, concludes is that what we are directly aware of is not the table itself, but the appearance of the table to our minds. The appearance is a trapezium; the reality is a rectangle. The appearance will change with point of view, while the reality remains relatively constant.

Sense data

Russell calls these appearances SENSE DATA. Sense data are the immediate objects of perception. They are what we are directly aware of, as distinct from the physical objects which cause them. It is on the basis of our awareness of sense data that we infer the existence of the table, so that the table itself is only perceived indirectly. Sense data are thought to be certain. That is, I cannot be mistaken about how objects appear to me.

Let us give the name of 'sense-data' to the things that are immediately known in sensation: such things as colours, sounds, smells, hardnesses, roughnesses, and so on ... if we are to know anything about the table, it must be by means of the sense-data – brown colour, oblong shape, smoothness, etc. – which we associate with the table.
Bertrand Russell, *Problems of Philosophy*, Chapter I

Response to the perceptual variation issue

However, this may not mean that we are forced to reject direct realism. After all, we are rarely fooled by the perspective we take into mistaking the real colours or shapes of objects. Moreover, we can explain how it is that objects will appear differently from different angles because of the lighting conditions, the point of view taken, and so on. Monet's haystacks appear to be different colours because of the colour of the light at different times of day – but we still know that hay is yellowy-brown. So Berkeley and Russell may be wrong in their claim that we cannot privilege one of the perceived colours over any others. Certainly when it comes to solid physical objects like Russell's desk, we do privilege normal lighting conditions and perspectives in order to assert that the table is brown, even though it may sometimes appear white or some other colour. Moreover, the science of optics explains why the shape of a table will appear different when viewed from different points of view – but we still know it is rectangular. And while its apparent shape may vary between different observers, if required to provide precise dimensions, different observers will nonetheless converge on the very same ones. If they did not, it would be impossible for us to co-operate in the most basic of practical tasks, such as buying a table to fit into your kitchen.

So while direct realists must concede that we do not perceive the world precisely as it is, they can deny that this implies that we do not perceive it directly or that we directly perceive appearances. Defenders of direct realism accuse Russell of making an unwarranted inference from the fact that a table appears different from how it is, to supposing that we must be immediately aware of an apparent table and only indirectly aware of the real table. But to say that the table appears different from how it is does not commit us to saying we are not directly aware of it or that there is something distinct from the real table, its appearance, which we *are* directly aware of. Rather we can say that the table appears differently from how it really is because of the way it relates to an observer. The apparent properties, then, emerge because of the relation between the object with its intrinsic properties, and the person perceiving it. In this way, we can distinguish the properties that it has whether or not anyone is observing it, and those that emerge when it relates to some observer without the need to invoke sense data.

Issue 2: illusion

The second problem is one we have already begun to consider: the fact that our senses are subject to illusions. It happens on occasion that I perceive an object which appears to be one thing, when in reality it is another. A straw half-immersed in my glass of water may appear to be bent when in fact it is straight, or a tower which appears round from a distance looks square when observed from close to.[7] The conclusion is drawn that what we immediately perceive cannot be what is in the world, since what we are perceiving is not the same as what is really there. Moreover, because I am directly aware of appearances, or sense data, I cannot be mistaken about them. In other words, it is not possible to go wrong when making judgements about how things appear to me. I can therefore be certain that the straw appears bent, even though I may be uncertain of what it is really like. So errors only occur when I make hasty judgements on the basis of misleading sense data about what causes them (see **Figure 1.17a**).

Response to the illusion issue

It may be that the direct realist can respond by claiming that in such situations the senses do reveal reality directly to us, but it is just that we can occasionally misinterpret what we perceive. Normally, we are not fooled by the way water refracts light differently from air; indeed, as children we quickly become used to such illusions. But if we are ever fooled, it is because we have misinterpreted the information given to us by our eyes and have made a rash judgement.[8]

▶ ACTIVITY

Can you think of occasions when you have been deceived by your senses in this way? Make a note of your own examples of perceptual illusions.

Figure 1.17 Illusions and hallucinations according to critics of direct realism. According to critics of direct realism, when I perceive an oar as bent when it is straight in reality, this is because I do not directly perceive the oar itself, but an appearance of the oar. And when I hallucinate, what I am directly perceiving is an appearance indistinguishable from the perceptions I might have when not hallucinating. The only difference is that there is no real object corresponding to the perception.

As with the perceptual variation argument, this response involves questioning the assumption that if we misperceive something, we must be immediately perceiving an appearance which is distinct from the reality. But the direct realist can insist that it is perfectly possible to perceive a straight straw as bent without this implying that we directly perceive a bent straw and only indirectly a straight one. The bent appearance of the straw is not a sense datum, rather it is a property of the straw which emerges in relation to an observer. So we should say that the straw '*appears* bent', not that there '*is* a bent-straw appearance'. The mistake is to turn the way it appears to an observer into a distinct thing – the appearance (or sense datum) – in the observer.

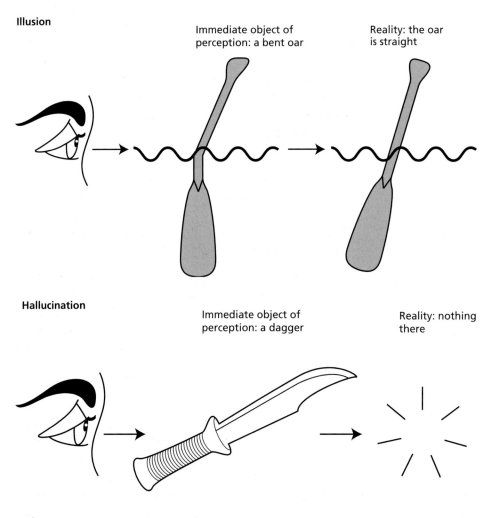

Illusion

Immediate object of perception: a bent oar

Reality: the oar is straight

Hallucination

Immediate object of perception: a dagger

Reality: nothing there

Issue 3: hallucinations

During a hallucination it may not be possible to distinguish my experience from a genuine perception. And if the two are subjectively indistinguishable, then the visible appearance of the dagger is exactly the same to Macbeth as if he were seeing a real dagger. The argument concludes that what I am immediately aware of, even when not hallucinating, must be a "dagger of the mind" or sense datum. (see **Figure 1.17b**).

Response to the hallucination issue

One response to the hallucination argument is to point out that we can, as a matter of fact, identify when we are hallucinating. Macbeth knows the dagger is not real precisely because he cannot grasp it with his hands. In other words, another sense helps him detect the deception. Indeed, if we could not detect hallucinations, then we would remain unaware that we were ever subject to them. It seems to follow that if hallucinations were really subjectively indistinguishable from VERIDICAL (that is, truthful or accurate) perception, then we would not know we had had them and so the hallucination argument could not get started.

Another response is to deny that hallucinations are really perceptions at all. Even supposing that a hallucination and a veridical perception are indistinguishable to the person having them, it does not mean they are not in reality distinct kinds of phenomenon. While I may be unable to tell that I am hallucinating at the time, this does not mean that hallucinations are not very different in terms of how they are produced from genuine perception. Macbeth's vision proceeds from his 'heat-oppressed brain', not from light entering his eyes reflecting off the surface of any real dagger. Thus there is no reason to suppose that genuine perception must involve the same kind of immediate object of perception as we are aware of when hallucinating.

In his *Meditations*, Descartes explores a similar train of thought when suggesting that dreams are often indistinguishable from real life. When immersed in a vivid dream, I may be unable to determine whether it is a dream or reality. And if such dreams are qualitatively indistinguishable from real life, I may conclude that I cannot be certain that I am not dreaming now. It appears to follow that what we are immediately aware of is not the same as what is real.

In the same way, we could complain about Descartes' dreaming argument that the fact that the person enjoying their dream cannot distinguish between the dream and reality does not mean that there is no difference. And if dreams are different in nature from veridical perception, again we have no reason to conclude that perception generally must involve an immediate awareness of an appearance as distinct from reality.

anthology
1.5

Issue 4: time lag argument

The light which reaches us from the stars has travelled across trillions of miles and taken many years to arrive. For example, there was a supernova explosion that became visible on earth in 1054 and was recorded by Chinese astronomers. We can still see the remnants of this explosion in the Crab Nebula in the constellation of Taurus. But the Nebula is over six thousand light years away, which means that the explosion those astronomers saw actually took place six thousand years before they recorded it. What we observe today is similarly out of date, so that we cannot even be sure of whether the Crab Nebula still exists. But if it might no longer exist, then we cannot really be perceiving it now. If we are not perceiving the real Crab Nebula now, then what we are perceiving must be an appearance: a mental image, not the real thing.

Now, while the time lag between us and the Crab Nebula is very great, there is also a time lag, albeit a very small one, between us and the physical objects around us. The light from the table in front of me takes some time to arrive and so, it appears to follow, we are not directly perceiving the objects around us.

anthology
1.6

Russell makes the same observation in the *Problems of Philosophy* when drawing the distinction between sense data and objects (see Anthology extract 1.6).

Response to the time lag issue

In response, the direct realist can accept that there is a time lag in perception, but deny that this implies that we do not directly perceive physical objects or that we must introduce something distinct from the object which we are directly aware of: a sense datum. All that follows from the fact of a time lag is that we perceive objects as they were. And this is exactly what astronomers say: 'We can see today the Crab Nebula as it was over six thousand years ago'; 'Chinese astronomers recorded the supernova explosion six thousand years after it happened.' But they still saw it. So while this argument shows that we must give up the naïve view that we perceive objects instantaneously and therefore that we cannot be aware of objects as they are now, but as they were, this does not refute direct realism. We are not aware of the Crab Nebula as it is now, but we are nonetheless directly aware of it as it was.

▶ **ACTIVITY**

There is a 'blind spot' in your vision. This is caused by an area on the retina without light receptors where the optic nerve takes the information to the brain. To find your blind spot, follow these instructions.

In the margin we have printed a circle and a square. In a moment:

- tip the book on its side so that the square is on the right and the circle on the left
- close your right eye
- hold the book at arm's length and focus on the square
- move the book slowly toward you
- at some point the circle will 'disappear' as the light bouncing off it falls on your blind spot.

So you can see that you have a blind spot. However, if you walk around with only one eye open, there is not a constant gap in your visual field and this is because the brain fills in this gap for you. The brain adds missing information from your eyes in other ways too, so that what is perceived is a less patchy view of the world. Now, if we accept that the brain is processing information before you perceive it, then it would appear that there must be at least two elements involved in perception: 1) the world as it is and 2) the world as it appears.

1.2.2 Indirect realism

The arguments we have looked at above have led many philosophers to conclude that direct realism is untenable. The indirect realist agrees with the direct realist that the world consists of material objects which occupy a public space and that these material objects possess certain independently existing properties. This commitment to the real existence of matter is what makes them both realists. However, the indirect realist disagrees with the direct realist over whether we perceive the properties of matter directly. What we are immediately aware of is not the objects themselves, but rather the way they appear to our minds. So indirect realists distinguish what Russell calls sense data from the objects perceived. In other words, the claim is that there is, on the one hand, a mental component – namely, the way the object appears to the observer – and, on the other, the object as it is in reality. For the indirect realist, sensations are a REPRESENTATION or image of mind-independent objects in the external world. It is as if we had pictures in our minds which represent for us the real world outside of our minds.

INDIRECT REALISM introduces a third term between the perceiver and thing perceived – sense data – in order to explain how perception works. Physical objects cause us to become aware of sense data, such as colours or shapes. It is these, and only these, that we are directly and immediately aware of. But these sense data do represent the world that causes them so that we can be indirectly aware of reality. So we now have two worlds: the world as it is in itself, and a picture of the world as it appears to our minds. Our perception of reality is mediated by sense data, so that we must infer the existence and nature of the external world on the basis of the way it is represented to us in the mind.

By using the distinction between appearance and reality, the indirect realist hopes to explain perceptual variation. The same object can appear different to different observers or to the same observer from different angles, because what we are immediately aware of is not the object as it truly is, but as it appears. Similarly, the theory explains illusions. When the image I have in my mind, for whatever reason, does not accurately correspond to the way things are in the world, I am subject to some sort of illusion. Indirect realism can also explain how hallucinations are possible. They occur when a sensation occurs in the mind, but there is nothing corresponding to it in the external world.

Primary and secondary qualities

Many of the arguments against direct realism hinge on the idea that some of the properties we perceive, such as colours, tastes and smells, do not exist in the objects themselves as we perceive them to be. Such properties depend on a mind being present in order for them to appear. Other properties, such as size and shape, are thought to have real existence independently of our minds. This is the distinction between PRIMARY AND SECONDARY QUALITIES. To begin to see why this distinction might be drawn, consider the activity below.

Consider the property of value. Does a pound coin actually have that property? Could an alien place the coin under the microscope and discern that it has the property of value? No, is the obvious answer. The alien would be able to tell its size, the metals from which it is composed and its density, but would not be able to measure its value. Value does not actually inhere in the object itself, but is caused by the role the object plays in a human society. So while we talk of the coin having a certain value, its value is not strictly a real property of the coin at all.

The same can be said for other supposed properties of the coin. Consider its colour. Remember, the alien only perceives light in black and white. The alien would measure the pound coin, would know all of its physical properties and would know how it absorbs and emits light waves. But the alien would not know that humans perceive this coin as gold-coloured, as it would not know how humans perceive the various wavelengths of light; nor would the alien even have the concept of gold-coloured. So even if the alien produced a complete physical description of the coin, it would not include the colour of the coin, only the wavelength of light the coin bounces back. Yet the alien's description would not be lacking in any important way, so it seems we must conclude that the coin does not have the property of being coloured in the same way that it has other properties such as shape and density.

Essential Terminology

▶ **ACTIVITY**

Imagine that an intelligent alien lands on earth. The alien has a very different set of senses from the ones we use to navigate reality. He has a sonic sense like a bat, and an electric sense like a dolphin. He has no colour vision and can only see in black and white. When he touches objects, his nerves and brain translate the touches into noises that he hears in his mind. The alien is about to examine some objects from earth and see what properties the objects have.

What would the alien write down as the real properties of the following objects?

1 A pound coin.
2 A cup of tea.
3 A piece of sandpaper.

Now consider smell. One theory is that different smells are caused by the different shapes of airborne molecules. On the inside of our noses are thousands of receptors. When we inhale, millions of molecules whizz up through our noses and, if they are the right shape and size, some of these molecules will lodge briefly in these receptors. If enough molecules of the same type do this, then we perceive a particular odour. So molecules are not coated with a smelly property that we somehow perceive. They merely have a shape which, in humans, causes the subjective experience of a smell, and there is no resemblance between our sensation of smell and the shape of the molecule.

Descartes argues that the sensation of heat also cannot accurately resemble any real property of fire. Rather we should suppose that there is something in the fire which causes us to feel heat, but which is of a completely different nature from the sensation. He points out that we do not suppose that the pain fire may cause us when we get too close is really in the fire, so by the same logic, we ought to reckon that the heat it causes in us is also not in the fire.

[A]lthough I feel heat when I approach a fire and feel pain when I go too near, there is no good reason to think that something in the fire resembles the heat, or resembles the pain. There is merely reason to suppose that something or other in the fire causes feelings of heat or pain in us.

Descartes, Meditation 6

anthology
1.7

Locke agrees. He supposes that the qualities of objects that cause certain sensations in us have something to do with the minute particles from which they are composed and their movements. The relationship between these qualities of the object, which cause us, for example, to see blue or smell a sweet scent, is an *arbitrary* one, meaning that there is no resemblance between the sensation of blue and whatever it is in the flower that causes it. Locke points out that we can conceive that God might have arranged things differently. The fact that we can imagine whatever it is that causes us to see blue actually causing a different sensation shows that the relationship between the sensation and the objective property is not one of resemblance.[9]

He tells us that the relationship between the immediate objects of perception and the qualities in objects causing them is like that between a word and the idea it invokes in our minds. Just as the word 'flower' does not resemble a real flower, but is arbitrarily associated with it, so too the blue colour does not resemble the quality of the flower which produces it. So the common opinion that the immediate objects of perception are 'images and resemblances of something inherent in the object [...] is quite wrong. Most ideas of sensation are (in the mind) no more like a thing existing outside us than the names that stand for them are like the ideas themselves'.[10] For this reason, we cannot directly know what it is that causes us to see blue.[11]

anthology
1.8

Thus it would seem that objects physically possess some properties, whereas other properties are related to the minds experiencing them. Primary qualities are those that exist independently of our perceiving them, while secondary are those that require a perceiving mind. So Locke defines secondary qualities as those 'qualities that are, in the objects themselves, really nothing but powers to produce various sensations in us by their primary qualities, i.e. by the size, shape, texture, and motion of their imperceptible parts. Examples of these are colours, sounds, tastes, and so on.'[12]

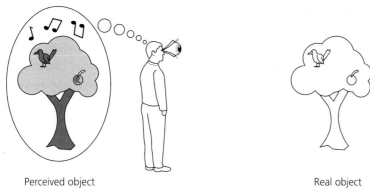

Perceived object   Real object

Figure 1.18 Indirect realism and primary and secondary qualities. Indirect realism distinguishes what we are immediately aware of in sensation from the world itself. The immediate objects of perception are mind-dependent sense data, which represent for us the mind-independent reality. But only some aspects of the representation are accurate. Our perception of primary qualities gives us an accurate picture of the size, shape and position of objects. But our perception of colours, smells and sounds does not. These are imperfect representations of the secondary qualities which cause them. Locke likens the relationship between sensations of secondary qualities to the relationship between words and ideas because it is arbitrary.

Leibniz wrote an extended commentary of Locke's *Essay Concerning Human Understanding*, published as the *New Essays on Human Understanding*. He has an interesting response to Locke's primary/secondary quality distinction. In Leibniz's view, nothing happens without a reason (this is his Principle of Sufficient Reason); or, as he puts it, to make an arbitrary decision on how to link the sensation with the secondary quality is not God's way. So, he argues, there must be a resemblance between our sensations and what causes them, even though we may not be able to recognise it. Leibniz's disagreement hangs on the fact that he denies the Cartesian assumption that Locke adopts that sense data are simple and that we have a complete idea of their true nature. Leibniz believes instead that sensations are compounds of smaller and unperceived sensations, or 'minute perceptions'. So the sound of the sea is not a simple sense datum, but is compounded out of smaller perceptions which lie below the threshold of consciousness. Since our sensations of secondary qualities are complex, not simple, there is no reason to suppose that there is not some relationship of resemblance between them and the secondary qualities, it is just that we cannot bring this resemblance to consciousness in the way we can with primary qualities.[13]

anthology
1.9

▶ **ACTIVITY**

Here are some possible properties of things. Which of these properties do you think are primary – properties that actually belong to objects? Which are secondary – reliant on humans or minds?

Primary and secondary qualities are not always defined or divided up in precisely the same way by philosophers. But a traditional division is set out in the table below. Do you agree? How would you place these various qualities?

	Primary qualities (that is, real, physical qualities)	Secondary qualities (that is, the 'powers' of the object to produce experiences in humans, and other animals)	Other associated properties (often a social concept, but in part a result of the primary or secondary qualities)
Position (where the object is)			
Number (how many there are)			
Shape			
Size (how big it is)			
Motion (how fast it is moving)			
Colour			
Heat and cold			
Smell			
Sound			
Taste			
Beauty			
Value			
Addictive			
Important			
Disposable			

People often find it difficult to recall which are the primary and which the secondary qualities. One way to think about the difference and so remember the terminology is to regard the primary qualities as those that are in objects from the beginning or primarily – that is, before anyone comes along to perceive them. By contrast, the secondary qualities are those which appear only secondarily, when minds arrive on the scene to perceive things. In a world without perceivers, there would be lots of objects with primary qualities reacting to each other; they would collide, melt, dissolve and so forth. The objects in this world can also be said to have secondary qualities as they would still have the potential to produce subjective experiences in perceivers should any appear. But without the perceivers there would be no experiences of the secondary qualities, and no sensations of colour, sound or smell (see **Figure 1.18**).

Also, note that for Locke, secondary qualities ultimately boil down to primary qualities. Consider the example of smell given above. A smell is a secondary quality – the power of a molecule to produce a subjective experience in a perceiver. However, a molecule has this power in virtue of the organisation of its parts, and this organisation is a matter of the primary qualities (shape, size and so on) alone. So although objects can be said to have secondary qualities, in terms of physics alone, they have only primary qualities. These primary qualities have the potential to cause specific experiences in humans, and it is this potential that we term a secondary quality. Thus it can be said that a secondary quality is simply the potential of a primary quality to produce an experience in a perceiver.

Locke lists the properties he considers to be primary: 'I call them original or primary qualities of body, which I think we may observe to produce simple ideas in us, viz. solidity, extension, shape, motion or rest, and number'.[14] However, the list changes slightly later in the *Essay*, when he adds texture, size and situation, and leaves out number, extension and solidity.

There are other considerations which have led philosophers to draw the primary/ secondary quality distinction.

1 All the primary qualities lend themselves readily to mathematical or geometric description. They are measurable. The positions of any objects relative to any others can be precisely described, as can their number, shape, speed and so on. So I can say that one object is moving three times as fast as another, that it is twice as big, and so on. And I can meaningfully say that a hexagon has twice the number of sides as a triangle. However, subjectively experienced smells, colours and so on just do not behave like this. We cannot add, subtract, divide or multiply tastes, flavours, colours, touches or smells in the same way that we can sizes, shapes, speeds, masses and quantities. In Meditation 6, Descartes draws the primary/secondary quality distinction in this way. Only those qualities that can be represented geometrically are real and this leads him to exclude weight and hardness, which have no shape, position or size.

2 Developments in natural science may also lead us to suppose that the world cannot be precisely as it appears to be. We have seen that Locke adhered to the corpuscular physics of his day, according to which the universe is made up of imperceptible atoms or corpuscles which possess the properties of size, solidity and shape.[15] Secondary qualities are the microstructures of these particles which cause sensations in us. And contemporary science is not so far removed from this sort of view. For example, physics tells us that light is a form of electromagnetic radiation, and that what we perceive as different colours are, in reality, simply light waves of different lengths reflecting off the surfaces of objects. Light in itself, in other words, is not coloured. In reality, it possesses only the primary qualities of having a certain magnitude of wavelength, of travelling at a particular speed and so on. Similarly, heat in objects cannot properly be said to be hot or cold. Rather, our experience of hot and cold is produced by our coming into contact with physical objects with differing mean kinetic energy levels among their component atoms and molecules. The sounds we experience are not things with independent existences. Rather they are produced in us by compression waves of air impacting on our eardrums.

3 Another way of marking the distinction between primary and secondary qualities is to reflect on which properties appear to be essential to objects and which do not. Essential properties are those an object cannot be without and remain an object, so these must be primary. Secondary qualities, by contrast, since they only appear in conjunction with perceivers, are inessential. There are different ways of distinguishing the essential from the inessential properties of an object. One very attractive method can be performed in your imagination now. You simply need to reflect on which properties you can or cannot conceive of an object lacking. Inessential properties will be those that you can imagine an object without. And the essential properties will be those you cannot.

To illustrate this approach, consider the following thought experiment about a bachelor. Can you imagine a bachelor who is hungry? Would he still be a bachelor if he were bald? Clearly, yes. So being well-fed and having a full head of hair are not essential properties of a bachelor. However, would a man still be a bachelor if he got married? Clearly not. You cannot be a married bachelor. Such a thing is inconceivable. So we have shown that being unmarried is an essential property of being a bachelor.

Now let us apply this same method to physical objects and their properties. Think of an object, say, an apple. If you imagine it is making no sound (which is not difficult to do), then you are still thinking of an object (a silent apple). So making a noise cannot be an essential property of an object like an apple. Similarly, if you suppose it to have no odour, then you are still thinking of an object. Next, subtract its flavour. Still you are thinking of an object, albeit not a very appetising one. You may say that it is no longer an apple, but certainly it is still an object of some sort. But now let us go further and imagine it without any colour. Again, it is plausible to argue that you are still thinking of an object, only now it is invisible. Perhaps it has been 'cloaked' by some alien technology that bends the light waves around its surface so that our eyes cannot detect it, or it has had a wizard's invisibility cloak thrown over it. So here we have subtracted sound, odour, flavour and colour, but we are still thinking of an object. This suggests that these qualities are inessential and so that it is possible for an object to exist without them.

But let us return to our apple and imagine it devoid of any shape, size, position or motion, neither still nor moving. Here, it seems, our imagination fails us. An object cannot lack these properties and remain an object. An object cannot be neither moving nor still. It cannot be completely without shape. It must have a particular size and occupy a specific position in space. It would seem, then, that these properties are not properties an object could lack in reality. If they are essential to the object, they cannot be properties that we merely perceive in it, but which are not really there. It follows that they must be primary qualities. At the same time, those qualities that we can imagine an object doing without must be inessential, so plausibly, they exist only through their relations with perceiving beings like ourselves. (Does this example convince you? We will return to it later.)

Locke makes a similar point when he asks us to imagine dividing up a grain of wheat. He says that the primary qualities will remain, no matter how small we cut it up – even when we can no longer see the parts – and therefore that they are essential to any portion of matter.[16]

> *Qualities thus considered in bodies are of two kinds. First, there are those that are utterly inseparable from the body, whatever state it is in. Qualities of this kind are the ones that a body doesn't lose, however much it alters, whatever force is used on it, however finely it is divided. Take a grain of wheat, divide it into two parts, each part has still solidity, extension, shape, and mobility; divide it again, and it still retains those qualities; go on dividing it until the parts become imperceptible, each part must still retain all those qualities. ... I call them original or primary qualities of body, which I think we may observe to produce simple ideas in us, viz. solidity, extension, shape, motion or rest, and number.*
>
> Locke, *An Essay Concerning Human Understanding*

4 Locke also draws our attention to the apparent fact that primary qualities are accessible to more than one sense. So I can both see and hear the movement of a bus. And I can feel and see the shape and position of a die. However, secondary qualities can only be picked out by one sense. I cannot hear the redness of an apple, smell the song of a blackbird or see the warmth of a cup of tea. Since a primary quality detected by one sense admits of an independent check, it must have real existence, independent of the way a particular sense organ happens to be constituted.

▶ **ACTIVITY: HOW CONVINCING DO YOU FIND THE DISTINCTION BETWEEN PRIMARY AND SECONDARY QUALITIES?**

I   Does the fact that primary qualities are accessible to more than one sense necessarily show that they are objective? Would shape be a secondary quality if we were all blind?

2   Does the fact that they are amenable to mathematical description show they are objective? Just because judgements in maths provide us with NECESSARY TRUTHS does not itself show that objects in the world necessarily obey these rules.

3   Does the fact that we cannot imagine them without primary qualities show that objects must have those qualities? Perhaps our imaginations are limited.

4   Is it really possible to imagine an object with no secondary qualities? When you imagined the colourless, odourless apple earlier, did the image in your mind's eye not have to have *some* colour for it to be an image at all?

> Essential Terminology Aa

Indirect realism readily accommodates the primary and secondary quality distinction. Some of those properties that we perceive to be in objects really are there, and some are not. So the former are accurate reflections of the way the world is in reality and so should form the basis for our scientific knowledge of it, while the latter are a kind of illusion. This is not to say, however, that they are not useful or that they tell us nothing of interest about the world around us. Our sensations of colour, sound, smell and so on are not completely misleading, since they do map onto real differences in the objects, but at a scale too small for us to detect. Matter might not be coloured in the sense that redness as we experience it is out there on the surfaces of things. But an apple does have certain properties to do with its ability to absorb, emit and reflect light that we succeed in picking out by seeing it as red, and it is often useful to be able to recognise these properties. For example, the ability to see red helps us pick out ripe fruits from a leafy background. Similarly, foodstuffs might not be objectively bitter, but foods that taste bitter are often poisonous to us. And the sweet taste of an apple signals to us that it is rich in energy-giving sugars.

A final way to understand what the indirect realist is saying is to imagine yourself reduced to the size of a molecule of air inside some miniature flying ship in which to get around the world. Imagine observing what happens when a person smells a smell, hears a sound or sees a colour. Nothing in what you observe would be smelly, noisy or colourful. The molecules producing the smell would not themselves smell; nor would the compression waves of air you observe have any sound. The wavelengths of light entering someone's eyes would have a particular length, but no colour, and the surfaces of the things that reflect these wavelengths would also have no colour. (How precisely one would observe the real world if so reduced in size is a difficulty we will ignore.) So, from the point of view of this microscopic ship, the real world is odourless, colourless and silent: a world describable only in the language of particles and forces. However, you would be able to see how the arrangements of the normally invisible parts which compose physical objects produce certain reactions in human sense organs. The powers to produce these reactions are the secondary qualities.

Indirect realism has been the preferred view of most modern philosophers since Descartes. Locke distinguished between sensations occurring within the mind (which he called 'ideas') and external, publicly observable physical objects. We can only come to know about the latter through observation of the former, and so long as we know when and which aspects of our sense data are accurate representations of mind-independent objects, we can use our senses to build up an accurate picture of the external world.

Russell's view, as expressed in *The Problems of Philosophy*, is very similar. He calls what we are immediately aware of within the mind a 'private space' consisting of sense data. The spatial relations between the sense data within this private space map onto those that exist out in the world of real physical space, so that there is a systematic relationship between the perceived table, which may be a trapezium, and the real table, which is rectangular. In other words, the shapes we perceive and the relative distances between the objects will vary between different individuals' private spaces, and within my own as I walk around the table. But because there is a correspondence between our private spaces and physical space, we can make reliable judgements about the shapes and relative positions of real objects.[17]

Russell also distinguishes private and public time. Each of us is immediately aware of 'our feeling of duration', or how time appears subjectively to pass, and this can appear to move more quickly when we are enjoying ourselves, or more slowly when we are bored. Related to the subjective experience of duration outside of the mind, there is an objective or public time, and we make judgements about the sequence of events based on our immediate awareness of our private times.

The strength of indirect realism as a theory is its ability to deal with the problems faced by direct realism: namely, perceptual variation, illusions, hallucinations, the colourless world of the scientist, the time lag in perception and so on. That is not to say it is without criticisms of its own, as we will explore below. But before doing so, let us return to the question we raised on page 54.

► **ACTIVITY**

If a tree falls in a forest with no one there to hear it, does it make a noise?

a) Having done a little philosophy, what do you now believe?

b) What would an indirect realist say?

According to indirect realism, the answer to the question is 'Yes and no'! Yes, in as much as the noise is a secondary quality – that is, a power to produce an experience in humans. But no, in the sense that if there were no perceivers, then there would be no subjective experience of a noise, but only compression waves of air. The same must also go for the colours, smells and tastes of the tree.

Issues with indirect realism

What we have been developing in this discussion of indirect realism is a 'two-world' view of perception. There is 'world number one' – the world as it really is. Here, objects with primary qualities happily obey the laws of physics in their colourless, soundless, tasteless and odour-free world. It is this world, in conjunction with the human perceptual system, that causes us to perceive 'world number two' – the colourful, smelly, tasty world of our everyday experience. World number two, the world we directly perceive, is a representation of world number one, the world as it is. World number two contains our perception of both primary qualities and secondary qualities, and while the latter do not resemble what causes them, our perception of primary qualities provides us with a pretty accurate picture of reality.

Issue 1: scepticism about the nature of mind-independent objects

However, indirect realism is accused of leading directly to a sceptical worry. If all that I directly perceive is a representation of reality in my mind, then I can never directly perceive objects outside of my mind. But if I cannot have immediate access to reality, then how am I to determine how accurate the representation of it is? In other words, how can we determine how well our perception of the world (world two) resembles the world as it is (world one)?

We have seen how indirect realists like Descartes, Locke and Russell claim that our perceptions of secondary qualities do not resemble what causes them, but that our perceptions of primary qualities do. However, if we can doubt that our perception of secondary qualities resemble reality, what is to prevent similar concerns being raised over the primary qualities? The fact that primary qualities are more amenable to mathematical description does not itself guarantee that they are objective.[18] Locke relies on the corpuscular physics to defend the distinction. However if the link between our perceptions of secondary qualities and reality is not one of resemblance, as Locke claims, as far as we can know, it could be anything that causes them. However, in this case, we cannot be sure that secondary qualities are constituted by minute particles with primary qualities. This, then, may lead us to question how we can be sure that our sense data of ordinary-sized objects resembles the primary qualities. Could objects in reality be very different, not just in terms of their colours and sounds, but also in terms of their positions and shapes?

To determine just how good our perceptual system is at representing the world, we would, it seems, need to compare reality with the representation. But without independent access to reality, we cannot place our sensations and the physical objects side by side in order to make a comparison. In other words, we cannot get out of our own minds and adopt a 'God's-eye view', as it were, from which to observe both our sense data and the world. But without such a point of view, we cannot establish when we are being deceived or how accurate our representations are.

For empiricist philosophers such as Locke and Russell, whether there is a relation of resemblance between our sense data and the external world will not be something that can be proved conclusively. This is because they are committed to the view that all knowledge of the world can only come to us through experience.[19] However, since we only have immediate and therefore certain knowledge of our sense data, we cannot have experience of the relationship between those sense data and reality. Hume makes this same point:

Are the perceptions of the senses produced by external objects that resemble them? This is a question of fact. Where shall we look for an answer to it? To experience, surely, as we do with all other questions of that kind. But here experience is and must be entirely silent. The mind never has anything present to it but the perceptions, and can't possibly experience their connection with objects. The belief in such a connection, therefore, has no foundation in reasoning because the reasoning would have to start from something known through experience.

Hume, *An Enquiry Concerning Human Understanding*

Figure 1.19 Indirect realism faces a problem. To determine how accurate our perception of the world is, we would have to compare our representations of it in our minds with the world as it is in itself. But to do this, we would need to get out of our own mind and adopt a 'God's-eye' point of view. This, of course, is impossible.

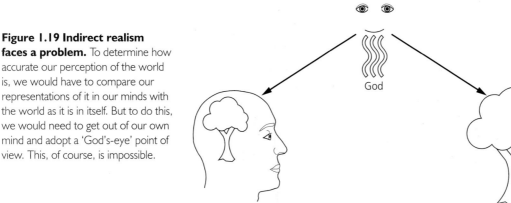

Perception in the mind   God   Real world

The veil of perception

In separating the world as it appears from the world as it really is, indirect realism risks making the external world inaccessible to our senses. The two-world account of perception creates a gap between the world as it appears and the world as it really is, which sceptics claim is impossible to cross. One common analogy used to describe this sceptical worry is the 'veil of perception'. It is as though a veil has dropped down between us and the world, meaning that we only ever have access to our representations and cannot peer beyond the veil to see the world as it really is (see **Figure 1.20**).

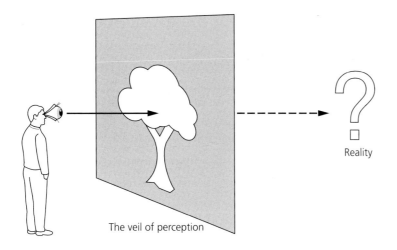

The veil of perception

Reality

Figure 1.20 The veil of perception and the trap of SOLIPSISM. All we have direct access to are our own sensations. We cannot peer beyond the veil of perception to perceive the world as it really is. But if we cannot penetrate the veil of perception, then not only can we not know what the world is really like, but we can never know that the real world exists at all. Perhaps something else entirely is causing our sensations.

So it appears we cannot know whether the world we perceive is an accurate representation of the world as it really is. The real world could be radically different from the way it appears to us, and because we cannot penetrate the veil, we will never be able to know what it is really like. One line of defence against this objection is that if the world we perceive did not, in important ways, match the world as it really is, then we would not survive. We would have been unable to hunt and catch animals, or find the nuts and berries needed to nourish and sustain ourselves, and our species would have died out long ago. We have survived, so our representation of the world must be fairly accurate. Our senses have evolved precisely to give us an accurate representation of the world as it is, so the correspondence between the two worlds must be pretty good.

This defence certainly suggests that our representations are correlated systematically with the world, and so seems to provide some assurance that they represent something real. However, it still does not tell us how accurate our perception is. It could well be that our senses are rigged up to help us survive in the world, but that in the process they distort it completely. There is no guarantee that the best way of ensuring a species' survival is for it to evolve an accurate perception of its environment. The way it is useful to perceive things need not be a good indication of the way things are. After all, different species appear to have very different ways of perceiving the world, none of which we can privilege over the others as the one that reveals reality as it truly is.

Another plausible response is to say that we can know that what we are perceiving resembles what is there by appealing to the testimony of other people. If everyone perceives the world roughly the same way as I do, then I have some other evidence that the world is how it appears. So if I see a banana as bent, and you see it as bent, then one would think that it must be bent. However, the sceptic may not be impressed by such a line of defence. The difficulty is that the perception of the second observer is plagued by the same difficulty as mine. If the human perceptual system distorts reality, then it will distort it in the same way for all humans. The fact that we both see bananas as bent tells us about the way we see bananas, rather than the way bananas are. Using another human does not get round the question of how accurate human perception is.

Issue 2: scepticism about the existence of mind-independent objects

But there is a worse problem for indirect realism. Recall Descartes' EVIL DEMON scenario, according to which our sense data could be caused by something entirely different from what we ordinarily suppose they are. If this were the case, there is nothing in our sense experience that would reveal it, so we cannot be certain that there really is a physical world out there.

Russell raises this 'uncomfortable possibility' in Chapter II of *The Problems of Philosophy*, accepting that we cannot strictly prove false the idea that 'the whole outer world is nothing but a dream'. Nonetheless, he does think we have very good reasons for rejecting it, and an initial solution he considers is, once again, to appeal to the testimony of other people. Surely, when we sit around the dinner table, we are all perceiving the same table. Since we all perceive something which is more or less similar, it seems reasonable to suppose that there is a real object there which causes our perceptions.

However, this solution will not do, argues Russell. For this presupposes that other people really do exist. But if I am questioning whether physical objects really exist independently of my sense data, I must also be questioning whether other people exist independently of my sense data. The sceptical worry we have been led into encompasses not just all the things around me, but all the people as well.

Thus, when we are trying to show that there must be objects independent of our own sense-data, we cannot appeal to the testimony of other people, since this testimony itself consists of sense-data, and does not reveal other people's experiences unless our own sense-data are signs of things existing independently of us.

Russell, *The Problems of Philosophy*, Chapter II

Responses to these issues

Locke concedes that we cannot attain complete certainty when it comes to knowledge of the external world, precisely because we cannot argue deductively from the appearance of a sensation in the mind to the existence of its cause: 'Merely having the idea of a thing in your mind no more proves its existence than the picture of a man is evidence of his existence in the world, or than the visions of a dream make a true history'[20]. But this concession does not mean he thinks knowledge of an external world is impossible. The evidence of the senses provides an assurance of the reality of a world beyond the mind which 'is still secure enough to deserve to be called "knowledge"'.[21] To show this, Locke draws our attention to two features of our sense experience which strongly suggest that they are caused by an external world,[22] and argues that in this area we cannot expect any better evidence. We will now examine two of these features.

The involuntary nature of our experiences

The first is that sense experiences cannot be controlled in the way that remembered experiences can. For example, I can conjure in my imagination the smell of a rose or the taste of sugar at will. However, sensations 'force themselves on me' so that 'I can't avoid having them'. '[I]f at noon I turn my eyes towards the sun, I can't avoid the ideas that the light or sun then produces in me'. The fact that I cannot control what sensations I have suggests that they 'must be produced in my mind by some exterior cause'.[23] Descartes makes the same point in his *Meditations*.[24]

anthology
1.10

Perhaps the obvious response to this argument is to remind Locke about Descartes' sceptical scenario about dreaming that we have already discussed. When we dream, we appear to have sense experiences over which we often have no control. But if we can sometimes have such experiences, then the claim that such experiences cannot come from within me is plainly false. Moreover, even if we grant that Locke's argument suggests that there is something external causing our sensations, it certainly does not show that it must be the physical universe or that it resembles our perceptions in any way. It might be that sense data are produced in me by a Cartesian demon, or the super-computer of an evil scientist who has kidnapped my brain. Berkeley will press this point against Locke, as we will see below.

To the dreaming hypothesis, Locke responds that dreaming of being in a fire is very different from being in a fire, so the fact that waking life is more vivid might be taken as evidence of its being caused by an external reality.[25] After all, even in the worst nightmare, while your fears may be real, any actual physical pain you suffer cannot really be compared to the real thing. Locke challenges the sceptic to test the hypothesis that a burning furnace might be a part of a dream.

> *If our dreamer wonders whether the glowing heat of a glass furnace is merely a wandering imagination in a drowsy man's fancy, he can test this by putting his hand into it. If he does, he will be wakened into a certainty – a greater one than he would wish! – that it is something more.*[26]

This evidence gives us 'all the assurance that we can want'; not a deductive proof perhaps, but such 'an assurance of the existence of things outside us is sufficient to direct us in attaining the good and avoiding the evil that is caused by them; and this is what really matters to us in our acquaintance with them'.[27]

This response may not impress the hardened sceptic in search of a cast-iron proof of the external world, and Locke himself recognises this, accepting that it remains theoretically possible that the pain of the fire is part of the extended dream. Nonetheless, for our purposes, Locke is satisfied that such scepticism is so extreme that we need not take it seriously. We may not be capable of a full proof here, but our conviction remains 'secure enough to deserve to be called "knowledge"'.[28]

Before considering the second feature of our experience, which Locke suggests is caused by an objective physical world, let us examine a puzzle which Locke introduced to the philosophical discourse of the eighteenth century, and which enjoyed a long subsequent history. Molyneux's problem concerns whether someone blind from birth, and who is able to recognise objects such as a cube and a sphere by touch, would be able to recognise them if their sight were restored, merely by looking at them. Now, Locke believes that we gain simple ideas of shape, size and movement from both our senses of touch and of sight. For we can both see that an object is a cube or that it is moving, and feel that it is. He writes: 'The ideas we get by more than one sense are of space or extension, figure, rest and motion. For these make perceivable impressions, both on the eyes and touch; and we can receive and convey into our mind the ideas of the extension, figure, motion and rest of bodies, both by seeing and feeling.'[30] This would suggest that having acquired the ideas of cube and sphere from touch, the newly sighted person might be able to recognise these ideas as the same when they are produced by sight.

▶ **ACTIVITY**

In *An Essay Concerning Human Understanding*, Locke discusses a thought experiment due to a friend and correspondent of his, William Molyneux (1656–98).[29] Suppose a person born blind were to regain their sight and were then shown a cube and a sphere. Would they be able to distinguish the two without handling them?

Discuss Molyneux's problem in small groups and try to formulate arguments for both an affirmative and a negative response.

Given what you know of Locke's philosophy, what do you think his answer was, and why?

Figure 1.21 Molyneux's problem

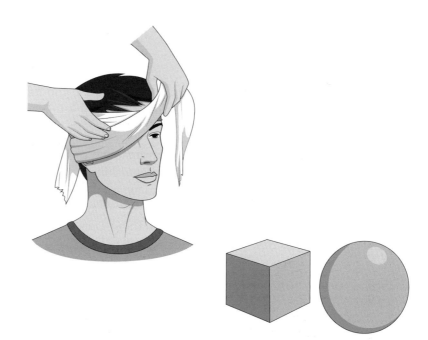

Locke's claim that the ideas of 'extension, figure, rest and motion' can be produced by different senses is closely connected to his claim that these ideas actually resemble the real properties of objects themselves – in other words, that they represent primary qualities. For if both the ideas of touch and of sight resemble primary qualities, then it seems that they must resemble each other. But in this case, there seems to be no reason why the newly sighted person, who is already familiar with these ideas by touch, should not be able to recognise similar ideas when first they first appear through sight.

The coherence of various senses

This claim about ideas common to different senses provides Locke with another feature with which to establish the reality of the external world. Elsewhere in the *Essay*, he notes that that 'our senses often confirm each other's reports concerning the existence of perceptible things outside us'.[31] Focusing on sight and touch, this can be interpreted as saying that these two senses back each other up when they give us the same ideas of primary qualities. We can both see and feel the faces and edges of a cube, and this agreement between the senses suggests there exists some object with those qualities independently stimulating both senses. It would seem to be an incredible coincidence if the very different senses of touch and sight agreed about the geometric properties of objects if those objects did not exist or had no such properties. After all, if two different witnesses independently give descriptions of a person leaving a crime scene, and the two descriptions are a detailed match, we have reason to be confident they are telling the truth and that their descriptions are accurate.

Given his view that the same ideas of extension come to us via sight and touch, it is puzzling that Locke does not reason as we have here when discussing Molyneux's problem. Instead, he agrees with Molyneux's view that the person would not be able to recognise the cube and sphere on first looking. To defend this judgement, he reasons that any connection between the ideas of sight and of touch would have to be learned through experience. Now, you might find this rather implausible, since it certainly appears as though sight produces in us images of shapes which match the way they feel. For example, I can see the straight edges and flat faces of the cube as well as feel them; there seems to be a clear resemblance between them – and Locke himself says as much elsewhere, as we have seen. Locke, however, responds that the sense that there is a resemblance here is down to the habit we have of associating the two sets of sensations after a lifetime of experiencing them together. Just as words immediately lead us to the idea of the thing they represent, without us even noticing the inference, so too with the connections between sensations of sight and touch. So the blind person, given their sight, would have to learn over time and through repeated experience to associate the way the cube feels with how it looks, and so to form a single concept of a cube based on both types of idea.

His response to Molyneux's problem presents a puzzle for interpreters of Locke, and Berkeley picks up on this point when criticising him. Berkeley writes that if, as Locke claims:

> *a square surface perceived by touch be of the same sort with a square surface perceived by sight; it is certain the blind man here mentioned might know a square surface, as soon as he saw it. [...] We must therefore allow, either that visible extension and figures are specifically distinct from tangible extension and figures, or else, that the solution of this problem, given by those two thoughtful and ingenious men [that is, Molyneux and Locke] is wrong.*[32]

So here, Berkeley is saying that if Locke and Molyneux are right, that we have to learn the connection between visible ideas and tangible ones, then Locke's claim that they both reveal the same ideas of shape and so on, must be wrong. Berkeley goes on to argue that the ideas gained through sight and through touch are of completely different sorts; there is no more resemblance between my sight of a cube and the feel of it as between the colour of an apple and its taste, or the sound of a bell and its shape. So while touch may give us ideas of shape, size, position and motion, sight alone cannot. As Locke said in discussion of Molyneux's problem, Berkeley says the sense we have that we can immediately see shapes and distances is illusory; in fact, we learn to connect visible sense data up with ideas of distance and shape by associating ideas of sight with those of touch, and only touch provides us with the ideas of extension. And this undermines the Lockean argument that the senses cohere, and so that they are most likely caused by an objective world which resembles their appearance.

Learn More

Cockburn's argument

We will examine Berkeley's account of perception in more detail below. For now, though, let us examine how a defender of Locke, Catherine Trotter Cockburn (1679–1749), develops the coherence of the senses argument to show that we can have knowledge of an objective reality.[33] In a short letter in which Cockburn questions Berkeley's theory of perception, she begins by conceding that if we had just one sense, we might well never come by the notion that there is a world beyond the inner world we are directly aware of. So if we had just one sense, we would not be able to escape solipsism. This is because the connection between any sensation in the mind and the object causing it outside the mind is arbitrary and a result of the constitution of our bodies and sense organs, and so gives us no basis for inferring that there is a world outside of the mind, nor what it is like.[34]

This is a point we are familiar with from Locke's discussion of our perception of secondary qualities. There is nothing in what causes us to perceive red which resembles the sensation. What causes it is something to do with the INSENSIBLE particles reflecting the light, but these are not themselves red.

Next, Cockburn maintains that there is no resemblance between the ideas of one sense and of another. For example, colours are completely unlike sounds. This is of a piece with Locke's claim that we cannot derive the idea of any sense experience without first having experienced it. For example, we cannot teach a blind person what red looks like by using sounds as an analogy. But Trotter also accepts Berkeley's claim that there is no resemblance between ideas of touch and of sight. This would mean that my perception of a cube as given by handling one, has no resemblance to my perception of a cube as revealed through sight.

Cockburn next argues that our experience of the connection between ideas of different senses provides additional evidence of the real existence of objects outside the mind, not because of any resemblance, as Locke had argued, but because we are able to learn the connection. Experience teaches us that a specific type of change in sensation from one sense is often correlated with a specific type of change from another sense. An example could be the way in which an object changes colour when heated. There is no resemblance between the sensation of burning and of glowing red, but I soon learn the connection from experience of touching the lighted hob. This is even true of the ideas of sight and touch, according to Cockburn. We learn how the visual appearance of objects changes when we alter their angles and positions by handling them. When a cube is turned in the hands, its visual appearance changes from a square to a hexagon, and the surfaces change their hue and brightness. And these changes conform to patterns that we learn through experience.

Now the ways in which the different sense experiences from different senses correlate is remarkably consistent and regular. So, for example, a small change in the visual appearance correlates to a small change in the feel of an object; and the greater the change in the feel, the greater the change in the look. The redder the hob, the hotter it feels, for example. The closer a cube is brought to the eye, the bigger the visual image. And I can correlate changes in the feel of a ball with the changes in the way it looks. So while it is an arbitrary matter how one sense correlates with the world and there is no resemblance between them, the fact that there is a regularity in the way they interrelate means we can conclude that these different sense experiences are produced in a law-like way by an objective reality.

Note that this argument may establish that some sort of world exists and that it correlates with our experience in law-like ways. But unlike the argument about the resemblance between sensations of touch and sight, it does not establish that our perception resembles reality. So knowledge of the true nature of the world causing our sense experience might still be beyond us.

anthology
1.11

Criticism

The coherence of our experience argument to justify belief in an external world can still be countered if we return to the example of dreams. For in dreams, it is quite common for different sense experiences to cohere, so that it seems we are aware of objects with different senses. I can, after all, dream that I eat an apple in which the bite I take correlates to a change in the visible appearance. The Cartesian demon could also be producing an experience in which my different senses cohere in the deception. To say that we would believe independent witnesses in their descriptions of a criminal presupposes that they are not involved in a conspiracy to frame an innocent person. But of course, an equivalent conspiracy is exactly what the evil demon scenario would involve: a concerted effort to make our sense experiences conspire to create the illusion of a physical world. So it seems that the radical sceptical worry about the existence of the physical world is not fully dealt with by Locke and Cockburn.

We have already seen that Locke is not overly worried by this, and dismisses the dream hypothesis on the grounds that, for practical purposes, we must suppose that mind-independent objects are real, as it is on this basis that we must live our lives and on which our wellbeing depends.

To conclude, then, Locke recognises that he cannot give a conclusive proof of the existence of the external world. What he hopes, though, is that these considerations will show that the supposition that there is a world of mind-independent objects which affect our senses in law-like ways is the best explanation of what we experience. As we will now see below, Russell tries to develop this line of defence.

Russell's defence: external world as the best hypothesis

Russell argues that we can justify belief in the external world as the best explanation going. In other words, a complete proof is indeed beyond us, but it is still reasonable to believe in mind-independent objects, as this explains why we have the sense data that we do and why they appear to us in regular and predictable ways.

I can explain why the apparent apple I hide in a drawer can be found again when I return to eat it, if I suppose that apples actually exist as independent objects. The reason I see it again is that apples are made of material stuff, and material stuff endures when no one is perceiving it, and causes us to perceive it when we are in its presence. If I forget about the apple for a few weeks, then come to open the drawer again, I may be shocked to find a rotten apple. If apples have no existence beyond my mind, what explains this experience? Again, the external world hypothesis has a very good explanation: the apple continued to exist while I had forgotten about it and slowly decayed. Apples rot, even when no one watches them. But if there is no material world, all this becomes mysterious.

Of course, Russell recognises that other explanations are possible. Perhaps there is a Cartesian demon causing my perceptions; perhaps I am a brain in a vat; perhaps I am stuck in the matrix or in some extended dream. But in the absence of any positive reasons to suppose that any of these is the case, it is rational to accept the alternative. So, for Russell, belief in the independent existence of a material world is a hypothesis which makes good sense of our experience and is therefore reasonable to accept. Since:

our instinctive belief that there are objects corresponding to our sense-data ... does not lead to any difficulties, but on the contrary tends to simplify and systematize our account of our experiences, there seems no good reason for rejecting it. We may therefore admit – though with a slight doubt derived from dreams – that the external world does really exist, and is not wholly dependent for its existence upon our continuing to perceive it.

Russell, *The Problems of Philosophy*, Chapter II

anthology
1.12

Russell develops the point, that it is far simpler to suppose that objects exist independently of us than that my experience is an extended dream, using the example of his cat. 'If the cat exists whether I see it or not, we can understand from our own experience how it gets hungry between one meal and the next.' But if we suppose it ceases to exist, just why the cat should become hungry in the interim becomes mysterious. Thus the hypothesis that the cat continues to exist makes best sense of the available evidence.

We cannot even talk about the real world

Some philosophers have gone further still in analysing the consequences of this gap between sensation and reality. Immanuel Kant argued that we cannot know anything about the 'real' world (which he called the noumenal world). Our mind receives data from this world, which it then processes. What we perceive (which he termed the phenomenal world) has been processed by the mind. This post-processed world is all we have access to. All the words and concepts we learn during our lives are learned by dealing with the world as we perceive it: the world of colours, smells, tastes and textures. As such, our concepts are designed to match and apply to this world of sensation. If this is the case, then there is no reason at all why our concepts should apply to the noumenal world – the world as it really is. For example, earlier we said that the real world is the cause of our sensations. However, can we really say this? After all, causation is a concept that (as far as we can know) applies only to the world of sense experience. It is only within our experience that we observe one event causing another, but we cannot observe the real world causing the perceived world, nor can we suppose the real world exhibits causal relations at all. The same applies to space and time. All of our sensations appear to us in space and time, but we cannot know whether the real world behind the veil is spatio-temporal. We, of course, cannot imagine what a world would be like that did not involve space, time or causality. But that is to be expected, since we can only understand and imagine the world of our experience. The real world lies totally beyond our comprehension. We should not even call it a world at all. We should say nothing about it whatsoever.

Kant suggests that we should call the perceived world the real world, as this is the world we inhabit and is the only world of which we can speak meaningfully.

Is there a physical world?

We have seen the indirect realist introduce a gap between the nature of our experiences and the nature of the physical world in order to account for the possibility of sense deception and the apparent fact that not everything we perceive is real. But in the process, it appears we have to accept that our claims to know things about a physical world that is supposed to exist independently of our experience cannot be fully justified. Sceptical doubts have forced us to retreat behind the veil of perception. If direct knowledge of the physical world is impossible and we can find no conclusive reason to suppose that the world exists at all, then belief in the external world begins to look like an irrational superstition, something which for practical purposes we cannot doubt, but which serious philosophers must reject. This is the position of the SOLIPSIST. The solipsist has a rich interior life of her own sense experiences, but denies that anything exists other than such experiences. The universe of the solipsist is a purely mental universe of one.

Few, if any, philosophers have defended solipsism. This may be because any sincere solipsists would have no reason to write down their arguments, since they would not believe there was anyone else around to read them. If I were ever to encounter someone defending solipsism, I could be sure that they were mistaken since if I could understand their arguments, then someone other than the solipsist (namely myself) must exist. But just because no one else could be correct in their solipsism does not refute it as a philosophical position. The possibility that no external world and no other minds exist remains a possibility for me – that is, for the subject of experience. If solipsism is true, then what you are reading was not written by someone else – it is nothing more than an aspect of your consciousness.

While it may be problematic to prove that the external world exists, for everyday purposes this appears not to matter to us a great deal. We cannot but believe that we are surrounded by independently existing objects and other people, and Hume and Russell have both pointed out that this belief appears to be instinctive.[35] So where philosophical arguments fail, perhaps we must make do with instinct.

Alternatively, rather than try to show that we are justified in believing in a world beyond our perceptions, some philosophers have opted to swallow the sceptical conclusion, and accept that we cannot know of the existence of anything independent of our experience. Anti-realists hope to overcome the sceptical problem by denying that there is any material world the existence of which we need to establish. The only reality is that of apparent objects; there is nothing left over, no EXTERNAL WORLD, for us to perceive indirectly. We will now look at an anti-realist theory of perception – Berkeley's IDEALISM.

▶ **ACTIVITY**

Imagine you actually believe that you are the only being in existence and everything else is some kind of illusion.

1 What would you do?
2 Would you change your life?
3 Can you think of a specific action that you might do differently?
4 Would you still have a sense of morality?
5 Is there a difference between genuine doubt and philosophical doubt?

1.2.3 Idealism

Idealism is the view that what is real depends upon the mind and, in the philosophy of perception, it amounts to the claim that the material world does not exist outside of the mind. According to the idealist Berkeley, all that exists are minds and their ideas, sensations and thoughts. We know we have a mind, we know we perceive various colours and shapes, and so on. But to suppose that there is a material world that causes these sensations is a leap of faith that we do not need to make. To be an idealist is to take an anti-realist stance regarding matter.

Berkeley's idealism

Bishop George Berkeley was born in Ireland in 1685 and died in Oxford in 1753. During his life, he made important contributions in the fields of philosophy, mathematics and economics. In philosophy, he is considered the second of the three great British empiricists (the first being John Locke and the third David Hume).

Following Locke, Berkeley called sense data, or whatever we are immediately aware of, IDEAS, and claimed that physical objects do not exist independently of minds, but in reality are collections of such ideas. In other words, the immediate objects of perception are mind-dependent and there is no external world beyond our perception. This position he termed idealism.[36] Berkeley advanced several arguments for this view.

The first follows from the empiricist principle he shared with Locke – namely, that all the contents of our minds must come from experience. Any concepts that we have, Berkeley is saying, have their origin in experience of SENSE IMPRESSIONS. This means that if we think we have a concept, but cannot find anything in experience from which it could have come, then we do not really have the concept at all. For example, a blind person, the empiricist argues, cannot have the concept of the colour red, since they have not had any experience of red.

With this point in view, let us consider the concept of matter, or physical stuff. Where could this concept have come from? What is its basis in experience? Well, according to the indirect realist, matter is something that we cannot experience, since it lies beyond the veil of perception. It is the cause of our experience, but not something we can actually experience directly. But, Berkeley argues, if we accept that we cannot experience matter, then it follows from the empiricist principle that we cannot have a concept of it. In other words, the concept 'material object' is empty of content, for there is no possible experience, no possible sensation, from which we could have acquired it. For this reason, he claimed that the indirect realist's talk about 'matter' was literally meaningless, and that the idea of an unperceivable thing was a contradiction in terms. From the claim that an object cannot exist unperceived, Berkeley concluded that its being or existence consists solely in its being perceived, or, as it is often put in Latin: *esse est percipi*, meaning to be (or to exist) is to be perceived.[37]

It is important to recognise that Berkeley did not intend to deny the existence of what we ordinarily think of as physical objects. Rather, he is denying that they have an existence independent of perception. He denies the existence of what the indirect realist terms 'matter': some mysterious stuff which it is impossible directly to perceive. So an object, on Berkeley's account, is no more and no less than a cluster of ideas or sense impressions. An apple is a certain smell, taste, colour, shape, position and size, somehow bundled together before the mind. This is not the same as saying that we imagine the apple. Berkeley is not saying that perception is really a kind of imagining. For there remains the key difference that Locke identified – namely, that you cannot choose what you are going to perceive next, no matter how hard you try. Perception is still the passive receiving of sense impressions; it is just that the sense impressions constitute the objects and so they depend on minds in order to exist.

Berkeley's attack on the primary/secondary quality distinction

On page 66, we suggested that one way of determining whether a quality was primary as opposed to secondary was to see if we can conceive of the object without that quality. We gave the example of an apple and suggested that it could be imagined without any colour, smell, taste, sound and so on (secondary qualities), but not without its shape, size, position or motion (primary qualities). Did you find this argument convincing?

Berkeley argues that you should not have. For an apple which could not be perceived by any of these secondary qualities would not be perceived at all. I can only have an idea of the apple via its SENSIBLE qualities, and if we take those away, nothing remains of it. Berkeley says he cannot conceive of an object which has no qualities other than the primary qualities.

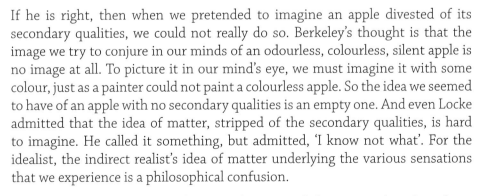

But I desire anyone to reflect and try whether he can, by any abstraction of thought, conceive the extension and motion of a body without all other sensible qualities. For my own part, I see evidently that it is not in my power to frame an idea of a body extended and moved, but I must in addition give it some quality which is acknowledged to exist only in the mind. In short, extension, figure, and motion, abstracted from all other qualities, are inconceivable.[38]

If he is right, then when we pretended to imagine an apple divested of its secondary qualities, we could not really do so. Berkeley's thought is that the image we try to conjure in our minds of an odourless, colourless, silent apple is no image at all. To picture it in our mind's eye, we must imagine it with some colour, just as a painter could not paint a colourless apple. So the idea we seemed to have of an apple with no secondary qualities is an empty one. And even Locke admitted that the idea of matter, stripped of the secondary qualities, is hard to imagine. He called it something, but admitted, 'I know not what'. For the idealist, the indirect realist's idea of matter underlying the various sensations that we experience is a philosophical confusion.

So where are the primary qualities of objects? Berkeley argues that if an object can only be conceived with both primary and secondary qualities, then our ideas of secondary qualities are inseparable from the primary. So if we accept that our perceptions of secondary qualities exist only in the mind, then our perceptions of primary qualities must be in the mind too.

Philonous *Therefore, since even the mind can't possible separate the ideas of extendedness and motion from all other sensible qualities, doesn't it follow that where the former exist the latter must also exist?*

Hylas *It would seem so.*

Philonous *Consequently the very same arguments that you agreed to be decisive against the secondary qualities need no extra help to count just as strongly against the primary qualities also. Besides, if you trust your senses don't they convince you that all sensible qualities co-exist, that is, that they all appear to the senses as being in the same place? Do your senses ever represent a motion or shape as being divested of all other visible and tangible qualities?*

Hylas *You needn't say any more about this. I freely admit – unless there has been some hidden error or oversight in our discussion up to here – that all sensible qualities should alike be denied existence outside the mind.*

Berkeley, *The First Dialogue*

anthology
1.13

Locke sometimes argues that our ideas of secondary qualities are those that are relative to the condition of the person perceiving. For example, when Locke discusses heat in the example of two hands, the fact that the water appears to be different heats suggests that heat is purely a subjective reaction and nothing in the water itself. Berkeley exploits this argument for his own ends by showing that primary qualities suffer the same variability. If we are going to argue that heat and colours are not real on the grounds that they can appear different from different perspectives or to different body parts, then, by the same logic, we should argue that our perception of shape and size are merely apparent. For if an object can appear different sizes to different-sized animals or from different distances, then the size cannot be real. And if the apparent shape of an object can vary, as in the example of Russell's table, then surely the shape, too, is only an appearance. But if these properties are purely apparent, then they exist only in the mind.

Criticism

A defence against Berkeley is to argue that his arguments rest on a misunderstanding of the nature of secondary qualities. Indirect realists are not saying that secondary qualities exist only in the mind, but rather that they are powers in objects which cause sensations in us. The precise nature of the sense experiences they cause may vary with changing conditions, both in the world and in our sense organs, and Locke's point was to argue that we cannot therefore suppose that our sense data accurately reflect what causes them. But although the sense data produced in us by secondary qualities may not be like what is out there, the secondary qualities still exist. So the temperature of the water is real – it has to do with the kinetic energy of the water molecules. It is just that the exact way in which we sense this temperature can vary with the conditions of our sense organs. Thus simple variability in our perception of a secondary quality does not show that it is not real. In the same way, the shape and size of objects may vary according to the conditions under which we encounter an object. But it does not follow from this that these primary qualities are only in the mind.

The likeness principle

Another argument Berkeley uses against indirect realism questions whether it makes sense to suppose that sense experiences within the mind can resemble physical objects existing outside of the mind. In the *Dialogues*, Berkeley's spokesperson, Philonous, reminds us that the indirect realist view involves the claim that 'our ideas do not exist without the mind; but [...] they are copies, images, or representations of certain originals that do'. These 'originals' are 'external things' or material objects.[40] Now, Philonous asks: 'how can that which is sensible be like that which is insensible'.[41] Something 'sensible' here means what can be sensed, so he is questioning whether a sense experience can be similar to or resemble something existing outside of sense experience. The claim that it cannot makes appeal to what is often called the 'likeness principle', which states that sense experiences can only be like other sense experiences and that we cannot make good sense of the idea that a sense experience might resemble something which is not sensed. In defence of the principle, Philonous asks: 'Can a real thing in itself *invisible*, be like a *colour*; or a real thing which is not *audible* be like a *sound*? In a word, can anything be like a sensation or idea, but another sensation or idea?'[42]

If the likeness principle is right, then our sensations and ideas cannot resemble anything beyond the mind, and so we cannot hold on to the indirect realist's claim that objects have primary qualities resembling our perception of them.

What Philonous's rhetorical questions above suggest is that Berkeley thinks it absurd to suppose that a sense experience could resemble what is not another sense experience or idea. But if it is indeed incomprehensible for sense experience to be like an object outside the mind, exactly why is not developed in the *Dialogues*. So what might Berkeley's reasons be for the likeness principle?

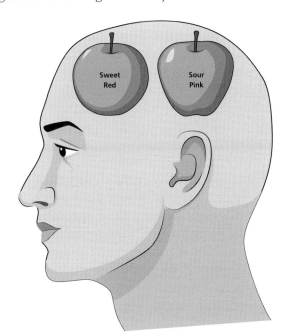

Figure 1.22 The likeness principle.
The sense experiences of these two apples are similar in various ways. But does it make sense to suppose that these sense experiences could be similar to something which is not a sense experience?

One consideration may be that to recognise a resemblance between two things requires that we be able to compare them. So in order to establish the claim that there is a resemblance between our sense experiences and mind-independent objects, we would have to compare the two. And yet any resemblance would have to be recognised within the mind by comparing our ideas or sensations with each other. But since physical objects necessarily exist outside the mind, it is impossible to compare them with ideas in the mind. And if no comparison between sense experiences and objects could ever be made, then no resemblance could ever be recognised. From here, Berkeley may conclude that we cannot make proper sense of the notion that our ideas might resemble objects outside the mind.

Criticism

The indirect realist may not be particularly impressed by this reasoning, however. For while it may well be that we cannot identify the resemblance between sense experiences and objects, this does not mean that such resemblance is incomprehensible or that it cannot occur. Locke, after all, insists that we can make sense of the notion that our ideas of shape correspond with real shapes out there in the world. In fact, Berkeley's examples in the *Dialogues* of sound and colour are accepted by Locke as not resembling anything in reality. Locke agrees that nothing in the external world is like a colour, and nothing in the real world is like a sound. Where he disagrees is with Berkeley's generalisation from these examples to the claim that nothing external can be like any sensation, for he thinks that our perceptions of primary qualities do resemble properties possessed by objects. On the face of it, at least, this does not seem a contradictory claim. Locke can concede to Berkeley that it may not be possible to demonstrate beyond any shadow of doubt that there really is such a resemblance, but this does not show that it is impossible.

Learn More

So if Berkeley's likeness principle is to stand, he needs a stronger reason for thinking that ideas can only resemble other ideas. It may be that he thinks that relations of resemblance or likeness can only occur within a mind since only minds can draw comparisons. If there were things existing outside of any mind, then they would not have real relations between them. Things in themselves just are; any likeness must happen through being compared in a mind. If this is right, then only ideas could ever be related to other ideas, so that no idea could resemble anything not in the mind.[43] A response to this would involve defending realism about relations: the view that two things may, for example, resemble each other without this resemblance being recognised. Defending this view would take us beyond the scope of this discussion, but we might just point out that, contrary to what Berkeley seems to suppose, it is not obviously nonsensical.

The master argument

As I was thinking of a tree in a solitary place with nobody there to see it, I thought that was conceiving a tree as existing unperceived or unthought of, overlooking the fact I myself conceived it all the while. But now I plainly see that all I can do is to form ideas in my own mind. I can conceive in my own thoughts the idea of a tree, or a house, or a mountain, but that is all. And this is far from proving that I can conceive them existing out of the minds of all spirits.

Berkeley, *The First Dialogue*

Whether or not we accept the likeness principle, Berkeley believes he has a final knock-down argument for idealism. This argument is termed the 'master' argument because Berkeley appears to think it is sufficient to establish idealism without the others – Philonous says he is prepared to set aside the other arguments and allow the whole debate to be settled on the basis of this one consideration.[44] We have already seen that he thinks that the idea of an object which exists independently of a mind is incoherent. And to show this, he asks us to try to conceive of a tree which exists outside of any mind – a tree of which no one has any awareness. Now this seems fairly straightforward. Try now to imagine a tree hidden deep in some uninhabited forest where no one can perceive it. Did you succeed?

anthology
1.14

Figure 1.23 Berkeley's master argument. If I try to think of a tree which is independent of any mind, I must think of it, and so it is in the mind after all.

You may have thought this was a pretty straightforward thing to do. However, if so, Berkeley thinks you are confused. For what is clear is that this imagined tree is being conceived in your mind. And if it is in your mind, then it is not the idea of a tree independent of any mind after all. He concludes that since any supposed thought of an object outside of any mind can only take place in someone's mind, the idea of a mind-independent object is contradictory.

Let us now return to the question of the tree in the forest.

Idealism (as we have described it so far) would say the tree makes no noise. Noises are ideas or sense data. They exist only in minds, so if no mind is perceiving one, it does not exist. For similar reasons, there will be no colours, smells or tastes. However, the idealist goes further and claims that there would be no actual tree falling at all unless someone experienced it. It is not just the noise which is mind-dependent, but also the whole event of the tree falling, consisting purely of the colours, the smells, the vibrations and so on. The falling tree is no less something

▶ **ACTIVITY**

If a tree falls in a forest and no one is there to hear it, then does it make a noise?

a) What do you personally think now?

b) What would an idealist say?

perceived than the noise we suppose it to make. We like to imagine that such a tree could still fall down unobserved, but when we do so, we always do it from the point of view of an imaginary observer. So to imagine the tree falling unobserved is implicitly to imagine its being observed. We are incapable of conceiving of the tree falling without at the same time conceiving the experience of the tree falling. For Berkeley, this reinforces his point that to be is simply to be perceived.

Criticism

However, Berkeley appears in this argument to conflate mind-independent objects with their representations in our minds. He is correct to say that whenever we conceive of a mind-independent object, the idea of it must be in the mind. But it does not follow from this that the thing itself is in the mind. So when I imagine a tree standing unobserved in a distant forest, it is quite possible for me to be thinking of an object which exists outside of any mind, even though I am using my mind to represent this thought.

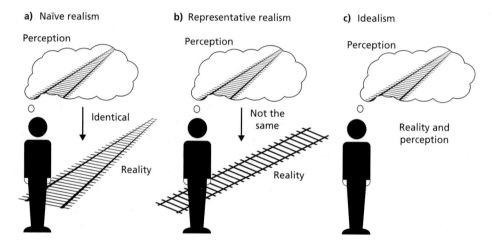

Figure 1.24 The problem of hallucinations. For a) the direct realist and c) the idealist, physical things are the immediate objects of perception. This makes it difficult to account for illusions and hallucinations, since whatever we appear to see is real. The indirect realist b) claims the only immediate objects of perception are sense data, and physical things are known only indirectly. This provides an account of perceptual error when our perception does not match reality.

Issues with Berkeley's idealism

Issue 1: illusions, hallucinations and dreams

An initial difficulty with idealism is that it seems unable to explain the distinction between illusion and veridical perception. If the whole of reality is in the mind, as the idealist seems to be saying, then there would appear to be no essential difference between seeing something as it really is and being mistaken; between hallucinating and veridical perception; or between dreams and reality. Indirect realism seems to have the advantage here. It can make sense of all these in terms of the failure of our sense experiences to match up accurately with the real world. The idealist does not have a 'real world' that can feature in their account of illusions, hallucinations or dreams, and if there is no distinction between veridical perception and illusion, then idealism seems to lead to scepticism about our knowledge of reality.

To focus on illusions for a moment: we normally suppose an illusion occurs when I perceive an object to have properties it does not really have. According to indirect realists, this is because the perception does not match up with reality. But if there is no mind-independent object, does this not mean that whatever I perceive is real and so that the illusion is the same as reality? This seems to mean that Berkeley is committed to saying that when I see an oar appear to bend in water (as on page 58), that it really is bent, and surely this is absurd.

But before we get too carried away with this apparent flaw in idealism, note that perceptual error represents a problem for the indirect realist too. The indirect realist admits that we cannot distinguish illusions and hallucinations from veridical perception by appeal to the way the world really is in itself, since we have no direct access to such a world. This means that the distinction has to be made from within one's experience. Somehow or other we must make the distinction by examining the inner world of sense experience – that is, by examining the contents of our own minds. In admitting this, the indirect realist is obliged to allow a similar solution to the idealist – one that looks for some feature of our experience which allows us to make the crucial distinction.

Given this, how does the idealist make sense of perceptual error? Berkeley begins by pointing out that we are able easily to distinguish what we imagine from veridical perception without appeal to an external world, for what we consider veridical perceptions are more distinct and less faint than imagination. Moreover, we can (at least sometimes) control what is imagined, unlike veridical perception. Dreams, too, he argues, are less vivid than waking life.

Vivid dreams

Now while this is doubtless generally true of what we imagine, and often true of dreams, what of illusions and hallucinations which take us in, or of vivid dreams of the sort that convince us we are awake? Here, Berkeley argues that we are also able to distinguish them because such illusions, hallucinations and dreams do not cohere with the overarching regularity of our experience. To develop the point, consider that what we regard as real are those features of what we perceive which fit well with the regularities displayed in our past experience, while those features which do not fit in well may be regarded as aberrations or errors. So, for example, if while reading these words, you suddenly see them leave the page and turn into writhing snakes, you have a choice: you can either regard this as a veridical experience or as a hallucination. But how are you to tell? You cannot work it out by comparing your experience of the snakes with the way the world is (as both the idealist and the indirect realist admit), since you only have access to the experience within your mind. So you have to ask yourself how well this experience fits in with your past experiences. Is this the kind of experience which coheres well with the way your world has been up to now? Clearly not. Printed words, for the most part, have remained stuck to the pages of the books you have read, and never (or at least very rarely) appeared to snake up towards your face. So past experience suggests this present experience is an aberration, not to be treated as a real feature of the world.

The same is true of dreams. If, for example, you recall a recent dream, in which you went about your everyday life, say, getting up and having breakfast, you might find it hard to tell whether it was a dream or whether you actually did this, precisely because it fits so well with the rest of your life. But if you recall that for breakfast you ate giraffe's eggs, or that after breakfast you caught a space shuttle to Venus, then you would be able to identify this as a memory of a dream, since these recollections do not fit in with how the world of your experience normally behaves.

Berkeley accounts for illusions in a similar way. When I see an oar appear to bend in water, there is no illusion here. This is just a perceptual experience like

anthology
1.15

any other. But the error comes, argues Berkeley, if I then try to draw conclusions about the rest of my experience on the basis of this perception. So if I conclude that the oar should also *feel* bent, or that it will continue to look bent when I raise it out of the water, then I would be making a false inference. And it is in these false inferences that the error lies, not in the perception itself. So again, for Berkeley, recognising veridical perception is all a matter of judging whether experiences cohere with the rest of our experiences. Those experiences that do not fit are regarded as illusory in one way or another.

Issue 2: the continued existence of things

While the idealist seems to have explained the difference between illusions and veridical experiences, she still faces an obvious difficulty: what happens to objects when no one is perceiving them? The answer seems to be that they cease to exist. An apple, for example, no longer exists as soon as I hide it in a drawer, and yet, no sooner do I open the drawer once again than it miraculously returns to existence. Similarly, the apple has no smell or taste until someone smells and tastes it. Indeed, before someone bites into it, it has no inside at all! But does this not seem patently absurd? You light a fire and it roars into life. You leave the room and so it ceases to exist. You come back in the room and, lo and behold, not only does it come back into existence, but the logs are gone and in their place are hot embers and ashes. Idealism seems to imply there are gaps in the fire's existence when it is not perceived. But if fires are so 'gappy', how come the fire has dwindled as if it had existed all the time? What can the idealist say to explain this? Consider also the tree which falls unobserved in the forest. If we saw it standing one day, and on the ground the next, how did it get there? How do we explain this if there has been no process, no unobserved falling over, that brought the tree to the ground?

It seems that the world inhabited by the idealist is very different from the one we thought we lived in. Physical things have no hidden sides, no interiors and no secret aspects. They disappear and reappear without explanation, and there are no unobserved processes going on to explain the changes they undergo in the interim.

Issue 3: regularity of the universe

A related difficulty is that idealism appears not to be able to give any explanation of why there is such regularity and predictability in our experience, nor where our ideas come from. Why, for example, do I expect to see the apple once again on reopening the drawer? Why can I be pretty sure of how this apple will taste? Indeed, why do I see and hear things at all? The realist, of whatever stripe, claims to have a good explanation for why we have the sense impressions we do, and why they are so regular and predictable. There exist material objects which impact upon our sense organs and cause us to see, hear or taste them. Matter retains certain properties when we are not perceiving it, so when we do come to perceive it, we can expect it to produce the same sensations in us. It is because of the independent existence of matter that our experience hangs together as it does. Idealism appears to have no parallel explanation, and the whole world of ideas we inhabit appears nothing short of miraculous.

Issue 4: the trap of solipsism

We have seen that the indirect realist's commitment to the idea that I only have direct access to sense data within my mind can lead to scepticism about the existence of anything beyond the mind. Since idealism is effectively embracing this sceptical conclusion, then it, too, seems to fall into solipsism. The whole of my experience amounts, it would seem, to an extended dream, and I cannot know about the existence of anything beyond my own experience – namely, the external world and other people. The master argument itself is often held to lead directly to solipsism: if it is impossible to conceive of anything beyond my own mind, then only my mind can be known to exist.

Berkeley's defence

In response to the complaint that idealism cannot explain the regularity of our experience, Berkeley would simply question the materialist's use of matter to this end. Why, he would ask, should we suppose matter to behave in a regular way? What account does the materialist have of this? Is this not at least as miraculous as Berkeley's claim that our sensations exhibit regularity? So when it comes to explaining regularity, realism and idealism are in the same boat.

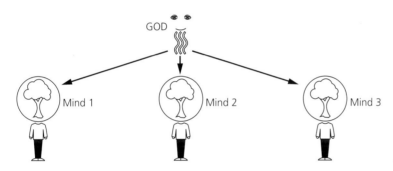

Figure 1.25 Idealism. Nothing can exist unperceived. So physical objects are just collections of 'ideas' or sense data appearing to minds. God plants these ideas in all of us and perceives the world, thereby keeping it in existence.

But what of the gappiness of objects? Berkeley's idealism as so far characterised appears to fly in the face of our common-sense understanding of the nature of physical things, and threatens to reduce idealism to absurdity. Given that Berkeley believes his position to be in accordance with common sense, he could hardly be claiming that the world disappears every time I close my eyes – and indeed he does not.

He claims that objects do continue to exist when not perceived by me, because they continue to be perceived by God. God is a permanent perceiver of all that exists and, by perceiving the universe, Berkeley's God ensures that physical objects retain the kind of continuous existence that realists and common sense would claim for them. Berkeley's God also deals with the other issues we identified above: the questions of where my perceptions come from, why they are regular and whether anything exists outside of my mind. Berkeley recognises that the origin and regularity of our sense data need an explanation, but believes he has shown that they cannot come from matter – for reasons we have discussed. So could they come from within me? If so, solipsism would be true. Berkeley rejects this possibility too, on the grounds that I have no control over my sense experiences. So what other external source could there be for my sense experience? Well, the regularity and predictability of experience strongly suggests the involvement of a good and extremely powerful intelligence. So he concludes that sense data are originally in the mind of God and that he produces them, in me, in a manner that makes them regular and predictable.

anthology
1.16

Berkeley's considered position is neatly summed up in a limerick by Ronald Knox:

There was a young man who said, 'God / Must think it exceedingly odd / If he finds that this tree / Continues to be / When there is no one around in the Quad.'[45]

to which the reply is:

Dear Sir: Your astonishment's odd; / I am always about in the quad. / And that's why the tree / Will continue to be / Since observed by, / Yours faithfully, God

Issue 5: problems with the role played by God

The use of God to shore up a philosophical position is often regarded as evidence that there is something seriously wrong with it. And Berkeley is often accused of bringing God in purely so that he can escape from the difficulties that idealism leads to. Yet, arguably, there is no independent reason to suppose either that there is a God or, if there is, that he plays the role Berkeley casts him in. To use God in this way expressly to solve a problem is often regarded as intellectually dishonest, since it masquerades as an explanation while in fact it explains nothing. If, whenever there is something that we cannot explain, we turn to divine intervention, then we could eliminate all mysteries. All philosophical difficulties could be explained away as miracles, a bit like 'solving' a puzzle about the world by explaining sagely that God moves in mysterious ways.

Moreover, we might complain that positing the existence of God goes against Berkeley's principle that we cannot conceive of anything beyond the mind. And worse, since all that we can conceive of must come from sense perception, it would seem to be impossible to have a coherent idea of God, or any other minds.

Berkeley is aware of this difficulty and accepts that his idea of God (and other minds) is not like other ideas – not, that is, an image of some set of perceived qualities. Nonetheless, he believes the inference to the existence of God is justified, in the same way as we are justified in believing in other minds generally. I can be fairly certain that other people and their minds exist on the basis of their use of language: language is a complex series of signs organised to convey thoughts, and it is inconceivable that combinations of words merely appear to refer to such thoughts in minds other than my own. It is inconceivable just because it would be impossible to construct complex sentences unless there were some understanding of their meaning; they could not come about just by chance or without some intelligence at work. In the same way, the regularity of our sense experience is like a language, indicating the presence of an intelligence orchestrating it. God, in other words, is continually speaking to us through our senses. And I can have the idea of other minds, including God's, by analogy with my own mind, which, even though I do not have a perception of it, I intuitively recognise as that which has my ideas. Given that matter is an incoherent concept, and yet that there is nothing contradictory in the notion that minds can have perceptions, it follows that a mind must be the basis of all that exists.

While the materialist thinks his use of God is dishonest, at least God is supposed to be an intelligence, and so it makes sense that he would do things in an orderly way. So he provides a good explanation, argues Berkeley, of the regularity and predictability of experience. The idea that some mindless substance called 'matter' should behave in a regular and orderly fashion and so account for the origin and regularity of experience is, according to Berkeley, a far bigger cop-out than an appeal to God. Moreover, Berkeley points out that he and the materialist are in agreement that there must be some power outside the mind which produces our sensations, so the disagreement is over what kind of a power it is. And he argues it makes far more sense to suppose it is a mind which actively produces sensations within us than that it is some passive material substance. For our idea of a mind is precisely something which is capable of actively willing – for example, when we choose to act in one way rather than another – and so can be what produces sensations in us. It is worth being clear here that, as far as Berkeley is concerned, God does not enter his theory to save it. Rather, Berkeley's whole argument amounts to a demonstration of God's existence – which is why he subtitles his *Dialogues*, '*In Opposition to Sceptics and Atheists*'. If his arguments succeed in showing that matter cannot exist, then the only way to explain the orderly appearance of sense experiences is by positing the existence of some intelligence producing them.

An imperfect God?

But there is another difficulty with Berkeley's use of God which Berkeley considers in the *Dialogues*. 'But', complains Hylas, 'you have asserted that any ideas that we perceive from outside ourselves are in the mind that affects us. It follows that the ideas of pain and discomfort are in God; or, in other words, God suffers pain. That is to say that there is an imperfection in the divine nature, which you agreed was absurd. So you are caught in a plain contradiction'.[46] In other words, if God is the cause of all ideas or sense experiences, and these sense experiences are in him, then he must suffer from sensations such as pain and so be imperfect. So Berkeley seems to be caught in the contradiction of saying, on the one hand, that our sensations come from the mind of God, and yet that his mind cannot contain pain or other sensations because of his perfection.

Berkeley's response is to argue that the way in which we are subject to sensations such as pain is very different from the way in which they can be said to be in the mind of God. This is because we suffer sensations against our will, as, for example, when God produces a sensation of pain in me. That is, if I hit my thumb with a hammer, I do not have any choice over whether I will experience pain. And God ensures that we experience such sensations in accordance with regular laws which he has instituted, and that are systematically connected to the make-up of our (perceptible) bodies. So not only do I have no choice about feeling the pain when I hit my thumb, but there is a regular, God-given law which determines me to feel pain whenever I hit my thumb. But God does not suffer sensations against his will, nor does he have a body which determines the appearance of sensations in his mind. He is not subject to any laws of nature which would impose sensations upon him, since he creates these laws and imposes them upon us. So God can be aware of what sensations are like, as is befitting his omniscience, but he does not himself passively *suffer* from them. Rather, he actively creates them and governs the manner and order of their appearance.

Berkeley's view of space and time

But the idea that is in my mind can't be in yours, or in any other mind. So doesn't it follow from your principles that no two people can see the same thing? And isn't this highly absurd?[47]

Berkeley rejected the scientific orthodoxy of his day, according to which space and time are absolute – that is, the view that they exist independently of the spatio-temporal relations between objects as if they were infinitely great containers in which objects and events take place. He argued that absolute space is an abstraction from our ideas of bodies and their relative positions, and absolute time is an abstraction from our experience of successive events, and since space and time cannot be perceived in themselves, then we cannot have a genuine idea of them.

According to Berkeley the spatial and temporal relations between objects are generated from within my sense experience, so the space and time of which I am aware is essentially private to me. Since my ideas of spatial relations are as subjective as colour, space is nothing more than the product of the spatial relations that we perceive and has no existence beyond this. Time, similarly, is nothing except the perception of the succession of ideas within each mind.

Criticism

But if space and time are private, and each of us occupies a world completely distinct from everyone else's, then it is difficult to make sense of our common-sense view that when, for example, we arrange to meet on the 18.25 from St Pancras, we succeed because we converge on the same point in an objective spatio-temporal order.

So how does Berkeley account for the public time of clocks and the public space of maps, which are so fundamental to the way we arrange our ordinary affairs?

For practical purposes, Berkeley argues that there is no problem. Even if no *objective* time exists, we can still operate with a *public* time since we can use our perception of standard measures of time, such as the revolution of the earth or clocks. God underwrites our perception of such standards so that they are inter-subjectively regular enough to allow us to arrange to meet, catch trains and so forth. There is no need to suppose there is an objective time over and above this.

Similarly with space. My space is private to me; yours to you. Yet God arranges things so that these different private spaces cohere sufficiently to allow our experiences to match up when we arrange to meet in a specific location. When we shake hands, we may not in a philosophically strict sense of 'same', meet in the 'same place', but for the purposes of everyday practicalities, we can speak of the 'same' here, since both subjective spaces resemble and cohere with each other, just as they do when we meet as two players in the virtual environment of a video game. And when we sit at the same table, strictly the table is a different idea in each of our minds. And yet, the fact that the two ideas resemble each other so precisely, and that our experiences cohere, fully justifies our ordinary usage of the word 'same' in such contexts. What is more, the table in my mind and in your mind are both copies of the table in the mind of God, which further justifies us in considering it the same.

We can see from this that God may be able to establish an objective spatial order by perceiving all of his creation and so sustaining them and their relations in existence. It is more difficult for God to provide an objective framework of this sort for time. This is because there can be no succession of ideas in the mind of God since he is thought to be immutable or unchanging. Moreover, if time is purely subjective and exists only in finite minds like ours, then when I am not conscious of its passage, it does not pass. Indeed, the very idea of time passing while no ideas are perceived to succeed one another is contradictory for Berkeley, so that no time can pass while I am in a dreamless sleep. This, however, seems problematic, in part because the clock appears to show that time has passed while I was unaware. Consider also watching someone else sleeping. In Berkeley's view, there is no passage of time for them – it is as though their time has frozen while mine continues. And yet, common sense strongly suggests that time is passing while they are blissfully unaware of it. After all, if I make a loud noise and wake them up, this event seems to have taken place in time and causes the person to go from a state of unconsciousness to consciousness. Yet, for Berkeley, there is no such thing as an unconscious state, since a mind without ideas it is conscious of is not a mind at all. At the very least, this understanding of time appears not to square with Berkeley's claim that his philosophy is in accordance with the common understanding.

Chapter summary

In this chapter, we have examined various considerations raised against the idea that we perceive the world directly: the facts that:

- our senses are sometimes deceptive
- we may perceive the same thing differently from different positions or under different conditions
- our perception of something does not occur simultaneously with what causes it.

All are taken by indirect realists to show that what we are directly aware of cannot be things as they are in themselves. Rather, they have urged, perception involves a direct awareness of a mental component – the sense data or appearance – which mediates between us and reality. The world as it appears to us becomes a representation of reality, which may be fairly accurate in some respects, but highly misleading in others (as if we are watching a movie of the world, rather than looking directly at the world itself). The arguments for indirect realism, however, are not universally accepted, and there are some strategies that we have explored by which direct realism may be defended. Moreover, indirect realism also leads us into serious difficulties. In particular, it raises sceptical concerns about our knowledge of reality because of the gap it introduces between the immediate objects of perception, which are held to be certain, and the world beyond them, the nature of which must be inferred. Berkeley's idealism is one striking attempt to cut to the heart of such concerns by questioning the indirect realists' right to maintain a belief in a world beyond experience. If we only have access to ideas in our own minds, argues Berkeley, then we have no reason to suppose there is anything beyond the mind. Indeed, the very idea of a non-mental reality is incoherent. Idealism is the view that all that exists are minds and their ideas, a position which may appear counter-intuitive, but which Berkeley himself claimed was in tune with common sense. This is because he is not denying that what we think of as physical objects exist, as it is often mistakenly supposed. Rather, he is saying that objects just are what is perceived, and no more. In other words, he is denying the existence of what indirect realists call 'matter': that unperceivable 'I know not what', which Locke and others claim causes our perception.

1.3 Reason as a source of knowledge

Introduction

If you are like me, then your mind will be full of stuff: hopes, dreams, colours, shapes, beliefs, knowledge, anger, imaginary snakes and so on. But where does it all come from? What is the source of the contents of our minds?

Most philosophers would assert that many of your ideas come from your senses – from hearing, seeing, tasting, smelling and touching. This could be directly sensing the world or hearing/reading about the beliefs of others (who in turn directly witnessed events with their senses). Some philosophers (empiricists) go further. They claim that ALL your ideas must come from the senses (counting both your outer senses and inner senses, such as emotions). This claim goes hand in hand with the belief that we are born with no formed ideas. At birth, our minds are like a blank slate, so all of the ideas in your mind must have come from the input of the senses. Empiricists also claim that experience and evidence from the senses provide us with most if not all of our knowledge. However, other philosophers disagree. There are different schools of thought regarding the origin of knowledge.

Experience as the source of knowledge: empiricism

As outlined above, EMPIRICISM is the view that the ultimate source of knowledge is experience. Empiricists argue that we are born knowing nothing. Everything we know, they claim, comes to us through our five senses. All our knowledge, indeed all our thoughts, must ultimately relate to things we have seen, smelled, touched, tasted or heard.

Reason as the source of knowledge: rationalism

RATIONALISM is the view that the ultimate source of knowledge is reason. Rationalists often look to the world of mathematics as a template for their theory. Mathematical knowledge can be gained with reason alone and without the direct use of the senses. Alone in a room, cut off from the world, in theory it would be possible for me to work out substantial truths about geometric shapes and numbers just by thinking very hard. The knowledge that is gained in this way appears to be eternal, or outside of time. In other words, while everything in the physical world comes in and out of existence, two plus three will always equal five. Moreover, mathematical knowledge seems to have a kind of certainty that exceeds other forms of knowledge. It is difficult to see how one could be wrong about a simple sum. For these reasons, many rationalists thought that the model of mathematical knowledge, with its clarity and certainty, should be applied to all human knowledge. Through the application of reason, they argued, it would be possible to understand a significant body of knowledge about the world and how it operates. This knowledge, like that of maths, would be certain, logical and endure for all time. The evidence of the senses should agree with the truths of reason, but it is not required for the acquisition of these truths.

Innate ideas as the source of knowledge

Some philosophers believe that we are born knowing certain things; in other words, we are born with INNATE KNOWLEDGE. Is this true? It is undeniable that we are born with certain instincts: to suckle, to cry when hungry, and so on. However, whether these count as knowledge is debatable. After all, do swallows

► ACTIVITY

Consider the following list. Some are ideas or concepts, others are beliefs. Where did you get these ideas and beliefs from? What is the source?

1 The belief that two plus two make four.
2 The idea of the colour red.
3 Your belief that parallel lines never meet.
4 Your concept of beauty.
5 Your belief that every event has a cause
6 Your idea of a god
7 Your moral belief that killing innocent people is wrong.

know that they must fly south in autumn? Do squirrels *know* that the winter is coming and that they should store nuts? It seems likely that they have no explicit understanding of these facts, but simply act instinctively. However, believers in innate knowledge argue that beyond instinct, certain other elements, such as a moral sense, a knowledge of God, of abstract principles, or of mathematics, may also be known innately. The belief in innate knowledge is traditionally associated with rationalism, since rationalists often claim it is reason that reveals the knowledge buried within our minds that we were born with.

This section of the book explores where our knowledge comes from. Specifically, it will look at whether reason, by itself, can be a source of knowledge. Can we generate knowledge just by thinking about how the world *must*, logically, be, as opposed to observing how it actually is?

The distinction between knowing something through experience or independently of experience (usually through reason) is captured neatly in two Latin terms (which are used quite frequently in philosophy).

The terms A PRIORI and A POSTERIORI refer to the way in which we acquire and justify knowledge. Truths that can be known independently of experience, without the use of the senses, are said to be *known a priori*. The term can also be applied to the truths themselves: an *a priori* truth is one which can be known *a priori*. Truths that can only be known via the senses and so are dependent on experience are termed *a posteriori*.

Although we may use experience to see that 2 + 3 = 5, our knowledge that two plus two will always make five is gained by reason, independently of the senses. Because of this, we can be certain of *a priori* knowledge **prior to any experience**. So I know that two apples and three pears will make five fruits, **before** I put them together in a bowl. (A good way of remembering these terms is that *a priori* knowledge can be known *prior* to any experience.)

It is acknowledged that we need experience in order to understand language and concepts, but the key point is that *a priori* knowledge is not generated on the basis of experience.

However, truths that can only be known via the senses (or inner feelings) and so are dependent on experience are termed *a posteriori* – for example, my belief that Leicester won the Premier League in 2016. This claim is based on the experience of watching the Premier League, so the belief is justified *a posteriori*. Also, I could not have known this certainty at the beginning of the season – I had to wait until the end to gain the knowledge.

The main differences between the two can be summed up as:

A priori knowledge	*A posteriori* knowledge
Justification is independent of experience	Justification is based on experience
Can be known with certainty in advance of experience	Cannot be known with certainty in advance of experience

In essence, this section explores whether it is possible to know anything substantial about the world *a priori*. Firstly, we will explore the idea of innatism – which argues that you have ideas in your mind, possibly from birth, which do not come from the senses. Secondly, we will look at the claim that we generate knowledge just by reasoning alone.

Essential Terminology

▶ **ACTIVITY**

Which of the following truth claims can be known independently of experience (*a priori*)?

For this activity, put to one side any questions about how you have come to acquire ideas and language. Just focus on whether the truth claim can be justified using reason (independently of experience), or whether the claim can only be justified by experience of the world. Do you need to check on the world to justify these truth claims or can you be confident of their truth independently of experience?

1 2 + 3 = 5
2 Arsenal's home kit is red and white.
3 Water consists of hydrogen and oxygen atoms.
4 It is wrong to kill the innocent.
5 This moment, on the pavement outside your door, it will either be snowing or not snowing.
6 All triangles have three sides.

1.3.1 Innatism

Nearly all philosophers would agree that *most* of our ideas and concepts come from our senses. The question we will explore in this next section is whether *all* ideas are produced this way or whether some ideas pre-exist 'innately' inside us. In particular, we will look at the views of Plato, Descartes and Leibniz.

Innate ideas: arguments from Plato

Plato wrote many dialogues, all concerned with philosophy (see page 9 for more on Plato). Despite this, it can be hard to piece together the philosophy of Plato from these dialogues, as the main character, Socrates, mainly questions others, rather putting forward a clear positive theory. However, across several of the dialogues, a distinct theory emerges, known as Plato's THEORY OF FORMS. Plato was puzzled by the problem of universals: of the relationship between a concept and an individual instance of that concept. We seem to have a concept of beauty, but never witness beauty in its pure form, only imperfectly in different people and objects. So what is beauty itself? If two objects are both red, where is the redness they share? Consider similarly our idea of a circle. We may never encounter a perfect circle in experience, yet the concept of a circle is clear in our minds. Also puzzling is that concepts such as numbers are eternal and unchanging, whereas everything in the world is temporary and fleeting.

To account for these puzzles, Plato believed that our souls were immortal and that, in a prior existence, we apprehended these perfect concepts or forms in their pure state. We have forgotten most of these forms, but they are in us innately, and Plato believed that through a process of reasoning, we can achieve a perfect understanding/apprehension once again.

Although this theory has elements that may seem far-fetched, Plato's account contains some of the classic features of innatism that have been repeated through the ages.

A INNATE IDEAS are 'in' us, although we might not be aware of them (exactly like a forgotten memory is 'in' us).
B We can realise these innate ideas through reason.
C Innate ideas provide timeless truths.

Plato's argument from the 'slave boy'

Plato shows how these innate ideas can be realised through reason in his dialogue, the *Meno*. Socrates engages a slave boy in discussion, and through question and answer draws out of him a proof about squares. The suggestion is that the boy was not learning from Socrates' words, but rather the questioning was helping the boy to recall knowledge that was in him 'innately'.

If Plato's argument from the slave boy were put formally, it might resemble something like this:

P1 The slave boy has no prior knowledge of geometry/squares
P2 Socrates only asks questions; he does not teach the boy about squares

▶ **ACTIVITY**

1 Read anthology 1.17 in the Anthology extracts. The suggestion is that the boy has this mathematical knowledge 'in' him innately – although he was not aware of it. By being encouraged to reason, he is able to access this innate knowledge.
2 Do you believe the ideas were in the boy all along?
3 Does this excerpt suggest that we have innate ideas/ knowledge?

anthology 1.17

P3 By the end of the questioning, the slave boy is able to grasp an eternal truth about geometry/squares

P4 This eternal truth was not derived from the boy's prior experience, nor from Socrates

C1 This eternal truth must have existed innately in the boy to begin with

Do you agree with this argument? If not, a) do you think one of the premises is wrong, and/or b) do you think that the conclusion does not follow from the premises?

Criticism: Memory or the faculty of reason?

The example of the slave boy does not necessarily show that knowledge exists in us as a type of forgotten memory. And the theory that our souls existed before birth in another realm is not needed to explain the slave boy's performance. It could be argued that the story of the slave boy simply shows reason in action. It shows the faculty of reason working out what must be the case given certain features of lines and shapes. And an understanding of these features could be derived from experience. If the boy is simply reasoning, following the hints from Socrates, then P4 is wrong – the boy *can* derive the truth by reasoning from his prior experience of shapes.

Plato and universals

The example of the slave boy illustrates a broader argument that Plato draws elsewhere. Like the boy in the dialogue, once we understand such a proof, we recognise it to be true not just of the particular square drawn, but of all squares. This suggested to Plato that such knowledge cannot derive from our experience, since our experience is only ever of particular squares. So how is such an understanding possible?

Plato's answer was that our minds see the essential nature or *form* of the square and recognise truths about this, rather than truths about the particular example of a square I see with my eyes.

Along with other later thinkers such as Descartes and Leibniz, Plato thought that we have an innate faculty which recognises such truths as eternal and NECESSARY. This furnishes us with genuine knowledge. By contrast, our understanding gained by the senses lacks certainty. Such ideas are only ever CONTINGENTLY true; that is to say, they might not have been true. For this reason, we can only have beliefs about them, not knowledge.

The precision of our mathematical thoughts contrasts with the imperfection of the world, which led Plato to suppose that mathematical and geometrical concepts do not correspond to objects in the physical world. Since he thought they must nonetheless correspond to something, he posited a realm of intelligible objects which is unchanging and perfect. In this way, Plato draws a distinction between a world of ideal forms – the objects of knowledge – and the physical world of which only belief or opinion is possible. Such knowledge is not restricted to maths and geometry, but also applies to moral and aesthetic concepts, such as justice and beauty.

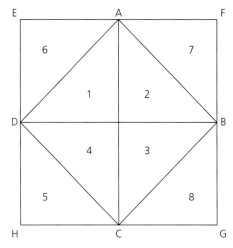

Figure 1.26 Socrates' experiment with the slave in Plato's *Meno*. This diagram shows that the total area of the square EFGH is twice that of the square ABCD. This can clearly be seen since each of the four triangles (1, 2, 3 and 4) which divide ABCD is equal in area and equal to each of the eight triangles (1, 2, 3, 4, 5, 6, 7 and 8) which divide EFGH, and eight is twice four.

Essential Terminology

This approach can be constructed as an argument, which adds more detail to premise 4 in the slave boy argument above.

P1 The senses can only reveal particular instances (usually imperfect examples)
P2 The mind can grasp perfect, universal concepts (often through a process of reasoning)
C1 The concepts (forms) cannot be derived from the senses
C2 These concepts must be contained within us to begin with (they are innate)

Criticism

One difficulty is that while it may be easy to give a clear definition of geometric shapes, when it comes to moral or aesthetic concepts such as justice or the beauty, things are much harder and Plato arguably fails to provide clear and complete definitions of such forms. Additionally, empiricist philosophers would argue that we produce the ideas we have of 'perfect' objects, such as a perfect circle, simply by thinking about shapes we have experienced and removing the imperfections. There is no need to say that the idea is innate, or is apprehended as a 'form' existing in an intelligible realm.

Summary: innate ideas and Plato

We can summarise Plato's theory of innatism as follows:

- **What ideas are innate?** Mathematical objects, such as *numbers* and *shapes*. Abstract concepts such as *justice* and *beauty*. Some interpret Plato as implying that *any* concept must be held innately – even concepts such as *horse* or *cloud*.
- **How are innate ideas held in the mind?** Innate ideas existing inside us as a sort of forgotten or hazy memory, from a time when we apprehended them in a previous existence. The innate ideas (or forms) are accessed through a process of reasoning.

Innate ideas: arguments from Descartes

Like Plato, Descartes also believed that some ideas are contained innately within us. In the *Meditations*, Descartes makes a suggestion that ideas can have three sources: 'Among my ideas, some seem to be innate, some to be caused from the outside, and others to have been invented by me'.[1] He continues by considering where his idea of God came from, concluding, 'The only remaining alternative is that my idea of God is innate in me, just as the idea of myself is innate in me'.[2]

Elsewhere, Descartes gives more detail on the sort of ideas he considers to be innate, which include mathematical ideas as well as very general principles of thought:

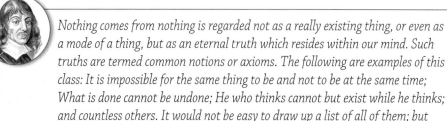

Nothing comes from nothing is regarded not as a really existing thing, or even as a mode of a thing, but as an eternal truth which resides within our mind. Such truths are termed common notions or axioms. The following are examples of this class: It is impossible for the same thing to be and not to be at the same time; What is done cannot be undone; He who thinks cannot but exist while he thinks; and countless others. It would not be easy to draw up a list of all of them; but nonetheless we cannot fail to know them when the occasion for thinking about them arises, provided that we are not blinded by preconceived opinions.[3]

Descartes, *The Philosophical Writings of Descartes*

John Cottingham suggests that Descartes' account of the way we hold innate ideas can be compared to the way information is held in a book. The ideas are in us, though not always present to the mind. It is only through careful 'reading' (thinking) that we can come to understand which ideas are innate and which come to us from elsewhere.

Summary: innate ideas and Descartes

We can summarise Descartes' theory of innatism as follows:

- **What ideas are innate?** Descartes does not present a detailed theory of innate ideas. But we know that he believed that the ideas of God, his own existence, the concepts of *mind* and of *extension* could all be known innately, as well as logical principles such as *nothing comes from nothing*.
- **How are innate ideas held in the mind?** The ideas are there and ready to be found via reason – much as the written words in a book are waiting to be read.

Innate ideas: arguments from Leibniz

Gottfried Wilhelm von Leibniz (1646–1716) was one of the world's greatest polymaths (meaning he was good at lots of things). Most of his life was spent working in the royal courts of various European countries, and consequently his studies in philosophy, maths and science were all conducted in his spare time. Much of his philosophy was carried out with correspondents through the exchange of letters – he wrote over 16,000 in his lifetime. He was also a great mathematician and discovered calculus at the same time as Isaac Newton. Leibniz even has a biscuit named after him – the Choco-Leibniz. Not many philosophers (or people) can boast that!

Leibniz, like Descartes, was a rationalist. He believed that the human mind could gain knowledge of the world through reason alone (though it needs to be prompted by the senses). Part of his belief rests upon the claim that we have innate ideas – which he called 'principles' – which are revealed by reason.

Innate principles: the argument from the necessity of truth

Leibniz puts forward a specific argument for the existence of innate principles which is based on the idea that there are different kinds of truths which have different kinds of status. Like Plato, Leibniz felt that the universality of some truths, such as those of maths, could not be established by the senses alone.

> *The senses never give us anything but instances, i.e. particular or singular truths. But however many instances confirm a general truth, they aren't enough to establish its universal necessity; for it needn't be the case that what has happened always will – let alone that it must – happen in the same way.*[4]

Leibniz is suggesting that the senses can only reveal individual instances and cannot confirm a general truth. To unpack what he means by this, consider the following events that your senses might reveal:

A You see the sun go down and rise the next day.
B You let go of a stone in your hand and see it drop.
C You see a right-angled triangle and, by measuring the sides, see that in this case $A^2 + B^2 = C^2$.
D You see two apples and three pears which together make five pieces of fruit.

We might be tempted to generalise from each of these instances to a more universal truth:

1 The sun will rise each morning.
2 Heavy objects fall towards the earth.
3 On a right-angled triangle, the square of the hypotenuse is equal to the sum of the squares of the other two sides.
4 $2 + 3 = 5$.

Leibniz claims that seeing individual instances is never enough to establish the necessity of a general truth. Consider A and 1. People might be tempted – having seen every sunset followed by a subsequence sunrise – to claim that their senses have shown that the sun will *always* rise. But this need not be the case. Indeed Leibniz points out that a) at the North Pole the sun does *not* rise for some of the winter, and b) there may come a time that the sun ceases to exist. Seeing lots of instances of a phenomenon does not prove that the phenomenon *must* happen in the future. Likewise with B and 2. Gravity is 'observed' every day; however, a (very) large gust of wind may prevent a released stone from falling. Indeed the so-called 'laws' of gravity might cease to operate at any moment and everything in the universe might just drift away. All we can know is that in the past this is the way the universe has worked, but, as Leibniz claims, 'it needn't be the case that what has happened always will – let alone that it must – happen in the same way'.[5]

The point is that the senses might provide a guide to the future, but they do not prove that any generalisation *must* be the case or will *always* apply (for more on this, see the discussion on induction on page xiii).

In contrast, consider the example of general truth number 4 above. This seems different from examples 1 and 2. Surely it *can never* be the case that we wake up one day and two apples and three pears make six fruits, and this is because two and three *necessarily* make five? This general truth has a status that examples 1 and 2 seem to lack. In cases 1 and 2, we might have different degrees of confidence in the status of the claim, but with 4 we can have certainty, and this is because the claim that $2 + 3 = 5$ is *necessarily* true. But if example 4 is necessarily true and we earlier suggested that generalisations based on the senses *cannot* show that any truth is necessarily true, then this would suggest that we cannot grasp the necessity of this truth from our senses alone. We must grasp the truth another way. For Leibniz, the truth is held innately and it is revealed by reason.

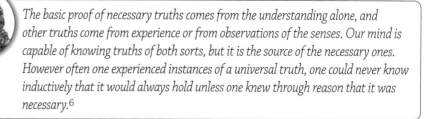

The basic proof of necessary truths comes from the understanding alone, and other truths come from experience or from observations of the senses. Our mind is capable of knowing truths of both sorts, but it is the source of the necessary ones. However often one experienced instances of a universal truth, one could never know inductively that it would always hold unless one knew through reason that it was necessary.[6]

Put formally, Leibniz's argument would look something like this:

P1 The senses only give us particular instances
P2 A collection of instances can never show the *necessity* of a truth
P3 We can grasp and prove many necessary truths (such as mathematics)
C1 Therefore the necessary truths that we grasp with our mind do not derive from the senses
C2 The mind is the source of these necessary truths
C3 These ideas are known innately

Leibniz's approach is fairly similar to Plato's. Both held up mathematical truths as cases where truths were necessary/universal and grasped by the mind, not the senses. However, Leibniz's approach does not involve a belief in a past life. Also, Leibniz did not claim that innate principles exist within us at birth, like a forgotten memory or even as words in a book waiting to be discovered. Instead he used a metaphor of a block of marble – one that has specific 'veins' running through it.

Leibniz compares our minds to a block of marble that is veined in such a way that when stuck with a chisel it will readily take a specific shape. The block of marble does not contain the fully formed statue, but has the 'inclination' or 'tendency' to take a particular shape when struck. Likewise we are not born with innate ideas fully formed, since we need the experience of the senses to gain ideas (the equivalent of the marble being struck), but our minds are structured such that certain ideas and principles will appear once prompted by the senses (though these ideas and principles are not derived from the senses). 'This is how ideas and truths are innate in us – as inclinations, dispositions, tendencies, or natural potentialities, and not as actual thinkings'.[7]

anthology
1.18

Unlike Plato and Descartes, Leibniz acknowledges the role of the senses in filling and forming the mind, but argues that the senses are not sufficient to give us the necessary truths we are capable of possessing. 'Although the senses are necessary for all our actual knowledge, they aren't sufficient to prove it all'.[8]

As well as certain principles and dispositions being innate, Leibniz added a list of concepts that are not derived from the senses but from our awareness of ourselves. These include unity (as *you* are a singular thing), duration (as *you* exist in time), change (as *you* change), action (as *you* act) and pleasure (which *you* experience).[9]

What do we mean by innate ideas, according to Leibniz?

Leibniz's conception of innate ideas raises questions about what we might class as ideas and also about what we might class as innate. With regard to those ideas, he claims we gain from an awareness of ourselves; empiricists such as Locke and Hume would argue that these are still ideas gained from experience. They grant that they may not be derived from the senses, but would claim they are derived from reflective experiences about yourself. Does this make them innate or not? They are innate in the sense that you are the source (innate to you), but according to Locke and Hume, they are not innate in the sense that you are born with them. They are derived from experience, albeit experience of yourself.

The question of what counts as an idea is trickier still. Is the ability to reason an innate idea? What about the ability to understand that 2 + 3 = 5, or that an object is identical to itself?

▶ **ACTIVITY**

Calling abilities and tendencies innate does raise the question about whether these count as innate *ideas*. Consider A–H.

1 Do you believe any are innate?
2 Would you count these as innate *ideas*?

A Beavers 'knowing' to build a dam to flood a river.
B The concept of self.
C The ability to understand geometry.
D Your sense of moral outrage.
E Swallows 'knowing' to fly south in autumn.
F A baby's ability to suckle.
G The ability to recognise two objects as the same.
H The concept of 'identity'.

In recent times, new thinkers have again revived the notion of innatism (though now referred to as Nativism). The broad claim is similar to that made by Leibniz – that is, the mind does not contain fully formed ideas, but structures, which might have evolved over long periods of time. The philosopher Noam Chomsky (1928–) has argued, with good evidence, that it would be impossible for any human to learn language simply on the basis of what they hear as they grow up, if their minds did not already possess certain innate organising principles. He argues that we have an innate capacity to learn language, which enables us to pick up the structure and grammar of language much more quickly than would otherwise be possible. The mind, in other words, brings an innate structure, a type of conceptual scheme, to our language impressions. In this sense, Chomsky suggests that we do have an innate ability to learn language, but this only comes into play if we are exposed to other language speakers.

Summary: Leibniz and innate ideas

We can summarise Leibniz's theory of innatism as follows:

- **What ideas are innate?** Truths of mathematics; logical principles such as the law of non-contradiction (for example, an object cannot be blue and not blue at the same time); the concept of identity. Leibniz includes concepts derived from our awareness of ourselves; these include unity, substance, duration, change, action and pleasure.
- **How are innate ideas held in the mind?** They are not held as fully formed ideas at birth, but as inclinations and tendencies to think. With sufficient, careful attention, we can reveal these innate principles using reason.

Empiricist responses to innate ideas

Above we have seen three different philosophers articulate accounts of how some of our ideas are innate. In contrast, empiricism is the branch of philosophy which claims that *all* of our ideas and concepts are derived from experience. Roughly, the idea is that we are born with no concepts or ideas, so all of our concepts and ideas must be derived from the input of our senses. This directly counteracts the claim that we are born with innate ideas.

Locke's arguments against innatism

John Locke was one of the first philosophers to put forward a detailed account of empiricism. The first section of his *Essay Concerning Human Understanding* (1690) is devoted to refuting the view that we are born with certain 'innate ideas'. The rest of the *Essay* attempts to show how the human mind is able to acquire all of its knowledge and ideas exclusively from sense experience and from the mind's ability to reflect upon itself.

At the time of his writing, innatism was a commonly held belief among both philosophers and the general population.

Nothing is more commonly taken for granted than that certain principles ... are accepted by all mankind. Some people have argued that because these principles are (they think) universally accepted, they must have been stamped onto the souls of men from the outset.[10]

Locke presents a range of arguments against innatism, which can be divided into the 'positive' and the 'negative'. The positive arguments rely on the strength and simplicity of empiricism to show that innatism is an unnecessary theory. The negative arguments attempt to show that innatism is incoherent and based on false claims, and it these 'negative' arguments that we explore first.

Locke's main approach in undermining innatism is to attack the idea of universal consent. A very brief version of his argument is this: universal consent, although used as an argument *for* innate ideas, is in fact an argument *against* innate ideas as, in reality, there are no universally held ideas and so there are no innate ideas.

... this argument from universal consent which is used to prove that there are innate principles can be turned into a proof that there are none; because there aren't any principles to which all mankind give universal assent.[11]

By denying that any idea is universally held, Locke wants to 'prove' that there are no innate ideas. In the text, Locke does not set out his overall argument formally, but if he did it would look something like this:

P1 Any innate idea, x, if it exists, would be universally held
P2 Children and idiots do not have the idea of x
P3 The notion of a person having an innate idea, x, and not being aware of it, does not make sense (This is really a sub-argument supporting P2)
C1 So x is not universally held
C2 Therefore x is not innate

Previously, we explored Leibniz's account of innate ideas. Leibniz was a contemporary of Locke and, as a believer in innate ideas, found some of the empiricist ideas of Locke very challenging. To counter these, he published a defence of his own philosophy entitled *New Essays on Human Understanding*. As Leibniz was responding directly to Locke, we will explore the strands of Locke's argument and Leibniz's counter-criticisms at the same time.

1 No ideas are universally held, so none is innate

Many people in the past (and even today) have used the idea of universal consent as a justification for believing that certain ideas are innate. The idea behind this argument is that all humans have different upbringings and experiences and so have different ideas. Some people like music, some do not; some are optimists, some pessimists; and each person has a unique set of tastes and preferences. Given this diversity of thought, if some ideas are held by *all* of humanity, then these ideas cannot be derived from our different experiences. Instead, they must have been 'stamped on our souls from the outset'. In other words, they must be innate.

One of Locke's key arguments is to attack this idea of universal consent. He wants to show that in reality, there are no universally held ideas and so there are no innate ideas. To do this, he selects two commonly held candidates for innateness.

▶ **ACTIVITY**

1 Can you think of any ideas or beliefs that are held by everyone in the world? Perhaps basic mathematical beliefs? Moral beliefs?

2 If such universal ideas do exist, do you think they would have to exist in all minds innately or could they be drawn from experience?

I shall begin with speculative principles, taking as my example those much vaunted logical principles 'Whatever is, is' [and] 'It is impossible for the same thing to be and not to be', which are the most widely thought to be innate. They are so firmly and generally believed to be accepted by everyone in the world that it may be thought strange that anyone should question this.[12]

The two ideas Locke selects are, 'Whatever is, is', which is known in logic as the law of identity, and 'It is impossible for the same thing to be and not to be', which is known as the law of non-contradiction. The particular detail of these claims is not really important. Locke wants to use what he thinks are the most likely candidates for innateness, as if he can show that *these* are not universally held, then the claim that *any* idea is universally held will be severely weakened. Locke later argues that other key candidates for innate ideas, such as the idea of God or of key moral principles, such as 'do not steal', are also not universally held.

Locke proceeds to assert that universal consent does not exist, even for these principles:

Children and idiots have no thought – not an inkling – of these principles, and that fact alone is enough to destroy the universal assent that any truth that was genuinely innate would have to have.[13]

Certainly if you asked a young child whether they believe that something can both be and not be, they are likely to stare at you in a confused manner and be lost for an answer. Similarly for knowledge of geometry or the idea of God: a child who has not been taught geometry may not be able to answer questions on it, and one who has not learned about God would have no idea of him. Because 'children and idiots' seem to lack these ideas, Locke claims they are not universally held, and so not innate.

However, there are several potential weaknesses in Locke's argument. First, it could be the case that 'children and idiots' do possess these innate ideas, but they are not aware that they possess them. We explore this possibility in Strand 2 below. Secondly, Leibniz claims that 'children and idiots' *do* actually employ the law of identity and the principle of non-contradiction in their everyday actions, even though they would not be able to articulate these ideas in words.

… we use the principle of contradiction (for instance) all the time, without explicitly attending to it; and everyone, however uncivilized, is upset when someone lyingly contradicts himself concerning something he cares about. Thus, we use these maxims without having them explicitly in mind.[14]

A child might not even be able to say the phrase 'law of non-contradiction', but she knows that her favourite teddy cannot both be in her hand and in the loft at the same time. So, contrary to Locke, these ideas may still be held universally.

Lastly, it is not clear that innate ideas need to be universally held in the first place. Certainly, not all universally held ideas are innate. Leibniz makes this point humorously by claiming that 'the practice of smoking tobacco has been adopted by nearly all nations in less than a century'.[15]

Presumably, even if everyone in the world smoked, it would not make smoking an innate desire! In other words, universality is not a sufficient condition for innateness. It is not even clear that universality is a necessary condition for innate ideas either. It could be the case that God has given innate ideas to specific people only. Maybe we are born with memories and ideas from a previous life; these ideas would be innate, but there is no reason why they would be universally held.

To come to Locke's defence, part of his motive was to undermine the reason people gave for believing in innate ideas, and at the time of his writing, many thinkers *did* in fact argue for the existence of innate ideas on the grounds of universal consent (as some do today). However, undermining the idea of universal consent does not necessarily undermine the theory of innatism.

2 Transparency of ideas

As we explore later (page 136), Descartes claims that the idea of God must be innate within him (as only God could cause his idea of God). This may work for Descartes, but Locke argues that not everyone has the idea of God and that most people learn about God through others – not innately. A classic defence of the innatist is to claim that we *do* all have the idea of God (and other innate ideas) within us, but some of us (children and 'idiots' included) may not be aware of this yet.

Locke takes issues with this defence and argues that the possibility of possessing an innate idea but not being aware of it makes no sense.

> *To imprint anything on the mind without the mind's perceiving it seems to me hardly intelligible. So if children and idiots have souls, minds, with those principles imprinted on them, they can't help perceiving them and assenting to them.*[16]

Locke is saying that any innate idea, if held, would be 'perceived' by the mind. In other words, that our minds are transparent and we are able to perceive all of the ideas they contain. For Locke, this does not mean you are constantly aware of all your ideas at once, but that for any idea to be 'in' your mind, you must at least have thought of it, or been conscious of it at some point in the past. After all, if you have never had an idea/thought, then in what sense could it be 'in' your mind? Could you have had a pain that you never felt?

However, maybe there *are* ideas/concepts/memories 'in' your mind that you have never been conscious of, or experienced at any point. Perhaps you have observed events without realising (subconsciously), and can recall these at a later stage. Maybe you 'absorbed' a song that was playing in the background, without being consciously aware of it. That song is not immediately accessible and transparent in your mind, in that you cannot recall it, but it may be recognisable if you heard it again. So it must have been 'in' you somewhere. If these examples are possible, then surely an innate idea, too, could be 'in' your mind, without you being aware of it yet.

Leibniz puts forward this very idea in his *New Essays*. In articulating this view – the idea of taking in information subconsciously – Leibniz was substantially ahead of his time (although he does not actually use the term *subconscious*). If this idea is plausible, then it would seem to undermine one of Locke's key arguments, as it may be possible to have innate ideas of beauty, or of mathematics, that are only awoken by the appropriate stimulus later in life.

anthology
1.19

3 How can we distinguish innate ideas from other ideas?

So an innatist might be able to claim that an idea is in you, perhaps as a capacity, which you are unaware of, but which becomes active later in life, given the right stimulus.

Locke rejects this by arguing that this approach could be true of all ideas/ capacities, so how can we distinguish the innate ones from the non-innate? Why not say that the idea of blue, or the capacity to see blue, was in you from birth, but only when you see the colour blue does the idea/capacity become active. Likewise with the taste of chocolate, concepts of geometry, the idea of a cat and so on. Everything the mind could ever know would be 'innate' in this sense. Even innatists, such as Leibniz, do not hold this. So the problem for the innatist is that if it is possible that we have innate ideas, but that they only come into our minds in later life, then how can we tell which ideas are the innate ones and which are the ones derived from experience?

Once again, Leibniz takes issue with this criticism of Locke's. As we saw on page 99, Leibniz suggests that we *can* distinguish innate ideas from the non-innate ones, even if they emerge later in life, because innate ideas are true in a different way – they are *necessarily* true.

Leibniz claims that although young children may not be able to know many of the truths of mathematics (even most adults do not!), once they do understand a truth, the mind immediately recognises that this truth has an eternal application and that such truths are different from truths of fact. In this way, contrary to Locke's claim, Leibniz claims that there is a way of distinguishing innate ideas from non-innate ideas, even though the ideas may not be made aware to the mind until later in life.

On this view, all the propositions of arithmetic and geometry should be regarded as innate, and contained within us in a potential way, so that we can find them within ourselves by attending carefully and methodically to what is already in our minds, without employing any truth learned through experience or through word of mouth. Plato showed this, in a dialogue where he had Socrates leading a child to abstruse truths just by asking questions, not telling him anything. [We explored this dialogue on page 96.] So one could construct the sciences of arithmetic and geometry in one's study – with one's eyes closed, even – without learning any of the needed truths from sight or even touch.[17]

The mind as *tabula rasa*

So far we have explored some arguments from John Locke's *Essay Concerning Human Understanding* – specifically his attempt to refute the theory that we are born with certain 'innate ideas'. Most of Locke's *Essay* is a positive attempt to show how the human mind, starting as a blank slate, is able to acquire the knowledge and ideas of which it is capable exclusively from sense experience and from the mind's ability to reflect upon itself and its own operations.

The idea that the mind can be compared to a *tabula rasa* (which is Latin for blank tablet or slate) goes back to the early days of Western philosophy, where we find it in the writings of Aristotle, but it was Locke who gave the theory its first clear articulation.

This idea of the mind starting as a *tabula rasa* has considerable appeal. After all, it does seem that we have to learn what we know about the world through our life experiences. A newborn baby knows nothing of colours, sounds, tastes and smells, except perhaps what it recalls of its limited experiences in the womb. It gradually learns to recognise faces, where to find milk, which foods it likes, and so on. What we as adults consider the most basic pieces of knowledge about our world, such as that objects fall downwards, or that day follows night, would at one point in our lives have been novel discoveries.

anthology
1.20

The *tabula rasa* theory works as a powerful argument against the theory of innate ideas. For if it can be shown that our ideas come from experience, then claiming that we have innate ideas would seem to be an unnecessary theory and so it would be unreasonable to hold it.

This argument implicitly relies on a principle known as Ockam's razor, which is the idea that, wherever possible, we should always go for the simplest explanation. (The idea of the 'razor' is that we should shave off any unnecessary elements to an explanation.) Locke uses the example of our idea of colours to make the case, but suggests that it will apply to any supposedly innate idea. He argues that it *could* be the case that:

anthology
1.21

a) we are born with an innate idea of each colour.

And it certainly *is* the case that:

b) we see colours with our eyes.

The question is, why would God, or even nature, bother with a), given that b)? It is a simpler explanation to say that our idea of colour is derived from b). Claiming a) seems to add no extra explanatory value and so, according to Locke, is an 'absurd' additional claim. The general principle in play here is that that we should go for the simplest explanation – in other words, Ockham's razor.

In this section, we will explore whether it *is* possible to explain all of our ideas by reference to our experience alone and see whether the *tabula rasa* theory is workable. In doing so, we will also draw on the ideas of another famous empiricist philosopher, David Hume.

Sense impressions and concepts

To see how the *tabula rasa* theory is supposed to work, we first need to make clear an important distinction between sense experiences and concepts (which some philosophers, such as Locke and Hume, call ideas). At any given moment, much of what we are conscious of is what we are actually sensing. So I am now aware of the tea I am drinking because I am actually seeing, tasting and smelling it. But I am also able to think about tea when I am not actually in its presence. This is an important ability, since without it we would only ever be conscious of what we are sensing at the present moment. If we could not think about tea while we were not actually experiencing it, then we could not recognise it on the next occasion, nor could we hold any beliefs about it, such as that it is a good drink to wake up to, or that it is made by pouring boiling water onto dried leaves. So concept formation is crucial to knowing about the world.

Empiricism claims that all our concepts, like that of tea, are formed out of sense experiences. It is only because I have encountered tea that I can have the concept of tea, and so can form beliefs about it. We also have various inner impressions, ranging from physical sensations of pleasure and pain to emotions such as jealousy or sadness. These are also an important source of concepts.

At first glance, this view seems inadequate to account for the complexity of the mind, since we surely possess all kinds of concepts of things we have never experienced. For example, we are able to imagine all kinds of fantasy creatures, such as unicorns and dragons, which do not exist in reality and which we have never encountered. I am able to imagine green aliens with eyes on stalks and spiky legs, which I have never actually witnessed with my senses. However, on closer inspection I have to concede that the elements out of which I have composed my imaginary alien do indeed come from my own experiences. Its colour is derived from my perception of grass and leaves; the antennae are obtained from seeing butterflies; and its spiky legs are stolen from crabs. It seems that all the elements of my imaginary alien friend have, in one way or another, come from my sense experience of the world. The only novel thing is the arrangement of the elements. And this, argues the empiricist, is true of anything I can imagine or conceive. As Hume writes:

> *But although our thought seems to be so free, when we look more carefully we'll find that it is really confined within very narrow limits, and that all this creative power of the mind amounts merely to the ability to combine, transpose, enlarge, or shrink the materials that the senses and experience provide us with.*[18]

anthology
1.22

Locke and Hume both distinguish between simple and complex concepts, or what they call 'ideas'. Simple ideas consist of a single element, such as the idea of red. Complex ideas involve various simple ideas merged together – for example, a gold mountain or a unicorn. All simple ideas must ultimately derive from simple impressions. For example, my idea of red must have come from my sense impressions of red.

Like Locke, Hume also claims that we have inward impressions (feelings) and outward impressions, such as seeing a tree. In other words, not all impressions are sense impressions; my emotions such as anger or feeling pain count as impressions too. And my idea of anger will come from my impression of anger. So not all our ideas are derived from sense experience, as some ideas, such as sadness, will be derived from our inward impressions.

One important consequence of this theory is that all of our ideas, our concepts, thoughts and imagination, must have come from our impressions. This, of course, is the central claim of empiricism. But for a moment, consider its consequence. The claim is that everything in our imagination must have come from an impression.

Locke and Hume claim that our imaginations can rearrange the basic elements we acquire from experience, but that we cannot invent these elements for ourselves. With this, we can flesh out the details of this picture of how our

▶ **ACTIVITY**

To help you consider the theory of empiricism, try the questions below:

1 Is it possible to imagine a brand new colour you have never experienced before?
2 Do you think someone who is colour-blind from birth could ever know what red is?
3 Construct your own made-up creature and then identify how your construction is derived from experience.
4 Can you think of any ideas that are not ultimately derived from experience?
5 Do your answers to these questions tend to support empiricism? Or do they raise difficulties with it?

minds work. We have, on the one hand, simple impressions – that is, the information gained through experience, typically via the senses (sometimes called sense data). These are the basic elements that come into the mind, which cannot be broken down further into smaller elements. Examples of simple impressions might be the sight of red, the smell of tea or the sound of a trumpet.

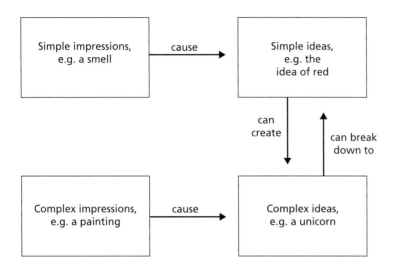

Figure 1.27 Where our ideas come from. Following the arrows backwards, we can see that all ideas, both complex and simple, derive from impressions.

On the other hand, we can also think about the things we experience when we are not actually perceiving them. I can think of the colour red or a nice cup of tea even when I am not presently experiencing them – in other words, I can form concepts. To do this, according to the empiricist, the mind retains the basic sense experience as a kind of copy or image. This copy is stored in the mind so that we can think about things we are not experiencing and recognise them when we encounter them. For example, I acquire the concept of red from first observing it, and my mind stores the concept as a kind of image of the original sensation. Armed with this concept, I am able to recognise some new experience as being an experience of red.

In the same way, my concept of tea is formed from the various sense experiences I have had of tea from seeing, smelling and tasting it. My concept of tea, therefore, unlike that of red, is complex, since it is formed out of the various simple elements of its smell, colour, taste and so forth. Once I possess the tea concept, the next time I encounter some tea, I can recognise it. Having the concept of tea also enables me to distinguish it from coffee, biscuits and everything else. Simple concepts, like red, can be acquired only if one has experienced the relevant impression, and so for every simple concept there must correspond a simple sense experience. This means a person born blind cannot have the concept of red, or any other colour, because they have not had the simple impression of red. But, as we have seen, I can concoct new, complex concepts of things I have never experienced by rearranging simple elements.

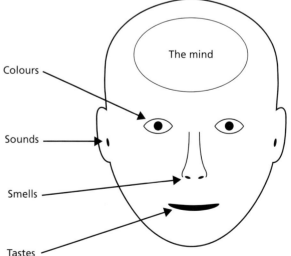

Figure 1.28 No concepts without impressions. The *tabula rasa* thesis is saying that all our ideas or concepts are derived from impressions, so that there can be nothing in the mind that does not originate with impressions.

Experimenting with ideas

To see if this theory of no concepts without impressions works, try to trace the following complex ideas back to the impressions from which they derive:

1 Sherlock Holmes   5 Chocolate pizza
2 Dragons   6 God
3 The number   7 Friendship
4 Beauty   8 Justice

Are some of the ideas harder than others? Later we discuss some of the difficulties with the empiricist account of concept formation that this activity raises.

Hume on innate ideas

After espousing his theory of how our ideas are derived from our impression, Hume adds a short passage concerning innate ideas. (He thinks the whole debate is a bit of a red herring, so only touches on it in a long footnote.) Hume claims that much of the disagreement between Locke and Leibniz (and others) arises from ambiguities in the terms 'innate' and 'ideas', which different writers use in different senses. Hume acknowledges that many of our passions and desires, such as disliking pain, are innate to us. They are not copies of any particular impression. Indeed he claims that *all* of our *impressions* can be considered innate, in the sense of being original and not copied. However, our *ideas* are formed from copies and combinations of these impressions. In this sense, none of our ideas is innate – we are not born with them because they are all derived from our impressions.

Tabula rasa versus innate ideas

Empiricism claims that all of our concepts, ideas and imaginings are derived from our impressions. If this is the case, then what happens to the theory of innate ideas? It would seem to be a pointless theory. Why claim an idea is innate if it can be shown to be derived from experience?

For example, several philosophers have claimed that we are born with the idea of God – it is innate. As an empiricist, Hume rejected this claim and offered a different account of where the concept of God, as a supremely powerful, infinitely wise, all-loving being, comes from. Clearly we have not encountered God, so it cannot come directly from him. Instead the concept comes from our experiences of powerful, wise and loving people whom we have encountered. Having witnessed such qualities in people, we then imagine their being extended without limit.

The idea of God – meaning an infinitely intelligent, wise and good Being – comes from extending beyond all limits the qualities of goodness and wisdom that we find in our own minds.[19]

According to many, God made man in his own image. However, according to Hume, God is made in *man's* own image. This invites the conclusion, radical in Hume's day, that God does not exist.

Put formally, the *tabula rasa* theory against innate ideas would look something like this:

P1 The theory of innate ideas claims we are born with innate ideas
P2 All of our ideas can be shown to be derived from experience (*tabula rasa*)
C1 The theory of innate ideas is redundant

Firstly, we should note that this argument centres on ideas and not capacities, such as the ability to reason. Locke and Hume are primarily concerned with showing how we derive our ideas, although the distinction between ideas and capacities can be vague. Secondly, this argument only works if premise 2 is true – in other words, if it *is* the case that all of our ideas are derived from our experiences. We will now turn our attention to some issues that might make us doubt the truth of the *tabula rasa* thesis.

Issues with the empiricism/*tabula rasa* responses to innatism

Criticism 1: do all simple ideas come from impressions?

An important consideration in favour of the empiricists' account is that someone who has not experienced the colour blue (for example, perhaps because they were born blind) cannot have an idea or concept of it. But suppose a person born blind were to gain their sight and, on first opening their eyes, were to stare straight into the bright blue sky. Having seen sky blue, are they then able to form the *general* concept of blue, in all its varieties – including aquamarine, navy blue, turquoise – or are they confined to a grasp of the sky blue they have so far experienced? Is it possible to imagine any shade of blue having only seen one? Hume discusses a similar case where someone has seen a range of blues from which one is missing and asks whether they would be able to form the concept of the missing shade (we have used grey to illustrate the point):

> *Can he fill the blank [shade] from his own imagination, calling up in his mind the idea of that particular shade, even though it has never been conveyed to him by his senses? Most people, I think, will agree that he can. This seems to show that simple ideas are not always, in every instance, derived from corresponding impressions. Still, the example is so singular that it's hardly worth noticing, and on its own it isn't a good enough reason for us to alter our general maxim.*[20]

Figure 1.29 Is there a missing shade of grey? Can you imagine a shade of grey or blue that you have never seen?

The problem here for the empiricists is that if they concede that you can form the concept of the missing shade of grey or blue, it means that it is possible to form a concept which has no corresponding impression, and this goes against their principle that nothing can exist in the mind that has not come through the senses. And yet it does seem plausible to suggest that one would be able to imagine the missing shade. Indeed Hume actually allows this to be an exception to the general rule, but in doing so he is often taken to have undermined this most basic tenet of empiricism. If we can form this concept without having had an impression, why should we not be able to form others? Perhaps the missing shade of blue *is* 'in' us innately at birth. Maybe the theory of innate ideas explains how this is possible.

One defence for the empiricist is to say that we can form the concept of this shade because it is actually a *complex* one. According to this view, the missing shade would be formed from the simple concept of blue-in-general and the concepts of dark or light. In the imagination, we could somehow mix some light with the adjacent shade of blue and so form the missing shade. The problem with this response is that all our concepts of shades of blue would then become complex ideas: mixtures of light and dark with the general concept. But this makes it difficult to see how we form the simple concept since it is no longer straightforwardly derived from any particular sense impression.

Another defence open to the empiricist is to insist that we *cannot* form the concept of the missing shade. We have a blue-in-general complex concept formed from the collection of all the shades of blue I have experienced, but we cannot form the concept of a shade of blue not so far encountered. Another odd implication of this would be that none of us has the full concept of blue; that the concept is constantly evolving as we encounter new blues; and that each of us, having experienced a different array of blues, has a slightly different concept.

This highlights a more general problem of how we move from the particular experiences of different blues, to the concept of blue in general. Does a copy of particular shade come to represent all blues? In other words, how does the specific image recorded in the mind come to function as a general concept?

Plato's 'innatist' answer would be that all blues in the world are imperfect versions of the pure form of 'blue'. It is this form that we refer to when talking of blue and that exists in us as hazy memory. Plato's theory of forms, in part, is an early attempt to solve the genuine puzzle concerning how we form general concepts from particular examples.

On a related point, you may think that that the empiricists' claim that we cannot imagine a colour we have never seen is fairly plausible. However, this is not the same as to say that we cannot form the *concept* of this colour. To see the point, take the example of ultraviolet, a colour in a wavelength too short for the human eye to detect. Now, we are able to form the concept of such a wavelength of light even though we cannot see it, suggesting that the concept here is not to be identified with a copy of any sense experience. In a similar way, a blind person could form the concept of red as being that colour which occurs in a particular part of the light spectrum, without ever being able to imagine what it is like to see this colour. So, again, the concept need not be identified with a copy of any impression.

Criticism 2: do all complex ideas/concepts relate to impressions?

Concepts do not have to relate to experience

Difficulties arise when we consider that we seem able to have a concept of something without ever having experienced it. I can have the concept of tea even if I have not tasted it; and, similarly, I can form the concept of Spain even though I have never been there. Consider also the concept I have of an atom, something that is too small for us ever to have any sense experience of it. How is this concept formed? Certainly, while such concepts might have their source in experience, the way in which they are derived from experience seems to be

▶ **ACTIVITY**

1 If you had only seen crimson, could you imagine scarlet and magenta?
2 If you had never seen pink or purple, could you imagine them on the basis of having seen red, white and blue?
3 Do you think a child who has never seen blue and yellow paint mixed can predict what colour they will make? Could you imagine green if you had only ever seen blue and yellow?
4 Do you think a child who has never seen yellow and red mixed can predict what colour *they* will make? If this case is different from the blue/yellow case, how is it different?

more complex than a simple matter of copying sense impressions, whether they be inner or outer. With the concept of Spain, it seems implausible to say that my concept is a series of images of Spain gleaned from travel brochures, and when it comes to abstract concepts the difficulties get worse. How do I acquire the concept of justice or freedom? It seems very difficult to relate such concepts merely to patterns within experience, and ultimately to patterns of sense impressions. After all, neither justice nor freedom looks or smells like anything; nor can they be equated with inner emotions or feelings. In fact, they do not seem to be things that we have sense experience of at all. Again, the innatist might claim that our sense of justice and of freedom is innate and not derived from experience at all.

Note here that it is possible that you have some sort of image in your mind when you think of justice – the scales of justice perhaps, or a wise-looking judge in a wig. Similarly, the thought of justice might produce a certain feeling within you – a warm, righteous glow in the chest perhaps. But even if you do enjoy such images and feelings when contemplating the concept of justice, they cannot be identified with it, since the concept involves all kinds of connections with other concepts that cannot be explained in terms of such impressions. Indeed, it is quite likely that other people will have very different images and feelings in mind when they think of justice, and yet they still have the same *concept* as you. So it seems that what we *imagine/picture* when thinking of justice is not the same as what we *think of*, and therefore that the concept is not reducible to a copy of any impression of inner or outer sense. Again, this brings us up against the obscurity of the relationship between the concept and experience which the innatist might exploit by claiming that we have an innate sense of justice.

An empiricist could argue that the fact that it is very difficult to explain abstract concepts in terms of sense experience is why such terms are notoriously vague. They could claim that if we could pin them more closely to experience then we would have greater clarity. The empiricist might also argue that if we lived in a world without fair/just behaviour of any kind, in some kind of anarchic dystopia, we would be unable to form the concept precisely because we would have no experience of it. Again, the innatist might claim that we are born with a moral sense or a sense of justice, and would have the concept of it even if we never experienced justice in the world.

Do relational concepts derive from impressions?

Further difficulties arise with relational concepts (these are concepts that describe relationships between objects), such as 'being near', 'sameness', 'next to' or 'on top of'. If I form the concept of a cat from seeing a cat, then how do I form the concept of the cat being *on* the mat? I cannot actually see the 'on-ness': all that appears in sensation is the cat and the mat. (After all, what colour, sound or taste and so on relates to 'on-ness'?) Obviously it is on the mat, but the recognition of this fact and the understanding of the relationship involved is not something we acquire by simply copying any sense impression. Likewise consider the concept of 'sameness'. 'Sameness' does not have a particular colour or taste and so on. Indeed 'sameness' cannot be related to any *specific* impressions, as it could apply to any or *all* impressions. Do we derive the concept of 'sameness' from our impressions? Or do we have it innately, prior to experience?

Criticism 3: do some concepts have to exist in the mind before sense impressions can be properly experienced?

This criticism is really a set of related criticisms that suggest that our minds/brains must have some concepts or structures in place in order for our impressions to make 'sense' in the first place. If this is the case, then these concepts themselves cannot be derived from our impressions. The arguments involved at times can be very abstract and difficult to follow, but the best place to start is by revisiting the *tabula rasa* thesis. Is the idea that all of our concepts and ideas are derived from our impressions really believable? The eighteenth-century French philosopher Etienne Bonnot de Condillac (1715–80), a disciple of Locke, certainly believed so, and tried to prove it through a thought experiment. He asked his readers to imagine a statue that is organised like a human on the inside but devoid of any sensations. In his book *A Treatise of Sensations* (1756), Condillac describes the process whereby the statue experiences a series of sensations and is brought from having no ideas at all to forming concepts and acquiring beliefs about itself and the world around it. Is this believable?

 Experimenting with ideas

Imagine a human-sized statue. It is made of marble and at the moment cannot let any sensations in. Then imagine that we add the five senses and place basic structures inside the head – for example, the statue now has a memory and can store copies of the sensations it starts to receive.

1 Would this statue eventually be able to develop all the concepts you have? Can you think of any concepts that would be beyond a being who was confined to sensation alone?

2 Could the statue develop into a being with a fully fledged belief system like your own? What problems would it face? Are there things you believe or know that such a statue could not?

Figure 1.30 Condillac's statue.
Would an 'empty' statue bombarded by a stream of sense data be able to make sense of it all? Would it be able to form concepts and beliefs about the world?

Some would argue that Condillac's whole approach is doomed. The statue would just receive a flow of uninterpreted sensations: noises, shapes, colours and tastes. But to even begin to form concepts, the statue would, at the very least, have to recognise that two sensations are similar. How could it do this without already having a concept of similarity or 'sameness'?

Many would reject this approach. Human beings are not like Condillac's statue and the mind is not like a *tabula rasa*. Rather the mind at birth is at least partially formed and has a structure or architecture that enables it to make sense of the raw sense data it receives.

Another way of understanding this criticism is to consider if we can ever be wrong about our sense impressions. It is generally thought that while we *can* be wrong about what the world is like, we *cannot* be wrong about the fact that we are having particular sense impressions. Even if you are dreaming this very second, and there is no actual book before your eyes, you cannot deny that you are having certain sense impressions resembling a white page and black ink in the shape of words. In this way, many claim that our sense impressions are certain – we cannot be mistaken about them.

Learn More

However, it does seem possible that sometimes we might be unsure as to how to characterise a particular sense impression. For example, I may see a flashy car and be unsure of whether the colour is metallic purple or magenta. Or I could taste a crisp and believe it is smoky bacon flavoured, when in fact it is prawn cocktail. These errors and uncertainties have to do with how I categorise or describe my impressions. Since these are examples of possibly mis-describing what one perceives, the defence goes, they do not touch the certainty one can have of the immediate sense impressions themselves prior to any description. I may not be sure of what this colour or taste is called, but I can nonetheless be certain of what it is like here and now for me.

So, it is claimed, we can avoid error so long as we resist the inclination to 'translate' the immediacy of experience into categories, or to put them into words. While we may go wrong in trying to conceptualise such experience, surely the immediacy of present sensation remains INDUBITABLE. The empiricist maintains that this original preconceptual GIVEN is the ground for any ordered experience.

However, without some sort of interpretation, it is difficult to see how such experience could be anything more than what the American philosopher William James (1842–1910) calls a 'blooming, buzzing confusion': an undifferentiated stream of sensations. It is only by placing what is given – the stream of sense impressions – within certain categories that beliefs can be held and knowledge claims made *about* one's experience. In other words, we need some kind of conceptual scheme in place before we can make sense of experience. The German philosopher Immanuel Kant (1724–1804) pushed this thought further, summing up his position in the well-known statement:

Thoughts without content are empty; intuitions [impressions] without concepts are blind.[21]

▶ **ACTIVITY: RAW DATA VERSUS CATEGORISED DATA**

MY WIFE AND MY MOTHER-IN-LAW
They are both in this picture — Find them

Look closely at the illustration. You can see the image in one of two ways: as an older woman or as a younger woman turning her head away.

1 Can you see the image in two ways?
2 Can you easily switch between the two ways?
3 Now try to see it as neither – just as meaningless lines on a page. Is this possible?

Consider the activity above. For most people it is hard, if not impossible, to see the image just as raw sensations – as lines on a page. Even then, this would not properly be 'raw', as you are categorising the experience as *lines* and the whiteness as a *page*. It is not easy to separate the 'raw' sense data from your experience of seeing the image as a young or old woman. This is because your brain/mind has processed the data and what you experience has already been classified in certain ways. Just like the letters on this very page, once your brain has been trained, it is very hard to see these just as meaningless scrawls of blackness on whiteness.

Kant's point is similar to this but on a global scale. He claims that all of our experience has been classified in certain ways. There is no such thing as experiencing raw data. Kant claims, for example, that you experience the world as a series of *objects* in *space* and *time* interacting in *causal* ways because your experience has the concepts such as *unity*, *space*, *time* and *causation* already applied to it. Sense impressions (which he terms intuitions) prior to any form of conceptual ordering cannot yet form any part of any experience. The mind would be 'blind' to them because they have not yet been classified.

Drawing these strands together, we can see that both a consideration of Condillac's statue and an exploration of how we might misclassify our experience point towards the idea that some form of conceptual organisation of sensations is needed, prior to any experience, to make experience possible. But if this is the case, then it appears that not all of our concepts can be derived from experience and some may be innate.

Criticism 4: the mind is born with innate structures

Earlier we saw Leibniz compare the mind to a veined block of marble. He claimed that our minds are not born with fully fledged ideas (like a fully carved statue), but with 'inclinations, dispositions, tendencies, or natural potentialities', which, like the veins in the marble, enable the mind to realise certain truths and think in certain ways.

The thought experiment of Condillac's statue also points to the mind not being a blank slate. It can be argued that certain ways of thinking, perhaps such as the ability to recognise 'sameness', might have to exist innately in the mind in order to make sense of experience. Kant further suggests that our mind contains specific innate categories that are not derived from experience. Indeed, he suggests that experience is impossible without them.

All these arguments give weight to the idea of innate capacities – not necessarily existing in the form of specific ideas, but as structures that enable ways of thinking and experiencing the world. These theories dispute the concept of the mind as a *blank slate* – not by claiming that the slate comes with lots of marks already sketched on it, but more by suggesting that the slate has hidden features (or veins, in Leibniz's analogy) that shape the way we think and experience the world.

As we saw earlier, the claim that the mind contains innate structures has been revived in recent time through the ideas of Chomsky, who claims that our exposure to language is not sufficient to account for our ability to learn to speak (page 102). This can only be explained in terms of an innate capacity to learn. Interestingly, Chomsky claims that this innate ability is universal and seen in all cultures, which echoes the claim by early innatists that universality is an indicator of innateness.

These different theories arguing for the existence of innate structures/categories pose a serious challenge to the *tabula rasa* thesis.

1.3.2 The intuition and deduction thesis

This section explores a philosophical debate about how our knowledge of the world is formed. On the one hand, a philosophical movement called *rationalism* argues that knowledge should begin with undeniable truths and proceed, using a process called *deduction*, to produce further truths; all of which can be known with certainty. On the other hand, a movement called *empiricism* argues that substantial knowledge of the world can only be generated by observing the world and using a process called *induction* to generate laws and theories. These laws, as with observations of the world, can never be known with certainty. This section explores some of the arguments between these two schools of thought. Specifically, we explore Descartes' method of using intuition and deduction and examine how successful this is.

Historical context

Descartes was born into a period of intellectual upheaval. The existing approach to science was based on a merging of medieval thought with some ideas from Aristotle. Often termed as 'scholastic science', this approach tried to explain how objects and chemicals behaved by reference to 'hidden' properties. For example, objects fall to the ground because they have the property of *heaviness*, or a potion may make you drowsy because it has the property of *sleepiness*. This approach did not yield many results and some grew frustrated at this way of thinking.

From the sixteenth century onwards, a new scientific approach emerged that increasingly applied mathematics to the world through measuring, weighing and generally quantifying objects. In 1543, Copernicus, using observation and mathematical modelling, gave new life to the revolutionary idea that the sun, not the earth, was at the centre of the solar system. The ideas of Copernicus were taken further by Galileo, who added new observations by peering through the world's most powerful telescope (which he designed). A new wave of thinkers emerged who rejected the idea of mysterious 'hidden' properties and instead focused on applying mathematics to the world. Galileo even proclaimed that the universe 'is written in the language of mathematics, and its characters are triangles, circles, and other geometric figures'.

Galileo's ideas contradicted those of the Catholic Church (which was very clear that the earth was at the centre of the universe). In 1633, Galileo was tried by a Roman inquisition and placed under house arrest for the remainder of his days.

Descartes' method

Descartes (see page 26) was a key part of the new scientific movement, which had gathered momentum with the work of Galileo. Indeed, Descartes had been preparing a large book at the time of Galileo's arrest, but since this also placed the sun at centre of the solar system, he decided against publication! Instead, Descartes chose to publish three short essays, each showing the application of the new science to a particular field of inquiry: *Geometry*, *Optics* and *Meteorology*. He accompanied these with another essay – *Discourse on Method* – which gave a summary of his philosophical views, along with an account of the particular method he had devised, which he claimed could be used to reach the truth on any topic. He enjoyed some success. *Geometry*, although baffling for many readers, established Descartes as a mathematical genius.

In the *Discourse*, Descartes set out his new approach for seeking the truth. Essentially it involves following these four rules:

1 Accept only beliefs that can be recognised clearly and distinctly to be true.
2 Break down every problem into the smallest parts.
3 Build up the arguments systematically in the right order.
4 Carefully check through to ensure no steps are left out.

Descartes had shown that these principles could produce results in geometry and mathematics and wanted to extend his approach to other areas. The *Meditations*, published four years later in 1641, is Descartes' attempt to apply his own method to the field of philosophy.

Two aspects of Descartes' method are worth noting. Firstly, using stage one of his method, Descartes rejected the alchemist approach of creating 'hidden' properties to explain events. Properties such as *heaviness* and *sleepiness* were too hazy and vague (they later became labelled negatively as 'occult' properties). In Cartesian terms (meaning *of Descartes*), such properties were not *clear* and *distinct*. Descartes claimed that the only clear and distinct properties that objects possess are size, shape, quantity, motion and duration (all of these are 'geometric' properties). Only these properties are sufficiently clear and distinct, and Descartes argued that science could explain the world with reference to these alone. These properties are properly understood by the intellect rather than the senses, which is why reason, rather than sense experience, is needed to understand the world.

Secondly, Descartes, along with other rationalists, was greatly inspired by the work of the Greek mathematician Euclid. In his book, *The Elements*, Euclid sets out what is known as an axiomatic system – that is, a system in which all the propositions are derived from a small set of initial axioms and definitions, which in turn are thought to be self-evident. For example, among Euclid's axioms are the following:

- *All right angles equal one another.*
- *A circle is a plane figure contained by one line such that every point on it is the same distance from the centre.*[22]

From these axioms, Euclid then proceeds to prove a host of further propositions, for instance:

- *If a straight line falling on two straight lines makes the alternate angles equal to one another, then the straight lines are parallel to one another.*[23]

If the initial axioms are accepted, then the subsequent truths are all 'proved' using a process of deduction, which keeps the certainty of the original claims. Through the careful use of reason, Euclid is able to establish a large and systematic body of truths. Many thinkers, even today, have been inspired by the beauty and detail of Euclid's proofs. They represent a pinnacle of rational thought that (it can be argued) was not matched for over a thousand years.

Euclid's system is more or less the blueprint for Descartes' method. First, one establishes a series of clear and distinct truths that cannot be doubted (axioms), and then one uses argument (deduction) to build out from this point and establish a complete system of truths. Descartes believed this approach could be used for all human knowledge.

These long chains of perfectly simple and easy reasonings by means of which geometers are accustomed to carry out their most difficult demonstrations had led me to fancy that everything that can fall under human knowledge forms a similar sequence.[24]

Although Descartes thought that observations from the senses could play an important role in validating scientific theories, he believed that reason was the key tool. By rejecting all previous thought and starting again using only clear and distinct ideas, Descartes thought that reason could bring a new level of certainty to all human knowledge.

Descartes' method gave a clear voice to this new wave of scientists. His approach represented a break from the medieval ways of thinking and placed epistemology at the heart of philosophy. Method became the focus, for both philosophy and science, and this emphasis on method is one defining feature of what is termed the modern era. (Descartes is one of the first philosophers of the modern era – which might seem an odd thing to say, given that he was writing nearly 400 years ago!) Descartes was one of the founding fathers of the ENLIGHTENMENT, a period of intense optimism in the ability of human reason to both understand the universe and create a better world.

Descartes' notion of 'clear and distinct ideas'

The *Meditations* begins with Descartes subjecting all his beliefs to extreme levels of doubt, culminating in him supposing that the whole physical universe, including his own body, could be illusory (see page 163 onwards for more on Descartes' doubt). The purpose of his scepticism is to see whether he can discover any beliefs which are beyond possible doubt, for if there are, he hopes these can be the basis on which to establish the new science. Eventually he finds one belief that he cannot refute – that he exists. He argues that he cannot doubt his own existence because in the very attempt to do so he must be doubting, and if he is doubting, he cannot be nothing.

This argument is often termed the *COGITO*, after the Latin formulation from Descartes' *Principles of Philosophy*, namely: *cogito ergo sum*, meaning 'I am thinking therefore I exist', or 'I think therefore I am'. Here, Descartes has reached the Archimedean point which enables his epistemological enterprise to make some headway in the sea of doubts into which he was plunged. For just as Archimedes claimed that, if given a long enough lever and a fixed fulcrum on which to turn it, he could move the whole earth, so too Descartes hopes that by starting with this one certainty, he will be able to discover others and ultimately rebuild his system of knowledge. To this end, he tries to establish whether there is an underlying reason for this certainty that could then be applied to other beliefs.

> *Doesn't that tell me what it takes for me to be certain about anything? In this first item of knowledge* [the *cogito*] *there is simply a vivid and clear* [clear and distinct] *perception of what I am asserting; this wouldn't be enough to make me certain of its truth if it could ever turn out that something that I perceived so vividly and clearly* [clearly and distinctly] *was false. So I now seem to be able to lay it down as a general rule that whatever I perceive very vividly and clearly* [clearly and distinctly] *is true.*[25]

In this quotation, Descartes attributes the certainty he has of his existence to how 'clearly and distinctly' he is aware of it, and concludes that any similarly clear and distinct idea must also be true.

Before exploring Descartes' conception of *clear and distinct ideas*, look again at the quote above and notice that it contains four sets of square brackets []. This shows words that are not in the original text. The first set of brackets, [the *cogito*], helps the reader understand what Descartes is talking about. This sort of information is useful, as many quotes carry on from a prior discussion, and so the SUBJECT of the sentence needs clarification. The remaining brackets all contain variations of the phrase, *clear and distinct*. Descartes wrote some of his works in French and many others, including the *Meditations*, in Latin. He did not write in English, so the above quote is a translation. The different translations of Descartes vary in terms of the style of writing, but also in the choice of key words. Most translators use the phrase *clear and distinct* when referring to those ideas that Descartes claimed could be held with certainty. However, Jonathan Bennett, who translated the version of the *Meditations* recommended to you (and quoted above), thinks the phrase *vivid and clear* gets closer to Descartes' meaning. Bennett provides a detailed note about this at the beginning of Chapter 3 in his translation of the *Meditations*. However, as your course uses the terms *clear and distinct* in the syllabus, we have included this phrase in square brackets alongside Bennett's preferred choice of *vivid and clear*.

What are clear and distinct ideas?

Descartes does not give definitions of these terms in the *Meditations*, although he offers an account in *The Principles of Philosophy*.

> *I call a perception 'clear' when it is present and accessible to the attentive mind – just as we say that we see something clearly when it is present to the eye's gaze and stimulates it with a sufficient degree of strength and accessibility. I call a perception 'distinct' if, as well as being clear, it is so sharply separated from all other perceptions that it contains within itself only what is clear.*[26]

Descartes gives the example of a leg pain, which might be very *clear* to one afflicted, but is not *distinct*, as it may be hard to separate and distinguish the pain from the true cause. The sufferer may make a false judgment about what is causing it, and for this reason it is not distinct. So clarity is about how bright and present an idea is in the mind (which is why Bennett prefers to use *vivid* for this), and distinctness is about how pure the idea is and whether it is sharply separated from other ideas (which is why Bennett prefers to use the term *clear*).

Descartes does not give many examples of ideas that are clear and distinct, other than *I am thinking* and *two and three make five*. He no doubt has the axiomatic method in mathematics in mind when suggesting these terms. Euclid starts his *Elements* with axioms such as 'all right angles are equal'. These are supposed to be so obvious as to be impossible to doubt which is why they are selected as the basis for the construction of his system. Such basic judgements of mathematics or truths evident to reason are those we are able to 'see' or 'intuit' the truth of with our mind's eye.

Criticism 1: not clear and distinct enough!

Later thinkers, such as Leibniz, criticised Descartes' use of 'clear and distinct', suggesting that a more detailed account of these terms is needed if they are to be usefully applied as a criterion of truth. Relying on a feeling is not enough. In other words, Descartes does not give a sufficiently clear and distinct account of what is clear and distinct!

Criticism 2: quick generalisation

Descartes puts the success of the *cogito* down to the fact that its truth can be grasped clearly and distinctly. He then generalises this principle and claims that any belief he can conceive clearly and distinctly must also be true. But is this a valid generalisation to make? One concern we may have is that it is based on very thin evidence. Although one belief may be knowable because it can be grasped clearly and distinctly, this can hardly be a sound basis on which conclude that any belief grasped in this way must also be true. After all, would this not be a bit like observing one pink pig and then concluding that all pigs must be pink?

121

Criticism 3: only internal criteria for truth

In the quote from the *Meditations* on page 120, notice that Descartes starts talking about what it 'takes for me to be certain about anything', and ends up concluding that 'whatever I perceive very vividly and clearly [clearly and distinctly] is true'. He moves from the idea of certainty (a subjective, inner feeling) to the idea of truth (which is external and objective). This is quite a leap and one that has been widely criticised. (Descartes later tries to bridge this chasm by arguing that a good God would not make him such that his most clear and distinct ideas were false, as this would be to deceive him.)

In general, what makes a belief true or false is not how strongly you believe it, but how the belief relates to the world outside of your head. Beliefs such as 'There are five cows in the field' or 'Molly is pregnant' are true or false because they correspond (or not) to states of affairs in the world (at least according to the correspondence theory of truth – and there are other theories; see page 17 for more on this).

However, Descartes, in suggesting that any clearly and distinctly apprehended belief must be true, is doing away with the any correspondence criteria. He claims that just by examining the belief alone we can tell if a judgement is true or not. If the idea is clear and distinct enough, it is true. Under this system, there is no need to check the judgement against any corresponding fact. The philosopher Gilbert Ryle (1900–76) has strongly criticised this position. Ryle compares the concept of truth with the act of scoring of a goal in football. To score a goal, you need a) to kick/head the ball, b) for the ball to end up in the net. And in the same way, for a belief to be true, you need a) a belief, b) the belief to correspond to the fact. Descartes believes that we can establish the truth just by examining a) the nature of the belief, and by seeing how clear and distinct it is. Ryle suggests that this is like trying to tell whether you have scored a goal by focusing on the shot alone. But this plainly does not work. You may have struck the ball beautifully, but this does not necessarily mean it will end up in the goal. You cannot tell you have scored by focusing on the strike of the ball alone. Likewise you cannot tell whether a belief is true just by focusing on the belief itself. Descartes is using only 'internal' criteria to establish whether a belief is true and can count as knowledge – that is to say, he looks exclusively within the belief itself. However, in doing so, Descartes is going against most theories of truth which, like the correspondence theory, require an 'external' criterion.

It can be argued that the *cogito* is an exception to this criticism. It seems we can know the *cogito* is true just by examining the belief itself. This might be because the belief 'I am, I exist' is confirmed in the very act of asserting it. The same utterance simultaneously acts as the belief and proves the relevant fact which is being claimed. So, in the case of the *cogito*, the belief and the fact coincide – as such it might be termed 'self-verifying'. But even if we accept this for the *cogito*, this is emphatically not the case for most other beliefs. The *cogito* is a very special kind of belief: one for which thinking it makes it true, but this character cannot be generalised to other beliefs.

Criticism 4: can we be sure clear and distinct ideas are true?

Having concluded that 'whatever I perceive very vividly and clearly [clearly and distinctly] is true', Descartes then attacks his own position by wondering whether 'Perhaps some God could have made me so as to be deceived even in those matters that seemed most obvious'.[27] Perhaps his nature is such that even clear and distinct ideas are false? Descartes concludes that the only way out of this doubt is to show that God exists. A good God would not make a being whose clearest and most distinct thoughts are false. This approach has been accused of making a fundamental error – known as the Cartesian circle – which we explore on page 141. In short, it is that Descartes uses clear and distinct ideas to show that God exists, and only then can he conclude that clear and distinct ideas must be true.

Regardless of this argument, it can also be charged that Descartes requires the supernatural (God) to make his theory of knowledge workable, which for some is a weakness. A non-supernatural approach could perhaps be used instead, arguing that EVOLUTION has ensured that clear and distinct ideas must be true (otherwise humankind would have died out a long time ago).

Intuition and deduction

Earlier, we saw Descartes propose a distinct method to gaining knowledge, which, in part, involved only accepting clear and distinct beliefs as true. Descartes believed that the natural 'operations' of the mind will always be able to reach the truth; however, in reality, humans all too often stray from the path because of impatience, prejudice, passions and so forth. His method is designed to keep the 'operations' of the mind in check and ensure that the right path is followed. For Descartes, the two key 'operations' of the mind are intuition and deduction. These are the 'actions of the intellect by means of which we are able to arrive at a knowledge of things with no fear of being mistaken'.[28]

Intuition

In modern times, the term 'intuition' has connotations of a hunch or guesswork. However, this is not the sense in which Descartes employs the term. Descartes uses the Latin term *intueri*, which literally means to 'look upon'. So, by *intuition*, Descartes means an act of the intellect whereby it inwardly 'looks upon' an intellectual object, such as a straight line or a triangle, and instantly sees its true features.

By 'intuition' I do not mean the fluctuating testimony of the senses, or the deceptive judgement of the imagination as it botches things together, but the conception of a clear and attentive mind, which is so easy and distinct that there can be no room for doubt about what we are understanding. Alternatively, and this comes to the same thing, intuition is the indubitable conception of a clear and attentive mind which proceeds solely from the light of reason … Thus everyone can mentally intuit that he exists, that he is thinking, that a triangle is bounded by just three sides, and a sphere by a single surface, and the like.[29]

So intuition is the ability to behold intellectual objects and grasp basic truths. This is contrasted with the evidence of the senses, which 'fluctuate'. As intuitions are independent of the senses, the truths they reveal can be known *a priori*.

Descartes' conception of an intuition has strong overlaps with his notion of a clear and distinct idea – which the mind also sees instantly as true. Indeed, in some of his writings, Descartes characterises an intuition as a clear and distinct

123

perception of the mind. The difference between the two phrases is not very important, but you may find it useful to think of an *intuition* as one of the key operations of the mind, and a *clear and distinct idea* as the object 'perceived' by the intuition. So, for example, *'two and three make five'* would be the clear and distinct idea which the mind intuits is true.

Deduction

The second key operation of the mind is *deduction*, which Descartes describes as 'The inference of something as following necessarily from some other propositions which are known with certainty'.[30]

Descartes' use of the term *deduction* is more or less the same as our modern usage. Deduction is the ability to infer what *must* follow from other facts. For example, if you know with certainty that Hector is taller than Ahmed and that Ahmed is taller than Sally, then you can deduce with equal certainty that Hector is taller than Sally. (See page xi for more on deduction.)

For Descartes, each stage of a deduction involves the mind 'intuiting' that the next truth necessarily follows. The mind, however, cannot 'intuit' the final stage of reasoning immediately, but only through intuiting each stage at a time. This process of intuiting each stage is deduction. For example, your mind may be able to intuit that a triangle has three angles; however, you would need a series of intuitions to see that in any right-angled triangle, the sum of the square of the hypotenuse is equal to the sum of the squares of the other two sides (Pythagoras' theorem). This series of intuitions is called a deduction. In Plato's *Meno*, the slave boy engages in a deductive process (page 96). At each stage in the deduction, the boy intuits what follows from the previous stage.

The intuition and deduction thesis

Descartes claims that these two operations of the mind, intuition and deduction, if used in accordance with his method, will enable the truth to be reached in any field of knowledge. All beliefs are questioned; problems are broken down into their smallest parts; the mind intuits the truth of those ideas that are clear and distinct and then proceeds to deduce other truths from these initial starting points.

This more or less describes the process of thought in the *Meditations*. Descartes doubts all his beliefs until he reaches the clear and distinct idea that he exists. From this point, he attempts to deduce the existence of God, who, as a good God, would not deceive him.

The intuition and deduction thesis is a theory of how knowledge is gained – it is an *epistemology*. The first key feature is of Descartes' epistemology is that it is based around reason. The initial intuitions are perceived by the intellect, not the senses. As such they are known *a priori*. The subsequent deductions are all also known *a priori*. Descartes is claiming that we can gain substantial knowledge of the world using reason alone, independent of observation. This makes Descartes an archetype rationalist. As we see below, empiricists will challenge this claim that reason alone can deliver substantial truths about the world. For empiricists, the bedrock of our knowledge is not reason, but the senses.

The second key feature of Descartes' epistemology is that it is a foundationalist approach. This means that all of our knowledge has underpinning foundations which, for Descartes, are the clear and distinct ideas intuited by the mind.

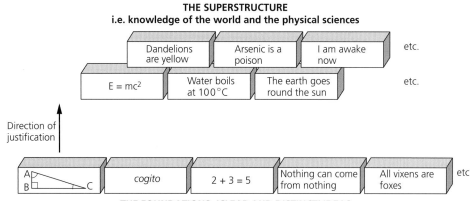

THE SUPERSTRUCTURE
i.e. knowledge of the world and the physical sciences

Dandelions are yellow | Arsenic is a poison | I am awake now | etc.
$E = mc^2$ | Water boils at 100°C | The earth goes round the sun | etc.

Direction of justification

A B C | *cogito* | $2 + 3 = 5$ | Nothing can come from nothing | All vixens are foxes | etc

THE FOUNDATIONS: 'CLEAR AND DISTINCT' IDEAS
i.e. knowledge of my existence, of maths and geometry; truths of reason and analytic truths

Figure 1.31 Descartes' foundationalism – the intuition and deduction thesis. All knowledge is based on a foundation of beliefs which are knowable *a priori*. These are the clear and distinct ideas which the mind intuits. The rest of our knowledge can be deduced from these basic starting blocks. The view that all genuine knowledge is grounded in reason is termed rationalism.

Descartes' rationalism contrasts with empiricism, which is also a foundationalist epistemology, but one which claims that the bedrock of all our knowledge is our impressions. It is from these that all of our ideas and knowledge are derived.

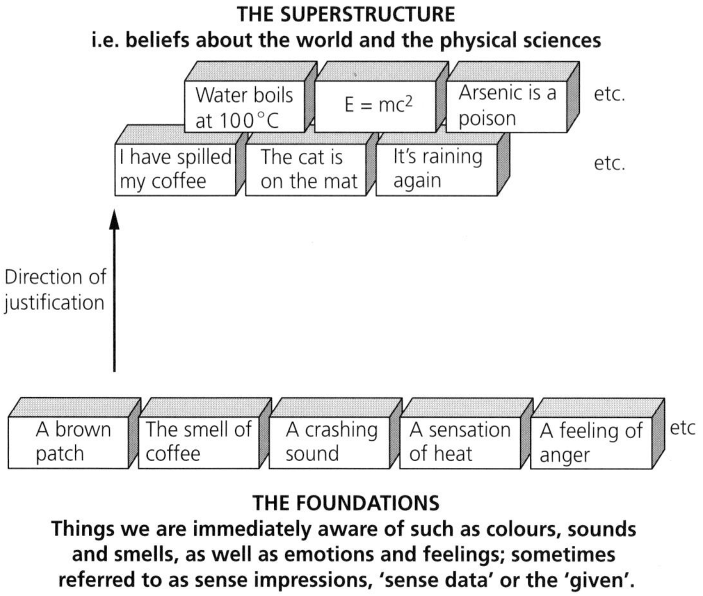

THE SUPERSTRUCTURE
i.e. beliefs about the world and the physical sciences

Water boils at 100°C | $E = mc^2$ | Arsenic is a poison | etc.
I have spilled my coffee | The cat is on the mat | It's raining again | etc.

Direction of justification

A brown patch | The smell of coffee | A crashing sound | A sensation of heat | A feeling of anger | etc

THE FOUNDATIONS
Things we are immediately aware of such as colours, sounds and smells, as well as emotions and feelings; sometimes referred to as sense impressions, 'sense data' or the 'given'.

Figure 1.32 The empiricist foundationalist regards impressions as the basis for all our factual knowledge about the world. Knowledge of sense impressions is immediate and INCORRIGIBLE. On this basis we infer the existence of the physical world.

125

Empiricist responses: Hume's fork

Earlier, we outlined the *tabula rasa* theory, associated with empiricism, which claimed that all of our ideas must come from experience. Many empiricists, including Hume, thought the truth of the *tabula rasa* thesis meant that Descartes' rationalist approach was doomed to fail, as the senses are needed to generate knowledge. Hume claimed that all our ideas must come from our senses or from our inner feelings. The process of deduction might be able to tell us about the relationship between these ideas – such that all bachelors are unmarried, but it cannot add new knowledge to the world. Deduction can only work out the consequences of what we already know. If we want to find out about the world, we have to observe it.

In his famous book *An Enquiry Concerning Human Understanding*, Hume provides a very different account to Descartes about how our reasoning relates to the world. Hume divides the areas of human understanding into two distinct camps.

All the objects of human reason or enquiry fall naturally into two kinds, namely relations of ideas and matters of fact.[31]

Hume articulates these two areas of thought in more detail.

The first kind include geometry, algebra, and arithmetic, and indeed every statement that is either intuitively or demonstratively certain. That the square of the hypotenuse is equal to the squares of the other two sides expresses a relation between those figures. That three times five equals half of thirty expresses a relation between those numbers. Propositions of this kind can be discovered purely by thinking, with no need to attend to anything that actually exists anywhere in the universe. Matters of fact, which are the second objects of human reason, are not established in the same way; and we cannot have such strong grounds for thinking them true. The contrary of every matter of fact is still possible, because it doesn't imply a contradiction and is conceived by the mind as easily and clearly as if it conformed perfectly to reality.[32]

Relations of ideas

Hume suggests that our attempts to understand the world can be divided into two areas. 'Relations of ideas' concern logic and mathematics and, although we need sense experience to form the concepts, Hume suggests that our reasoning in this area does not depend on how the world actually is. Two and three will always make five and we do not have to check this by observing facts in the world. The truth of such claims lies in deduction alone. Such truths are true by definition and the opposite would be impossible. Consider the example of triangles. We do not have to observe every triangle in the world and then make the generalisation that they all have three sides. Triangles have three sides by definition and we can work this out by analysing the meaning of the terms alone. Because these truths are not derived from observing the world, they do not tell us anything new about the world. Such truths consist of working out what must already be the case from a given starting point (deduction). The truths generated are certain, as they are true by definition.

Matters of fact

In contrast, 'matters of fact' can only be derived from experiencing how the world is. It may seem obvious that (most) objects fall down toward the earth or that fire burns, but this is only known through experience. Hume claims that our knowledge in this area consists of a) observing how the world is, and b) generalising from experience (induction). Matters of fact can never be certain; we can only achieve degrees of probability or confidence. We may feel absolutely certain that the sun will rise tomorrow – but maybe it will not. All of our scientific laws are based on observations of how the world has been in the past, and there is always the possibility that this will change tomorrow. We assume that the past will resemble the future, but again, this is only on the basis that in the past, the future has previously resembled the past. So we are generalising from experience again.

Hume defines the difference between the 'matters of fact' and 'relations of ideas' using several different, but related criteria which we outline in the table below. (Note that some of the terms we use in the table were actually not used by Hume, as they were coined afterwards. However, Hume was referring to the same concept, albeit by another name.)

	Relations of ideas	Matters of fact
Covers	Mathematics, geometry, logic	Facts and generalisations about the world
Examples	2 + 4 = 6 All bachelors are unmarried	Barack Obama was a US president Water can turn into ice
Certainty level	Absolute	Not 100 per cent certain; different levels of probability
How we know	By thinking about the concepts alone (can be known *a priori*)	By experience (can be known *a posteriori*)
Reliance on how the world is	None: truth does not rely on how the world is, or even the existence of objects	Complete reliance on how the world is; relies on the existence of objects and how they operate
Is the opposite conceivable?	No – it is true by definition (an analytic truth)	Yes – the opposite is conceivable and possible; it is not true by definition (a synthetic truth)

A few decades after Hume made his distinction between relations of ideas and matters of fact, Kant coined the terms ANALYTIC and SYNTHETIC to refer to ways in which sentences can be true. Some sentences are true simply through *analysing* the meanings of the terms involved. Kant termed such truths *analytic*. An analytic truth is true by definition and so cannot be denied without contradiction. For example, it is analytically true that a square has four sides. To say that a square does not have four sides is to contradict oneself. That a bachelor is unmarried is also an analytic truth. I can tell this is true just by looking at the terms involved; I do not need to go out into the world and conduct a survey of actual bachelors.

Essential Terminology

Kant explored how this process works. He claimed that for all analytic truths, the PREDICATE (the describing term) is already contained within the subject of the sentence. So in the sentence *a square has four sides*, the concept of four-sidedness (the predicate) is already contained in the concept of a square (the subject). When the predicate is already contained the subject, this makes the sentence an analytic truth. Likewise with the sentence *the bachelor was a man who had never been married*; the predicates (of being unmarried and being a man) are already contained in the subject (the concept of a bachelor), so the sentence is true by definition. It is an analytic truth. Analytic truths are also known by other names – TAUTOLOGIES or *logical truths*. A tautology is a statement that can only be true no matter how the world happens to be, such as 'Either it is raining or it is not raining.'

Essential Terminology

In contrast, consider the sentence, *John the bachelor is miserable*. Here, the subject (John the bachelor) does not contain the predicate (the idea of misery). So the sentence is not true by definition – it is a *synthetic truth*. As synthetic truths are not true simply by definition, they can be denied without contradiction. For example, it is a synthetic truth that the dinosaurs died out, or that John, a 43-year-old bachelor, is miserable. Dinosaurs might have continued to dominate the earth if the asteroid that ultimately wiped them out had been on a slightly different course. John might not have been miserable if he had met the woman of his dreams. These possibilities are conceivable since there is no contradiction in them.

Hume, in dividing our knowledge into *relations of ideas* (known by reason) and *matters of fact* (known by experience), is claiming that all relations of ideas will just be analytic truths – truths that can be established just by thinking about the concepts alone. On the other hand, all matters of fact require experience of the world and are not true by definition. This suggests that reason alone cannot tell us anything new or substantial about the world – we need experience (matters of fact) for this. This is an important claim. This whole section of the book is exploring whether reason can be a source of knowledge. Hume is suggesting that reason alone can only tell us things that are true by definition, all other 'substantial' knowledge has to be gained by experiencing the world.

Hume's division of human thought into these two areas is one of the most influential passages of philosophy. By separating out the areas of human understanding and clarifying what each is capable of, Hume sets out the limits of what each area can achieve. 'Matters of fact' (including science) cannot achieve absolute certainty and also can never *fully* explain why the world is as it is. We can explain some aspects of the world in terms of other generalisations – for example, explaining a light bulb shining in terms of electricity and electromagnetic radiation. But in the end, all of our explanations are based on observing how the world actually is, and generalising from it.

On the other hand, 'relations of ideas' can achieve absolute certainty – but only because they tell us nothing new about the world. This form of reasoning only concerns definitions and logical truths.

These two distinct areas of thought make up the two prongs of what has become known as Hume's fork.

Figure 1.33 Hume's fork. Hume suggests that our understanding is limited to these two areas – matters of fact and relations of ideas.

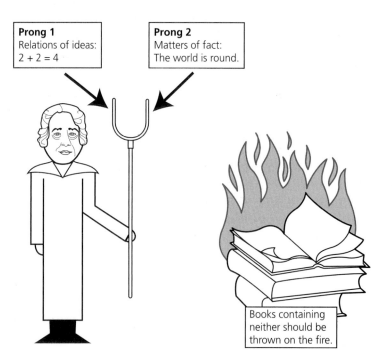

Prong 1
Relations of ideas:
2 + 2 = 4

Prong 2
Matters of fact:
The world is round.

Books containing neither should be thrown on the fire.

Hume's fork became a key discussion point in philosophy. Many rationalist philosophers, including Descartes, had tried to use reason alone to show how the world must be. This was partly in the hope of achieving certainty, and partly because they thought that reason could penetrate the ultimate truths about the world, in a way that our unreliable senses could not. According to Hume, these rationalists were simply wasting their time. You can only learn about the world by experience, and you cannot have certainty. On the one hand, we can study maths and logic using reason, and on the other, we can observe the world and see how it is. Reason alone cannot tell us about the world. Once we have observed the world, reason may be able to help us deduce some further elements and truths, but by itself reason cannot tell us about the world.

Hume realised that his 'fork' had powerful consequences for the writings of many other philosophers, and he was not frightened to spell this out.

> *When we go through libraries, convinced of these principles, what havoc must we make? If we take in our hand any volume – of divinity or school metaphysics, for instance – let us ask, Does it contain any abstract reasoning about quantity or number? No. Does it contain any experiential reasoning about matters of fact and existence? No. Then throw it in the fire, for it can contain nothing but sophistry and illusion.*[33]

Hume is suggesting that books that try to tell us what the world is like using reason alone should be burned!

See the activity below. Hume's claim is that all relations of ideas (prong 2) will be true or meaningless (sophistry and illusion). The challenge for the rationalist is to prove Hume wrong. To do this, a rationalist would need to show that thinking alone can produce knowledge (*a priori* knowledge) that is NOT just true by definition (so is synthetic, not just analytic). In fancy terms, the rationalist needs to show that synthetic a *priori* knowledge is possible. Hume's fork is a powerful claim. The following sections explore Descartes' attempts to produce knowledge using reason alone via his intuition and deduction thesis. Will Descartes succeed, or, as Hume argues, will he fail to produce anything other than statements that are true by definition? To answer this question we explore Descartes' famous *cogito*, his arguments for the existence of God and his proof of the external world.

Experimenting with ideas: Hume's fork

Is Hume right? Should all books about the world be based either just on maths (pure reason) or on experiments (senses)? What about trying to find out about the world using reason alone? Hume suggests that all attempts to use reason alone will either a) only involve ideas that are true by definition, or b) be 'sophistry and illusion' (which we are classing as empty or meaningless). To test Hume's bold assertion:

1 Try to stick each of the propositions below on one of Hume's two prongs.
2 Are all the relations of ideas (prong 2) true by definition, or meaningless as Hume claims?
3 Did you have difficult in classifying some of the propositions?

Propositions	Prong 1: matter of fact Needs observation to establish Tick/Cross	Prong 2: relation of ideas Can be established by thinking about the concepts alone Tick/Cross	Is this true by definition? Tick/Cross	Is this empty or meaningless? Tick/Cross
1 London is the capital of England				
2 God loves the world				
3 Time will always move on				
4 You exist				
5 2 + 3 = 5				
6 All bachelors are unmarried				
7 The sun will rise tomorrow				
8 It is wrong to kill the innocent				
9 Water boils at 100 °C at sea level				
10 Some bachelors throw wild parties				
11 Every event has a cause				
12 The amount of energy in the universe is constant				

The *cogito (a priori* intuition)

In the *Meditations*, Descartes doubts his beliefs until he finally reaches a point of certainty (see page 163 onwards for more on Descartes' doubt). He concludes that he cannot be deceived about his existence.

> *Now that I have convinced myself that there is nothing in the world – no sky, no earth, no minds, no bodies – does it follow that I don't exist either? No it does not follow; for if I convinced myself of something then I certainly existed. But there is a supremely powerful and cunning deceiver who deliberately deceives me all the time! Even then, if he is deceiving me I undoubtedly exist: let him deceive me all he can, he will never bring it about that I am nothing while I think I am something. So after thoroughly thinking the matter through I conclude that this proposition, I am, I exist, must be true whenever I assert it or think it.*[34]

In this paragraph, Descartes discovers the first certainty that he has been searching for. But how does the *cogito* work as an argument and is it successful?

Does the *cogito* succeed?

One of the problems in deciding whether the *cogito* succeeds is trying to work out what sort of argument or claim it is. Much has been written on this matter. Descartes believes that the truth of the *cogito* is so clear and distinct that it can be instantly 'intuited'. But while it is 'intuitively' convincing for many, articulating exactly how it works is not as simple as it seems.

Is the *cogito* a deductive argument?

We might be tempted to see it as some sort of deduction from the premise that *I am thinking* to the conclusion that *I exist*. This interpretation is certainly suggested by the *therefore* of the *Discourse* and *Principles* versions of the *cogito* (I think *therefore* I am).

However, a deductive inference from the premise that *I am thinking* to the conclusion that *I exist* would not be valid as it stands – there would seem to be a missing premise, in the same way that *I am reading, therefore I must be wearing my glasses* does not work, as I may not need glasses to read. To make this work, I would need to add a hidden premise, such *as I cannot read without wearing my glasses*. Similarly, if the *cogito* is to work as a deduction, we would need to add a premise such as *I cannot think without existing*, or something more general, such as *all thinking things exist*. So a complete version of the argument would be a syllogism like this:

P1 I am thinking
P2 (hidden) I cannot think without existing
C Therefore I exist

If Descartes did intend the *cogito* to be a syllogism, then why does he not mention this hidden premise? In fact, in a later work, Descartes states that at this stage of doubt the thinker is not in a position to claim something as bold as P2, and rules out the possibility that the *cogito* is a syllogism.

> *When someone says 'I am thinking, therefore I am, or I exist', he isn't inferring existence from thought by means of a syllogism [deduction]; rather, a simple intuition of his mind shows it to him as self-evident.*[35]

Is the *cogito* a transcendental argument?

Another possibility is that the *cogito* is a transcendental argument (a term first used in this sense after Descartes by Kant). Transcendental arguments work by claiming that a specific feature of the world (in this case, my existence) is necessary to enable a particular experience (in this case, my doubt) to occur. If it is the case that you need to exist in order to doubt, then it is impossible to doubt that you exist, as existence is a necessary precondition for doubt to occur in the first place. So the very act of doubting actually proves that you exist, and the attempt to doubt your own existence becomes self-defeating.

The interpretation of the *cogito* as an argument of this sort is backed up by the text of the *Discourse*:

I noticed that while I was trying in this way to think everything to be false it had to be the case that I, who was thinking this, was something. And observing that this truth I am thinking, therefore I exist was so firm and sure that not even the most extravagant suppositions of the sceptics could shake it, I decided that I could accept it without scruple as the first principle of the philosophy I was seeking.[36]

▶ **ACTIVITY**

Consider the following items and ask yourself which of them would have to exist or be in place in order for doubt to happen. In other words, which of these are preconditions of doubting?

1 The capacity to use language
2 The physical world
3 Self-awareness
4 A reliable memory
5 The existence of French wine
6 A mind
7 The ability to reason reliably
8 Time

But the *cogito* is not merely based on the fact that I am doubting my existence, but on the possibility of thinking in general – that is, that my existence is a precondition of my consciousness. So if you are thinking at all, then you must be existing. Again this has textual support. In the second replies to the *Meditations*, Descartes suggests that the thinker 'learns it by experiencing in his own case that it isn't possible to think without existing'.[37]

There is, however, a difficulty with this interpretation. Recall that at this point in the *Meditations*, Descartes cannot rely on his most basic reasoning processes. He has told us that he cannot even be sure of adding three to five accurately or counting the sides of a square. So we may wonder whether he could work through the steps of a transcendental argument of this sort with any confidence of not going astray. What Descartes really needs is for the *cogito* to work as a simple item of knowledge: a thought so clear and distinct that its truth is immediately intuited.

Cogito as a self-verifying thought

Another aspect of the *cogito* is how Descartes emphasises its temporary and fleeting nature: 'I am, I exist, must be true whenever I assert it or think it'.[38] This suggests that the truth of the *cogito* is revealed in the act of performing it. So perhaps we should consider that doubt is overcome through the process of thinking the *cogito*. The thought that 'I do not exist' is self-defeating in its performance. In this way of seeing the situation, the transcendental nature of the argument – the recognition that my existence is a precondition of my thinking – is immediately revealed in having the thought. Compare the doubts about my existence with claims such as 'I am not here' or 'I am not speaking' which are similarly self-defeating.

The content alone 'I do not exist' when, say, written down, does not have the same effect, as one day I may not exist and the written words will not be self-defeating. So it is not the thought itself that leads to any contradiction, but the act of having the thought. It is what may be termed an 'assertoric inconsistency', which is the same as saying it is performatively self-defeating. As thinking 'I do not exist' cannot be true when it is thought, it must be the case that the thinker exists.

This interpretation focuses on the negative statement 'I do **not** exist' being self-defeating, which Descartes sometimes emphasises in his writing. It could also be claimed to work in the positive version too. The very act of asserting 'I think' also verifies that 'I exist', as existing is a precondition of thinking. This leads to two similar ways in which the *cogito* is self-verifying:

A In having the thought 'I think', it is clear and distinct that you must exist as a precondition of thought. The *cogito* is self-verifying. (This is the positive version focusing on the precondition of thought.)

B Thinking 'I do not exist' would be a contradiction, as existence is a precondition of doubt. (This is the negative version. The *cogito* is self-verifying because the opposite is an assertoric inconsistency.)

Descartes' different versions of the *cogito* seem to support either A or B. Again, whether either can work as a single intuition, or only as a deduction involving stages, is a point of discussion.

Has Descartes produced *a priori* knowledge?

Many would concede that the *cogito* works on some level and that Descartes can know that he exists. In this chapter, the overriding question is whether reason alone can be a source of knowledge. It appears that Descartes' *cogito* has produced some level of knowledge, and seemingly using reason alone. To be sure of this, we need to answer two further questions:

1 Exactly what knowledge has the *cogito* established?
2 Is this knowledge established *a priori* (independently of experience)?

In regard to the first question, it may seem obvious what knowledge the *cogito* produces – that 'I' exist (whoever is thinking it). But what is meant by the 'I'? A person that endures through time? Is it the same 'I' that thinks about the *cogito* the next day? Descartes seems to think so – 'I am, I exist, must be true whenever I assert it or think it'. But others have doubts as to whether he can claim as much as this.

Criticism 1: different thinkers

At this stage in the *Mediations*, Descartes is still in the throes of his radical doubt. If he can only be sure that he exists when he is actually thinking about it, then is it possible that he may cease to exist while he is not thinking about it. Consequently, at this stage, the existence of the SELF has a rather provisional and temporary character. Perhaps every time the 'I am, I exist' is thought, it is a different person thinking it – but each has been created anew that second and given the memories of Descartes.

The philosopher Bertrand Russell (1872–1970) articulates a similar position, claiming that the *cogito* fails to establish the existence of an enduring thinker at all.

> *When I look at my table and see a certain brown colour, what is quite certain at once is not 'I am seeing a brown colour'; but rather, 'a brown colour is being seen'. This of course involves something (or somebody) which (or who) sees the brown colour; but it does not of itself involve that more or less permanent person whom we call 'I'. So far as immediate certainty goes, it might be that the something which sees the brown colour is quite momentary, and not the same as the something which has some different experience the next moment.*[39]

This doubt may seem highly radical; however, it is in keeping with Descartes' mission to establish absolute certainty. Descartes takes an infallibilist position in regard to knowledge (see page 26); as such it seems reasonable to say that he has **not** proved, beyond any doubt, that there is an enduring 'I' that exists in between thinking about his own existence.

► **ACTIVITY: WHO IS THE THINKER?**

How well do you know 'yourself'?

1 Are you sure you are the same thinker who was thinking thoughts yesterday?
2 If so, what makes you sure? Is it your memory? An ongoing awareness of your 'self'?
3 Is it possible that you were created one second ago, but with a full set of memories?
4 If you do not think you are the same thinker as yesterday, then what is it that links the thoughts of yesterday (by someone else, presumably) to thoughts of today (which *you* are having?)
5 Does there need to be a 'thinker' at all? Could 'your' existence just be a sequence of thoughts?

133

Criticism 2: no meaningful self – just a bundle of thoughts

In a famous passage opposing Descartes, Hume claims that he has no consciousness of himself:

> *There are some philosophers who imagine we are every moment intimately conscious of what we call our self; that we feel its existence and its continuance in existence ... For my part, when I enter most intimately into what I call myself I always stumble on some particular perception or other, heat or cold, light or shade, love or hatred, pain or pleasure. I never can catch myself at any time without a perception and never observe anything but the perception.*[40]

As we saw earlier, Hume believes that all our concepts must originate in experience, and more specifically in impressions. Hume is asking us to perform an experiment: to look into ourselves in search of our self. If we have a genuine concept of the self, it must originate in some experience or perception. But, looking into himself, all he is aware of are perceptions of various sorts, none of which is a perception of himself. The self, then, is nothing over and above the perceptions we have. There is an awareness of perceptions, but none of any owner of the perceptions. Hume concludes that the concept of 'self' merely refers to a bundle of perceptions without anything in which these perceptions occur. If Hume is right, then this is a dangerous criticism for Descartes. For he goes on to argue that his self is indeed a thing, or substance, which has various conscious experiences and is not simply reducible to those experiences.

Criticism 3: radical doubts – no thinker at all

Do thoughts even need a thinker? Is it not possible for thoughts to just exist like puffs of steam? Is it necessary to have some sort of steam engine producing these puffs? How can Descartes be sure? Perhaps the *cogito* should read, 'there are thoughts, therefore some thoughts exist'. This is considerable less catchy and also an analytic truth – it is true by definition. The Canadian philosopher Barry Stroud (1935–) argues that the problem with transcendental arguments is that the sceptic can always deny that any property is a precondition of experience. It may seem obvious that you need to exist in order to think, or to doubt, but maybe you do not?

It does seem very obvious that, for there to be conscious experiences, there must be a mind or thinker which is having those experiences. However, Descartes has put himself in the arena of highly radical doubt. Just how clear and distinct does Descartes need to be to shake even the radical doubt that thoughts do not require a thinker?

Critics may say that the infallibilist position of equating knowledge with certainty is a mistake. We can have knowledge without requiring absolute certainty. I genuinely know that my cat exists, even though she cannot perform the *cogito*, nor can I on her behalf. If the concepts of knowledge and certainty are decoupled, then of course we can know that the *cogito* shows that there is a thinker, me, that has thoughts.

The exact nature of the thinker, though, is still mystery, in particular the question of whether there is a permanent, enduring 'I' that exists over time. After all, do you not change each moment of each day? Are you the same thinker that you were a moment ago?

Is the *cogito* an *a priori* intuition?

So far we have seen that the *cogito* seems to generate some form of knowledge. The question now is whether it does so by reason alone – independently of experience. This is a very difficult question to answer and there is no agreement amongst philosophers. To explore the debate, we will present different strands of the considerations in the form of an imaginary discussion between someone arguing that the *cogito* is known through experience of the world (*a posteriori*) and someone claiming that is it known, through reason, independently of experience (*a priori*).

1 The use of concepts/language

Mr Experience (*a posteriori*): Experience is definitely needed to generate the *cogito*. Descartes draws on many fundamental concepts – for example, what *thought* is, what *doubt* is and what *existence* is. He may want to claim these are innate concepts, but they are derived from experience.

Ms Reason (*a priori*): But deriving our concepts from experience does not invalidate the claim that the *cogito* is justified by reason. Leibniz acknowledged that we need experience to generate our concepts and our language. The key is whether the knowledge is **proved/justified** by thought alone; by thinking about the concepts. Or whether it is justified by experience, by observing the world. And in this case, it is justified by thought alone.

2 The intellect

Ms Reason: The *cogito* is the result of the intellect alone. No evidence from the senses or the imagination is used at any point. So the truth of the *cogito* is not reliant on the senses in any way.

Mr Experience: But remember that Locke and Hume claimed that reflection and inner sensations count as experience. The *cogito* is based on Descartes' awareness of thinking, which is a reflection on the experience of thinking.

Ms Reason: But the thought 'I think' is not based on reflections about sensation or inner emotions. It is a thought about thoughts. It is a kind of pure reason, so is devoid of empirical content. Indeed the *cogito* could be thought even if the world did not exist, so it is not derived from experience.

Mr Experience: Your awareness that you are thinking is still an experience. A fact about the world that you become aware of.

3 Level of certainty

Mr Experience: Most *a priori* knowledge is true for all time and can be known in advance of experience. That Descartes exists, he claims, is only known when he thinks about it. I know that triangles have three sides all the time, but my knowledge is not dependent on having a specific thought about it. In contrast, I can only know it is raining at the time of the rain. The *cogito* seems much more like this second case, which is an example of *a posteriori* knowledge.

Ms Reason: Descartes claims 'I am, I exist, must be true whenever I assert it or think it'. He is making a universal claim, but because this is a self-verifying form of knowledge, it can only be known when thought. But it will always be true that it can be known when thought.

4 Method of argument

Mr Experience: The evidence base for the *cogito* is drawn from our experience – in this case, thought. It claims that whenever a specific experience occurs (thought), then we can know that we exist. Also as a self-justifying thought, it has some of the features of an experiment about the world; it is something you have to do (think), to generate the truth. So the *cogito* has some of the hallmarks of *a posteriori* knowledge – knowledge gained by experience.

Ms Reason: Just because the *cogito* is *about* experience, this does not mean that it is *justified* by experience. Descartes is NOT making an inductive generalisation from past experience – for example, every time he has thought in the past he has also existed, so it is reasonable to claim that this will be true in the future too. He is making a claim, based on reason, which is that one must exist in order to think (possibly as a transcendental argument). In this sense, it is an *a priori* claim, albeit one that is about experience itself.

Mr Experience: Not so fast. In the second set of replies to the *Meditations*, Descartes writes, 'what actually happens is that he learns [the *cogito*] it by experiencing in his own case that it isn't possible to think without existing. Constructing general propositions on the basis of our knowledge of particular ones is something that we just naturally do'.[41] This seems to imply that it is an INDUCTIVE ARGUMENT, moving from a single case to a general case on the basis of experience.

Ms Reason: What Descartes writes is ambiguous. Also, Descartes presents and writes about the *cogito* differently in his various works. We are not engaged in a guessing game about what Descartes might have thought and whether he is consistent; we are supposed to be philosophising ourselves about how the *cogito* works.

As an aside, it is worth noting that the debate about *a priori* versus *a posteriori* knowledge only really flourished after Descartes' time. Also, some philosophers have questioned how meaningful or useful the concepts are anyway.

Whether the *cogito* is born out of reason or experience is not really the issue. Overall, Descartes is concerned with establishing certainty. Whether we class the *cogito* as being derived from experience or pure reason is not vital to his project.

Is the *cogito* a successful *a priori* intuition?

Hume's fork suggests that all substantial knowledge must come via the senses; reason alone can only tell us about the relations between ideas. Does the *cogito* prove this wrong? The *cogito* does seem to produce some form of knowledge, though exactly what is debatable. It is also debatable whether this knowledge is derived independently of experience or not.

Descartes' proof of God 1: the trademark argument

Having established the *cogito*, Descartes concludes that he can be certain of its truth because it is so clear and distinct. He then makes the tentative claim that 'whatever I perceive very vividly and clearly [clearly and distinctly] is true'.[42]

Descartes then proceeds to question this claim by wondering whether an evil demon may have made his nature such that even clear and distinct ideas are false. Descartes concludes that the only way out of this doubt is to show that God exists, as a good God would not make a being whose clearest and most distinct thoughts were false ones.

Descartes' first argument for the existence of God is a classic example of his intuition and deduction thesis in action. From his initial clear and distinct ideas of God and himself (intuitions), Descartes attempts to deduce God's existence through a series of steps.

The basic idea of the argument is that Descartes' idea of God can only have appeared in his mind if there really is a God. Much as the hallmark stamped on a silver spoon, or even the logo on a T-shirt, reveals its maker, so the idea of God within his mind also reveals its maker, namely God himself (see **Figure 1.34**). To show this, Descartes argues that the idea of an infinite being (that is, God) cannot be produced from within the mind of a finite being like himself or anyone else. The cause of such an idea, he argues, can only be a being that really is infinite.

In the *Meditations*, Descartes does not present his argument in a formal style; instead he presents his reasoning in the manner of someone debating an issue in their own mind. However, if he did present a formal argument, it might look something like this:

P1 The cause of anything must be at least as perfect as its effect
P2 My ideas must be caused by something
P3 I am an imperfect being
P4 I have the idea of God, which is that of a perfect being
Intermediate conclusion (IC)1
I cannot be the cause of my idea of God (From P1, P2, P3 and P4)
IC2 Only a perfect being (that is, God) can be the cause of my idea of God (From P1 and P4)
Main conclusion (C) God must exist (From P4 and IC2)

If you managed to read through Descartes' text, you may feel rather confused about the details of his argument, as he seems to rely on many ideas that might not seem obvious. Here we will work through one or two elements of the argument in greater depth to try to clarify some of the intricacies.

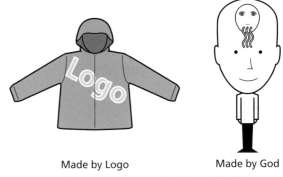
Made by Logo   Made by God
Figure 1.34 A designer imprints his clothes with his logo. God has 'imprinted' the concept of God in our minds.

> ▶ **ACTIVITY**
> If you have a copy, read through Meditation 3 and identify where each of the premises and conclusions can be found in the text.

Idea of God   Caused by   God himself
Figure 1.35 Descartes is moving from knowledge of his idea of God in his mind, to the cause of that idea outside of his mind. This cause must be God, so God must exist.

137

The causal principle (P1 above)

In this argument, Descartes introduces a general principle which he thinks is self-evident. He writes:

> *Now it is obvious by the natural light that the total cause of something must contain at least as much reality as does the effect.*[43]

Descartes is saying that the cause of anything must, in some sense, be *adequate* to its effect. So, you cannot cause something to happen unless the cause is sufficient to make the effect. A corollary of this principle is that 'something can't arise from nothing'.[44] The thought here is plausible enough: if something occurs, what caused it has to have enough power or *oomph*, as it were, to produce the effect. To illustrate the basic idea, imagine that a window shatters. Now, we can tell that whatever caused it to shatter must have had enough power – what Descartes here calls 'reality' – to make it shatter. So it could not have been shattered by something too small or weak, such as a grain of sand or a fly. It would have to have been something big and powerful enough, or with sufficient 'reality', or *oomph*, such as a brick or an escaping criminal.

Descartes gives an example to illustrate his point. He asks us to consider the production of a stone. Whatever it was that caused a stone to come into existence would have to be sufficient to have produced it.

A stone, for example, can begin to exist only if it is produced by something that contains – either straightforwardly or in some higher form – everything that is to be found in the stone.[45]

What must have caused my ideas?

Armed with his causal principle, Descartes proceeds to consider the possible causes of his various ideas. Our ideas, after all, must be caused by something, and the causal principle suggests to Descartes that this cause must have at least as much reality as the ideas themselves. In other words, our ideas cannot be more perfect than what has caused them. Descartes argues that his ideas of humans or animals could be made up by himself out of his ideas of material things, even if these things did not exist. The thought here is that, so long as he has an idea of physical things, he can make up men and animals in his imagination just as we make up the idea of a unicorn. However, when Descartes considers how wonderful his idea of an infinite God is, he concludes that it would have been impossible for the idea to have originated in him.

Descartes claims that since the cause of his idea of God must have at least as much reality as the idea has reality, the only thing that can be the cause of it is God himself. For the idea of an infinite substance could not have originated from within him, as he is only a finite substance. The only cause with sufficient reality to produce the idea of an *infinite* being would have to be an infinite being. It follows that the idea of God must have been planted in him by God himself, and so God must exist.

Moreover, Descartes elaborates, the notion of the infinite must *precede* that of the finite (that is, the notion of God must precede that of myself) since the latter could only be recognised by contrasting it to the former.

The only remaining alternative is that my idea of God is innate in me, just as the idea of myself is innate in me. It is no surprise that God in creating me should have placed this idea in me, to serve as a mark of the craftsman stamped on his work. The mark need not be anything distinct from the work itself.[46]

Criticism 1: is the causal principle true?

Descartes' causal principle states that 'total cause of something must contain at least as much reality as does the effect'.[47] Descartes clearly believes this is self-evidently true. Part of his thinking is that you cannot get more out of the effect than was already in the cause, otherwise you would be getting something for nothing. Since it is self-evident that nothing can come from nothing, this must be impossible.

This idea, in part, is borne out in the first law of thermodynamics, which roughly states that the amount of energy in the universe remains the same. If effects, on the whole, were 'greater' than their causes, then the amount of energy in the universe would increase (and perpetual motion machines would be possible). As a scientist, Descartes was one of the earliest thinkers to articulate a theory of the conservation of momentum (which is a pre-runner to the first law of thermodynamics), so the idea of effects not being greater than their causes would have seemed obvious to Descartes.

Superficially, however, there do appear to be all kinds of examples where it does seem possible to produce something with more perfection or reality than there was originally in its cause. Can we not light a bonfire with a match? Or cause an avalanche with a whisper? Here the causes appear to have markedly *less* reality than what they are able to produce. Consider also the effects of a long process such as evolution. Incremental changes over billions of years can produce complex creatures such as ourselves out of disorganised matter. Here the effect surely has vastly more 'perfection' than the original cause.

The key challenge, however, is in applying the causal principle to ideas. The principle may have some credibility in regard to the physical world, but seems far less credible when it comes to the world of ideas. It is not clear at all that the physical cause of an idea must be greater than the idea itself. It is not even clear what this would mean in terms of relating the physical world to the mental in terms of causation.

Empiricists argue that all our concepts come from experience, including our idea of God. We saw on page 110 how Hume argued that our idea of God is derived from considering virtues in other people and augmenting them without limit. In this way, our ideas do not have to be caused by something with more reality or perfection. We can simply augment our existing ideas to create better versions of things we may have experienced.

Criticism 2: do we really have an idea of an infinite being or of infinity?

A premise of Descartes' argument is that he has the idea of God as a 'substance that is infinite, eternal, unchangeable, independent, supremely intelligent, supremely powerful, which created myself and anything else that may exist'.[48]

But can we really grasp such an idea? God may be just too great for us to understand. So, it can be argued that Descartes is able to use the word 'God' without having a genuine corresponding idea in his mind. The idea of an infinite being, like that of infinity, may be something we can express in words, but not truly understand. If I try to conceive of infinity, my mind fails me; the idea is really only a negative one, namely the opposite of finite. Now if this is right, and we do not really have the idea of an infinite being, then the issue of where the idea comes from does not arise, and so the trademark argument does not get off the ground.

▶ **ACTIVITY**

Descartes has an idea of God as an infinite, supremely intelligent, supremely powerful creator of the world. List all the possible causes of these ideas – where might Descartes (or any other believer) have got these ideas from?

▶ **ACTIVITY**

1 Do you possess an idea of infinity?
2 Have you ever experienced infinity?
3 How might this idea be derived from experience?
4 Is this idea innate?

Criticism 3: the idea of God is incoherent

Another reason for thinking that we do not have a proper idea of God in the first place is that it is contradictory. Note that in Descartes' account of his idea of God, he mentions that God is all-powerful. This is problematic: can God set himself a task that he cannot perform? If he *can*, then there is a task he cannot perform; and if he *cannot*, there is a task he cannot perform (namely set himself a task that he cannot perform), so either way he cannot be all-powerful. This PARADOX in the very notion of omnipotence suggests that Descartes' idea of God is unclear. And if Descartes has an unclear idea of God, the cause of this idea is not likely to be a perfect God. It would be far more likely to have originated within Descartes himself.

Essential
Terminology   Aa

Criticism 4: the idea of an all-powerful God is not universal

It often occurs to those encountering this argument for the first time to point out that people from other religions do not have an idea of an all-powerful God. And if they do not have such an idea, then Descartes is surely wrong to say that it is planted in our minds. Similarly, it can be argued on EMPIRICAL grounds that we know that the origin of the idea of an omnipotent God is not divine, since it has a historical genesis around 500 BCE in Palestine.

In Descartes' defence, he could claim that people *do* have an innate idea of God, but do not always think hard enough about METAPHYSICAL issues to be fully aware of it. Much like the slave boy (page 96) may have an innate understanding of geometry without realising it.

Does the trademark argument show that reason alone can produce knowledge via the intuition and deduction method?

As we have seen above, the trademark argument has many criticisms. However, even if it did work, would the argument show that reason alone can be a source of knowledge? Specifically, would this count as an example of an *a priori* deduction – as envisaged by Descartes' intuition and deduction thesis? There are two strands to this question. Is it a deduction? Would the knowledge be *a priori*?

Is it a deduction? Just like the *cogito*, Descartes is trying to move from a thought to the existence of something. Descartes claims to have an innate idea of God and that from this idea (along with the causal principle) he can deduce that God must exist. This has two hallmarks of a classic DEDUCTIVE ARGUMENT: a) If the premises are true, then the conclusion *must* be true too, as opposed to just being probable, and b) all the necessary information is contained in the premises (in this case, the idea of God and the causal principle).

Is the knowledge *a priori*? The conclusion of any deduction can be known *a priori* given that the premises are true. For example, if the following premises are true: *Ahmed is taller than Sally* and *Sally is taller than Robin*, then I can deduce that Ahmed is taller than Robin. I can know this conclusion *a priori* – I do not need it revealed by experience. However, in this case, the premises themselves can only be known via experience (*a posteriori*). So, overall, the knowledge that Ahmed is taller than Robin cannot be known *a priori*. The two premises were known via the senses and the additional claim deduced, *a priori*, from these. For the knowledge to be truly *a priori*, the premises would *also* need to be knowable independently of experience. This, of course, is exactly Descartes' plan. To start with intuitions, 'seen' by the intellect alone, and then use reason to deduce further truths. So is the knowledge of God's existence, via the trademark argument, fully *a priori*?

Again, we present this as a debate.

Ms Reason (*a priori*): Descartes was moving from an idea in his head to the existence of God. Each stage involved the intellect and not the senses; as such, the knowledge was established independently of the senses, by reason alone.

Mr Experience (*a posteriori*): Descartes drew on several ideas during his musings, such as the causal principle (*something cannot come from nothing*), and, in doing so, drew on many examples from experience (such as the example of a stone).

Ms Reason (*a priori*): The causal principle is either innate or is so obvious that it can be intuited. As such, Descartes' 'proof' only involved innate ideas (God and the causal principle) and his intellect (not his senses).

Mr Experience (*a posteriori*): The principle that *something cannot come from nothing* is gained from experience of the world. It is not innate, nor is it true by definition (just considering the concepts of *something* and *nothing* alone). I can easily imagine something being created out of nothing, which suggests the opposite is not an inherent contradiction and so the principle is not one that is true by definition.

Further, the general structure of the argument is to move from an observed effect (the idea of God) to the suggested cause (God). This is an argument based around the principle of causation. Hume would argue that all causal connections can only be established by observing how the world is and so would say that this argument relies on experience, so is not an example of a pure *a priori* deduction.

Again, this debate is not essential to Descartes' project. He was more interested in establishing certainty than guaranteeing the *a priori* nature of the argument.

Cartesian circle

There is a claim that the trademark argument fails, not just because of its content, but also due to where it fits in the bigger picture of the *Meditations*. Descartes has just established the *cogito* and concludes from this that whatever he perceives clearly and distinctly will be true. He then proceeds to doubt this conclusion by remembering that an evil demon could still be deceiving him into thinking that his clear and distinct thoughts were true, when they are not. Descartes' way out of this doubt is to show that God exists and a good God would not make a being whose clearest and most distinct thoughts were false ones. This approach has been accused of making a fundamental error, known as the Cartesian circle. The charge against Descartes is that he uses clear and distinct ideas to show that God exists, and only then can he conclude that his clear and distinct ideas must be true. But if his clear and distinct ideas are not 'validated' until after the proof, then how can he be sure that a demon is not deceiving him in making the proof? Take as an example the causal principle that there must be at least as much reality in the total cause as in its effect. This is crucial to Descartes' argument and Descartes takes this to be clearly and distinctly knowable. Now, quite apart from whether it really is actually true, the fact that he has not yet dismissed the demon hypothesis means it is still possible for the

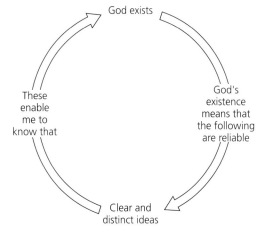

Figure 1.36 The Cartesian circle

demon to deceive him into thinking it is true when it is not. Descartes' reasoning here appears to be circular – that is, it presupposes what it sets out to prove. He relies on clear and distinct ideas to show that clear and distinct ideas are reliable.

A more familiar example of such a circular justification occurs in the following chain of reasoning:

Q   How do you know that God exists?
A   Because it says so in the Bible.
Q   How do you know what the Bible says is true?
A   Because it is the Word of God.

We could construct a similar line of reasoning from the above passage of the *Meditations*.

Q   How do you know that God exists?
A   Because I proved his existence using clear and distinct ideas.
Q   How do you know that clear and distinct ideas are reliable?
A   Because a non-deceiving God exists.

It is perhaps unlikely that Descartes could have been guilty of such an obvious error. One line of defence against the charge of circularity is to claim that there are some propositions of which I can have self-evident knowledge while I am attending them and which do not need the divine guarantee (such as the *cogito*). Specifically, the realisation that a non-deceiving God exists would have to be of this category. This suggests that doubt is not supposed to extend to cover basic intuitions of clearly and distinctly perceived truths. However, this defence will only help Descartes if he could claim that his awareness of God's existence, which he derives from his idea of God, can be held as a single intuition, rather than a series of intuitions that make up a deduction. A series would require our memories to be free from deception and Descartes has yet to establish this.

Descartes' proof of God 2: the contingency argument

In Meditation 3, after the trademark argument, Descartes produces what appears to be a second argument for God's existence. He asks whether the fact of his own existence is enough to show that there must be a God. To answer this, he investigates where his own existence might have come from. The possibilities that suggest themselves are that he created himself, that he has always existed, that his parents or some other cause less perfect than God created him, or that God created him. So he considers these possibilities in turn.

Does my existence derive from myself?

Descartes reasons that if he were the author of his own being, and so depended on nothing else for his existence, then he would have made himself perfect and so he would be God. But clearly he is not God, since he has so many imperfections – for example, he does not know everything, as is shown from the fact that he doubts so much – and so he cannot have created himself.

Have I always existed?

So is it possible that he has always existed? Descartes answers that even if he had, this would not mean that he was himself the author of his own being, for since his past existence is not sufficient to guarantee his present existence, there must also be something which conserves his existence at every moment. Now, clearly he does not conserve himself in existence since, if he did, as a conscious being, he would be aware of this. So it follows that he must be conserved by something other than himself.

Does my existence derive from my parents?

Could his parents or some other cause less great than God be the author of his being? Well, in some sense, of course they are, since it is because of them that he was born. But, for Descartes, his parents do not create him out of nothing; they are simply the architects of a certain organisation of the matter of which he is composed. Nor do they conserve him in his existence and so they cannot be the ultimate explanation for his existence. Moreover, looking to his parents does not provide any ultimate explanation for his existence, since we are now left with the question of where they derived their existence, so we end up in an INFINITE REGRESS.

Does my existence derive from God?

Since Descartes and his parents (or any similar imperfect cause) have been rejected and there must be an ultimate cause for his existence, he has to suppose that God is the ultimate explanation. As we have seen, since 'there must be at least as much reality in the cause as in the effect', and since he is a thinking thing, he must be caused by something with at least as much reality as a thinking substance. And in Descartes' terminology, that substance must contain formally the perfections that his idea of God possesses objectively. Now although his physical being may have come from his parents, his conscious being as a thinking substance can only have come from another thinking substance. Thus, Descartes can conclude that God exists.

Put formally, Descartes' argument resembles something like this:

P1 The cause of my existence as a thinking thing could be a) myself, b) I have always existed, c) my parents, or d) God

P2 I cannot have caused myself to exist for then I would have created myself perfect. Nor can I sustain myself in existence, for then I would be God

P3 Neither have I always existed, for then I would be aware of this

P4 My parents may be the cause of my physical existence, but not of me as a thinking mind

C (by elimination) Therefore, only God could have created me

Criticism 1: could I not be what created and conserves me?

We might object that even though Descartes is not aware of having the power to sustain himself in existence, he might nonetheless have it. Descartes' response would doubtless be that if as a conscious being he were always conserving his own existence, he could not but be conscious of this activity going on within himself. So if he is not conscious of the activity which preserves him, he cannot be its author. Nonetheless, this defence is not particularly convincing, since Descartes has accepted that dreams have a cause of which we are not conscious and yet which may come from within us, so it seems possible that we may have aspects to our own nature of which we are unaware.

Criticism 2: could we have been created by a less than perfect being?

Could we not have been created by another conscious being less great than God, say, an evil scientist or an angel, or even a process of evolution? Why must our

▶ **ACTIVITY**

Does this argument strike you as a sound one? If not, which of the premises would you say is suspect; and/or which step would you say was not justified? Would you class this argument as a deduction, an ABDUCTION, or both?

143

author be either ourselves, our parents or a perfect being (God)? After all, these options are not exhaustive (they are not the only ones). Descartes does look at the possibility that we could be put together by a series of less than perfect causes. His response to this invokes the original trademark argument about the source of his idea of God. He writes:

That can't be right, because God's simplicity – that is, the unity or inseparability of all his attributes – is one of the most important of the perfections that I understand him to have. The idea of his perfections as united in a single substance couldn't have been placed in me by any cause that didn't also provide me with the ideas of the perfections themselves.[49]

In other words, if he were created by a being lesser than God, or which was only perfect in some ways, he could not have the idea of a God which is perfect in every way. For this reason, the trademark argument is the more important one, as the contingency argument cannot work alone without relying on the same underlying causal principle.

Does Descartes produce *a priori* knowledge via a deduction?

As the causal principle is again drawn upon, the previous discussion of this question in relation to the trademark argument still applies (page 140).

Descartes' proof of God 3: the ontological argument

In Meditation 5, Descartes presents another proof for the existence of God, known as the ONTOLOGICAL argument. He was not the first (nor the last) philosopher to present this argument. It is one of the more famous proofs for the existence of God and is explored in more detail in Unit 3 of the A-level.

By this stage in the *Mediations*, Descartes has argued that, with careful attention, his intellect can take any intelligible object and work out which features are essential to it – for example, a triangle having three sides and straight lines. He cannot conceive of a triangle without three sides, so it must be the case that having three sides is an essential feature of a triangle. Descartes claims that he is aware of such things clearly and distinctly, so they must be true. Once we are aware of the essential features of the triangle, he claims we are then able to deduce other features that also must be the case – such as Pythagoras' theorem.

Descartes then takes this approach to the idea of God. It follows that any properties of God that he clearly and distinctly perceives to be part of his idea of God must really be part of God's essence.

So what is Descartes' idea of God? Well, it is the idea of a supremely perfect being. Now, one property that he perceives as belonging to God's nature is *existence*, and therefore God must exist.

In general, understanding the essential feature of an object (say a triangle) does not tell you whether that object exists or not, and Descartes accepts this principle. However, Descartes claims that in the case of God things are different. Unlike the case of a triangle, God's existence cannot be distinguished from his

anthology
1.23

essence. For if we try to subtract the property of existence from the idea of God, we take away something essential, much as to subtract the property of three-sidedness from the idea of a triangle is to subtract something essential from it. Thus Descartes claims that he cannot think of God as not existing, just as he cannot think of highlands in a world with no lowlands.

Descartes claims that the idea of a non-existent God would not be an idea of God at all, as a perfect being must have all perfections. Descartes elaborates why he believes that the very concept of God entails his existence. The idea is that God is the supremely perfect being and a perfect being must be perfect in every way. This means he must be omnipotent (all-powerful), omniscient (all-knowing), all-good, all-loving, and so on. In other words, he must have all perfections. Now, Descartes claims, existence is itself a perfection. That is to say, it is more perfect for something to exist than not to exist. And this means we must include it in the list of perfections possessed by God. And so it follows that God must exist. Put more formally, Descartes' argument would resemble something like this:

P1 I have an idea of God, that is to say, an idea of a perfect being
P2 A perfect being must have all perfections
P3 Existence is a perfection
C God exists

Experimenting with ideas

Who is the greatest? Have a look at the two different scenarios in **Figure 1.37**.

There are two possibilities. Either God, the greatest possible being, exists only in our minds, or he exists in our minds and in reality as well.

1 Which scenario do you think is true? (Which universe do we live in?)
2 Which scenario do you think contains the greater being?
3 Are your answers to 1 and 2 the same? If they are different, how can you account for the difference?

Scenario 1: The greatest possible being only exists in people's understanding.

Scenario 2: The greatest possible being exists in people's understanding and in reality.

Figure 1.37

▶ ACTIVITY

Most people, when they hear the ontological argument, are inclined to think that there is something fishy going on. However, it is not obvious what exactly has gone wrong, and it is a controversial matter to identify where the flaw lies – if indeed there is a flaw. Before reading on, consider what you think may be the error Descartes makes here. Take note of your thoughts.

Figure 1.38 The perfect island

Gaunilo's objection: 'The perfect island'

Gaunilo of Marmoutiers, a Benedictine monk (active eleventh century), responding to an earlier version of the ontological argument (by St Anselm (c.1033–1109)), argues against it by producing a gentle parody.

P1 I have an idea of a perfect island
P2 A perfect island must have all perfections
P3 Existence is a perfection
C The perfect island exists

Gaunilo's point is that, by using this form of reasoning, we should be able to prove the existence of a perfect anything, such as the perfect island. But obviously it is unlikely that a perfect island does exist, and so it follows that there is something wrong with the reasoning leading to this conclusion. Therefore, Descartes' argument cannot work for proving the existence of God. In response to this, Descartes would probably argue that the idea of God is not like that of an island. Earlier, Descartes had argued that objects have essential features which can be understood by the mind. This is why we can have clear and distinct knowledge of truths about these objects – for example, that the internal angles of a triangle are equal to the sum of two right angles. Now the idea of a perfect island is not like this. It is not an idea we discover within us simply by thinking. It is what we might call a 'made-up' idea, in the sense that it depends on our thinking in a way that the idea of a triangle does not. For this reason, what a perfect island would be like is not an objectively discoverable matter that all minds would agree on. I cannot simply contemplate the idea of a perfect island and work out what it would have to contain. In fact, its qualities will tend to depend on the particular mind which considers the question and what sorts of things you look for in an island – whether you prefer sunbathing, snorkelling or the nightlife, for example. Now, Descartes claims that the idea of God, the perfect being, is more like that of a triangle, and so we can discover truths about it which are mind-independent and discoverable *a priori*. The idea of God is not like that of a triangle.

Criticism

However, proving that the idea of God really is more like that of a triangle than an island may prove problematic for Descartes. For while there is universal agreement about the meaning of the term 'triangle', and consequently necessary propositions involving the term, this is not so with the concept of God. The concept of God, we can plausibly argue, is vague; there are many different definitions, and much historical disagreement concerning the significance of the term. But if there is no 'true and immutable nature' to the idea, then it looks more like a 'made-up' idea which depends on Descartes' mind for its existence, much like Gaunilo's perfect island. If this is right, then for Descartes to claim he has proved God's existence from his idea is no different from making up the idea of the perfect island, the perfect song or the perfect goat, and demonstrating its existence.

Kant's objection: 'existence is not a predicate'

Kant's famous criticism of Descartes' version of the ontological argument has become the standard objection. Kant argued that Descartes wrongly treats existence as a property (which Kant terms predicate, meaning a describing term) of individuals in the same manner as, for example, a colour can be a property. In other words, Descartes' mistake is to think that existence is a property that we can imagine things as either having or not having, just as we can think of dandelions as being yellow or not being yellow. By treating existence in this way, Descartes is able to argue that existence must be one of the properties or perfections a perfect being would have to have. But there is an important difference between saying that something is yellow and saying that it exists. In the former case, I am describing it. To say that dandelions are yellow is to give information about what they are like. To say they exist does not tell you anything about what they are like; it merely tells you that there are such things in the world. If I tell you that some cows have horns and some do not, I am telling you about a property possessed by some cows and not by others. But if I tell you that some cows exist and some do not, I seem to be saying something strange precisely because I seem to be implying that there is a property – existence – that some cows have and others do not. But which ones do not? The only answer here is the non-existent ones. But surely there are no non-existent cows, so how can they lack a property? Existence cannot be a property that some things do not have, because if they do not exist, they do not have any properties at all. And if existence cannot be a property that things can lack, then it cannot be a property that they can have either.

The French philosopher Pierre Gassendi (1592–1655) makes a similar point in his Objections (fifth) to the *Meditations*, where he says:

> What doesn't exist has no perfections or imperfections; what does exist may have various perfections, but existence won't be one of them ... We don't say that existence 'exists in a thing' as perfections do. And if a thing lacks existence, we don't say that it is imperfect or lacks a perfection; rather, we say instead that it is nothing at all.[50]

▶ **ACTIVITY**

To begin to see what Kant means by this, try the following exercise.

I Imagine a piece of paper.
2 Picture it in detail in your head: what does it look like, where is it, what is it made of, how big is it? Write down a description of the paper, starting with the phrase, 'The piece of paper I am imagining is ...'
3 Now add the following features to your picture-image of the paper:
   • is splattered with chip grease and batter
   • is made of eye-catching lime-green paper
   • says the words, 'Congratulations, you have won a trip of a lifetime' at the top
   • is scrunched up in a gutter
   • exists.
4 Which of these further features change your image of the paper?

In the activity above, your initial description of the paper contained a number of predicates, to which we invited you to add some more. These additional predicates should have enriched your original idea of the paper: in other words, they have added to the concept by giving it new properties. However, what happens when you add the last feature and imagine the scrunched-up, greasy paper existing? Does this make any real difference to your idea?

Kant thinks not. He proposes that a genuine predicate is one that really does describe the thing we are talking about and so adds a descriptive property to it and enriches our concept of it. However, 'existence' does not do this. If I think of something as existing, the idea is the same as if I think of it as not existing. The properties it has are the same in both cases. This means that existence is not a property that a thing can either have or not have.

If he is right, then Descartes' ontological argument must fail. It fails because it is essential to the argument that 'existence' is a part of what we mean by 'God'. But if 'existence' is not a predicate, then existence cannot belong to our definition of anything, including 'God'.

Issues raised by Hume

As an empiricist, Hume was temperamentally opposed to the idea that we could acquire knowledge concerning what exists by the use of reason of alone. If we are to establish whether there is a beast living on Bodmin Moor, then we will have to make empirical enquires; in the same way, if we are to establish that there is a God, we can only do so by reference to our experience. Arguments which try to show that God's existence can be established *a priori*, therefore, must fail. To show this, Hume has a simple argument which he regards as 'entirely decisive':

> There is an evident absurdity in claiming to demonstrate – or to prove by any *a priori* arguments – any matter of fact. Nothing is demonstrable unless its contrary implies a contradiction. Nothing that is distinctly conceivable implies a contradiction. Whatever we conceive as existent, we can also conceive as non-existent. So there is no being whose non-existence implies a contradiction. So there is no being whose existence is demonstrable.[51]

Here Hume is wielding his fork. As we saw earlier, according to this doctrine, all claims we can make must be of two kinds: either they are 'relations of ideas' or they are 'matters of fact'. Relations of ideas can be recognised as true by analysis of the meanings of the terms involved and so can be known *a priori*. Hume claimed that all true relations of ideas are true by definition, which means that the opposite of any relation of idea is inconceivable. Try to imagine a triangle with two sides, or ice that is not frozen. Impossible. But it *is* clearly possible to imagine any existing object as non-existent. If this is the case, the existence of any object *cannot* be true by definition, but only discoverable by experience.

Also, relations of ideas are not derived from experience; this means that they remain true (or false) no matter what happens to be the case in the actual world. It would still be true that a bachelor is an unmarried man, even if every man in the world was married. Such propositions only tell us about the definitions of words, and nothing about the world. According to Hume's fork, the most that Descartes' ontological argument could show is that the idea of God contains the idea of existence. This does not actually tell us if God exists however.

Does the ontological argument show that reason alone can produce knowledge?

As we have seen, there are many strong criticisms of the ontological argument. But putting these to one side, would the knowledge of God's existence be gained *a priori*? As with the *cogito* and the trademark argument, Descartes is trying to move from a thought to the existence of something. The trademark argument moved from the effect (the idea) to the cause, so there is a strong case to say this cannot be established reason alone. In contrast, the ontological argument focuses squarely on the idea of God alone. It is a clear attempt at a deductive argument. As with all deductive arguments, the conclusion *must* follow, rather than be probable, and the knowledge is 'contained' in the premises to begin with (the idea of existence being contained within the idea of God). So *if* idea of God is innate, and *if* the concept of existence is an essential part of the idea of God, then, indeed, the knowledge would be the product of the intellect alone and would be classed as *a priori* knowledge.

Descartes' proof of the external world

At the beginning of the *Meditations*, Descartes doubts his belief in a bid to establish certainty. Amongst the beliefs 'rejected' are those based on the senses and the very existence of the material world. Through the *Meditations*, he slowly rebuilds his beliefs on a platform of certainty. By the time Descartes reaches his final Meditation, he claims to be certain that both he and God exist. He then attempts to prove that the external world exists too.

Proving the existence of the external world has proved quite a challenge over the years, and some idealist philosophers, including Berkeley, claim that the existence of an external, material world is simply not justified. All that exists are minds and their ideas and this is a sufficient ontology to account for our experiences (see page 80 for more on this).

The intellect and the imagination

Descartes begins by making a distinction between the imagination and the intellect.

He notes that although he can imagine a triangle (that is, he can visualise it in his mind), he cannot really imagine a chiliagon (a 1,000-sided figure), for the image he conjures is rather hazy and confused and indistinguishable from the image of a myriagon (a 10,000-sided figure) or some other many-sided shape. But this does not mean that the *intellect* understands the essential nature of a chiliagon any less than that of a triangle: he understands perfectly well what a thousand-sided shape is in the same way as he understands what a three-sided shape is. Because of this difference, Descartes concludes that the intellect is a distinct faculty from the imagination, with distinct capacities. He goes further and claims that the imagination is not an essential part of him, as he would be the same mind without it. (He earlier established that thinking/the intellect was an essential part of him.)

Descartes' thought here seems to be that he could still establish his own existence as a thinking thing – that is to say, perform the *cogito* – whether or not he were

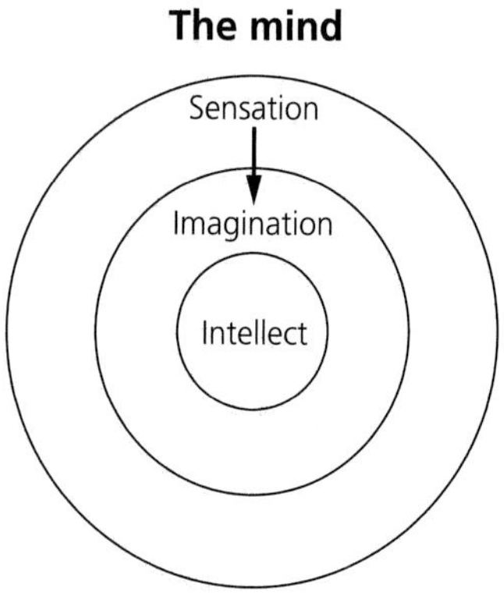

The mind

Figure 1.39 The intellect is the essential core of the mind. Imagination is inessential, meaning I would be the same mind without it. Our capacity to imagine material things comes from sensation. So where does sensation come from?

able to conjure up images of material things in his mind's eye. In other words, if he did not have any imagination, he would still be able to think and to reason and still be aware of his own existence as a conscious thing. Descartes concludes from this that the imagination must depend on some object other than the self. His reasoning here is simply that any property of something which does not derive from its own (essential) nature must derive from something else.

What, then, might be the origin of imagination? Descartes puts forward a plausible idea based on what he used to believe before he began his sceptical meditations, namely that his mind is able to contemplate a physical body to which it is joined. Perhaps this is how physical objects are imagined. Thus the imagination would consist in the mind turning towards the body and apprehending resemblances of things perceived by the senses; while the intellect would simply consist in the mind turning towards itself. While the imagination deals with images of material things, the intellect is purely intellectual, dealing with *a priori* truths which require no empirical input.

The existence of material things

If the imagination finds its origin in sensation, then this leaves Descartes with a new question: where do our sensations come from? Descartes' attempt to answer this question heralds his proof for the existence of material things. The argument is quite complex. To make it more manageable, we have divided it into two key steps.

Step 1: sensations come from outside of me

Other than those (clear and distinct) features which are the subject matter of mathematics and geometry (shape, position, size, number), there are other (obscure and confused) qualities of objects which are the principal subject matter of imagination. These qualities (colours, smells and so on) appear to originate in sensation. Descartes recalls his initial (pre-doubt) view of sensory ideas and their origin. On this view, all his ideas, both the clear and distinct, and the obscure and confused, are caused in him by the existence of material things outside of his mind. Physical objects were thought to be the source of these ideas, and they projected representations of themselves into his mind. Can he now prove that this was basically a correct view? What in it is true and what misleading?

To answer these questions, he points to two features of his sensations which suggest they do not emanate from his essential nature as a thinking thing. For if he can show that they do not come from within, it must follow that they must come from somewhere else. The first feature he points to is the fact that sensations are not subject to his will. That is to say, he is unable to control their appearance (after all, you cannot look at this page and choose to see the ink as red). He cannot see or hear whatever he pleases. But since his will is part of his essence as a thinking thing, this suggests that they are not produced from within him, but by some other power.

Secondly, he observes that his sensations are (in a sense) extended (which means that they occupy some space). That is, they appear to represent things which have size and shape. But he himself (that is, his mind) is unextended. It has no size or shape and cannot be divided into pieces, since different faculties of the mind (the will, the intellect and so on) are not different parts of him, but are all aspects of the same mind. So although sensations occur within his mind, in the sense that they are aspects or 'modes' of his consciousness, they do not and cannot arise spontaneously within such a mind. For mind is non-spatial and whatever is non-spatial, Descartes maintains, cannot create something which is spatial. So, again, sensations must come from outside of him.

Step 2: sensations originate in matter

So where could sensations come from? Two possibilities suggest themselves. They could come from the material world, where he had always thought they came from, or they could come from God. However, Descartes has a strong natural inclination to believe that there is a physical world and has no faculty or means by which to discover that this is not so. So if there is a belief that I have no means of correcting, then God would not allow me to be deceived about it, and therefore my sensations must originate in material objects, just as they appear to. And these must contain those properties which I clearly and distinctly perceive. For Descartes, these are the primary qualities of size, shape, position, quantity and motion which are apprehended by the intellect. Secondary qualities, such as colours and sounds, are apprehended in a confused and obscure way by the senses. In this way, Descartes holds a version of REPRESENTATIVE REALISM (see page 61).

Put more formally, Descartes' argument would look something like this:

Step 1: Descartes argues that sensations must have their origin outside of him

To this end, he produces two parallel arguments leading to the same conclusion.

Step 1a:

P1 The will is a part of my essence
P2 Sensation is not subject to my will
C Sensations come from outside of me

Step 1b:

P1 My nature or essence is unextended
P2 Sensations are ideas of extended things
C Sensations come from outside of me

Step 2: Descartes attempts to prove that their origin is in material bodies

P1 There are two possible sources for the origin of sensation: God or matter
P2 I have a strong natural inclination to believe they come from matter, and I have no faculty by which to correct this belief
IC So if their origin were in God, God would be a deceiver
P3 God is not a deceiver
C Sensation originates in matter

Problems with step 1a: dreams are not subject to my will

Descartes claims that sensations cannot come from within him since they are not subject to his will. However, we could argue that dreams are not subject to our will any more than our sensations are, and yet they certainly come from within us. This shows that not everything that is not subject to my will must come from outside of the mind. So perhaps sensations come from a part of me of which I am not conscious.

151

► ACTIVITY: DOES YOUR MIND OCCUPY SPACE?

1 Think of a green elephant.
2 Does that thought occupy any physical space?
3 Think of a bigger elephant. Does the new thought occupy more space?
4 If I froze your brain while you thought of a green elephant and sliced it into small pieces (this is just a thought experiment!) would I find any elephants? Or anything green?
5 If not, *where* was the green elephant you were thinking of? Did the thought exist in space?

Problems with step 1b: why could an extended thing not create extended ideas?

Descartes also claims that sensations cannot come from within him as they are representations of extended things, while he is an unextended thinking thing. However, it is not clearly and distinctly obvious that an unextended thing could never produce the idea of an extended thing. Descartes' thought involves appealing, once again, to his causal principle, claiming that we cannot produce something from nothing and so cannot get extension out of an unextended thing. But if this is the case, we might wonder how it is possible for an unextended thing to have perceptions of extended things at all. If the mind is truly unextended, then in what sense can its perceptions be extended? And if we are able to perceive representations of extended things although we are unextended, why not be able to dream them up too?

Problems with step 2: are we inclined to believe sensations come from matter?

Must we follow Descartes in step 2 of the argument when he claims that our sensations cannot come from a non-deceiving God? Why could God not be the origin of sensation? Perhaps God feeds the ideas of material things directly into our minds. This is exactly the view held by Berkeley (page 90). It could be argued this is a far more efficient way of arranging things, since it produces the same effect without having all the bother of creating and maintaining a material world. Descartes rejects this possibility on the grounds that it would be a grave deception on God's part to make us think there is a material world, when there is not, whilst at the same time giving us no means to correct this view. But for Berkeley there is no deception. He claims to use reason to establish that there is no ground for believing in a material world. So, contrary to Descartes' claim, God *has* given us the tools to work out the truth, and Berkeley, for one, is not under the illusion that his sensations come from matter. There is no material world and no deception is involved on God's part.

Berkeley argued that the very idea of a material world, in the sense of something lying beyond our perception, is a philosophical confusion. We cannot make coherent sense of this idea of matter, since it is the idea of a thing of which we could never have any experience. What we perceive are our own sensations or 'ideas', and what we mean by a material object is nothing more than a collection of such sensations. It is the supposition that there is something more, something lying beyond the sensations of which I am directly aware in my mind, that is the error.

Problems with step 2, premise 3: is God a deceiver or not?

Perhaps God is deceiving us about the existence of matter. This thought is given added credence when we consider that we already know that we are deceived about the independent existence of secondary qualities. We tend to believe that objects really possess colours, smells, tastes and so on, and yet, according to Descartes – who is a representative realist – this is an error. Yet it is an error into which we naturally seem to fall, so surely God might also allow us to be deceived about the independent existence of the external world.

Moreover, we also know, as Descartes points out in Meditation 1, that our senses are often deceptive. Does this not show that God is a deceiver anyway? And if he deceives us, how can we possibly rely on him to ensure our senses are reliable about anything? David Hume makes this criticism of Descartes in his

Enquiry Concerning Human Understanding: 'To have recourse to the veracity of the Supreme Being, in order to prove the veracity of our senses, is surely making a very unexpected circuit. If his veracity were at all concerned in this matter, our senses would be entirely infallible; because it is not possible that he can ever deceive'.[52]

Descartes' response to these points would be to accept that we have a natural inclination to believe that objects actually possess colours as real qualities. However, the key point is that in this case, God has allowed us to escape from this deception by the use of our reason, which is to say, by relying on clear and distinct ideas. And similarly with illusions and sense deception: in these cases, we are able to detect the error.

A final point on the issue of deception is this: Can Descartes really know what would be for the best in such matters? It might be that supposed existence of the material world is a deception, but one that is in our best interests, and Descartes does not seem to be in any position to be able to determine the matter.

General criticism: God might not exist

Even if we accept that an all-powerful, all-good God would not deceive us about the existence of the material world, this simply throws us back onto the question of the success of Descartes' proofs for God's existence. If we have good reason to suppose that these do not succeed, then there is no guarantee that we are not being radically deceived, and so the world may be very different from the way it appears, or worse, it may not exist. Descartes' reliance on God to escape scepticism means that any failure to prove his existence has a heavy price.

Indeed the extent to which many of Descartes' deductions rely on the existence of a good God may strike you as a little odd. Descartes' whole plan was to start the project of science and philosophy again – free from the dogma and assumptions of the past. Given this, it may seem a little paradoxical that the existence of God is needed so early on his project, and that a non-supernatural grounding of human knowledge is not possible.

Does the proof of the external world show that reason alone can produce knowledge?

Is it a deduction? The approach taken by Descartes is very similar to an inference to the best explanation (an abduction); he considers what might cause his ideas of the world: Is it himself? Is it God? Is it the material world itself? He considers each in turn, concluding that it must be the material world. In an abduction, the conclusion is only *probable*, but as Descartes has attempted to show that the cause cannot be God or himself, he concludes that it *must* be the material world. Descartes could have bypassed God and argued that the reality of the external world was the best hypothesis, which would be an abduction (this is the approach taken by Russell; see page 77). However, this approach would have lacked the certainty that Descartes' deductive approach seeks to gain.

Is the argument fully *a priori*? Well, it draws on the idea of God as a non-deceiver, but also on Descartes' sense experience and his natural inclination to believe that there is an external world beyond his mind. As such, the argument clearly draws on evidence gained *a posteriori*. After all, if there are no impressions of an external world, then there is no need to prove its existence.

As with the trademark argument (but NOT the ontological), Descartes is working from an effect to the possible cause. It can be argued that this means it is an argument based on experience, as we need experience to establish causal relations.

Chapter summary

In this chapter, we have explored the sources of ideas and of knowledge. Asserting the *tabula rasa* model of the mind, empiricism claims that all of our ideas and much of our knowledge comes from our impressions. In contrast, rationalism is the view that reason is the true source of knowledge. Rationalists often associate knowledge with certainty and, impressed by the certainty established in mathematics, seek to extend the reach of deductive reasoning to other areas. Rationalism often denies the idea of the *tabula rasa* and suggests that we possess innate ideas that can be drawn out through reason. Rationalists such as Plato, Descartes and Leibniz have tried to use reason to reach these innate ideas/intuitions and use deduction to establish further truths. However, it is not clear that they established the certainty they sought.

It is, however, an appealing image, that the human mind, shut off from the world, using reason alone, would be able to work out what must be the case regarding many features of the world. But it seems that no one has achieved this so far. Hume appears to be right in that that we can only find out features of the world by observing it, not by reasoning about what must be the case.

As a postscript to this debate, the great German philosopher Kant started out as a rationalist, but after reading the work of Hume rejected this path and became convinced that experience must be the source of our knowledge. Kant was (more or less) persuaded by the division of knowledge set out by Hume's fork. His famous masterpiece – the *Critique of Pure Reason* – argues, along with Hume, that pure, deductive reasoning will only establish statements that are true by definition (analytic).

However, he also put forward the idea that our senses alone cannot account for all of our concepts, and argued that we need concepts in order to interpret our raw sense data and so experience a world in the first place. His work made other philosophers question the simple, perhaps naïve idea of the *tabula rasa*, and since then many have suggested that our experience of the world is not a passive one whereby sense data simply fall into our minds. Rather, they suggest our experience is active and shaped by our language, culture and the structures of our brains/minds.

1.4 The limits of knowledge

Introduction

In everyday life, we reckon we know all kinds of things. For example, if you are reading this book, you probably know how old you are, what the capital of France is and what you get if you add three to five. So much seems fairly obvious. But as we have seen, philosophers are concerned to ask what it is that enables us to know such things as these. They demand that we provide a justification for our knowledge claims and seek to discover the ultimate sources of our knowledge. In this way, it is hoped that we can distinguish when we really know something from when we merely think that we do.

In Chapter 1.1, we explored philosophers' attempts to define knowledge and discussed the role of justification. We saw there why it has traditionally been thought (by Plato, for example) that a genuine knowledge claim needs some kind of rational support or evidence. After all, an unsubstantiated assertion is just that, unsubstantiated. So even if it happens to be true, if it lacks justification it would appear to have nothing to recommend itself to us. However, it also seems that the evidence we appeal to when justifying a claim needs to be true if it is to count as proper evidence. We cannot, after all, expect to support a piece of knowledge with false evidence. This is perhaps obvious. Yet appreciating this point can very quickly lead us into an important difficulty. To introduce this difficulty, consider the following dialogue. Sasha and Esme are holidaying in Wales in August; they are discussing over breakfast how to spend the day.

Sasha: The forecast today is looking good. It should be sunny all day. Let's climb up to Mount Snowdon to see the view.

Esme: I don't know about that. Forecasts can't be relied upon. Once I went for a walk when they had forecast only light rain and I got drenched. If they have been wrong before, they can be wrong again.

Sasha: That is the exception rather than the rule. And while it can be quite hard to forecast just how hard it will rain, when it comes to predicting clear weather, forecasts are actually very reliable.

Esme: But not perfectly reliable. Today could be the day that the weather system suddenly behaves differently. We could have a snowstorm!

Sasha: Don't be ridiculous! There has never been a snow fall here at this time of year. It would be impossible.

Esme: How do you know for sure that there hasn't been a snowstorm here?

Sasha: Well, as it happens, I have been reading the guidebooks and there is no record of a snowfall here in August.

Esme: That information is based on people's testimony, but we know that people sometimes lie and that they can be mistaken. So we can't know it hasn't snowed before. And even if it is true that it has never snowed here in August, there is nothing contradictory in the idea of a freak snowstorm. The past does not fix the future, after all.

Sasha: Okay, I can't at the moment see a fault in your reasoning, but still I am pretty convinced that it is not going to snow. So I tell you what. Let's live dangerously! We can chat as we walk and if we think hard enough, perhaps we will work out just how it is that we can have knowledge here. And if it does snow, I will buy you a coffee.

Read through the knowledge claims A–H below. Working with a partner, one of you is going to argue that you *know* the claim, while the other person should be sceptical and is going to argue that you *do not know* the claim. Take it turns to be the sceptic.

A That bird over there is a robin.

B Paris is the capital of France.

C It is wrong to steal sweets from the corner shop.

D Sherlock Holmes was killed by Moriarty.

E The floor outside this room is solid, and I will not fall through it.

F The population of the United Kingdom in 2017 was just over 65 million.

G Postboxes in England are red.

H Either the earth is the only planet to contain life forms in the whole universe, or there are aliens somewhere out there in space.

There are a few things to note about this dialogue. What probably strikes you immediately is the silliness of Esme's doubts. She appears interested in being sceptical simply in order to irritate Sasha, or perhaps to find an excuse to avoid the walk. Moreover, she has no very good reasons for supposing that the forecasting is wrong. In fact, her sceptical scenarios are increasingly unlikely as the dialogue progresses, so her line of argument is not one we would be inclined to take seriously in everyday life.

While all this is true, there are still some useful philosophical lessons about scepticism that we can draw from the dialogue. The first concerns how different philosophical scepticism is from scepticism in everyday life. Esme's doubts do indeed look rather silly, and philosophers' doubts can appear silly too. But there is a more serious purpose that we should make clear. So, let us examine the nature and purpose of philosophical scepticism.

Philosophical scepticism and normal incredulity

Ordinary doubts are sensitive to evidence

One important difference between philosophical scepticism and normal incredulity is that in ordinary life we tend to doubt a claim only when we think it could well be false. So normal incredulity arises only when there is some good reason to doubt a belief. For example, suppose I am taking a walk in the countryside and spot what appears to be a group of field mushrooms. I pick and inspect one and note that it looks and smells not unlike the mushrooms you can buy at the grocer's, and so conclude that the mushroom is edible. But is this a safe conclusion to draw? Can I *know* the mushroom is edible? Well, there are good reasons to be sceptical here. I have heard that mushrooms can be poisonous and that people have been made very ill, and even died, from mistaking edible for poisonous varieties. I may even have heard that the so-called Death Cap looks very like a field mushroom, that it smells and tastes good, but that it can kill. Here are some powerful reasons for me to be sceptical, and because so much is at stake, I would be unlikely to take the mushrooms home and put them into an omelette and feed them to my family. This, then, is a case of ordinary incredulity. Notice that such scepticism arises because I have reasons to doubt my initial judgement that the mushrooms are safe to eat; the fact that they look like the ones in the shops and smell all right is not sufficient evidence to justify the belief that they are edible. In this case, my background beliefs about mushrooms are taken for granted; they are the context within which my ordinary doubts arise.

Suppose I now take the mushrooms home and get out my copy of the well-respected *Mushroom Collectors' Guide*, and learn that the Death Cap has white gills, whereas the mushrooms I have gathered have brown gills. Suppose I also read that all white-capped mushrooms with brown gills are safe to eat. In this case, this new evidence may well be sufficient to dispel my doubts, and as a result I cook up the mushrooms and feed them to my family. In this case, my incredulity has given way as further evidence has been collected. The fact that it is sensitive to further evidence in this way, so that the reasons for doubt can be removed, is typical of ordinary incredulity.

However, suppose now that I push my scepticism further. Perhaps the *Mushroom Collectors' Guide* has a misprint where it says the Death Cap has white gills?

Misprints do happen, after all. So I decide to cross-check this advice with a reliable website. Does this satisfy? Perhaps not. I might worry that the website had also been fooled by the same misprint in the normally reliable *Guide*. Unlikely perhaps, but surely it is *possible*. And if it is possible, then not only can I not know that these mushrooms are edible, but it may also seem that I cannot know for sure any fact I might read about in textbooks or on the internet. This more extreme sort of conclusion now leads us into the realms of philosophical scepticism, where the doubt covers a whole set of beliefs. Such scepticism can lead to the point where it appears impossible to remove. Philosophical doubt, in other words, by giving up a whole class of our beliefs, takes away the context of accepted beliefs needed to allow us to remove the doubt. We cannot check other textbooks to dispel our doubts because *all* text books are now suspect.

So, to sum up, when it comes to normal incredulity, if I am doubtful about some claim and the grounds for that doubt are removed, my doubts should also be removed. Once a renowned guide to foraging confirms that a mushroom is safe, this ought to dispel any concerns. This is because ordinary incredulity involves using other background beliefs to raise doubts about some belief. I doubt this mushroom is safe because I have heard of poisonings in the past. However, if it turns out that this mushroom has brown gills, then I can now be confident enough to give up my doubts. But as our doubts become deeper, this aspect of normal incredulity fades away. Philosophical scepticism does not raise doubts about one belief because of another belief taken to be true, which, if given up, would remove the doubts. Rather, it raises doubts about all beliefs of a certain sort, such as any information gleaned from books.

Philosophical scepticism is extreme

Another difference between philosophical scepticism and ordinary incredulity concerns the kinds of things that are doubted. In ordinary life, we might well doubt whether a mushroom found in a field is safe to eat, whether the weather will stay dry today, or whether the train will be on time. But philosophers go further. Philosophers tend to doubt things that in ordinary life are very difficult, if not impossible, to doubt. For example, they may question whether or not their own hands really exist, whether other people could really be zombies with no thoughts or feelings whatsoever, or whether we can know that the sun will rise tomorrow. By attempting to doubt such basic and everyday beliefs as these, epistemologists hope to come to an understanding of what underlies our most fundamental beliefs, such as those concerning physical objects, other people and the future.

Philosophical scepticism remains theoretical

Indeed, when philosophers doubt something, they may actually believe it to be true, and any reasons for doubt may well be weak and questionable themselves. So while a philosopher may doubt the existence of the physical objects that she sees around her for the sake of argument, this does not imply that she really thinks they do not exist. Rather, her doubt is being used as a tool to establish whether the reasons we have for thinking they exist are good ones, and so her doubts will normally have no impact on how she behaves. The philosopher will continue to lean on the very table she pretends to doubt exists, and will continue talking to you, even while she doubts that you have a mind. In this sense, if

Esme's doubts from the dialogue on page 155 do impact on her behaviour and she refuses to go out, then she would not be being properly philosophical. But if she agrees to discuss the problem as they walk, then she is treating her doubts as a theoretical exercise and this is typical of philosophical doubt. This is one reason why philosophical doubt often appears silly. The philosopher's doubts appear pointless, since they have no bearing on the practicalities of life. They also seem far-fetched, and even insane. But their doubts do not arise because philosophers suffer from paranoid delusions. Rather, philosophical doubt is a theoretical exercise designed to discover what we can know.

Philosophical scepticism is used to test knowledge

Another point to make about philosophical scepticism is that it is often used to test the strength of our knowledge claims. The sceptic asks questions of the evidence supporting the knowledge claims we hold, and if we cannot provide adequate answers, the sceptic demands that we give up the claims. At the same time, if we can refute the sceptic, we will have vindicated our claim to know. This was what Descartes was attempting to do by using scepticism in his *Meditations*. By trying to defeat sceptical arguments, Descartes and others have tried to clarify what we can and cannot know and to establish the certainty with which we can claim knowledge. Also, through dialogue with scepticism, epistemologists hope to come to a better understanding of the nature of knowledge and justification.

Table 1.4.1 The differences between normal incredulity and philosophical scepticism

Normal incredulity	Philosophical scepticism
Normal incredulity happens when we encounter ordinary evidence which challenges a belief or makes it appear unlikely.	Philosophical scepticism happens even when the ordinary evidence makes a belief very likely to be true. It involves invoking a radical sceptical scenario, in itself unlikely, to raise its doubts.
Because it is grounded in ordinary evidence, normal incredulity will often mean altering our behaviour.	Philosophical scepticism has a theoretical rather than a practical purpose: to test the justification for our knowledge claims and to develop our understanding of the nature of knowledge. So it tends not to impact on how we act.
Normal incredulity about a particular belief occurs against a background of other beliefs which are taken for granted.	Philosophical doubt is infectious, so tends to extend to a whole set of beliefs of a certain sort.
Normal incredulity is sensitive to ordinary evidence and so can be overcome if the grounds for doubt are removed.	The philosophical sceptic demands such a high burden of proof for beliefs that the grounds for doubt may be very hard or even impossible to remove.

The infinite regress of justification

With this in mind, it becomes clear that the force of Esme's scepticism in the dialogue does not rely on her scenarios being likely or believable, but only on whether they are remotely possible, and as yet unrefuted. If they are even a remote possibility, then Sasha's claims to know are in some way undermined. Esme, instead of being merely an irritating cynic trying to avoid going for a walk, may well be interested in seeing whether any of our justifications are completely foolproof. She may be concerned by the idea that if our beliefs are not ultimately grounded in certainty, then they cannot count as knowledge.

Another aspect of the dialogue concerns its *structure* and the general sceptical point that this structure reveals. Sasha has to appeal to evidence – to further beliefs – in order to support her claims to know. But the beliefs she appeals to must themselves count as known if they are to play an adequate supporting role. She must believe that past experience of the behaviour of seasonal weather systems is a reliable guide to the future. She must believe that the forecasters are honest, that their instruments are not faulty and so on. As we have seen, if I justify a belief by appeal to a further belief, then this further belief must itself be worthy of assent. This seems to mean that this further belief will also have to be known. But if Sasha needs to have knowledge of her evidence, then she will need to be able to justify that evidence in turn by appeal to further evidence. And yet, Esme is always able to question this further evidence. This means that the process of producing evidence to justify one's beliefs can have no end. So any claim to knowledge is caught in a vicious infinite regress: there seems to be no way of providing a complete justification for our beliefs. But if our beliefs cannot be justified, knowledge must be impossible to come by, so we seem forced to draw the sceptical conclusion that *we cannot know anything*.

This infinite regress argument suggests that, in the final analysis, none of our beliefs is justified. The whole of our belief system rests on nothing. It is as if we have suddenly discovered that the ground had been pulled from under us and we no longer have reason to believe anything at all. This is a serious problem not only for philosophers interested in understanding how we justify our beliefs, but also, it would seem, for anyone who holds any beliefs at all!

What sceptical arguments such as the infinite regress argument do is present us with a DILEMMA. A dilemma is a situation where we are forced to make a choice between two options, but where both options are difficult to take. In this case, we must either accept the sceptical conclusion or reject it. If we accept it, we will have to try to fit in with the rest of our beliefs the claim that knowledge is impossible, in such a way that we can be comfortable with it. But if we reject it, we must find something wrong with the argument that leads to it. Accepting the sceptic's conclusion that knowledge is ultimately impossible puts us in a difficult position. If all justifications are unfounded, then it seems as though we have no good reason to believe one thing rather than another. If any justification is as groundless as any other, we might as well flip a coin to decide what we should believe. Clearly, if this argument is sound, it threatens to undermine our whole belief system. Is it possible for us to resist the sceptical argument and so avoid this conclusion?

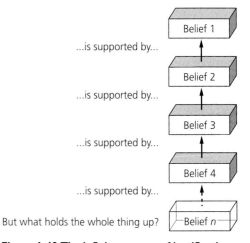

Figure 1.40 The infinite regress of justification. For a belief to be known, it must be supported by a good reason or evidence, and the reason will be something else we believe. This second belief must also be supported by some further reason. This leads to an infinite regress, and it seems that there can be nothing to give any ultimate support to our knowledge claims. So the sceptic concludes that nothing can be known.

Essential Terminology Aa

Stopping the infinite regress

There are different possible reactions to the problem posed by infinite regress of justification. The classical response to this dilemma is to search for 'regress-ending' beliefs that could be known to be true without evidence or supporting reasons. Such beliefs would have to be knowable without the need for further justification, perhaps because they are able to justify themselves. If such beliefs could be found, then the regress could be stopped and we would have a firm basis on which to establish our knowledge claims. The beliefs that justify themselves or need no justification we can call *foundational* beliefs, since they are the basic ones on top of which all others are built, or in terms of which all the others are justified. This is the classical reaction to the regress argument, and any theory of knowledge and justification that is committed to the existence of such foundational beliefs is termed FOUNDATIONALISM. We examined two foundationalist approaches to epistemology in Chapter 1.3. Rationalist philosophers search for beliefs which can be known *a priori* simply through the application of reason and treat these as the self-justifying basis for all knowledge. Empiricists, on the other hand, argue that experience is the basis for knowledge and that the immediate data of sense represent the indubitable basis for knowledge of the world.

▶ ACTIVITY: PHILOSOPHICAL SCEPTICISM

Below are five examples of sceptical arguments (A–E). Each makes us question the nature of our beliefs about the world, and casts doubt on our claims to knowledge. A sceptical argument presents us with a dilemma. Either we reject the conclusion, in which case we must find something wrong with the argument, or we accept the conclusion, in which case we have to try to fit it in with the rest of our belief system.

Read through each argument. Then ask yourself whether you find the sceptical conclusion (**in bold**) acceptable.

1 If you reject the conclusion, try to think of ways in which the conclusion might be avoided. Where does the argument go wrong? Does it make any dubious assumptions? Is there something wrong with the reasoning process? Note your thoughts.

2 If you accept the conclusion, try to explain why the conclusion is not as unpalatable as it first appears. What impact does the sceptical conclusion have on your belief system as a whole? Does the conclusion require you to give up much of what you usually take for granted? Is it compatible with a considered understanding of what we can and cannot know? Note your thoughts.

A Scepticism about knowledge of the future
(cf. Hume's *Enquiry Concerning Human Understanding*[1])

In our ordinary lives, there are certain things about the world that we take for granted. For example, I expect the sun to rise in the morning, objects to fall when dropped, the neighbour's dog to bark as I leave my house and not suddenly to start speaking Chinese, and so forth. But what evidence do we have for these beliefs? Why do we suppose we know that dogs will not suddenly start to speak to us in Chinese, or that gravity will not suddenly work in reverse?

The obvious answer is that gravity has always worked that way, and dogs have never spoken Chinese, so we have no reason to think that such things will change now. But is this a good response? Notice that it presupposes that the future resembles the past, since it is saying that dogs will continue to behave as they always have and that objects will fall down just as before. But why should we suppose that the future will resemble the past? Maybe tomorrow things will be very different. After all, think of a poor turkey fed grain for 364 days, who wakes up on Christmas morning expecting the same again, only this time it is to be tragically disappointed. In blindly assuming that the future must resemble the past, we may end up as disappointed as this turkey.

In response to this, we might accept that it is *possible* that things will change, but nonetheless insist that, generally speaking, the past is a good indicator of what the future will hold. After all, this supposition has worked well so far, so it is sensible to stick with it. Unfortunately, the fact that (generally speaking) the future has resembled the past *in the past* goes no way to establishing the claim that it will continue to do so *in the future*. To think it does is once again to use evidence from the past to make claims about the future, and this move is the very thing being questioned. So our general belief that past experience is a reliable guide to the future cannot be justified, since any appeal to past experience inevitably begs the question, or presupposes what it is trying to prove. In other words, it amounts to saying that the future resembles the past because the future resembles the past and argues in a circle. **Therefore we cannot gain knowledge of the future.**

B Scepticism about knowledge of other minds

We can all recall occasions when other people have fooled us about what is really going on in their minds. Perhaps someone has lied to you about what they think of your new haircut, or pretended to be sorry about your misfortune when secretly they were amused. The reason they can fool us is that people's outer behaviour does not necessarily reflect what they are thinking and feeling. So while we can directly see and hear what people do and say, these outer signs can easily disguise what is really going on inside. This shows that the inference we make from people's behaviour to what they are thinking and feeling is not foolproof. It also makes clear that we do not have direct awareness of what goes on in other people's minds. If you do not want to reveal your thoughts to me, then I have no way of knowing them, as they are private to you. But if the inference from your behaviour to your mind is not infallible, how can I ever be sure that I know what you are truly thinking and feeling? Indeed, since I cannot access your mind directly, it is even conceivable that you have no mind at all. You could be a mindless automaton. It is impossible to prove that this is not the case, and so **I cannot know that other people have minds**.

C Scepticism about religious claims

For a claim to be meaningful, it needs to tell us something about the world. This means that we need be able to check whether or not it is true. So if you tell me that there is a rabbit in the field outside, then this is meaningful because I know how to check whether you are telling the truth. I simply need to look out of the window to see. On the other hand, if I do not know how to tell whether a claim is true or not, then it is not really telling us anything about the world. And if it is not telling us about the world then it has no content, or is not really saying anything. When it comes to religious claims, such as claims about God, we have to question whether they tell us anything that could be checked. If, for example, you claim that God loves us, then there must be something about the world which would reveal whether or not this is true. But our experience is compatible both with this claim being true and with it being false. And there is no experiment we could conduct which might prove it either way. Similarly, even to claim that God exists cannot be proved and tells us nothing about how the world is. So this, too, is a meaningless claim. So **religious claims generally cannot be known**.

D The infinite regress of reasons

Suppose someone claims to know that the Amazon is the longest river in the world. How can you be sure she knows? The obvious way is to ask her what evidence she has for her belief. Perhaps she was told so by a competent and honest geographer or read it in an encyclopaedia. But then how does she know that the geographer has not made a rare mistake, or that the encyclopaedia has not misprinted the length of the Amazon? Again, supporting reasons need to be provided. She might cross-check against maps, other encyclopaedias and geographers, and so forth. But the sceptic could point out that the original measurement on which all these records are based could have been mistaken. So perhaps to be sure that she knew, she would have to travel to South America and measure the river for herself. But again, the sceptic could ask how she could know that her measuring equipment is accurate. This process of sceptical questioning would appear to have no end. So any claim to knowledge is caught in a vicious infinite regress, and so knowledge about the physical world is impossible.

This example argues that if I claim to know something, then I must be able to justify it by appeal to evidence, since otherwise I am simply making an unsubstantiated claim. Moreover, a claim to knowledge is only as good as the evidence supporting it. So it would appear that I need to be sure of my evidence and consequently need to have knowledge of that, too. But if I need to have knowledge of my evidence, then I will need to be able to justify that evidence, in turn, by appeal to further evidence. Since the process of justification has no end, the sceptic's conclusion is that **we cannot acquire knowledge**.

E The closed belief system[2]

Imagine you have a friend who begins to develop paranoid delusions. He believes that the government is watching him and plans to do away with him because of what he knows about alien plans to take over the world. He is convinced that his phone is bugged, the newspapers have secret coded messages about him, and that people are following him wherever he goes. You try to convince him that none of this is true. For example, you open up the phone to reveal that there are no bugs. Your friend, however, responds that they must have special methods to hide them in the wires, or perhaps MI5 have people working undercover for the phone company. You point out that the people he thinks are following him are different people each time. But he responds that this is because they are all masters of disguise. Whatever you say or do, he remains unconvinced. He even begins to suspect that you are saying all this because you are in on the conspiracy.

Imagine, further, that your friend is a member of a strange cult, which is convinced that aliens are taking over the world. Members of the cult have all kinds of weird evidence to support their belief. If you try to point out that such evidence is silly, they argue that you are too brainwashed to recognise it. If you point to contrary evidence, they reject this as being part of the government cover-up. Nothing you say or do will sway them from their belief.

The belief system of your friend and of his cult seems immune from revision, yet they are obviously crazy. But is your system of beliefs not equally immune from revision? Are you not also in the grip of a self-sustaining set of beliefs? If so, how can you be sure that your belief system is not equally crazy? Maybe the cult is right and it is you who is brainwashed! Perhaps most of your beliefs are as baseless as those of your friend. If this is possible, then the sceptic argues that all your beliefs might be part of a closed belief system that is false, so **you do not know anything**.

Local and global scepticism

From the exercise on philosophical scepticism, we have seen some of the variety of weapons the sceptic has at her disposal to undermine our claims to know. What they have in common is that they question whether the justification condition can be fulfilled so that someone can have sufficient justification for beliefs for them to constitute knowledge.

What we can also see from this activity is that sceptical arguments may suggest that knowledge is impossible within some particular area, or they may cause us to doubt the possibility of knowledge as such. For example, arguments A, B and C are restricted versions of scepticism. Scepticism about the future is restricted since it allows that we can have knowledge about the past and present. Scepticism about other minds, similarly, is directed at a particular subset of our beliefs, rather than at knowledge as such, since it accepts that we can have knowledge of our own minds, and of the physical world around us. Argument C raises doubts about religious claims, but leaves our knowledge of empirical reality untouched. Such scepticisms may be termed 'local', meaning they concern some particular and restricted domain of knowledge, but do not raise doubts about knowledge as a whole. Arguments D and E, though, seem to raise doubts about all of our knowledge. They conclude that knowledge in any area is impossible. Such arguments are far more radical and lead to 'universal' or 'global' scepticism, meaning they threaten to undermine the whole of our belief system.

Descartes' use of scepticism: the 'method of doubt'

The central Anthology text that employs philosophical doubt is Descartes' *Meditations*, so we will now turn to this work in order to explore the way scepticism is used within epistemology. In the first few paragraphs of Meditation 1, Descartes outlines his reasons for employing scepticism and explains what he hopes to achieve by it. He tell us that he has noticed that many of the beliefs he had held from an early age had turned out to be false, and that his ordinary belief system appeared to be full of errors and contained little of which he could be certain. Because if this, he felt he needed to start again and see if he could build a system of beliefs that was completely free from error. The best way to do this, he decided, would be to tackle scepticism head-on. For if he could defeat it and so dispel even the most extreme doubts about his beliefs, then he would have good reason to claim to have knowledge. So he used a method that began by employing the most radical sceptical arguments he could muster. This method – the so-called METHOD OF DOUBT – tried to suspend judgement about *all* the things he previously took for granted. Everything that could possibly be doubted was treated as false for the purposes of argument. So the very possibility of doubt about a belief was, for Descartes, sufficient for treating it as false. If, after following this method, he arrived at something that could not be doubted – that is, something that was indubitable – then he would have reached a point of absolute certainty. At that point, he hoped, he might start to rebuild a new system of beliefs which would be free from errors.

What Descartes is proposing here is to use doubt as a tool to uncover those beliefs which, by surviving scepticism, prove themselves to be beyond any possible doubt. This 'method of doubt' entails suspending judgement about everything he previously took for granted. All that can be doubted is treated as false for the purposes of argument. So Descartes says he does not have to prove that any of his previous opinions are false in order to reject them. For the slightest ground for doubt that he finds will be sufficient for him to treat them *as if* they were false. So the burden of proof is on his beliefs to show that they cannot be doubted; not on him to show that they must be false. Now, clearly such a standard of proof is very fierce and will lead him to reject very many (if not all!) of his beliefs. But it is precisely because it is so fierce that if anything survives which cannot be doubted, then this must be absolutely certain. For this reason, the beliefs that survive his radical scepticism should be solid enough to be the foundations upon which he can reconstruct a new body of knowledge free from error. What this means is that Descartes is not himself a sceptic: he does not raise doubts simply for their own sake. Rather, his scepticism is a means to an end. He uses sceptical arguments precisely in order to give security to his theory of knowledge by uncovering unshakable first principles.

anthology
1.24

The last point Descartes makes about his method is that it need not involve going through each of his beliefs in turn and subjecting it to doubt. He has, after all, so many beliefs that this would take him for ever. Rather, he decides to doubt what he calls the 'basic principles' – that is, the most fundamental beliefs 'on which all my former beliefs rested' (Descartes, Meditation 1, page 1). Since his whole belief system rests on just a few such principles, by doubting them he can demolish the system more efficiently.

Summary of the method of doubt

1 Descartes' project is to eliminate error from his system of beliefs, and establish certain and enduring knowledge.
2 To do this, he will destroy all his previous opinions by rejecting any that have the slightest grounds for doubt.
3 He will not go through each belief individually, but will destroy the 'principles' or most basic beliefs, so that the rest will collapse of their own accord.
4 Whatever beliefs survive this method must be indubitable, and so can be the foundations on which to build human knowledge anew, free from error.

The first paragraphs of the *Meditations*, then, outline Descartes' intentions and make clear how he intends to use scepticism to clear the way for him to rebuild a body of knowledge. The nature of the doubt he employs is clearly *philosophical*, a kind of scepticism which, as we have seen, is very different from the ordinary doubts that we have in everyday life. To recap, everyday incredulity occurs when you have clear grounds for withholding your assent from some claim; perhaps the source of the claim is questionable, or the nature of it makes it seem unlikely to be true. But Descartes' doubt involves rejecting beliefs if he has any grounds *whatsoever* for being suspicious of their truth, not just if he has reasonable grounds.

Figure 1.41 Descartes' method of doubt. Descartes thinks of his present belief system as like a badly constructed building. It has been built haphazardly on shaky foundations and so is full of errors. To remedy the situation, he will demolish the building, find secure foundations, and carefully rebuild so that the new building will be free from error.

Descartes is dismayed that his belief system is so shaky.

Descartes, using the bulldozer of doubt, demolishes his old house of beliefs.

Descartes reduces all his beliefs to rubble.

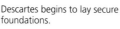
Descartes begins to lay secure foundations.

Descartes carefully begins to rebuild a new house of beliefs – one that will last forever.

Experimenting with ideas

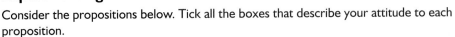

Consider the propositions below. Tick all the boxes that describe your attitude to each proposition.

	A It is not possible for me to doubt this claim.	B I have genuine doubts about this claim.	C It is theoretically possible for me to doubt this claim.
Humans have landed on the moon.			
Jesus Christ was the son of God.			
Teresa May is a politician.			
Shakespeare wrote *Macbeth*.			
I have just read the world 'elephant'.			
The sun will rise tomorrow.			
I am awake.			
Apples do not exist.			
England will win the next football World Cup.			
19 is a prime number.			

Column B represents our ordinary, run-of-the-mill doubts. Column C represents philosophical doubt. Hopefully, for every tick in column B, you also put a tick in column C, as *genuinely* to doubt a belief implies that it is possible, *theoretically*, to doubt it. However, the reverse is not true. There will be many beliefs that can be theoretically doubted, but which, in the ordinary course of life, you hold no genuine doubts about. It is important to remember this distinction when reading the opening Meditation, as Descartes is primarily concerned with column C, not B. He wants to shake off any beliefs that are even theoretically doubtful, so that he can start building a new system of knowledge based only on doubt-free beliefs. But he does not mean to suggest that he harbours genuine doubts about the beliefs in question. Indeed, if Descartes genuinely doubted most of his beliefs, it is unlikely that he would have bothered to write the *Meditations* at all. For if you genuinely doubted that you were awake, or the very existence of ink, pens or other people, it would certainly make you think twice about putting pen to paper. Philosophical doubt is a useful tool for examining the nature of beliefs, but if genuinely held it would make ordinary life impossible.

The gulf between the philosophical doubt and more ordinary mundane concerns is neatly mocked by Woody Allen: 'What if everything is an illusion and nothing exists? In that case, I definitely overpaid for my carpet.' (*Without*

Feathers, Warner Books, 1976) We need to be clear, however, that Descartes is not saying that his suspension of judgement is *merely* an academic exercise which can have no implications for his ordinary beliefs. On the contrary, if he finds good reason to reject his common-sense assumptions, he has resolved to do so. However, in the meantime, he cannot genuinely discard all beliefs. For without them, he would have nothing to guide his everyday conduct. He would be paralysed, having no reason to do one thing rather than another. While some sceptics might be attracted by such an option, Descartes was not, because, as we have seen, his scepticism is ultimately at the service of his quest for certainty. Consequently, he needs a set of rules by which to live until his sceptical meditations are complete. In the *Discourse on Method*, Descartes proposes that during this interim he will:

> [O]bey the laws and customs of my country, constantly retaining the religion which I judged best, and in which, by Gods grace, I had been brought up since childhood, and in all other matters to follow the most moderate and least excessive opinions to be found in the practice of the most judicious part of the community in which I would live.[3]

In other words, the suspension of judgement about previous beliefs actually leaves a whole set of prejudices in place until they are refuted. These prejudices cannot be abandoned, since they are required for one to continue to live.

Issues with Descartes' scepticism

Issue 1: is Descartes' doubt sincere?

But these remarks may raise a worry about the sincerity of his method. Could it be that the doubts are just a sham, and that Descartes had a pretty good idea of what he wanted to prove from the outset? Or, more generously, is there not a risk that his prejudices might reassert themselves – even unconsciously – in the process of rebuilding a system of supposedly perfectly indubitable beliefs? If so, we might accuse Descartes of not taking his method seriously enough. For the method to be effective, it may be argued, Descartes needs *genuinely* to destroy all his opinions. A purely theoretical doubt cannot achieve this, since beliefs left in place inevitably prejudice the inquiry. This is certainly the suspicion of many on completing the *Meditations*, for by the end, the new system of beliefs appears, in most essentials, identical to the system he claimed to demolish. Whether or not you will harbour such suspicions will have to be seen.

Issue 2: can Descartes really doubt all his beliefs?

There are various serious difficulties with Descartes' pronouncement that he will 'devote myself, sincerely and without holding back, to demolishing my opinions' (Meditation 1, page 1). For one thing, to entertain the possibility that all his opinions could be doubtful invites the question of whether the possibility that all his opinions are doubtful is *itself* doubtful or not. If it *is*, then it suggests that not all his beliefs are doubtful after all. But if it is *not* doubtful, then there is at least one opinion that is not doubtful, namely that all his opinions are doubtful. So he cannot doubt *this* belief at least, and so not literally *all* his beliefs are doubtful. Either way, it seems, not all of his beliefs can be doubted at once.

To put the problem another way, consider the claim that 'nothing can be known'. Either this claim can be known or it cannot. So can it be known? If it can, then there is one claim that can be known, namely that 'nothing can be known', and so the claim is false and it cannot be known. Therefore it cannot be known that 'nothing can be known'. This is an important discovery made by the ancient Greeks. It shows that not everything can be doubted at once, and if we are to doubt one set of beliefs, we are also going to have to take certain other beliefs for granted.

In a similar vein, consider that if Descartes wants to doubt *all* his beliefs, he would have to abandon the belief that he had previous beliefs to doubt. But if he were to doubt *this*, it would disable him from doubting any of his other beliefs, since he would not believe he had them. What we are seeing here is that in order to doubt something, one has to believe at least that one has beliefs that can be subjected to doubt; that these beliefs can be more or less certain or well-justified; that they may be true or they may be false; that one can raise sceptical difficulties which make them doubtful, and so on. In other words, to use sceptical arguments at all, Descartes is bound to take certain assumptions for granted. One needs certain beliefs about the nature of belief, evidence, certainty, truth and so on, in order even to call beliefs into question. So, there appear to be certain necessary limits on how far scepticism may be pushed.

Actually, Descartes is not unaware of this fact about the very possibility of doubt. In the *Rules for the Direction of the Mind*, he writes:

> *If Socrates says he doubts everything, it follows necessarily that he knows this at least – that he doubts. Likewise he knows that something can be either true or false, and so on, for all those consequences necessarily attach to the nature of doubt.*[4]

What this suggests is that Descartes' scepticism is not really as all-encompassing as the opening lines of the *Meditations* suggest. There are limits to how sceptical one can be, and Descartes must retain the basic framework of beliefs concerning the nature of doubt, certainty and evidence which allow his method to operate.

Issue 3: is indubitability too much to ask of our beliefs?

We may also question another aspect of his method. Is it really reasonable to reject all beliefs about which there is just the slightest doubt? This is a very fierce standard to apply to our beliefs, as we have seen. Surely it would be far more sensible to reject those beliefs about which there is a 'reasonable' doubt, as in a court of law. Think how impractical it would be to demand absolute certainty of our beliefs before we acted. Someone who is overly sceptical never gets anything done, since they are always waiting for conclusive evidence. Refusing to believe what is not absolutely certain may ensure that you do not believe anything false, but the downside is that very few beliefs are admitted into your belief system. If, as it may plausibly be argued, we are never going to get conclusive evidence and absolute certainty, then the best option is to accept beliefs which are reasonable given the evidence.

To illustrate the point, suppose Descartes were a defence barrister at a criminal trial at which he asked us, as jury, to adopt his method. Before we could convict, he would demand that we establish the defendant's guilt beyond any possible doubt. In such a case, we would have to admit that even though the defendant had the motive; even though his fingerprints were on the gun; and even though a dozen witnesses saw him pull the trigger, it is still *theoretically* possible that he is innocent, say, if there were an elaborate conspiracy against him. Even though there is no evidence of any conspiracy, it *is* theoretically possible, and so, according to Descartes' standard of proof we could not convict.

Clearly, if we were to accept Descartes' method in a court of law, we would never convict anyone and this would be extremely impractical. Perhaps, then, things should be the same in philosophy. This is the way the empiricist philosopher David Hume reasoned in his attack on Descartes' method in his *Enquiry Concerning Human Understanding* (1748). 'Cartesian doubt, therefore, if someone could attain to it (as plainly nobody could), would be entirely incurable, and no reasoning could ever bring us to confident beliefs about anything'.[5] Hume's point is that extreme scepticism, once embarked upon, cannot be escaped, since most, or even all, of our beliefs can be doubted *theoretically*. If we begin by demanding so much of our beliefs, we will end up not having very many, so Descartes' method leads us into a sceptical dead end. We will be turning shortly to see how Descartes does try to escape from the scepticism he initiates, and then we will be able to judge better whether Hume is right.

Issue 4: why not doubt our beliefs one by one?

If we cannot reject all our beliefs in one fell swoop, would a more piecemeal application of the method of doubt not be more reasonable? Should Descartes not proceed by criticising his opinions one by one, using other opinions as a basis for doing so? Those that were found to be wanting could then be discarded, and the ones that could not be doubted could be retained. Descartes rejects this approach as too time-consuming. He claims that he does not need to examine his beliefs one by one because he can question the *principles* upon which they are based. If these principles are found to be worthy of doubt, then all the beliefs that are based upon them can be abandoned as well. This way of thinking is really part and parcel of his *foundationalism*: the view that our system of beliefs is structured like a building, with basic beliefs supporting the rest. If this is how our beliefs are structured, then clearly undermining the foundational beliefs will mean that those based upon them will collapse also. However, not all philosophers accept foundationalism. Rather than a building, a simile used by anti-foundationalists for our belief system is that of a boat on the open sea. We cannot destroy the boat and rebuild it from scratch, since we would drown; rather, we must rebuild it piece by piece. In the same way, it may be that the process of ridding our belief system of error is necessarily a piecemeal affair, since the destruction of all our beliefs leaves us with nothing to operate with. Without beliefs of any sort we cannot function.[6]

The application of the method of doubt (Meditation 1)

Now that we have discussed the method Descartes has elected to use, we can turn to his application of the method in Meditation 1. Descartes presents us with three distinct sceptical scenarios or 'waves of doubt', each more radical than the last.

1. He doubts the testimony of sense experience by pointing out that it can be deceptive.
2. He doubts the nature of waking life by blurring the distinction with dreaming.
3. He doubts the existence of the physical world and his judgements about simple mathematics by positing the existence of an all-deceiving demon.

> *Whatever I have accepted until now as most true has come to me through my senses. But occasionally I have found that they have deceived me, and it is unwise to trust completely those who have deceived us even once.*
> Meditation 1

Doubting the senses

In the first wave of doubt, Descartes argues that because his senses have sometimes deceived him, it would be prudent no longer to trust them. The possibility of perceptual error is sufficient to lead him to doubt the whole of sense experience, since his method demands that the slightest doubt about beliefs will lead him to reject them. No example of such deception is given in Meditation 1, but in Meditation 6 Descartes recalls how:

> *A tower that had looked round from a distance appeared square from close up; an enormous statue standing on a high column didn't look large from the ground. In countless such cases I found that the judgments of the external senses were mistaken.*
> Meditation 6

The possibility of error undermines the principle that one can trust the senses. And if one abandons this principle, then all the beliefs that rely upon it will collapse with it. So he does not need to question the beliefs about the world obtained through his senses one by one. He does not ask, 'Is this tower *really* round as it appears?' 'Is this stick *really* bent?' and so on. That would be 'an endless task', as he points out in the second paragraph. Rather, if one doubts that the senses are trustworthy *as such*, the whole edifice of beliefs resting on this foundation stone can be swept aside in one fell swoop.

Issues with doubting the senses

We see straightaway that Descartes' application of his method is directed against the senses. This is because his plan is to undermine empiricism and the view that knowledge comes ultimately from sense experience. What he is trying to do is make us realise that the senses, far from being the most reliable and important source of knowledge, as we might ordinarily think, are in fact the main source of error. It is our unthinking faith in the senses which leads us astray, so he begins by trying to raise doubts about the senses as the basis for our knowledge of the world.

However, there is an immediate difficulty with Descartes' doubt about the senses. The issue concerns the move Descartes appears to make from saying that his senses are occasionally unreliable to his decision not to trust them at

► **ACTIVITY**

A Try to think of a situation where your senses deceived you.

B How did you come to realise that they were deceiving you?

C Is it possible that the way you came to notice the deception was also a deception?

all. For while our senses do *sometimes* deceive us, it does not follow that they may *always* deceive us. In fact, we can argue that the only reason we are able to tell that our senses are sometimes deceptive is precisely because on other occasions we take them to be accurate. For example, if I recognise that a stick appears bent when half-immersed in water (but is not really bent), this must be because I am able to use my senses to check. I may pull the stick out of the water and look again, or I may immerse my hand to have a feel of its shape. In other words, I use the very same senses to detect the deception. This point is sometimes illustrated through an example of a similar argument which is clearly fallacious. From the fact that some paintings are forgeries, it does not follow that all paintings could be forgeries – in fact, quite the contrary. For since a forgery is a copy of a genuine (non-forged) painting, you cannot have forgeries unless you have genuine paintings. If Descartes' argument is indeed of this type, then this suggests that it may be self-refuting. To notice that the senses *sometimes* deceive, itself depends on being able to correct errors by appeal to other sensory evidence. Thus the conclusion that the senses might always be deceptive actually relies on the assumption that they are only sometimes deceptive.

However, this objection probably misunderstands Descartes' intention at this stage. Descartes' argument intends to infer from the fact that the senses have deceived us in the past only that they are not entirely trustworthy and could deceive us again. Thus he is not yet suggesting that the senses might *always* deceive him, but just that he cannot tell when to trust them and when not, and therefore that he should not trust them completely. Descartes is not saying that it is possible that every one of his beliefs based upon the senses could be false, but rather that not one of his beliefs based on the senses is guaranteed to be true. This means that each of his beliefs may be false, although not all of them. The key distinction here is between 'possibly all false' – meaning that all of his beliefs may be false (a claim which appears to be incoherent, as we saw above) – and 'all possibly false' – which implies that some are true, even though we may not be able to tell which ones. An analogy may help to make Descartes' point. If I know that either the ones with white gills or the ones with brown gills are deadly, I have a good reason to abstain from eating both sorts of mushrooms. In the same way, Descartes has good reason to withhold assent from all beliefs based on the senses just because he knows some are false, without needing to claim that they could all be false.

In fact, Descartes' own response to his doubt about the senses shows that it is not intended to raise global doubts about the possibility of knowledge gained through the senses. He states that some of his beliefs based on the senses must surely be true, namely those about things which are close at hand, like the fact that he is in his sitting by the fire.[7] This suggests that Descartes thinks this initial argument does not lead to global scepticism about empirical knowledge, but rather only a local scepticism about his ability to discern accurately via the senses those things perceived at a distance or which are very small. And he is using beliefs derived from his senses in order to make this observation. Such scepticism may be considered not so very different from normal incredulity in that it is grounded in an acceptance of the general reliability of sense experience as a basis for knowledge, and uses such background knowledge to cast doubt on a relatively small subset of beliefs which are grounded on sense experience.

> *Often in my dreams I am convinced of just such familiar events – that I am sitting by the fire in my dressing-gown – when in fact I am lying undressed in bed!*
> Meditation 1

The dreaming argument

Descartes now suggests that the previous doubts about the senses only really affect objects at a distance or things which are difficult to perceive properly. We surely can be absolutely certain that we are not being deceived about objects which are right in front of us. Unless, of course, we are mad. However, Descartes now pushes the process of doubt even further to cover even these apparently fundamental perceptual beliefs. For are we not rather like mad people when in the grip of a dream? When dreaming, I have often supposed that I am going about my ordinary daily business, and when in such a dream I am convinced that I am awake. But if I can have dreams which are just like being awake, then I cannot be sure that I am not dreaming now. The sceptical point of the argument is that if I cannot know that I am not now dreaming, any belief I have about what I can perceive around me may be false. So even Descartes' belief that he is sitting by the fire in his dressing gown, a belief which seems so self-evidently true, may not be.

Issues with the dreaming argument

Issue 1: dreams can be distinguished from waking life

Many find this argument unconvincing because they have never had dreams which are at all similar to waking life. Surely, we might think, dreams are very different in character from real life, so it is relatively easy to tell the difference. And so one might try to mount an objection to Descartes' dreaming argument by identifying certain signs or criteria by which one can tell whether or not one is dreaming. For example, one could try pinching oneself to see whether it hurts, or try to read something, since it is supposed to be impossible to feel pain or to read in a dream.

Descartes anticipates this objection and claims that it misses the point of his argument. For no matter how good I may normally be at distinguishing dreams from waking life, whatever criterion I apply in drawing the distinction, whatever test I use to tell that I am awake, it remains possible that I merely *dream* that the criterion is satisfied or the test passed. For I could always *dream* that I pinch myself and that it hurts, or *dream* that I can read the words on the page in front of me. That is, I could always dream that this experience I am having has all the hallmarks of waking life. Descartes concludes that there can never be 'any reliable way of distinguishing being awake from being asleep' (Descartes, Meditation 1).

Issue 2: dreams must come from waking life

Similar objections to those against the argument from perceptual illusion have often been levelled against Descartes' dreaming argument too. For example, it might be pointed out that from the fact that I am *sometimes* unaware that I am dreaming, it does not follow that I might *always* be unaware that I am dreaming.

▶ ACTIVITY

A Have you ever had a dream which was so real it felt like real life?

B Have you ever dreamt you have woken up, got out of bed and got on with your normal life, only to wake up for real later?

C Have you ever been awake and thought you might be dreaming?

D How do you know that you are not dreaming now?

Also, one might point out that the concept of a dream is that of a kind of copy of waking life. And so, as with the forged painting example above, to be able to say that one has had dreams which are just like waking life presupposes that there is a distinction. If all life were a dream, then there would be no contrast with waking life on which the very concept of a dream depends, and so it would make no sense to call it a 'dream'.

A similar line begins by noting that the contents of my dreams ultimately come from waking life, in the sense that what I dream about is not totally made up, but rather composed out of memories of real-life experiences. So while I might dream about flying on a carpet, such a fantasy is nonetheless based in reality: I have, after all, experienced carpets and seen things fly when awake. It follows from this that if I am dreaming, then I must have been awake at some point, otherwise I would have nothing to be dreaming about.

In the same vein, against the claim that I might always be dreaming, it can be pointed out that in ordinary language we are perfectly able to distinguish dreaming from waking. Such terms only gain currency by being used in a fairly consistent way. Now, if I were always dreaming, I should not be able to distinguish dreaming from waking, so one of the terms would be redundant. For 'dreaming' to have any reference, there must be a state with which to contrast it. And therefore I can know that I am not always dreaming.

However, while such arguments might show that I am not *always* dreaming, they do not show that I am not dreaming *now*. And it is doubtful that Descartes actually wants to claim at this stage that he might always be dreaming. To question whether I am dreaming now may raise enough doubts about the *veracity* (that is, truthfulness or accuracy) of sensation for his present purposes. This interpretation is given support by the fact that Descartes suggests that the dreaming argument does not raise doubts about the existence of physical objects *as such*. For the most basic constituents from which our dreams are made are not themselves mere figments of our sleeping life, amongst which he lists 'body, and extension; the shape of extended things; their quantity, size and number; the places things can be in, the time through which they can last, and so on' (Descartes, Meditation 1, page 2).

Issue 3: you cannot know you have had dreams indistinguishable from waking life

The feeling that Descartes' argument may be self-refuting, however, may persist. Can Descartes even use the premise that he sometimes has dreams which are indistinguishable from waking life? How could he ever know this? For, on the one hand, to know this premise to be true is to know such dreams to be indistinguishable. And yet if you *know* you have had such dreams, they *must* be distinguishable (otherwise you would not know you had had them). So, paradoxically, you cannot know the truth of the claim to know that you have had dreams which are indistinguishable unless it is false.

However, this objection does not show that the premise actually *is* false; only that one cannot know that it is true. But Descartes does not need to *know* the premise for his doubts to get going. Simply believing, or even entertaining the possibility that he may have had dreams which were indistinguishable from waking life may be enough to raise doubts about whether he might be dreaming now. Moreover, Descartes' argument relies only on the premise that he has had dreams which are indistinguishable from waking life *while he was having them*. They may well have become distinguishable upon waking. So this premise can raise the doubts he needs: namely that he might be dreaming *now*, even though this dream may well be identified as such when he wakes.

In keeping with the interpretation that Descartes is not suggesting that he might always be dreaming, Descartes next points out that, even if he is dreaming, there must be a real world out there from which has got the materials to compose his dream. A dreamer is like a painter who makes up the creatures populating his or her landscape, but the basic colours and shapes are still originally gained from real life. This suggests that whether or not I am dreaming some very general truths about the world must be knowable: perhaps that it is coloured and has spatial dimensions. Pushing this line of thought further, Descartes figures that, whether or not his present experiences are real, the basic truths of mathematics and of geometry remain true. 'For whether I am awake or asleep, two plus three makes five, and a square has only four sides. It seems impossible to suspect that such obvious truths might be false' (Descartes, Meditation 1, page 2). I can clearly see that these claims are true, regardless of whether I am awake or asleep.

> *I have for many years been sure that there is an all-powerful God who made me to be the sort of creature that I am. How do I know that he hasn't brought it about that there is no earth, no sky, nothing that takes up space, no shape, no size, no place, while making sure that all these things appear to me to exist?*
>
> Meditation 1

The evil demon argument

However, Descartes now reasons that an all-powerful God would be able to deceive him about the very existence of the physical universe, for there would be nothing to prevent such a being from making the world appear to me as it does, even though it does not really exist. Moreover, even with mathematical truths there may be room for doubt. I have, after all, made mistakes in arithmetic before. Could it be that I am mistaken now, even in things that seem as obvious as that $2 + 3 = 5$? Could I go wrong when counting the sides of a square, so that what seem to be four sides might really be three or five? There is no difference that we experience between believing the right, or believing the wrong answer to a sum; so if there were an all-powerful God, he would be able to deceive me into thinking I was right, when I was in fact wrong. Descartes' point here seems to be that while mathematical truths are knowable *a priori* – that is to say, simply by thinking about them, regardless of any knowledge we have gained through experience – nonetheless, we are prone to error about them. And if it is always possible that we be mistaken in our judgements, then we can always doubt their veracity.

However, Descartes continues, my idea of God is of a being which is not only omnipotent, but supremely good. And to deceive me in this way about simple mathematics would surely be INCONSISTENT with such goodness. In other words, the beliefs that God is good and that I am deceived cannot both be true. And yet it would seem to be no less inconsistent with his goodness for him to deceive me about other things I used to take to be obvious, and yet I clearly *am* deceived in some such things, as has been shown.

Essential Terminology

anthology
1.25

These considerations lead Descartes to abandon the notion of a deceiver God. After all, it may be that no God exists. If not, then it is possible that there is an extremely powerful and malicious demon who employs all his energies to deceive him. Descartes imagines that such a demon would be powerful enough to deceive him about the very existence of the physical world. The appearance to him of the sky, and earth, of colours, shapes and sounds may all be illusions. Even the appearance of his own body may be part of the demon's deception. With this final and most radical wave of doubt, the first Meditation concludes. In the metaphor which opens the second, the whirlpool of doubt is all-engulfing and bottomless[8] – until Descartes manages to find his first firm foothold: the proposition 'I exist'.[9] It is from this that the positive rebuilding phase of the epistemological enterprise begins.

▶ ACTIVITY

In the film *The Matrix*, the hero, Neo, lives in a world very much like this one, where he goes to work, goes home, gets on with life and so on. However, early in the film, Neo makes a terrifying discovery. The world he inhabits is not real; it is part of 'the matrix', a computer-generated simulation world. Neo takes a pill to remove him from the computer simulation and wakes up to find that he has cables going into his spine that had been feeding false information to his brain and making him believe that he had a home, a job and so on. Neo pulls out the cables and sees the world as it really is – a world controlled by computers who have enslaved human beings.

1   Do you think that this scenario is a possibility? Is it possible that the world in front of you now is not the real world, but is just being 'implanted' into your head?
2   How do you know that you are not in 'the matrix' at this very minute?
3   How does Neo know (when he 'woke up' and pulled the cables out of his spine) that this new world (that is, the one where he sees computers enslaving human beings) is not also an illusion?

Brain in a vat

A more recent version of Descartes' evil demon argument is the thought experiment known as the 'brain in a vat'. A version of this might run as follows.

Imagine the year is now 2720. Somewhere in an evil laboratory, an evil scientist is undertaking an evil experiment. He has placed a human brain in a vat of chemicals. Connected to the brain are thousands of wires which carry electro-chemical signals to and fro between the brain and a vast computer. The scientist is feeding images, sounds, noises and sensations to the brain to make the brain think it is in fact a person living at the beginning of the twenty-first century. The brain even thinks that at this precise moment they are reading a philosophy book on Descartes.

Is this a possibility? If so, could *you* really be a brain in a vat? Even if this is only 0.00001 per cent likely, if you accept that it is theoretically possible, does that not mean that you can never be 100 per cent certain of anything?

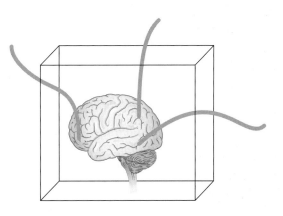
Figure 1.42 A brain in a vat

You may be tempted to think that, one way or another, at least you have a brain and that the earth still exists, even if you are in a vat being controlled by an evil computer. But even these thoughts are not certain. The world as you know it might only be a creation of the scientist, and the very idea of a brain simply another illusion that has been fed to you by the scientist. You could be anything in that vat: some kind of slug, a cloud or something totally unimaginable. Once the scenario is established, the possibility for doubt seems endless. Is there anything you could be certain of?

▶ ACTIVITY
Look again at the list of propositions on page 156. In the light of Descartes' demon argument or the brain in a vat or *Matrix* scenarios, ask yourself whether any of the propositions are free from doubt?

Issues with the evil demon argument

Issue 1: doubting reason is self-defeating

It seems that Descartes is saying that the dreaming argument is limited in that it cannot throw doubt on *a priori* knowledge, or on knowledge of the reality of the most fundamental units of our waking experience, namely the existence of shape or extension, sounds, colours and so on. Only a deceiving God or an evil demon can call these truths into question too. Thus the third wave of sceptical reasoning is presented as a reason for doubting even these minimal beliefs about real existence and about the most basic mathematics. However, the doubts about his basic mathematical judgements lead to an important difficulty for Descartes, which we will be returning to. If the demon hypothesis can cast doubt on such simple reasoning processes as are involved in counting the sides of a square and adding two to three, it should also cast doubt on our capacity to make basic logical inferences, such as the inference that a supremely good God would not deceive us about mathematics and geometry. So if the demon could be fooling me into thinking that 2 + 3 = 5 when it does not, surely he might also be fooling me into thinking that God would not deceive me, when he would. As we shall see, the idea that God would not deceive us about such basic reasoning processes is crucial to the development of Descartes' argument, but the point runs deeper than this. For if I cannot trust my basic reasoning processes, then I must give up my belief in argument as a means of acquiring the truth. If the reliability of reason is doubted, then how can we hope to use reason to overcome doubt? It seems that in pushing his scepticism thus far, Descartes' whole enterprise must grind to a halt.

It would seem that while Descartes can engage in doubt about a particular domain – namely, what the senses teach – he cannot seriously doubt the possibility of rational thought itself, since he has to use reason to do so. As we saw above, there is a certain basic logic to the very use of the concept of doubt such that in order meaningfully to doubt something, something else needs to be taken as certain. In other words, at the very least, the possibility of doubt is premised on the distinction between truth and falsehood. If I can doubt something, I must know what it means to say that something may be true or false.

Issue 2: the demon hypothesis is empty

Critics have complained that the supposition of an evil demon deceiving me about the existence of the physical world is empty if the demon's trickery is undetectable. The idea here is that if I could never tell the difference, *even in*

175

principle, between the demon deceiving me and my having a true experience, then for all practical purposes there is no difference. It is, as it were, a difference which makes no difference, since there are no criteria (or at least none available to me) for drawing the distinction between deception and reality. To illustrate the point, consider the idea of a counterfeit ten-pound note, which is so perfect that it is impossible to tell it from the real thing. No conceivable test would ever be able to detect anything to indicate that it was anything other than a genuine note. This would be a case of a perfect deception. But if the deception is this perfect – so perfect that it cannot be detected even in principle – then surely it is no different from a real note. Certainly, one would have no trouble using the note and it would pass unnoticed into circulation like all other notes, and, the thought goes, there is no real sense in which a fake which does all that the real thing does can meaningfully be called a fake. An undetectable counterfeit is effectively the same as a genuine note. In the same way, if Descartes' demon is able to produce a perfect illusion, one which we can never detect, then surely its creation is identical with what we call reality.

It is worth pausing to draw parallels here between Descartes' demon argument and the *Matrix* films (mentioned in the activity above), in which late twentieth-century reality is an illusion generated by a race of machines which have in fact enslaved humanity. In this case, there is a way of detecting the difference between the illusion and reality. It is possible to escape the illusion, as the heroes of the films do, in order to wage war with the machines in their efforts to liberate humanity. And things are similar in the *Truman Show* (1998), in which Jim Carrey's character, Truman Burbank – unbeknownst to him – has been a soap-opera character all his life. The lake-bound island where he lives is actually a film set, and his friends and family merely actors. But he is able to detect the deception by finally sailing across the lake and touching the painted wooden sky. In these scenarios, the deception is meaningful because those deceived can – at least in principle – expose the illusion for what it is. But if, as seems to be the case, Descartes' demon is so cunning that no such discovery is possible, then it is surely an empty hypothesis.

Descartes' response to scepticism

Despite these problems, Descartes' demon hypothesis, or the 'brain in a vat' or *Matrix* scenarios, although perhaps improbable, certainly appear to be possible. And if we concede even this much, then it seems we cannot be 100 per cent sure of anything. So, perhaps, we will be forced to give in to scepticism and accept that nothing can be known. At this point, Descartes produces a response that is probably the best-known philosophical argument of all and one which will be familiar to you: the *cogito*.

[L]et him deceive me all he can, he will never bring it about that I am nothing while I think I am something.
Meditation 2

anthology 1.26

Descartes argues that while it is possible to doubt the existence of the physical universe, my own existence cannot be doubted because, when I attempt to doubt it, I recognise that there must be something doing the doubting, and that something is me. So at the time of thinking, I cannot be nothing. My own existence can be known for certain in the face of the most radical doubts.

Meditation 2: the *cogito*

We have seen how Descartes' desire for a way of defeating the sceptic led him in search of a belief that could escape any possible doubt. The *cogito* represents the first such belief. It is impossible to doubt your own existence. What is so significant about the *cogito* is that it can be known to be true just by thinking it. Here, my conviction in my own existence appears unshakable. It does not depend for its truth upon anything else, and so appears to justify itself. This is precisely what Descartes was looking for: an indubitable belief from which to rebuild a body of knowledge. But has Descartes really defeated the sceptic? And, if so, what exactly has he established?

Focusing on the latter question, Descartes is claiming to have established that 'I exist', but what exactly does the word 'I' refer to? What am I? What is the self? Descartes is clear that he has not yet established the existence of himself as a human being, for the evil demon could still be deceiving him as to his earthly form. He may not even have a body. But he claims that the *I* must nonetheless be something, and that at the very least it must be a thing that can think. So he claims knowledge of himself as a thinking thing – in other words, a conscious being.

We have already examined the *cogito* in some detail when looking at Descartes' project in Chapter 1.3. The discussion of the *cogito* there is directly relevant to his efforts to overcome scepticism that we are now engaged in, and so you should reconsider those arguments now before moving on. The key question to ask is whether the *cogito* succeeds in arresting scepticism and whether it establishes as much as Descartes claims, in particular concerning the existence of an enduring thinking substance: my self.

Clear and distinct ideas

Satisfied that he has established his own existence in the face of radical scepticism, Descartes tries to discover further truths that have the same indubitable character possessed by the *cogito*. Given that the *cogito* can be known clearly and distinctly (or as Bennett's translation has it 'vividly and clearly'), he writes that 'I now seem to be able to lay it down as a general rule that *whatever I perceive very vividly and clearly is true*'.[10] Descartes' hope is that the *cogito* is not alone in its ability to defeat scepticism and that he can uncover a good number of beliefs that have the same clear and distinct character which makes them self-evident. If he is right, then he can rest his foundationalism upon these items of knowledge and rebuild a system of beliefs which is free from error.

We have already raised four criticisms of Descartes' use of clear and distinct ideas in Chapter 1.3. See if you can recall these objections and explain how they can be used to attack Descartes' efforts to defeat scepticism.

Criticism 1: clarity and distinctness do not guarantee that a belief is true

The first problem with this is establishing why a belief that appears clear and distinct would have to be true. The fact that a particular belief appears self-evident to me is not on its own enough to guarantee that it is actually true. I may have a subjective conviction that two added to three must equal five, but what exactly guarantees that this is more than a subjective conviction and that there is any objective certainty that this judgement is actually correct? The inner feeling of conviction is not the same as objective certainty; 'I am certain that p' is not the same as 'It is certain that p'.

We explored this problem above (page 121), where it was pointed out that the apparent clarity and distinctness of a belief does not guarantee that it corresponds with any of the facts that would make it true. In other words, Descartes' use of a criterion which is internal to the mind – the subjective conviction that this belief could not possibly be false – is not enough to establish that the belief is objectively true.

Descartes might defend himself here by pointing out that the *cogito* can indeed be known to be true just by its being thought. The belief 'I am, I exist' is confirmed in the very act of asserting it, so the belief and the fact that it proves coincide, which is why we called it 'self-verifying'. But even if we accept that in the case of the *cogito* (clearly and distinctly) recognising it as true is what makes it true, it does not follow that this characteristic can be generalised to other beliefs. So at best, Descartes might be able to say that all self-justifying beliefs must be true, but not all beliefs are recognisable clearly and distinctly. Analytic truths and mathematical truths may well be recognisable in a single intuition of the mind, but it is not the clarity and distinctness of this recognition that makes them true, so it cannot be used as a general criterion by which to identify items of knowledge.

Criticism 2: how can we be sure which beliefs really are clear and distinct?

Even if we were to accept that recognising a belief clearly and distinctly is enough to guarantee its truth, there are still problems. For how precisely can Descartes be sure that he really does clearly and distinctly understand a belief? Is it not possible that he may *seem* to understand something clearly and distinctly, but not in fact do so? After all, it is quite possible to make mistakes, even in simple judgments, as Descartes himself points out in Meditation 1. So could I not be mistaken into thinking a belief is clear and distinct when it is not? Could the demon not kid me into thinking I can clearly and distinctly recognise 2 + 3 = 5 when I do not? Indeed, Descartes appeared to be making this very point in Meditation 1 when considering basic judgements of mathematics and geometry, so surely he has not really found a way out of such an extreme scepticism.

To avoid making such a mistake, Descartes would appear to need some criteria to apply by which to distinguish those beliefs which he understands clearly and distinctly from those he does not. But if he could find such criteria, the same problem would loom again: how can he be sure he is applying *these* criteria correctly. Again, the difficulty is that it is always possible that what seems to be making the distinction properly may not in fact be doing so. To answer that he can clearly and distinctly perceive that he is applying them correctly obviously will not do, as this simply invites the question of how he can be *sure* of this, and in doing so, a vicious infinite regress looms.

We could defend Descartes by suggesting that such criticisms take scepticism too far; that we have no option but to use reason in our enquiries; and so that the most basic and simple judgements of reason have to be relied upon. If we do not trust our most basic judgements of this sort, then we cannot hope to continue philosophising and so the whole enterprise would be self-defeating. Certainly to doubt that 2 + 3 = 5 is hard to take seriously. We can have no coherent idea of what else they might make, and doubt about it depends on the most extreme of Descartes' sceptical scenarios. He himself calls the doubt that depends on the power of a deceiving God or demon 'slight and theoretical'. We may want to urge that we can recognise this truth in a simple intuition of the mind and so there is no room within it for doubts to get any real purchase.

Criticism 3: Descartes needs to prove God exists to dispel his radical doubts

However, Descartes is not satisfied to take this line in defence of his clear and distinctness criterion. Instead, he tries to dispel the remaining doubts by establishing some sort of guarantee that what is perceived clearly and distinctly really is true and reliable. Only in this way can his further epistemological progress be immunised from error.

> I shall want to remove even this slight reason for doubt; so when I get the opportunity I shall examine whether there is a God, and (if there is) whether he can be a deceiver. If I don't settle this, it seems, then I can never be quite certain about anything else.[11]

And so Descartes embarks in the remainder of Meditation 3 on a proof of the existence of God. His thought here is that if he can establish the existence of an all-good and powerful God, then he can eliminate the possibility that he is being radically deceived. This is because an all-good and powerful God would neither create him with such a deceptive nature nor allow him to believe with such conviction what is actually false. For, according to Descartes, deception is a mark of weakness or evil, and so if God exists, then the idea of a deceiving demon no longer holds force and all clear and distinct ideas can be taken as reliable. So proving God's existence becomes a way of guaranteeing that the foundations of his new system of knowledge – his clear and distinct beliefs – really are true and so of dispelling scepticism.

Criticism 4: the Cartesian circle

So can Descartes' proofs of the existence of God finally dispense with the radical sceptic who continues to doubt the veracity even of beliefs which seem self-evident or clearly and distinctly recognisable as true? To answer this, we will not re-examine the actual arguments Descartes adduces to prove God exists; we have already done so in detail in Chapter 1.3. However, it will be worth revisiting a key criticism of the strategy that Descartes employs here, a criticism known as the Cartesian circle.

Recall that Descartes intends to prove that a non-deceiving God exists in order to show that he could not be deceived about beliefs recognised clearly and distinctly. But in order to establish God's existence, he has to put forward arguments. And how are we to be sure that these arguments are sound? If you were not persuaded by the trademark and ontological arguments, you might well have thought that Descartes was duped – if not by an evil demon, then perhaps by the prejudices of his upbringing – into thinking that such arguments succeed. If you can have doubts, how can he or anyone else be so sure that somewhere in all this reasoning there is not a mistake? It is certainly not obvious that none is possible. And if we are to take seriously the possibility that we could be mistaken when counting the sides of a square or adding two to three, then how

179

▶ ACTIVITY

1 Do you remember what is meant by the Cartesian circle? (See page 141.)
2 How does this criticism undermine Descartes' efforts to defeat scepticism?

much more probable is it that these two proofs of God's existence are flawed in some way?

Earlier, we used a key premise of the trademark argument, the causal principle, as an example to drive home this point. Descartes tells us that we can know that 'the total cause of something must contain at least as much reality as does the effect' because 'it is obvious by the natural light'.[12] It is, in other words, knowable clearly and distinctly. Now, the very fact that we raised concerns about this principle is enough for us to question whether it really is knowable clearly and distinctly. But even if we accept that it seems obviously true, the fact that Descartes has not yet dismissed the evil demon hypothesis surely means that it is perfectly possible for us to be deceived into thinking the principle is self-evident, while it is actually false. It follows that we cannot rely on the soundness of the arguments for the existence of God, and so cannot dismiss the radical scepticism of the evil demon hypothesis.

The upshot of this is that Descartes' strategy to defeat scepticism appears to be circular: that is, it presupposes what it sets out to prove. He wants to prove that judgements he understands clearly and distinctly must be true, and to do this he needs to prove the existence of a non-deceiving God. Yet the arguments he uses to prove God's existence depend upon the truth of the premises made in their construction. So until he has proved that these premises are true, he cannot prove that God exists, and he cannot prove God exists until he knows the premises are true.

So Descartes seems unable to use God to defeat the radical scepticism of Meditation 1. Indeed, it would seem that once we push scepticism so far as to undermine our most basic judgements and reasoning abilities, then we destroy the only tools we can possibly use to escape scepticism. A plausible conclusion to draw from this is that if he is to avoid circularity, Descartes will be forced to retreat from the most extreme scepticism of Meditation 1 and accept that I can have self-evident knowledge of, at the least, some very simple propositions and judgements.

Descartes' efforts to overcome scepticism about knowledge of a mind-independent reality

In his efforts to overcome scepticism, proving God's existence is just one step. By the sixth Meditation, Descartes is ready to make good the move beyond the subjective realm of his own thought and establish both the existence of the physical world and an account of its true nature.

Descartes argues that certain properties of matter are clearly and distinctly perceived – namely, those amenable mathematical and geometric descriptions (their shapes, sizes, positions and movements), and Descartes thinks this means they may actually exist in objects themselves. For, in contrast to our confused ideas of colour, smell and so forth, we know what such properties would represent in reality. In other words, I have a clear idea of what it would be for something to be square or spherical in itself, independently of my perception of it. By contrast, I have no real idea of what it is for something to be red, or hot. My perception of red could be caused by anything and I cannot work out what kind of thing it is to be red, just by analysing my idea of red.

Descartes recalls his initial (pre-doubt) view of sensory ideas and their origin. On this view, all his ideas, both the clear and distinct, and the obscure and confused, are caused in him by the existence of material things outside of his mind. Physical objects were thought to be the source of these ideas, and they projected representations of themselves into his mind. Can he now prove that this was basically a correct view? What in it is true and what misleading?

To answer these questions, he points to two features of his sensations which suggest that they do not emanate from his essential nature as a thinking thing. For if he can show that they do not come from within, it follows that they must come from somewhere else. The first feature he points to is the fact that they are not subject to his *will*. That is to say, he is unable to control their appearance. He cannot see or hear whatever he pleases. But since his will is part of his essence as a thinking thing, this suggests that they are not produced from within him, but by some *other* power.

Second, he observes that his sensations are (in a sense) *extended* – that is, they appear to represent things which have size and shape. But he himself (that is, his mind) is unextended. It has no size or shape and cannot be divided into pieces (since different faculties of the mind, the will, imagination and so on, are not different parts of him, but are all aspects of the same mind). So although sensations occur within his mind, in the sense that they are aspects of his consciousness, they do not and cannot arise spontaneously within such a mind. For mind is non-spatial and whatever is non-spatial, Descartes maintains, cannot create something that is spatial. So again, sensations must come from outside of him. Descartes quickly dismisses the possibility taken seriously by Berkeley that God could be the origin of my sensations (on the grounds that this would implicate God in a deception which is contrary to His nature) and thus concludes that they originate in matter.

We examined the proof of the external world in some detail above in Chapter 1.3 and explored key criticisms that are relevant here. By revisiting that discussion, you should ensure you have a full grasp of the question of whether Descartes succeeds in overcoming the radical scepticism of Meditation 1.

Primary and secondary qualities

The next question to raise is what the material world is actually like. It certainly is not quite like it appears to be, as has been established by the arguments from illusion of Meditation 1. Descartes' answer is that only some of the perceived features of objects are actually in them, while the remainder are mere effects made upon the mind by these objects. In other words, he draws a distinction between the primary or real qualities of objects and the secondary or merely apparent ones. The way he draws the distinction is to claim that he can be certain that those features he clearly and distinctly perceives to be in objects must really be in objects since God would not allow him to be deceived about what he clearly and distinctly perceives. So those features of his sensations, those that are amenable to mathematical and geometric description, must be the real qualities of objects. However, those qualities which he perceives only obscurely and confusedly, such as colour, smell, heat and so on, and which do not lend themselves to mathematical description, cannot be relied upon to make judgements about. So we should not jump to the supposition that they exist in objects.

anthology
1.27

In this argument, Descartes establishes a form of indirect realism – the theory we explored above (page 60), according to which our sensations are private representations of physical things. Such things have primary qualities such as extension, mass, motion and quantity (the subject matter of mathematics and geometry). These qualities are inherent features of matter itself. In addition to primary qualities, there are secondary qualities such as sounds, smells, colours, tastes and textures, which are simply the way matter appears to a perceiving mind. Our perceptions of secondary qualities are not directly representative. Thus matter itself is not coloured; rather, there are powers or dispositions in matter which cause us to perceive colours.

Empiricist responses to scepticism

Chapter 1.2 on perception examines the arguments of the empiricist philosophers, Locke and Russell, in their efforts to vindicate our common-sense assumption that we can acquire knowledge of the world through our sense experience. The basic problem that each philosopher was grappling with was essentially the same as Descartes'. They accepted Descartes' view that knowledge of our own sense data cannot be doubted. I may be dreaming, or subject to the deceptions of an evil demon, but nonetheless I can be assured that what I am directly aware of within my own mind is immune from doubt. So while I may doubt that I am really walking through an orchard, picking and eating an apple, I cannot doubt that it *seems to me* as though I am. Even if life is an extended dream, immediate sense certainty puts an end to any conceivable doubt.

But such certainty is only a starting point, for empiricist philosophers hope to use this experience as the basis for knowledge of a reality that lies beyond the individual's mind. How can this be done?

> *If we can find out what the scope of the understanding is, how far it is able to achieve certainty, and in what cases it can only judge and guess, that may teach us to accept our limitations and to rest content with knowing only what our human condition enables us to know.*[13]

Locke's response to scepticism

Like Descartes' *Meditations*, Locke's *Essay Concerning Human Understanding* is centrally concerned with scepticism and how to contend with it. But the tone of the opening paragraphs of the *Essay* contrasts markedly with Descartes' *Meditations*. Whereas Descartes' ambition was to construct a comprehensive body of scientific knowledge on foundations that are beyond any possible doubt, Locke concedes to the sceptic that there is a great deal in the universe about which we must remain ignorant. At the outset, Locke adopts a sceptical attitude towards our cognitive abilities, arguing that we must accept their limitations and not expect to find certain knowledge in all matters.[14]

Locke sees Descartes' project as overly ambitious. By undertaking to employ human reason alone to establish certain and substantive claims about the world, Descartes set himself up for a fall. Human reason just is not up to the task of finding such certainty, for the reasons we have seen. But Locke's scepticism about our cognitive abilities is not purely negative. Rather, he believes that a more modest enterprise is more likely to meet with success. If we recognise

► **ACTIVITY**

Read Chapter 1.2, or remind yourself of it if you have already read it. Then see what you can recall of these three philosophers' attempts to overcome scepticism about our knowledge of a mind-independent reality.

1 How does Locke try to establish knowledge of a mind-independent reality?

2 How does Berkeley try to deal with scepticism about our knowledge of a mind-independent reality?

3 What is Russell's argument to the best hypothesis (explanation)?

our cognitive limitations, we may be able to chart those areas of human understanding where we may establish knowledge, and distinguish them from those where only opinion is possible. And once we become aware of 'where the line falls between opinion and knowledge',[15] Locke hopes that we will become content with our own cognitive limitations and cease to pursue enquiries beyond the point where they can reach. The reason why he thinks we ought to be satisfied with accepting our ignorance of certain matters is that he claims that we are capable of knowing all that we need to know for 'the conveniences of life'.[16] So even if full knowledge is impossible, we can nonetheless attain sufficiently well-founded opinions that are perfectly adequate for our purposes – namely, allowing us to get on with the practical business of ordinary living.

One aspect of Descartes' optimism is his desire to show that human reason could uncover the true nature of material substance. The essential nature of matter, according to Descartes, is *extension*. In other words, it is extended in three-dimensional space, so its defining characteristics can be described by the science of geometry, making them amenable to rational demonstration. For Locke, however, reason alone cannot tell us what the essential properties of material substance are. This is because we are necessarily confined to the way it appears to our senses, and our senses cannot penetrate through the veil of perception to reveal the essence of reality. This means he remains sceptical about our capacity to acquire knowledge of the nature of material substance. Thus substance can be 'only a supposition of he knows not what support of such qualities which are capable of producing simple ideas in us'.[17]

For Locke, we can explain the perceived qualities of objects, both primary and secondary, in terms of the primary qualities of the 'corpuscles' or atoms that compose them. The shape of an apple, as perceived by me, is caused by its actual shape. And the colour, smell and taste are to be explained in terms of how the shapes, sizes and movements of the imperceptible atoms of which it is made impact on my sense organs. But if we then ask a further question, 'What is it that gives these atoms their primary qualities?,' then it is unhelpful to appeal to a general notion of 'substance', as Descartes had. Here we are searching for something which lies beneath any possible experience and therefore we cannot have any idea of it. To illustrate the point, Locke recounts the view of an Indian philosopher which explains how the earth is supported in space by claiming that it is carried on the back of an elephant. When we ask the philosopher how the elephant is supported, the response is that it stands on the back of a great tortoise. Then, 'being again pressed to know what gave support to the broad-backed tortoise', he replies, 'something, he knew not what'.[18] Locke concludes:

> The idea then we have, to which we give the general name substance, being nothing but the supposed, but unknown, support of those qualities we find existing, which we imagine cannot subsist ... without something to support them, we call that support substantia; which, according to the true import of the word, is, in plain English, standing under or upholding.[19]

So the best our understanding can achieve when it comes to substance is to identify specific substances, such as gold, in terms of the sensible qualities it produces in us. And Locke's scepticism about our knowledge of material substance also applies to our idea of mental substance. We are aware of the contents of our minds and of how they work, such as when we perceive, feel, imagine and reason. But we have no clear idea of what it is that underlies or produces these experiences. So we have no knowledge of the true nature of the self. In this, Locke is prepared to accept a far more sceptical position than Descartes, for whom the substantial nature of the self was a key discovery he hoped to establish in the *Meditations*.

Locke and knowledge of a mind-independent reality

When it comes to the central sceptical problematic – the veil of perception problem – true to his modest approach, Locke concedes to the sceptic that we cannot establish the existence of a world of mind-independent objects with total certainty. The certainty I have concerning the appearance of sense data within my mind cannot be extended beyond the mind. However, Locke does not conclude that we must remain in total ignorance about the existence of a physical world and about its nature. Rather, he thinks that the nature of our experience gives us sufficient, if not conclusive reasons to infer that a physical world exists. And, as we saw in Chapter 1.2 (pages 72–77), there are two features of our sense experience in particular that he draws our attention to.

The first is the fact that our sense experiences are not subject to our voluntary control. That is to say, I cannot look out of the window and see whatever I please. Rather, sense data seem to force themselves upon me. Locke thinks that the fact that they are not controlled makes it most likely that they are caused by something outside the mind. Second, our sense experiences cohere with each other. If I spot an apple on a tree, walk over, pick it and then bite into it, my ideas of sight, touch and taste seem independently to have homed in on something outside of me; something which has caused each sense to be affected in a specific way.

Such arguments show that, for practical purposes, we have some reliable strategies by which to distinguish illusions, hallucinations, dreams and so on, from veridical perception. I can tell I am daydreaming and imagining being on holiday on the beach because the daydream is subject to my voluntary control. I can tell the dagger before me is a hallucination because when I go to grasp it, my hand clutches only thin air. But while these strategies are all well and good for practical purposes, they deal only with fairly ordinary and local sceptical worries. The philosophical sceptic is not going to be impressed, since these observations about sense experience do not conclusively establish that sense experience is caused by a physical world. They assume that the senses are reliable some of the time in order to identify the hallucination. Indeed, they do not really seem to address the possibility that I might be dreaming, since dreamed experiences are normally involuntary, and also involve a certain agreement between what the different senses seem to observe. Moreover, it does not dispel the global scepticism of the evil demon or brain in a vat scenarios. After all, if a demon or supercomputer is causing my sensations, I could expect them to cohere and be beyond my control. But the force of Locke's argument here is not to refute scepticism on its own terms. Rather, he is asking us to consider whether the sceptic is expecting too much. Sure, we cannot provide a deductive proof to dismiss the demon hypothesis, but we do not need to. Our lived experience of our sensory experience provides sufficient evidence for our purposes.

As we saw in Chapter 1.2, Locke further tries to undermine the sceptic by pointing out that a scepticism that relies on the merest possibility of doubt is not a good basis for giving up on a set of beliefs and denying the existence of the external world. And to expose the lack of genuine conviction in the sceptic's doubts, he points out that, for practical purposes, we are incapable of taking seriously the idea that we could be dreaming. If we could, we would surely be capable of risking our physical safety. Yet if we were actually to put a hand into the fire, the pain would soon dispel any doubt. What greater certainty could we ask for? So, while deductive reasoning may fail us here, we can still attain a kind of lived conviction, which, Locke suggests, is actually more solid than reason could provide.[20] We have seen that Descartes' philosophical doubt is conducted at a theoretical level, so it has no practical impact on his everyday actions. What Locke is suggesting here is that, while scepticism about the external world may be possible at this theoretical level, it is not possible at the practical level. And since the practical business of living is what really matters to us, we should be content with this.

So Locke's strategy involves questioning whether we should accept the sceptic's insistence on theoretical reason and argument as the only basis for accepting beliefs. A sceptical scenario may be logically possible, but this does not imply that we cannot be as sure as we need to be that it does not obtain. So we may say that Locke is a fallibilist about empirical knowledge of the physical world. He is saying that we can have knowledge just as long as we believe a true belief for which we have sufficient, although not conclusive or indefeasible, evidence.

Hume's mitigated scepticism

However, a more moderate degree of such scepticism can be quite reasonable, and is a necessary preparation for the study of philosophy.[21]

It is common to suppose that to know something truly, you must be absolutely certain of it. After all, it may seem that you cannot really know something so long as you harbour doubts. Descartes went along with this common way of thinking and so searched for an indubitable basis for knowledge. However, we have seen that his method of doubt may mean that he cannot escape scepticism. He may be able to discover with certainty the reality of his own existence, and perhaps also of the basic claims of maths, geometry and truths of reason, but beyond this, knowledge of the physical world may well become impossible.

Hume argues that Descartes' style of scepticism is necessarily self-defeating. To seriously doubt the reliability of our most basic reasoning processes amounts to casting away the only tools we have available to us with which to construct a system of beliefs. Descartes, in other words, would be stuck in the solipsistic whirlpool of doubt into which he has fallen at the beginning of Meditation 2, with no possibility of establishing any knowledge beyond the confines of his own consciousness.

However, Hume does not despair. Influenced by Locke's down-to-earth approach, Hume appeals to the fact that we seem to be psychologically incapable of accepting solipsism during our everyday lives. He draws attention to the fact that ordinary doubts inevitably impact on how one lives, so that the purely theoretical doubts of

anthology
1.28

the philosophical sceptic are divorced from and irrelevant to belief formation in everyday contexts. The sceptic claims to doubt that there is a dog before her, yet flinches when it snaps at her hand, thus betraying the fact that her doubts are irrelevant to the way she acts. In such cases, our instincts force upon us the conviction that our sense experience provides a pretty accurate representation of a world of mind-independent objects. We are just not capable of living out theoretical doubts about such fundamentals as the existence of our own bodies and the physical things that surround us. Hume concludes that the extreme philosophical scepticism of Descartes has to be mitigated, and instinct accepted as a force equally important as reason in advising us what to believe. In this, he moves beyond Locke's position, which still respects the role of reason in providing us with a strong probabilistic argument for the existence of the world, and instead emphasises Locke's involuntarism – the idea that we have no choice about how we form beliefs and that reason is therefore not the most important force in belief formation.

So, Hume concludes, we possess certain natural dispositions which force us into holding certain beliefs, such as belief in the existence of our own bodies and the physical world. From a purely rational point of view, this may not be a fully justified hypothesis. We may not be able to find any rational arguments to defeat the sceptic. But here we do not need strong justification, because we are incapable of acting in any way other than in the complete conviction that there is a physical world. While *reason* appears to lead us into a sceptical hole, luckily our natural instincts or passions will not allow us to remain sceptical for long. It follows that while reason may be useful for certain enquiries, it has its limits. We cannot expect reason alone to give us sufficient grounds for us to claim knowledge of the physical world. If we were to wait for reason to do so, we would be paralysed, having no basis for action. Instead, we need to put our faith in instinctive convictions.

So although the sceptic may seek to undermine our most natural and mundane beliefs, she must leave such argument to one side as soon as life demands action. Rather than produce a *rational* refutation of scepticism, something Hume regards as impossible, he relies on the principles of our nature, our instincts, to undermine it.

The great subverter of excessive scepticism is action, practical projects, the occupations of everyday life. Sceptical principles may flourish and triumph in the philosophy lecture-room, where it is indeed hard if not impossible to refute them. But as soon as they come out of the shadows, are confronted by the real things that our beliefs and emotions are addressed to, and thereby come into conflict with the more powerful principles of our nature, sceptical principles vanish like smoke and leave the most determined sceptic in the same believing condition as other mortals.[22]

Russell and the rejection of infallibilism

What Descartes' experience may teach us is that if we insist on being absolutely certain, then we may end up with very little that we can really know. What empiricists such as Locke and Hume have argued is that the way to deal with this impasse is to reject Descartes' infallibilism. If we are less strict about what counts as knowledge, then we can allow ourselves to know a bit more. Although in the past, philosophers have tended to value certainty very highly, most philosophers these days do not think you need to be certain of something to know it, as we have seen in our investigation of the concept of knowledge.[23]

It is worth remembering this, as sceptical arguments can have a tendency to make us search for certainty as a way of overcoming them, because beliefs that are absolutely certain can never be undermined. Having resisted the sceptic in this way, the tendency can then be to take the further step of supposing that in order to know something, you must be absolutely certain of it, and that you cannot really be said to know if you are not certain. But while this is a possible position, it is important to be aware that it is not the only one.

Russell recognises that we cannot demonstrate conclusively the existence of the material world. But, importantly, I cannot demonstrate conclusively that it does not exist either. So we are presented with a choice. To accept that the physical world does exist or that it does not. When thought of in this way, Russell thinks, it is clear that the physical world hypothesis has far more to recommend it than the alternative. This is because if there is a physical world, this will explain why our sense experience behaves in regular and predictable ways. An example would be what happens when I place an apple in my desk drawer, intending to eat it for lunch, but forget about it. What happens when I open the drawer again several months later? Well, we can predict with some confidence that I will experience a shrivelled and rotten apple. But why is this? The obvious answer is that the apple has undergone a transformation during the period that I was not thinking about it and that the changes are now detected by my sense organs when I open the drawer. The alternative hypothesis, that there is no mind-independent physical object, the apple, provides no explanation for my experience. The rotten apple experience would be a complete mystery. It follows that it is reasonable to suppose that there is a physical world.

Berkeley's response to scepticism

Berkeley not satisfied with Locke's efforts to avoid the sceptical conclusion that the veil of perception problem seems to point towards. If the picture which Locke and indirect realism paint were correct, then, so far as Berkeley is concerned, scepticism would be inescapable and knowledge of the world as revealed to us through perception would indeed be beyond us. Berkeley's reaction to this, though, is not to capitulate to the sceptic and accept that our beliefs about physical reality must lack certainty, but to look again at the model of perception which has led us into this sceptical dead end.

Berkeley' follows Descartes and Locke in accepting that we can have certain knowledge of what we are directly aware of – that is to say, the contents of our own consciousness. But his solution to the sceptical worry that we cannot move by any deductively valid argument from knowledge of our sense data to the existence of a mind-independent physical world is to collapse the distinction between appearance and reality. For if there is no mind-independent reality, then there is no longer any problem of how we can come to have knowledge of it. So, by denying the existence of matter, Berkeley hopes to defuse the scepticism of the veil of perception problem.

Because Berkeley accepts that we cannot have knowledge of a mind-independent reality, it can seem as though his position embraces scepticism. But this can only be regarded as a sceptical position if we suppose that there is a mind-independent

▶ ACTIVITY

1 Can you recall Berkeley's arguments to show that matter does not exist?
2 What difficulties do these arguments and Berkeley's idealism face?

▶ ACTIVITY

Examine an object in front of you. You can pick it up, look closely at it, sniff it, listen to it, taste it even.

As you examine it, try not to focus your attention on the object itself, but just on the sense data it produces in your mind.

Did you succeed? Could you ignore the physical object and just focus on the sense data? Which properties do you find you can identify as merely part of your own consciousness? Which seem inseparable from the object itself beyond your consciousness?

reality that we would like to have knowledge of, but cannot. By denying that matter exists, Berkeley is able to insist that we have secure knowledge of reality precisely because that reality is within the mind, so that we are directly aware of it. If physical objects are no more than what they appear to be, then there is nothing that is hidden from our view – no gap between perceiver and perceived – and so no room for sceptical arguments to gain purchase.

We discussed Berkeley's arguments against indirect realism above, so we will not go over them again here. But these arguments and the difficulties they face are both important to the current topic, scepticism and how to overcome it, and can be employed when writing about this in the exam. So it will be worth your while reconsidering them here.

Direct realism

Berkeley's attempted solution to scepticism about our knowledge of the physical world is supposed to work by claiming that we perceive it directly. And there is another theory of perception that we have examined which makes the same claim: direct realism. So it will be worth revisiting this view to see whether it might provide an alternative route to overcoming scepticism about the external world.

Recall that for indirect realists such as Locke, we infer the existence of mind-independent objects and their properties on the basis of our immediate sense experiences. Now, this raises an obvious question. Why is it that we are unaware of making this inference? For when I examine my experience, I seem to be directly aware of a mind-independent reality. It does not appear as though I am aware of something called 'sense data' existing only within my own consciousness, and that I make a more or less shaky judgement on the basis of these data about what lies outside my mind. Indeed, in everyday life, it is very hard, if not impossible, to focus on your sense data and not 'see' real objects. To remind yourself of this fact about sense experience, try the activity below in the margin.

We examined some fairly persuasive philosophical arguments for indirect realism which aimed to convince us that what we directly perceive are only sense data (the arguments from illusion, hallucination, perceptual variation and time lag). But the activity in the margin may have helped you to reconsider just how odd this conclusion is and just how out of kilter it is with our everyday experience. So how does Locke explain the fact that our experience appears to be at odds with indirect realism?

Locke's answer is that our minds automatically make the inference from sense data to mind-independent objects without our conscious awareness. Now, on the face of it, this claim may seem rather implausible. Surely, if we were continually making such inferences, we would be well aware of doing so. To persuade us that unconscious inferences are indeed possible, Locke points out that we make them all the time when we use language. When you hear or read a word, your mind is transported directly to the word's meaning, without you being aware of any inference taking place. And yet, clearly there is an inference here. Words are arbitrarily associated with what they stand for, and when we acquire a language, we must learn what each group of letters and sounds mean. As children, we must learn the meanings of words, but when we are fluent, we no longer need to think about what a word means – the meaning appears to come immediately to mind. In the same way, Locke suggests, we must learn to perceive, and once we become proficient at it, we seem to perceive objects immediately.

However, this analogy with language learning is not fully convincing. For while we may not normally pay much attention to the sounds of words, as fluent speakers we are still very much aware of them. Hearing a word certainly immediately triggers the idea it stands for, but for all that, I never fail to notice that I have heard the word. And yet with sense data, things are not like this. It actually seems rather hard to bring the sense data to consciousness. Russell argues that we can train ourselves to do so. Artists, for example, have to consciously attend to the appearance of a scene in order to learn how to reproduce the true appearance of objects. But while this example may support the claim that we are directly aware of sense data, it may also be used to question whether the indirect realist picture has things the wrong way round. The experience of artists learning to copy appearances, suggests that we are first aware of mind-independent objects in sense perception, and only secondarily, through arduous training, become aware of sense data.

Moreover, it may be argued that if we really only had access to the world of sense data, then we could never even form the idea of a mind-independent reality. On empiricist principles, we can only have access to sense data, so the very idea of a world lying beyond sense data would be impossible for us to make any sense of. The fact that we do appear to have a pretty clear idea of a mind-independent reality suggests that we are able to perceive it directly, and not indirectly through our sense data.

But while direct realism may be more in keeping with our experience, how can it deal with the philosophical arguments in support of sense data? If we see the world directly, how do we explain illusions and perceptual variation? For surely direct perception implies that we see things as they truly are?

Direct realists respond to this by saying that just because there is a mismatch between the way reality appears and the way we believe it is, this does not mean we see it indirectly. They argue that it is perfectly possible to perceive things differently from how they are, while still seeing them directly. When we perceive something, the way it appears to the observer is a property which it has in virtue of being perceived. It is true that appearing white in a particular light, or trapezoid from a particular angle, cannot be an intrinsic property of the table, but this does not mean that these are purely mind-dependent properties of our sense data. Rather, these apparent properties are those which the object produces when it relates to a perceiver. We see the rectangular table directly, but we see it as a trapezoid. By denying that sense data mediate between the perceiver and reality, direct realism may be able to dispose of the veil of perception problem, and with it the sceptical worry about knowledge of the world.

The appeal to ordinary language

An alternative strategy which may be employed in the effort to resist scepticism involves an appeal to the ordinary way in which we talk about perception and knowledge of the world. In everyday life, we are happy to say that we are *certain* or that we *know* that grass is green, that dogs do not speak Chinese, and that Everest is the tallest mountain on earth, and we are rarely challenged when we do so. Ordinarily speaking, to see a table is good enough reason for affirming that one knows it exists. It is only philosophers who question our use of such words as 'know' and 'certain' in these and other everyday contexts, when they depart from ordinary incredulity and dabble in philosophical scepticism. In the process, they often claim that we need to refine our concepts of certainty and knowledge, and give them a philosophically strict meaning.

In the twentieth century, however, so-called ordinary language philosophers questioned this approach and in so doing hoped to find an alternative route to defeating the sceptic. So how does ordinary language philosophy attempt to overcome scepticism? To answer this question, let us begin with the example of the term 'knowledge'. Remember that the sceptic claims that I cannot 'know', just because I *see* a table before me, that there really *is* a table before me. The possibility that there exist Cartesian demons or mad scientists deceiving us shows, according to the sceptic, that we cannot have knowledge of the nature or existence of the physical world. In other words, the sceptic argues that, because it is possible for me to be mistaken, I cannot really have knowledge.

Notice, however, that in ordinary language, the merest possibility of error does not warrant avoiding the use of the words 'know' and 'knowledge'. In everyday life, we say we know all kinds of things about which it is at least conceivable that we may be mistaken. For example, if, in the ordinary course of things, someone were to ask you if you *know* that there is a table before you, you would doubtless think she were joking. But if she were insistent that your knowledge claim might be ill-founded, you might be led to make some straightforward checks. You might make sure that it was no hologram by rapping your finger against it; or you might pick it up to ensure that it was indeed made of solid wood and not a fiendishly clever fake fashioned out of paper. Having conducted these tests, you would – according to the ordinary use of the word – be quite justified in claiming that you *knew* that this thing was indeed a table. This is just the kind of situation in which the word 'know' or 'knowledge' is typically used. If the sceptic insists that you still do not know, even after these various checks have been made, then she is inviting you to buy into a radical departure from the way the word 'know' is normally used. This shows that the philosophical tradition uses the concept of knowledge (and of certainty, doubt and so on) in a different way from our ordinary usage.

Having made this clear, the ordinary language philosopher can now claim that traditional sceptical arguments only have force if we accept this departure from our ordinary usage of terms like 'knowledge' and 'know'. But, the argument goes, the sceptic has given us no reason to accept this new usage. If we reject this departure and continue to use language in the ordinary way, then the sceptical arguments lose their force. Instead of responding to the sceptic by trying to prove that we really do know – even according to the new, stricter definition of knowledge – the ordinary language philosopher insists on keeping the old definition, and so can claim to know according to it.

But why should the ordinary usage of words like 'knowledge' be preferable? The ordinary language philosopher points out that words are meaningful because there is social agreement about their meaning. Words acquire their meaning from their use in everyday contexts. To rip them from those contexts and try to make them do work for which they are not designed is literally to start talking nonsense. Imagine trying to use the word 'biscuit' to do the work of the word 'the'. If others do not agree to accept your new usage, no one will understand you and you will very quickly start talking gobbledygook. You cannot just use words to mean whatever you please. It is the same with philosophers who try to use words in the wrong way. In claiming to have grave doubts about the existence of physical objects, we have departed radically from ordinary usage of the word 'doubt', and in so doing we have raised confusions about how the word works. The sceptic is no longer talking about 'doubt', 'certainty' and 'knowledge', but rather about some peculiar philosophical versions of them.

In sum, philosophical doubt, by trading on the mere possibility of being mistaken, has little to do with the original or proper meaning of doubt. If we stick to the generally accepted understanding of the concept, then the sceptic's argument is invalid.

The Austrian philosopher Ludwig Wittgenstein (1889–1951) claimed that all manner of philosophical muddles could be avoided if only people paid more attention to how language works in ordinary contexts. Philosophical difficulties arise when, as he put it, language is allowed to go on holiday – that is, when terms become used in inappropriate ways.

Ordinary language user

Philosopher

Here, the word 'doubt' is at home.

But here doubt has gone on holiday, which can lead to confusion.

Figure 1.43 Language goes on holiday. Words like 'doubt' or 'know' begin life as ordinary words used in ordinary contexts. When being used in these contexts – when they are at home, getting on with their everyday work – everyone understands how to use them and no puzzles arise. However, when words like these are taken out of their ordinary context – when they are taken off 'on holiday' by unscrupulous philosophers – they are no longer able to do the work for which they are suited and all sorts of confusions arise. The sceptic, when talking about 'knowledge', is no longer talking about the same thing that we are talking about ordinarily.

191

The appeal to common sense

In a similar move, philosophers have also tried to defeat scepticism by appealing to common sense. Again, the idea here is that philosophers are mistaken if they claim that we do not really know what we normally think we do. So the philosopher of common sense argues that the first task of any theory of knowledge is to account for the fact that we do know all kinds of ordinary things, rather than fabricate a peculiar philosophical definition of knowledge which drastically restricts what can be known.

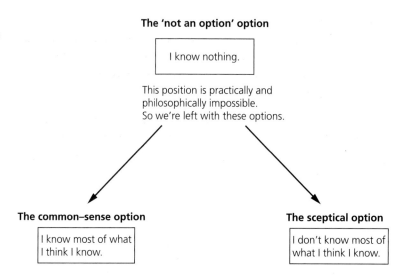

Figure 1.44 What is more reasonable to believe? In life, we do not really have the option of believing nothing at all. Rather, we have a choice about what to believe. So the question boils down to which beliefs are more reasonable. Given the options, is it more reasonable to believe that we know most of what we think we know, or that we do not? The philosopher of common sense argues that we have compelling reasons to believe common sense rather than what the sceptic offers.

In the twentieth century, G.E. Moore (1873–1958) pointed out that we have to take some beliefs for granted. We cannot hope to prove everything, since the process would be endless. As we saw above with the infinite regress of justification, some beliefs must be basic and not in need of any further proof. Moreover, we cannot doubt everything at once. Believing nothing is not a real option, since even the sceptic has to retain some beliefs, for reasons we have discussed above. So where does this leave us? Which things should we believe? Well, why not believe the basic claims of common sense? Do these not have as good a claim to our assent as any other beliefs? And while it may well be that we cannot *prove* them, this, for Moore, shows just how basic they are. Perhaps they are so basic that they do not need to be proved, but rather simply accepted. Moore argued that it is more reasonable to believe common sense than any weird belief you might be led to by doing too much philosophy.[24]

The defender of common sense argues that she knows certain things (the existence of physical objects, for instance), even though she is unable to give any explicit justification for the claim. In other words, we can know things without knowing how we know. At some point, she argues, we have to accept that we reach rock bottom and doubting comes to an end. The Scottish philosopher Thomas Reid, like Hume, recognised that anyone who took radical scepticism seriously would be disabled from carrying out even the most mundane day-to-day business. How can you be certain that, with the very next step you take, the ground will not collapse? How can you be sure this book will not suddenly burst into flames as you turn the page? Scepticism, taken seriously, would make every single act a leap into the unknown. Since even the most committed sceptic has no trouble conducting their everyday affairs in their non-philosophical moments, we must assume that we are all incapable of sincere doubts about certain basic common-sense beliefs. Among these beliefs would be our conviction that the physical world exists and that it has the various properties that we perceive it to have, that other people have minds, and that the future will resemble the past. Such beliefs about the world, while not strictly provable rationally, are nonetheless so fundamental to our way of thinking as to be impossible to reject. Reid's point is that although it is possible (in one's theoretical moods) to raise doubts about the basic beliefs of common sense, they are not *doubt-worthy*, nor could anyone doubt them consistently.

The assumptions of common sense are so basic to our lives that it is pointless to doubt them. They constitute the very fabric of our belief system, and the merest possibility of being mistaken about them does not give us good reason to doubt them. In the absence of any good reason or evidence for us to doubt them, we are justified in continuing to believe them.

> *To what purpose is it for philosophy to decide against common sense in this or any other matter? The belief of a material world is older, and of more authority, than any principles of philosophy. It declines the tribunal of reason, and laughs at all the artillery of the logician.*[25]

Experimenting with ideas

Armed with the tools we have considered for defeating or moderating scepticism, consider the three sceptical arguments A–C. How might you defeat them? In constructing your case against these arguments, consider the following points:

1   How might the arguments be self-defeating?
2   Do they trade on a distinction which they go on to deny?
3   Do they presuppose knowledge, which they go on to claim is impossible?
4   Do they depart from the ordinary use of language?
5   Do they go against the basic tenets of common sense?

A The light coming from the sun takes about six minutes to reach us. So what you are seeing when you glance up at the sun is actually an image of the sun as it was six minutes ago, not as it is now. So, it could be that the sun exploded five minutes ago and that what you are seeing no longer exists. Worse still, the same must go for the ordinary objects you see around you. For the light reflected from them takes some time to reach you, and in the interim they may have ceased to exist. It follows that you cannot know that anything you see around you exists.

B How can we be sure that any of the evidence we have about the past is reliable? Indeed, it is conceivable that the world came into existence only yesterday, complete with apparent memories, history books and fossil records, all as a cosmic prank made up by some unthinkably powerful deity. Since we cannot know that this has not happened, we cannot have knowledge of the past.[26]

C We are becoming better and better at creating computers that can simulate reality. Virtual reality is often indistinguishable from the real thing. As our wizardry increases in sophistication, we can expect virtual reality machines to be able to mimic more and more aspects of our lives. Indeed, one day it may well be possible for the whole of one's life to be reproduced by some very fancy virtual reality machine. If this happened, once you were plugged into the machine, you would no longer be able to tell the difference between living a virtual life and living a real life. But if this is right, then this may already have happened. Perhaps your life is not real, but part of a virtual reality program created just for you. But if this is possible, then you cannot be sure that any of your life is real.

Reliabilism as a response to scepticism

In our discussion of the concept of knowledge on page 31, we saw that according to reliabilism, the subject of knowledge (S) knows a proposition (p) just if they hold a belief that is true and that is arrived at by a process which is reliable. Acquiring a true belief by luck – for example, by guessing because of wishful thinking – cannot count as knowledge, and this suggests that the belief needs to be produced in an appropriate way – in other words, in a way that reliably produces true beliefs. So, for example, according to reliabilism, an expert mushroom collector may know that a certain mushroom is edible just if she employs her senses and the identification techniques she has learned properly, since these have proved to reliably produce true beliefs about mushrooms. (Now, the expert may make a mistake and be poisoned, but then this does not count as knowledge either, because the belief turned out to be false.) If, however, I, who have little experience of mushroom collecting, assume a mushroom is edible just because it looks like the ones in the supermarket, even if I (luckily) turn out to be right, because my belief-forming process is not reliable, I cannot be said to have knowledge.

So, reliabilism rejects the traditional view of justification, which says that that knowledge requires the knower to be able to provide evidence or reasons for their belief for it to count as knowledge. As long as the process which produces a belief reliably produces *true* beliefs, then it is to count as knowledge, irrespective of whether I am aware that the process is reliable or that I can provide any justification for my belief. If I collect mushrooms based on techniques handed down by my grandmother – avoid those that stain blue when you cut them, avoid those with white gills or which produce a burning sensation when pressed to your lips and so on – then I may be said to have knowledge that a certain mushroom is edible, just if these techniques reliably identify edible mushrooms. What I do not need to be able to do is explain why these techniques work. I may have no understanding of toxicology and no knowledge of the science of mycology. And I may not be able to justify my faith that my senses are not deceiving me. Just as long as they are reliable, then I can have knowledge. This is why reliabilism is called an externalist account of the nature of knowledge. For there need be no internal or conscious process that I can access by which to defend a belief for it to count as knowledge.

Considerations in favour of rejecting the internalist justification condition include the fact that we may want to accept that we often have knowledge, even though we may not be able to give any account of how we know. For example, I may rightly claim to know that the Battle of Hastings took place in 1066, but have no clue as to how to defend this claim, as I know nothing else of English history. Nor can I recall any reliable source from which I may have obtained this information. Nonetheless, unbeknownst to me, I may well have come about this information via a reliable process – perhaps I gained the belief from a teacher at school, who in turn read about it from a conscientious historian who had studied the archive material which ultimately led back via a complex causal route to the original event. Thus the process which ultimately caused my belief may have been a reliable one and so should count as knowledge. Consider again my mushroom-collecting grandmother. Suppose she has never been able to explain how she identifies safe mushrooms, but nonetheless has unerringly done so all her life. According to reliabilism, we can say she knows the safe from the unsafe mushrooms because her identification process is reliable, even though she may have no idea what she does or why it works.

Using reliabilism to overcome scepticism

Now, how can this account of knowledge help us to overcome scepticism? Well, sceptical arguments try to show that a necessary condition for knowledge cannot be established. For example, the infinite regress argument maintained that we need to be able to give a justification for any belief we claim as knowledge, but then pointed out that the justification itself needed to count as knowledge. This then leads to an infinite regress, meaning that we seem incapable of giving any of our beliefs an ultimate justification and so cannot know anything. However, reliabilists deny that we need to be able to provide a justification for our beliefs, so the sceptical argument does not get off the ground. I can know that a mushroom is edible, just if my belief is produced through a reliable process, even though I may be unable to offer any coherent justification for my belief.

The other sceptical arguments we have been looking at say that we cannot have knowledge of the external world because the evidence of the senses is unreliable and so cannot provide a sufficient justification for our beliefs. If I cannot provide conclusive evidence to show that my senses are not subject to an illusion, or that I am not now dreaming, then this undermines my claim to know propositions about the physical world. However, reliabilism says that being able to provide an internalist justification for my knowledge claims is not necessary for me to have knowledge. Beliefs can count as knowledge even if we are unable to provide a cogent defence of our belief. The reliabilist response to the sceptical challenge is to say that it may well be the case that I cannot give sufficient reasons to believe a proposition, yet I may still have knowledge, so long as the belief is true and produced in the right kind of way – a way that generally produces true beliefs. So, if my senses are reliable most of the time, if I have reliable techniques for identifying when I am awake, then I can be said to have knowledge of true beliefs formed through the senses when I am awake. The key point here is that the force of the sceptic's argument relies on the assumption that I must be able to know that I know before I can be said to know, or failing this, at least that one has some conscious access to the reasons that would justify the knowledge claim. If we deny this needs to be the case, then the force of the sceptical arguments is blunted.

But what of the kind of global scepticism presented by the evil demon or brain in the vat scenarios? The sceptic claims that the evidence from the senses is compatible with my being a brain in a vat, and so that I cannot know that I am not a brain in a vat. The sceptic concludes that I cannot know that my body or the physical universe exists. However, as far as reliabilism is concerned, although I cannot tell simply by inspecting my own sense experience whether or not I am a brain in a vat, this does not show that I do not have knowledge of the physical world. For if I am not a brain in a vat, then my beliefs about the physical world are produced by a reliable process, and so count as knowledge. And if they count as knowledge, then it follows that I am not a brain in a vat. Notice that if reliabilism is right, then I can know that I am not a brain in a vat, just if the beliefs I have about the reality of physical objects around me are produced by a reliable causal process. I may not be able to provide evidence of this myself, so I cannot necessarily know *that* I have knowledge here, but nonetheless I may still have such knowledge. In other words, I do not have to be able to prove I am not a brain in a vat in order to know that the physical world exists (contrary to standard definitions of knowledge).

Conclusion

In this chapter, we have looked at how the philosophical sceptic casts doubt on knowledge claims, and at different strategies for resisting or defeating scepticism. An important lesson to draw from all this is that the battle with scepticism is fought on a continuum between, on the one hand, the blind acceptance of beliefs, and on the other, an extreme scepticism in which very few, if any, beliefs are accepted. If we are extremely gullible, we will believe all kinds of things, and so have a large stock of beliefs. But gullibility is not a very sensible strategy in life or in philosophy. If we believe things on very little evidence, then much of what we believe will inevitably be false. On the other hand, if we are overly sceptical, and refuse to believe things that are even slightly doubtful, then we will end up believing very little. This is equally impractical as a strategy. If I harbour doubts about the reality of my body, or refuse to believe that the world will continue to obey the basic laws of physics, I will be unable to step out of my front door for fear that my legs may melt away beneath me, or that the pavement may turn into blancmange. And the philosopher who refuses to believe anything ends up an incurable sceptic with a failed epistemology. So, it seems, in order to get on, we need to decide where to operate on this continuum. How sceptical should we be? Where should we draw the line?

Figure 1.45 How sceptical should we be? There is a continuum between the extremely sceptical and the extremely gullible. The more gullible one is, the more beliefs one can hold; the more sceptical, the fewer. We have to decide whereabouts on this continuum we should arrest the sceptic.

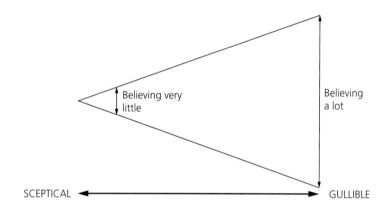

Chapter summary

In this chapter, we began by exploring the differences between scepticism in philosophy and scepticism in everyday life. Philosophical scepticism is essentially a tool by which philosophers test their knowledge claims and how well they are justified, and try to determine what we can and cannot know. We examined a range of sceptical arguments, some of which led to the global sceptical conclusion that no beliefs can be properly justified, and so that we are incapable of acquiring genuine knowledge. Foundationalism is the traditional reaction to such scepticism. It is the view that there must be certain basic beliefs that justify themselves and in terms of which all other beliefs are justified. Descartes' *cogito* argument, for example, appears to establish one's own existence beyond any possibility of doubt. Descartes hoped he could find further indubitable beliefs and so defeat the sceptic once and for all.

However, there are difficulties with Descartes' efforts to establish a body of indubitable truths in the face of radical scepticism. One central problem is that global scepticism appears self-defeating, as one cannot consistently doubt all of one's beliefs at once, doubt the nature of doubt itself, or doubt one's capacity to reason without undermining any chance we may have of developing an epistemology. So we explored alternative accounts of how scepticism can be resisted. Empiricist philosophers such as Locke, Hume and Russell try to limit scepticism by accepting that we can have knowledge without certainty. Berkeley takes an alternative route and, by collapsing the distinction between appearance and reality, hopes to show that we can have unmediated access to the external world. Ordinary language philosophers and philosophers of common sense try to defend our everyday belief system against the sceptic, claiming that it is more reasonable to believe what we ordinarily reckon is true than to allow the sceptic to persuade us that we actually know very little. Finally, we returned to reliabilism to see how an alternative definition of 'knowledge' may allow us to overcome scepticism. If we do not need to be able to justify our knowledge claims for them to count as knowledge, but only arrive at them via a reliable process, then we may know a good deal.

2.1 Introduction to ethics: how do we decide what it is morally right to do?

We *all* want to do the RIGHT thing, surely? Do we not? Well, maybe you do, maybe you do not. The problem is, though, what *is* the right thing to do? *Do not steal, do not lie, eat your greens, do not speak back, be honest, clean behind your ears* and so on. There is no shortage of advice for what the right thing might be, from parents, friends, teachers, preachers, politicians and celebrities (among others).

Ethics is the branch of philosophy that explores what the right thing to do might be. This section will explore several ethical systems that attempt this project. In ordinary language, and in many textbooks, the word *morality* is sometimes used instead of *ethics*. Indeed, in the world of philosophy, *ethics* is sometimes called MORAL PHILOSOPHY. The distinction between morality and ethics is not very clear, nor is it very important. The term *morality* tends to be associated more with an individual's beliefs about right and wrong, whereas *ethics* is more associated with systems that articulate right and wrong. However, this distinction is not universally held and often the two terms are used synonymously. We will also use the terms 'MORAL PHILOSOPHY' and 'ETHICS' interchangeably.

As a topic to study, moral philosophy is not just of 'philosophical' relevance; it also has a clear, practical application. There are times in everyone's life when they face big ethical dilemmas: should you put your ageing mother in a care home? Should you lend a large sum of money to a friend in need? Other ethical dilemmas may be encountered on a more regular basis: should I buy free-range eggs? Should I recycle? It can be argued that ethical dilemmas surround us at every moment, although we may not be consciously aware of them. Should I study a bit harder? Should I speak to Zach after what he said? Should I look at this picture of a semi-naked person? What should I do with my life? Studying ethics should shine some light on these and other questions. At the very least, it should help to clarify your thinking.

Ethics and the self: the scope of morality

Experimenting with ideas: the wipe-out

Imagine humanity has succumbed to a deadly virus and you are the only person left in the world. You survived because you were alone on a remote desert island at the time, as part of a soul-searching retreat. Does this new situation change the ethical world you inhabit? You might still face lots of dilemmas in your life: should I sleep in a cave or on the beach tonight? Should I keep myself fit? Should I have one more coconut before bedtime? Tough choices! However, would these count as *moral* dilemmas?

Imagine you are the last person on earth.

- Would you have any clear-cut ethical dilemmas?
- Would there be anything morally wrong with just following your desires all the time?
- Could you do anything morally wrong?
- Is morality a human invention?
- Do the terms 'good' and 'bad' only have meaning in a society?
- There are monkeys on the island. Would you kill and eat them?

It is not easy to answer these questions without already having an account of what an ethical action is. Maybe it is possible to do wrong as the last surviving human: perhaps self-harm? Blaspheming? Having nasty thoughts? Hurting the animals? Some would argue that you still face the key decision about how you *ought* to live your life. Yes, you want to eat nice food and stay alive, but what would you ultimately aim for? Pleasure? Self-improvement? Trying to help the animals? Morality in the widest sense includes this big question of what you should pursue in life. If this fundamental decision is a moral one, this, in turn, makes most actions morally relevant.

Ethics and others

Experimenting with ideas: the wipe-out revisited

Imagine that after two years of living alone on the island, with no one but Ruffles, your faithful parrot, to talk to, a large boat arrives carrying four people. These people were at sea when the virus struck and have survived all this time on the ship's resources. They are severely malnourished and are pleased to be on dry land. They are also insistent that you have to kill all the birds on the island, as they can spread the deadly virus.

- Would you welcome these people?
- Would you have any ethical dilemmas going forward?
- Would there be anything morally wrong with just following your desires all the time now?
- Could you do anything morally wrong?
- Would you be willing to kill Ruffles, your parrot?

Most people would suggest that with the arrival of more people, your ethical universe expanded. This is to be expected, as ethics, in the narrower sense, can be seen as how we *should* interact with others. These new people on the island have desires too and these may conflict with yours. You may have to modify your behaviour.

Character and virtue

After two years alone, your behaviour would no doubt be different from how it was before the virus struck. Your table manners may have lapsed a bit. You may not take much pride in your physical appearance. Your conversation may be very limited. Growing up in civilisation, through training, education and habit, you would have acquired certain ways of behaving. Some of these might be good (VIRTUES), some might be less good (VICES). However, it is likely that many of these habits have changed since you have been alone. Another feature of the strangers arriving on the island is that you may have to redevelop some characteristics (or acquire them if you never had them to begin with) in order to interact well. You may have to make yourself polite, or a better listener.

Figure 2.1 The three levels of ethics. (A) Meta-ethics asks questions about morality itself. (B) Normative ethics seeks to answer questions about good and bad in general. (C) Applied ethics works out how to apply the answer from (B) to specific cases.

Three levels of ethical discussion

Some of the questions we asked above probe different aspects of ethics. Traditionally, these are divided into three areas. One area explores what makes for morally good and bad behaviour in general. What are the underlying reasons why we might call an action a GOOD one? This area is known as NORMATIVE ETHICS. A second area applies the answers from the first area to very specific MORAL DILEMMAS. This area is known as APPLIED ETHICS. A third area takes a step back from the discussions above and, instead, focuses the attention on moral discussion itself, asking questions such as: *is morality a human construction? Do moral words have meanings?* This area is known as META-ETHICS.

This section explores all three areas of ethical thought. The first chapters examine some of the big normative theories of ethics – UTILITARIANISM, KANTIAN ETHICS and VIRTUE ETHICS. The last part of each of these chapters applies these theories to a series of specific topics and dilemmas (PRACTIC AL ethics or applied ethics). The final part explores some of the key questions of meta-ethics.

Normative ethics: different approaches

The bulk of this section is devoted to examining three key ethical theories. These theories differ in several ways, but a key distinction is that they focus on different aspects of what might make an action a *moral* one. Some actions in life clearly belong in the moral arena (*stealing* or *lying* and so on), whereas others do not appear to have any moral relevance (*scratching your ear* or *staring at the extra full stop at the end of this sentence*).. So what makes an action a moral one (good *or* bad), as opposed to a morally neutral one (PRACTICAL ethics or neither good nor bad)?

Experimenting with ideas

For each of the ten scenarios A–J below:

1   Decide if it is morally relevant (good or bad) or morally neutral.

2   For those that are morally relevant, decide what makes the scenario a moral one.

3   For those that are morally neutral, decide what makes it neutral.

A   A deer is caught in a forest fire caused by a freak lightning strike and is burnt to death.

B   A killer whale toys with a seal that it has half-killed – batting it into the air with its tail and catching it with its teeth. It takes 20 minutes before the seal finally dies. The whale leaves it to rot on the ocean floor.

C   You deliberately step on someone's toe in a lift but pretend it was an accident.

D   You accidentally poison your neighbour's dog.

E   You beat your friend in an ant-killing competition (with a winning combination of bleach and boiling water).

F   You persistently bullied a classmate at school.

G   You successfully pass the ball to members of your team 15 times in a 1-1 draw at a friendly local hockey match.

H   An orphanage is set up to help victims in a war-torn country.

I   You stop to help a blind man cross the road, but fail to notice the unstoppable juggernaut that injures you both.

J   An evil scientist releases a new biochemical into the water supply of a large city, intending to kill millions. However, this agent, when diluted, turns out to be a harmless cure for cancer and countless lives are saved.

▶ **ACTIVITY**

Revisit the questions in the 'wipe-out' scenarios on pages 198–199.

Which questions belong to the area of normative ethics, which to applied ethics and which to meta-ethics?

Many would label scenarios A and B as morally neutral, as neither event was caused by a moral **AGENT** – a being with sufficient awareness to carry out moral actions. In this way, we do not hold very young children, or those with severe brain damage, morally responsible for their actions – as they are not moral agents. Scenarios C and D explore the idea of intentions. Not only do you need an agent, but most would claim that to make an act a moral one, the agent must have intended to do the act. Situations E and F seem to have agents with intentions, but the question of morality may hinge on what you classify as a moral patient (that is, a thing capable of being at the end of moral actions). For some, this would not include ants. Scenarios G and H involve intentional agents and patients, but explore the idea that the consequences of an action may dictate whether it is moral or not. Scenario H involves helping the suffering, whereas scenario G does not seem to have any morally relevant consequences. Finally, scenarios I and J involve intentional agents, patients and relevant consequences, but explore the idea that the motive (the nature of the intention) is the key factor.

Overall, the key features that seem to make an action a *moral* one are:

- AGENCY
- intentions/motives
- consequences
- moral patients.

Each of the three theories of normative ethics examined in this chapter puts a different emphasis on these features:

- Utilitarianism claims that the consequence of an action is the important element. Only the consequences determine the moral worth of an action (that is, whether it was good or bad).
- For Kant, motive is the key. Only actions carried out for the right motive have moral worth; the consequences are irrelevant.
- For virtue ethics, it is the agent and their character that is key. As we briefly explored in the virus scenario, having new people come to the island may require you to (re)develop virtues in order to be a good person. For virtue ethics, the character of the PERSON/agent is the key, not specific actions.

Intuitions

Each of the theories we explore will tell us what is good or bad; however, you will already have your own thoughts on these issues. We all have moral intuitions. The status of these intuitions is itself an area of philosophical discussion (which we will not go into) and these intuitions will play an important part in the examination of the theories that follow. We should not expect an ethical theory to match your intuitions *exactly*, but if a theory claims that certain actions are good, whereas you completely disagree, then this presents a problem. Do you ditch your intuitions and go with the theory? Or should you try to modify the theory to better match your intuitions? A theory that strays too far from intuitions will never have appeal, but a theory that resembles them too closely can be seen as supporting the status quo, rather than aiming for a better world. Probably the most significant ethical philosopher alive today is the Australian,

Peter Singer (1946–). His claims frequently challenge people's intuitions, but he makes no apology for this:

> *If we have a soundly based moral theory we ought to be prepared to accept its implications even if they force us to change our moral view on major issues. Once this point is forgotten, moral philosophy loses its capacity to generate radical criticism of prevailing moral standards, and serves only to preserve the status quo.[1]*

Moral dilemmas

Before exploring any of the three ethical theories, read the scenarios in the Activities below and make a note of what your intuitions tell you. Note, we will return to these scenarios after exploring each theory and you can compare the results to your intuitions. Maybe your ideas will change as a result, or maybe you will reject each theory as not matching up to your own moral ideals.

Stealing

Ethics has a close association with crime (and punishment). The morality of a society is often reflected in what is classed as a criminal offence, and the law slowly changes to reflect the evolving moral climate (often lagging behind). For example, homosexual sex was punishable by death in the UK 150 years ago, but now has the same legal status as heterosexual sex.

Though laws change over time, some have remained fairly constant. The oldest record of laws (around 2000 BCE) comes from the Sumerian civilisation of Mesopotamia (roughly where Syria and Iraq are today). The first two laws are:

1 If a man commits a murder, that man must be killed.
2 If a man commits a robbery, he will be killed.

Theft is one of the oldest crimes known to man, though the sentencing has softened a little over time. That said, as recently as 200 years ago there were hundreds of offences that were punishable by death in the UK (including 'being in the company of Gypsies for one month'). A large proportion of these offences were for stealing of one kind or another, from pickpocketing through to poaching. Critics saw these laws as being made by the wealthy for the protection of the wealthy.

Wealth and property have always been political issues. Even today, half of Scotland (in terms of land) is owned by less than 500 people, often the result of gifts to individuals made by non-democratic, despotic kings, and subsequently handed down from generation to generation. Is this fair? Should one person be able to 'own' so much of the earth that we are all born on? The French anarchist Pierre-Joseph Proudhon (1809–65) went as far as to declare that all 'Property is theft!'

It is a catchy slogan, but we all like our possessions – even most anarchists. It is hard to imagine someone stealing your possessions and you being morally fine with it. But is stealing always *morally* wrong and, if so, what makes it morally wrong?

Might some types of stealing even be morally justified? Perhaps if a law was unfair, and you feel that justice is better served by stealing? Perhaps when you believe that the theft is completely 'victimless'?

▶ **ACTIVITY**

Test your moral intuitions on these two fictional scenarios.

ST1 (This example is adapted from Lawrence Kohlberg's famous Heinz dilemma.[2]) Your partner has liver cancer. The chances of survival are 50 per cent at best. For the last few months, your partner has been on a new medication, Tastaphon, which seemed to be helping. Last week, the NHS decided to stop using Tastaphon as the results are inconclusive and, at £30,000 a year per patient, it is deemed too expensive. Since ending the medication, your partner has deteriorated. You cannot afford to buy the drug privately. This evening a friend, who works on the cancer wing of the hospital, is staying over at your house to help. You notice that their hospital pass and keys are on the table. You know the hospital well, and where the drugs are kept. There is a very good chance that you could get hold of lots of Tastaphon this evening, while the cancer wing is quiet. *Should you steal the drug?*

ST2 File sharing is just so easy, innit? Nathan, over the years, has acquired over 2,000 albums and not paid a penny for the privilege. Most of the music is from artists who are already very wealthy. But this is not always the case. What Nathan is doing is illegal, *but is it immoral?*

Simulated killing (within computer games, plays, films)

Violence in films, in plays and on television has become a common source of public outrage. Since the 1980s, the outrage has been increasingly focused on video games, particularly those that place the ability to violently kill in the hands of the player. No one is being hurt when playing these games and no RIGHTS seem to be infringed, yet the games have produced moral outrage. Some feel that gaining pleasure in this way is morally dubious; others believe that the games may have negative effects on the player, and, in turn, on society. Both video games and violent films have been blamed in a large number of killings and massacres; for example, the Columbine High School massacre (1999) was linked to the killers' obsession with the game *Doom*; also, the film *A Clockwork Orange* (1972) was withdrawn from release in the UK by its director, Stanley Kubrick, after several copycat events of 'ultra-violence'.

But on the other hand, such moral outrages have been commonplace in history. From the ancient Greeks to today, older generations have a well-documented tendency to look at the pastimes of the youth and believe that the world is getting worse.

▶ **ACTIVITY**

Test your moral intuitions on these two fictional scenarios.

Read the following fictional scenarios and see what your intuitions tell you.

SK1 *Crime Spree 6* involves stealing cars and causing mayhem in a 'free to wander' world, while vaguely engaging with a plot. A team of underground programmers have taken the programme's engine and spent a lot of time releasing an altered version. In this version – called *Psycho-Tick* – you have a limited time and score points for each killing you inflict, with extra points for killing children and the elderly. You only have a baseball bat and a screwdriver as your weapons. *Is it morally wrong to play* Psycho-Tick?

SK2 The latest use of technology at the Théâtre National has seen the introduction of 'Feelies' (predicted by Aldous Huxley in *Brave New World*). Audiences sit in rows of special chairs, wearing hooded suits and visors that are networked into the actors on stage. Everything the actors see, feel and touch, the audience also sees, feels and touches. The Théâtre National has decided to launch this technology with a new performance of *Oedipus-X* by the late playwright Susan Cain. This revival has been the most successful play in the history of the theatre. Audiences have queued round the block to witness this contemporary Greek tragedy – thrilled to experience for themselves the blood-soaked suicide of the queen, the horrific self-blinding of Oedipus and the murderous slaughter of the king. The production's tag line says it all: 'Ever wondered what it's like to kill someone … well now you'll know.' *Is it morally wrong to enjoy watching and experiencing a dramatised murder?*

Eating animals

The moral status of animals has long been a source of philosophical controversy. In the UK, around 4 million people are vegetarian, with the numbers in the 14–16 age bracket being particularly high (up to 20 per cent in some surveys). Many of these people are vegetarian for moral reasons. Many meat-eaters also find the treatment of animals in factory farms shocking and repulsive, though not necessarily wrong. But even non-vegetarians would find the deliberate and slow torture of a dog, or horse, to be morally wrong. So, what moral status should we accord to animals? You may have well-rehearsed moral views on these issues already.

▶ **ACTIVITY**

Test your moral beliefs against the scenarios below.

EA1 Every day, millions of chickens are born into complete darkness. They have been selectively bred to the point where many grow so quickly that they cannot stand. The conditions are so cramped that many cannot move. After 40 days of this existence (chickens normally live for seven years) the chicken is killed for its meat, having never seen grass, felt sunshine or been comforted by a mother. *Is it wrong to eat chickens that are reared this way?*

EA2 I am Gilbert. After 15 years as a merchant banker, I escaped the city and now run a free-range, organic cattle farm. The cows have both shelter and the great outdoors. Yes, I know that the people from PETA still make noise about overcrowding and overfeeding, and calves being taken from their mothers. And that on organic farms, medicines and antibiotics cannot be used if the animal is suffering. But compared to the majority of farms in the world, my cows have a much better life. *Is it morally okay to eat Gilbert's cows?* As an additional thought, what if Gilbert were running a free-range ape farm, raising great apes to eventually be sold as meat. *Would it be morally okay to eat these apes?*

Telling of lies

This sentence tells at least one lie.

Well … does it? … Not sure? On the face of it, it does not seem to tell any lies. But if it does not tell a lie and it says that it does, then surely *that* is the lie! So it does tell a lie after all! But if it does tell a lie, and it says it tells a lie, then it appears to be telling the truth, there is no lie after all. But this would mean that there is a lie, as the sentence claims there is one …

Still here? To free you from your thoughts, the sentence is a paradox: a proposition whose truth implies its falsity and whose falsity implies its truth. There is no easy way out of this one.

What is the point of putting it in the book? Well, it is here, (a) to keep you concentrating, (b) to warn you that lying does not just get you into ordinary trouble, it can get you into logical trouble too, and (c) the section on lying does not really need an introduction. After all, we have all been there! In fact, thinking about your day so far, have you lied to anyone? Have you deceived anyone? Be honest!

But what would you do in the following two scenarios?

► **ACTIVITY**

Read the following fictional scenarios and see what your intuitions tell you.

TL1 Shelly has been married to Jacob for 25 years. They have three children and live a supposedly good life. But Jacob has been an absent husband – he has worked away from home for most of his career, and for much of the year he plays golf at the weekend. He is nice enough, but has done very little to help around the house, or raise the children, or show much love or affection to Shelly. Their children have long since grown up and moved away and Shelly is desperately lonely. Recently, Shelly has fallen in love with a neighbour who has shown her genuine kindness and taken an interest in her concerns and her hopes – they have talked about getting married. Jacob has noticed Shelly is anxious and suggests that she has a weekend away with a friend, as a treat. Shelly has asked the neighbour to join her, and when Jacob asked who she was going with, Shelly lied and said it was with one of her old school friends. *Is it wrong for Shelly to explore this new relationship? Was it wrong for Shelly not to tell the truth?*

TL2 You answer the door to your friend Bob. He takes off his muddy boots outside, rushes into the kitchen and slams the door, shouting, 'Do not tell anyone I am here!' A few minutes later, there is another knock at the door. It is a man with an axe in his hand, explaining that he is knocking on all the doors in the street looking for someone. He is sweating and panting and looking very agitated. As he swings his axe from one hand to the other, he explains that he is very keen to find this man and that he just has a couple of questions to ask him. He asks you if a man wearing muddy boots has just come into your house. Bob was not wearing his boots when he came into your house, so you say, 'No'. *Have you told a lie? Should you now tell the truth about where Bob is? (Why? Why not?)*

We revisit each of these dilemmas (ST1, ST2; SK1, SK2; EA1, EA2; TL1, TL2) when we apply three normative ethical theories to these situations: utilitarianism (page 212), Kantian ethics (page 284) and Aristotelian ethics (page 349).

2.1.1 Utilitarianism

Introduction

On page 198 we asked you to imagine you were alone on a desert island. How would you behave? Could you be immoral? Many people would try to look after their basic welfare needs – food, shelter, warmth and so on. But after these had been established, what would you do? Perhaps you would try to enjoy yourself: go swimming, train a parrot, work on some new coconut recipes. In other words, you would try to seek pleasure or happiness. Of course, things will get more complicated when more survivors join you on the island and they too seek happiness. Sometimes compromises will be needed. Utilitarianism is an ethical theory based around the idea that trying to maximise happiness is the right thing to do.

Utility

The word utilitarianism is derived from the idea of UTILITY or usefulness. In general, any object or action is useful only in so much as it helps us achieve a specific goal (or goals). Is a stone useful? Does it have utility? The only way in which it might be is if you can think of a goal or purpose that it could be used for (such as breaking a window). A bottle opener is only useful because we sometimes want to open bottles. If we never wanted to open a bottle, or bottles had never been invented, then a bottle opener would not have much usefulness or utility.

I might invent a unicorn whistle – which attracts only unicorns. But this has little use/utility, as there are no unicorns. However, if the whistle also attracted horses, then it might have a use. The same is true with actions. If a bath plug becomes wedged, I might try to empty out the bath water using a sieve. But, however well-intentioned, given my goal, the action would have little utility.

So an object, or an action, has utility if it helps to bring about something we want/are aiming for. Note that for objects and actions to have utility, we must have goals and desires in the first place. But how many different goals do we really have in life? Consider this example.

The other day I found myself walking down the street. What was the purpose of this? Did my walk have any use/utility? It could be that I enjoy walking as an end in itself and so this was the purpose/use, but on this occasion I was walking to get to a shop. My walk had utility in as much as it got me to the shop. But why stop our analysis here? What was the purpose of going to the shop? Well, I went to the shop to buy a razor. So my walk really only had utility in as much as it helped me to get a razor. But why did I want to buy a razor? I wanted to buy a razor because I wanted to shave. But why did I want to shave? It could have been because I wanted to 'look smart' or impress someone, but in truth it was because my beard had become very itchy and I just could not stand it anymore. But why did I want to stop myself itching? It could be that our explanation ends here – wanting to stop an irritation or pain is an end itself, rather than just a stage or means to reaching a further aim or end.

What was the ultimate aim of this walk? This analysis of a simple action suggests that the goals of reaching a shop and of buying a razor were not the ultimate ends or purpose of my action (walking). The ultimate purpose was to stop an itch. The walking and the buying of a razor, however well-intentioned, had no utility unless they did help me to stop the itch. If the shop had been shut, I would have been wasting my time. Luckily, the shop was open and the plan worked, so my action of walking had utility.

Can all actions be analysed like this? And, if so, what are the ultimate ends of our actions?

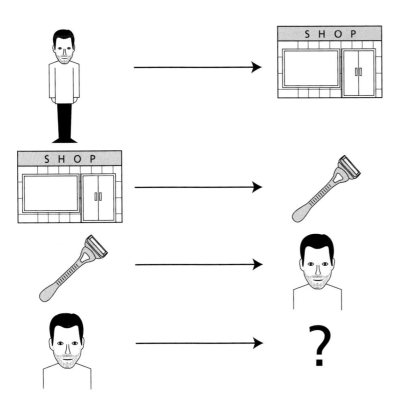

Figure 2.2 What is the ultimate aim of the walk to the shop?

Experimenting with ideas: what are your ultimate goals?

For each of the activities below, attempt to work out the ultimate end for the action. To do this, take one of the initial actions from below and insert it as X into one of the following formulae.

I did X in order to Y

or

I did X so that I could Y

Then use Y as the new X and repeat using one of the formulae. Repeat this until you reach a circle/or a clear goal that is an end in itself and not just a means to some other end.

- I got out of bed …
- I ate my breakfast …
- I read this philosophy book …
- I cleaned my teeth …
- I bought my friend/family member a present …
- I gave money to Greenpeace/Save the Children …

Did you find that some of the ends were the same in the activity above? Perhaps to gain knowledge or to make someone else feel good or for your own pleasure? For classic utilitarians, such as Jeremy Bentham (see below) and John Stuart Mill (see page 213), the ultimate aim of our action is pleasure (which they equate to happiness). The idea that pleasure is the ultimate goal is at the heart of three different, but related theories:

- *Psychological hedonism*. This is not a moral theory, but a DESCRIPTIVE theory of human motivation. It claims that the individual's potential pleasure and the avoidance of pain are the sole aims of the individual's action (HEDONISM comes from the Greek work *hedone*, which means 'pleasure').
- *Hedonism*. This is a moral theory which claims that for each individual, pursuing pleasure and avoiding pain is the right thing to do. One *ought* to seek pleasure. This theory has its roots in ancient Greek philosophy. Some writers also refer to the *paradox of hedonism*, which is the loose claim that the more a person pursues pleasure, the harder it is to obtain.
- *Classic (or hedonistic) utilitarianism*. This is a moral theory that claims that a right action is one that increases the general happiness (not just the individual's).

Figure 2.3 Three related theories.
The three theories all relate to pleasure/happiness, but in different ways.

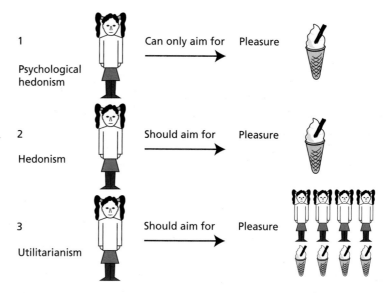

In this section, we will be exploring utilitarianism. Some utilitarians, such as Jeremy Bentham, also believed in psychological hedonism and used this to justify the theory of utilitarianism. However, it is not clear that psychological hedonism and utilitarianism need to go together. It may be possible to believe in one without the other. Indeed, believing in both together can generate some philosophical problems. For if you believe that humans *are* motivated solely by their own pleasure and pain (psychological hedonism), then what is the point in telling them that they *ought* to maximise the general happiness (utilitarianism), when they are, in fact, only capable of maximising their own?

Jeremy Bentham

The moral theory of utilitarianism has roots which go back to the early Greeks; however, its first formal articulation was in the work of Jeremy Bentham. Bentham (1748–1832) was a member of a group of thinkers known as the British philosophical radicals, who wished to transform the British legal, parliamentary and penal systems. He was a child prodigy (he went to Oxford at the age of 12) and went on to engage in a wide range of political and philosophical issues. These included designing a prison (which was never built) and helping to found University College London (UCL) – England's first non-religious university and the first to treat female students equally. After his death, Bentham's body was specially preserved and dressed, and can still be seen sitting in a corner of UCL today. He is even wheeled out to attend the occasional meeting!

Jeremy Bentham lived in London at a time of rising population and widespread poverty. In the absence of a police force, alleged criminals were often rounded up on the words of informants or victims, and sentencing was swift and harsh. Over 200 crimes carried the death penalty – including the chopping down of trees and even the theft of rabbits. With overcrowded prisons, many were sent on prison ships to America or Australia for fairly minor offences. Bentham thought that the criminal justice system was harsh, arbitrary and unjust. He campaigned to reform it. In his seminal utilitarian work, *An Introduction to the Principle of Morals and Legislation* (1780), Bentham attempted to provide a rational underpinning to the justice system. To do this, he outlined the theory of utilitarianism, which he then applied to ideas of punishment and sentencing.

Bentham wanted to fix criminal justice system

anthology 2.1

His book begins with powerful and poetic claims (a longer extract is included in the Anthology).

Nature has placed mankind under the governance of two sovereign masters, pain and pleasure. It is for them alone to point out what we ought to do, as well as to determine what we shall do. On the one hand the standard of right and wrong, on the other the chain of causes and effects, are fastened to their throne. They govern us in all we do, in all we say, in all we think: every effort we can make to throw off our subjection, will serve but to demonstrate and confirm it.[1]

In the first sentence, Bentham proposes that pain (avoiding it) and pleasure are our two masters. In the second sentence, he puts forward both a descriptive and a PRESCRIPTIVE theory. He claims that avoiding pain and seeking pleasure are the ends of human action (psychological hedonism) and also suggests that pain and pleasure can form the basis of an ethical or prescriptive theory – utilitarianism. This is the theory that suggests that bringing about pleasure and avoiding pain is the right thing to do.

Utilitarianism: maximising utility

According to Bentham's reasoning, if psychological hedonism is true, and our actions are aimed at pleasure and avoiding pain, then the only reasonable moral theory is one that seeks to make such actions as consistent and effective as possible. In other words, we must follow a moral system that invokes us to maximise happiness and minimise pain – for both the individual and the sum of individuals in a community. This is the UTILITY PRINCIPLE.

Earlier we saw that an object is useful (has utility) if it helps to bring about a specific goal. Bentham claims that pleasure (which he also equates with happiness) and the avoidance of pain are the goals we pursue. As such, any action has utility if it helps to bring about pleasure/happiness or the avoidance of pain. When we consider the effects of actions not just on ourselves, but on others too, we can then judge how much utility an action has by seeing how much more happiness than pain it brings into the world. If an action does this, then Bentham says that this is what we mean by a good act. The more an action brings about happiness, the more it maximises utility, the more moral worth it has.

Bentham states his principle slightly differently throughout his writings, although the same point (more or less) is being made.

An action then may be said to be conformable to the principle of utility, or, for shortness sake, to utility, (meaning with respect to the community at large) when the tendency it has to augment the happiness of the community is greater than any it has to diminish it.[2]

... it is the greatest happiness of the greatest number that is the measure of right and wrong.[3]

Bentham claims that morally good actions are those that bring about happiness, and morally bad actions are those that bring about more pain than pleasure. He claims that this principle – which is variously called the *utility principle*, the *greatest happiness principle* or *utilitarianism* – not only is the correct system of ethics, but is also the principle underlying all other systems.

In other words, all other systems of moral rules (including Christianity) are really just striving to bring about general happiness and the avoidance of pain.

Bentham's utility calculus

Bentham offers us a guide as to how we are supposed to apply the principle of utility – in other words, how we are supposed to measure the amount of pleasure and pain an action brings and so maximise happiness. Bentham termed the method of calculating, measuring and weighing up the pleasure/pain of individual actions, the 'hedonic calculus' (also known as the utility calculus).

One of the advantages that utilitarians claim for their theory is that by using a universal feature of human life (pleasure and pain), their theory can be applied to all of our day-to-day actions. To apply the utility principle, we simply weigh up the amount of pleasure and pain an action might create and then select the action which brings the most amount of pleasure over pain. **Figure 2.4** shows Bentham's suggested utility calculus – that is, the steps for measuring the pleasure and pain that result from an action.

Simple! Or maybe not. Bentham's approach is intended more as a guide than a practical tool. Even as a guide it faces some objections.

All moral systems are based on utilitarianism.

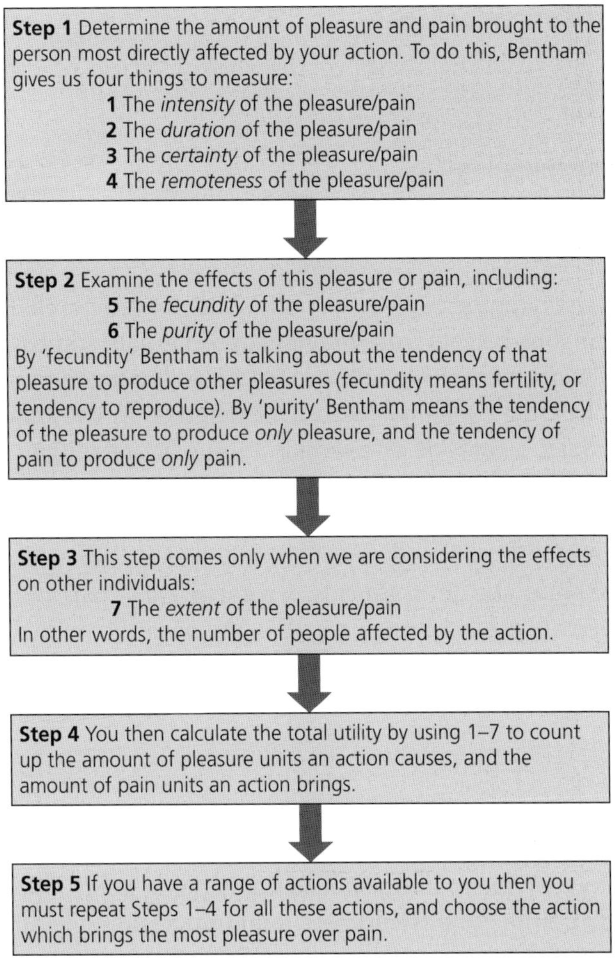

Figure 2.4 Bentham's utility calculus

Step 1 Determine the amount of pleasure and pain brought to the person most directly affected by your action. To do this, Bentham gives us four things to measure:
    1 The *intensity* of the pleasure/pain
    2 The *duration* of the pleasure/pain
    3 The *certainty* of the pleasure/pain
    4 The *remoteness* of the pleasure/pain

Step 2 Examine the effects of this pleasure or pain, including:
    5 The *fecundity* of the pleasure/pain
    6 The *purity* of the pleasure/pain
By 'fecundity' Bentham is talking about the tendency of that pleasure to produce other pleasures (fecundity means fertility, or tendency to reproduce). By 'purity' Bentham means the tendency of the pleasure to produce *only* pleasure, and the tendency of pain to produce *only* pain.

Step 3 This step comes only when we are considering the effects on other individuals:
    7 The *extent* of the pleasure/pain
In other words, the number of people affected by the action.

Step 4 You then calculate the total utility by using 1–7 to count up the amount of pleasure units an action causes, and the amount of pain units an action brings.

Step 5 If you have a range of actions available to you then you must repeat Steps 1–4 for all these actions, and choose the action which brings the most pleasure over pain.

Criticism 1: impossible to compare pleasures

Some would claim that we cannot compare the pleasure of, say, watching tennis, with that of eating an apple, with that of helping a friend learn to drive. They are such different things that there is no common currency with which we could compare them. This difficulty is just within one person. Comparing the amounts of pleasure between people may be equally meaningless. How can anyone know if you gain more pleasure from eating spaghetti than me? Perhaps we should all have pleasure-ometers attached to our heads, so that we can compare. However, even if this were possible, it would be treating pleasure/happiness just as an internal sensation, which some argue is a mistake (page 229).

Criticism 2: is quantity the only factor?

Using Bentham's utility calculus, it is the quantity of pleasure that is the key indicator of the utility of action. His utility calculus can be called quantitative hedonistic utilitarianism: if two different pleasures are compared, the one that has the highest quantity is the one we should aim for. As we will see on page 222, John Stuart Mill thought that some pleasures, such as those gained from poetry or opera (he called them higher pleasures) were better to pursue – even though they may be less pleasant. Bentham, though, did not make this distinction – he thought that only the quantity mattered. He once famously wrote that 'the game of push-pin [a game played in pubs at the time] is of equal value with the arts and sciences of music and poetry' and therefore that both should be treated equally in the utility calculus.[4]

► ACTIVITY: CALCULATING
PLEASURE

Make a rough calculation of
whether the following acts, A–F,
bring more pleasure or pain into
the world.

1 What difficulties did you have
   in trying to work these out?

2 Do you agree that the acts
   that bring pleasure are good
   acts?

A Giving money to a charity

B Volunteering to visit an old
   people's home

C Playing a hilarious practical
   joke on a friend

D Buying clothes that were
   made in a 'sweat shop'

E Poisoning your neighbour's
   cat, as it kept soiling your
   garden

F Stealing from the rich to give
   to the poor

Utilitarianism in action

So now that we have the basics of the theory, let us road-test a couple of examples.

Example 1: the mugging

Reuben is walking home when he is mugged. The mugger takes Reuben's mobile phone and money.

Let us add up the happiness/pleasure points this act generates. The mugger may enjoy the adrenaline he gets from mugging, so may gain some notional pleasure points from the act (say, 5). He sells the phone and uses the money to buy some drugs, which he then consumes with some friends. In the short term, they all gain pleasure (say, a total of 20 points). So, the act of mugging has added 25 happiness points to the world. Now consider Reuben. He will suffer immensely. Violent acts, such as muggings, can live in the mind for a lifetime and be a regular source of discomfort. Reuben's family and friends will all be distressed too, as will others as the news spreads. A total of 1,000 pain points may emerge as a result. Overall, the act brings about 1,000 negative points and 25 positive points, giving a total 975 negative points. The act introduces more pain than pleasure to the world, and so is a bad act.

Example 2: pizza!

An uncle gives you restaurant vouchers worth £80 on your birthday. You treat your four closest friends to pizza. The meal is enjoyed by all; more so because it is free for four of them, and you also enjoy being host. This gives a total of 100 happiness points. One friend gets mild indigestion, yielding 1 pain point. A grand total of 99 happiness points. Overall, the act introduced happiness into the world and so was a good act.

Consequentialism

One of the key difficulties you may have faced is in deciding what the consequences of an action might be and when, if ever, they come to an end. Because utilitarianism claims that something specific (namely pleasure/happiness) is a 'good', then this makes it a consequentialist theory of ethics. A good act is one that brings about the 'good' (pleasure/happiness). So the moral worth of any action lies in the amount of pleasure it brings into the world, and to work this out you need to examine the consequences of the actions. CONSEQUENTIALIST ETHICS are also sometimes called teleologicial ethics – as they involve working towards a specific end (or *telos* in the Greek). One big problem for all consequentialist ethical theories is that they can feel counter-intuitive (see pages 244–245 for more on this), and for philosophers such as Kant, the motive/intention of an action is the source of its moral worth, not the outcome. For Kant, only actions carried out for the right motive can be called good.

Bentham on motive and government

For Bentham, as a psychological hedonist, the issue of 'motive' is a red herring, as everyone is motivated by pleasure anyway. We all have the same motive. People may have different intentions in terms of how they will achieve pleasure, but their motive is the same. Bentham was writing primarily for governments when he first articulated utilitarianism. After all, why appeal to citizens? If everyone is motivated to maximise their own happiness, what is the point of telling them to maximise the general happiness? They will not do it! This is where the government comes in. By making laws and tweaking crime and punishment, we can modify people's intentions and align the pursuit of individual happiness with the pursuit of general happiness.

For example, Billy may enjoy drinking a lot and singing loudly on the street in the middle of the night (which his neighbours find very annoying). If a law is introduced which makes this sort of behaviour a criminal offence, then Billy will be less inclined to sing at night, as he wants to avoid the pain of prison. In this way, how he pursues his happiness will be better aligned with the general pursuit of happiness.

Criticism: utilitarianism as social engineering

One criticism of this approach is that the goal of utilitarianism seems to be best achieved by a kind of social engineering. In the seminal novel *A Brave New World*, Aldous Huxley portrayed a society where people are educated and trained in different ways. The 'Alphas' are trained to rule and to enjoy this, whereas the manual workers – the 'Gammas' – are trained to hate books and enjoy manual work. In addition, everyone takes a drug called *Soma* to keep them even happier. Hey presto, everyone is happy! A perfect utilitarian world. Yet some people think that this would not be an ideal society. Human AUTONOMY and freedom seem to be diminished and replaced by a government trying to socially engineer happiness. This idea that the goals of utilitarianism are best achieved by the state manipulating the masses (without the masses necessarily knowing) is sometimes referred to (critically) as 'Government House Utilitarianism'.

[handwritten margin note: Government social engineering is the best way to make sure utilitarianism is followed and create an ideal society. This takes away freedom and autonomy which makes it not an ideal society.]

John Stuart Mill

John Stuart Mill (1806–73) was not only a moral philosopher, he was also a social reformer, a Member of Parliament and, in his day, a logician of great eminence. As a child, he was the subject of a famous experiment in education by his father, James Mill, and Jeremy Bentham. The young Mill was hot-housed in philosophy, the classics, economics and maths and duly became a child prodigy, although at a cost. Throughout his childhood, Mill did not spend any time in the company of other children. At the age of 20, Mill suffered a nervous breakdown, feeling that the emotional side of his upbringing had been neglected. Mill recovered, with a renewed interest in not just the intellectual but also the emotional side of his life. In 1863, he published *Utilitarianism*, which continued the work carried out by his father and Bentham. He also wrote *On Liberty* in 1859, which has become one of the most influential texts in the history of philosophy.

Mill agrees with Bentham that the 'one fundamental principle ... at the root of all morality' is the utility principle:

> *Utility, or the Greatest Happiness Principle, holds that actions are right in proportion as they tend to promote happiness, wrong as they tend to produce the reverse of happiness. By happiness is intended pleasure and the absence of pain; by unhappiness is intended pain, and the privation of pleasure.*[5]

So Mill, like Bentham, proposes happiness as the foundation for his ethical theory.

Mill's proof of utilitarianism

Bentham did not think that the theory of utilitarianism could be 'proved' as such. He thought it was obvious that maximising pleasure is the right thing to do, as this is what everyone tries to do all the time. Mill was also sceptical about whether a formal proof for the theory could be provided.

Questions about ultimate ends can't be settled by direct proof ... [but] considerations can be presented that are capable of determining the intellect either to give or withhold its assent to the doctrine; and this is equivalent to proof.[6]

Despite this scepticism, in Chapter 4 of *Utilitarianism*, Mill attempts to clarify the foundations underpinning his and Bentham's theory. This one short chapter has generated an enormous amount of controversy ever since.

Mill claims that the ultimate principles of morality, like all first principles, cannot be proven, but that reasons can be given for believing these principles, particularly if these reasons are simple matters of fact. So the question is, what simple matters of fact can Mill find to provide the foundations for utilitarianism?

To explore Mill's 'proof', we have divided it into three stages; 1) happiness is a good (as in an end) for each person; 2) general happiness is a good for all; 3) happiness is the only good we seek.

anthology
2.2

Step 1: from desired to desirable

1 The only evidence that something is visible is that it can actually be seen, likewise audible and heard.
2 Similarly, the only evidence that something is desirable is that it is actually desired.
3 Each person desires their own happiness.
4 Therefore *Each person's happiness is desirable* (this is implied, from 2 and 3 above, but not stated).

A much criticised move occurs in line 2. Mill is arguing by analogy that the property of being 'desirable' is *like* the properties of being 'visible' and 'audible'. However, we do not have to buy this analogy. It can be argued that desirability is crucially different from visibility or audibility.

Criticism: equivocation – two senses of desirable

G.E. Moore (amongst others) leapt on this part of Mill's argument. 'Well, the fallacy in this step is so obvious that it is quite wonderful how Mill failed to see it'.[7]

Moore thinks he has discovered a FALLACY in Mill's argument, which is the mistake of identifying 'what is actually desired' with 'what ought to be desired'.

We would all agree that visible does, indeed, mean 'able to be seen', and audible means 'able to be heard'. But 'desirable' does not mean 'able to be desired' – a point which becomes clear when we consider that not everyone's desires are 'desirable'. It is possible to think of all manner of gross things that people happen, as a matter of fact, to desire; for example, there are some

▶ **ACTIVITY**

Read anthology 2.2. Try to identify each stage of Mill's argument, perhaps by giving each stage a number. Does his argument convince you? Why, or why not?

(Please note that the anthology extract does not include the final stage of Mill's argument, in which he attempts to show that happiness is the only good we seek. However, the full text is easy to find online.)

people in the world who desire to drink their own urine in the morning. But it is not the case that such a desire is desirable. Usually when we say something is 'desirable', we are recommending it as something that is fit or worthy to be desired – something that we *ought* to desire. So there are two possible senses of the term 'desirable':

- Sense 1: A factual sense, meaning *that which is able to be desired* (which could be anything – even morally questionable things/people).
- Sense 2: A more moral sense, meaning *that which ought to be desired* (which tends to be worthy things/people – that is, not 'undesirables').

The charge is that Mill is using 'desired' in sense 1 to suggest something is 'desirable' in sense 2. That is to say, he is guilty of equivocation (using a term with more than one meaning misleadingly). If this is the case, then we can see that the analogy with visibility and audibility does not hold. 'Visible' does not mean 'fit to be seen' and audible does not mean 'fit to be heard'. So in this part of the argument, Mill has not proved that just because X is, as a matter of fact, desired, it ought therefore to be desired.

In Mill's defence, he is not trying to deduce, by definition, that anything we desire is worthy of desire. But how else are we to decide what is desirable, if not by looking at what is desired? Mill is an EMPIRICIST, so believes that only experience is capable of telling us what is desirable. He is making an induction based on what people actually desire. Mill is not religious, so cannot look to God to tell us what we ought to desire; nor can he look to innate ideas or intuitions. All we have is the evidence of what humans actually desire. No one would be convinced that something was a suitable goal, unless it was already, in practice, a goal.

Further criticism: the is–ought gap

This, however, leaves Mill open to a criticism which claims that you cannot argue for morality on the basis of actual behaviour or experience. You cannot say how we *should* behave just on the basis of how we *do*. (Historically, owning slaves has been desired by many people, but it would be hard to argue this was desirable!). This criticism was suggested by Hume a century before. Hume claims that many moral thinkers start their arguments by discussing what is the case in the world (making factual claims), and then end up concluding what ought to be the case in the world (making prescriptive/moral claims). Hume suggests that moving from an is to an *ought* always involves a logical error. For more on the is–ought gap see page 391.

Criticism: naturalistic fallacy

Moore makes a second, somewhat related, criticism of Mill. Moore's point involves the claim that the term 'good' is indefinable, and any attempt to equate 'good' with a property in the natural world (such as happiness) is a mistake. If 'good' literally meant 'happiness', then it would be a meaningless question to ask if happiness is always good. And this is not a meaningless question. For more on what Moore termed the NATURALISTIC FALLACY, see page 381.

However, Mary Warnock argues that Mill does not attempt to *define* desirable or good at all.[8] According to Warnock, Mill's project is primarily an empirical one: he is simply setting out for us what sorts of things are, as a matter of fact,

215

considered good. Mill is trying to persuade us of the truth of utilitarianism by informing us that people already consider happiness to be good (and desirable). But that is not to say (as Moore believes) that Mill therefore considers the 'good' to *mean 'happiness'* or 'pleasure' and so on. If it turned out that people considered something else say, pain) to be fundamentally desirable, then it would be this thing, pain, that was the good. Again, Mill is an empiricist and basing his argument on evidence alone.

Step 2: from individual happiness to general happiness being desirable

4 Each person's happiness is desirable.
5 The general happiness is desirable. (Mill claims that 3 is the only reason that can be given for 4.)
6 (Presented as a restatement.) Each person's happiness is a good to that person.
7 The general happiness is a good to the aggregate of all persons.

Mill is saying here that if happiness is good to you as an individual, then the general happiness is *good* to the aggregate of all people.

Criticism: fallacy of the composition

Mill argues that general happiness is desirable (5) because each person desires their own happiness (3). But who is it who desires the general happiness? You and me? It does not follow that if each person wants their own happiness, then each of us also wants the general happiness. This is known as the fallacy of composition – just because something applies to each part, it does not necessarily apply to the whole as well. For example, this week, each person in the UK might want to win the National Lottery, but each person does not want everyone to win the lottery this week. In fact, I want to be the only winner so that the jackpot is not shared.

So, it does not follow that general happiness is desirable to each individual. Perhaps the general happiness is desirable to the general people (the collective us). But the collective us is not the sort of thing that has desires.

This same point arises in arguing that because happiness is a good for each of us, that (8) the general happiness is a good to the aggregate of all persons (7). Bertrand Russell gives an absurd example of the apparent mistake here: it is true that every member of the human species has a mother, but it is a fallacy to conclude from this that our species as a whole must have a mother.[9] Likewise, from each person having happiness of a good, it does not follow that the aggregate of us also has happiness as a good.

In Mill's defence, it can be argued that he is not making a claim, from a psychological viewpoint, that the mystical 'aggregate' of the people desires the general good. Rather he is making the point that if each of us thinks of happiness as our good, then from an *impartial* point of view, overall general happiness is the good.

Also, it can be seen that again Mill is simply being an empiricist. The fact that for each person happiness is a good, is evidence for the claim that general happiness is a good. It is not meant as a definition or proof, but as inductive evidence for a general claim.

Step 3: happiness as the sole end/criteria for morality

8 Happiness is one of the ends of conduct.

9 Happiness is one of the criteria for morality (the extract in the Anthology ends here).

10 Other elements (such as virtue, music, health and money) can be ends of conduct too (though these are not universally held).

11 However, these other elements start as a means to gaining happiness for the person, then, by association with pleasure/happiness, become ends in themselves.

12 Through association, these other elements become a part of what happiness is for that person. Only in this way do they become ends in themselves.

13 Because these elements were initially sought as means of happiness, then happiness should be seen as the sole end of our conduct (even though these elements are now part of it).

14 Happiness is the sole good.

Mill here relies on the principle of psychological association (which was popular when he was writing). The claim is that we are do not 'naturally or originally' desire things such as money. After all, for a baby, money is just a kind of funny paper. It is only through culture and socialisation that we come to see money initially as a means to happiness, and then, in time, as a constituent part of this happiness. In this way, money can become an end itself (for some people), not initially, but through its association with happiness. As such, we should see happiness as the ultimate end.

A full discussion on this would stray somewhat into the realm of psychology. It is worth nothing that the general theory of association (that our mental life starts out in disarray, and then, through gradual associations, becomes coherent) is questioned by many. However, it is possible to question the claim that happiness is our sole end on more philosophical grounds (page 226).

Summary: Mill's proof

Mill was an atheist and extreme empiricist. His proof does not rely on intuitions or innate ideas and appeals only to factual evidence. It also uses generalisations (induction) from experience of how the world is. Critics often treat Mill's 'proof' as a kind of formal deductive argument, where each line *must* follow from the last. However, it is important to remember that Mill starts the chapter by saying that matters of ultimate ends cannot be proved, and ends it by saying, 'Whether the doctrine [of utilitarianism] is true must now be left to the judgment of the thoughtful reader.'[10] So Mill's lack of certainty in the proof is evident. For empiricists, there are very few certainties, just ideas that are supported by evidence to a greater or lesser degree.

Act utilitarianism

Bentham's version of utilitarianism is a form of 'act' utilitarianism. Although Bentham was writing primarily for lawmakers, others took his theory to be an ethics that can be used by all. In other words, we should all appeal directly to the 'principle of utility' in order to judge what is right in any particular situation. We must calculate the effects of each potential action, or 'act', on its own merits.

However, this form of act utilitarianism is susceptible to a certain number of problems, which we shall now look at.

Criticism 1: act utilitarianism has counter-intuitive implications

A major criticism of act utilitarianism is that the goodness or badness of an act is based solely on the consequences. The nature of the act is not important. In this way, the ends can justify the means, as long as the end result is happiness. However, this goes against our intuition that the nature of the act itself (the means) is also important in the moral calculation. In this way, act utilitarianism can sometimes feel very counter-intuitive.

Experimenting with ideas: testing utilitarianism against your intuitions

Consider the decisions made in situations A–E and answer the questions below:

A The Colosseum. In ancient Rome, the Colosseum was built mainly for the purposes of enjoying blood sports. The crowd of 20,000 people regularly derived a huge amount of enjoyment from watching the spectacle of gladiators fighting, slaves being killed and Christians being eaten by lions. Most of the time, only a few people would die, and thousands would gain pleasure.

B The DVD. You borrow a DVD player from a rich friend, promising to give it back. A few months later she has forgotten she even lent it to you, yet you use it all the time, so you decide that you will keep it.

C The scapegoat. A serial killer is on the loose. Thousands of citizens are in a state of panic and fear, and they march on the town hall, demanding that the killer be brought to justice. This mob is getting out of control, but local police and magistrates have no idea who the killer is. Eventually the mayor selects someone at random from the mob, a man with a known criminal record who is widely disliked. This man is quickly tried and found guilty, and the mob disperses, feeling happy and secure again.

D Bodily organs. A surgeon is desperate to receive some organs (one heart, one lung, two kidneys, one liver) to save the lives of five well-loved patients. He asks his assistant to find a healthy man with no family or friends, kills him painlessly, and take his organs so that the five can be saved.

E Nude pictures. A couple split up. A year later the ex-boyfriend puts various nude pictures of his ex-girlfriend on the internet. She does not discover this. The pictures bring pleasure to others.

For each situation or policy:

1 Do you think that the utility principle can be used to justify the situation?

2 Does the situation go against your own moral intuitions?

3 If so, explain why you believe the utilitarian decision is the wrong one.

One key difficulty with act utilitarianism is that it appears to recommend courses of action that go against our moral intuitions. Take the example of the innocent scapegoat. If we could demonstrate that, in order to prevent massive harm (perhaps further rioting or a civil war), we must execute an innocent person, then it seems as if Bentham thinks we should kill that person. But this seems fundamentally unjust, and Bentham, as we have seen, is keen to ensure that there is justice in the penal system. It goes against all our intuitions to say that it is morally good to kill, torture or deprive people of their freedom, even if it does lead to beneficial consequences for the majority.

Bentham might argue that we must consider not only the immediate pleasure brought to the majority, but also the pain brought by the fear that we too might one day be arrested and tried for a crime we did not commit, simply to placate the mob. But it is possible to adjust the example so that the crowd would not know that an innocent person had been executed – say, if the police and judicial system were able to orchestrate a perfect cover-up – and therefore that there would be no risk of generating any fear of future injustices.

Criticism 2: impossible to follow

This criticism claims that act utilitarianism is impossible to use in practice:

- It is often impossible to work out how much happiness each action might bring (more on this below).
- Even if this were possible, it would take too long to work out for some actions.
- Sometimes happiness involves being spontaneous, not working out what would maximise general happiness.

For these reasons, many utilitarians suggest that for most/all actions, we follow basic rules that will, in general, maximise happiness. Act utilitarianism may be the right way to judge whether an action is a good one or not, but is not really fit for purpose as a method of deliberation.

Rule utilitarianism

Imagine that traffic lights did not exist. At busy crossroads it would be up to each driver to decide whether to go or not. Naturally, people would try to maximise their own happiness and go as soon as they could. Chaos and gridlock would ensue. Imagine, instead, that everyone behaved as a good act utilitarian and tried to maximise the general happiness. What would this involve? Each driver would have to consider whether staying or going would generate the most happiness/avoid the most pain. Obviously crashes would be avoided. If there were more cars queuing one way than another, it would make sense to let the longer queue work down a bit. But what about the people inside the cars? Some may be in a real rush. One could be a doctor trying to get to the hospital – surely she should get priority? How on earth would you know this? It would be impossible to work out the exact implications of pulling out or not.

What is needed is a set of rules – in this case, traffic lights – that we can all follow. There may be one or two occasions when it would be better to ignore these (as happens when ambulances approach); however, it will raise happiness overall if we all follow the rules.

Rule utilitarianism suggests just this. Ethical rules and norms, such as *Do not lie* and *Keep your promises*, act as moral traffic lights. If followed by all, they will generally provide the best result.

Mill specifically introduces the idea of 'secondary principles' for this purpose. These secondary principles, or rules, are ones which experience has shown tend to produce the greatest happiness, and they should be adhered to, even though in particular cases breaking the rule might have better consequences. In another of his great works, *On Liberty* (1859), Mill lists some of these rules: for example, we should not encroach on the rights of others; we should not lie or deceive or cause injury to others. By applying the greatest happiness principle to general rules rather than individual actions, Mill avoids many of the problems of act utilitarianism.

In this way, rule utilitarianism also becomes a useable moral theory for individuals: there is no need to make complex calculations in order to take a moral decision; you can simply follow a moral rule. Rule utilitarianism can also be defended on utilitarian grounds by saying that it is only by our acting for the most part according to rules, rather than attempting always to evaluate situations on their own merits, that the greatest good is served.

Rule utilitarianism and rights

One key advantage of rule utilitarianism over act utilitarianism is in its ability to justify the adoption of human rights (and rights in general) as moral rules. In the 'bodily organs' example on page 218, an act utilitarian could argue that killing one man to save five would maximise happiness – and so be the right thing to do. However, for many people, this seems intuitively wrong. A rule utilitarian, though, would claim that having a moral rule about 'not killing', perhaps in the form of a right to life, would be a rule that, if followed by all, would maximise general happiness. It would be wrong, therefore, to break the rule. Even if on this one occasion it may seem as if more happiness could be brought about through the killing, people generally feel much safer and happier going about their business knowing the rule/right to life will not be broken in this way.

Strong and weak rule utilitarianism

Rule utilitarianism offers a two-level account of right and wrong. An action is right if it is in accordance with a moral rule, and a moral rule is right if, overall, it maximises utility (see **Figure 2.5**).

▶ **ACTIVITY: RIGHTS AND RULES**

Revisit the scenarios in the Experimenting with ideas task on page 218.

- In each case, what rule/ right could be put in place to prevent the situation/act from occurring?
- Are these rules that would maximise happiness if everyone followed them?
- Is rule utilitarianism more in tune with your ethical intuition than act utilitarianism?

Figure 2.5 Act and rule utilitarianism. For rule utilitarianism, it is following a rule that makes an act good or bad.

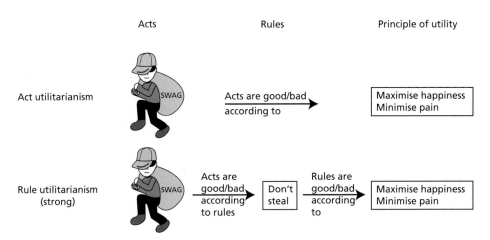

However, if utility is the ultimate judge of whether rules are morally right, should we not use this as our guide for action, rather than following a rule – particularly when following a rule may seem wrong? Consider this example:

Example 3: the axeman

A friend, Thierry, has asked if he can stay with you for a few days. On the first night, a deranged-looking man with an axe knocks at the door and asks if Thierry is staying with you. Do you lie or tell the truth?

Most rule utilitarians would say that *Do not lie* is a rule that would maximise general happiness. However, here it would seem that breaking the rule would produce greater happiness. So it seems perverse, given that the rule is itself set up in terms of the principle of utility, not to break it on this occasion. This way of thinking leads from a 'strong' version of rule utilitarianism to a 'weak' version.

A strong rule utilitarian claims that we ought to keep to a rule no matter what the consequences of breaking it may be in a particular circumstance. It is *following the rule* that gives an act its moral value, so in the example above, telling the truth would be the right thing to do. In contrast, a weak utilitarian allows that there may be exceptions to the rule and sometimes the rule needs to be broken to maximise happiness. For a weak utilitarian, it is the *principle of utility* that gives an act its moral value, and so lying would be the right thing to do.

Both versions, though, have their problems. Strong utilitarianism is a bit like DIVINE COMMAND ETHICS – you must always follow the rule, not matter what. The philosopher J.J.C. Smart (1920–2012) characterises this as 'rule worship'.[11] This, as in the example above, can lead to counter-intuitive examples. Also, it can involve claiming that some acts were the right thing to do (as they followed the rule), even though they may do more harm than good – which goes against the principle of utility.

Weak utilitarianism claims that you should make exceptions to rules, to maximise utility. However, in taking this approach, critics argue that you have a DUTY to check each time you apply a rule to see whether the application would maximise happiness or whether you should make an exception. But of course, this is (more or less) to revert to act utilitarianism – which is not really fit for purpose as a method of deliberation. Also, what is the status of these moral rules if the principle of utility is the ultimate judge of whether an act is right or wrong?

Although these are presented as criticisms of rule utilitarianism, Mill (often classed as a weak utilitarian) also sees them as a strength. The dilemma of 'lying' can also be seen as a clash of different rules – or secondary principles, as Mill called them. There is a rule that says lying is wrong, but there is also a general rule to prevent harm to others. When these secondary principles clash, then we should appeal to the primary principle – the principle of utility. One of the strengths of the theory of utilitarianism is that there *is* a primary principle to appeal to. Without this, what could people appeal to when moral rules or commandments clash?

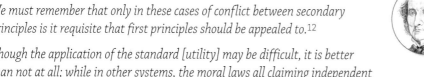

We must remember that only in these cases of conflict between secondary principles is it requisite that first principles should be appealed to.[12]

Though the application of the standard [utility] may be difficult, it is better than not at all; while in other systems, the moral laws all claiming independent authority, there is no common umpire entitled to interfere between them.[13]

Criticism: does rule utilitarianism collapse into act utilitarianism?

Continuing from the example above, a rule utilitarian might argue that *Do not lie* is still a good rule, but that it needs refining. The rule should be something like, *Do not lie, unless it is to a potential murderer*. This looks promising, but the difficulties with this approach are that the process of refining could go further still. We could always imagine other scenarios where the best outcome is to lie, and we could always refine the rule further – for example, *Do not lie unless to potential murderers, or to partners when they ask if you like their new haircuts*. Every time there is a set of cases where lying may produce more happiness, we could make an amendment to the rule. However, this process, taken to its logical CONCLUSION, would effectively end up with a version of act utilitarianism, but with rules that apply to very, very specific sets of circumstances. J.J.C. Smart argues that it would in fact become act utilitarianism.

 Whatever would lead the act utilitarian to break a rule would lead the ... rule utilitarian to modify the rule. Thus an adequate rule-utilitarianism would be extensionally equivalent to act-utilitarianism.[14]

Also, the advantage of rule utilitarianism is that the rules are simple and easy to follow. If refinements to each rule are needed to better maximise utility, then the theory loses its usefulness and appeal. Ultimately, Smart suggests that to be a good utilitarian, the rule utilitarian would need to keep modifying the rules in order to maximise happiness. However, in doing this, a point is reached whereby the rule utilitarian is effectively thinking like the act utilitarian, and following just the one important rule – which is that you should maximise happiness.

Two-tier utilitarianism

The English philosopher Richard Hare (1919–2002) outlined a two-tier version of utilitarianism. Act utilitarianism is the judge, and rule utilitarianism is the principle of deliberation for humans (most of the time). In other words, the moral value of each act is still decided by the amount of happiness it brings/pain it avoids, but for humans we should follow moral rules most of the time, as this will result in maximising happiness. However, there will be times in all of our lives when we need to question a rule, or think harder about a specific dilemma. In these instances, we should revert to act utilitarianism and try to work out the best action based on the likely outcomes.

Mill's qualitative hedonistic calculus: higher and lower pleasures

In the decades after Bentham first introduced the theory, utilitarianism attracted a wide range of criticisms, and in his book, *Utilitarianism*, Mill wanted to address these concerns. Some had claimed that utilitarianism involved too little pleasure. The term *utilitarianism*, even today, has connotations of something being plain and functional. Someone might describe a plain, but hard-wearing plate or dress as being *utilitarian*. Mill rightly rejected this criticism as a misunderstanding of the theory. More telling, though, was the opposite criticism: that utilitarianism is focused too much on pleasure, and, specifically, on bodily pleasures. At the time, the overcrowding in London had led to the poor living very cramped, uncomfortable lives. Many sought comfort in drinking gin, which became very popular. Critics of utilitarianism saw the theory as advocating the pursuit of

► **ACTIVITY: TWO-TIER VIEW**

Draw a diagram representing this two-tier view of utilitarianism.

mindless drinking (and so forth) as a morally good thing to do (as it gave pleasure). Mill sought to defend the theory against this charge. Part of his defence involved introducing a new distinction between 'higher' and 'lower' pleasures.

Previous utilitarian writers had also claimed that pleasures of the mind were superior to physical ones, but they did so on the grounds that such pleasures were likely to last longer and so, overall, give more pleasure. Mill, although agreeing with this, also claimed that the 'quantity only' approach is not really necessary.

It is quite compatible with the principle of utility to recognise the fact, that some kinds of pleasure are more desirable and more valuable than others. It would be absurd that while, in estimating all other things, quality is considered as well as quantity, the estimation of pleasures should be supposed to depend on quantity alone.[15]

Bentham saw all pleasures as equal, so the pleasures of the body (for example, having a massage) were of the same value as pleasures of the mind (for example, reading a book). A good act is one that simply maximises the overall quantity. Mill, however, argued that many humans would prefer the pleasures of the mind over those of the body, *even if* the pleasures of the body were more pleasurable. He called the pleasures of the mind *higher* pleasures. And although not every human would prefer such pleasures, those who have experienced both would choose the higher pleasures over the lower ones – even if they were not as pleasant. Further, being able to experience both kinds is better than only being able to experience the lower kind.

It is better to be a human being dissatisfied than a pig satisfied; better to be Socrates dissatisfied than a fool satisfied. And if the fool, or the pig, are of a different opinion, it is because they only know their own side of the question. The other party to the comparison knows both sides.[16]

J.J.C. Smart suggests that as a sheep you would be content (have your desires satisfied) and enjoy yourself, but there is more to happiness than this. He argues that, in part, happiness also involves having a positive attitude towards *how* you gain your pleasures/contentment. The Socrates/pig puzzle (right) shows this requirement. While we might genuinely be content and happy as the pig, we (from the perspective of a human thinking about it now) might not be content about being content in such a way. There may be other desires we want fulfilled in life. So to be happy, we must not only fulfil our first-order desires (itches, scratches, food, books and so on), but also our desires about how/which desires are satisfied.

Mill's solution is to suggest that some of our first-order desires/pleasures are inherently better than others. And that someone who has experienced both would value higher pleasures more, even though sometimes they may be less pleasant. The pig may be content, but only the human is able to access these higher pleasures and would choose these, even knowing that she may be more satisfied as a pig.

> ▶ ACTIVITY: SOCRATES OR A PIG
>
> Which would you rather be?
>
> **A** A happy and contented pig
> **B** An unhappy human
> Why?
>
> What might a pig say (if it could talk)?
>
> If you chose A, then could you argue it would be better if we got rid of most humans and filled the world with happy pigs? (You still need some humans to keep the pigs safe and happy and so on.)

223

Experimenting with ideas

Savour the following pleasures (A–F) and then answer the questions below.

A Drinking a warm mug of hot chocolate on a cold day.

B Reading and understanding a piece of difficult philosophy.

C Laughing until you cannot breathe from watching a comedy on television.

D Having a thoughtful discussion with friends about how to change the world.

E Reading a version of the Harry Potter books, in which no one dies, and the tone is much more light-hearted.

F Reading the real version of the Harry Potter books, which includes the death of several key characters, including **SPOILER ALERT** Dobby.

1 Which of the above are the most pleasant?

2 Are the ones that are most pleasant the ones that you think are worth pursuing more?

3 Which of the above pleasures do you think Mill might call 'higher' and which 'lower'?

4 Which of E or F would bring you more pleasure?

anthology
2.3

An easy criticism of this approach is that Mill is just thinking of the pleasures that he personally likes and wants to claim that they are somehow superior to the pleasures that some others prefer. However, Mill claims that only those who can appreciate both are in a position to say which is the better. A pig would not be in a position to say that reading Shakespeare is, or is not, a valuable pleasure. Mill claims this enables him to preserve a degree of objectivity in utilitarianism. We can draw on the pronouncements of 'competent judges' – that is, people who have had experience of both higher and lower pleasures.

Mill believed there would be substantial agreement between these judges, but if there were not, then we should stand by a majority decision.

 On a question which is the best worth having of two pleasures, or which of two modes of existence is the most grateful to the feelings ... the judgment of those who are qualified by knowledge of both, or, if they differ, that of the majority among them, must be admitted as final.[17]

Criticism 1: is this hedonistic utilitarianism anymore?

The gist of Mill's distinction is that some pleasures are somehow better, even if they give less pleasure. Does this make sense as a hedonistic utilitarian? It would seem that if something could be less *pleasant*, yet *better*, then we are no longer seeking to maximise *pleasure*. Going back to the idea of the pleasure-ometer attached to the head, activity A may record a lower pleasure score than activity B, yet somehow be better. If this is so, then surely a utilitarian needs a new type of '-ometer', perhaps one that measures the preferences of competent judges, rather than pleasure. Measuring pleasure seems to be the wrong thing.

In Mill's defence

Mill does think you can argue that higher pleasures are actually more pleasant than lower, when you take into account the duration and so on. For example, a good book will give you pleasure for a long time, whereas it seems unlikely that you really remember that lovely cup of tea and muffin you had last September.

But Mill thought that utilitarianism does not need to be quantity-only in its approach.

Mill may be claiming that higher and lower pleasures are simply incommensurable – rather than one being less pleasant than the other. For example, blue is different from red. No amount of blue will be the same as any amount of red; they are simply different. Mill does indeed claim that even for lower pleasures/pains, we cannot really compare two side by side; we can only ask someone who has experienced both, which is the better or worse.

> *What means are there of determining which is the acutest of two pains, or the intensest of two pleasurable sensations, except the general suffrage of those who are familiar with both?*[18]

So Mill seems to be claiming that we need the competent judges for *all* pleasures and pains and not just to settle the higher/lower debate.

Mill did not see happiness just as a question of pleasure. In his view, a society of people plugged into some kind of pleasure machine would not be a good thing. Humans have capacities to reason, to develop and they enjoy these aspects of life in a different way. These aspects would be overlooked if we were all just busy getting physical pleasures. A competent judge is able to say which pleasure she would prefer precisely because she has developed her capacities. The fact that competent judges do prefer higher pleasures (most of the time) points to the direction we should all be pursuing – and this is to develop our capacities so as to enjoy these higher pleasures. In his earlier work, *On Liberty*, Mill gave a different account of utility which reflects this broader view of human pleasure.

> *I regard utility as the ultimate appeal on all ethical questions; but it must be utility in the largest sense, grounded on the permanent interests of man as a progressive being.*[19]

Some have argued that this approach is to move away from hedonistic utilitarianism; however, Mill saw it as a more sophisticated development of our account of happiness.

What this criticism (and defence) points to is that there may be something a bit odd about comparing pleasures. In part, this may be because there is something suspicious about the very concept of pleasure (see page 228). Furthermore, if we are reliant on competent judges to say which of two options they *prefer*, then perhaps we should be aiming to maximise people's *preferences*, rather than guess what will give them pleasure. We explore PREFERENCE UTILITARIANISM on page 229.

Criticism 2: utilitarianism loses its simplicity

Mill, in trying to make Bentham's utilitarianism more sophisticated and acceptable to the critics, has created enormous problems for himself. What makes utilitarianism so appealing is its simplicity and practicality: it tells us that we can calculate what actions we should take by weighing up the quantity of pleasure (and pain) that different acts produce. However, once Mill introduces the notion of quality into the discussion, then some of the simplicity disappears.

For example, imagine a council is trying to decide whether to build a gym or a library. Under Bentham's system, the council only has to think about the overall quantity of happiness either would bring (which is hard enough!). Under Mill's regime, they now have to compare not only the quantity, but also the quality. It may be that most competent judges would prefer the pleasure a library would bring, but how are we to factor this into the equation? Does it make the library infinitely better than the gym? Does one library = 100 gyms? Is it only up to the competent judges to decide what the right thing is? What if 75 per cent of the local residents would prefer a gym?

The quality distinction seems to make the application of the hedonistic calculus harder still. Again, we might be tempted to conclude that what the council should do is find out what people would prefer and try to maximise the preferences.

Criticism 3: cultural snobbery

Should the BBC spend public money on buying a 'trashy' new Australian soap opera, or should it spend money on a series addressing the problems of philosophy? The philosophy series would only attract a tenth of the viewers of the soap, but would bring about much higher quality pleasure, though less quantity. (Unless, of course, you are the sort of person who gets as much pleasure per minute from reading this book, as from, say, eating a cream cake.)

But even where it seems obvious which is the higher and which is the lower pleasure, the question remains: what should we do, as good utilitarians, when the lower pleasure is felt by millions of people and the higher pleasure by only a select few? We are left wondering whether 'higher pleasures' really just means 'the things that Mill and his friends like to do'.

Issue: is pleasure the only good?

Above we saw how Mill introduced a distinction between higher and lower pleasures. The suggestion was that activity A could be less pleasurable than activity B, yet somehow be better and the one we should pursue. This raised the question of whether it is pleasure that we should try to maximise, or something else.

Earlier still, we looked at the theory of psychological hedonism, which claims that pleasure and pain are our sole motivations, such that we are *'fastened to their throne'*. In this section, we will question the PREMISE that we do, in fact, pursue pleasure (psychological hedonism) and also that we should pursue pleasure (utilitarianism).

Psychological hedonism

The idea that pleasure is the ultimate end of our actions is a fairly simple idea, although some would argue it paints an unpleasant view of the human condition – that of pleasure-seeking animals with brains acting as a sort of computer to work out how to maximise pleasure.

Simple, psychological hedonism can be a very difficult theory to argue against. You might claim that a particular act is not pleasure-seeking – for example, staying in and doing your homework rather than going out and having fun.

However, Bentham (were he alive today and not merely stuffed) would come back at you by saying that you are either driven to do your homework by fear of punishment (pain) or by the prospect of future pleasure (praise from a teacher/parent, the pleasure of better grades, getting to the right university or even getting a better job). By staying in and working hard, you are sacrificing shorter-term pleasures (going out) for longer-term ones, but pleasure (and the avoidance of pain) is still your goal.

Some religious believers, as well as others who consider themselves very upright and moral, have claimed (and still do) that seeking pleasure is not good, but is actually wrong. Instead, these people have chosen to live simple lives that avoid pleasure. Some religious sects have even used self-chastisement (whipping oneself) as part of this overall philosophy of avoiding pleasure. This would seem to be a clear counterexample to psychological hedonism. However, Bentham claims that even these people are still driven by pleasure and pain. They may be driven by the prospect of pleasure in the next life, or the avoidance of pain through the punishment of God.

Criticisms of psychological hedonism: the pleasure machine

> ▶ **ACTIVITY: IS PLEASURE THE ULTIMATE END?**
>
> Look back to the Experimenting with ideas box on page 207 (What are your ultimate goals?):
>
> Is it possible to argue that each of these activities is ultimately aiming at gaining personal pleasure and avoiding pain?
>
> Can you argue that any/all of the activities are not aimed at gaining pleasure or avoiding pain?

Figure 2.6 The pleasure machine.
The machine will give you guaranteed pleasure. But would you enter if you knew that you could never come out?

Experimenting with ideas: the pleasure machine version 1.0

The following idea is adapted from the philosopher Robert Nozick (1938–2002) and his idea of the experience machine (also called the pleasure machine).[20] Imagine that scientists have developed an amazing new pleasure machine. You enter the wardrobe-like machine, get hooked up with lots of wires, and hey presto, the machine gives you guaranteed pleasure! These pleasurable sensations will vary in intensity from mild pleasures (akin to sitting next to a fire, warming your feet) to medium pleasures (such as the taste of marshmallows), to more intense pleasures (the equivalent of racing downhill on skis). It can give you *other* intense pleasures too – ones that it would not be appropriate to describe in a textbook. The only downside is that once you have stepped into the pleasure machine, you cannot come back out (but then again, you will not want to!). You will live a long and healthy life of guaranteed pleasurable sensations.

1 Given that the pleasure machine is completely safe, with no side effects whatsoever, and no threat to your health, would you plug yourself in for the rest of your life?

2 Why, or why not?

If you are happy to sign up to the machine, then this thought experiment seems to prove the truth of psychological hedonism. On the other hand, if you are not ready to sign up, does this mean that psychological hedonism is wrong? Or perhaps there is something missing from the machine? John Stuart Mill might claim that this machine focuses only on what he calls lower pleasures – tastes, physical sensations and so on – whereas many humans want higher pleasures, such as the pleasures of reading poetry, or difficult and sad books. To overcome this potential shortfall, consider this ...

▶ ACTIVITY: THE ALL NEW IMPROVED PLEASURE MACHINE VERSION 2.0

Perhaps the new version of the pleasure machine can tempt you. In this version, you are plugged into a virtual-reality machine – as real as the world you now inhabit. You are guaranteed to live a pleasurable life – maybe win an Oscar, or become an acclaimed pop star or footballer. You can also read all the difficult, sad books you want to read! Your memory will be tinkered with a little, so that you will not even know that you are in a machine, a bit like being in the film *The Matrix*, though a much, much happier version. Again, once you step in, it will have to be forever.

1 Would you step into the new improved pleasure machine?

2 Why, or why not?

Again, this could point towards the truth of psychological hedonism, but it might also count against it. If you would *not* step into the machine, is it because you think that the machine would not give the right sort of pleasures? Or is it because you believe that pleasure is not our only goal, or is not even a meaningful goal? If you are hesitant to step in, then the criticisms of psychological hedonism below may articulate some of your concerns.

Criticism 1: it is not *pleasure* that we seek, but states of affairs in the world – things outside of our heads

Nozick created the thought experiment of the pleasure machine (the one we refer to as 'version 2.0') to show that the idea of humans just seeking things inside our heads (that is, pleasure) may be wrong. What people often want are specific states of affairs in the world. They want their children to be happy, or for people to think well of them, or for there to be more dolphins. People want these states of affairs in the world, and not just for the sensations that might then result in their heads. If it were just the sensations you were after, then surely you would have stepped into the machine (or maybe you *have* stepped into the machine and stopped reading this!). But many would refuse the machine, as what they seek are things in a real world, not sensations and deceptions.

Criticism 2: it is not *pleasure* that we seek, but the specific actions, activities and objects themselves

Imagine you have been collecting football/Hello Kitty/*Hunger Games* stickers. You only have one missing and have been trying to get it for ages. You *really* want this missing sticker. Bentham would claim that the sticker is just a means to your ultimate aim, which is the pleasure it will give you. However, you may feel strongly that what you actually want is the sticker, not the pleasure it will give. For example, if I offered to give you the equivalent amount of pleasure that you would gain from getting the missing sticker, but from another source (say a Michael McIntyre DVD), then you might be tempted, but would still probably claim that it is the sticker you want, not just a certain quantity of pleasure.

Another utilitarian, Henry Sidwick (1838–1900), claimed that it is the specific activities/objects in life that we desire and not pleasure itself. I might want to play football for the intrinsic qualities of the game, the smell of grass, the crunch of the tackle, and so on – not for any specific sensation called pleasure. If it were just pleasure I wanted, then I might just settle for the Michael McIntyre DVD after all, and not bother getting muddy and tired.

Criticism 3: pleasure is a way of talking about behaviour, not sensations

I gain pleasure from lots of things: a cup of tea, watching football, a nice walk, reading Harry Potter books. These are all things I seek to do, but there does not seem to be a specific mental sensation linking them all. In seeking pleasure, there is not a specific thing – say, Easter eggs – that I am hunting. But if it is not a specific thing, then what is it? Behaviourists and others would claim that pleasure is not a specific sensation. Instead, they claim it is a way of talking collectively about all of those things that we seek to do. In other words, calling things pleasurable is really just a shorthand way of talking about *what we seek*. If this is true, then psychological hedonism can be seen as an empty theory. If we can define *pleasure* as *what we seek*, then the sentence 'We seek pleasure' really means 'We seek what we seek', which is a tautology (that is, it is true by definition), and tells us nothing new about the world. This may be why Bentham thought it was always possible to show that we seek pleasure – because it is true by definition.

What emerges from this discussion is that it is not clear that pleasure is a mental sensation, it may just be a way of talking about activities we *prefer* to do. Because of this, some utilitarians believe that we should focus on satisfying people's preferences rather than maximising their pleasure.

Non-hedonistic utilitarianism

Hedonistic utilitarians suggest that we should aim to maximise pleasure/happiness. However, we have seen above that this aim is questionable. These concerns have given rise to other forms of utilitarianism. They share with the original theory the idea that we should aim to maximise something (utility), but argue that this is not just pleasure. Because of this, they are collectively termed non-hedonistic forms of utilitarianism, the most famous of which is preference utilitarianism.

Preference utilitarianism

As well as articulating two-tier utilitarianism, Richard Hare also developed a new version of the theory, known as preference utilitarianism.

Preference utilitarianism acknowledges the issues with the concept of pleasure and puts the emphasis on our preferences instead. It suggests an action should be judged by the extent to which it conforms to the preferences of all those affected by the action (and its consequences). In other words, the morally good thing to do is whatever maximises the satisfaction of the preferences of all involved. So, for example, when considering whether to turn off the life-support machine of someone terminally ill, rather than aiming to maximise happiness, you should find out what all the relevant parties would prefer. Furthermore, in line with classic utilitarianism, you are required to think of the general good – so you should count your preferences in the same way as those of other people – no more, no less.

As we saw, it can be argued that act utilitarianism might lead to a world where giving everyone wonder drugs and forcing them to watch Michael McIntyre DVDs was the right thing to do. Pleasurable as it might be, most people would not specifically desire this. It would not be their preference. As a preference utilitarian, it would be wrong to do this. By focusing on what people actually want, rather than on someone else's (say, a government's) idea of what makes people happy, preference utilitarianism also avoids the criticism that utilitarianism can lead to social engineering (see page 213).

Preference utilitarianism also has an advantage in that preferences are easier to find out – you can ask people. We do not need to have a hedonistic calculus or pleasure-ometer, although some system of ranking preferences is still needed, as not all preferences are equally strong.

Differences between classic and preference utilitarianism

Many moral decisions will be the same whichever form of utilitarianism you choose, but the reasons for the decisions may be different. Classic utilitarianism may claim that lying is wrong as it often leads to *unhappiness*. For a preference utilitarian, lying is also often wrong, but this is because it goes against the *preference* we have to know the truth.

▶ **ACTIVITY: BIRTHDAY TIME**

It is your birthday! But what are you going to get? When people buy you presents, they generally try to maximise your happiness (within their budget); however, there are different deliberation processes that might be involved. A buyer might:

A Think about what makes them happy, and buy you the same thing
B Think about what makes people happy in general, and buy accordingly
C Think about what might make you happy, and buy that
D Think about what you might want, and buy accordingly
E Ask you what you want, and buy that.
I Which is the best strategy?
2 What do you prefer on your birthday?

A classic utilitarian might use any of these strategies. A preference utilitarian would use D and E. Strategies A–C may involve buying you something you have never thought about, which could turn out to be the best way to make you happy (although you might end up with a lot of Michael McIntyre DVDs!). However, over time, it can be argued that it would be better to use D and E to get you what you would prefer, as this will avoid lots of unwanted and unused gifts.

Please note that this example is not a perfect case study, as often people *prefer* to be surprised by gifts, and also, young children might have silly preferences (*I want a baby elephant!*). So strategies A–C may be preferable or in the best interest of the birthday boy/girl. However, the thought experiment shows how preference utilitarianism puts the emphasis on *your* preference – *your* conception of the good life – rather than options A–C, which involve someone else's idea of your happiness.

The focus on preferences can also be seen as solving some counter-intuitive utilitarian puzzles. From the perspective of act utilitarianism, a husband who cheats on his wife can be seen as doing a good thing – as long as his wife does not find out. Likewise with borrowing a friend's precious coat without asking, or reading someone's secret diary. However, in each of these cases, a person's preference would be thwarted – as the wife would prefer the husband to be faithful, and a friend would prefer you not to borrow their coat or read their diary.

Criticism 1: bad and crazy preferences

Preference utilitarianism claims that it is good to maximise/satisfy people's preferences. But is this always the case? Consider the following examples.

A Tas wants to drink the wine in her glass (she does not know it is poisoned).
B Little Johnny, aged four, is having a meltdown because he wants a fourth lollipop.
C David has become increasingly psychotic and wants to punch strangers.
D Sim is quite depressed and wants to self-harm.

In these cases, it would seem wrong to try to satisfy their preferences.

However, the preference utilitarian has some defences they can mount. In example A, if Tas knew about the poison, she would not want to drink the wine. In these cases, we can try to imagine what Tas would prefer from an 'ideal viewpoint' position – in other words, if she knew the wine was poisoned. In this case, she clearly would not drink it. Preference utilitarianism sometimes makes the distinction between a person's manifest preference (to drink the wine) and their true or idealised preference (to not drink the wine, if they knew it were poisoned). In such cases, we should seek to fulfil their true preference.

In example B, Little Johnny clearly is capable of preferences, and may even be aware that sugar is bad for his teeth, so has some knowledge base. However, preference utilitarians may argue that young people, or people with severe mental restrictions, will lack sufficient understanding of the world to reach their true or idealised preference. As such, adults should sometimes seek to act in their interest, rather than satisfying their every preference.

In example C, the preference utilitarian has three lines of defence:

C1 Other people's preference not to be punched would be much stronger than David's desire to punch, so it would be wrong for David to punch others, or for us to help him do so.
C2 Because David's mental health is becoming a problem, we should not seek to satisfy his preferences, but rather what his preferences might be after a suitable course of therapy. Again, this would be to argue that his manifest desire to punch others is not his true or ideal desire.

C3 As with the classic version, there is rule preference utilitarianism – which claims that we should follow the rules which, overall, will satisfy people's preferences. In this case, 'Do not punch people' would clearly be a rule.

In example D, as with C2 above, it could be argued that this is not Sim's true or idealised desire and that a course of therapy would change the desire. However, if this were not the case, then a preference utilitarian would say that it is right that Sim satisfies her preference.

Criticism 2: preferences from a distance

Consider the following preferences:

A James is now dead. He told his son (Bobby) to scatter his ashes on his favourite football club's pitch. The club charges £10,000 for this.
B Sammy would prefer that indigenous Amazonian tribes stay in the rainforest and avoid modern life.

Should a preference utilitarian take account of these preferences when making decisions?

In example A, an act utilitarian would say that Bobby could probably spend the money maximising happiness in better ways. After all, James is no longer alive to experience happiness. A rule utilitarian might say that Bobby should keep his promise (if he made one), as keeping promises, in general, will maximise happiness. A preference utilitarian may say that we should still try to fulfil the preference, even if James is not alive, as fulfilling preferences is the right thing to do. This may (or may not) seem counter-intuitive; indeed, some count this as a strength of preference utilitarianism and some a weakness.

In example B, Sammy may have a strong preference about this, but he never intends to visit the Amazon basin; it is just a preference about how he wants the world to be. Should Sammy's preference be a factor in any individual's or government's decisions? How should we weigh this against the preferences of the Amazonian tribes people themselves? It seems a bit odd that we should take into account someone's preferences about things when they have no direct causal connection to the people involved. (Note that this problem applies to hedonistic utilitarianism too.)

Criticism 3: weighing up of preferences

Bentham's hedonistic calculus was an attempt to quantify different pleasures and pains to help facilitate moral decision-making. Preference utilitarianism needs something equivalent to this. If people have different preferences – for example, if some are for, and some against, building a proposed airport, then how are we to know the morally right thing to do? Is it a question of numbers, or does strength of preference make a difference? Also, what about the preferences of people who are not directly affected by the airport, or even expressed preferences of those who have died – should these all count? In the gladiatorial arena, thousands of baying Romans want to see a Christian die at the claws of a lion. The Christian though, would prefer to live. Does this one person's preference override the thousands? These are not insurmountable problems for the preference utilitarian. Act utilitarianism also faced these problems, and rule utilitarianism – for example, in the form of a right to life – can be seen as a good solution. Likewise, rule preference utilitarianism can find solutions, although the question of weighing preferences still remains.

Preference utilitarianism and pleasure

The focus on pleasure at the core of utilitarianism can be seen to give moral value to counter-intuitive acts. The gruesome killings in the Colosseum entertained thousands – yet most would say they were not a good thing. Stand-up comedians bring pleasure to thousands, yet few would want to claim that their work has the same moral value as the hard toil of doctors and nurses volunteering in a war zone.

Preference utilitarianism provides a solution to some of these issues. Most people's preference to be pain-free and not suffering is far, far stronger than their preference for gaining pleasure. Ask someone in great pain if they could choose between pain relief and watching an amusing video, and they will give you a very swift answer. (Note, it is probably not a good idea to ask this question to someone in great pain.) This is why it is morally better to help those suffering and in pain than it is to make non-suffering people happier. The rise in happiness levels of both might be the same, but the strength of preference is definitely on the side of the sufferer.

In this way, preference utilitarians argue that our moral priorities should be to relieve pain and suffering in the world.

Other forms of non-hedonistic utilitarianism

As we have seen, preference utilitarianism is not based solely around pleasure. However, this is not the only form of non-hedonistic utilitarianism. G.E. Moore, despite his attacks on Mill's proof of utilitarianism (see page 214), developed his own brand of the theory that embraced several non-natural values.

Moore believed that it was a fallacy to define 'good' as happiness or pleasure, or any naturalistic concept (that is anything found in this world – see page 381 for more on this). Instead, Moore believed that the 'good' and the other values were indefinable ideals that could be grasped only by our intuitions. This version of the theory became known as ideal utilitarianism, and was associated with Moore, amongst others, because of his definition of 'ideal' as 'the best state of things conceivable' or the highest good. Amongst Moore's list of these greatest goods were not just moral, but also aesthetic and emotional values, in particular beauty and friendship. He argued that we should aim to maximise these ideas in the world – not because they bring pleasure, but because this would help to bring us closer to the best state of things conceivable.

Moore produced several arguments to show that we cannot equate pleasure with moral good. One argument is that we can think of pleasures that are not good. J.J.C. Smart updated a thought experiment of Moore's to explore this idea.[21] It goes (roughly) like this (see activity in the margin - 'The deluded sadist').

Many would be inclined to think that scenario B is the better of the two options. The pleasure gained in scenario A is somehow wrong and it would be better if it did not occur. But if you think this, then you are evaluating the worth of the pleasure (saying it is good or bad), and if you say it is bad then you cannot be using the concept of pleasure as the basis of your evaluation (as any pleasure

▶ **ACTIVITY: THE DELUDED SADIST**

Imagine a world in which only one person exists. This one being is falsely led to believe that others exist and, further, that these other people are being tortured. Which of these two scenarios is morally better?

A The one existing person is not distressed at the thought of the suffering of others, but actually delights in it and gets a great deal of pleasure imagining it.

B The one existing person is quite upset at the thought of others being tortured.

233

would then be good). In other words, you must have a prior understanding of good and bad and are applying this to the gaining of pleasure. This means that pleasure is not the same thing as good, contrary to what Bentham's version of hedonistic utilitarianism claims.

J.J.C. Smart (a utilitarian) thinks that A is the better option. It is better for the one person to be gaining pleasure. He argues that, in general, we rightly think of sadistic pleasure as bad, as sadists are likely to harm others. We have been conditioned from early on to think this. But in this scenario, we can see that no harm can come of the sadist's pleasure, as there is no one else in the world to harm. Using reason, we can overcome our conditioning and see that this thought experiment does not disprove hedonistic utilitarianism.

Strengths of utilitarianism

So far we have seen that hedonistic utilitarianism is based on a very simple idea: *that happiness is the good*. Thinking this simple idea through has led to a number of variations of the theory – but the core remains. This gives the theory a number of strengths. Basing the theory on something tangible(ish) allows reason to compare and contrast different actions and provides a common moral 'currency' that is flexible, universal, non-religious and transcends culture.

Bentham initially intended his theory to apply to governments, as a way of measuring which laws/policies were good ones (those that raised happiness). This approach has been adopted by governments throughout the world. When considering any policy or potential spending, governments will frequently undertake some form of cost–benefit analysis. This is essentially a utilitarian method of deliberation. Will building a new road in town A or B add more to the general happiness? When deciding whether a new, expensive cancer treatment should be available on the NHS, the government has to think how the money could be otherwise spent and whether this new treatment is a cost-effective way of reducing suffering. These are difficult decisions, but without utilitarianism, how could we even go about thinking them through?

So, utilitarianism has been hugely influential, but the quantitative and consequentialist approach it takes to morality raises some serious questions; and it is to these that we now turn. The main issues are:

- whether pleasure is the only good (see page 226)
- fairness and individual LIBERTY/rights
- problems with calculation, including which beings to include
- issues around PARTIALITY
- whether utilitarianism ignores the moral integrity of the individual
- whether utilitarianism ignores the intentions of the individual.

Issue: fairness and individual liberty/rights

Earlier (page 218), we saw that act utilitarianism could lead to some counter-intuitive moral JUDGEMENTS – for example, sacrificing scapegoats to please the masses or killing one person to use their organs for five others. Rule utilitarianism can avoid many of these problems by arguing that following moral rules makes an act right or wrong, and these rules would include having rights – such as the right to life, liberty and freedom of speech. In this way, ideals such as justice and human rights can be seen as useful ideals, because, if followed by all, they will raise overall happiness.

But in taking this approach, utilitarians argue that rights/values such as liberty and the right to life have no moral worth in themselves, but are useful devices *only* because they are a means to bringing about overall happiness. However, some people object to this approach. They claim that ideals and rights such as liberty, honour and justice have value as ends in themselves and not just as side effects of the quest for pleasure. Such ideals have their own moral worth.

Consider these examples.

Example 4: flatmates

Zach lives with four housemates (while studying philosophy at university). All of the housemates hate cleaning and tidying, but Zach does not mind it as much as the others. As utilitarians, they work out that Zach should do all of the cleaning and tidying, as this would maximise utility. Zach agrees, but has a nagging doubt that this is not fair.

Example 5: slavery

A family kidnaps an orphan boy from a very poor country and keeps him as their slave. He is prevented from ever leaving the house. The boy is well-fed, not beaten and the work he is made to do greatly increases the happiness of the family.

These situations can be seen as maximising utility, but are they fair? Rule utilitarians might argue that they are wrong as they breach moral rules that in general would maximise happiness. But critics would claim that these cases are wrong – not due to the fact that they breach a rule which overall would maximise happiness, but because example 4 is not fair and example 5 denies someone their liberty. And both liberty and fairness (justice) are worth pursuing as ends in themselves – independently of whether or not they maximise happiness. Such ideals/rights have moral worth in themselves. They are morally primitive and do not derive their moral worth from their ability to maximise happiness.

People have undergone great hardships, including sacrificing their own lives in the name of liberty, democracy and justice. It *could* be argued that these people were just trying to maximise happiness – but do people really sacrifice their lives for the ideal of maximising happiness? Many socialists would claim that a society where wealth is more evenly distributed is better than a society that is overall richer and *happier* but more unequal. What is important is not the happiness, but the *fairness*.

Mill on liberty: the 'tyranny of the majority'

The case of liberty is an interesting one. If you were reluctant to step into the pleasure machine (page 227), it could be because you did not like the idea of being trapped inside. Perhaps you valued your liberty more than your happiness. John Stuart Mill was a passionate advocate for liberty. He was concerned that utilitarianism (and democracy) can see the desires of minorities crushed under the weight of the majority. For example, the UK is a democracy, so if there were a majority vote at a referendum to ban homosexual sex, should we do so?

Mill noted how history is littered with examples of unelected leaders tyrannising the masses. Many revolutions came and went, and slowly democracy started to win the day in the West. However, this did not end the problem of tyranny. Although democracy is considered the 'will of the people', in theory, and practice, it is only the will of the majority of the people, and there is always the potential for the majority to govern in their own interests, even to the point of oppressing others. The tyranny of kings and despots, even today, could become the 'tyranny of the majority' (a phrase popularised by Mill, though it predated him).

Mill was concerned about this and argued that the *only* reason governments and other individuals should interfere in your life is to prevent you causing harm to others (this is known as Mill's *harm principle*). As long as what you are doing does not harm others, then individuals should be left to pursue their own lives in the way they see fit. His account of liberty has been hugely influential (most accounts of liberalism are based around it). Mill claimed it is consistent with the principle of utility – that is, adopting a 'hands-off' approach will lead to more happiness in the long run. However, many dispute whether this is the case and would claim that *liberty* is an end in its own right.

▶ **ACTIVITY: THE TYRANNY OF THE BABY BOOMERS**

The UK has an increasingly ageing population, and older folk are far more likely to vote than their younger counterparts. With this voting advantage, a recently formed 'Back to the 1950s' party is swept into power. The new, democratically elected government introduces: food rationing, compulsory national service and compulsory lessons in British cooking, tea-making and cricket. Long hair for men is illegal and no woman with school-aged children can work full-time. Oddly, because of the enforced rationing and cricket training, the health of the country increases quite dramatically.

Does this scenario challenge the truth of utilitarianism? Choose one (or more) of the following:

A No. Utilitarianism is right, this would increase overall happiness and so would be a good thing.

B No. Utilitarianism is right. However, this set-up would be wrong precisely because it would never increase overall happiness. It would increase overall misery.

C Yes. Utilitarianism is wrong. This set-up is wrong even if it *does* increase overall happiness. People should be free to do/eat as they wish (without hurting others), even if this does **not** increase happiness. This is because liberty is morally important, regardless of whether it increases happiness.

D Another answer (one that is different from A, B or C).

Issue: some problems with calculating utility

This next set of criticisms involves difficulties, both theoretical and practical, with assessing how much happiness/avoidance of pain an action may bring about.

It is impossible to compare pleasures

Bentham thoughtfully provided an ingenious utility calculus to aid our moral thinking (see page 210), but he did not explain how we are supposed to go about measuring things like the 'intensity' or 'remoteness' of the pleasure or pain. Should we issue a questionnaire to the people involved? ('On a scale of 1–10, how would you rate the pain of exam revision?') As outlined earlier (page 225), it is hard enough to compare and rate two of your own pleasures in your own head, let alone compare the value of pleasure between people.

Average happiness versus total happiness

Have a go at the activity in the margin. World A has a higher happiness total, but world B has a higher average. When we aim to maximise utility, is it average utility or total that we should aim for? This is a difficult (and real) question for utilitarians and also for governments. Is it better to have large populations who are less happy (perhaps because of overcrowding and limited resources), or smaller populations who may be happier per person, but with a lower total happiness? The answer makes a moral difference. If you are trying to maximise the total, then providing free contraception might be morally wrong (as it stops children being born, who would add to the total happiness), whereas if you were maximising the average, then providing free contraception may be the right thing to do.

Both approaches have their problems. Going for the total may end up with an overcrowded world of barely happy people; going for the average could (theoretically) involve killing anyone less than averagely happy (as this would raise the average). Though taken to its logical conclusion, this would end up with a world with just one person in it – who is fantastically happy!

Strict versus progressive accounts of utilitarianism

This problem is not really one of calculation, but rather a problem as to what to describe as a good action in relation to the calculation.

The pizza example (page 212) involved you treating friends to a meal. We imagined that this added happiness to the world (a notional 99 points) and so was a morally good act. However, you *could* have used that money differently; perhaps by giving it to a charity, you could have treated 100 starving people to a decent, hot meal. This, surely, would have provided more than 99 happiness points. If this is the case, was treating your friends to pizza a good or right thing to do?

A strict utilitarian would claim that a good action is one that *maximises* general happiness. So treating friends to pizza would not be good, as there are many better options in terms of bringing about happiness. Our moral duty is to maximise happiness with our actions.

A progressive utilitarian would say that treating friends to pizza was a good act as it *increased* general happiness, though other acts would be better as they would have increased general happiness more. Our moral duty is to increase general happiness (though it would be good to maximise it).

Both versions have problems. The strict version would mean that a non-wealthy single mother who gives away half of her income to charity is still not doing the right thing. It is not a good act, as she could have given even more. This seems too strict. The progressive version would mean that any act that adds happiness is morally good – even telling a joke. Or perhaps a sadistic surgeon[22] who fixes broken bones, but does so deliberately in a way that makes the recovery more painful. He is still performing good acts, as over time his acts relieve more pain than they cause. But to call his actions good seems too lenient. Some argue for a compromise version.

▶ **ACTIVITY: TWO WORLDS**

Imagine two worlds:

World A has 10 billion people who are not particularly happy, but not sad either. Let us say they have a net worth happiness of 1 point each. This gives a world with a total of 10 billion happiness points, at an average of 1 point per person.

World B has 1 billion people, but they are much happier – say, an average of 9 happiness points each. This gives a total of 9 billion happiness points at an average of 9 points per person.

Which is the better world?

Distribution of happiness

All our happiness should be equally weighted when making decisions. We all count for one. Nevertheless, most actions only affect some people; they have no impact on the vast majority. This raises some difficult questions in our deliberation. Is it better to make one person 100 points happier or ten people 10 points happier? The total happiness is the same in both cases.

Left-leaning thinkers argue that a wider, more even distribution is the ideal to aim at. The wealth of the richest few could be better used to raise happiness for all. Right-leaning thinkers disagree; they argue that we are all better-off with a liberal, capitalist system that encourages wealth and protects individual property. Yes, some people will be richer than others, but overall this system will make us all happier.

Even within your own life, the question of the distribution of happiness is a dilemma. Is it better to have lots of highs and lows, or a quieter life with less fluctuation (but with the same total of happiness)? Is it better to have a life that starts with less happiness and gets better, or a life that starts with lots of happiness that gets worse? (Again, the total is the same.) Which would you prefer?

Where do consequences end?

Example 6: young Hitler

You are walking alongside an Austrian river in January 1900, as the new century is beginning. You see a young boy, about 11 years old, fall into the river, and you wade out and rescue him from drowning. This boy is called Adolf Hitler and he goes on to cause the deaths of millions of innocent people.

From a utilitarian perspective, this would initially look like a good act, as the young Hitler and his family would be very happy. In the end, it turned out to be a very bad act, as millions went on to suffer and die. So the act would be classed as a bad act. The problem is that if the moral worth of an act is based on its consequences, then the moral worth of the act has to be constantly revised and there is no final moral value that can be assigned. If this is the case, can we ever say whether an act is definitely good or bad?

Please note that this is not a problem for deliberation – for example, *Should I save the boy or not?* Saving the boy would always be a praiseworthy act, as you could not reasonably foresee the longer-term consequences. And it is good to follow the rule, *Save life when you can.* The problem lies in deciding the moral worth of an act.

Whose happiness? Humans or animals?

Is it only human happiness/suffering that we should take into account? Earlier we looked at preference utilitarianism. The theory was adopted by Richard Hare, but is most commonly associated with the one of his former students, the Australian philosopher Peter Singer. For Singer, happiness and the avoidance of pain are still at the core of the theory, but these should be gained/avoided by thinking about people's preferences. Singer applies his version of preference utilitarianism to a range of ethical issues, most famously to the treatment of animals.

► **ACTIVITY: DISTRIBUTION OF HAPPINESS**

Read the example of the flatmates on page 235.

How might this be a problem of the distribution of happiness?

Bentham, some 150 years earlier, had raised the issue of whether animals' suffering should count in a utilitarian's thinking.

> *The day may come when the rest of animal creation may acquire those rights which never could have been withholden from them but by the hand of tyranny ... The question is not, Can they reason? nor Can they talk? but, Can they suffer?[23]*

Singer has developed this line of thinking much further. The basis for our moral equality is our sentience, our ability to feel pain and pleasure – which we all share. Singer argues that as animals are also sentient, we should also take their interests into account when making decisions. To not take into account their ability to suffer would be an example of speciesism (treating species differently for no good reason).

Singer's key argument is based on a consideration of the equality of moral interests among humans (this is known as the argument from *marginal cases*). He argues that this cannot be based on intelligence or sporting prowess and so on, as these are not shared by *all* humans – and we want to give *all* humans moral consideration. He claims that the equality of moral interest can only be based on sentience, which is also shared with animals. Formally, his argument looks like this:

P1 If only humans have full and equal moral status, there must be some special quality that all humans share that enables this

P2 All human-specific possibilities for such a quality will be a quality that some human beings lack

P3 The only possible candidates will be qualities that other animals have too

C Therefore, we cannot argue that only human beings deserve moral status

It may be contended that humans do have some unique qualities that grant us special moral status – for example, our DNA – and therefore we should be treated differently. However, this can be countered by the following consideration: a) not all humans have the same DNA; b) what about intelligent, sentient aliens with different DNA – should they have moral status? and c) selecting DNA as the quality seems arbitrary and not morally relevant.

Singer presents another argument for the equality of moral consideration, using the analogy of racism. Racists (say, white supremacists) claim that, because of a particular factor, say, greater intelligence, white people are morally superior to non-white. Their pain counts for more, their lives are worth more, they have greater moral importance and so on. Now it is simply not true that all white people are more intelligent than all non-white people, so a factual mistake is being made here. But another fundamental mistake is also being made. Even if it were true that all white people were more intelligent than all non-white people, it would still be wrong to assign different moral value on the basis of intelligence. For example, we could ask everyone to take an IQ test and divide the world into those with a score above 100 and those with a score below. Should those with a score below be treated differently? This would be wrong. We should not assign moral worth on the basis of intelligence.

This type of argument works for all qualities that admit of degree, such as intelligence and sporting prowess. It does not work so well for other qualities, such as DNA or having a soul. But in the case of DNA, the moral relevance must also be shown, and the arguments about souls have their own weaknesses.

Using this argument, as well as other similarities in human behaviour, Singer sees our treatment of animals as akin to racism – calling it *speciesism*.

Singer, though, does not argue that animals should have all of the same rights as humans – for example, the right to vote. In the same way that men do not have the right to an abortion – as it is irrelevant because of their bodies – animals should not have rights such as the right to vote or freedom of speech, as this would be irrelevant. Indeed, as we discuss later, Singer argues that in certain circumstances, eating animals is not wrong. What *is* morally required though is that we take their interests/welfare equally into account when making decisions.

In his seminal work, *Animal Liberation*, Singer outlines various experiments that seem needlessly cruel. Many of these would be too distressing for this book, but we include one example featuring dogs.

In 1953 R. Solomon, L. Kamin, and L. Wynne, experimenters at Harvard University, placed forty dogs in a device called a 'shuttlebox', which consists of a box divided into two compartments, separated by a barrier. Initially the barrier was set at the height of the dog's back.

Hundreds of intense electric shocks were delivered to the dogs' feet through a grid floor. At first the dogs could escape the shock if they learnt to jump the barrier into the other compartment. In an attempt to 'discourage' one dog from jumping, the experimenters forced the dog to jump one hundred times onto a grid floor in the other compartment that also delivered a shock to the dog's feet. They said that as the dog jumped he gave a 'sharp anticipatory yip which turned into a yelp when he landed on the electrified grid'. They then blocked the passage between the compartments with a piece of plate glass and tested the dog again. The dog 'jumped forward and smashed his head against the glass'. The dogs began by showing symptoms such as defecation, urination, yelping and shrieking, trembling, attacking the apparatus, and so on; but after ten or twelve days of trials dogs who were prevented from escaping shock ceased to resist. The experimenters reported themselves 'impressed' by this, and concluded that a combination of the plate glass barrier and foot shock was 'very effective' in eliminating jumping by dogs.[24]

▶ ACTIVITY: ANIMAL EXPERIMENTATION

1 Is the pain and pleasure of animals morally relevant?
2 Is this experiment described in the quotation above immoral?
3 Would *you* be able to carry out such an experiment?
4 Do you think carrying out such experiments would make you more or less empathetic to the suffering of humans?
5 Would it be morally different if the experiments were being carried out on primates?

Singer is not an absolutist about animal experimentation; for a utilitarian, the end *can* justify the means. However, he is very sceptical about whether the ends ever *do* justify the means. It is very hard to imagine in the case above that the experiment is adding to the sum of happiness in the world.

Singer notes that people arguing *for* animal experimentation often put forward hypothetical questions such as, *What if one experiment on an animal could save a thousand lives?* His reply is to pose another hypothetical question.

> *Would the experimenter be prepared to perform his experiment on an orphaned human infant [baby], if that were the only way to save many lives? ... If the experimenter is not prepared to use an orphaned human infant then his readiness to use non-humans is simple discrimination, since adult apes, cats, mice and other mammals are more aware of what is happening to them, more self-directing and, so far as we can tell, at least as sensitive to pain as any human infant.*[25]

Criticism: an alien way of discussing animals

In her article, 'Eating meat and eating people', Cora Diamond (1937–) takes issue with the way Singer argues for animal rights. The approach Singer takes of 'lining up' all beings and saying we should take their interests into account according to their level of sentience does not do justice to the complexities of our concepts and attitudes to animals or to humans. Diamond adopts an approach similar to that of the later Ludwig Wittgenstein – who argued that words and concepts resist easy definition and we have to look at the complex ways in which we use them to gain a fuller understanding. Diamond argues that if sentience were the only factor, then we should have no problem in eating dead humans who were healthy and died in accidents, or even of eating amputated limbs. No sentience is involved. Yet this *is* a problem, and to understand why, we have to start from a deeper understanding of our current concepts and attitudes to humans and animals. Animals can be pets, companions, meat, vermin, predators, cute, dangerous, pests and so on. Our attitudes to animals are complex and conflicting in some ways, but this complexity is an important part of our moral landscape. Just lining up all living creatures and applying the abstract universal concept of sentience does not do this justice, and is not likely to persuade a farmer to treat animals differently. Arguing from within our existing conceptual understanding and teasing our patterns would be a better approach. We have similarly complex and conflicting attitudes to our fellow humans. They can be friends, lovers, enemies, slaves and so on. Cora analyses a moment described by Orwell from his experience of fighting in the Spanish civil war. When the moment came, Orwell found himself unable to shoot at a half-dressed man who was running away, topless, holding up his trousers with both hands. 'I had come here to shoot at "Fascists", but a man who is holding up his trousers is not a "Fascist", he is visibly a fellow-creature, similar to yourself, and you do not feel like shooting at him'.[26]

Diamond notes how Orwell sees a fellowship in the enemy and is unable to shoot. Similar moments of realisation may occur to individuals in relationship to animals – they may suddenly see not just a sheep, but a fellow creature, and are then unable to stomach a lamb casserole. It is in these moments that vegetarians are made, from within our complex conceptual understanding and not in the application of abstract and alien concepts.

In Singer's defence, many see this approach to philosophy as a kind of anti-philosophy. Defenders of Singer's more traditional approach might argue that philosophy is *precisely* the attempt to define concepts and apply abstract universal principles to organise/clarify our understanding, and philosophers such as Wittgenstein and Diamond are attempting a different discipline entirely.

Issue: partiality

As a reformer, Bentham was passionate about equality, especially complete equality for women. The utilitarian morality sees everyone as equally important: 'every individual in the country tells for one; no individual for more than one'.[27]

Bentham was writing primarily for governments, and most of us would want our government to treat each citizen's welfare and happiness as having equal worth. But does this also apply to individuals making moral decisions? Should a good utilitarian treat all people as moral equals? If so, this seems to imply that we should never be partial – that is, to favour yourself, or those close to you, when making moral decisions. Mill seems to support this 'impartial' approach:

> [T]he happiness which forms the utilitarian standard of what is right in conduct, is not the agent's own happiness, but that of all concerned. As between his own happiness and that of others, utilitarianism requires him to be as strictly impartial as a disinterested and benevolent spectator.[28]

This view, taken from a strict utilitarian stance, would seem to make our moral duties far-reaching. Given that there are people in the world who are starving and in need of shelter, it would seem to be that I should give nearly all of my money to help these people – and I should do this every time I get money. This is the view adopted by a young Peter Singer. Writing about a humanitarian crisis in Bengal, he argued that people:

> ought to give as much as possible, that is, at least up to the point at which by giving more one would begin to cause serious suffering for oneself and one's dependants.[29]

But is it right to treat everyone equally? When considering how to act morally, am I really obliged to treat people I have never met in Bengal equally with my family and friends? Consider the following example.

Example 7: burning house

Your house is burning. You bravely rush inside to help. Breaking down a door, you find two people lying unconscious. You can only carry one out. One is a young and brilliant scientist who is working on a cure for cancer; the other person is your son. Who should you save?

An act utilitarian would say that saving the scientist would be the most likely way of maximising general happiness; however, most people would save their own son. This, they would argue, was the right thing to do, because we have moral obligations to our family and friends. In other words, you have a moral duty to be partial, **not** impartial in some circumstances.

How could a utilitarian respond to this difference between what their theory says is the right thing and many/most people's intuitions?

There are two elements to this:

The judgement about what is the right thing to do (J) (be impartial and save the scientist)

and

The intuition about what is the right thing to do (I) (be partial and save your son).

J is right, I is wrong. A utilitarian could maintain that saving the scientist is the right thing to do (J) and explain that it is understandable to want to save your son (I), but wrong. They may add that the instincts we have to look after family are driven by evolution, but that they are morally wrong.

J is wrong, I is right. Critics may argue that it is right to save your son, on every level. It is right because we have special moral obligations to our family. This could be because we have duties of care and/or because relationships have moral worth, and not, as a rule utilitarian may argue, because looking after families is just a useful way of maximising happiness. Looking after families is an end in itself, not a side effect of maximising happiness.

J is right, I is right. A rule or two-tier utilitarian might try to claim that saving your son is the right thing to do, as the rule of looking after family is a good one (as it ensures that everyone is looked after and this will maximise happiness). However, in this instance, saving the scientist would have maximised happiness. So the judgement is that saving the scientist is better, but the rule – the method of deliberation – says that saving the son is better.

Singer later argues for this point of view.

> *It is from an agent-neutral point of view that we determine whether an action was right; but it is a mistake to focus always on the rightness of individual actions, rather than on the habit or intuitive ways of thinking that can be expected, over a lifetime, to do the most good.*[30]

Whether a utilitarian can maintain this seemingly contradictory position is debatable.

How impartial should governments be?

We suggested above that we want our government to treat each citizen's welfare and happiness as having equal worth. We want governments to be impartial. But how impartial should they be? Why should the government favour the citizens of the UK in particular? This question is similar to the issue of the burning house above, but writ large, on a societal level.

A rule utilitarian may argue (as in the case above) that the best overall rule is that every country looks after its own population (after all, the UK government's money comes from UK taxpayers). Others think this is unfair and that rich countries should not sit back and watch fellow humans starve and suffer. More should be achieved through increased foreign aid.

Even within this country, should all people's happiness be treated equally? For example, some people feel it unfair that recently arrived refugees get some form of access to housing (often very limited) when they themselves have found it very difficult to gain social housing. Should the government take everyone's welfare into account equally? Or should those who have lived here 'longer' get more priority?

Issue: does utilitarianism ignore the moral integrity of the individual?

Bernard Williams (1929–2003) argues that ethical systems such as utilitarianism (and KANTIAN ETHICS) may require us to do things that go against our intuitions, and this challenges our sense of personal integrity. The following example illustrates a difficult choice.

Example 8: Jim in the outback (adapted from Bernard Williams[31])

A botanist, Jim, is working in a South American country that is fairly lawless. Jim ends up in a small town, where the local warlord treats him as a guest of honour. The warlord has recently taken 20 people from local tribes and is going to kill them as a way of keeping all the tribes fearful. The warlord says that if Jim personally shoots one of them, he will release the others as a sign of good will. If Jim does not do this, he will kill them all.

What should Jim do?

An act utilitarian would say there is no dilemma here. You kill the one to save the 19. However, Jim does not want to harm, let alone kill anyone. It goes against one of his key principles. He has lived his life around this principle and it defines, in part, who he is. What should he do? Utilitarianism, as a consequentialist ethic, would have us do anything in the name of maximising happiness. There is no act so bad that we cannot invent a scenario where this is the right thing to do. Furthermore, a utilitarian would say that if Jim did kill the one man, he should not have any guilt or regret, as it was the right thing to do.

The problem is that consequentialist ethics never allow you to draw a line in the sand and say, *I will not do that*. Yet Williams argues, for many people, their personal integrity demands that there are such lines in the sand. If Jim did shoot one person, then his sense of self, of purpose may be destroyed.

In this way, utilitarianism can undermine our personal integrity. The character of the person committing the act may not reckon in the moral value of the act, but it does matter to the person committing the act. More formally, Williams' argument would look something like this.

- Personal integrity requires that there are things that you would not do (X and Y).
- Using a utilitarian framework, a scenario can always be created that shows that doing X and Y is the right thing to do.
- Therefore utilitarianism undermines our personal integrity.

In defence of this, you could argue that a person's sense of personal integrity is culturally acquired. The difficulty is that if we cede to our intuitions or even our sense of personal integrity, then this gives too much weight to a person's upbringing, which in turn can work to maintain the moral status quo, which is not always good (see Singer quote on page 201). Utilitarianism does not ask us to give up personal integrity completely, but instead requires us to develop core, defining values around the principle, such that there would be not conflict between personal integrity and utilitarianism.

In Chapter 2.3 on virtue ethics, we explore a different approach to ethics entirely. This approach, deriving from ancient times, focuses moral worth not on consequences, nor on the motive, but on the people who carry out the actions themselves. What is important is to be a good person, as this is the key source of moral value.

Issue: does utilitarianism ignore the intentions of the individual?

In judging an action as good or bad, utilitarianism focuses solely on the consequences of the action – weighing how much pleasure or pain the act adds to the world. This has advantages in as much as consequences are more transparent than motives. For example, a prime minister may introduce a new policy to win favour with voters, or for reasons of personal ambition, or to annoy the opposition. The true motives may never be known. In contrast, what *can* be seen is whether the policy has utility – whether it maximises happiness. It is on this basis alone, according to utilitarians, that we should judge the policy as good or bad. However, one big problem for utilitarianism (and all consequentialist ethical theories) is that they can feel counter-intuitive precisely because they focus solely on the consequences and seem to ignore the intentions.

Example 9: visiting Grandma

A   Simra visits her elderly grandma once a week. She buys a few groceries, tidies up a little, helps Grandma with her post and reads to her. Grandma loves the visits; Simra does not particularly enjoy them, but she visits out of a sense of duty to the family.

B   Maisie visits her elderly grandma once a week. She buys a few groceries, tidies up a little, helps Grandma with her post and reads to her. Grandma loves the visits; Maisie does not particularly enjoy them – she visits to increase the chances of getting lots of money in Grandma's will.

Which of these two, almost identical acts, has the most moral worth? Many would argue that A does. A utilitarian would calculate the pleasure that each of the acts brings – which is roughly the same in both cases. Both acts are equally good. However, this feels counter-intuitive. Surely the motive for carrying out the act plays a part in the moral worth of the act. A utilitarian would disagree. They would claim that the acts have the same moral worth. Utilitarians often argue that we can still use the concepts of blame and praise, as distinct to the moral worth of the action. In this way, the intention of the agent can be acknowledged in our moral language. Consider these two cases.

Example 10: the evil scientist

Evil scientist Jake decides to poison the water supply of a town (to avenge his horrible childhood). However, it transpires that the poison, when diluted, has no harmful effect, and in fact it acts as a mild pain relief for those with arthritis. Good or bad? A utilitarian would say that because of the consequences, the act was good. A good thing happened that day. The utilitarian would argue, however, that we would not want to praise Jake. In fact, he should be morally blamed as he was trying to cause pain.

Example 11: the elderly lady

Jaspreet saw an elderly lady struggling up some steps to get to a shop. She tried to help, but in holding her arm she made the old lady lose her balance and fall, breaking her hip in the process. Good or bad? In this case, a utilitarian would say that a bad thing happened – pain was added to the world. The utilitarian would not blame Jaspreet, however, as she was trying to do good and could not reasonably have foreseen the pain caused. (Though if she could have reasonably foreseen the fall, then she might be considered negligent and so could be blamed to some extent.)

So, although utilitarianism can be criticised for not weighing up the intentions in the moral value of any action, this can be mitigated to some extent because intentions can be acknowledged through concepts of praise and blame. By praising and blaming people, we can encourage people to act in ways that help people. In general, acting on the intention of causing pain will result in causing pain, and trying to help result in more happiness. Praising those who try to help people will therefore contribute to increasing happiness, so it is important to do this. However, the moral worth of the action is based on the consequences alone.

Summary of utilitarianism

Despite the many problems with Bentham's and Mill's versions of utilitarianism, the theory captures a powerful intuition: that morality is not just about following rigid rules and principles, irrespective of the consequences (as Kantian deontology tells us). For many policymakers, utilitarianism is the only moral theory in town: it does not depend on any metaphysical system (such as the belief in God); it is flexible (unlike Kantian ethics); and it seems to describe much of what we do mean by a morally good act (one that increases the amount of happiness and decreases the amount of pain in the world). It is a firmly humanistic and practical system, even if it is not the whizz-bang moral-calculating machine that its originators first thought.

Because of its power, utilitarianism has become influential in policymaking around the world. When economists and politicians try to determine policy, they will, in general, perform a cost–benefit analysis on the different courses of action available to them. In other words, they weigh up the costs and the benefits, to help them to decide which policy or decision will maximise the benefits.

2.1.2 Applying utilitarianism

In this section we will apply the theory of utilitarianism to four specific areas: *stealing, simulated killing, eating animals* and *telling lies*. In each area, we refer back to the ethical dilemmas presented in the introduction (pages 202–205).

Stealing

For an act utilitarian, stealing would be morally good if the happiness gained from the theft outweighs the pain caused. For an act utilitarian, the end (happiness) can justify the means, even when the 'means' is illegal. However, before you are tempted to steal, consider these points:

In general, theft is wrong, as the pain caused to the victim far outweighs the pleasure gained by the thief.

Stealing is nearly always illegal and people get upset when others break the law, so this adds to the total pain caused. Having laws around property ownership makes us all feel more secure, and this lawfulness is a big source of background happiness. Because of the strong disapproval of law-breaking, the default position of an act utilitarian is that law-breaking is morally wrong.

As stealing is illegal, if you are caught, you may well be punished, and this too adds to the pain in the world.

But in some cases it can seem as if stealing might be a morally good thing. Consider this modern-day Robin Hood.

Example 12: Robin Hood

A close associate of Mr Amveryrich (the billionaire owner of Madchester football club), through some clever accounting, steals £10 million from Mr Amveryrich's account (who never finds out). He uses the money to fund an orphanage in Lithuania.

Is this a good act? An act utilitarian might say this is a good act as it adds happiness to the world. However, oddly, were the thief to be caught, it would become a bad act, as the money might be reclaimed and the victim and the criminal will suffer. The moral worth of the act depends on the thief getting away with it.

For many people, this is counter-intuitive: what makes illegal acts bad is committing the act itself, not the consequences. It is just bad to break the law.

This is exactly the position of strong rule utilitarianism: it is always wrong to break a rule/law (as long as the law is one that overall maximises happiness), as the moral value of an act comes from its observance of the rule. Because many laws *are* moral rules (do not kill, steal, drive dangerously and so on), the law *is*, in effect, rule utilitarianism.

For a strong rule utilitarian, the only time it might be right to steal is if you think the law protecting the property was unjust. For example, in 1930 Mahatma Gandhi encouraged thousands to march with him in India and extract salt directly from the sea, without paying the salt tax to the British, which he thought unjust. This is stealing from the state, but because the law mainly benefited the wealthy, imperialist rulers, then breaking this law/rule could be morally justified.

▶ **ACTIVITY**

Read ST1 and ST2 on page 203.
What would a utilitarian say?

A weak rule utilitarian might argue that stealing is both illegal and wrong, apart from those very few occasions when happiness will clearly be gained by the theft: then it is morally right to steal (though not legally right) – perhaps in the Robin Hood case above.

A rule utilitarian, however, would *also* argue that utility is best achieved by us all following the law and not making exceptions, which would be to set a meta-rule about rule-following itself. So the utilitarian would not only have to feel that stealing would maximise happiness, but also take into account the general way that this undermines laws and so makes us less happy. This makes the act of law-breaking even harder to justify.

Regarding ST1 (page 203), a utilitarian should not place the value of his wife's happiness above that of anyone else (which, again, some feel is counter-intuitive; see page 242). It would only be right to steal the drug for his wife if it is also right to steal it for a stranger he has never met. The NHS has analysed the situation and obviously feels that the money the drug costs could be used more efficiently to make people happy. This is the rule that has been set. From an act utilitarian perspective, it would seem wrong to use the drug, as the money could be better used elsewhere (presuming the NHS would get the money back from the drug company for the leftover drugs). Also, drug companies need to sell their drugs to fund research into new drugs. Stealing drugs means reducing this research, which in the long term may result in less reduction of suffering.

From a rule utilitarian perspective, the rule has been set by the NHS on the basis of maximising utility. This would seem to be a just rule and so it would be wrong to break it.

An act utilitarian might argue that ST2 is morally good, as Nathan gains pleasure from the music, pleasure he otherwise would not have had. Some of the musicians he listens to might even agree. Others would say that if no one paid for the music then they could not make it (even though, *It is all about the music, not the money*, and so on!), so there would be less music to listen to and less happiness overall.

Nathan might make a (reasonable?) assumption that most people are law-abiding and will pay money, so then his gaining it for free does not stop the music being made, it just adds to the total pleasure in the world as he enjoys listening to it. But if enough people thought like Nathan, then … (some of the avenues of possible discussion lead to complex areas of game theory).

A strict rule utilitarian would acknowledge that stealing is illegal and that breaking the law is wrong. The only justification for breaking the law is if you could argue that the law was morally unjust. Is copyright law in music morally unjust? Would abolishing copyright law in regard to music make the world a happier place? Could you argue this? A world of free, but possibly not very well-produced music?

Also remember that not only do people not like having money stolen from them, they also get very unhappy when ideas are taken. With no copyright laws, this could happen all the time.

Simulated killing

For a utilitarian, there is something paradoxical in the 'pleasure' gained from watching people being killed. On the one hand, there is the pleasure, and on the other, the portrayal of pain and death. Presumably people would think very differently if real death were involved (although public executions were always well-attended historically).

This links to Nozick's analysis of the pleasure machine – what we want in life (and want to avoid in this case) are real events in the world, not just sensations in our head. The physical sensations of watching a fake or real death may be almost identical for the viewer; the difference is knowing that one is real and the other is not.

All pleasures are equal for the utilitarian (not quite for Mill though, as we shall see). The pleasure of watching a fake killing is of the same worth as that gained from listening to opera or that gained from watching a real killing. The pleasure counts for the same in each case; what determines whether it is a good or bad thing overall is whether the sum total of pleasure outweighs the pain, or whether pleasure is maximised (this depends on your interpretation of utilitarianism; see page 237).

So, does watching deaths on stage, screen or in a video game overall produce more happiness than it does harm? Could alternatives be produced that are more pleasurable, with less harm caused? Would the world be happier without simulated death, or with it?

These are the key questions for the utilitarian. There is no question of such entertainments being intrinsically wrong, as wrong is defined entirely by ends (pain or less happiness), not the means.

On the positive side (happiness) are the following considerations:

- These entertainments produce a lot of pleasure. They are very popular.
- There are often secondary pleasures gained from engaging with a part of a specific culture – chatting with friends about games, conventions and so on.
- They are also part of successful industries that supply jobs, create wealth and advance technology.
- Video games can have beneficial effects in terms of motor skills.

And on the negative/harm side:

- Violent video films, and in particular video games, have been linked to increased antisocial behaviour in the short and longer terms (however, there is also evidence that shows there is very little link).
- Too much time spent on video games can have harmful effects on health (in terms of sedentary lifestyle).
- People disapprove of these activities and this causes some sadness.

Simulated killing is hugely popular. An immense amount of pleasure is being caused every second by these sources. In the last 20 years, violent crime has decreased in the UK and in other Western countries too, and this is at the same time that violent video games and films have boomed. This, on the face of it, suggests that any causal link between video games and violence cannot be strong.

▶ **ACTIVITY**

Read SK1 and SK2 on pages 203–204. What would a utilitarian say?

It would be very hard to argue that such entertainments cause more harm than good. Rock climbing, horse riding and even football cause far more average harm per hour to the player. And football is also associated with a level of violence in and around stadiums (though less so in recent years).

Higher/lower distinction

For Mill, the sorts of pleasure produced by violent films and video games may well be the wrong sorts of pleasure (see page 222). These entertainments may be classed as lower pleasures, which, though still good, are of lower worth. A 'competent judge' may prefer other sorts of higher pleasures and Mill thought that we should prioritise these. Mill wanted utility not just to be about physical pleasure but *'utility in the largest sense, grounded on the permanent interests of man as a progressive being.'*[32]

Mill may argue that the pleasures gained from simulated killing appeal to our baser, animal side and not to our progressive, intellectual side. Although they are pleasurable, maximising such pleasures is not as morally good as enjoying the less 'pleasant' higher pleasures of, say, reading Tolstoy, or even this book!

Holding a higher/lower qualitative distinction may alter the result of the utilitarian calculus on simulated killing entertainments. By how much is not clear: do we halve the pleasure total on the 'gained' column? The fact that there is no easy answer to this question is a criticism of having such a distinction in the first place. Also, it is questionable whether such entertainments are, in fact, lower pleasures. They are cultural, engage the brain and so are not just the equivalent of, say, drinking gin.

The question of the competent judge is an interesting one too. Mill never played video games; he may have taken to *Grand Theft Auto* like a duck to water. There are many competent judges who can appreciate both video games and Tolstoy, and prefer the former. So the higher/lower distinction (itself questionable), does not necessarily downgrade the status of the pleasure gained from these entertainments, as they are not clearly lower pleasures.

Liberty

Many people are offended by the existence of violent video games. Should their displeasure (or their preferences) be taken into account in the utility calculation? Also, could it not be argued that the same amount of pleasure could be gained by alternative methods of entertainment that offer less offence/harm? If so, it could be argued that playing violent games may not be so good (like the sadist surgeon on page 237).

The problem with taking into account the offence of others is that this approach places too much power in the moral sentiments of the majority. Perhaps all things that the majority find displeasurable or offensive should be considered immoral? Mill argued passionately that the secondary principle (or rule) of liberty should play a central role in utilitarianism. We should all be free to pursue our own pleasures, as long as we do not harm others (the extent to which offence counts as harm has to be fairly minimal). A society committed to liberty, freedom of expression and the pursuit of different goals will be happier in the long run. And this is a society that does not allow the moral sentiments of some to dictate the non-harmful pursuits of others. So, for Mill, allowing people to play video games is a good thing, as this follows the rule of liberty, which is the rule that will enable utility to be best maximised. Exceptions to the principle of liberty are made in the cases of children. Parents and the state are permitted to restrict freedom, and freedom of access, for children, for their own benefit.

In summary, for a utilitarian, simulated killing is morally good as long as the pleasure outweighs the harm. The distinction between higher and lower pleasures is ambiguous, both in general, and in its specific application to the case in question. Mill would also claim that pursuing pleasures that are not harmful to others is, in general, a good thing. Simulated killing is a clear source of happiness for millions; for a utilitarian, such things are morally good.

Eating animals

As we saw on page 239, Peter Singer has argued that the pain and pleasure of animals has moral weight. However, he claims that eating meat is not always wrong.

Singer is a preference utilitarian, which means that we should try to maximise preferences. Animals are limited in their rationality and (as far as we know) do not hold specific hopes and thoughts about the future (with the possible exception of great apes). As such, animals do not have conscious preferences, which makes a difference to how we might treat them morally.

What makes killing humans morally wrong is not specifically the potential loss of pleasure, but that the killing goes against the preference of the victim (and the preferences of the victim's family and friends). Staying alive is (generally) the strongest preference that anyone has, and this is what makes murder so bad. Also, in killing someone, you are also not just overriding one of their preferences (to stay alive), but also their preference to learn Spanish, write a novel, learn to make bread, watch all of Jim Carrey's movies and so on. You are going against thousands and thousands of their wishes and desires.

However, can we say the same of animals? It is highly unlikely that animals have similar conscious preferences (after all, most have never heard of Jim Carrey!). We might reasonably infer that animals prefer not to be in pain, as their behaviour suggests this, but can we even say that an animal has a conscious preference to stay alive? Probably not, as the animal would lack the necessary conceptual framework. In which case, the painless killing of an animal does not go against its preference, so is not morally wrong on this account. However, if someone killed your family pet, then this would go against the preferences of the family and so it would be a wrong act.

(Controversially, Singer extends this line of thinking to young (and unborn) babies. They do not have conscious preferences, so ending their lives does not go against their preference (though again, it is more than likely to go against the preferences of the family).)

In the case of EA1 (page 204), Singer claims that causing such suffering would be wrong if we could gain our food in other ways (which we can). Most forms of intensive food farming cause considerable suffering, and eating from these sources is morally wrong.

anthology 2.4

▶ **ACTIVITY**
Read anthology 2.4. Do you agree with Singer's reasoning?

Example EA2 is a harder case to call. If animals were genuinely being raised in a way that did not cause undue suffering (and in the example some doubts are raised about this) and are painlessly killed, then no specific preferences are being quashed (apart from the preferences of some vegetarians, but these are cancelled by the preferences of meat eaters). Singer would also want the farm to be sustainable, so that more cows could be raised. This way, even if one cow is killed, another is born, so the total amount of cow pleasure in the world would remain the same. (Note that this principle is not true for humans: my preferences are specific to me and different to yours. Humans are not replicable in the same way.) If these conditions are met, then eating the animals from Gilbert's farm may not be wrong.

The sub-question about a similar ape farm is different though. Apes and primates, Singer argues, also have 'interests' that other animals may not have. (Though it is all a matter of degree.) So killing apes has a different moral weight to killing other animals.

The great apes are intelligent beings with strong emotions that in many ways resemble our own. Chimpanzees, bonobos and gorillas have long-term relationships, not only between mothers and children, but also between unrelated apes. When a loved one dies they grieve for a long time. They can solve complex puzzles that stump most two-year-old humans. They can learn hundreds of signs and put them together in sentences that obey grammatical rules. They display a sense of justice, resenting others who do not reciprocate a favour.[33]

Telling lies

As in the other examples, for an act utilitarian, the end justifies the means. So lying is completely morally acceptable if it maximises happiness/minimises harm. In fact, in such instances, not only would lying be morally acceptable, but it is the right thing to do – we *ought* to lie. (Remember, though, that it is general happiness that is to be maximised, and not just your own.) For some, this seems an odd conclusion. Consider this example.

Example 13: American tourists

Two American tourists stop you in London. They have just got into town, have never been to London before and ask you for the quickest way to get to St Paul's Cathedral. You do a very hasty utilitarian calculation, and instead of telling them the quickest way, you tell them the most scenic route, which is to walk across Waterloo Bridge (see the Waterloo sunset), hop along the South Bank and then cross the Millennium Bridge to St Paul's. Though a good ten minutes longer, than the quickest route, it is the easiest to describe and you strongly believe they will gain more pleasure this way. They ask you again if you are sure this is the quickest way. You lie and say yes.

Is this right? Surely you should just come clean, but if you do, they will take the trafficky, stressful, ugly, quickest route, rather than stroll along the beautiful South Bank.

Some criticise utilitarianism for this approach, claiming that telling the truth (as well as keeping promises) comes with its own moral obligation, regardless of the consequences. A utilitarian would naturally disagree, but would note that lying and breaking promises are highly likely to cause upset in many/most cases, as, in general:

- people do not like being lied to
- people do not like being accused of lying
- people want to be trusted and lying undermines this
- lying frequently causes hurt when discovered
- lying often causes stress to the liar (having to remember lies, the thought of being discovered and so on)
- lying weakens people's general faith in humanity, and so lowers happiness.

For these reasons alone, lying comes with an inbuilt negative outcome, so the benefits of the lie clearly need to outweigh this too. Because of this, everything being equal, it is generally wrong to lie and break promises. It is also hard to predict what the outcome of a lie may be. The American tourists above may have a particular need to get to St Paul's in a rush, and the delay may lead to a lot of stress. Also, the positive benefits of the lie often rely on the lie not being uncovered, and it can be very hard to know if this will happen or not. Again, this uncertainty makes the default position of truth-telling much stronger. So, although an act utilitarian would deny that truth-telling (and promises) comes with an inherent moral obligation, they would acknowledge that truth-telling, in general, should be the default position.

To test your intuitions about the inherent wrongness of lying, consider the example of a lie that would never be discovered – a lie that has no positive or negative consequences either way. Imagine that someone whom you will never meet again (and never do meet again), in passing, asks how old you are. You lie, by one year. Is this wrong? Or is it morally neutral? Some would say the former, some the latter; it all depends on your moral intuition about whether lying is inherently wrong, or only wrong if it has consequences.

Rule utilitarianism

Above we saw the argument that lying has a default position of being wrong. This way of thinking leads naturally into rule utilitarianism. We can conclude from these considerations that, in general, lying will cause more harm than good. The rule, *Tell the truth*, is one that will maximise utility. So, for a strong rule utilitarian, it is always wrong to tell a lie (as the moral value of the act depends on whether it is in accordance with the rule). A weak rule utilitarian would, in general, tell the truth, but occasionally lie if it was clear that lying would maximise happiness.

For many people, weak rule utilitarianism is the position that best describes their intuitions. Few would argue that telling the truth is *always* the right thing to do (as in TL2, page 205).

A final mention should go to preference utilitarianism. Rather than focusing on whether a lie would bring more happiness, the theory suggests we should focus on whether a lie would satisfy more preferences. This is significant, as most people have a preference to be told the truth, which further justifies the default position of truth-telling. However, there are times (*Does this suit look nice? Did my speech go well?*) when the questioner would prefer to be lied to, in which case, lying is the right thing to do. The position of the preference utilitarian is also different, as someone's preference to be told the truth is frustrated when a lie is told, and this does not rely on whether the person finds out they are being lied to or not. Whereas for plain old utilitarianism, some lies may only become wrong when the lie is discovered, as this is when the upset is caused. See the example of the new friend, on page 271.

In TL1, an act utilitarian may argue that the affair should be pursued. It certainly seems as if pleasure would be gained in the short term. The longer term is harder to gauge: guilt, mistrust and disillusionment may result if it does not work out. The pleasures they are pursuing are fleeting and high-risk, the key risk being whether the husband will find out. It is a difficult decision to make using reason alone (you suspect the decision to lie may not have been fuelled by reason alone). This is why act utilitarianism is not a good method of deliberation, as there are too many unknowns. Rule utilitarians may have different answers to this, depending on the different rules that they think would generally maximise happiness. Would the world be a happier place if no affairs ever occurred? Or is it happier for having affairs? A preference utilitarian may have a slightly different take on this too, as the husband may well have a preference for his wife being faithful. In which case, the affair goes against this preference, so this needs to be added into the equation from the start. From a traditional utilitarian perspective, if the affair is not discovered and pleasure is gained, then the act is a good thing. The displeasure of the husband is only relevant to the moral value of the act if he finds out. From a preference utilitarian perspective, it is relevant to the moral value whether or not he finds out, as his preference is not being satisfied from the outset.

TL2 is much easier for a utilitarian – you lie! No sensible rule utilitarian would have a rule that says 'Never lie', as following this would not maximise happiness. In this scenario, the utilitarian approach seems to work well, as the consequences seem obvious. However, if it turned out that Bob were saved by your lie, but himself became a serial killer, then your act would have been a bad one. You would not be blameworthy though, as you could not reasonably have foreseen this. Your decision to lie would be praiseworthy and be the right one based on the circumstances.

2.2 Kantian deontological ethics

2.2.1 Kantian ethics

Background

Immanuel Kant is one of the most important philosophers of all time. Unfortunately, he is also one of the most difficult to understand!

Kant was born and lived for most of his life in the town of Königsberg (then part of Germany/Prussia, now part of Russia). He was an academic and wrote on a wide range of subjects, including geology, mathematics, science, religion, aesthetics and philosophy. It is his work on philosophy and ethics for which he is most famous.

Kant was writing during a period of intense intellectual activity in Europe, a period that became known as the Enlightenment. Thinkers of this 'age of reason' were beginning to liberate themselves from the restrictive ties to the Church that had characterised most of the Middle Ages, and which had still been felt by the father of modern philosophy, René Descartes. There was a confidence in human reason, boosted by the growing successes of 'natural philosophy' (what we now call science) in explaining the physical laws of the universe. Religious authority could no longer determine what people ought to think about the nature of the universe, nor about what was right or wrong. Human beings had come of age and were sufficiently 'enlightened' to realise that they had to discover their values for themselves, rather than expect them to be delivered by a higher power.

Kant, however, was sceptical of the optimistic claims made by some 'RATIONALIST' philosophers about the extent to which human reason alone could grasp truths about the universe. Kant thought that our knowledge is pretty much limited to that which we can experience. However, he also thought that by analysing the nature of human thought and morality, we could unravel their inner structures or forms. This would reveal an important kind of knowledge – knowledge that did not derive from any specific experience of the world, but that would apply to all experiences. In this way, much of Kant's philosophy is concerned with discovering the hidden rules and laws that govern how our mind understands the world, and how morality functions.

Two things fill the mind with ever new and increasing admiration and awe, the oftener and more steadily we reflect on them: the starry heavens above and the moral law within.[1]

Kant was a Christian, but he did not believe that ethics could be founded on the commands of God. He believed that morality was independent of God's and everyone else's will. The moral law is something that each of us can discover within us, through the use of reason, rather than being instructed from another source. Kant outlines his ethical theory in two important works, *Groundwork of the Metaphysics of Morals* (1785) and the longer *Critique of Practical Reason* (1788).

Introduction

The philosophy of Kant is particularly difficult to understand. There are several reasons for this.

- Philosophy, by its very nature, can be quite difficult. After all, it tackles the problems that have not yet been solved.
- Kant's approach in philosophy is very abstract, and he always wants to go back to first principles when exploring any issue.
- Kant developed a complete philosophy that fits together as a whole. This often makes looking at a part of it complicated, as it was not intended to stand in isolation.
- Kant invented a lot of new terminology – much of which has remained in philosophy – but it can make his writing hard to follow.

That said, all of what follows comes down to a fairly simple idea, which is that when we perform a particular moral action, we must be able to consistently assert that everyone should act in that way too. In other words, we must be able to assert that this is the right thing for anyone to do, not just me.

Kant came from the tradition of rationalism, which claims that we can gain substantial knowledge through reason alone. In the section on utilitarianism, we saw Mill, the empiricist, attempt to justify morality on the basis of what people actually desire – that is, on the basis of experience. Kant's approach is different. He attempts to work out what the moral laws must be, just by thinking about the nature of morality and laws. His arguments do not depend on what humans desire. Kant presents his philosophy as part of a series of arguments that fit together into a whole. At times, it can feel a bit empty or circular, but like a good jigsaw, the pieces do fit together and make sense in the end. In **Figure 2.7**, we have represented the key steps that Kant makes and we will refer back to this diagram as we proceed.

As **Figure 2.7** shows, Kant is going to argue for something called the CATEGORICAL IMPERATIVE, which we have a duty to follow. This categorical imperative will enable us to work out how we should and should not act. In prose form, Kant's approach is roughly this: *Doing something for the right reason makes it a moral action. The right reason is making sure you only act in a way that you could consistently will that all other people do too. This rule (known as the categorical imperative) acts as a test for the different rules we follow in life. By applying the test we can work out which rules we should follow and which we should not.*

Good will is the source of moral worth

It is impossible to conceive anything at all in the world, or even out of it, which can be taken as good without qualification, except a good will.[2]

anthology
2.5

For Kant, someone with a GOOD WILL is someone who does things for the right reason. Think of your will as your motivator/driving force. So what is a good motivation? What are the right reasons to act? Well, we will see below that for Kant, having a good will is being driven, by duty, to act in accordance with the moral law.

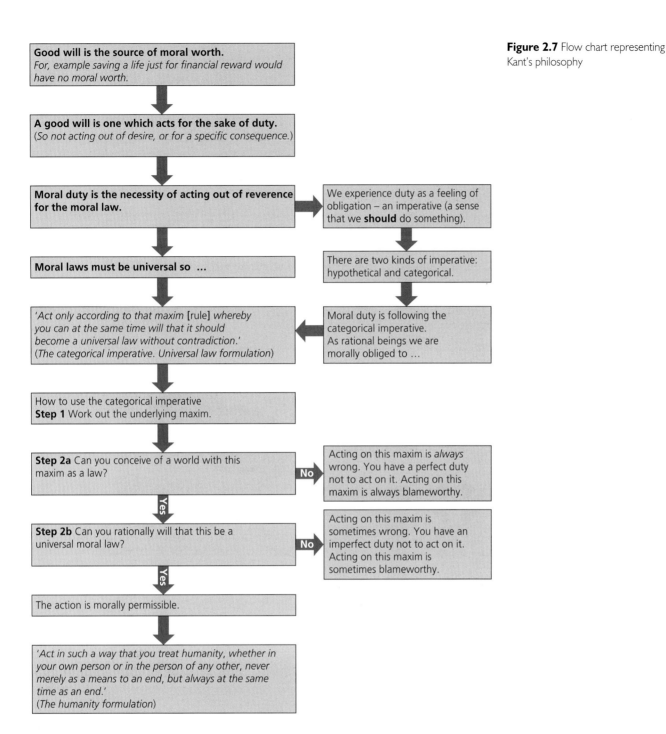

Figure 2.7 Flow chart representing Kant's philosophy

For Kant, a good will represents the only 'pure' good in the world. He also believes it is the source of all moral good/worth. This is quite a difficult idea and needs some unpacking. Most of us pursue ends that we think of as 'good'; this could be the pursuit of say happiness, health or money, or even the pursuit of virtues such as intelligence or creativity. Kant argues that each of these supposed 'goods' can sometimes be bad – in other words, they are not good 'without qualification'. For example, someone may gain happiness from torture, or use intelligence to swindle money from pensioners, and we would not call these ends 'good'. (Bentham, however, would still say that the pleasure gained was good.)

For Kant, no 'end' that we pursue can be thought of as morally good in itself. Happiness, intelligence, money and so on can only be considered good if they are accompanied by, or result from, a good will. In this way, a good will is the source of good. This may sound a little empty; surely a *good* will is good by definition? Thankfully, Kant does give an explanation of what he means by 'a good will': *A good will is one which acts for the sake of duty*.

We will explore what is meant by duty later, but for now think of it as 'doing the right thing for the sake of doing the right thing'. Consider the following example.

Example 1: the drowning man

A man is drowning in a river. You could walk on by or you could help. You decide to help, but what is motivating you?

A You might want to help because you may receive a reward.
B You might want to help because you will receive praise (and maybe some attention from the press!).
C You might help because it is the right thing to do, and you feel it is your duty to do the right thing.

Figure 2.8 The drowning man.
What is your motive for saving the man?

Kant would argue that although helping to save the man is the right thing to do (it is in accordance with duty), if you saved the man for motives A or B, then your action would have no moral worth. Likewise, with example 9 (page 245). Visiting your grandma to potentially gain money would have no moral worth, whereas visiting her because you believe it is the right thing to do, and you feel you have a duty to do the right thing, *is* morally worthy.

Note how this contrasts with utilitarian ethics. Utilitarians claim that the amount of happiness produced is what gives actions their moral value. Happiness is a particular 'end' that we seek to bring about, and a right action is one that brings about this end, regardless of how or why. For a utilitarian, motives play no part in the moral value of an action. Kant's view is the complete opposite: morality is not about the particular ends that we seek to bring about. The only acts that have moral worth are ones that are carried out from a sense of duty – a duty to do the right thing. For Kant, it is the motive, not the consequence, that is key. Because of this, Kant's ethics are often labelled as being DEONTOLOGICAL. This is the general term for ethics that are based on duty (it derives from the Greek *dei*, meaning 'one must').

▶ ACTIVITY: GOOD WILL HUNTING

It is hard to know what a person's motive for an action might be. After all, even if you ask someone, they might be lying. Which of the following actions, if any, do you suspect might be done from good will alone (and without a self-interested motive)?

A Josie enjoys spending time with her children and helps them to practise the piano every day.

B As part of his community service, Colin carefully sets aside four hours every Saturday to work in his local 'Making the World a Better Place' Youth Centre.

C In the weeks running up to his birthday, Marlon always makes an extra special effort helping out his parents, checking they are okay and whether they need anything.

D Leonie gives Friends of the Earth £1. She loves watching the coins whirl round and round the hole before falling into the charity box.

E Samsia notices a large, unaccompanied rucksack by the door of a train, and asks the crowded carriage who owns it.

F Jane keeps her promise to show off her latest dance moves to her philosophy class, despite just having been promoted to head of department.

Criticism: is a good will always good?

Firstly, it can seem a bit circular to say that a good will is good; after all, is a good meal not always good? Secondly, it is not obvious that a good will *is* always good. Imagine a person, Billy, who is very well-meaning and tries to help everyone, as he believes it is the right thing to do. But Billy is very clumsy and keeps accidently hurting people and breaking things as he helps others cross the road or carries their bags. After a while, people might think that Billy's good will is not such a good thing after all.

Humans as imperfectly rational beings

Another way of seeing why it is important to have the right motive is to consider Kant's view that humans are imperfectly rational beings.

Kant believed that, like animals, humans are driven by desires and instincts. However, unlike animals, we can also reason. We are a mixture of reason and desires; this is what he means by being imperfectly rational. As we shall see below, Kant thinks that it is reason that reveals the moral laws that we have a duty to follow. So it is the rational part of us that reveals how we *should* behave morally. On the other hand, our desires and appetites (when mixed with some reason), tell us how we *should* behave non-morally. Our desires give us the goals that we then try to achieve.

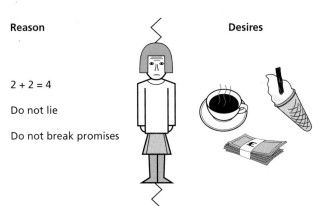

Reason

$2 + 2 = 4$

Do not lie

Do not break promises

Desires

Figure 2.9 Humans are imperfectly rational beings. Our desires tell us how we should behave (non-morally). Our reason tells us how to behave morally.

Acting from desires is to act out of self-interest. Self-interested motives are subjective, particular to the individual and often in conflict (though not always) with the interests of others. Kant believed that moral laws, like scientific laws, are objective and universal, insofar as they apply to all individuals, no matter what differences in personal circumstances, character, wishes, hopes, desires. These laws are revealed by reason.

If we were perfectly rational, we would always do the morally right thing. On the other hand, if we acted on our desires all the time, we would often do the wrong thing. We may sometimes do the right thing (by accident), but it would have no moral value (as we saw in the examples above). Within humans, there is often a tension between these two parts of us: reason and desires. The fact that there is a tension creates the possibility of duty. We may want to walk past the drowning man, or may want to save him for money. However, we have a duty to do the right thing, and that is to assist those in need, when we can. Saving the man, *because* it is the right thing to do, is to act for the sake of duty, and this is what is meant by a good will.

Note that God, or any perfectly rational being, would not do the right thing for the sake of duty. Such beings would not experience the tension between desire and reason and so not need the 'call of duty'.

Further, Kant believed that it is our ability to reason and follow moral laws that gives humans their autonomy. An animal that follows its instincts all the time cannot really be said to be free. It is a slave to its passions. In this way, animals lack autonomy: they are not able to reason, to understand rules and apply these to situations.

Not that following laws by itself gives freedom (although it is the sign of reason). After all, a human who unquestioningly follows the rules of others also cannot be said to be free (for example, a slave may do this). Morality is only possible because we have FREE WILL (and do not have to follow our passions), and autonomy is only achieved when we use reason to create our *own* moral laws. Following laws that we have worked out ourselves using reason is to be our own master and to have autonomy.

Acting in accordance with duty versus acting out of duty

In example 1 of the drowning man (page 258), we saw that acting on your desires will sometimes coincide with doing the right thing (options A and B in the example), but that this is not good enough to make it a moral act. Doing the right thing, but acting on desires, is to act in *accordance* with duty, but not *out* of duty. However, saving the drowning man, not for personal gain but because it is the right thing to do, is to *act out of duty*. Only acting out of duty has moral worth.

This has considerable implications. For example, Jasmin regularly donates to charity – and she may do so simply because it has become a habit, or because she feels like it, or because she hopes that if she is ever in trouble someone will be similarly generous. If she acts from any of these motives, then her action is not, properly speaking, a moral act. She is acting in *accordance* with duty, but not *out* of duty.

Moreover, according to Kant, someone who, through the use of dispassionate reason, recognises her duty to help others in distress, even though she has no compassion for her fellow human beings, is more praiseworthy than someone who would have helped others whether it were his duty or not, because of a compassion for others. For the former must act, as it were, against the grain of her inclinations, while the latter is slavishly led by his emotions. For Kant, the moral person is someone who, among all the noise and demands of our emotions, is able to think through what principles underlie any action, and make sure they act on the right principles. It may help you to imagine a calm, thoughtful person, who always makes sure they do the right thing.

Kant himself gives the example of a shopkeeper who does not rip customers off because he wants a good reputation. For Kant, his actions are not moral. They are not carried out because they are the right thing to do, but because of the shopkeeper's desire for a good reputation.

anthology 2.6

At times, this requirement for a moral act to be motivated by a duty to do the right thing can seem counter-intuitive.

ACTIVITY: FATHERHOOD

Example 2: the dutiful father

Consider these two contrasting fathers:

- Father A spends his evenings developing his son's talents (football and music). He does this because he loves his son, enjoys spending time with him and wants him to flourish.
- Father B spends his evenings developing his son's talents too. He does not love his son and really does not like spending time with children. He does this out of a sense of duty.

Which of the two fathers' dedication is more morally worthy?

Kant would say it is Father B; however, many would have an intuition that it is Father A. It is sometimes held as a criticism of Kant that it would seem to be easier to be moral if you are a bad person, as it is clear that in acting according to duty, you are going against your desires. However, most commentators interpret Kant as saying that in these cases the motive of duty is more clearly seen, not that it is preferable. When your duty and interest coincide, the motive of duty is less clear to see, but as long as you are motivated by duty, then the act is a good act. Kant's idea of duty as the source of good does seem counter-intuitive at times. Philippa Foot (1920–2010) argues that a sense of duty alone does not give us enough reason to act; instead, she claims that people, like Father A, are motivated by moral ends which are not self-interested, and this makes the acts have moral worth (see page 280).

Duty as reverence for the law

So far we have interpreted duty as *doing the right thing for the sake of doing the right thing*. Although this interpretation is in line with Kant's thinking, his definition appears somewhat different, and this again needs some unpacking. For Kant 'Duty is the necessity of acting out of reverence for the law'.[3]

To understand this definition, consider the following scenario.

Experimenting with ideas: the island

You are king of a small island. You make the laws. As a good king, you try to make laws that enable everyone to rub along together and get on with their own lives. Some of your citizens are troublemakers and break the law, but most abide by them. Let us examine these law-abiding citizens in more detail. There are three groups. Group A like the laws and follow them because they think they gain from them. In Group B, some like the laws and some do not, but they abide by them as they fear being caught and punished. In Group C, some like the laws, some do not, but they follow them anyway out of respect for the law. The people in Group C follow the laws, not for what the laws bring, but because they are the laws.

1 As a ruler, do you think Group A, B or C are better citizens?
2 Why?
3 In the UK, which Group of citizens do you belong to: A, B or C?

The problem with saying that group A is better is that some of these citizens may stop following the law if their circumstances change and the law no longer suits them, or if a new law goes against their interest. Group A members are only following the law out of self-interest. Group B is also self-interested. With this group, there is always the risk that they may break the law if they are *certain* they can get away with it. The good thing about group C is that they follow the laws out of duty, out of respect for the law. In this way, they are not acting out of self-interest. Group C can be relied on to be good citizens, come what may.

This is only an analogy, based on political laws, but this is the idea of duty that Kant was articulating: duty as reverence for the law.

The additional thought experiment below may be useful for the discussion ahead, where we explore Kant's attempt to articulate the moral law. Again, this is only an analogy – though it is very closely related to the actual ideas of Kant.

Experimenting with ideas: trouble on the island

A group C citizen, Immanuel, writes a letter to you, his king. Immanuel expresses how he is law-abiding out of respect/reverence for the law, but that he disagrees with some of the rules. He also does not like having to follow them as it makes him feel like a prisoner on the island. He feels he has lost his autonomy.

How might you address his concerns?

You may be tempted to move to a democracy. This would enable the islanders to agree rules when there are differences of opinion. Nevertheless, this would not satisfy Immanuel. The citizens will propose laws from self-interested perspectives and the subsequent discussion and voting would just be a bonfire of the interests to see which emerges from the flames victorious. If Immanuel did not personally vote for the law, he would still be living under someone else's laws. As the king, you come up with an even more radical idea. The islanders are all rational people, so you let them work out and follow their own laws – basic laws that will apply to everyone. The temptation, though, would be for individuals to come up with laws that are in their interest, but clearly such rules will not work for all. In fact, laws based around any specific interest will not work, as not everyone may share this interest. The only rules that will work, for all, are those laws that are drawn from the mere fact that everyone is a rational agent. Anyone coming up with laws that work for all would then feel autonomous as they would be following their own laws. Also, they would feel obliged to follow them, as these would be the rules that all rational agents should follow.

What laws might you come up with?

If we are all rational beings, would we come up with the same rules?

Universal moral laws

Figure 2.10 illustrates what we have seen so far.

This all seems very abstract; to become more practical, we need to discover what these moral laws are. At this stage, you might expect Kant to give a long list of moral laws that we should follow. Unfortunately, he does not do this. Instead, he shows how there is one general principle/rule that itself can be used to find out what the moral laws are (and are not). Also, if Kant gave a list of rules or commandments, this would run counter to the idea of autonomy outlined above. It is only by using reason to work out and follow our own rules that we have autonomy.

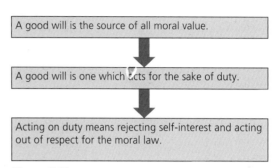

Figure 2.10

So, what would a moral law look like? What features would it have? Well, scientific laws are *objective* and *universal* (in that they apply to the whole universe equally). Moral laws, Kant reasons, should have similar features: they should be objective (not based on your specific viewpoint) and universal (apply equally to all people). A scientific law is often in the form of a formula (for example, $F = ma$) or a principle that you can apply to a specific instance, perhaps to predetermine the outcome. In a similar fashion, a moral law would be in the form of a rule outlining how you should act in a general set of circumstances, which you then apply to your particular circumstance. For example, potential moral laws might include: *When you are hungry, steal property from others* (not a good rule!) or *Help others when they are in need, and no one else can.*

As suggested, the rules need to be universal, they need to apply everywhere. Now it may be the case that when considering potential moral rules (which Kant calls MAXIMS), some of them are impossible to apply consistently in all cases; they *cannot* be rationally UNIVERSALISED. In which case, these potential laws are not fit to be a moral law and we should not follow the rule. So, just by considering what a moral law must be like, Kant is able to conclude that 'I am never to act otherwise than so that I could also will that my maxim should become a universal law.'[4] In other words, we should not act on rules which are incapable of becoming universal laws. For example, consider this potential rule: *I will make promises that I cannot keep.* What would happen if everyone acted on this rule? There would be no institution of promises, and so the rule would undermine what it seeks to do. It is not fit to be a moral law as it cannot be a universal rule.

Hypothetical and categorical imperatives

So, just by considering the nature of a moral law, Kant concludes that we should not act on any rule unless we can universalise it. Kant reaches a similar conclusion through a different line of reasoning: by considering the nature, not of *laws*, but of moral *imperatives*.

Kant believed that morality is experienced as a command or 'IMPERATIVE'; in other words, it tells us what we ought to/should do. An imperative is an inner 'tug' on our will, a compulsion to act in one way rather than another. But there are two different types of imperative, which is to say, two distinct senses of the term 'ought', both of which are related to uses of the word 'good'.

Hypothetical imperatives

One kind of 'ought' is conditional, or (in Kant's terminology) a HYPOTHETICAL IMPERATIVE. An example of this use might be: *If you want a cup of tea, you should boil the water.* Note that this kind of *ought/should* depends upon your having a certain goal or aim, namely getting a cup of tea. The first part of the statement gives us the condition we aspire to; the second part tells us what to do to meet this condition. In other words, the *ought* is conditional upon the desire – which not everyone will have.

Many of the imperatives we encounter in life are based on this type of self-interested, or prudential, reasoning. Not all of them have the same 'if X, then you should Y' formula – sometimes the elements are hidden or implicit. For example: *You should get your pawns out early in chess.* This really means, *If you want to win, then you should get your pawns out early in chess.*

Hypothetical imperatives are often linked to the word *good*, as in: *It is good to get your pawns out early in chess*, or *It is good to boil the kettle when making tea* – although *good* is not used in a moral sense here. This is because hypothetical imperatives are not moral imperatives. After all, consider this example: *If you want to burgle a house, you should wear gloves*, or *It is good to wear gloves when you burgle a house.* This is hardly moral!

Imperatives and reason

Kant believed that as rational beings, if you genuinely have the desire, and the imperative is a sound one, then you are rationally committed to follow it. For example, consider the hypothetical imperative: *If you want to lose weight, then you should exercise more and eat less.* Kant believed that if you genuinely do want to lose weight, then your reason commits you to exercise more and eat less. (Kant is sometimes accused of overlooking weakness of the will – when you accept the imperative and want the end, but still do not do it.)

Categorical imperatives

Kant, however, is not really interested in hypothetical imperatives, as they are not moral imperatives. They lack the universality to be moral imperatives because they rely on desires/ends that not everyone wants (or are not permanent). Not everyone wants a cup of tea, so it is not the case that everyone should boil a kettle. The sorts of imperative Kant thinks are central to morality are ones that are not dependent on any set of conditions or desires. These types of *oughts* are unconditional and absolute, or (in Kant's terminology) categorical imperatives.

An example might be, *You ought to keep your promises*. Note that this use is not dependent on any goals or aims you may have – the 'if you want X' bit of the imperative disappears, leaving only 'you ought to do Y'. These sorts of imperatives tell us that we have a certain obligation or duty regardless of the consequences. This is what is meant by saying they are unconditional or categorical. And it is this sort of *ought* which Kant regards as the only genuinely moral *ought*. That is to say, any action which we perform because we are trying to achieve some practical or personal end has no moral worth.

▶ ACTIVITY: YOU *OUGHT* TO SORT THE IMPERATIVES

Read commands A–I and answer the questions that follow.

A I should do more sit-ups.
B I ought to be more loyal to my friends.
C I should pay more attention to my charming philosophy teacher.
D I ought to buy flowers and grapes for my sick aunt.
E I ought to start revising soon.
F I ought to give more money to Children in Need.
G I should not lie as much as I do.
H I should get up earlier.
I I should stop eating meat.

1 Which commands are hypothetical imperatives? In other words, which rely on a hidden 'if' and a hidden goal/desire?
2 Which commands are moral commands?
3 Which commands are unconditional, or categorical imperatives?
4 What connection, if any, is there between the answers you gave for 2 and 3?

The categorical imperative

So moral imperatives will be categorical ones, but what are they and how can we discover them? Well, as we shall see, there is only one categorical imperative (although Kant gives at least three versions of it). Hypothetical imperatives are based on desires and 'ends'. Categorical imperatives are not, as desires are not universal. Stripped of desires and 'ends', the categorical imperative can only be based on the idea of reason and rationality itself. It is the imperative that I should act in a way that is consistent with rationality – in other words, in a way that all rational beings could rationally act. And so I should only act on principles that I can consistently universalise that other rational beings should follow. In Kant's words:

> *Act only according to that maxim [rule] whereby you can at the same time will that it should become a universal law without contradiction.*[5]

This is the categorical imperative (the *universal law formulation*). It is an imperative, as a rational being, to be logically consistent. As we shall see, Kant thinks that this imperative can be used as a test – a test we can use to work out how to behave morally.

Another way to conceive of this is to think back to the idea of man as an imperfectly rational being. All hypothetical imperatives relate to our appetites and desires (the animal part of us). Categorical imperatives are the actions that a purely rational person would follow (although a purely rational person would not feel them as a sense of duty, as there would be no other desires to 'tug' against). A purely rational person would only act in a way that it is possible for all purely rational people to act.

Universalising and the golden rule

All of this is very complicated; however, at the core is a simple principle. When any of us say 'we did the right thing', what we mean is that anyone in a similar position should act in that way too. In other words, moral rules apply universally. Kant thinks this idea alone is enough to guide moral behaviour, as you should only act in ways that can actually be universalised with consistency.

Sometimes people compare Kant's position to one of the world's oldest moral ideas: the GOLDEN RULE. *Do unto others as you would have them do unto you*, or *Treat others as you would have them treat you*. This, in essence, is a call to act, not just from self-interest, but from a position that you can universalise. The problem with the golden rule is that people like odd things, which other people do not. For example, Lenny might like being punched, so according to the golden rule, it is okay for Lenny to punch people, as he, in turn, is happy to be punched. This clearly will not do! To be truly universal, we have to transcend individual desires. Kant's categorical imperative does this. His version of the golden rule would be something like this: *Do unto others that which you can rationally will that they can do unto anyone.*

Using the categorical imperative to determine our duties

We have now seen the central idea behind Kant's approach to ethics, namely that in moral terms we are bound by the categorical imperative – this is our moral duty.

Once again, this system still sounds a little empty. As yet, there are no clear rules for action. Kant believes that the categorical imperative can help us to determine what these are. It will allow us to distinguish truly moral rules from amoral or immoral ones.

The process is roughly this. Underlying an action there is a rule (which you may or may not be consciously aware of). Kant calls these rules 'maxims'. Strip out the particulars and make this maxim as general as possible, then ask yourself: *Could this be a universal law?* If yes, then the action is morally permissible; if no, then there is a problem and you should not (as a rational being) act on that maxim. For those where there is a problem, the negation of the maxim becomes a duty.

The process is a bit more complex, as there are two ways in which a maxim may fail as a universal law:

- Because we cannot conceive of a world in which this was a law – it is inconceivable. This is a *contradiction in conception* and leads to a perfect duty.
- We can conceive of such a world; however, we cannot rationally will such a world. This is a *contradiction in will* and leads to an imperfect duty.

The two ways in which a maxim may fail are important, as it is in *failing* the test that the moral duties arise. We have a duty not to follow maxims that fail the test. Maxims that pass the test are merely morally permissible, they are not duties.

The process is presented as a flow chart in **Figure 2.11**.

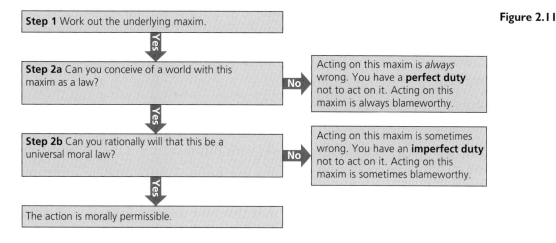

Figure 2.11

Let us test-run this process using two of Kant's own examples.

Example 3: the false promise – *a perfect duty to others*

A man needs some money. He intends to get hold of it by promising to pay it back, even though he has no intention of doing this. Is this right?

Step 1: Work out the underlying maxim. (A maxim is a sort of rule of action.) They normally have the form of an *action* in a *circumstance* with an *end or motive*. We should try to make the maxim as general as possible; in this case, the maxim would be something like: *When in need, make promises with no intention of keeping them to gain help.*

Step 2a: Can you conceive of a world with this maxim as a law? What would happen if everyone followed this maxim as a law and made promises that they had no intention of keeping? Presumably, as suggested earlier, no one would trust promises anymore. Kant argues that this maxim cannot be a universal law without contradiction; the maxim relies on the institution of promises, whereas if everyone followed this maxim, there would be no institution of promises. The man, in willing this maxim, is willing that we all live in world with no promises, but simultaneously willing that he gains money via giving a false promise. This is willing the impossible.

> *Should I be able to say to myself, 'Every one may make a deceitful promise when he finds himself in a difficulty from which he cannot otherwise extricate himself?' Then I presently become aware that while I can will the lie, I can by no means will that lying should be a universal law … Hence my maxim, as soon as it should be made a universal law, would necessarily destroy itself.*[6]

Following this maxim would be wrong. Because the problem happens at the conceiving stage, it is a contradiction in will and the maxim generates a perfect duty – in this case, a perfect duty *not* to do it. A perfect duty is one that we are always obliged to follow. We have a perfect duty to keep promises. Breaking a perfect duty is always wrong and your action would always be blameworthy.

In this way, Kant believes that the categorical imperative can be used to work out the moral law. Note that the categorical imperative does not generate the moral law, nor are laws derived from it; rather, it is a test that we can apply to any maxim, to see if it could be a universal moral law.

Example 4: not helping others – *an imperfect duty to others*

Someone who is doing pretty well in life sees that others need help. He is inclined not to help.

Step 1: Work out the underlying maxim. This would be something like: *I will not help those in distress, when I easily could, through selfishness.*

Step 2a: Can you conceive of a world with this maxim as a law? Kant thinks that it is possible to conceive of a world where people do not help each other, so the maxim is not ruled out at this stage.

Step 2b: Can you rationally will that this be a universal moral law? Kant says 'no'. Everyone will have been in situations (as a baby, for example) when they were unable to help themselves and needed the help of others, and we would not want to be in a situation where we need assistance and yet no one will help us. Because this maxim was conceivable as a universal law, but could not be consistently willed, it is a *contradiction in will*, which generates an imperfect duty – in this case, an imperfect duty not to not help others, which means that in situations when we can easily help, we cannot always ignore those who need help. Breaking an imperfect duty is not always wrong, and is not always blameworthy. So you will not always be blamed if you fail to help others. Quite how much of a duty this becomes – how much we should help others – is not clear (see page 275 for more on this).

Kant offers two more examples. The ones above concern more than one person, so Kant labels them examples of our *duties to others*. The next two concern just the one person, so are examples of *duties to ourselves*. We will cover these in brief.

Example 5: suicide – perfect duty to ourselves

Someone miserable is contemplating committing suicide. Kant seems to imply that the maxim underlying this possible action is, *I will end my life if there is more pain than pleasure because of self-love.* Kant thinks this cannot be a universal law as this fails at the first stage, so it is a contradiction in conception: we cannot conceive of a world with this as a law. As such, we have a perfect duty not to kill ourselves. This is generally considered to be the weakest of Kant's examples and he does not go into much detail in his explanation; he seems to assume that to kill yourself from the motive of self-love is contradictory. Sometimes people are tempted to analyse this by saying that if we all acted on the maxim, *Kill yourself*, then there would be no one left in the world to kill themselves, so the action cannot be rationally willed (stage B). However, Kant does not produce this argument; he also feels it fails at stage A – the conception stage. Kant's argument seems to be that self-love is the motive that keeps us wanting to stay alive, so it cannot also be the motive for killing ourselves. (Kant seems to overlook the fact that many people may kill themselves for self-loathing – which probably would not fail as a rule at the conception stage.)

Criticism of this example, though, does not mean that Kant's approach is wrong – just that he failed to apply his own ideas correctly to his own example. However, if you think there is something wrong with all of the examples, then it might point to a broader problem with the system.

Example 6: lazy, but talented – *imperfect duty to ourselves*

Someone with natural talents lets them go to waste because they are lazy. Kant sees the underlying maxim as something like this: *I will not develop my talent, when I discover one, so as to remain comfortable* (laziness). Kant thinks that a world with this as a universal maxim is conceivable, but believes it cannot be rationally willed – it is a contradiction in will. So we have an imperfect duty to develop at least some of our talents. It is an imperfect duty, so we can choose to let some of our talents rust; the reasoning being that we have all relied on other people's talents (doctors, teachers and so on) and so we cannot consistently will that no one has talents.

Experimenting with ideas

Have a go at generating moral laws yourself using the categorical imperative. For each of the examples, answer the following questions:

1 What is the maxim? (Try to make this as general as possible)
2 Can you conceive of a world where this is a moral law?
3 Can you rationally will that this should be a moral law?
4 Is the action morally permissible, or is there a duty not to perform it?

A The queue. You have been eagerly awaiting the publication date of the new Harry Potter/*Game of Thrones*/A-level Philosophy book. You wake up early to head to the bookshop before it opens. When you get there, you are dismayed to see that the queue is half a mile long! As you walk past the queue, you see a friend. She leans over and whispers in your ear – suggesting you pretend you are together. That way, you can join the queue quite near the front. You consider her offer.

B Surrender. You are a military commander. Unfortunately, your enemy has made significant military gains. There is no point facing them in the battlefield – you will lose. One option is to pretend to surrender, lay down some of your ground weapons, and then, a few days later, launch a deadly counter-attack from the air when they are not expecting it. You consider taking this option.

C Exams. It is exam time (again). You are really struggling with the maths paper. However, you are clearly able to see the answers on the paper of the person next to you. You consider copying their answers.

D Vows. You married very young (18). You said your vows in front of over a hundred people, which involved promising to be together for ever. However, after two years of living together you have (both) realised that you made a mistake. You are considering getting a divorce.

E Waiter. You are a waiter in a restaurant. A very wealthy man spends a fortune (£1,600) on a meal for business clients. He is loud, rude and does not leave you any tip. However, he miscounts the notes when he hands them to you. He overpays by £100. You believe he will not notice the money is gone (as his wallet was literally stuffed with cash). You are considering keeping the £100 and not pointing out his mistake.

Different formulations of the categorical imperative

Kant argued that there is only one categorical imperative; however, he believed it can be expressed in different forms. He claimed there are three important formulations (although you are only required to study two of them). The version discussed so far is known as the *universal law* formulation. The second formulation is known as the *humanity* formulation; it is one of the famous elements of Kant's philosophy and has a profound legacy in the field of ethics and also in the development of human rights.

Learn More

The argument for the second formulation

This passage briefly summarises Kant's argument for the second formulation. However, it is not crucial to know this, so feel free to skip to the next section.

Kant argues that the categorical imperative (the version we discussed in the previous section) is a theoretical imperative. However, all practical action needs a specific end that is pursued. What end are we pursuing when we use the categorical imperative? Unlike hypothetical imperatives (discussed above), this end must be universal, and it must be contained within the idea of the categorical imperative itself. In this way, the end is achieved simply by using the categorical imperative. It becomes an end in itself (otherwise the ethic would be a consequentialist one). Free will and autonomy arise precisely because of the ability to reason and to use the categorical imperative to generate one's own laws and so escape acting on desires. By considering the first formulation, we can see that it would be logically impossible to will that there is no will. As such, we should never act in a way that overlooks another person's (or your own) will/autonomy. Kant argues that it is the idea of an autonomous agent or 'will' that provides the end (as an end in itself) that we pursue when using the categorical imperative.

Another way of seeing this is to think of each human will as its own moral legislator (making its own moral laws). This idea is implicit within the categorical imperative (as the categorical imperative is the means of making one's own moral laws). To treat someone as a means but not as a rational free agent themselves, would be to treat that other human's will as not being its own moral legislator. I cannot make a rule (using my autonomy) that involves others not having autonomy. This is clearly a contradiction, which cannot be universalised. In this way, Kant argues that the autonomy of the human will is the supreme principle of morality.

Jeremy Bentham claims that pleasure is universally pursued, so this should be the universal end which generates the imperatives that should be followed by all. However, for Kant, the seeking of pleasure is an EMPIRICAL FACT (which can be disputed) and this is not good enough for the basis of morality. For Kant, the supreme principle of morality (human autonomy) is contained within the idea of morality itself, and so is an *a priori* principle that will apply universally.

The second formulation: The humanity formulation

Having put forward a complex argument, Kant presents his second formulation of the categorical imperative. He claims that there is a categorical duty to:

Act in such a way that you treat humanity, whether in your own person or in the person of any other, never merely as a means to an end, but always at the same time as an end.[7]

Kant believed that this formulation has the same meaning as the *universal law* formulation, but that it presents the ideas in a way that is more intuitive. Consider the following example:

► **ACTIVITY**

Example 7: the new friend

Quite suddenly, you acquire a new friend, Sam. Sam goes out of her way to be nice to you, pays you compliments, lets you borrow her fancy camera and even buys you a thoughtful (yet inexpensive) birthday present. However, you find out that, in reality, Sam does not like you at all. She only became friends with you so that she could meet your cousin, who is an up-and-coming journalist. Sam thinks your journalist cousin could help move her career forward.

1 How does this make you feel?

2 Was Sam's behaviour wrong?

In general, we feel very strongly if we suspect we are being used or deceived in some way. If Sam had been upfront in saying she wanted to meet your cousin, then maybe you would have acted differently towards her. However, she deceived you, and in doing so she overrode your autonomy, using you as a means to an end. For Kant, this is always wrong.

The humanity formulation expresses the idea that it is always wrong to treat you (or any person) in a way that involves you in an action that you do not, in principle, have a chance to consent to.

This does not mean you can never use people as a means. Every time I go to a restaurant, take a taxi or call a plumber, I am using a person to further my ends. However, this person has consented to the arrangement, and they too are using me as a means to an end – to make money. The moral problem arises when you do not have a chance to consent, so your autonomy/rationality is undermined. When this happens, you are being used *merely* as a means to an end.

Example 8: fake notes

A man comes round to buy your old bass guitar. He deliberately gives you fake £20 notes, which you do not notice.

This action is wrong because the man is bypassing your autonomy. If he told you the notes were fake, you would not accept them. In keeping it secret, he is acting in a way that does not give you a chance to consent. He is treating you merely as a means to get the guitar and not as a person with your own ends.

Figure 2.12 The humanity formulation. In (A) the photographer makes money by taking photos without permission. He uses the couple merely as a means to this end. In (B) the photographer makes money, but he takes photos with the permission of the couple, who want the photos to be taken. In doing this, he treats the couple as people with an end themselves, while also pursuing his end.

So stealing from me, lying, deceiving, drugging, kidnapping, forcing me into slavery or murdering me (and so on) would be to involve me in acts that I have not had the opportunity to consent to. In doing any of these, the person would be using me merely as a means to further their own ends, and not as an autonomous being with my own ends.

Using the humanity formulation

As the humanity formulation of the categorical imperative is (allegedly) the same as the universal formulation, we should expect the same moral duties to emerge when considering the same scenarios. So, in the example of the new friend on page 271, using the universal law formulation Sam would be acting on some sort of maxim like this: *When I need to I will fake friendships in order to further my cause.* What would happen to the institution of friendship if everyone acted on this law? Likewise, what would happen if everyone used fake £20 notes? Neither of these actions/maxims would be fit to make a universal law, so we have a duty not to do them. These two cases seem to arrive at the same answer on both formulations of the categorical imperative. In the *Groundwork,* Kant revisits his own examples to see if the humanity formulation yields the same results.

The clearest case is that of borrowing money with a false promise (see page 267). Here you are using the lender merely as a means to further your end. By making a false promise, you are denying the lender the right to make an appropriate autonomous decision about lending. As you are using them merely as a means to an end, you have a perfect duty not do this.

The other case of a perfect duty – that of not killing yourself – was not very convincing using the universal law formulation. It is also not very convincing using the humanity formulation (so there is consistency here at least!). Kant argues that in deciding to end your life when it becomes insufferable, you are treating yourself, in the meantime, as a means to an end. Kant also argues that just as killing another person is to treat that person as a means to your end, so is killing yourself. Commentators dispute how convincing this is.

The two cases of imperfect duties (examples 4 and 6) introduce a slightly different interpretation of the humanity formulation. Both cases are permissible, in that not developing your talents and not helping others do not contradict the humanity formulation (you are not treating anyone as merely a means to your end). However, they are not in *harmony* with the formulation. The humanity formulation has the autonomy/rationality of humanity at its heart, as the supreme moral principle. To be in harmony with this would require you not only to respect, but to develop human autonomy/rationality, and this would involve furthering your skills and helping others. Failing to do these things (help and develop) does not contradict the humanity formulation, so you do not have a perfect duty to do them. However, failing to do them is not in harmony with the humanity formulation, so you have an imperfect duty to carry them out.

Experimenting with ideas: testing the humanity formulation

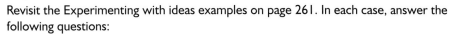

Revisit the Experimenting with ideas examples on page 261. In each case, answer the following questions:

1   Would acting on the maxim contradict the humanity formulation? If so, you have a perfect duty not to act on the maxim.
2   Would acting on the maxim be out of harmony with the humanity formulation? If so, you have an imperfect duty not to act on it (meaning you can act on it sometimes).
3   Are your answers the same as you derived using the universal law formulation?
4   Is the humanity formulation easier to use?

As an extension activity, revisit the Experimenting with ideas examples on page 218. Use both the universal law formulation and the humanity formulation and answer the questions above.

The humanity formulation and human dignity

The humanity formulation places a great emphasis on respecting autonomy, which for many people is the key to dignity. Consider again the example of the nude photos (page 218). Utilitarians struggle somewhat with articulating why this is wrong. A strict act utilitarian may even say that it is a good thing, especially if the photos are widely viewed and enjoyed. A rule utilitarian may be able to construct a rule which this act violates, which, if generally followed, would maximise happiness. However, this would still treat the rights of the girlfriend as just a side effect of maximising happiness, not as valuable as an end in itself. A preference utilitarian may be able to say that the act would be against the ex-girlfriend's preference; however, the preferences of all the online viewers also need to be factored in. For Kant, though, this represents a violation of the supreme moral principle: human autonomy. The ex-girlfriend is being treated as a means to an end and not as a person with ends herself. She has had no opportunity to consent. The ex-boyfriend has a perfect duty not to act in the way he did. Kant's theory seems to cut right to the core of what is wrong in this situation.

The humanity formulation and human rights

The two formulations of the categorical imperative do not look the same on paper; however, Kant's belief is that in committing to the universality of moral law, we are committing to the value of rationality and autonomy in all of us, for it is through the ability to create universal laws that human autonomy exists. This focus on autonomy has been very influential. The development of human rights is closely associated with the belief in the importance of human autonomy, and it was Kant's work that placed autonomy at the heart of ethics.

The relationship between Kantian ethics and human rights can be seen by revisiting the example of the scapegoat (page 218). An act utilitarian would be very tempted to kill the innocent person. A rule utilitarian might claim that having a rule about a right to life, in the long term, would make us all happier (though not on this occasion). For the rule utilitarian, this would not be based on the intrinsic worth of humans, but rather the fact that rights may make us happier. Rights are a sort of side effect in our quest for happiness, a means to an end.

In Kantian ethics, the innocent scapegoat is clearly being used as a means to some other end. This is something he has not had any opportunity to consent to (and would not consent to if he had). Killing the man would undermine his rational autonomy (in quite a serious way!). Slavery, false imprisonment, torture and so on, are all extreme ways of treating people as a means to some other end and undermining their autonomy, which is an end in itself. The basis of all human rights is to enable individual, rational autonomy, and Kant's philosophy played a significant part in their development.

Strengths of Kantian ethics

Kant's system of ethics, though complicated, has many strengths. It is based on reason, so the moral laws should be universal, not culturally dependent. It rationally articulates and places a central importance on the worth and dignity of human autonomy. It is not ends-based, so avoids some of the criticisms of consequentialism. As there is no singular 'end' that we have to maximise, Kant's system of ethics allows for individuals to pursue their own projects/ends. Despite these strengths, Kant's ethics have also raised many problems, and it is to these criticisms that we now turn. The main issues are:

- clashing/competing duties
- non-moral maxims
- the moral value of consequences
- the value of other motives
- morality as a system of hypothetical, not categorical imperatives.

Issue: clashing/competing duties

For Kant, we are all creators of our own moral laws. The categorical imperative enables us to work out what is morally permissible and what our moral duties are. Using this system, we can create our own metaphorical book of moral laws. However, just because a maxim gets into our book, that alone does not tell us where it goes and what weight to attach to it. What happens, for example, when our duties seem to contradict each other?

Consider the example of the axeman on page 220. Kant, most agree, would say that it is wrong to lie. You cannot universalise lying. However, we also have a duty to care for others, so we might see this axeman scenario as a clash in our duties: a perfect duty to tell the truth, and an imperfect duty to care for others. In general, perfect duties have no exceptions, and imperfect duties do not have to be performed all the time. So this gives us some direction.

For Kant, however, clashing rules represent a serious problem. His whole moral system involves not acting on rules that cannot be consistently universalised. Inconsistent rules give rise to duties, so duties are all about consistency. If it is the case that two moral duties are rationally inconsistent, then, by definition, they cannot be duties, and his system collapses. In his own words, this is actually inconceivable:

two rules opposed to each other cannot be necessary at the same time, if it is a duty to act in accordance with one rule, to act in accordance with the opposite rule is not a duty but even contrary to duty; so a collision of duties and obligations is inconceivable.[8]

So, for Kant, duties cannot clash, by definition. However, we can sometimes be wrong in thinking through our grounds of obligation. If I made a promise to a friend that I would lie for them, then it would seem that I have two conflicting duties: a) I should keep my promises, and b) I should never lie. However, it is clear that I am not obliged to keep the promise in this case; we cannot rationally will a maxim whereby we keep promises to lie. It was wrong to make this promise; in fact, we have a duty not to make such promises. In this case, revisiting my grounds of obligation shows that the duties do not in fact clash, as I do not have a moral duty to keep this promise.

Competing imperfect duties

This approach may work for some 'alleged' clashes of duty – particularly those involving two perfect duties. However, the situation is less clear when imperfect duties are included, such as our imperfect duties to help others, to develop our own talents and so on. These are duties we do not have to follow all of the time. We are praised for following them, but, unlike perfect duties, we are not always blamed for not following them. This seems to leave us with a very vague moral duty. We seem to need more guidance on when I should help people, and how much self-improvement I should undertake and so on. Having an imperfect duty alone does not seem to tell us when to perform the imperfect duties. Also, knowing which of these duties to prioritise can be difficult, and sometimes these duties seem to compete.

Utilitarians seem to have an advantage here, as by using the common currency of happiness, they can weigh up different actions and see how they compare. Kant's approach is less clear; instead of looking at the consequences, we need to examine our reasons – our grounds of obligation – and see which is stronger. However, it is not easy to do this. But this weakness can also be seen as a strength. Utilitarians can be seen as treating humans as a means to an end, or treating them not as individuals, but as numbers of quality-adjusted life years of pleasure, to be weighed and measured when making decisions. This might render decision-making easier, but at a cost. For Kant, human dignity and respect are absolute and so cannot be weighed and calibrated. For Kant, we have a duty to treat everyone as an end in themselves; the downside is that this can make decision-making harder.

Jean-Paul Sartre (1905–80)[9] criticised Kant, using an example from his own experience during the Nazi occupation of France, of a young man torn between his duty to his country, which impelled him to join the Resistance and which would probably lead to his death, and his duty to care for his mother, who had already lost her other sons to the war. He suggests that Kant's ethical theory is of no use in helping him to resolve this conflict between two duties, and that the young man had to go on instinct. The suggestion here is that when our duties clash, we have to use desires and feelings to decide which to choose. Kant, of course, would disagree. He claims that we have to look at the grounds for obligation and assess the strengths.

Consider this case. I come across someone collapsed on the road. Do I help? I know that I have a general duty of care towards others, but if I see that some people are already helping, then there is no blame in me not helping. However, if I come across someone collapsed and there is no one else there, then the rule in question may be different. Do I treat my duty in the same way as before, as a general duty to help? I may even kid myself and say that someone else will come along soon and that other people may help. If I choose to ignore the person, what rule would I be following? The change in circumstance suggests that it may be a different maxim, perhaps: *I will not help someone in need, even though I am the only person that can, because I am in a rush.* Even though I can conceive of this world, I cannot rationally will it. In this case, there seems to be a stronger ground of obligation than before.

This approach is not easy to follow, and Kant does not offer much guidance (although other philosophers have developed elaborate Kantian systems). However, it can be argued that this complexity is just part of the world that we live in. After all, human rights lawyers spend years arguing about the hierarchy of competing rights. Does freedom of speech mean I can say anything? What about when it undermines other people's right to practise religion? Or if I incite hatred, might this undermine people's right to freedom of movement? And so on. On a personal level too, competing obligations can be a minefield. On page 226, we discussed the dilemma of staying in and doing your homework or going out with friends. For Bentham, this would be all about weighing up the pleasure; for Kant, this would be about negotiating obligations. For example, you may have promised friends that you would join them later that evening, and also have homework and know that you have a general duty not to waste your life and develop your talents, but you may also have promised your parents that you would tidy up and know that it would be wrong to lie to your parents about completing the homework ... and so on. The world is complicated, and balancing our competing duties is hard. But Kant, at least, presents a theory that helps us to think through our duties in a rational way.

Issue: universalising maxims and morality

Another line of criticism is that the link between UNIVERSALISABLE/non-universalisable maxims and morality is not very clear. For it would appear that a) not all universalisable maxims are moral and, more importantly, b) not all non-universalisable maxims are immoral.

Not all universalisable maxims are moral

A criticism commonly levelled at Kant is that many trivial acts, which themselves do not seem to be moral, can be successfully universalised. For example: *I will chew food 32 times before eating, to aid digestion.* However, for Kant, those maxims that *can* be universalised are just morally permissible; we have no duty to do them. It is those actions that we *cannot* universalise that generate moral duties (a duty not to perform them or a duty to do the opposite). This, though, leads to a different criticism – that Kant's ethics only tell us what we *cannot* do (lie, deceive and so on); it does not give a positive account of what we *should* be aiming for. On the other hand, this can also be seen as a strength in that it allows for people to pursue their own projects and ends.

Are all non-universalisable maxims immoral?

Something odd can happen when we try to universalise maxims that include relative or 'norm'-related positions (comparing ourselves to others).

For example, consider the maxim, *When taking an exam, I will come in the top 50 per cent*. This seems fair enough, yet a world where this is a law is impossible to conceive, as we cannot all, by definition, be in the top 50 per cent. This would mean we have a perfect duty not to try to come in the top 50 per cent (before you stop revising, note that we also have a perfect duty not to come in the bottom 50 per cent). I can, however, universalise the maxim, *When taking an exam, I will always try to gain over half of the marks, to push myself*, as everyone could get over half the marks. The problem lies in fixing outcomes in relation to other people, in ways that cannot be universalised. Perhaps we should never compare ourselves to others. Maybe this is to treat them as a means to an end. Nevertheless, on the face of it, acting on the maxim of coming in the top 50 per cent does not seem to be immoral. It is worth noting that these norm-related problems also occur for some forms of utilitarianism (see page 237), so maybe there is something wrong with applying norm-related positions to all people equally.

On a similar note, consider this rule: *I will always help the poor when I can afford to, to ease their plight*. It can be argued that this cannot be willed to be a universal law, as if everyone did this, there would be no poor. So we have a duty to *not* help the poor! However, this would seem wrong.

Here we seem to have clear cases where the non-universalisable maxims are clearly not immoral to act on. Indeed, we *should* help the poor and you *should* at least try to come in the top 50 per cent in your philosophy A-level, even though it seems we cannot universalise the maxim.

The categorical imperative also seems to generate trivial duties. Consider the rule, *On trick or treat nights, I will go and collect sweets, but will not provide any at my house, to save money*. I might be able to conceive of a world where this is the rule (it would be a dull Halloween!), but I cannot rationally will it, as following the maxim would destroy the institution of trick or treat, on which the maxim relies. It would seem that, as a rational being, I have an imperfect duty not to do this. But, although I would agree that I cannot universalise just collecting the sweets, this does not seem to be a moral issue – just an issue of cultural practice. (Many of Kant's examples of perfect duties involve acting in a way that would undermine a social/cultural institution that the act also relies on – for example, promising. In the case above, the institution is 'trick or treat', which does not seem to be a moral one.)

Do we have a duty to offer sweets at Halloween if we also collect them? According to Kant, it might seem so. But if this is not a moral duty, then how can we distinguish moral duties from non-moral duties, unless we have a prior understanding of what morality is – an understanding that is not derived from the ability to universalise maxims?

Issue: the moral value of consequences

One of the key objections to Kantian ethics is that it places all of the moral worth on the motives of an action. Just as utilitarianism is criticised for placing all of the moral worth on the consequences, so Kant is criticised for placing all of the emphasis on the motive. It seems our moral intuitions want to have it both ways – to attach some of the value to the consequence and some to the motive.

Consider again the example of the axeman on page 220. Lying to a murderous-looking axeman seems to be the right thing to do. However, in concluding this, it appears we would be thinking about the consequences of the act – and, for Kant, the moral value lies solely in the reason for acting. For Kant, it would be wrong to lie, as you cannot consistently conceive of a world in which this is the moral law. Using the second formulation, to lie would be to treat the potential murderer as a means to some other end (saving your friend's life). To lie would be to undermine his autonomy to make decisions himself, and so it would be wrong. However, most people would have no hesitation in lying and would believe that to be the right thing to do. The apparent requirement to lie seems very counter-intuitive.

Now, there are various Kantian ways of avoiding this seemingly counter-intuitive conclusion (see page 289 for more on this), but the fundamental point seems to be that telling the truth will have bad consequences – and this is what makes it wrong, not whether you can universalise the maxim underlying the act. On this occasion, the moral value of the act (lying or not) seems to reside in the consequence, not the motive.

Kant's larger claim, in essence, is that we all need to focus on our own sphere of control: make sure that *I* do not lie, deceive and so on, and only act on maxims that *I* have worked out to be universal laws. If we all did this, then we would end up in a world where we all had freedom and autonomy. However, in the example above, I might be busy doing the right thing, but the mad axeman certainly is not, and this would have disastrous consequences. This focus on my sphere of control seems to miss the bigger, and consequentialist, picture. It can appear that Kantian ethics are more concerned with being rationally consistent in our actions, than with whether a friend is killed. It may well be the case that if we all acted rationally consistently, the world would be a better place. However, we do not live in this ideal world; we live in a world with murderers and cheats. Just focusing on my own sphere of action would seem to have disastrous consequences in the real, non-ideal world in which we live. Because the world is non-ideal, some argue that we have to look at the consequences of our actions, and override the need to be rationally consistent in our willing.

On a different note, Kantian ethics is also criticised for having consequentialist tendencies (while claiming to be purely motive-based). Some suggest that to work out whether a maxim can be consistently willed relies on thinking through the consequences of having this as a law – and so is consequentialist. However, in Kant's defence, the moral value lies in the consistency of the will, and not in whether the world would be 'good' or 'bad' if the maxim were universalised. A harder criticism to defend is that Kant seems to be pointing towards a world where we maximise our mutual autonomy as the ideal. This is akin to saying there is an end that we should be aiming for, and this end makes actions good. This, of course, would be a consequentialist philosophy, and some argue that we should interpret Kant this way.

Issue: the value of other motives

Previously (page 261) we explored the example of two fathers (A and B). A common intuition is that Father A, who helps his son because he wants to, is the better dad. Kant, however, argues that only Father B's actions have moral worth, as they are carried out from duty, not desire. This seems counter-intuitive.

We seem to want to place value on the motive of Father A too, and more generally also on the motives of people who *want* to help others and devote their life to doing so. For Kant, these actions, though in accordance with duty, are not done for the sake of duty, so have no moral value. This seems to be at odds with our intuition that certain emotions have a moral dimension, such as love, compassion, guilt and sympathy, or pride and jealousy. Do we not regard the possession of such emotions itself as morally praise- or blameworthy, as having moral value?

Some also object to Kant's approach, claiming it encourages a cold and calculative approach to ethics by demanding that we put aside our feelings for the suffering of others. In Kant's defence, he is not against people *wanting* to do right actions, and positive emotions, but he is clear that acting from desire, not duty, has no moral worth. Happiness is worth pursuing, but for Kant it has no value unless it comes about for the right reasons – from acting dutifully.

Kant's account of duty as the source of moral worth also makes his concept of virtue a little counter-intuitive. For Kant, virtue is 'the moral strength of a human being's will in fulfilling his duty'.[10] A good will is one that acts out of duty, but this need not be virtuous, as the will might not require much strength to act out of duty. It may come easily to some people. This leaves Kant in an odd position, in that it seems that people who do not want to do the right thing, people who have strong desires to lie and cheat and so on, when they do act out of duty, are more virtuous than those people whose duties and desires coincide. It also means that a perfectly rational being (God) would not be virtuous at all, as there would be no desires to tug against when doing the right thing.

Issue: the value of other motives – care

There is a feminist critique of both utilitarianism and Kantian ethics (from Carol Gilligan (1936–)[11] and others). The argument is that the emphasis both systems place on reasoning from an abstract, neutral viewpoint, and the adoption of a dispassionate approach in how we assess our concern for different humans, represents 'male' patterns of ethical thought. Females, it claims, often put more attention on the subjectivity of situations, and on care and concern for others.

Consider this tale of the moles and the porcupine (adapted from Carol Gilligan, who adapted it from Aesop).

▶ ACTIVITY: MOLES AND THE PORCUPINE

A group of moles live in a system of tunnels and have developed ways of getting along together. One stormy day, a porcupine comes to shelter in the tunnels and stays for a while. This causes a bit of commotion as he is slightly larger, which makes squeezing past him in the tunnels quite difficult. However, he is a jolly fellow, which makes things easier. After a week, the moles get together and discuss what to do – specifically, whether the porcupine should stay.

1 Is it right that the porcupine stays?
2 If you were a mole, would you let him stay?
3 What sort of things would you consider in making this decision?
4 As a human, would you let a porcupine stay in your house?
5 Is it different for the moles?

During the council of the moles, some start to argue whether justice and duty apply across different species; others debate whether they can universalise the maxim of sending him away; others look to see if applying their moral rules would maximise utility. In amongst all this abstract discussion are still more voices. These moles want the porcupine to stay because they care about him. They care about this specific porcupine. For them, this is the most important factor. All of the abstract discussion misses the point. Morality is about individual situations and about care. The problem with Kant and with utilitarianism is that they overlook this very different way of ethically thinking. Nearly everyone would lie to the axeman (page 220) and that is because they care about the person in the house. Only someone who really did not care, or cared but did not place moral value on care, would tell the truth.

We cannot adopt an impersonal perspective

We may doubt whether it is even possible for us to set aside the interests, concerns and desires that make us individuals, and to think of ourselves, as Kant wants us to, as purely rational autonomous beings engaged in universal lawmaking. Bernard Williams[12] argues that the impartial position that Kant wishes us to adopt may be possible for factual considerations, but not for practical, moral deliberations. For example, if I ask, 'I wonder whether strontium is a metal?' it is possible to remove the personal 'I' from this question, and seek an answer that is independent of my own perspective on the world. This kind of deliberation means that it is possible for anyone to take up my question and be given the same answer; there is what Williams calls a 'unity of interest' in the answer. This is because deliberation about facts is not essentially personal, but is an attempt to reach an impersonal position (where we all agree that these are the facts). In contrast, Williams maintains that practical deliberation is essentially personal and it does make a difference whether it is me or someone else (for example, the madman's mother, his intended victim, the victim's life insurer or the madman himself) asking the question, 'Should I lie to this man?' We cannot and should not strive for the same impersonal position as in the factual case. With moral deliberations there is no longer a 'unity of interest', and a different person, with a different set of desires and interests, who is now standing in my shoes, might seek a different answer. The position from which we ask this practical question is a personal position, and the answer will affect us very much. Williams argues that Kant is wrong and that we cannot adopt an impersonal perspective (the perspective of the categorical imperative), because by doing so we lose our place in the world, our interests and any sense of self.

Issue: Morality is a system of hypothetical (not categorical) imperatives

Above we saw the claim (critical of Kant) that motives such as the desire to help others do have moral worth. The philosopher Philippa Foot agrees wholeheartedly with this – in fact, without such motives, we do not have a good reason to behave morally. In her paper, 'Morality as a system of hypothetical imperatives',[13] Foot argues that the moral law, as Kant conceives it, does not give sufficient reason to follow it. Only end-based, 'hypothetical' imperatives give us sufficient reason to act.

All imperatives command either hypothetically or categorically.[14]

Earlier, we saw Kant make the distinction between hypothetical and categorical imperatives, both of which 'command' us to act. Hypothetical imperatives are based around our desires/ends:

- *If* you want to win the match, you *ought* to practice.
- *If* you want to earn loads of money, you *should* work in the city.

But why *ought* you to do these things? In these cases (and for all hypothetical imperatives), the reason to act is clearly given – *because* you will win the match/ earn lots of money. Your action is motivated by an end/goal. In this sense, if you have the desire, then the imperative is the 'command' to act. In contrast, Foot contends, the reason to act on categorical imperatives is not so evident.

Previously, we saw Bentham claim that all of our actions stem from the desire for our own pleasure/self-interest (psychological hedonism), and Kant largely agrees with this. However, for Kant, a) following our desires has no moral worth, and b) sometimes we can escape acting on our desires and use reason to work out how we *should* act, *independently* of whether you have any particular desire/ end. This is because reason can reveal categorical imperatives:

- You *should* not steal.
- You *ought* to help others.

With hypothetical imperatives, there is a clear reason to act (to earn money and so on). With categorical imperatives, the reason is not so clear. Why *ought* I not steal? What is the reason to obey the 'ought'? In her article, Foot explores and rejects different possibilities. In ruling out the idea that moral oughts somehow 'command' us all to act, Foot pre-empts Mackie's argument from queerness, which we explore later (page 399). It is not essential to know the full details of her arguments, so you can skip to the solution section below, if you prefer.

Non-hypothetical 'oughts'?

One possibility is that the command of moral imperatives comes precisely because these imperatives are not based on our individual desires. The moral 'ought' is not an 'if-based ought' which stems from having a particular desire (*if* you want to win, *if* you want money and so on). In this way, the moral 'ought' is universal, it applies to all of us, and that is why we ought to not steal. No 'ifs', no buts!

In other words, the binding force of the moral 'ought' comes from the fact that it is a non-hypothetical 'ought'. However, Foot claims that there are other examples of non-hypothetical 'oughts' that are based on convention, not morality. She gives two (somewhat dated) examples of etiquette about how one *should* not bring women into the smoking room at a club, and how one *should* reply in the third person when written to in the third person.

A (slightly) more updated version would be that one *ought* not to split infinitives. In general, rules of spelling and grammar should be observed to aid the understanding of the reader; however, some rules have no obvious goal/ end. For example, when writing, you are not supposed to put any words in the middle of an infinitive arrangement:

- *To quickly swim* – This is wrong.
- *To swim quickly* – This would be acceptable.

Learn More

281

■ *Boldly, to go* – Good.
■ *To boldly go* – Wrong.

To openly split an infinitive is considered wrong (see what I did there!). One *ought* not to do it.

Foot contends that the person issuing this sort of 'ought' does not do so in relation the listener's desires. Regardless of whether you do not care for grammar or want to annoy the reader, you still should not split infinitives. The *should* in these contexts is used in a sense that is independent of desire fulfilment; it is just a question of how one *should* write/behave. It is not a hypothetical 'if-based ought', but a non-hypothetical 'ought'.

However, Foot claims that just being a non-hypothetical 'ought' alone does not give us a real reason to follow the imperative. It does not really 'command' us to follow the rule. From this, she concludes that moral 'oughts' do not derive their binding force from the fact that they are non-hypothetical and do not depend on 'ifs'.

Rational consistency?

For Kant, moral laws are generated because some maxims cannot be rationally conceived or consistently willed as universal laws. So I should not steal/lie/ignore others because I cannot *consistently* will this as a way for everyone to act. So could the binding force, the 'command', of a moral 'ought' come from the need, as a rational being, to be consistent? Is this why we *ought* not to steal, as we have a duty to be rationally consistent? Foot rejects this possibility. The immoral man, she claims, is not inconsistent.

The fact is that the man who rejects morality because he sees no reason to obey its rules can be convicted of villainy but not of inconsistency. Nor will his action necessarily be irrational. Irrational actions are those in which a man in some way defeats his own purposes, doing what is calculated to be disadvantageous or to frustrate his ends. Immorality does not necessarily involve any such thing.[15]

Should we follow moral 'oughts' for their own sake?

Perhaps we should follow moral laws for their own sake? Out of respect for the moral law itself? But we do not *have* to behave morally out of respect for the moral law, any more than we *have* to follow etiquette for the sake of convention. People, though, claim that somehow we are 'bound' to follow the moral law, unlike matters of etiquette. But are we? We are not *literally* bound, forced or pulled. Even metaphorically, these terms do not seemingly apply to morals, as I cannot escape the force, pull or binding when it comes to ropes, but can when it comes to morality. Yes, there is social pressure to be moral, as there is to follow etiquette, but this cannot provide the sort of moral 'ought' that Kant and others are seeking. Foot suggests that in using the metaphors of being 'bound' by morality, people 'are relying on an illusion, as if trying to give the moral "ought" a magic force'.[16]

Foot's solution: morality as a series of hypothetical imperatives

For Foot, the key is to reject the theory of psychological hedonism, which claims that we always act out of *self*-interest. Some people genuinely want to help others, not for fame, fortune or their own benefit, but just to help others. If we accept that this is a suitable moral goal, then we have the proper motivation to be moral.

Likewise a person might genuinely aim to be fair and just, not for their own reward, nor for self-gratification, but for the love of truth and liberty and a desire for everyone to be respected. If we accept that people have these as moral ends, then they are a suitable reason to act. Indeed, people fight hard for liberty and justice; these are ends that people find highly motivating.

> A moral man has moral ends and cannot be indifferent to matters such as suffering and injustice[17]

So moral 'oughts' are not categorical, but hypothetical 'oughts', depending on 'if' you have the relevant moral ends. The downside to this is that moral 'oughts' are not universal, but contingent on you thinking that specific moral ends are worth pursuing. For some, this is a worrying conclusion. Surely the 'oughts' of 'we *ought* to help others' is a universal ought. We *all* ought to help others, not just those who happen to have this as a moral end. Surely morality applies to all of us and you cannot escape the duty of morality by claiming to not have moral ends/desires?

Foot is not concerned by this. In some senses, you cannot choose to escape morality, as we are all raised in a society that encourages moral behaviour; a society that literally and metaphorically boos and hisses those who behave immorally. So people cannot completely 'get away' with being immoral. But does having morality as a universal duty really help? Foot suggests that categorical 'oughts' cast humanity as forced conscripts in a moral army. A better vision is to see us not as conscripts, but as 'volunteers banded together to fight for liberty and justice and against inhumanity and oppression'.[18]

Foot sees morality as a series of imperatives: *you should not steal, you should help others* and so on. There is no single overall imperative to be moral. For this reason, she thought the question, *Why should you be moral?* is either meaningless or obvious by definition. The meaningful questions are: *Why should you not steal? Why should you help others?* And so on. In others words, morality is a *series* of imperatives, not an overarching single one. Foot claims that these imperatives are hypothetical ones, so depend on you having the relevant moral end. You might have some moral ends, but not others. Collectively, this series of imperatives constitutes morality.

Summary of Kantian ethics

Utilitarianism places the emphasis on human (and non-human) sentience, whereas for Kant, it is rationality and autonomy that form the basis of morality. Kant's approach to ethics requires us to determine what is right and wrong for ourselves by the application of reason, and not expect it to be delivered by any higher authority. Kant argues that a moral action is one which proceeds from the proper motive, namely the 'good will' which is a recognition of *duty*. Moral duties are unconditional (or categorical) demands on our behaviour – for example, 'You should give up your seat to the elderly and infirm'. They are unconditional or categorical because they do not depend on any conditions that need to be met; they are imperatives that apply to us all the time, whatever our personal desires and goals. We can work out what duties are determined by the use of reason by considering whether it is possible to universalise the maxim underlying an action. The ultimate duty is always to act in accordance with the categorical imperative, and so act in accordance with a maxim that you will everyone to act by. A second version of the categorical imperative states that we should always treat others as ends in themselves and never as means to our ends. Kant's approach to ethics is quite complex and not without criticism. However, his approach of giving human autonomy a central role in ethics has been highly influential and underpins the conceptual framework for human rights.

2.2.2 Applying Kantian ethics

In this section we will apply Kant's deontological ethics to four specific areas: *stealing*, *simulated killing*, *eating animals* and *telling lies*. In each section, we refer back to the ethical dilemmas presented in the introduction (pages 202–5).

Stealing

So far we have looked at Kant's ethics – this concerns our internal reasons for acting (sometimes called our internal behaviour). The goodness or badness of actions relates entirely to these reasons for acting. In examining stealing, we will also draw on Kant's politics – his theory of juridical rights (rights relating to law). These concern our external behaviour, so some of the ideas will be a little different, but linking both is the concept of freedom. Freedom is gained *internally*, by being able to follow maxims and use reason, and *externally* (politically), by being able to set and pursue our own ends, without being impeded by the choices of others (as long as my ends do not impede others' too).

Experimenting with ideas: there are no laws

Imagine a world without laws. Imagine today, this very day, this very moment, that all government simultaneously gives up. All police forces/courts/armies are disbanded. All prisons are closed down. There are no more crimes, as there are no laws. What would you do?

- In the first hour?
- In the first week?
- In the longer term?

Some people see laws as inhibiting their freedom (speed restrictions, illegal drugs and so on) and so we would be freer without them. But would you be freer with no laws?

Kant, in common with other philosophers, calls this idea of a lawless world a 'state of nature'. In a state of nature, we lack external freedom as other people's choices may be imposed on us and there is no way to deal with this – except through violence. Consider possessions. In a state of nature, if I leave my precious Zippo lighter in the woods and someone comes across it, then what is to stop them from taking it? What actually makes it 'mine'? How can I get it back without violence? Only laws can enable this. Living in a state of nature has a kind of wild, anything-is-possible freedom, but it lacks real freedom, the freedom to pursue my ends without other people's choices being imposed on me. We need a civil society for this.

In a civil society, I have a means of getting my Zippo lighter back. We can settle disputes with reason, not violence. Laws allow us each to have the maximum freedom that can co-exist with everyone else's freedom. Kant calls the idea of a civil society 'a rightful condition', and rational beings have a duty to enter into it.

In a rightful condition, my possessions and freedoms are upheld by the law. When someone acts illegally by stealing, it is not just the victims whom it affects, but the law/state is also damaged. The criminal's act pushes us all towards the wild state of nature, and in so doing damages the state.

▶ **ACTIVITY**
Read ST1 and ST2 (page 203). What would Kant say, and why?

> *Whoever steals makes the property of everyone else insecure and therefore deprives himself … of security in any possible property. [In this way, crimes] endanger the commonwealth and not just an individual person.*[19]

In ST1, stealing is morally and legally wrong for Kant for the following reasons:

▪ Categorical imperative – universal law formulation
   You cannot rationally conceive that people should steal property. What would happen in a world where people acted on the maxim, 'Steal when in need'? The concept of property and ownership would break down, so stealing, as such, would not exist. It is therefore inconceivable to act on a maxim if the concept would be meaningless if everyone did it.

▪ Categorical imperative – humanity formulation
   By 'borrowing' your friend's hospital pass without asking, you will have bypassed your friend's autonomy, so treating them as a means to an end. In stealing the medicine, you would also be treating the hospital manager as a means to your end. This is a violation of the second formulation of the categorical imperative.

▪ Kant's political theory
   If you choose to steal, you would be moving us all away from the rightful condition towards a state of nature. This cannot be consistently willed.

Overall, Kant is very clear on this. Do not do it. Stealing is morally wrong, and further, it is morally wrong to break the law. Laws need to be followed, otherwise you are willing that we all enter a wild state of nature.

The case of ST2 is slightly different. Making copyrighted material freely available to others is a criminal offence. The act of downloading such material for your own use is illegal in the UK, but is not a criminal offence (a crime against the state); it is a civil offence and you could be sued. However, these nuances would not matter to Kant.

You cannot rationally conceive that people should steal copyrighted material. What would happen in a world where people acted on the maxim, 'Steal copyrighted material'? The concept of copyright would break down. It is therefore inconceivable to act on a maxim if the concept would be meaningless if everyone did it. Morally, Nathan has downloaded songs without the musicians' permission, so has bypassed their autonomy and, as such, is treating

285

the musicians as a means to his own end. This is a violation of the second formulation of the categorical imperative. Also, as an illegal act, Nathan is moving us all away from the rightful condition towards a state of nature. This cannot be consistently willed.

Kant is very strict about not stealing. However, this strict approach for Kant leaves his system in a difficult position when it comes to unjust laws. What if a government passed laws that handed all wealth and land to the rich? (Perhaps like the salt tax laws in India; see page 247). Should these laws be obeyed?

Kant argues that lawmakers have a duty not to pass such laws, but unjust laws are still a problem, as there is no higher system that enables a citizen and government to rationally settle a dispute over an unjust law, and not obeying the law is to will us to return to a state of nature, which you cannot rationally do. Kant would have suggested that Ghandi was fine to organise a peaceful protest march against British Rule in India, but taking the salt without paying tax would be immoral. However, others would argue that the law was immoral and Ghandi did the right thing.

Simulated killing

▶ **ACTIVITY**

Read SK1 and SK2 (pages 203–204). What would Kant say?

Kant's morality is based around following rules that we can rationally will everyone to follow, and acting in ways that respect other people's autonomy (for Kant, these are the same thing). This usually requires working out if we have a duty to behave in a certain way, which in turn can be equated to whether you or other people have rights. (Having a right, say, to free speech, creates a duty in others – in this case, to not censor me. Duties are the 'flip-side' of rights.) For Kant, the moral value (right or wrong) of watching/playing simulated killing is not dependent on the consequences of such activities, but on whether it is possible to consistently will that you should watch them, and whether watching them is consistent with treating others as rational autonomous beings.

Not surprisingly, Kant wrote *literally* nothing about the morality of video games or violent films. So it is up to other commentators to work out what an appropriate Kantian position might be.

When I watch a violent film, or play a violent game, on the face of it, I do not seem to be reneging on anyone's rights. The actors were free agents who chose to be in the film. The pixels on the video screen are not real people. Other people may claim to have rights to not be offended by such sights, but as long as such films are not shown in outdoor places, where they cannot be avoided, then those who may be offended are not having their freedom curtailed.

There is a claim that in SK1 the game has been illegally altered and this does affect its moral status. In altering the game, the programmers were not respecting copyright. The original creators of the game did not have the opportunity to agree to this, so their autonomy was undermined and this is wrong.

This aside, the watching of simulated killing does not seem to infringe upon the rights of others. However, it may be that I have a duty to myself to not be entertained by simulated killing. An argument along these lines can be constructed from the work of Kant. Kant argues that morally we can treat non-human animals as a mere means to our ends, as animals lack the rationality required to have ends in themselves. However, he does not think this gives us a licence to be cruel to animals.

> *If a man shoots his dog because the animal is no longer capable of service, he does not fail in his duty to the dog, for the dog cannot judge, but his act is inhuman and damages in himself that humanity which it is his duty to show towards mankind. If he is not to stifle his human feelings, he must practise kindness towards animals, for he who is cruel to animals becomes hard also in his dealings with men.*[20]

Kant believes we have a duty to show our humanity towards mankind. This stems from having a duty to perfect our own moral nature. Our moral nature is our ability to treat others as ends in themselves – to see them as rational, autonomous beings. I cannot will that my ability to do this should diminish, as, when universalised, I would be willing that other people's ability to see me as an autonomous being should diminish. This is inconceivable, as the act of willing *is* the act of being autonomous, so we cannot will not to will.

So we have a perfect duty to treat others as ends, and this means we have a perfect duty to encourage our own ability to treat others as ends. For Kant, this involves an imperfect duty to sympathise with the suffering of other creatures and to 'cultivate the compassionate natural (aesthetic) feelings in us'.[21]

Kant's argument relies on there being an empirical connection which shows that being cruel to animals makes a person less likely to treat others with moral respect. Whether this is true or not is a matter of debate. There is research showing a link between the two; in other words, those who are violent towards animals are more likely to be violent towards humans. Being cruel to animals is widely used as a test for potentially dangerous conditions, such as psychopathic personality disorder. However, establishing a link does not show that being cruel to animals *causes* people to be cruel to humans. It could (and probably does) show that there is an underlying condition that causes the cruelty both to animals and to humans.

These arguments can be translated fairly easily to the issue of simulated killing. Kant claims that we have a perfect duty towards moral perfection and an imperfect duty to cultivate compassionate feelings in ourselves. It could be suggested that watching people violently die on films, or killing them violently in video games, makes us less compassionate towards others. Such entertainment may encourage us to see other people as a means to an end, as cannon fodder, without ends in themselves. If this were so, then we have a duty not to watch these films or play these games.

Again, this would seem to be an empirical matter and rely on there being a causal connection between simulated death as entertainment and being less compassionate to humans. The evidence does not have to directly suggest that such activities make us more violent, just that it makes us less compassionate (though violence would be an indicator of this).

There is some evidence pointing to this; however, there is also evidence pointing against it. There is also the problem that showing a link does not always show a causal link. Although society has become less violent in the last 20 years, studies have shown that general empathy levels have decreased during this time. The cause of this is not clear, and commentators are keener to suggest that wider societal changes such as capitalism and parenting have had a much greater impact than films/video games.

So Kant's position for both SK1 and SK2 is not fully clear. Engaging in such activities is not treating others as a means to an end (apart from the piracy element). However, it can be argued that it diminishes our ability to treat people as autonomous ends in themselves.

If it is shown that this is the case, then we have an imperfect duty not to do such things, and acting on the maxim of watching video games for pleasure can be blameworthy (but not always). If there is no causal connection between such activities and the diminishing of our compassion, then entertaining ourselves in this way is morally permissible, but not morally good, which utilitarians may claim.

Eating animals

For Kant, humans are different from other animals. Kant thought that we can escape our animal instincts through reason (see page 260). Humans can use reason to work out what they ought to do – in both senses of 'ought' : what is prudent, given our desires, and also what reason alone demands that we *ought* to do (the moral sort of 'ought'). As we know, reason alone demands that we only act in ways that we can rationally will that others do too. This ability to work out our own moral laws, and act on them, gives us freedom and autonomy. Animals lack this ability.

For Kant, this makes a striking difference. The only source of good is a good will. Freedom/autonomy is the supreme moral principle. For Kant, animals lack this autonomy. They are driven by instinct and do not have the ability to reason: to weigh up options and ask themselves what they *should* do. Animals act on the world, but they do not 'will'. Because they do not have the ability to conceptualise what they should do, animals do not pursue ends. And because of this, we do not have to treat them as beings with ends themselves – as beings with moral status. In essence, the moral law only applies to those beings capable of making moral laws.

The fact that the human being can have the representation 'I' raises him infinitely above all the other beings on earth. By this he is a person ... that is, a being altogether different in rank and dignity from things, such as irrational animals, with which one may deal and dispose at one's discretion.[22]

Whereas Bentham, in discussing animals, suggested that 'The question is not, Can they reason? nor Can they talk? but, Can they suffer?',[23] Kant is firmly suggesting that 'Can they reason?' is, indeed, the key question.

Criticism

One key difficulty with this position is that it would seem to require us to treat humans who cannot reason, who lack the ability to work out what they *should* do, as having no moral worth. For Kant, we also have no reason to treat them as autonomous beings with ends in themselves.

As we saw above (page 287), Kant believed we have an imperfect duty not to be cruel to animals, because we have a duty towards moral self-perfection. In this way, animals do sort of have rights – a right not to be cruelly treated. However, for Kant, this would be an indirect right, as the right only occurs as a

▶ **ACTIVITY**

Read EA1 and EA2 (page 204). What would Kant say?

▶ **ACTIVITY**

Read the account of the dog experiment on page 240.
● Do you think the suffering of the dogs is morally relevant in itself?
● Or do you agree with Kant that the suffering of the dogs is only morally relevant as it may undermine the experimenters' ability to treat other humans with sufficient respect?

consequence of a duty towards ourselves (humans). His argument, even for this right, relies on there being a causal connection between being cruel to animals and treating humans less morally. As outlined above, there is certainly evidence of a link, but proving a causal connection is harder.

In case EA1, Kant would argue that we should avoid being deliberately cruel, but not because of any harm caused to the animals. This may rule out some particularly cruel farming methods – but only for the farmer, as it is *his* duty to work towards moral self-perfection that is potentially threatened. It would not be morally wrong for the consumer to eat the meat.

Regarding EA2, Kant would consider this absolutely fine.

Telling lies

As with promises (page 267), it would seem that you cannot universalise a maxim of telling lies. The whole concept of lying relies on the concept of truth-telling. If everyone lied, then lies would not deceive. The wrongness of lying can also be clearly seen using the humanity formulation. Recall the example of the American tourists (page 252). In lying to the tourists, you are undermining their ability to pursue their own ends. Although you are not treating them as a means to your end (after all, it is their happiness you were pursuing), you are not treating them as rational people with their own ends, as their end may have been to get to St Paul's as quickly as possible. In telling the truth, we allow people to pursue their own ends, make up their own minds. In lying, we prevent this.

In the case of TL1, there are several Kantian problems with the idea of the affair. In lying to her husband, Shelly is undermining his autonomy. Maybe he would consent to an affair, maybe he would not; but if Shelly lies, he has no choice. Furthermore, in getting married, Shelly would have made a promise (either explicitly or implicitly) to be faithful – this would break the promise. You also cannot universalise the idea of infidelity, as the institution of marriage would be meaningless.

Kant also found the idea of sex outside of marriage problematic. Although Kant was not against the idea of sex *per se*, he believed that if it was not within a marriage (where you legally 'own' each other's bodies), then you would be treating the other (consenting) person's body as a means to your end.

The case of TL2 is quite complicated and controversial. Most people's moral intuitions about TL2 are that you should lie to the axeman. However, it seems as if Kant would be committed to telling the truth. Much has been written about this, in part because Kant himself wrote about a very similar example to this when defending his theory from criticism. Kant claimed that you have a duty to tell the truth in this scenario, which most people find odd. Consequently, many philosophers have revisited this dilemma to try to resolve the difference between our intuitions and what Kant said.

It is important to note that there is no moral requirement for you to speak at all in this scenario. You could simply stay quiet and so avoid lying. This would be an ideal solution for Kant. However, when Kant explored this scenario, he stipulated that you are forced to answer by the axeman (though it is not revealed exactly how). So the scenario is really: *given* that you have to answer, should you lie or tell the truth?

▶ **ACTIVITY**

Read TL1 and TL2 (page 205). What would Kant say?

289

Universal law formulation

Many philosophers suggest that the universal law formulation of the categorical imperative does not require you to tell the truth at all times. It seems perfectly possible to rationally will that everyone should follow maxims such as *I will always tell the truth, except if in telling the truth I put someone's life at risk*, or *I will always lie to a would-be murderer*. These do not seem to lead to any contradictions, as I would be happy to be lied to in these circumstances. Furthermore, we have an imperfect duty to help others, so not only is lying morally permissible, it may also be the right thing to do. So, according to this interpretation, Kant is wrong in applying his own theory, and lying in some circumstances is morally permissible.

Humanity formulation

The situation seems less flexible when we look at the humanity formulation. When we lie to someone, we are overriding that person's ability to make rational choices. We are using them as a means to our end (in this case, saving Bob's life). This is always wrong, so we should tell the truth. This leads to a few potential criticisms. Firstly, that the two formulations cannot mean the same thing (which Kant claimed they did), as they seen to produce different answers to this question. Secondly, if true, this requirement to always tell the truth points to a flaw in Kant's system, as the *consequences* of telling the truth seem to be disastrous in this case. As outlined earlier (page 278), by only focusing on *motive* and making sure our own 'sphere of action' is rationally faultless, we leave ourselves open to the faults in others' reasoning. On the plus side, having a moral system where some acts are *always* wrong means that our personal integrity is never compromised by doing the right thing. Kant's system enables lines to be drawn in the sand that you are required not to cross, whereas utilitarianism might require you to do *anything* to justify the ends (see page 244). The negative side of this is that the system seems inflexible and cannot deal with encountering evil in the real world, as in the case of TL2.

Telling the truth seems so wrong in this case that some philosophers have tried to find more ways in which Kant's system might allow lying in this case. One approach is to suggest that the moral status of the axeman may be altered because of his intention to kill. The axeman has clearly chosen to leave the rightful condition and enter a state of nature (page 284), as, whatever issues he has with Bob, he clearly wants to settle them by force rather than by reason. In a state of nature, we do not have full autonomy, as other people, through force, may override our choices. The axeman, in choosing to enter the state of nature, has then given up his entitlement to be treated as a person with full autonomy and so we can lie to him. For Kant, we have a duty to leave the state of nature and enter the rightful condition, so doing this would break that duty and so be wrong. However, something similar happens with war. When a country is attacked, it may defend itself, and in doing so the country enters a state of nature, but does so with the intention of leaving it as soon as it can (in other words, we can fight, but only do so with the aim of getting peace). In the same way, it is suggested we may lie to the axe murderer, with the intention of getting back to the rightful condition as soon as possible, perhaps by calling the police and getting the state involved at the earliest possible moment (which most people would do in the circumstances).

This seems like a reasonable Kantian way of solving the dilemma and showing that even the humanity formulation can have exceptions. If this solution seems fair enough, then why was Kant so insistent that telling the truth was the right thing to do in the axeman scenario?

Moral and legal lies

Learn More

Several philosophers have suggested that Kant's insistence that telling the truth was right should be interpreted in light of his views about legal rights, not just moral rights. When Kant wrote about this scenario, it was in the context of a discussion about the law.

Kant thought that lying is always morally wrong, but it is not always legally wrong (for example, you might lie to yourself and there is no law against that). Lying to others, though, always runs the risk of leaving the liar (partly) legally responsible for the subsequent events, but telling the truth never does; and it was this point that Kant was making when he said that telling the truth is always the right thing to do. It is always legally right. To understand this point, consider some of the following lies.

Experimenting with ideas

Rank each lie (A–F) on a scale of 1–10, based on how morally bad you think it is (10 being very bad).

A A friend asks you what the weather will be like today. You know the forecast says it will rain, but you lie and say it will be sunny as a joke.
B You lie about your age on a car insurance form – to get cheaper insurance.
C Two American tourists ask for the shortest way to St Paul's. You lie and tell them the prettiest route instead.
D You borrowed £30 from a friend. The friend cannot remember if you paid it back. You did not. You lie and say you did.
E A school window is broken. You lie to a policeman about where Reuben was the night it was broken.
F The prime minister lies, saying he never knew about a critical report before it was published.

Lie A does not seem to be illegal. However, imagine that your friend takes you at your word and goes out in a dinghy at sea. He is caught unprepared in a rain storm, contracts hypothermia and dies. If this were to happen, then it can be argued that you are legally responsible (in part) for your friend's death. In lie C, imagine that the tourists followed your route and in doing so are killed in a terrorist bomb attack. They would not have died if they had taken the quickest route. Would you feel guilty? Probably yes. Would you feel equally guilty if you had told the truth and they had died on that route? Probably not. By telling the lie, it is no longer *their* end that they were pursuing; your will altered their end and, in doing so, in part, it becomes your end that they were pursuing. Hence your feeling of guilt. In cases B and D, your lie denies people what is rightfully and legally theirs (money) and so is illegal from the outset. Case E is also illegal. The state is the means of settling disputes rationally; by lying, you are willing that we return to a state of nature – this is legally wrong and morally wrong. Case F is worse still for Kant. Lawmakers cannot act in this way, as this would be to will us into a state of nature – they have a perfect duty to tell the truth. This is illegal and immoral.

In light of this analysis, some interpret Kant's insistence on telling the truth in the axeman scenario as making a specific point about law. If you tell the truth, you will never break the law and will never be held legally responsible for any subsequent event. If you lie to others, then you are either breaking the law directly, or could be held legally responsible if events turn out badly. For example, you might lie to the axe murderer and say that Bob had gone to the pub. Unknown to you, Bob had heard the murderer at the door and ran immediately to the pub for safety. The axeman goes to the pub and kills him. Kant's point is that telling the truth is always legally right.

Kant did believe that lying is morally wrong, but it is suggested that his strong insistence in the murderer case is making a legal, rather than a moral point. So, what would Kant say about TL2? Well, you can say nothing. This avoids many issues. But if you were forced to answer, then we know that Kant would say that from a legal perspective, telling the truth will not lead to any legal responsibility for any subsequent events. Kant also seems to say that lying is always morally wrong (not just legally so); however, several 'Kantian' approaches can be constructed to show that it is not necessarily morally wrong to lie on this occasion.

2.3 Aristotelian virtue ethics

2.3.1 Aristotelian ethics

How is virtue ethics different from other ethical theories?

I'm talkin' about friendship. I'm talkin' about character.
I'm talkin' about – hell, Leo, I ain't embarrassed to use the word – I'm talkin' about ethics.

The opening lines from the labyrinthine gangster film *Miller's Crossing,* directed by Joel Coen, 1990

Virtue ethics is the name given to those moral theories that focus on the individual person, rather than an individual course of action. This difference in focus is an important one, and may appear to be at odds with our ordinary understanding of ethics. So, it might help if we consider what utilitarian and Kantian theories share, and then we can see how theories of virtue ethics differ from these.

It may seem as if the two types of normative theories we have already looked at, deontological (Kantian ethics) and consequentialist (utilitarian ethics), have very little in common with one another.

Take the example of the potential axe murderer who is looking for your friend (page 205). The utilitarian, weighing up the consequences, would recommend that you lie; a Kantian, considering your duties, would recommend that you tell the truth. But when you have a closer look at the differences between these two theories, you notice that they are specifically disagreeing over how to act in this situation. So, what they agree on is that it is the *action* (lying or not lying) that carries the moral weight. Moreover, they also agree that we can specify the method by which we assess whether or not an action is a good or right one. For consequentialists like the utilitarians, the assessment is based on whether this action brings about the best consequences; for deontologists like Kant, the assessment is based on whether performing this action breaks, or adheres to, certain rules.

Despite the flaws in both utilitarian and Kantian ethics, both theories strike a chord with our moral intuition: the intuition that ethics is about working out whether the things we do are good or bad, right or wrong. But in the history of Western moral philosophy, such intuitions are fairly recent, and for two thousand years from the ancient Greeks until the Enlightenment, ethics was centred around a very different intuition: the intuition that ethics is about the kind of character you have, the kind of person you are.

Theories of virtue ethics approach morality by judging the person (the agent) who committed the act, rather than the action itself. Julia Annas describes virtue ethics as 'agent-centred' in contrast to deontological and consequentialist theories, which are 'act-centred'.[1]

So, within act-centred ethics, our judgements are made first and foremost of specific acts: we judge them to be right or good (see **Figure 2.13**). Agent-centred, or virtue, theories make judgements of character: of whether someone is a good or virtuous person. The kinds of questions that a virtue ethicist wishes to address are 'What makes a good person?', 'What sort of life should I be leading?' and 'How should I develop my character?'

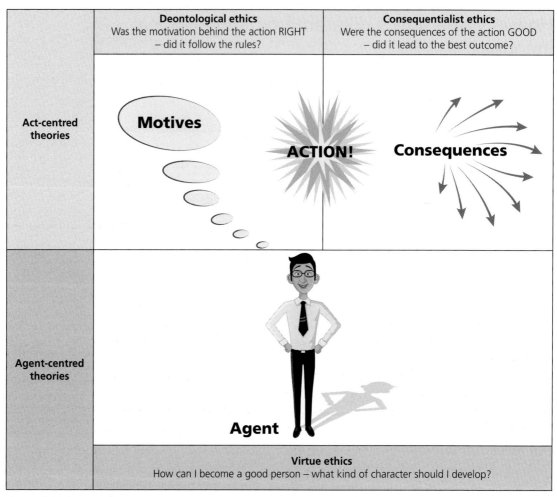

	Deontological ethics Was the motivation behind the action RIGHT – did it follow the rules?	Consequentialist ethics Were the consequences of the action GOOD – did it lead to the best outcome?
Act-centred theories	**Motives**	**ACTION!** **Consequences**
Agent-centred theories	**Agent**	
	Virtue ethics How can I become a good person – what kind of character should I develop?	

Figure 2.13 Some of the differences between act-centred and agent-centred theories

So, virtue ethicists take a more holistic approach when making moral judgements; they consider not just the present action, but the past and the future actions of the agent. However, as we shall see, this means that virtue ethicists find it difficult to offer simple rules or formulae about how we should live.

Virtue ethics has had its supporters throughout the centuries (notably Plato, Aristotle, Aquinas and Hume), but it is only in the last 50 years that it has been revived as a credible alternative to utilitarian and Kantian ethics and has even thrown light onto debates in epistemology (see page 40). We shall now look at the moral philosophy of one of the founding fathers of virtue ethics, namely Aristotle.

Background to Aristotle's *Ethics*

Aristotle (384–322 BC) was one of the greatest thinkers that the world has known; he was a genuine polymath – an expert in many different fields of knowledge. He held a TELEOLOGICAL view of the universe, the belief that everything in the universe has a purpose or function, and that the natural state of things is to move towards that final goal (*telos* in ancient Greek). This view governed his philosophical and scientific analysis of the world. Aristotle's writings are extensive, consisting of around 30 different treatises, but these represent only a fraction of what he originally produced. The surviving works appear to be lecture notes for his students rather than finished works for general consumption and consequently, compared to Plato's dialogues, they are rather prosaic. This is unfortunate as Aristotle was known in the ancient world for the beauty of his prose and the missing works, including many dialogues, represent one of the great losses to the philosophical canon. Aristotle wrote on a huge variety of subjects, from zoology and biology to logic and metaphysics, with detours via history, astronomy and psychology. In contrast to Plato's writings, Aristotle's are ordered and schematic, so the Roman editors who packaged his treatises together into books found it possible to divide his ideas up into chapters and sections.

Aristotle's exploration of virtue can be found in one of his most important works, the *Nicomachean Ethics*, or the *Ethics* as it is also known. It is worth noting some possible sources of misunderstanding that may arise when reading the *Ethics*. First, Aristotle's scientific leanings may have informed his empirical approach in the *Ethics*, as he presents this book as an investigation which must take into account our observations of people's behaviour and nature. Secondly, we also need to acknowledge that Aristotle had views on women and slaves that we no longer recognise as morally acceptable; nor are they generally considered relevant to his overall ethical theory; and so where Aristotle refers to 'men' we have applied his ideas to all humans (not just men). Thirdly, the Greek words used by Aristotle have a traditional translation, but throughout our analysis we will suggest alternative translations if we feel they are helpful. Finally, the *Ethics*, as we noted above, is best thought of as a series of Aristotle's lecture notes, to be used at his philosophy school (the Lyceum) rather than as a polished piece of literature. It is divided into ten books which explore several interconnected themes. However, it does contain a coherent ethical theory which we shall now investigate, and **Figure 2.14** should help us navigate through Aristotle's arguments and themes in the *Ethics* (at least those highlighted by the AQA specification). As you can see from the diagram, Aristotle's thoughts about the significance of virtue emerge from a much larger project, namely an investigation into the highest good for humans. So Aristotle's theory of virtue needs to be understood in this wider context: how virtue can help us in our pursuit of a life that is the best kind of life.

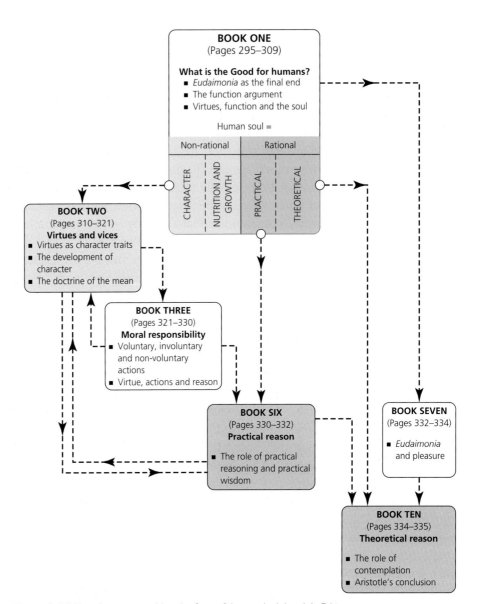

Figure 2.14 Flowchart summarising the flow of themes in Aristotle's *Ethics*

The Good for human beings (Book One of the *Ethics*)

Aristotle opens the *Ethics* with a bold generalisation that sets out his philosophical stall:

> *Every art, every procedure, every action and undertaking aims at some good; and for this reason the good has rightly been declared to be that at which all things aim.*
> Aristotle (1094a1)[2]

But what does Aristotle mean by 'good' here? As with other concepts that we shall encounter in his *Ethics* (such as 'virtue' and 'happiness'), we must be careful to clarify Aristotle's terms. 'Good' in this sentence does not refer to a utilitarian good (actions that maximise pleasure and minimise pain), or to a Platonic 'good' (which is an ideal existing only in the WORLD OF FORMS[3] see also, page 97), or to material goods (of the kind sold by shops). Nor does it refer to the functional concept of good that we will look at later on (the 'good can-opener'), although for Aristotle this is important too.

Instead, 'good' in the *first* part of Aristotle's opening sentence means something like 'our goal', in an individual sense. We can make sense of the word 'good' here because we believe that by achieving our goal we will add value to our lives, make our lives better in some crucial respect. We will return to this idea shortly, but before we do, we should note that 'the good', as it appears in the *second* part of the sentence refers to something slightly different, closer to the idea of the 'ultimate good', or the 'good for human beings': the thing that all humans are striving to reach. 'The Good' (which philosophers sometimes spell with a capital 'G') is also known by the Latin phrase the *SUMMUM BONUM*, the 'highest good', which is valued above all other goods. We saw above (page 209) that the utilitarians thought this 'good' was pleasure. But before we look at Aristotle's own account of the good, it is worth exploring our own intuitions as to what a good life (the best life) would consist of for us.

Experimenting with ideas: The Ideal Life Show

This is your opportunity to imagine your ideal life. Let your imagination run riot as you sketch the features that would make up your ideal life.

I   Under each of the categories in the table below write down several things that would be an essential part of your Ideal Life. What material objects (including money) would you have? What would you be like physically (health and appearance)? What mental, emotional or psychological characteristics would you have? What relationships would you like to have? What would you like to do or achieve in your Ideal Life? And finally what would the world around you be like?

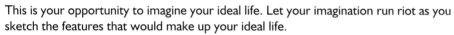

1. Material objects	2. Physical attributes	3. Mental attributes
✓ –	✓ –	✓ –
✓ –	✓ –	✓ –
✓ –	✓ –	✓ –
✓ –	✓ –	✓ –

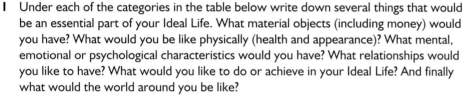

4. Relationships	5. Achievements	6. Environment
✓ –	✓ –	✓ –
✓ –	✓ –	✓ –
✓ –	✓ –	✓ –
✓ –	✓ –	✓ –

2   Now compare your Ideal Life with that of your friends or class mates. What features did they all have in common?
3   Do you think, as Aristotle and other philosophers suggest, that there is a unifying 'Good' or a single goal that we are all striving for in our lives? What kind of thing might this be?

Understanding 'means' and 'ends'

Let us now return to Aristotle's opening line in the *Ethics*: that everything we do is aimed at some good. His claim here is that everything we do has a purpose or an end, and that *this* end is itself also aimed at some further purpose or goal. Aristotle backs up his claim with various examples from everyday Athenian life. For example, a saddler makes bridles with the aim of controlling a horse; the aim of controlling horses is to improve military horsemanship; the aim of improving horsemanship is to develop the art of warfare (military science). Aristotle might extend this to say that improving our military science leads to a safer Athens (or Macedonia or Sparta). But is this claim true: is *everything* you do aimed at some meaningful goal; moreover, is that goal then aimed at some other further or higher goal?

Aristotle is drawing our attention to an important philosophical distinction between means and ends. Some things that we do, we do for their own sake (you may have reached this point at stage 3 in the Ideal Life Show), other things we do to bring about some end beyond the activity. Philosophers call those activities that are done for their own sake 'ends in themselves'. Those actions done for the sake of other things are simply the *means* to other ends, although, as was noted above, they are still aimed at some end (good). We can find out whether an activity is done a) for its own sake or b) for the sake of something else by asking 'Why did you do that?' And if there is no further answer than 'I did it for its own sake', then we have found an end in itself. Let's look at an example of this.

Why read this philosophy book? → In order to do well at A-level.

Why do well at A-level? → In order to go to university.

Why go to university? → In order to get a job.

Why get a job? → In order to earn some money.

Why earn some money? → In order to holiday in the Caribbean.

Why holiday in the Caribbean? → In order to feel the warm sun on my skin and the breeze on my face as I look out over a crystal blue sea.

For many of us, it wouldn't make sense to ask 'Why do you want to feel these sensations?' I just do. Therefore we could conclude that this must be a final end. So, in this example, the final end (the good) of reading this philosophy book is to have the pleasures of being on a tropical beach, and that is an end in itself. However, although we may think that pleasurable goals like these may be *a* good, we shall see that Aristotle would not agree with the utilitarians that they could be *the* Good.

Eudaimonia as the 'final end'

So Aristotle has plausibly shown that every activity aims at a good, an end. But at the end of this opening section (1094a19), he goes further by reiterating that there is one end that we all aim at. We saw on page 297 that he refers to this final end as the 'the Good', the *summum bonum*.

Some philosophers have argued that Aristotle is not offering a proof that everything is aimed at some end,[4] and that alternative translations of this passage reveal that he is merely offering a definition: namely that 'goodness' is what anything aims at. The 'bridle-making' passage suggests that Aristotle believes there is a hierarchy of goals, with each end in itself contributing to a goal that is more valuable (as the goal of keeping a country safe has more value than bridle-making). So Aristotle, in keeping with his teleological view of the universe, believes that by ranking goals we eventually arrive at a goal that is the highest: the supreme Good, which is good for all human beings.

▶ **ACTIVITY**

Revisit the activity on page 207 in the utilitarian section. Can you think of any examples of actions that don't have an 'end'?

▶ **ACTIVITY**

1 Go back to the Ideal Life Show on page 297 and identify each of your items as a means or an end.
2 For each item that is a 'means', use the method (from page 207) to work out what it is a means to.
3 Is there a single good which all your items, or those of your classmates, are directed towards?

But how are we to know when we have found an answer, when we have discovered something that really is the supreme Good, the final end that we are looking for? Aristotle outlines the following criteria for that supreme Good (1097a15–1097b21):

- It must be an **end**, and not a means to an end: 'we always choose it for itself, and never for any other reason.' (1097b2)
- It must be the **final end**, or the supreme Good: 'that for the sake of which everything else is done.' (1097a17)
- It must be **self-sufficient**, and it needs nothing more to complete it: the supreme Good is that 'which by itself makes life desirable.' (1097b17)
- It must be a life that we all want: it is 'the most **desirable** of all things.' (1097b18)
- Finally it must be something that is intimately related to us as **human beings**, which we shall see when we come to examine Aristotle's 'function argument' below.

The rest of the *Ethics* constitutes an examination of this supreme Good, and Aristotle is really searching for an answer to the question 'What is the good life?' Aristotle gives both a short answer and a much longer answer to this question. First, let us turn to the short answer.

> *What is the highest of all practical goods? Well … there is pretty general agreement. 'It is happiness' say both ordinary and cultured people.*
>
> Aristotle (1095a17)

We are in agreement, so Aristotle says, that the good life, the life we are all striving for as our final end, is *EUDAIMONIA* – normally translated as 'happiness'. Even after two thousand years, this seems to ring true; but once again we need to be careful about how we understand this translation, as our understanding of 'happiness' is not the same as the Greek concept of *eudaimonia*. The suffix *eu* (as in 'euthanasia', a good death) means 'good', and *daimon* refers to a spirit, so *eudaimonia* suggests a good spirit who could guide us through life.[5] This etymology, although not made explicit by Aristotle, points towards the ancient Greek conception of *eudaimonia* being different from our modern concept of happiness. Aristotle explains that *eudaimonia* is identified with living well and doing well in life (1095a18), in the way that we would fare well if a guardian angel really did guide each of us through it. Even though 'happiness' remains the conventional translation when writing about Aristotelian *eudaimonia*, a better translation might be 'flourishing', and we return to this when we examine the function argument, below.

We are now armed with the short answer to the question 'What is the good life?', namely 'It is *eudaimonia*', the sort of life that we all desire; a life that needs nothing added to it to make it more complete, one that is the final end of all we do. But that tells us very little, as what we really want to know is how in practical terms we reach *eudaimonia*, and what the good life actually consists of? This will give us the longer, fuller answer which will in turn help us to understand how Aristotle thinks we should live our lives.

Experimenting with ideas

A new marketing company Hipsters MORI has been commissioned by a multi-national tech giant, Facemazoogle, to identify customers for its new Aristotelian 'Good Life' app. This app takes information from across your online footprint to create a personalised online-life experience that enables you to reach the Good Life (which probably means you'll see more adverts!).

Hipsters MORI surveyed over one million people asking them 'What do you think you need to do to reach the Good Life?', and from this survey they identified the key groups/segments of customers for this new app:

- The *YOLO-ers*: life is all about **pleasure** and getting as much of it as you can.
- The *Gen-Y Wall-Streeters*: life is all about **money** and getting as much of it as you can.
- The *Click-'Like' Needies*: life is all about recognition, **honour**, respect and getting as much of this as you can
- The *Mid-life Wrist-Banders*: life is all about being morally **good** and helping others as much as you can (and wearing a wrist band for each good cause you support).
- The *New Millennial Elders*: life is all about reflecting on and **contemplating** life as much as you can

See **Figure 2.15** for a summary of their findings, and answer the questions below.

Figure 2.15 Chart showing the Hipsters MORI Good Lifers. Each of these groups represents a particular view of the good life and how it is reached

1 Which of the above groups is closest to your own view?
2 What's missing? Are there any other popular or important views about 'what makes the Good Life' that aren't represented in the five groups above?
3 Aristotle, as you might guess, would not allow his name to be associated with such an app – because most of these views do not in fact lead to the Good Life. Which of these views do you think he would reject and why? (You may want to refer back to the criteria for the Good Life outlined above.)

It is worth noting that in the *Ethics* Aristotle's empirical and descriptive approach (what do people think the good life is?) sometimes takes a more prescriptive approach (what *should* people do to reach the good life?), particularly in Book Ten. But, in these early chapters, Aristotle describes some populist answers to this question, the kinds of answers that he might have heard had he stopped people in the Athenian market place and asked them 'So, what do you think is the good life?' or 'What do you think Happiness consists in?' Although Aristotle was writing over two thousand years ago,

Key
- YOLO-ers
- Gen-Y Wall-Streeters
- Click-'Like' Needies
- Mid-life Wrist-Banders
- New Millennial Elders

the answers he considers aren't so different from answers we might hear today and which you may have encountered in the activity above, namely:

- Pleasure
- Wealth
- Honour
- Goodness
- Contemplation.

These are all plausible, rival, candidates for the good life – each of which fills in the details of the kinds of activities we should be engaged in if we are to be happy, and we shall now look at Aristotle's assessment of each of these ways of life.

The Good for humans: some possible candidates

Pleasure

Aristotle notes that the masses 'ask for nothing better than a life of enjoyment' (1095b15). The claim that *pleasure* is what we are all striving for in life is something that the utilitarians took for granted, and built their ethical theory upon (you may have come across it as 'psychological hedonism'). And perhaps when you think of 'happiness' you are thinking of the many pleasures that life can be filled with and that make life worth living. But early on in the *Ethics*, Aristotle dismisses the common claim that the Good, or happiness (in the sense of *eudaimonia*), is a life of pleasure. A life of pleasure and enjoyment is a 'bovine existence', a life fit only for cattle, writes Aristotle (1095b16). However, we shall see below (on page 332) that pleasure does have a crucial supporting role to play in a *eudaimon* life.

Wealth

Aristotle gives short shrift to the 'life of the business man', in other words someone who seeks to acquire wealth. The acquisition of money is simply a means to an end, to buy fancy meals, expensive goods, super yachts, once-in-a-lifetime experiences. Money is not an end in itself. *Eudaimonia*, we have seen, is by definition the final end in itself and so wealth cannot be 'the good we are seeking' (1096a4).

Honour

More refined people, according to Aristotle, claim that it is respect or *honour* that we are all striving for (eminence in public life was highly valued in Athens). But this is also rejected by Aristotle, because honour, or respect, is something that is bestowed on us by other people, and so is largely dependent on other people; *eudaimonia* isn't like that at all – it isn't given to us, but is something we gain ourselves and is not so easily lost as honour. Moreover, Aristotle points out that people seek honour in order to reach some higher good and so honour in itself can't be the final end: people seek to be honoured for their goodness (1095b27).

Goodness

Is, then, a life of *goodness* or virtue the kind of life we should all be striving for? We may be getting closer to the answer here, but for Aristotle, goodness alone cannot be *eudaimonia*. This is partly because we can imagine a situation in which someone who is good or virtuous is experiencing atrocious suffering or misery. Later on in the *Ethics*, Aristotle pushes home this point: 'those who maintain that, provided he is good, a man is happy on the rack … are talking nonsense' (1153b11). This may seem an obscure point for Aristotle to make, but he may be responding to a central claim made by his teacher, Plato, in the *Gorgias*: that it is better for someone to be tortured on a rack than to do wrong; and that a person who remains good, even though they are made to suffer, is happier than a person who avoids that suffering, but only by agreeing to become a criminal. These claims of Plato are what Aristotle describes as nonsense.

anthology
2.8

This is a rather extreme example, but it emphasises Aristotle's point very clearly. *Eudaimonia* is the kind of life we are all striving for, and goodness or virtue cannot by itself guarantee *eudaimonia* (although it may play a part). For our lives to go well, we need to have external goods (things we can't control, such as a life with some good fortune and luck, free from great disasters), as well as internal goods (things we can control, such as developing our character, honing our reasoning skills and learning to make the right decisions).

Contemplation

The final candidate for *eudaimonia* that Aristotle considers is a life of reflection or *contemplation*, but he promises to examine that later, which he does in Book Ten of the *Ethics*, and we return to it below (see page 334).

Concluding this part of the investigation, we now know Aristotle's short answer to the question 'What is the supreme Good?' *Eudaimonia* is the final end of all our actions and it cannot be bettered. We also know that neither pleasure, nor wealth, nor honour, nor goodness alone, will enable us to reach *eudaimonia*. But we still don't know what *eudaimonia* is, and Aristotle now sketches a methodology which should help us determine 'the long answer'. As you might guess, the long answer leads to a discussion of virtue; and the passage that bridges Aristotle's discussion of *eudaimonia* with his analysis of virtue is known as 'the function argument'.

To say happiness is the supreme good seems a platitude, and some more distinctive account of it is still required. This might perhaps be achieved by grasping what is the function of man.[6]
Aristotle (1097b22)

The function argument

Aristotle introduces the notion of 'function' (*ergon* in ancient Greek) quite out of the blue. We would probably agree with the first part of his statement that we do need a more distinctive account of *eudaimonia* and we would like a longer answer to the question of what the supreme Good is; but we may well ask what has function got to do with it? Aristotle's assumption is that, if we want to know how to be *eudaimon*, we must analyse how we can function well as humans: how we can be good humans. But what does the good life have to do with being a good (well-functioning) human? The connection between something being good and its fulfilling its function is brought out in the following activity.

▶ **ACTIVITY**

Consider each of the following pairs and answer the questions below.

A A good can-opener   An ordinary can-opener
B A good sheepdog   A satisfactory sheepdog
C A good musician   An okay musician
D A good video game   A mediocre video game
E A good person   An average person

1 What are the qualities and attributes that distinguish the good thing from the other, more ordinary, thing?
2 Which is better at fulfilling its function – the good thing or the more ordinary thing?
3 So, overall, what would Aristotle say made something good?
4 Imagine now that you were confronted with an unknown object 'Z' in a box. What method would Aristotle use to determine whether Z was a good object?

Hopefully, this activity will have teased out the connection that there is, even in English, between 'goodness' and 'function'. It should also have revealed the connection between 'good', 'well-functioning' and 'having qualities that enable it to be well-functioning'. We refer to something as 'good', in an instrumental or functional sense, first if that thing has a recognised function and secondly if it fulfils its function really well because it has those special qualities that enable it to do so. Thus a good can-opener fulfils its function well because it has the appropriate *arete* (excellence or virtues): it is sharp, safe, easy to handle, etc. (see **Figure 2.16**).

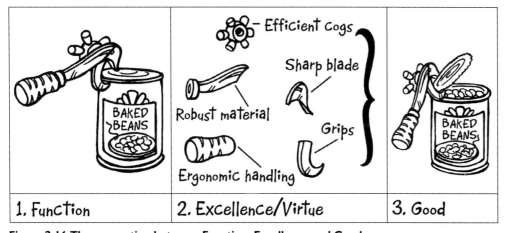

Figure 2.16 The connection between Function, Excellence and Goodness
A good can-opener has all the qualities (virtues) needed to open easily a can of baked beans.

However, now we don't really associate this instrumental sense of goodness with any moral sense of goodness. So why did the ancient Greeks connect good in its broader (moral) sense with the special virtues or qualities (*arete*) that enable something to fulfil its function (*ergon*) well? Why did 'being good at something' mean for the Greeks that you were actually 'good'?

Alasdair MacIntyre, in *A Short History of Ethics*, argued that in Homer's time, centuries before Plato and Aristotle, being a good person was linked to being good at whatever role you played in ancient Greek society.[7] Take the example of a soldier: for MacIntyre you were thought of as a good (in a noble or moral sense) soldier if you had all the qualities that a soldier needs in order to excel in your allotted role (*ergon*) as a soldier. As ancient Greek society developed after Homer, and as social roles became less defined, so the connection between instrumental goodness and moral value became less clear according to MacIntyre. But there remained that lingering association between noble (or moral) goodness, and *ergon* even in fourth century BC when Plato and Aristotle were embarking on their philosophical projects.

It should be clearer now why Aristotle brings in the idea of 'function': to his audience, this might have seemed natural, as goodness in what we understand as its instrumental sense was still connected with goodness in the sense of having moral value. Moreover, you may recall that Aristotle held a strongly teleological view of the universe: that nature and its occupants are directed towards a goal, a purpose, an end. He applied this to his biological studies and his astronomy as well as to his politics and his theories in the *Ethics*. So Aristotle believed that we have a function that goes above and beyond the one prescribed for us through any role we might have in society. This is our function *as human beings*, and Aristotle thought that by understanding our function as human beings we would understand how we could be good, and this was the key to happiness. If we could understand the life of a good human, then we would understand the good life for a human.

anthology
2.9

Let us turn to Aristotle's argument proper, which has become known as 'the function argument' and which follows from his assertion (at 1097b22) that we might better understand what *eudaimonia* is if we know the function of man. As we mentioned above, the function argument is a critical stepping stone between Aristotle's discussion of *eudaimonia* and his discussion of virtue. Aristotle has three aims in his function argument: first to show that the Good for humans consists in us fulfilling our function (*ergon*) well; secondly to show that humans do actually have a distinct function, and thirdly to say precisely what this function is.

The first aim is crucial to the success of Aristotle's project in the *Ethics*, namely showing us what type of life we should be leading if we want to reach *eudaimonia*. Aristotle draws a clear connection between the instrumental goodness of a human (whether or not we fulfil our function well) with the overall Good for a human (how we can flourish). Aristotle says that if we consider any class of people who have a specific function, for example flute players, sculptors or artists, then the goodness of the flute player, sculptor or artist is determined by their performance of that function. The same, Aristotle says, is true for humans; in other words, our goodness as humans is determined by whether or not we fulfil our function well as humans. The activity (below) may help us to clarify the connection Aristotle is making here.

Experimenting with ideas

Let's take a leaf out of Aristotle's botanical work, and focus on plants now rather than humans.

1   On a blank sheet of paper, draw two boxes side by side. In the left-hand box draw a *eudaimon* plant, i.e. a plant that is living a good life (for a plant) and is flourishing.[8]
2   Write down what you think the function of a plant is.
3   Write down a list of those qualities which a well-functioning plant has.
4   Now in the right-hand box draw the plant you have described, i.e. a Good plant (one that is fulfilling its function well), and on it label the qualities listed in 3.
5   Is there any difference between the two pictures that you have drawn, i.e. between a plant living the Good life and a Good plant?

You may have found that your drawings of a good plant and a *eudaimon* plant weren't that different, they may even have been identical, showing that there is a plausible connection to be made between the life of a good plant and a good life for a plant (see **Figure 2.25** on page 334). Although the example of the plant is our example, we hope you can see how it illustrates Aristotle's direction of thought. If Aristotle can show us that humans have a function, and describe what that function is, then what follows is a route map to *eudaimonia*: we must perform well to become a good human, and in doing so we will be living the good life for a human.[9]

Let us turn now to the second aim: how does Aristotle demonstrate that humans do in fact have a function? Aristotle gives two arguments to support this claim, although they seem more like rhetorical questions than arguments. First, we have seen that people with different occupations (flute players, sculptors, artists) have a function, so is it likely, Aristotle asks, that all these occupations have a function while 'man has none'? Secondly, we can see that the parts of a human body, our eyes, our hands and feet, all have a function, so shouldn't we assume that a human being as a whole has a function?

Criticism

Several criticisms have been levelled at Aristotle's argument in this passage, but we shall look at just two of them. The first criticism is that it appears as if Aristotle is offering a very weak ARGUMENT FROM ANALOGY to support his conclusion that humans have a function. You will see from your investigations into the argument from design[10] that an argument from analogy is at its strongest when the two things being compared are very similar to one another. So a strong analogical argument convinces us that because two things are alike in some respects, they are also alike in a further respect. But if this is indeed an argument from analogy then Aristotle seems to have selected a very small number of random things which have a function (the occupations people have, the parts of the body) and concluded that *like* these things, humans must have a function too. It is not at all clear why a human being should be compared to the occupations we have or to the parts of our body. The analogy would have been strengthened, perhaps, if Aristotle had listed a huge range of things (all living creatures, all human endeavours, all natural processes), shown that they had a purpose, and then asked 'Is it likely that human beings are functionless?' But he didn't do this, and so the purported analogy doesn't ring true.

A second criticism is that Aristotle may be guilty here of the fallacy of composition (which you may remember from your analysis of Mill's proof of utilitarianism (page 216)): just because the parts of something share a common feature does not mean that the whole has that common feature. Just because the parts of our body have a function does not mean that the whole body (the human) has a function.

One possible defence of Aristotle against both these criticisms is to say that he isn't providing an argument here at all, but he is simply articulating his teleological assumptions, namely that everything is directed towards some purpose. The parts that make up a whole (the parts of a body, the different occupations within human life) can only be seen to have a meaningful function if the whole to which they contribute (the body, or human life) itself has a purpose. Aristotelian teleology is no longer widely held, but you may be familiar with religious teleology: people who believe that God created the world generally believe that the world has a purpose and that humans also have a purpose.

But if we reject Aristotle's teleological view (which most scientists and philosophers now do), then his argument fails. Not because the argument commits the fallacy of composition or is a weak analogy, but because scientists no longer need teleological explanations to account for the processes of the natural world, and philosophers have long since lost their optimism that there is any external purpose to human existence! Without this purposive view of the world, we think very differently about function: something only has a function if it is specifically assigned a function (a can-opener, a sheep dog, a member of parliament), and unless you believe in God then it's hard to see how humans could have an assigned function.

In Alasdair MacIntyre's modern revival of virtue ethics, he retains certain aspects of Aristotle's teleology.[11] MacIntyre argues that we should understand moral goods in terms of how they are embodied in many different 'social practices', such as teaching, nursing, farming, football, musicianship. Each of these practices has its own sets of virtues, its own goals, its own *telos*, and these goods are realised through our attempts to reach that standard of excellence (virtue) that is established by those practices. For MacIntyre, then, our human 'function' is identified through our engagement in a plurality of social practices, but it is not identified with any one single activity.

An alternative way of proceeding with Aristotle's project, however, is by understanding *ergon* not in the sense of 'function' but in the sense of 'work' or 'characteristic activity'. Humans may, in this sense, have a characteristic activity which distinguishes them from other living creatures. So on this view it does make sense for Aristotle to ask 'What is our specific *ergon*?' 'What is the distinguishing characteristic(s) of a human being?' 'What makes us unique as a species?'

▶ **ACTIVITY**

1 Write a list of all the things that distinguish us from other species.
2 Now exclude from the list all those features that are shared by other species, to create a shortlist.
3 From your shortlist, which do you think is the single most significant distinguishing characteristic?

Aristotle's argument continues to his third aim as follows. The characteristic that distinguishes humans from other things cannot be mere nutrition or growth, because that is shared with plants; so even though a life of nutrition and growth is important to our survival, it isn't distinct to us and so cannot be our function. Nor can our function be sentience or perception, as that characteristic is also shared, namely with other animals. And so Aristotle comes to the following conclusion: 'There remains, then, a practical life of the rational part ... [a] life determined by activity' (1097a3–7). Aristotle is often misquoted as saying that 'man is a rational animal', a simple and memorable phrase which unfortunately doesn't appear in any of his surviving works. However, the misquoted phrase does capture the gist of this part of the argument, as Aristotle believed that it is our reason (*logos*) which distinguishes us from plants and animals (see **Figure 2.17**). In short, our function as human beings is to reason:

> *The function of man is an activity of the soul which follows or implies a rational principle.*
>
> Aristotle (1098a8)

Figure 2.17 What is the function of a human?
Humans share sentience with animals, and both humans and animals share nutrition/growth with plants. But Reason is the function (or characteristic activity) of humans.

But why the soul? Our function, according to the ancient Greeks, is determined by the kind of thing we are. So if we are a dog, then we have a doggy function, and our goals in life are very different from humans': to chase after balls, sleep a lot, guard our cave, eat as much as we can and have loads of offspring (actually they're not that different!). But what kind of thing is a human? For both Plato and Aristotle, we are creatures with a soul (in Greek *psyche*, which is where we get our word 'psychology' from), as this is what makes us human. Our function as human beings is determined by the makeup of our souls. So, if we want to understand our function, we need to understand our soul. Famously, in *The Republic*, Plato argued that our soul consists of three parts: reason, spirit/drive and desires, and it is the job of our reason to control the powerful impulses of our desires and our headstrong drive. Aristotle, however, had developed a more sophisticated, psychological view of the soul. When Aristotle talks about the 'soul' he is definitely not talking about a separate, spiritual, side of our self, or something that lives on after we die. For Aristotle, the soul was a kind of 'blueprint' or 'form' for a living being – the instructions for how it could develop over the course of its life. So our function, our characteristic activity, is determined by the kind of soul that we have. Humans have a rational soul and so our function is to exercise the rational parts of our soul. We shall see later how Aristotle views the different parts of the human soul.

The relationship between virtues, function and the soul

At the end of the function argument, Aristotle gives his clearest definition yet of the good life for humans. It is:

an **activity** of the **soul** in accordance with **virtue** (or if there are more than one kind of virtue, in accordance with the best and most perfect kind).
Aristotle (1098a15)

At last, we see the word 'virtue' appear, but once again, we need to understand what Aristotle means by virtue. On page 303, we encountered the idea that for something to be good, and function well, it needed certain special qualities, *arete*, which philosophers usually translate as 'virtue'. Unfortunately 'virtue' (derived from *virtu*, which was the Latin translation of *arete*) now has particular connotations in ordinary language: it suggests a sort of Victorian prudishness, a goody two-shoes or perhaps, even more narrowly, a kind of sexual purity. When thinking about virtue ethics, it is important that we throw out these connections, as they have nothing to do with 'virtue' in the philosophical sense. Remember that virtue has other more relevant cousins: 'virtuosity' and 'virtuoso' – in other words, being brilliant or excelling in a particular area of life. In fact, *arete* is better translated as 'excellence', and we shall use both 'virtue' and 'excellence' when talking about *arete*.

▶ **ACTIVITY**

Refer to the activity on page 303, and list the virtues (excellences) of the following things:

- a good can-opener
- a good sheepdog
- a good musician
- a good human.

You may have noticed that the 'good' things had attributes or qualities that the 'ordinary' versions lacked, which meant they were better able to fulfil their function – we can think of these qualities as virtues. So it is clear how virtue (in the sense of virtuosity) is connected to function and goodness for Aristotle: in order to be good, you need to fulfil your function well; but in order to fulfil your function well, you need to excel in the right ways – you need to possess virtues. And in order to be a good human, you need to excel in the characteristic activity of a human, which is determined by the rational parts of our soul.

The good life for humans, *eudaimonia*, is therefore achieved through virtue (*arete*): excelling in the rational parts of the soul.

Aristotle goes on to assess how closely his view of *eudaimonia* fits in with our commonly held ideas, and in doing so he expands on his own understanding of what it means to flourish, to live the good life.

- Happiness, or flourishing, is something that we work towards over our whole lifetime; it is not something that a single event can bring about – as Aristotle puts it, 'One swallow does not make a summer' (1098a20).
- Happiness, or flourishing, is reached in part through the exercise of reason, but it is something that needs external goods as well. It is much easier for people to flourish if they live in a comfortable, safe society (as Aristotle did) than if they live in a state of fear, or war, or hunger, or poverty. These external goods may be down to good luck, but without exercising our reason, we will not flourish, even if we do have an abundance of external goods.
- Happiness, or flourishing, is not something we are born with, but is something we strive to achieve through habituation and training, which we look at on page 310.

By the end of Book One of the *Ethics*, we can see where Aristotle's investigation in the *Ethics* is heading. Aristotle has used the first book simply to introduce the idea of happiness, and to prove that it is achieved by excelling at our function. We have seen that our function is closely related to our soul or *psyche* (the form of a human being), and so, if we really wish to understand how to be a good human, then we must understand how we can excel in the different parts of the soul. Aristotle views the soul as divided into a rational and a non-rational part, each of which is then subdivided (1102b10–b30). Aristotle clearly identifies two non-rational subsections: first, the section related to our body and governing growth and nutrition; and second, the section related to our character and governing our desires and emotions. Crucially, as we shall see, this second section can be shaped by reason. Then there is the rational part, including practical, day-to-day reasoning (which also shapes our character) and theoretical reasoning or contemplation (examined right at the end of the *Ethics*). We have seen that happiness is reached by excelling as a human being, which means exercising virtue, or excellence, in each of the parts of the soul, particularly its rational aspects.

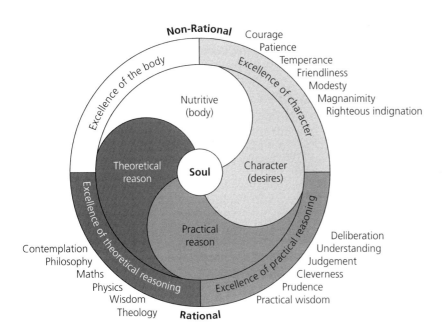

Figure 2.18 Aristotle's division of the soul

The remainder of the *Ethics* (apart from some important chapters on friendship) is primarily concerned with the detail of how we can excel in the different parts of our soul, and in so doing, how we reach *eudaimonia*. We have represented Aristotle's view of the soul in **Figure 2.18** as divided into four parts, and have given some examples of the associated excellences for each of its parts. However, you may choose to picture the division in a different way. In **Figure 2.18**, we have deliberately aligned excellence of practical reasoning close to excellence of character: like Plato, Aristotle believed that we could only be happy if the rational part of our soul were in control and our practical reasoning skills helped to shape our character to ensure our emotions and desires did not lead us astray. We shall now turn to the part of the soul that governs our desires and emotions, and the virtues or excellences that apply to this part.

Aristotle's account of virtues and vices (Book Two of the *Ethics*)

Virtues as character traits or dispositions

Book Two of Aristotle's *Ethics* begins a deep account of virtue that continues through the next five books of the *Ethics*. The themes explored in Book Two include: how we can develop virtues (through habituation and education, in a way that is analogous to the development of skills); the role of both the intellect and feelings in understanding virtues; how we can identify virtues (through the doctrine of the mean); and how we can apply this doctrine to specific virtues. Before we look at these themes, however, let us try to clarify further what is meant by virtue (*arete*).

▶ ACTIVITY: WHAT IS A VIRTUE ANYWAY?

1 Write down a list of characteristics (or personality traits) that people might say were 'virtues'.
2 Next to that list, write down another list of characteristics that people might call 'vices'.
3 Is there anything that the characteristics you have called 'virtues' have in common?
4 Is there any obvious way in which they differ from the 'vices'?

One simple way of thinking about what virtue is, is to think of it as a DISPOSITION or character trait possessed by good people – that is, by people we admire, value or praise. In contrast, a vice is a disposition or characteristic possessed by bad or 'vicious' people – that is, by people we condemn. What we mean when we are talking about a characteristic or a disposition or a trait is a *tendency to behave, habitually and reliably, in a particular way*, so, for example, we say someone is kind (has a kind disposition) when they are habitually, and reliably, thoughtful and generous to others. The key idea here is that a disposition is not a one-off act (which utilitarians and Kantians seemed happy to pass judgement on), but a description of how someone has acted in the past, and how they will probably act in the future.

So a virtue (*arete*) is what philosophers call a 'thick' concept. In other words, it is complex, multi-layered and contains both descriptive and prescriptive elements. We have already identified at least three key elements of virtue above: first, a virtue is a disposition – a habitual and reliable way of behaving; second, a virtue is a highly developed and skilful characteristic ('virtue' in the sense of 'virtuosity' or excellence; page 308); and third, a virtue is a characteristic or disposition which has a high social or moral value placed on it (for example, having integrity, courage or wisdom).

The role of education and habituation in the development of a moral character

The debate about whether we are who we are, and have the character traits that we have, through nature or through nurture, is an age-old debate extending at least as far back as Book Two of Aristotle's *Ethics*. In your answers in the activity (left), you may have identified at least some character traits that have emerged as you have grown older, suggesting that you were not born with that

▶ ACTIVITY

1 Think about how your family would describe your character – what words would they choose? (Are you kind, lazy, careful, greedy, late, modest, loyal, passionate, angry, calm, conscientious, patronising, self-reliant, cynical, friendly, honest, witty, etc.?)
2 What words would your friends choose to describe your character?
3 Finally, how would you describe yourself? (If you need more inspiration, or more words, look up 'list of virtues and vices' on the internet.)

particular disposition. For example, you may remember a time when you lacked confidence but now you have it, and so in class you can assuredly defend your belief that Jediism is a genuine religion. Or you may remember a time when you had only a small degree of control over your desires (ask your family to reminisce about your tantrums when you were 2 or 12), but now you have more control (although chocolate may still be a particular issue). You may have been patient as far back as you can remember, or you may have always had a short fuse and angered easily. The question is, how did you, and how do we, acquire dispositions like these, and how can we develop excellence of character – is it through nature or nurture? Aristotle's answer is that:

The moral virtues are engendered in us neither by nor contrary to nature; we are constituted by nature to receive them, but their full development in us is due to habit.
Aristotle (1103a23)

So nature has a role to play insofar as we are born with certain predispositions or potential. But this potential only becomes actual through exercise, practice, action and habit. In other words, our character is not determined merely by having some predestined or innate 'personality' gene, or natural gift for courage or friendliness. For Aristotle, excellence of character, or moral virtue (two alternative translations of *ethica arete*), has to be developed by practice and training until it becomes a habit.

'Habit' is not quite the right word, as it suggests a passive, perhaps mindless, response to our situation. Picking your nose, or saying 'like', like all the time, is a habit; being courageous is not a habit in the same way – like all the virtues, it requires mental effort; there need to be reasons underpinning our behaviour. But 'habituation', a type of education we undergo through repetition, is certainly where the process of developing a virtue begins.

The skill analogy

Aristotle compares the development of a virtue (a disposition such as being courageous or being just) with the development of a practical skill, like learning an instrument or a craft.

The virtues we acquire by first exercising them, just as happens in the arts. For the things we have to learn before we can do them, we learn by doing them: people become builders by building and instrumentalists by playing instruments. Similarly we become just by performing just acts ... brave by performing brave ones.
Aristotle (1103a33–b1)

This may sound paradoxical, but we learn to play *Grand Theft Auto XV* or *Pokemon Go Go Go* not simply by sitting and watching someone else, but firstly by copying someone else, then by playing it ourselves (badly) and learning from our mistakes. Anyone who has ever successfully learnt an instrument began the process of learning by playing it (to the horror of their neighbours), and through practice and guidance (a teacher, a website, a friend) gradually improved. So there are some key elements in the development of the skill here:

- initial observation, guidance and input by an expert
- starting to practise the skill (which is difficult and painful)
- getting better through practice and habit (which may become more pleasurable)
- the move from dependence on the expert to independence from the expert.

This process helps us to develop a skill and exercise that skill independently, but that does not necessarily make us an expert. There is a widely quoted claim (made popular in Malcolm Gladwell's book, *Outliers*[12]) that in order to become an expert you need to devote 10,000 hours of practice to that skill: the best ice hockey players (practising all year round, from year 1 to year 13), the Beatles (who played live 1,200 times in Hamburg before they became famous), Bill Gates (who, as a teenager, spent thousands of hours programming computers). The precision of Gladwell's claim is contested (what about someone who only spent 9,000 hours practising?), but nonetheless we might agree that to become an expert in a particular skill, we need to devote a huge amount of hours to practising that skill – Minecraft replicas of the Eiffel Tower do not build themselves, you know.

According to Aristotle, the development of a virtue, or character trait, is similar to the process of skill development outlined above. When cultivating a particular character trait – for example, kindness – we may start slowly, perhaps even unwillingly, and we need to be told what to do: most of us, as children, had to be constantly reminded to consider the needs of others. But we can learn to become kind by repeatedly acting (and being reminded to act) in a kind way; in Aristotle's words, 'like actions produce like dispositions' (1103b22). Through this process of educating our emotions, we become inclined to kindness, independently of any parent or teacher. We start to recognise what would be the kind thing to do, in a particular situation, and we may even start to get pleasure from being virtuous, which provides further motivation for us to be virtuous in future, and for Aristotle, this habituation is how we start to develop *ethica arete*. So we can recognise, in the cultivation of a virtue, key elements similar to those found in the development of a skill:

- initial observation, guidance and input by an expert
- starting to practise the behaviour (which is difficult and painful)
- getting better through practice and habit (which becomes more pleasurable)
- the move from dependence on the expert to independence from the expert.

anthology
2.10

The last point, about independence and autonomy, is a critical one, and is one that Julia Annas (1946–) emphasises: mere habituation is not enough to create the genuine dispositions that we need to develop if we are to be *ethica arete*.[13] We begin by following rules, but the world is complicated and the rules do not always easily apply, so as we develop, we learn to recognise how to act in different situations and contexts. In other words, we exercise our reason: a virtue does not mean blindly following a habit, it means thinking through our reasons for behaving in a particular way.

Aristotle makes it clear that to be good and have *ethica arete*, you must not just act in a good way, but you must also act as good people act (1105a20–33). On this view, there is a psychological, as well as a behavioural, aspect to virtue. To be *ethica arete* then, it is not enough to do good acts and behave as a virtuous person would; you must do these acts in a certain way: with a depth of understanding, with a certain attitude, and with a history of similar acts behind you. Someone who has *ethica arete* has not merely done one, or a few, virtuous acts; they have learnt by habituation to do virtuous acts, they enjoy doing virtuous acts (they naturally want to do them) and they have a disposition (a firm character) to always act virtuously. They also know what they are doing, and choose to act virtuously. This ties virtue closely to practical reasoning and practical wisdom, which we look at in more detail on page 330.

Criticism

Julia Annas[14] argues that there are limits to Aristotle's skills analogy. When we are developing a skill, we are striving to achieve some particular end (to learn the drums, to pass an exam, to build a Minecraft replica of the Eiffel Tower), and we can detach ourselves from that end. We might give up on achieving these things or, once we have achieved them, we might cease to think that they are important. But when developing a virtue, we cannot give up on the end – because the end of virtue is the final end, namely our efforts to flourish and live the best life possible.

A further limit that Annas identifies is that, generally, the development of a skill is made independently of our emotions and feelings. You can be skilful whilst hating what you are doing, or being emotionally disinterested in what you are doing – quite a lot of adults go through their working lives in this state. However, for Aristotle and other virtue ethicists, a mark of virtue is that there is no internal conflict between your feelings: when you are generous, you are not fighting a desire to be selfish, you actually want to be generous. As we have just seen above, a virtuous person does not just act virtuously (ticking all the right boxes, in a Kantian way), but they act in a virtuous way that comes from the inside – they feel and want to act virtuously. Let us now look at this in more detail.

The importance of feelings

We have seen how, for Aristotle, we are striving for the good life and that a critical part of this consists in developing *ethica arete*, excellence of character or 'moral virtue'. But a virtue such as courage is not just about taking a courageous course of action; instead, it is about having a disposition towards courageous actions. And this makes it a very different type of moral philosophy from Kantian or utilitarian ethics, which make judgements about specific actions and situations. Virtue ethicists such as Aristotle take a more holistic view, and they expect us to strive not just to be courageous on this one particular occasion, but to develop a disposition for courage so that, whenever required, we will do the courageous thing (or the kind thing, or the generous or just thing …). However, Aristotle makes it clear that virtues, or dispositions, are not just about actions, but also about emotions: 'virtues are concerned with actions and feelings' (1104b15).

For Aristotle, a virtue is not just a disposition towards a certain kind of act, but also towards a certain kind of feeling. There is an interesting symmetry here between action and feeling (or 'passion', as philosophers used to refer to it), namely that actions involve us affecting something, whilst emotions involve us being affected *by* something. A virtue is our capacity to shape our behaviour both as active agents (through taking the right action) and as passive recipients (through having the right response to our emotions).

The importance of feelings in Aristotle's theory can be seen in the series of examples (listed in the table on page 320) which he uses to illustrate how someone with a virtue is able to navigate a path between excessive or deficient responses – a path that has become known as the doctrine of the mean (page 315). In this list, many of the examples are emotions such as shame, indignation, anger and fear. Someone who is virtuous is able to respond appropriately to the emotion – the feelings that bear down on us, that flow through us, that drive us – and is then able to act appropriately in the light of that emotion.

But why are feelings important to developing the right dispositions and becoming *ethica arete*? We mentioned above that a virtuous person does not have the internal conflict that is familiar to many of us who are still learning to be virtuous. Someone who is generous (who possesses the disposition or virtue to be generous) does not have to overcome the internal dialogue and struggles that are familiar to many of us. Apparently, generous people do not have conversations in their heads like this: 'I do not want to share the last slice of cake. I made it, so it is my cake ... but I suppose I ought to share it, as they did specifically ask me for cake... but they just will not enjoy it as much as me ... they will not savour every mouthful like I did with my first two slices – and after all, I made it, it is my cake. But I guess I am obliged to offer them the cake. They are my children after all. Oh all right then, offer them the last slice of cake ... Perfect: they have turned it down ... Mmmmm, my cake.' This is someone trying, and struggling, to be generous. Instead, the internal monologue of a generous person is probably more straightforward: 'I will offer them the last slice of cake.' To a utilitarian, this would be a good action, no matter what the internal dialogue. Whilst to a Kantian, this was the right action so long as it was motivated by duty. The internal struggle of the person trying to be generous is not morally relevant to Kant or Mill, as to both types of theory the action is being judged in isolation from the person's character. But to a virtue ethicist such as Aristotle, the internal struggle with conflicting emotions is a strong indication that someone has not yet developed the virtue – they are not yet a generous person (in fact, the author of this passage could be more accurately described as a greedy person). A truly generous person, as Annas notes, is wholehearted in their generosity.[15]

This is connected to the process of habituation and training outlined above – that practice helps us to shape our responses to an emotion, but it can also help us to shape the emotion itself. So we begin to *feel* generous, and to feel courageous, and to feel kind (not simply act in a generous or courageous or kind way). The development of these feelings, and a disposition towards these feelings, is as important to *ethica arete* as the development of our dispositions to act. So Aristotle's theory of *eudaimonia* is not only about how to act well, but also how to feel well.

There is a related issue at stake here. Aristotle argues that virtue involves choice, which is one of the marks of virtue (and which emerges from our capacity to reason – see below, page 328). We can see how actions are chosen, but surely feelings are not chosen? We just have them. How can Aristotle resolve these apparently contradictory claims: that virtues apply to feelings (which we cannot choose), and that virtue involves choice? One solution is to recognise that the process by which we become virtuous does involve choice after all. Initially, we choose to act kindly, generously, courageously – that is how we start to develop the habit – even if we do not feel kind, generous or courageous. But eventually, the actions become habituated and so does the feeling itself. So choice is involved – the choice to alter how we feel about something (such as sharing chocolate cake), even if that process takes years.

The doctrine of the mean and its application to particular virtues

Virtue, then, is a state of character concerned with choice, lying in a mean.

Aristotle (1106b36)

We now arrive at the most famous part of the *Ethics*, and one of the most famous, if misunderstood, moral principles in the history of Western philosophy. This principle is known as Aristotle's doctrine of the mean, and although Aristotle did not use the phrase himself, it is a term that usefully summarises how Aristotle thinks we can attain excellence of character.

Aristotle introduces his own doctrine of the mean by proposing that it is in the nature of some things to be destroyed by 'excess and deficiency' – for example, the physical qualities of health and strength. If we eat too much or too little, then our health is destroyed, and if we exercise too much or too little, then our strength is destroyed. But both the health and strength of our body are preserved and increased by finding the right quantity of food and exercise respectively. We avoid excess or deficiency by aiming at the intermediate – that is, the mean that lies in between both excess and deficiency, and this rule ('aim at the mean') applies as much to our character as to our body (see **Figure 2.18** on page 309). In the same way:

temperance and courage are destroyed by excess and deficiency and are preserved by the mean.

Aristotle (1104a21)

The doctrine of the mean also seems easily applicable to the virtue of courage. Courage means striking the balance between fear and confidence in the face of danger or threat: if you tend to feel and respond with too much fear, then you are cowardly; if you tend to feel and respond with too much confidence, then you are rash or foolhardy. But if you get the balance right, and are able to overcome your fear, while not doing anything stupid through overconfidence, then you are courageous (see **Figure 2.19**). Aristotle considers both rashness and cowardice to be a *kakia*, translated as 'vice'; but once again this translation lends itself to some unhelpful associations. The term *kakia* is better thought of as a type of deficiency, a flaw or a defect, rather than as a vice.

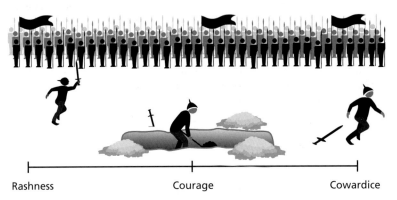

Rashness   Courage   Cowardice

Figure 2.19 Courage is midway between rashness and cowardice

Figure 2.19 shows courage as falling on a line somewhere between cowardice and rashness, a sort of point of moderation. Aristotle himself says, 'we have a bad disposition … if our tendency is too strong or too weak, and a good one if our tendency is moderate' (1105b26). Thus Aristotle's doctrine of the mean has been readily interpreted as a doctrine of *moderation*, sometimes recommended as the principle of 'moderation in all things' (which was how the Confucians applied their own version of the doctrine). Interpreting the principle in this way suggests that Aristotle is giving us practical advice on how we should *act* in any situation. This would bring Aristotle's virtue ethics in line with the other moral theories we have looked at, giving us a formula to guide our actions:

- Mill's utilitarian ethics: act in a way that maximises happiness and minimises pain
- Kant's deontological ethics: act in a way that conforms with the categorical imperative
- Aristotle's virtue ethics: act in a way that finds the middle ground between over-reaction and under-reaction.

On this account, the doctrine recommends that in any situation we should act in a way that avoids the extremes and instead displays a moderate amount of feeling, a moderate amount of indulgence, a moderate amount of pride and so on. We shall now assess whether Aristotle's doctrine of the mean should be interpreted as a 'formula' in this way.

Experimenting with ideas

Consider the following four situations and answer the questions below.

A A *resident* in an American town discovered that, for decades, her local power station had been pumping the waste products of its cooling system into nearby ponds. From the ponds, these waste products had found their way into the town's drinking water, which explained the very high rates of cancer in her town.

B *Doctors* become concerned about the possible side effects of a new, mild sleeping pill which also reduces morning sickness. Thousands of women who took this pill when pregnant gave birth to children with severe disabilities, and only half of these children survived.

C A well-known tobacco company introduced additional, carcinogenic chemicals into its cigarettes in order to make them more addictive. When *a researcher* working for the company challenged this practice, he was sacked and forced to sign a confidentiality agreement forbidding him from discussing this.

D On your birthday, *you* were given an album by your favourite band on CD, even though CDs are only listened to by old people and you do not even have a CD player, so that was a waste of money, wasn't it?

For each of the people in italics:

1 What would be an excessive response in each situation?
2 What would be a deficient response in each situation?
3 What would be the moderate thing to do in each situation?
4 Do you think that the moderate response in each situation is the right response?

Criticism

The question is this: should the doctrine of the mean be interpreted as a doctrine of moderation? Is Aristotle claiming that, in a very British stiff-upper-lip kind of way, we should display only a moderate amount of emotion or desire as we navigate our way through our lives? One of the emotions that could link the scenarios above is the anger felt by the people affected by them. The anger of the people affected by the contaminated water, or by the untested sleeping pill, or by the unfair dismissal, or, in fairness, by the uselessness of older technologies. If the doctrine of the mean is a recommendation for moderation, then should all these people show the same degree of anger? Is Aristotle claiming that they should all avoid an excess, or a deficiency, of anger and should display only a moderate amount of anger?

This seems absurd, almost irrational, particularly when we recall that excellence of character is shaped by reason. Moreover, sometimes a moderate response is not simply an appropriate response. It is more reasonable to expect that there will be different displays of anger according to the situation. We expect people whose lives are destroyed by an unsafe drug to be outraged; and people who cannot listen to a particular music format to be mildly put-out (and people whose ethical doctrine is misunderstood to be pretty cross). By applying the doctrine of moderation to even a few simple cases, we can see that 'act moderately' is not what Aristotle had in mind when talking about the mean.

Virtue discovers the mean and chooses it ... virtue is a mean; but in respect of what is right and best, it is an extreme.

Aristotle (1107a07)

Aristotle's words above direct us away from interpreting the mean as moderation by highlighting two important features of the concept of the mean and how it relates to virtue. The first part of the quote makes it clear that there is a certain intellectual skill to excellence of character: the skill in discovering what the mean is and understanding that this will vary from situation to situation. On these grounds, we can reject the interpretation of the mean as blanket 'moderation'. In the second part of the quote (which is echoed at 1107a22), Aristotle is telling us that the mean is also an extreme. This is a further indication that Aristotle is not thinking of the mean as the 'average' or the 'moderate' – that is, as the middle point on a line between two extremes (as in **Figure 2.19** on page 316). So instead of thinking of the mean as lying on a straight line, it may be more helpful for us to picture it as one corner of a triangle. **Figure 2.20** shows this alternative view – our emotions of fear and confidence can be felt as an internal pressure (like the build up of steam) and they are expressed in different amounts in different types of character: rashness = too much confidence, not enough fear; cowardice = too much fear, not enough confidence; courage = lots of confidence helps us to overcome the fear, but our fear prevents us from being rash.

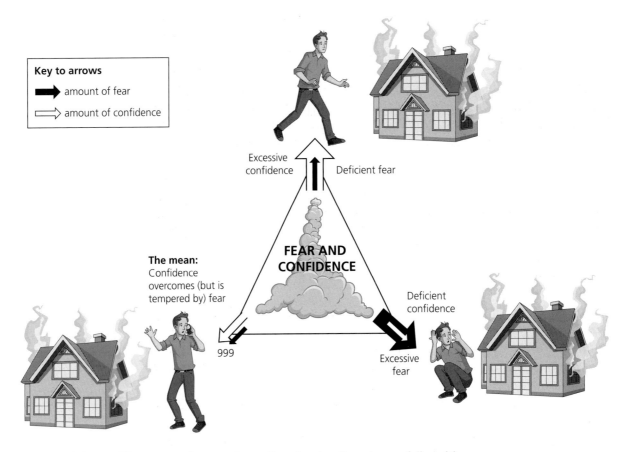

Figure 2.20 Three different reactions to a house fire, showing three types of disposition.
The courageous person overcomes his fear to call 999; the coward cowers; and the rash person marches into the burning house.

Already we can see there is far more complexity to grasping the doctrine of the mean than seeing it simply as a principle of moderation that can be applied as a moral rule to individual acts.

Aristotle gives an even clearer account of what he understands by the mean in Book Two, Chapter 6 of the *Ethics*. Yes, the mean is the 'intermediate between excess and deficiency' – that is, between two extremes, but that can be understood in two ways. First, the mean could be calculated in an objective sense, giving us a mean which is equidistant between two fixed extremes (for example, the mean lying between 2 and 10 is 6).

Secondly, it could be the mean relative to us, and in this sense the mean is something that is neither too much nor too little *for us*. Aristotle emphasises this last point by using the example of a coach considering how much protein two of his athletes should eat per day. Ten pounds is too much for most athletes, and two pounds is too little, but it does not follow that the trainer should give each athlete six pounds (that is, the trainer should not follow the first, objective, interpretation of the 'mean'). An athlete who is just beginning their career may need just three pounds, but Milo of Croton, who was a legendary ancient Greek wrestler, allegedly needed a hefty 20 pounds of protein a day. So the expert, the person with excellence of character, is able to determine the mean relative to the situation – whatever is appropriate – and sometimes that results in a mean that is itself an extreme.

anthology 2.11

In one of the most important passages in the *Ethics* (see the quote below), Aristotle describes what he believes to be the true mark of virtue, the brilliance of someone with *ethica arete*. We know that they are guided by their likes and dislikes (pleasures and pains) to do the right thing. We have seen that this is brought about by habituation, so that someone who has a kind, or courageous, or temperate character actually enjoys being kind, courageous and temperate. In this way, they are drawn towards the right and appropriate thing to do in any situation. For Aristotle, what characterises someone as virtuous is that they are able to:

> *feel or act towards the right person to the right extent at the right time for the right reason in the right way – that is not easy and it is not everyone that can do it. Hence to do these things well is a rare, laudable and fine achievement.*
> Aristotle (1109a26)

This is indeed difficult and we need to develop excellence of practical reasoning to assist us (see page 330). Practical wisdom and *ethica arete* combine to give us skills with which we can flourish. *Ethica arete* gives us the desires, the emotions and the goals, while practical wisdom uses these to drive our action towards exactly the right action and appropriate expression of that emotion. That is someone who really does have excellence of character. So the doctrine of the mean is best understood as a description of people who, by making the most appropriate decision in each situation, nurture the right kind of dispositions to equip them for future situations, and in doing so avoid inappropriate excessive or deficient responses. At 1106b36, Aristotle sums up his position, describing *ethica arete* as 'a settled state of choice, in a mean relative to us, this being determined by reason, as the wise man determines it'. People who are able to shape their character in this manner are well on their way to flourishing.

▶ ACTIVITY

Books Three, Four and Five of the *Ethics* look in detail at a wide variety of virtues, some of which are listed in the table below. Read through the list and (avoiding the mistake of interpreting the doctrine of the mean as 'moderation') for each *arete*, add in the appropriate excess and deficiency.

Sphere of action/feeling	Excess (*kakia*)	Mean (*arete*)	Deficiency (*kakia*)
Fear and confidence		Courage	
Pleasure and pain (likes and dislikes)		Temperance	
Giving and receiving		Generosity/ liberality	
Self-expression		Truthfulness	
Honour and dishonour		Proper ambition	
Social conduct		Friendliness	
Getting and spending		Magnificence	
Indignation		Righteous indignation	
Anger		Patience	

Now check your answers by looking in the *Nicomachean Ethics* or the *Eudemian Ethics* or by researching on the internet, to find out what Aristotle thought were the excess and deficiency for each *arete*.

Criticism

There are problems that emerge from Aristotle's efforts to apply the doctrine of the mean to the messy and complex subject of human emotions. Aristotle talks about the doctrine applying to a particular sphere, or field, of emotions – for example, the sphere of 'fear and confidence' (see **Figure 2.20** on page 318). We have seen that in this sphere, our emotions can be expressed with an excess or deficiency, leading to rashness or cowardice; or expressed in the appropriate amount, leading to courage. Aristotle makes every effort to identify a wide range of emotions, but at times his efforts to find the excess and deficiency of a connecting emotion seems artificial. For example, righteous indignation is analysed in this way (1108b1):

▪ The righteously indignant man is upset at the undeserved good fortune of others.
▪ The jealous man (who has the feeling in excess) is upset by the deserved fortune of others.
▪ The malicious man (who is deficient in this feeling) is pleased at the bad fortune of others.

Therefore what the three men are upset or pleased by is different in each case – and this undermines Aristotle's claim that the excellences and flaws are displays of the same feeling. Aristotle also admits that there is no word for some excellences or deficiencies, such as proper ambition; 'they have no name' he writes, which suggests that they may not exist as common character traits. Finally, Aristotle points out that some emotions (spite, anger) and some actions (murder, theft) are always wrong (although we examine his claims about theft in more detail below when applying virtue ethics, on page 349). He says that there cannot be a mean to what is permanently in excess or deficiency (spite, anger, murder, theft); but this admission also chips away at the universality of the doctrine of the mean. Taken together, these problems undermine the empirical nature of the doctrine. It seems as if Aristotle is searching for some character traits that do not exist, in order to fit his theory.

The strength of Aristotle's theory is the recognition that, if we want to be happy, we must develop our emotional skill set. We must get better at reading the situation we are in, at controlling the impulsive pressure of our emotions, and at acting in a way that is appropriate to our emotion and the situation. In modern psychology, this is known as 'emotional intelligence', and it is generally recognised as one of the most important skills you can develop.[16]

Moral responsibility (Book Three of the *Ethics*)

Voluntary actions

The question Aristotle now addresses is which of our actions should we be held responsible for? In Book Three of the *Ethics*, Aristotle provides the first attempt at a comprehensive account of human action and how it relates to responsibility, choice and judgement. We make judgements about people all the time: informally, we praise or blame people for their actions, and more formally, our legal system makes judgements about who to punish and who to release, while our honours system judges who to reward. But if we are to be successful in making judgements about people's characters, including our own, then we need to identify those actions that are relevant to determining our character and those that are irrelevant.

▶ **ACTIVITY**

Can you think of examples of actions that are irrelevant to our judgement of whether someone has a good or bad character? Why are they irrelevant?

Aristotle asserts that people are praised or blamed for voluntary (intended acts), but not for acts done contrary to intention. Therefore it is only in intended acts that excellences, and vices, are to be found. What we *intended* to do in any situation reveals our dispositions and desires, and thus our moral character; things that we accidentally did, or which we did against our wishes, do not reveal our character. For example, while surfing in rough seas, we noticed the Duchess of Cambridge was in danger of drowning and we deliberately swam to save her. This act of courage was intended and is an indication that we are courageous. If we intentionally stayed away from her because we were scared of drowning, this would indicate cowardliness. But if we were forced to stay away from her *against our intention* (perhaps an evil Bond villain threatened to kill us if we tried to save her), then this would not provide any evidence that we were cowardly. Similarly, if we only saved her by accident (as we were swept under a wave we *unintentionally* let go of our surfboard which she then managed to grab hold of), then this again tells us nothing about whether we are actually cowardly or courageous.

Aristotle identifies and analyses two main types of action – 'voluntary' and 'involuntary' – while also exploring a third type of 'non-voluntary' action.

Unfortunately, these traditional translations are confusing, and it is once again more helpful to use alternative translations of these three types of action: namely acts that are 'intended', 'contrary to intention' and 'unintended'.

It is by our intended actions that we can be properly judged, and therefore praised or blamed, as only they are representative of our dispositions. When we deliberately do something, we are striving to bring about a goal, or an end, that we desire, and in doing so we reveal our current dispositions, as well as shaping our future dispositions. What makes an action intended? We shall see that Aristotle believes an action cannot be 'intended' when its cause lies outside us, or when we are acting in ignorance. For Aristotle, an action is intended when its origin lies in us – in other words, there is a clear line we can trace between our internal decision processes (our initial beliefs and desires, the assessment of options and the selection of a choice) and our physical processes (the movement of our body) and the action itself in the world. Because of this clear connection between the action and our choice, we are responsible for our intended actions. Moreover, because our dispositions are the result of numerous actions (we become kind by doing kind things, cruel by doing cruel things), we are responsible for the development of our character through our intentional acts.

However, we shall now see that this clear connection between our actions and our responsibility for these actions becomes more complex, as Aristotle starts to dissect the different types of actions that we carry out.

Involuntary actions: compulsion and responsibility

Actions are regarded as involuntary when they are performed under compulsion or through ignorance.

Aristotle (1109a1)

There are two types of acts that we might classify as 'contrary to intention' (involuntary acts): those done under *compulsion* and those that are done in *ignorance*. We return to acts done in ignorance below (page 325). Aristotle firstly looks at acts which are clearly done as a result of an external force or compulsion; he then goes on to assess whether these acts are ones for which we should be held responsible. He gives a straightforward example of two actions that are the result of forces external to us: in the first, a voyager is blown off course by winds; in the second, a voyager is kidnapped and taken somewhere. In both instances, the voyager contributes nothing (no intention, no deliberate movement) to the outcome, and takes no responsibility for these acts. In fact, because of the complete lack of agency involved in these acts, we may agree with Aristotle and say that, strictly speaking, these are not proper actions at all.

However, there are actions done under compulsion which are more problematic, because they are acts which are partly contrary to our intentions and partly intended. Aristotle gives two examples of these 'mixed' acts: dumping your cargo overboard in a storm, or committing a robbery under the threat of blackmail. In this first case, the angry Athenian merchants who paid you to safely transfer their cargo across the Adriatic Sea might ask: 'Did you intend to throw the cargo overboard?' Well, when you set out across the calm turquoise waters, you did not have any intention of losing the cargo, as transporting it safely meant you would get paid. So, in the long-term sense, your answer is 'No'; losing the cargo was against your intention. But this will not wash with the angry merchants who are now throttling you: 'Did you, or did you not, throw the cargo overboard during the storm?'

In cases like the above the agent acts voluntarily [intentionally]; because the movement of the limbs that are the instruments of action has its origin in the agent.
Aristotle (110a16)

Aristotle argues that, strictly speaking, in the short term, yes, you did intend to lose the cargo. The origin of the action lies within you: you are the agent – you had control of your thoughts, you made a decision about priorities (cargo or survival), and you had control of the limbs that chucked the cargo overboard. This is very different from your colleague, the voyager, who was kidnapped and had no choice at all and no power over where she was heading. But it is also true that you *felt* that you had no choice, and most people, including a jury and hopefully the angry merchants, would be sympathetic to your claim that you had no choice because you wanted to live. So Aristotle calls such actions mixed, as they are both intended (in the short term) and contrary to intention (in the long term).

Experimenting with ideas

It is time for the captains of these three ships to face the music, as the Athenian judge wants to know what happened to the merchants' gold. Read through each of the excuses (all of them true) that the captains give to the judge and answer the questions below.

'I was kidnapped by pirates and forced to sail the gold to Sparta.'

'I threw all the gold overboard – it was either that or be drowned along with all the crew.'

'I spent all the gold – Aristotle was making a one-off appearance at the Lyceum and I had to see it.'

Figure 2.21 The captains' excuses for losing the gold

Now, for each captain:

1 Identify whether their action leading to the loss of the gold was voluntary or involuntary (through compulsion) or involuntary (mixed).
2 Do you think they are responsible for their action?
3 Do you think they should be punished or pardoned for the loss of the gold?

Acts done under compulsion, including mixed acts, share the feature of being involuntary acts (done contrary to our intention) because they contain strong elements of force which direct the actions away from what we intend. But what are the differences in the judgements we make between acts done under full compulsion and mixed acts? With the first type, Aristotle argues that we are not held responsible (and so should neither be praised nor blamed) because there is no choice. But with the second type, Aristotle believes that, despite the compelling circumstances, there is an element of choice: we are responsible for these actions and so can be judged, praised or blamed for them. After all, it was we who performed the action, and we were free to do otherwise – we could have let the blackmailer post those photos on the internet, but we chose not to, preferring instead to rob the bank. What is important is that such mixed acts demand understanding, and perhaps pardoning, by those around us, or by a judge or jury. Aristotle notes, however, that there are some things that are unpardonable, even if we feel forced into doing them (for example, matricide). So where there is no agency, there is no responsibility; and where there is agency, and the origins of the action lie within you, then there is responsibility, but you may be exonerated if the action is 'mixed' (unless it is matricide). Furthermore, where there is agency and an act is voluntary, then this helps us to identify a person as having a particular virtue (for example, courage); where there is no agency in an act, then this act tells us nothing about whether the person is a courageous or cowardly person.

anthology
2.12

Experimenting with ideas

You have been investigating the assassination of a politician, and have found that the assassin was systematically brainwashed by a mysterious organisation called the Parallax Corporation. This brainwashing was so powerful that whenever the assassin was told the trigger word 'Manchuria', he would kill the next politician he saw.

1 Do you think that the assassin had agency in the moments leading up to the murder?
2 Is his act of assassination a 'mixed' act, or one done from compulsion?
3 Do you think the assassin is responsible for his actions?
4 Should the assassin be punished?

A colleague is conducting the investigation with you, but starts to put on weight, eating more and more junk food (particularly an American cake called a Twinkle Bar). Finally, he is so large that he cannot get into his car or into your small office, and he loses his job. Eventually he sues the manufacturers of Twinkles, arguing that he was forced by his desire for sweet things to eat their product, and that the manufacturers are thus responsible for his dismissal from his job.

1 Do you think your colleague had agency when eating Twinkle Bars?
2 Do you agree that your colleague is compelled to eat Twinkles? Why/why not?
3 Do you agree that your colleague is not responsible for his actions?
4 Should the manufacturers be punished?

Aristotle does not deal with examples of brainwashing or hypnotism, which we may now acknowledge as causes powerful enough to qualify as examples of full compulsion, rather than as 'mixed' actions, even though the origin of the action lay in the agent.

anthology
2.13

However, he does dismiss the claim that some people may make (in order to avoid taking responsibility) that they were 'forced' by their desires to act in a particular way. For Aristotle, being 'forced' by your desires is exactly what an intended action is all about: we act in a particular way because we want something. So your colleague is completely responsible for eating all those Twinkles. Moreover, Aristotle notes rather cynically that people who offer this defence ('I was forced by my desire, so it is not my responsibility') only offer that excuse for the bad things they have done; we never hear them say, 'I was forced by my desire to do something good, so I should not be rewarded or praised for this good act'.

Non-voluntary actions: ignorance and responsibility

Aristotle introduces a further degree of subtlety into his analysis of involuntary action by looking at another class of acts that are not intended. These are acts done from ignorance. Translators usually refer to these acts done from ignorance as 'non-voluntary', but it might be more helpful to think of them as 'unintended' acts. There are aspects of all our actions which we are ignorant of; after all, we are not omnipotent and so would not know the details of every situation in which we have to make a decision. What Aristotle is focusing on is those material aspects of a situation upon which our decision is based, and which we may think we know, but which it transpires we were mistaken about. There are all sorts of ways in which we can be materially ignorant: lack of knowledge, mistaken identity, misinterpretation, errors of judgement or misunderstanding of a situation (1111a2ff.). What these examples share is this: our description of the situation at the time of the action is different from the description we would give of that same situation once we were made aware of certain other features.

One example of an unintended act can be found in the tragedy of Oedipus, who intended to 'kill the angry posh bloke in the chariot, and marry the Queen of Thebes'. He did not intend to 'kill his father and marry his mother', but that is exactly what happened (**Figure 2.22**). It was through his ignorance that this tragic event occurred; Oedipus was not aware who his real father and mother were (the angry posh bloke and Queen of Thebes, it turns out). So should Oedipus have taken responsibility for this awful outcome? He certainly felt he should, as when he discovered what he had done, he blinded himself with the

Figure 2.22 Oedipus's non-voluntary marriage

pin from his mother's brooch. If he had studied Book Three of the *Ethics*, he might have been a little more forgiving. Although Aristotle does not discuss Oedipus, the young man was clearly acting in ignorance and his actions were non-voluntary acts. The question remains: when, if ever, should we be held responsible for non-voluntary, unintended acts?

 Every act done through ignorance is non-voluntary, but is involuntary only when it causes the agent subsequent pain and repentance.
Aristotle (1110b17)

For Aristotle, whether we are responsible for our non-voluntary acts depends on whether the act was actually one that was contrary to our intention. And we can discover whether it was against our intentions by asking the question: 'Do you regret doing that, and would you have acted differently if you had been in full possession of the facts?' If the answers are 'Yes', then we would say that your act was *contrary to your intention*, not merely unintended.

An act done in ignorance can be unintended because it had unforeseen consequences or because we were not aware of all the facts (like Oedipus), but this does not remove our responsibility. After all, it was our action – we were the agent. What may lessen our responsibility is whether it was contrary to our intention to, say, marry our mother. This does not imply that we can repent and will receive guaranteed forgiveness, for remorse and repentance cannot change an action that has already been performed. What Aristotle means is this: at the time of the action we were ignorant of certain things, and whether that ignorance is relevant or not depends on whether we would have acted otherwise if we had known all the facts. If we would have acted otherwise, then we will reveal regret for our action ('If only I had known'), and our act will be shown to have been contrary to our intention. So remorse and regret are a very strong indication that a non-voluntary (unintended) act is actually involuntary (against our intention), and hence that we should be considered for pardon.

The flow chart (**Figure 2.23**) summarises Aristotle's analysis of action and responsibility. He has identified two types of action in which our responsibility for an act (and the praise or blame bestowed on it) may be repudiated or lessened: namely, mixed acts done with some compulsion, and acts done from ignorance of a particular fact. He has also identified those actions for which we have no responsibility at all, namely acts that are done under compulsion. The actions that we are fully responsible for are our intended actions, and it is in these that our character, and virtue if we possess it, is displayed.

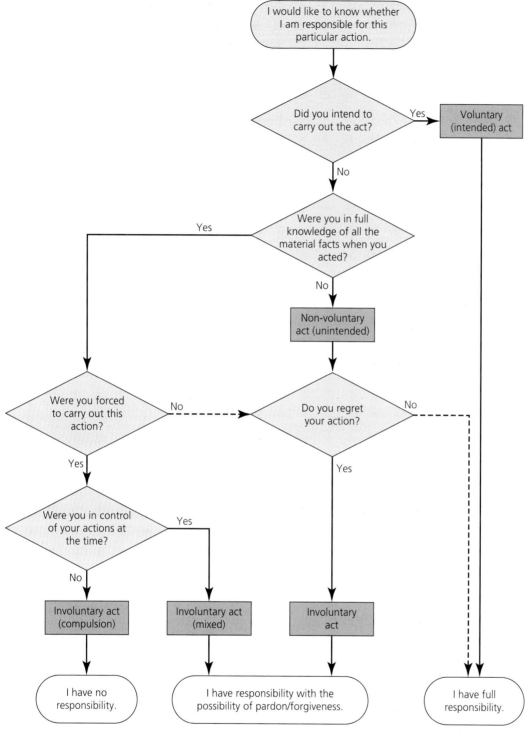

Figure 2.23 Flow chart summarising Aristotle's thoughts on responsibility and action

The relationship between virtues, actions and reasons

We have already looked at the role of feelings in the development of virtue and our dispositions to act – but what of the role of reason? Aristotle outlines in Book 3 (1111b5–1113b21) the technical part that reason plays in our voluntary, or intended, actions. If reason is essential to our voluntary actions, then it is also essential to virtue. This is because our virtues are dispositions built up, one by one, from those voluntary actions.

So what is the technical role assigned to reason in our voluntary actions? We noted above (page 322) that an act is intended when its origin lies within us, and its cause stems from our internal decision-making processes. But not all intended/voluntary actions are relevant when it comes to judging someone's character – for example, at 1111b6, Aristotle excludes voluntary actions that are done on the spur of the moment, or voluntary actions taken by children, and he excludes these for the same reason: because they are not chosen. Aristotle argues that virtue is formed by voluntary actions that are the result of a special kind of internal thought process, namely *choice*:

Choice implies a rational principle and thought
Aristotle 1112a16

We saw above (page 315) how choice is integral to the development of moral virtue, *ethica arete*, and reason is essential to the choices we make which underpin, and create, our dispositions. When we start to develop a virtue, such as courage, we have to choose to take a courageous course of action: we have to understand what we are doing, the risks involved, the management of our fear, the other possible courses of action, and yet still choose to be brave. Our disposition for courage (so that others would call us a 'courageous person') is built up, brick by brick, action by action, through the choices (that is, the rational decisions) that we have made and will continue to make (see **Figure 2.24** in the next section).

In Book 3, Aristotle goes further in his analysis of choice: an action is chosen if it is a result of prior thought and deliberation. According to Aristotle, there are certain things we cannot deliberate about; these are things over which we have no possibility of control – for example, unpredictable weather events or whether we will win the lottery. And there are certain things we do not deliberate about, including everyday matters or aspects of life governed by tightly prescribed rules, such as spelling. In other words, we deliberate about things which lie between complete certainty and complete uncertainty/impossibility; we are weighing up the possibilities and options and trying to determine for ourselves the best route to achieve our goal. Aristotle gives, as an example of deliberation, the process by which we reach a particular outcome we want to achieve (1125b10–26). Once we are clear about the outcome (our 'end'), we work backwards, step by step, gradually establishing the various means that will enable us to reach that end, until we arrive at an action that we can take here and now.

In addition to the role of deliberation and choice described above, our outline of Aristotle's theory has identified a number of other ways in which reason is critical to Aristotle's virtue ethics.

1   Reason is the defining characteristic of humans (in Aristotle's terminology, of our soul), and so is essential to our fulfilment of our function: to becoming a good human and living the good life for a human. **Figure 2.18** on page 309, which illustrates the different components of our psychological make-up according to Aristotle, shows the parts of our soul which are rational (in darker grey), and the part of our soul which is influenced by reason (in light grey). Reason is the golden thread that connects our soul to virtue/excellence, and virtue to *eudaimonia*: it is by exercising our reason and encouraging its influence upon us that we optimise our chances of flourishing.

2   Reason is essential to the true development of the virtues. It is possible to misconstrue Aristotle's account of virtue, to think of a virtue simply as the development of good habits and ways of behaving that is almost automatic, or mindless. However, we saw above (page 313) that developing a virtue such as generosity is not just about acting generously, it is also about acting as a generous person would act, which means knowing what you are doing and choosing what you are doing (1105a32). Both knowing and choosing are rational activities, and for Aristotle we cannot be virtuous without this understanding.

3   Reason underpins Aristotle's doctrine of the mean. We saw that this is not a doctrine of moderation (pages 317–318), but instead depends upon our ability to take the right action, avoiding an excessive or deficient response. As we move through life, the circumstances in which we find ourselves vary; what was a brave action to take in one circumstance (for example, whilst in a school playground) might be a foolhardy thing to do in another (for example, whilst in a strange city). Each situation we find ourselves in, each moral dilemma or decision we have to make, depends upon us successfully using our practical reasoning skills to work out what is the appropriate thing to do here. Practical reasoning enables us to feel or act towards the right person, to the right extent, at the right time, in the right way and *for the right reason*.

4   Reason is what binds together the intellectual virtues (wisdom and practical wisdom) and moral virtue (or excellence of character) – both of which are essential for virtue, and both of which are essential for *eudaimonia*. For Aristotle, it is not possible for someone to have moral virtue without having practical wisdom, and we shall now turn to examine this point.

We are now in a position to draw several threads together, from the first three books of the *Ethics*, to sketch Aristotle's account of virtue and its connection with reason and action. We start with a wish for the Good – in this particular example, we want an environment for us and our children which is healthy and free from pollution (see **Figure 2.24**). We deliberate about the various ways in which we could contribute to achieving this end (for example, if we stop using a car every day, and start walking, cycling or using a small scooter). Our successful deliberation results in the right choice (in this context, it is the choice to cycle) and this leads to a voluntary action to carry out that choice and start cycling. We repeat this process of rational deliberation (for example, on rainy days, when we really want to take the car, but when the right action is still to cycle), until our cycling becomes a habit. And through repetition we are no longer forcing ourselves to behave in an environmentally aware way, but instead our respect for the environment has become second nature, we are getting pleasure from this, and we are getting good at this – our environmental awareness is now a virtue (**Figure 2.24**), one that Rosalind Hursthouse (1943–) calls 'respect for nature' or 'being rightly disposed towards nature'.[17]

The role of practical reasoning/practical wisdom (Book Six of the *Ethics*)

According to Aristotle, the soul is divided into two parts: the rational and the non-rational parts (**Figure 2.18**), and in order to flourish we must excel (that is, be virtuous) in both parts of the soul. We have already looked at the most significant non-rational part of the soul, our character, and how we can develop excellence of character (moral virtue) through developing good habits and positive dispositions. But what about the rational part? This is subdivided into two distinct types of reasoning: first, practical reason, reasoning about our lives, our goals, and the means by which we can achieve our ends; and second, theoretical reason, which is a more abstract contemplation of the world – for example, in the way that philosophers and theoretical physicists do. We briefly revisit contemplation on page 335, but let us now turn to practical reasoning.

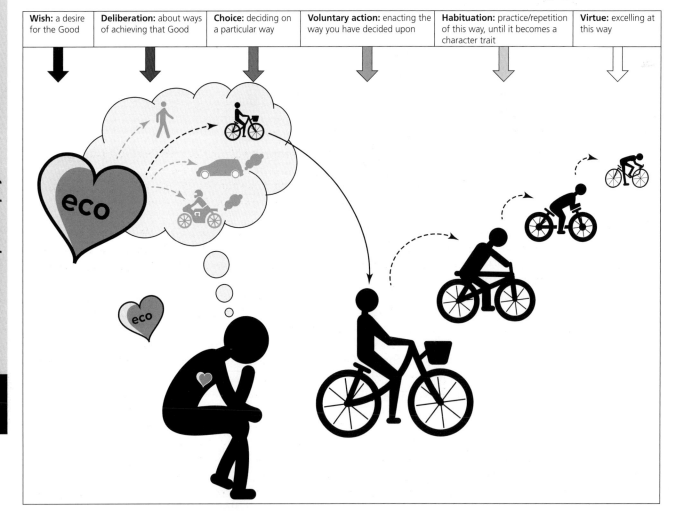

| **Wish:** a desire for the Good | **Deliberation:** about ways of achieving that Good | **Choice:** deciding on a particular way | **Voluntary action:** enacting the way you have decided upon | **Habituation:** practice/repetition of this way, until it becomes a character trait | **Virtue:** excelling at this way |

Figure 2.24 Aristotle's account of how virtue (in this case, 'respect for nature') emerges from rational deliberation, choice and voluntary action.

It is practical reason that lies behind making the right choice, so it involves deliberation and the skills of decision making that we have already outlined above. But the right choice is not just about working out what to do; it also means having the right desires, and these are determined by the non-rational part of our soul, our wishes and emotions, and shaped by our character. So reason and desire are inseparable aspects of making a choice – there is no choice without a desire for an end, and an effort of reasoning about how to achieve it. And if we want to make the right choice, then we need to excel both in practical reasoning, which is called practical wisdom, and in our character (*ethica arete*).

anthology 2.14

There are several ways in which practical wisdom manifests itself, intellectual traits which Aristotle outlines in Book 6 of the *Ethics*:

1 We are able to *deliberate* and plan our lives well – that is, we get what we desire, which is good ends.
2 We have a good *understanding* of a situation – we can see the Big Picture.
3 We have good *judgement* and know what is the right thing to do in a situation (remember that this is what links reason to *ethica arete* in the doctrine of the mean).
4 Furthermore, we possess *cleverness* – that is, the ability to accomplish our goals and execute our plans. This is also an ability someone who does not have practical wisdom can do: a flawed or a bad person can be clever, and have excellent project-planning skills, but they are not wise because they lack the other three skills.

Experimenting with ideas

Which of the following characters is exhibiting practical wisdom through their actions?

A Charlie 'The Fingers' Phipps and the Toad in the Hole gang mastermind the first billion-dollar robbery using only Bitcoins, a stolen laptop and his gran's wifi connection. High fives, champagne and luxury villas all round.

B Daniel 'Two Shoes' Hayward finally saves enough money to buy a pack of multi-coloured 'Bluntie' pens so that he can highlight each of his A-level topics in a different-coloured pen when he plans his three-month 'Countdown to June' revision timetable.

C Potone, Plato's forgotten sister, hears of a strange new plant that comes from distant lands in the West. It is said that the leaves, when chewed, produce for one hour the effect of comprehending the world of forms. Death follows immediately. Eager to impress her famous brother, Potone designs and builds a boat herself to journey across the ocean to find and taste this wondrous plant.

D Lisa, the forgotten daughter of the ancient poet Homer, invents a machine that transfers sound waves into marks on paper, thus enabling her father to speak into it and create in book format all 260,000 words of the *Odyssey* without him having to remember his poem word-for-word each time he tells the story.

E Robin Hood used to steal from the rich to give to the poor. But now he has a better plan: he will steal from the rich and invest it in a high-interest savings account, which over the ten-year life of the savings plan yields a much higher return on his investment, meaning that he will have more money at the end of the decade to distribute to the poor of Nottingham.

F Chloe is on a Students Against Climate Change march. She has realised that by organising positive, peaceful action on a mass scale, and by harnessing their sophisticated use of social media, she can help her generation to change the world and prevent global catastrophe. Unfortunately, once again, the heavy police handling of the march completely irritates her, and she hits one of the officers round the head with a placard (twice) and is arrested and charged with affray.

1 For each character, identify what is driving their plans – what end do they want to reach? What desires are fuelling them?
2 Is their end one that you would consider a 'good' goal? Is it an end that Aristotle would consider a good goal?
3 As they plan to achieve their ends, does each character display each of the intellectual traits outlined above? Which (if any) are they missing?
4 Finally, based on your answers above, is each character displaying practical wisdom? Why? Why not?

Character	What is their end?	Is their end a good end?	Do they display all the intellectual traits?	Which skill (if any) is missing?	Do they show practical wisdom?
A Charlie 'The Fingers' Phipps					
B Daniel 'Two Shoes' Hayward					
C Potone					
D Lisa					
E Robin Hood					
F Chloe					

In the exercise above, some of the characters who failed to display practical wisdom failed precisely because their ends, their goals, were not good goals: they had not developed the virtues of character that are needed to shape our emotions and desires, and to make our goals the right ones. Practical wisdom and moral virtue (*ethica arete*) are bound up with one another: we cannot have the right dispositions/virtues if we do not have practical wisdom that tells us how it is appropriate to act in those particular circumstances. In other words, the desire to be excellent is useless without the ability to achieve it. But having the ability to reason and determine lines of action without possessing any desires is equally useless.

According to Aristotle, the two excellences (of character and practical reasoning) are inseparable. We return to the question of what it is that 'drives' us to action – is it desire or reason – when we look at David Hume's theory of motivation below (page 388).

The relationship between *eudaimonia* and pleasure (Book Seven of the *Ethics*)

The role that pleasure has to play in the good life is something that Aristotle addresses throughout the *Ethics*. Alasdair MacIntyre (1929–) has proposed that Aristotle is arguing against two kinds of opponent.[18] Aristotle disputes the view taken by Plato and his followers that pleasure was not part of the good life in any way and even damaged the good; but he also wanted to avoid the claim made by other ancient Greek philosophers (such as Eudoxus) that pleasure was the supreme good. Aristotle, if you like, is threading his theory between these two extremes by finding the mean: acknowledging the importance of pleasure, but not giving it the rarefied status afforded it by hedonists, and later by utilitarians.

One school maintains that pleasure is the good; another, on the contrary, that it is wholly bad.

Aristotle (1172a26)

Let us remind ourselves about what we already know of Aristotle's thoughts on pleasure, and we will see a balanced view emerging.

On the one hand, we saw above (page 301) that Aristotle's investigation into the good for humans ruled out pleasure as the supreme good. It is a plausible candidate for the good, as people do seek pleasure as an end, and nearly everyone seeks pleasure of one kind of other. However, you will remember that Aristotle thought that seeking pleasure as the sole end is only a life fit for cattle, but not for humans, who have rational souls and who must excel in all parts of their soul if they wish to flourish. Moreover, one of the identifying features of the good life is that it needs nothing further to complete it (page 299), but there are many goods that we can add to a life of pleasure that would improve it, so pleasure cannot be the Good. What are we then to make of this quote?

> *Happiness is the best, the finest, the most pleasurable thing of all.*
>
> Aristotle (1099a27)[19]

There is a vast difference between happiness in the Aristotelian sense of *eudaimonia* and happiness as a hedonist might conceive of it. The difference can be brought out through an anecdote about the 1960s footballing genius, George Best. He loved to tell the tale of how, in the early 1970s, a room-service waiter came into his hotel room one morning. The footballer was in bed with one of the most beautiful women in the world, surrounded by thousands of pounds in cash that he had won at the races, drinking champagne from the bottle. The waiter looked at him, shook his head and said, 'So, George ... where did it all go wrong?' And it was true; something had gone wrong. From being hailed as the best footballer in the world, George Best had turned into an alcoholic playboy – he failed to fulfil his real potential. In a hedonistic sense, he was happy, but in Aristotelian terms he was not happy – he was not *eudaimon*; he was no longer flourishing. We saw earlier (page 301) that Aristotle specifically ruled out indulgence in pleasure as part of the good life. Like Plato, he saw the restraint of our desires as a virtue, namely temperance, and an excessive indulgence in our desires as a vice (licentiousness). So, for Aristotle, Eudoxus is wrong: pleasure is not the good life, and indulgence in our desires is not a part of the good life.

But on the other hand, we also know that Aristotle believed pleasure to be an important feature in the development of virtue. You may remember that Aristotle disagreed with those philosophers (including his teacher, Plato) who thought that goodness, even without pleasure – even when being tortured on a rack – was all that was needed for happiness (page 302). You may also remember that excellences or virtues are developed through habituation – the training of our dispositions (page 312). Pleasure has a crucial role here in the nurturing of *ethica arete*, by being part of a positive feedback loop. As we start out trying to develop excellent dispositions, it is difficult, and we have to force ourselves to be kind, just, courageous, generous and so on. Over time, we find that we begin to enjoy these actions, and get pleasure from acting kindly, generously, justly and so on. This pleasure makes us more inclined to do those types of actions in the future, and so we become disposed to kindness, justice, courage and the like. Moreover, although Aristotle rules out indulging in physical pleasures, he also rules out as a vice (*kakia*) the avoidance of all bodily pleasures. Aristotle advocates that some sensual pleasures (enjoying sport, art or music) should be actively encouraged, while acknowledging that other pleasures (food, sex, drink) are natural and necessary so long as any indulgence is avoided (1147b25). In which case, Plato and his followers are wrong, and pleasure is a critical part of *ethica arete* and the good life.

The middle way between the view that pleasure is the good, and the view that pleasure has no part to play in the good, is the route taken by Aristotle. For Aristotle, the good life cannot ignore pleasure, but nor is the good life a life of pure pleasure. So, what is pleasure for Aristotle? When Aristotle investigates this question in Book Ten of the *Ethics*, he concludes that it is not any *one* thing at all – it is not a single sensation (or *qualia*), for example. Nor is pleasure an end at all; rather it is something that arises from the activity itself. I aim to do an activity, and if it goes well, then I get pleasure from the activity, and there are as many possible pleasures as there are possible activities. Thus the hedonist is not actually saying anything concrete when they say we aim at pleasure, because 'pleasure' is too vague a term, and is dependent on the activity being done. For Aristotle, pleasure supervenes on activities; it does not exist separately from any activity. However, and this is an important point, Aristotle, like Mill, believed that some activities are superior to others, and hence some pleasures are superior to others. You may not be surprised to discover what activities Aristotle thinks of as the most superior.

Aristotle's Conclusion: the role of contemplation (Book Ten of the *Ethics*)

At the end of the *Ethics* Aristotle reveals his true colours as a philosopher. Prior to that, the picture of the good life that he has painted during the previous nine books of the *Ethics* is a complex, varied and persuasive one. It requires us to develop skills in practical wisdom, and at the same time to develop our character so that we can make the right decision in any given situation; it requires us to enjoy what we do, and take pleasures in the sensual world; it requires luck and good fortune and external goods; it requires love and friendship and participation in our community.

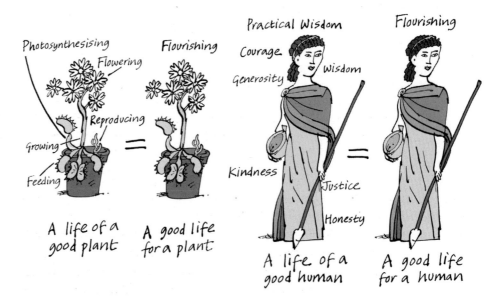

Figure 2.25 The good life for plants is the life of a good plant; and the good life for humans is the life of a good human.

Just as we saw that the good life for a plant was the life of a good plant (your drawings and activity on page 304), so Aristotle has shown that the good life for humans is the life of a good human (**Figure 2.25**). Aristotelian *eudaimonia* is a life of well-being, flourishing and happiness for us as individuals. And yet… Aristotle, in the final book of the Ethics, seems to take a step away from this rich and complex account of *eudaimonia* and offers another, much more self-centred, thesis. In Book Ten, Aristotle turns to look at the final excellences, or virtues, of the soul which had originally identified in Book One (see **Figure 2.18** on page 309). He has examined excellences of character (*ethica arête*), and excellence of practical reasoning (practical wisdom) and now turns to excellence of theoretical reasoning: contemplation and wisdom.

Criticism

It seems unfair to include the final part of Aristotle's positive thesis, given at the end of the *Ethics*, as a criticism of the rest of his theory. But the proposal made by Aristotle in Book Ten does seem to undermine much of what has gone before in the *Ethics*. You may remember that Aristotle set aside a question right at the beginning of Book One (page 302), saying he would return to it later. The question was whether contemplation (*theoria*) is the good life, and in Book Ten Aristotle's answer is a resounding 'yes'.

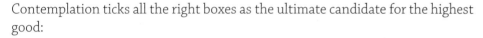

> If happiness is activity in accordance with virtue, it is reasonable that it should be in accordance with the highest virtue; and this will be that of the best thing in us.
> Aristotle (1177a11)

Contemplation ticks all the right boxes as the ultimate candidate for the highest good:

- Contemplation is the supreme exercise of reason.
- Contemplation is done for its own sake (1177b1).
- Contemplation is self-sufficient, it needs nothing to complete it and there is no end to it – it can go on for ever.
- Contemplation brings happiness in a real, long-lasting sense.

Moreover:

- Contemplation is greater than practical wisdom because the objects of contemplation are the highest objects of knowledge.
- Contemplation is of the highest objects because contemplation is Contemplation of God (i.e. pure-reason) and any activity that strives to do this will bring happiness greater than any mortal pursuit (1177b31).

And so the good life is the life of contemplation, a position held by many philosophers from both Eastern and Western traditions. But Aristotle had seemed to be different from all those other philosophers who claim that philosophy is the ultimate human activity: he seemed to be offering a view of the good life with which we could all agree and would all find persuasive, as outlined in **Figure 2.25**. The previous nine Books have been talking about what it is like to live in this world, not in some abstract world of ideas, yet in Book Ten we are told that, after all, the good life is philosophy. But that is hardly something that contributes to the well-being of our community, nor is it something that would help most of us flourish, nor is it something that would persuade non-philosophers that Aristotle is taking the right approach. Contemplation seems a self-centred activity that might benefit only the individual engaging in it, rather than benefiting the community he or she lives in. We return to look at the balance in the *Ethics* between the good for the individual and the 'moral' good, on page 344.

Issues with Aristotelian virtue ethics

We have encountered difficulties with Aristotle's arguments and ideas throughout our discussion of his theory of virtue ethics. We shall now turn to further criticisms of Aristotle's theory, which arise because virtue ethics is so unfamiliar to modern philosophers and to our own moral tradition of the past 200 years. Virtue ethics does not claim to have the precision of utilitarian or Kantian ethics, which attempt to be clear in their prescriptive rules. But virtue ethicists would reject Kantian and utilitarian ethics precisely because of this attempt at precision – the world is complex, moral dilemmas are messy, and ethical decisions are rarely straightforward. Over the last 50 years, philosophers like Elizabeth Anscombe (1919–2001), Peter Geach (1916–2013) and Alasdair MacIntyre have revived our interest in the virtue ethics of Aristotle, Aquinas and Hume, precisely because it is only a virtue approach that seemed to accommodate the complexity of our moral lives.[20] However, this lack of precision, together with the unfamiliar agent-centred approach, does leave virtue ethics open to criticism, as we shall see in the five issues raised below. Hopefully, the discussion of these issues and criticisms will help throw more light on Aristotle's theory and give us a better understanding of it, whether or not we agree with him.

Issue: can Aristotelian virtue ethics give sufficiently clear guidance about how to act?

One of the features that we expect to see in an effective ethical theory is some guidance on how we should act. Act-centred theories, like utilitarian and Kantian ethics, certainly aim to provide some sort of code or set of concrete rules prescribing how we should act and make judgements. At first sight, it appeared as if Aristotle's doctrine of the mean could provide the equivalent rule for his virtue ethics, and if the mean were interpreted as a doctrine of moderation – 'act moderately in any situation' – then this may have been a clear rule about how to act. But we have seen above (page 317) that Aristotle did not take the mean to be 'moderation'.

Instead, Aristotle's doctrine of the mean provides a complex analysis of virtue. It describes how virtuous acts are in a mean between an excessive and deficient response, and that this mean is relative to the situation. It describes how the mean response is the right response, leading to the most appropriate behaviour, which may even sometimes entail an extreme response – for example, being furious at the unethical behaviour of a large corporation. So, far from offering clear guidance, the doctrine of the mean suggests that every situation is different and there is no single rule.

To feel or act towards the right person to the right extent at the right time for the right reason in the right way – that is not easy.

Aristotle (1109a26)

The problem is: 'How do we know what the right behaviour is?' In other words: 'What is a virtuous act in any given situation?' Aristotle's theory is vague on this, and we shall see below (page 340) that attempting to define a virtuous act in terms of a virtuous person does not solve the problem of this vagueness.

Aristotle himself admitted that being virtuous was very difficult, and unfortunately, the doctrine of the mean does not provide a hard-and-fast rule that will simplify the decisions we have to take and the moral judgements we have to make. For a modern proponent of virtue ethics, the principles, rules and guidelines of Kantian or utilitarian ethics may be too good to be true, as there is no easy way of calculating right and wrong. For Aristotle, there is always going to be a certain looseness about moral decision-making, because experience tells us that for every rule of thumb we prescribe (for example, it is good to be courageous), we shall find exceptions (for example, occasions when the best thing to do is to run for your life as fast as possible). Life is complex, situations vary in subtle but significant ways, and no formula can accommodate these variations.

We know that Aristotle expected people with practical wisdom to develop roughly the same sorts of disposition: these are the virtues listed in the activity on page 320. Rosalind Hursthouse has argued that through the virtues Aristotle has identified, he does offer guidance on how to act after all. We know that Aristotle tells us that we apply practical wisdom in order to act virtuously and to avoid acting viciously (that is, in excess or deficiently); we also know that Aristotle gives us specific examples of the virtues that we should strive for, and the *kakias* (vices) we should avoid. Hursthouse says that, taken together, these virtues and vices do offer rules or principles for action, and she calls these 'v-rules'.[21] So virtues carry a positive prescription for action ('do X'), while vices carry a negative prescription ('do not do Y'). For example, the virtue of truthfulness entails the v-rule, 'Do what is honest', while the vice of meanness entails the v-rule, 'Do not do what is uncharitable'. According to Hursthouse, these v-rules do, after all, provide clear guidance on action (see also page 349, where we offer our own framework for applying Aristotelian ethics).

Even if Hursthouse is right, and coherent v-rules can be generated from Aristotle's virtues, we might still reject these rules by arguing that these virtues are culturally specific. In other words, these virtues may well have been valued in ancient Athens, but that does not give us any reason to value them today (or give us any reason to be guided by the corresponding v-rules). This criticism is one often aimed at virtue theorists, not just Aristotle. Even when we compare the virtue ethics of Aristotle with those of St Thomas Aquinas, or with David Hume or the Victorians, we can see that the list of virtues changes. Does this not suggest that the lack of any external criteria, telling us what counts as a virtue, means that virtues are culturally relative? In which case, there are no universal v-rules, no prescriptions in virtue ethics that are equivalent to the maxim of the utilitarians or the categorical imperative of Kant. However, James Rachels (1941–2003) argues that there are some virtues which all societies need – in other words, without which stable societies could not be sustained.[22] These foundational virtues include honesty, loyalty, generosity, courage ... a very similar list to the one that Aristotle gave in fourth-century Athens.

▶ **ACTIVITY**

Using the list of virtues and vices identified in the activity on page 320 and the list on page 349, generate one v-rule for each virtue, and one v-rule for each vice.

Issue: can Aristotle's virtue ethics deal with clashing or competing virtues?

The robustness of any ethical theory is tested through its application to 'hard cases' or moral dilemmas – in other words, situations in which there is no clear right course of action that can be recommended by the theory; and virtue ethics is no different from consequentialist or deontological theories in its vulnerability to moral dilemmas. Utilitarian dilemmas may emerge if we have to decide whether to maximise happiness or minimise pain in a situation, but we cannot do both. This can be resolved for utilitarians by deciding in advance which of these two outcomes is more important (leading to the distinction between positive and negative utilitarianism). Kantian dilemmas can emerge if there are situations which lead to conflicting duties, and these can be resolved by determining, in advance, which duties take priority.

Dilemmas for virtue ethicists seem to be less clear-cut than they are for utilitarians or Kantians. For any situation, there are many different responses that we could have, a range of virtues that we could display, a number of vices (excessive or deficient responses) that we might fall into. So, potentially, every situation could be one which is a dilemma for an Aristotelian virtue ethicist, as there is always more than one virtuous response available to us, which we could take. Only by developing skills in practical wisdom can we navigate our way through life successfully, making the optimum decision in each situation.

However, occasionally we will encounter situations not just where there is more than one virtue 'on the table', but where one possible response obviously conflicts with another possible response. Virtue ethics deals very well with that classic dilemma of Plato's and Kant's: the mad axe murderer (see TL2, page 205).[23] Imagine your neighbour has lent you their axe so that you can chop down a tree. They knock at your door one night and ask for the axe back, looking and sounding as though they are going to murder someone, and the question is: what do you do? On the one hand, you are an honest person, and have demonstrated the virtue of truthfulness throughout your life. On the other hand, you are a kind person, and hate to think of other people being injured (for example, by mad axe murderers). So, should you be honest here, and give back the axe, or should you be kind here and lie about not having the axe? It is pretty clear that Aristotle can deal with this potential conflict of virtues by saying that the right thing to do (the most appropriate thing to do) would be to lie. There is, in fact, no conflict at all. This is because, as Aristotle says, sometimes the mean (that is, what is appropriate) can itself be an extreme, so a deficiency of honesty here would be exactly what a virtuous person would do. We return to see how virtue ethics addresses cases of lying and deception on page 358.

What about a harder case, where there is no clear route that can be taken? Michael Haneke's film *Amour* (2012) is about a married couple, Anne and George, both ex-piano teachers in their eighties, living in a flat in Paris. Anne suffers a stroke and undergoes surgery, leaving her paralysed and unable to play the piano. Anne tells George that she does not want to go on living. George tries to look after her, but she suffers a second stroke and now has severe dementia and is incapable of speech. Both George, as a carer looking after his dying loved one, and his wife, Anne, are undergoing unbearable suffering. At the end of the film, George tells the non-responsive Anne a story and then kills her by smothering her with a pillow. He then adorns the bed with flowers – his last act of love for her. The issue for a virtue ethicist is: what was the virtuous thing to do here? There are clearly competing virtues: the charitable, loving virtue that leads George to kill his wife; and the virtue of justice which should prevent us from killing anyone.

Aristotle does not provide a hierarchy of virtues, but if he had, then justice would have been placed above charity. After all, Aristotle admits that while some virtues might be in an extreme, like lying to the axe murderer, there are some actions which are always vicious, like theft and murder, acts of intolerable injustice. But is George's act an act of charity – euthanasia – and not a murder at all? If so, then there is a genuine dilemma for the Aristotelian virtue ethicist. George's action seems to display not just charity, but kindness and love, and heart-breaking regret; but on the other hand, he could have displayed courage and justice by not killing her, and lived with the daily sharing of her suffering. In either case, there would be a residue of pain, what Hursthouse calls a 'moral remainder', which can be experienced as intense guilt or regret by the person making the decision. But, Hursthouse claims, one of the strengths of the virtue ethics approach is that it acknowledges this regret as morally significant, even life-changing (just watch or read *Sophie's Choice* (1982)). The moral significance of the remainder is the result of the impact that clashing virtues, and the resultant tough decision-making, have on the agent. Hursthouse contrasts this nuanced view with utilitarian or Kantian ethics, which fail to give any weight to moral remainders.[24]

Issue: the possibility of circularity in defining virtuous acts and virtuous persons in terms of each other

Let us return to the question raised above (page 337), namely 'What is a virtuous act?' If we can answer this question, then we may be able to apply Aristotle's ethics more readily as a guide to moral action. As an answer to this question, Aristotle directs us to virtuous people: it is the 'good man' who sets the standard – these are the people who find the mean and do the right thing, the people whose example we should follow. Aristotle clarifies this in Book Three when he is discussing the ends that our actions are aimed at.

> *the object of wish is the good, but for the individual it is what seems to be good to him; so for the man of good character it is the true good … For the man of good character judges every situation rightly … he is a sort of standard for what is right and pleasant.*
>
> Aristotle (1113a25ff)

In other words, for most of us, our actions are aimed at the apparent good, what seems good to us; but the good person, someone with *ethica arete*, chooses the actual good; they set the standard for us to aim at. Perhaps we are now making some headway here in our search to find, in among Aristotle's theory, some guidance on how we should act. We wanted to know what a virtuous act is, and Aristotle directs us to virtuous people: a virtuous act is done by someone virtuous. The question we should now ask is, 'Who are these virtuous people?' since if we can identify them, then we can follow their example. The problem of circularity immediately arises if our answer to this question is, 'Virtuous people are those who choose virtuous actions'. For example, if we want to know what the courageous thing to do is, then we should look towards people we know who have courage. And who are these people with courage? Well, they are the people who always act courageously. If that is Aristotle's answer, then we are left with an unhelpful piece of advice, as what we need is some external criteria that tell us what virtue is without referring to virtue.

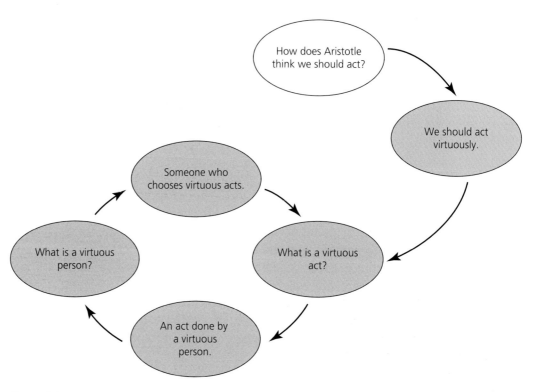

Figure 2.26 Is Aristotle guilty of this type of circular reasoning?

However, Aristotle does have more to say about virtuous people than simply, 'They are the ones who act virtuously'. We know at least two other things about virtuous people. First, for Aristotle, virtuous people are those who are *eudaimon*, the men (and they were definitely men) in Aristotle's classes studying philosophy, the wealthy Athenians who formed Aristotle's circle of friends, those people who were comfortably off, but had time to devote to contemplation of the good life. Second, we should remember (see **Figure 2.18**) that virtuous people are excellent in a number of different ways: they do not just have *ethica arete*, but they are also people with practical wisdom – that is, those able to make the right choice or wish about the goals they should choose. Practical wisdom (the virtue of practical reasoning) and *ethica arete* (the virtue of character) are bound up with each other, and both of them are needed for us to make the right decisions throughout our life that enable us to flourish.

So, first, can we free Aristotle from the charge of circularity by using the concept of *eudaimonia* to define a virtuous person? J.L. Mackie (1917–81), in *Ethics: Inventing Right and Wrong*, argues that Aristotle's account of *eudaimonia* is dependent on his account of virtue and so also leads to circularity.[25] Aristotle's function argument aims to show that the good life for humans (*eudaimonia*) is the life of a good human (that is, a human who fulfils their function well) – in other words, someone who excels and is virtuous. So a virtuous person is someone who flourishes, and someone who flourishes is someone virtuous – the circularity remains (**Figure 2.27**).

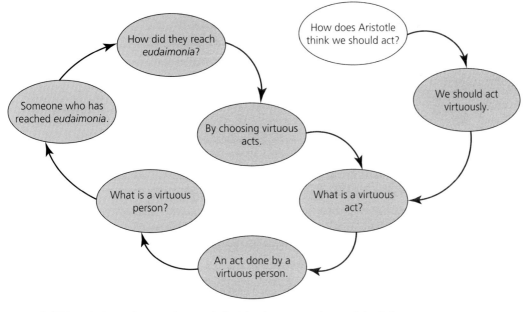

Figure 2.27 Introducing *eudaimonia* does not help Aristotle escape a charge of circularity

Perhaps, then, we can free Aristotle from the charge of circularity by finding an external criterion in the concept of practical wisdom. Unfortunately, this escape route fares just as badly, as St Thomas Aquinas (who revived the work of Aristotle in Western Europe) pointed out nearly 800 years ago.[26] A virtuous person has both excellence of character and practical wisdom: our character provides us with the desire and drive, and our practical wisdom enables us to direct our desires towards the right ends. So how do we identify someone with these excellences? Someone has practical wisdom because they choose the right ends; but to identify the right ends, they must have *ethica arete*. But to have *ethica arete*, someone must be capable of choosing the right ends – they must have practical wisdom, and again the circularity remains.

Aristotle must have been aware of this circularity himself, but he saw it as a fact about virtue, not as a problem with his argument, which meant the two excellences were so co-dependent. The external route that Aristotle would have taken to know who the virtuous people were was to look around him at the good people of Athens. He does not need to give a definition of 'virtuous person' which is free from circularity, because it would have been clear to him and his audience who these people were. The virtuous person is someone who has all the qualities that were valued by the middle classes in Athens: people with virtues we would also recognise in a moral sense (they are kind, courageous, just, generous, honest and so on); but also people with virtues we would not necessarily now value in a moral sense (pride, ambition, wit, righteous indignation and so on).

So Aristotle may avoid a charge of circularity by pointing to the virtuous people who live all around him. But closely following from this account is the criticism that has been made frequently of the supporters of virtue ethics (including Aristotle, Hume and Aquinas), namely that they are simply describing the values of their social class and age, and their lists of virtues are the preferred characteristics of that class and age. There just do not seem to be any accepted criteria for determining what is a genuine virtue and what is not. In fact, it seems as if deciding what is a virtue, such as friendliness, or a vice, such as rudeness, is a matter of personal opinion – perhaps a highly informed one (Aristotle was one of the most widely read and travelled intellects of his age), but an opinion nevertheless.

Issue: must a trait contribute to *eudaimonia* in order to be a virtue?

A virtue, in general terms, is a character trait, or disposition, that we admire, value and aspire to have. More specifically, for Aristotle: a virtue is a disposition (underpinned by reason) which means we aim, and are able, to act in the right way, towards the right people, at the right time and so on; and virtue is essential to our achieving *eudaimonia*. The connections between virtue and *eudaimonia* have been drawn in several places during this chapter, most notably in the section outlining Aristotle's function argument, in which he shows that in order to flourish, we must excel (be virtuous) in our function, which is to reason. So for Aristotle, we cannot live the good life for a human (and flourish) without being a good human (and being virtuous). But is it possible for us to identify traits that we might consider virtues, but which do not contribute to *eudaimonia*? Or is it part of the definition of a virtue that it must contribute to *eudaimonia*? First, let us address this question within an Aristotelian framework.

An Aristotelian response

It is worth remembering that not all character traits are positive traits: cowardice, meanness or dishonesty are all dispositions that we generally try to discourage in ourselves and others. But these are all recognisable flaws in our characters, developed as we regularly act in an excessive or deficient way, until they become habits, and until our reasoning processes are so flawed that we think that these responses are the right responses. For Aristotle, these traits (termed vices) certainly do not contribute to *eudaimonia*, and we can understand why: people who are liars, or cowards or cheats tend to do poorly in society: they may lack friends, they may not progress at work, they may anxiously look over their shoulder having broken the law – they do not flourish. However, Aristotle recognises that, on occasion, these deficient or excessive responses may be the right response – for example, sometimes lying, or running away, or cheating may be the most appropriate action to take. But 'on occasion' or 'every now and then' does not amount to a character trait, and Aristotle would expect the person who did occasionally have to lie or steal, to be honest and courageous in general if they are to flourish.

Can we imagine a situation in which these 'one-off' extreme responses become traits (we become liars, cheats, thieves), not contributing to *eudaimonia*, but nonetheless recognisable as virtues because they are the right thing to do? Primo Levi (1919–87), in *If This Is a Man*, describes the horrific experiences of life in a Nazi concentration camp during the Second World War and the actions he took to survive (see the quote on page 360).

It is possible to imagine that in the brutal, murderous environment of war, morality seems turned upside down and people develop traits such as those described by Levi (in this case, theft, but in other cases, cowardice, dishonesty or bribery); and it is possible to imagine that on every occasion in which this trait is exhibited, *it is the right thing to do on that occasion*. These things may be the right thing to do because the people you are lying to, cheating or stealing from are themselves a vicious and corrupt group who are destroying your community through their warmongering and brutality. So is this the counterexample we were looking for – that is, an example of how (negative) traits might be virtues, even though they do not contribute to *eudaimonia*? We can present the argument in support of this conclusion more formally in this way:

P1 A virtue, according to Aristotle, is a disposition to act towards the right person to the right extent at the right time for the right reason in the right way (let us call this condition the 'Right Five' or R5)

P2 In certain unique circumstances, acts such as stealing, lying, cheating, bribing may be R5

P3 If these unique circumstances are repeated over a number of years (for example, during war), then a disposition may be developed for stealing, lying, cheating and still be R5 – that is, virtuous

P4 Traits like stealing, lying, cheating and bribing do not contribute to *eudaimonia*

C (from P3 and P4) There exist traits (such as stealing, lying, cheating, bribing) which are virtues, yet these traits do not contribute to *eudaimonia*

Aristotle may reply to this argument by attacking premise 2: he writes in Book Two of the *Ethics* (1107a8) that some actions, such as murder and theft, can never be the right response, whatever the circumstances.

For the sake of this argument, let us imagine that your examples persuade Aristotle to accept premise 2, and he concedes that these actions could be justifiable under special circumstances (see page 350 for more on Aristotle and stealing). Can we then conclude that the traits developed during war which result in stealing, bribing and lying demonstrate virtue because in this unique context they are the right thing to do? Probably not. Even if Aristotle accepts premise 2, he may attack the argument at another vulnerable point, premise 4, by arguing that actions such as theft and dishonesty during war do in fact contribute to our *eudaimonia*. Perhaps not immediately, as they are actions only taken to survive, not to flourish, but they contribute in the long term by enabling us to stay alive so that we can get our lives, our honesty and integrity, back on track. So if we accept that premise 4 (or premise 2) is false, then we cannot accept the conclusion. Within Aristotle's account, then, a trait must contribute to *eudaimonia* in order to be a virtue.

But there are alternative theories of virtue which are not eudaimonistic, and they offer a different explanation of virtue. Let us turn to look at one of the most influential non-eudaimonistic theories of virtue, the one put forward in the eighteenth century by David Hume.

A non-Aristotelian response

Hume offers an account of the character traits we call virtues, but his account does not tie these traits to *eudaimonia*. He is interested in the question: what makes us call this type of behaviour a 'virtue'? which is a much narrower question than Aristotle's interest in: what is the good life for humans? Hume

▶ **ACTIVITY**
1 Can you imagine circumstances in which murdering someone would be the right thing to do on that occasion?
2 Can you imagine circumstances in which stealing something would be the right thing to do?

argues that when we make a moral judgement, such as *he is generous* or *she is courageous*, we are not talking about some feature of the world 'out there' that is good or right or virtuous. For Hume, if we think carefully about the moral judgements we make, then we discover that they are derived only from a feeling inside us. When someone does something kind, or generous or courageous, we have a general feeling of approval for such behaviour. So, for Hume, morality is not really a (rational) judgement at all; it is more of a gut feeling, it triggers our sympathy. So when we are talking about virtue, we are talking about our response to a behaviour, we are not describing any property of the behaviour itself.

Hume thought that there were two types of virtues, based on two kinds of positive responses we have to someone's behaviour. The first is a response to the usefulness of her behaviour, the pains and pleasures it generates, which Hume calls its utility and includes virtues like justice, benevolence and generosity. The second response is simply based on whether her behaviour pleases us, which Hume terms its agreeability, and includes virtues like wit, modesty, politeness. These qualities (of utility or agreeability) may either be extended to ourselves, or to other people. This is the principle that Hume believes governs morality: that we value those qualities which are 'useful or agreeable to the person himself or to others'.[27] Qualities that are neither useful nor agreeable to ourselves or others are not virtues.

Hume's account of virtue is subtle, detailed and influential: the utilitarians of the nineteenth century and the emotivists of the twentieth century (page 405) were inspired by Hume's theory. But on Hume's account, it is *not* part of the definition of virtue that they must contribute to our happiness or help us to flourish. Instead, virtues should be understood as traits that we are born with, or traits that society instils in us, which trigger responses of approval: either because they are useful or because they are agreeable.

Issue: The relationship between the good for the individual and the moral good

At the very start of this chapter, we noted how the ancient Greek approach to ethics, such as Aristotle's, is very different from a modern approach. The main focus of enquiry for Aristotle is: what do I need to do in order to flourish? emphasising the development of personal character traits and the goal of personal happiness. This seems very far removed from the moral concerns of philosophers like Mill and Kant; and virtue ethics has been taken by some philosophers to be a self-interested ethics, focusing on the good for the individual at the expense of the 'moral' good. In this section, we look at the basis of this criticism and assess whether it is justified.

There are several questions it would be helpful to address here:

1 What is meant by the 'good for the individual' and 'the moral good', and how do they differ?
2 Is Aristotle's virtue ethics focused only on the good for the individual? What reasons can be given to support this view?
3 If Aristotle's ethics is focused on the good for the individual, then in what way can it be reconciled with 'the moral good'?

Experimenting with ideas

Ministry of Righteous Action in Life

Aristotle is being put on trial by the government's Ministry of Righteous Action in Life (M.O.R.A.L.). The charges against him are being made under the Sales of Goods Act 1979 and the Misrepresentation Act 1967. The prosecution has brought the case on the grounds that Aristotle's book, the *Ethics* (read by millions of students over the past 2,000 years) has been mis-sold and misrepresented. They argue that the book makes the fraudulent claim that it is about ethics, when it is not at all, but instead is just about how we can be happy. The prosecution argues that Aristotle should recompense the millions of students for the time and money they wasted studying a book on ethics that was not, in fact, about ethics.

(**Authors' note**: the authors argue that they should also be recompensed on similar grounds, for writing a book on Aristotle's *Ethics*, which, it turned out, was not about ethics.)

1 What reasons might the prosecution give for claiming that the *Ethics* is not about ethics?

2 How might Aristotle defend himself?

What is meant by the 'good for the individual' and 'the moral good'?

Modern philosophy (and by 'modern', philosophers tend to mean philosophy since Descartes – philosophers have long memories!) has drawn a distinction in ethics between actions that are self-interested, done primarily for the benefit of the individual, and actions which are done primarily for the benefit of others. For example, Kantians and utilitarians may disagree on the foundations of morality, but they agree that the moral good is fundamentally about the good for other people, not the good for me.[28] This is the tradition (heavily influenced by Christian thought) of Western teachings on morality over the past few hundred years.

Within this tradition, moral goodness is contrasted with selfishness, or self-interest, or egoism. These are actions we take that benefit ourselves first and foremost. Self-interested acts are not moral acts; even if they have beneficial side effects, they are not valued in the way that morally good acts are valued. Some philosophers have embraced self-interest and there are interesting, albeit controversial, branches of moral philosophy that explore such -isms as egoism, existentialism and NIHILISM (see page 420) as an alternative form of ethics. Other philosophers, such as Thomas Hobbes (1588–1679), have warned us against the dangers of self-interest. Hobbes acknowledged that self-interest is a primary driver of human action, but our pursuit of each of our individual interests would drive us into a state of violent competition in which our lives would be 'nasty, brutish and short'.[29] Hobbes argued that we should appeal to this self-interest in order to bring about 'moral' outcomes. For example, given that we are all self-interested, and to avoid us descending into universal war, it is in all our interests to give up some of our individual freedoms (surrendering these to government, to law, to society) in order to be safe, protected and able to pursue our other interests. But this is merely a practical solution to our inherent selfishness.

Given this stark contrast between the moral good (good for others) and the good for the individual, which category does Aristotle's virtue ethics slot into?

Is Aristotle's virtue ethics focused only on the good for the individual?

Anyone encountering Aristotle's *Ethics* for the first time might be struck by how different, how 'un-moral', his approach actually is. Although Aristotle talks about the Good, he does so without reference to helping other people; and his analysis is frequently diverted into a discussion of all sorts of subjects (friendships, ambition, contemplation, project-planning skills), which we would not expect in a work of moral philosophy. In addition to these apparently off-topic diversions, there are a number of ways in which Aristotle's ethical theory seems to focus only on the good for the individual.

For example, Bertrand Russell highlights the character traits that Aristotle admires, but which make us feel uncomfortable: someone who is magnanimous, ambitious, proud, aristocratic, with a slow step and a deep voice. The sort of person we would cross the street to avoid, but whom Aristotle would invite round for a lengthy dinner party at his villa. For Bertrand Russell, Aristotle's theory promotes the type of person who is looking out only for themselves.

> *There is in Aristotle an almost complete absence of what may be called benevolence or philanthropy. The sufferings of mankind do not move him emotionally.*[30]

Aristotle's primary concern in the *Ethics* is to show us how we might each, individually, strive towards flourishing – *eudaimonia*. This does seem very far removed from the concerns of Mill or Kant, or other moral philosophers who are trying to make the world a better place. Aristotle's book is almost like one of those found in the 'Self-help' section of your local bookstore, as it aims to guide us towards happiness: our own happiness. So the overall purpose of the book seems to focus only on the good for the individual. When we look at the process by which we achieve this goal, namely the development of virtue, we might again be struck by how self-interested this process is. Aristotle sees virtues as valuable because they help us to achieve our goal of happiness – or rather they help *me* to achieve *my* goal of happiness.

If Aristotle's ethics is focused on the good for the individual, then in what way can it be reconciled with 'the moral good'?

Critics say that Aristotle's theory is not a moral theory, because it focuses on 'the good for the individual', not 'the moral good'. But Aristotle would not recognise the gap that more recent moral philosophy has placed between 'what is good for me' and 'what is good for others'. Within the ancient Greek tradition, moral behaviour does not conflict with self-interested behaviour; rather morality flows from self-interest. This is very far from Hobbes' claim that the pursuit of self-interest places human beings in a condition of universal war. For Aristotle, self-interest is defined by what is good, so we must seek an objective understanding of what is good if we are to really to do what is best for us. His analysis reveals that moral action is part of our good, and so it turns out that our true self-interests are best served by being moral.

Moreover, Aristotle's account of self-interest is a more nuanced account than his critics give him credit for. According to Aristotle, people are often mistaken about what is really the best life to lead, what is in our true self-interests: we can be wrong both about the ends (what we should be aiming for) and about the means (the methods by which we get there). We have seen Aristotle identify and critique some of the ends, or goals, that appear to be in our self-interest, but actually are not – these include pleasure and honour and wealth. So Aristotle is not concerned with 'selfish' ends; they do not lead to *eudaimonia*.

Aristotle's account of virtue does not mean that pursuing virtue is incompatible with what we would call the 'moral good'. It is true that Aristotle argues that we should aim to develop virtues, as these will enable us to flourish. But when we consider many of the traits that Aristotle considers (such as those listed on page 349), we recognise them as having moral value. Through the development of our practical wisdom, we become considerate, fair and reasonable people. Through the development of *ethica arete*, we also develop friendliness, courage, truthfulness, justice, generosity and a host of other virtues that, while benefiting our journey to *eudaimonia*, also benefit those people around us and contribute to the well-being of our whole community. It is even possible to argue that through the development of theoretical wisdom (via contemplation), we also contribute to the good of others – through the sharing of our discoveries and wisdom.

Therefore, if we are virtuous, then we will be both morally good (that is, consider others) and live a good life (that is, satisfy our self-interests and flourish). If we fail to be virtuous (and examples of such failure include habitual behaviour that we would label 'immoral', such as lying, killing and maliciousness), then we stand no chance of living a good life or flourishing in a community. Aristotle's understanding of virtue results in us living what we would now call a morally good life, and my happiness is inseparable from the people amongst whom I live. For Aristotle, humans really are social animals, and our *eudaimonia* is bound up in that of the other individuals among whom we live. My well-being contributes to the well-being of my community, and the pursuit of our proper self-interest, towards virtue and *eudaimonia*, results in (what modern philosophers would call) the 'moral good'.

Summary of Aristotle's virtue ethics

Virtue ethics takes an agent-centred approach to morality, in contrast to the act-centred approach adopted by utilitarians (and other consequentialists) and by Kantians (and other deontological theorists). The origins of virtue ethics lie in ancient Greece, most particularly in the philosophy of Plato and Aristotle. But virtue ethics has been revived in recent years as an alternative to consequentialist and deontological theorists.

Aristotle's virtue ethics is articulated in his *Nicomachean Ethics* (or simply, the *Ethics*) which is an edited collection of his lecture notes for his students at the

Lyceum. The *Ethics* begins with an exploration of the *summum bonum* – the Good that we are all striving to reach. Aristotle thinks we all agree on what this is, namely happiness (*eudaimonia*) – in other words, living well, doing well and flourishing. But we disagree on how to achieve *eudaimonia* and Aristotle rejects the usual suggestions (a life of pleasure, or wealth, or honour, or goodness). Instead, Aristotle opts for a psychological account of happiness, based on the type of beings we are and on the function or characteristic activity we possess as a species, namely reason. Aristotle argues that this function is determined by the activities of our soul, in particular our capacity to reason. If we excel at reasoning, and thus fulfil our function well (we are 'good humans'), then we will reach *eudaimonia* (living the good life and flourishing). Another term for 'excel' is 'virtue', which is a character trait or disposition, and Aristotle spends most of the *Ethics* investigating those virtues or excellences which we need to possess in order to flourish.

Book two of the *Ethics* gives an account of the excellences of character (or 'moral virtues'). Aristotle thinks that we develop these virtues through practice and habituation, like learning a skill, but these never become mindless habits. We also learn to take pleasure in acting virtuously. The 'virtuosity' of someone with virtue is an ability to develop responses to situations which are the right responses, and which avoid an excessive or deficient response – in other words, someone with virtue is able to find the mean. For example, someone with the virtue of courage is able to develop her character so that she avoids rash or cowardly behaviour, which are both 'vices'.

Our judgements of people's characters and virtues (including our own) are based on particular types of actions, ones which give us a clue as to the person's real character. Aristotle gives a clear account of what types of actions we should be judged on, and which types are irrelevant. Voluntary acts are ones that we intended to do, and we must take full responsibility for these. But some actions go against our intention (involuntary acts), and these include acts that we felt compelled to do (which we are partly responsible for) and acts that were beyond our control (which we are not responsible for). There is a further class of unintended acts (non-voluntary), which were the result of us not knowing the full facts of our situation: the key thing is that if we regret these actions once we find out the full facts, then these are treated as involuntary acts.

In addition to the 'moral' virtues (excellences of character), Aristotle also argues that the intellectual virtues most be developed if we are to flourish. When we excel at practical reasoning, this is termed 'practical wisdom', and it means that we are able to plan our lives and achieve our goals; we have a good understanding of any situation and are able to judge what the right thing to do is. But practical wisdom is inseparable from excellence of character (you cannot have intellectual virtue without having moral virtue).

The other intellectual virtue is 'theoretical reasoning' or contemplation. At the end of the *Ethics*, Aristotle revisits the Good and suggests that contemplation is the highest goal we can strive for. This seems to contradict the rich and varied life (of skilful and virtuous behaviour, of good fortune and health, of friendship and pleasure) outlined in the rest of the *Ethics*.

2.3.2 Applying Aristotelian virtue ethics

We have seen that both Kantian and utilitarian approaches were able to provide overarching principles to guide our actions and tell us what we ought to do. However, virtue ethicists like Aristotle do not give us clear rules to follow. In contrast, virtue ethicists urge us to take a more holistic approach, so that we are harnessing all the skills available to us in order to make a correct judgement; this also means balancing a number of different values that pull in different directions. For the virtue ethicist, each situation presents itself to us differently but, over time, someone who is virtuous will tend to conform to the sorts of values that deontologists and consequentialists espouse (trying to do good, trying to do what is right and fair and so on).

Virtue ethics has been accused of vagueness, but philosophers like Rosalind Hursthouse have defended virtue ethics, by arguing that it does offer us action guides in the form of v-rules (page 337). These rules are derived from the dispositions that we hold to be virtues and vices, in other words, dispositions that we value and praise, and dispositions that we condemn. Hursthouse lists a wide range of virtues, which include being compassionate, benevolent, generous, conscientious, fair, responsible, caring, courageous, public-spirited, having goodwill, empathy, integrity and self-respect. The list is long, but there is an even longer list of vices, which includes being self-interested, mean, callous, cruel, spiteful, dishonest, thoughtless, unjust, dishonourable, disloyal, lazy, unfair, irresponsible, uncaring, cowardly, materialistic, antisocial, greedy, envious, small-minded, arrogant and lacking integrity.[31] This is a useful list to start with and provides the foundations for virtue ethics (in the way that the categorical imperative is foundational for Kant, and the principle of utility is foundational for Mill). We should note that the list is not necessarily the list that Aristotle would provide, and although there is an overlap, there are significant differences. So, in applying virtue ethics to the dilemmas, we are actually applying an Aristotelian-inspired virtue ethics (such as can be found in Hursthouse or MacIntyre), rather than Aristotle's ethics itself.

A framework for applied virtue ethics: easy as ~~ABC~~ CBA

Unlike utilitarian and Kantian ethics, there may not be a formula for applying virtue ethics, but we have developed a *framework* (which is slightly more complex and open-ended than a formula) that you might find helpful when approaching moral dilemmas from a virtue ethics perspective. Our framework prompts a number of different questions that a virtue ethicist might ask, and clusters these questions into three steps. The questions you need to ask are about the behaviours and character traits, the virtues and vices, that are relevant to the agent(s) in this situation (we have called these virtues and vices V+ and V− for short). But the questions are also about using your practical wisdom to help you understand the context of the dilemma, to help you to multiply options (often a dilemma appears to offer only two choices), and to work out what the right, most appropriate, thing to do is. The framework is as easy as ABC, or rather, CBA, which are the letters that should help you remember the three steps in our virtue ethics framework. The letters stand

▶ **ACTIVITY**

1 What other character traits that are valued and praised (as virtues) would you add to Hursthouse's list?

2 What character traits that are condemned (as vices) would you add to the list?

for **C**ontext, **B**ehaviours and **A**nalysis/Action, and in **Figure 2.28** below we explain how to apply the CBA approach.

The CBA framework		Questions to ask at each step
Step 1		Circumstances: What are the special circumstances of this situation? (Do any specific values or responsibilities apply here?)
	Context	Choices: What are the options open to the agent? Can you use your practical wisdom to try to generate at least three options?
Step 2		V+ What are the virtues that are needed, expressed or reinforced in this situation?
	Behaviours	V− What are the vices that might be expressed, reinforced or avoided in this situation?
Step 3		Weigh up the V+ and V− for each option, taking into account the long-term impact on the agent's dispositions. What are the reasons behind each option (are they virtuous ones)?
	Analysis/action	What should be the agent's final decision – which option is the right/most appropriate one, given the circumstances?

Figure 2.28 Easy as CBA – a framework for applying virtue ethics

▶ **ACTIVITY**

Read ST1 (page 203). For this dilemma, try applying step 1 of our CBA framework, which is about context. What are the special circumstances of this situation? (Do any specific values or responsibilities apply here?) What are the options open to you? Can you use your practical wisdom to try to generate at least three options?

Stealing

Aristotle's doctrine of the mean proposes that nearly every action, or emotion, can be performed excessively, or deficiently, or appropriately (which is the mean). However, Aristotle goes on to say in the *Ethics* (1107a10) that for some actions, such as murder and stealing, there is never an occasion when these would be the appropriate course of action. What would Aristotle say about the two dilemmas on page 203, and how would a modern virtue ethicist approach them?

ST1

If you did the activity in the margin, then you may have noticed that there is a particular set of circumstances here that might have a bearing on the moral dilemma (and make it more complex than, for example, a simple Kantian application of duty). The circumstance is that it is your partner, rather than a friend or a colleague or a stranger, who is at risk of dying. For a virtue ethicist, we need to acknowledge that some relationships (those with our children and people we love) have a stronger demand on us than other relationships – we have an opportunity to express the virtues of generosity, loyalty and integrity with those closest to us, and we rely on them for our flourishing.

However, we know that on a strict Aristotelian view, it seems that Aristotle states that it is never appropriate to steal, hence it appears he would recommend that you should not steal the drug, even though your partner may die as a result.

This may not be the view taken by modern virtue ethicists, who have been inspired by Aristotle's comments that we should judge the appropriate thing to do on a case-by-case basis, and that sometimes even the mean (that is, the appropriate) thing to do can be an extreme (see page 319 above). In the case of stealing the Tastaphon, you may be acting out of benevolence: your desire to help people, to reduce the amount of pain in the world and possibly increase the amount of pleasure or happiness. However, a single action is not enough to judge whether you are benevolent – the virtue ethicist would want to know: is benevolence a part of your character? Are you habitually benevolent? It is possible that you are only acting benevolently in this case because it is your partner whose life is at risk, but that generally you are a thoughtless or inconsiderate person? Even if your action were a benevolent one, it would at the same time be a dishonest one, and it would deprive other patients of the drug who might then go on to suffer. Are you a dishonest or thoughtless person, or is this theft a one-off act of criminality motivated by love, compassion and benevolence?

It seems, in this case, that the dispositions of honesty and thoughtfulness (consideration of those people who would be affected by your theft of the drug) are competing with your disposition for benevolence and love (of your partner). Partiality, or bias, is a special feature of certain relationships that we have, recognised in virtue ethics;[32] the question is, does our partiality towards our immediate loved ones outweigh our consideration of other people in the community? You may have to utilise your practical wisdom to find an alternative, and legitimate means of getting this drug (a crowd-sourcing website to raise the money, an internet campaign to change NHS rules on this drug, a charitable event held by your friends...).

ST2

What is Aristotle's problem with theft? On the one hand, Aristotle thinks that there are no hard-and-fast moral rules, but that we must use our virtues (of character and practical reason) to decide what is the right thing to do on any one occasion. On the other hand, he appears to give us a moral rule by instructing us that some acts (such as theft and murder) are always wrong. This tension between two opposing beliefs may be resolved when we look at another of Aristotle's significant works – the *Rhetoric*. Here he expands on what he means by 'theft' (*klope* in ancient Greek), and he acknowledges that judges do need to take the context into account – for example, when someone admits having taken something without the owner's knowledge (which is generally called theft), but denies taking it with the intention of keeping it or using it to harm the owner.[33] But in general, for Aristotle, theft is a vice (a flawed character trait) because it damages us, and damages our chances of reaching *eudaimonia*. We must make

▶ **ACTIVITY**

Read the dilemma ST2 (page 203), and apply both step 1 and step 2 of the CBA framework to it – that is, make notes about the context and options, as well as about the virtues (V+) and vices (V−) that are attached to each option.

the right choice at the right time, using the right means, but stealing, even with the right intentions in mind, is nearly always the wrong means.

First of all, let us think about the context of ST2. There is a question raised, mostly by those people who engage in file-sharing, about whether file-sharing is stealing at all. There is a warm fuzziness about the expression 'file-sharing': it sounds like you are actually being helpful; whereas on the other hand, 'stealing' (unless you are Robin Hood) is generally not helpful. As part of sketching the context, it might be helpful to agree a broad definition of stealing – for example, as 'depriving someone of something they own and value without their permission'. So does file-sharing music count as stealing? Those, like Nathan, who defend the practice, might say that file-sharing of music is more like copying than stealing because you are not actually depriving the musician of anything – they still have the original song or album. All you have done is to copy it.

If part of the job of a virtue ethicist is to influence people's behaviour, then we need to understand why people do not think of it as theft, and how they can change that behaviour. And this is another critical aspect of the context of file-sharing: that most people like Nathan who engage in it do not recognise it as theft, even though they would morally disapprove of 'real' theft. Rather than use the hammering music and message that appears at the start of all DVDs ('You wouldn't steal a car ... you wouldn't steal a DVD ... downloading pirated films is stealing'), the virtue ethicist might want to appeal to other parts of Nathan's character and practical reason.

So what of the virtues and vices that may be engaged in this situation. There are few virtues, few positive character traits that Nathan is exhibiting in this dilemma; at a pinch, we might say he has the virtue of music appreciation, but that is about it. He is also being frugal, which may be a virtue in some contexts (for example, where Nathan is trying to reduce his carbon footprint), but not in this context. Nathan has a habit (a vice) of not paying for music – his frugality is a character flaw which is not appropriate in this context. Aristotle might say it is in 'an excess'; and this is made worse when combined with Nathan's dishonesty, as he knows that albums cost money to make, and part of that money should eventually make its way back to the artist. There is research showing that for smaller artists, without the backing of large record studios, illegal file-sharing is taking money away from them disproportionately. So by indulging in his dishonesty and exercising his frugality, Nathan is also failing to engage his practical wisdom: 1) he has a desire to listen to a particular artist; 2) but he is taking money away from that artist (by not paying for their albums); and 3) that artist relies on money to make new albums; then it is possible 4) that at some stage the artist will not have made enough of a profit to continue; and 5) Nathan's desire to listen to their music will no longer be fulfilled – thus undermining 1). This lack of practical wisdom is evidence of another vice: that of Nathan's thoughtlessness: he has not thought through the effects of his file-sharing habit, and its impact on the particular musicians who are being deprived of income, and on potentially new musicians who might give up as the music industry haemorrhages money.

The virtue ethicist might conclude the following: Nathan could carry on file-sharing, and in doing so he displays the virtue of 'music appreciation', but against this are the character flaws of dishonesty, excessive frugality and thoughtlessness. Or he could stop file-sharing, delete the files and buy them legitimately (an honest and thoughtful approach that still retains his music appreciation). Hey, Nathan could even write a song about it: the 'Don't Preach to Me About File-Sharing Blues'. I would buy it.

Simulated killing

SK1

In his seminal paper, 'Is it wrong to play violent video games?', Matt McCormick examines the response to this question from a utilitarian, Kantian and virtue ethics perspective. As technology has increased, so has the graphic realism with which violence and murder on screen can be represented, and McCormick points out that the desire for faster-paced games has led to killings not just being more graphic, but more numerous as well; that would certainly be true of *Psycho-Tick*. But simulated killings, however graphic, are just that – simulated; no one is actually being hurt, which is why the act of simulated killing poses such a dilemma for most moral theories.

A utilitarian and Kantian approach may emphasise the impact the game has on real people in the real world after the game has finished, but McCormick concludes that, of all moral theories, virtue ethics is best able to articulate why it may be wrong to play violent video games, whatever their impact. He draws this conclusion on the following grounds: first, that our moral intuitions tell us that there is 'something morally objectionable' with people playing a game that graphically mimics the murder of children – even if nobody is affected. Second, that neither utilitarianism nor Kantian ethics can provide compelling reasons for why playing the game *itself* (not the eventual effect that the act may have on other people) is wrong. Only virtue ethics, according to McCormick, is able to articulate what is objectionable about taking part in the virtual murder of video games: 'engaging in simulated immoral acts erodes one's character and makes it more difficult for one to live a fulfilled eudaimonic life'.[34]

So virtue ethics, especially of the Aristotelian flavour, does have something to say about virtual murder, even if the action does not affect other people. As you know, virtue ethics is agent-centred and not act-centred, but acts are still important to Aristotelian virtue ethics: actions contribute to habituation, which contributes to our character, which in turn contributes to how we will be inclined to behave in the future. We saw above (page 312) that building a virtuous character does not come easily, but requires careful cultivation. McCormick argues that by indulging in the excessive, indulgent and wrongful acts of games like *Psycho-Tick*, we are 'cultivating the wrong sort of character'. This sounds convincing, but there is an important empirical question here that McCormick does not address: whether cruel or callous behaviour in the virtual world of *Psycho-Tick* is actually converted (however unconsciously) into cruel or callous behaviour in the real world, which certainly would be the 'wrong sort of character'.

McCormick may not need this empirical evidence for his argument still to work. After all, actions that do not contribute to habituation of the virtues are an 'opportunity cost' – in other words, time spent doing one thing is a cost against time spent doing something more valuable. Let us imagine that

> ▶ **ACTIVITY**
> Read SK1 (page 203). Apply all three steps of the CBA framework to this dilemma: make notes about the context and options; draw up a list of V+ and V− for each option; then decide which course of action is the most appropriate.

353

empirical research has conclusively shown that there is no harmful impact on your character as a result of playing video games, thus time spent playing the games is 'morally neutral' time – the habits you are developing, in McCormick's words, are 'virtueless'. Even in this case (which may not be true), time spent on reinforcing virtueless dispositions, like gaming skills, is time taken away from developing virtuous dispositions (like volunteering in the community, or developing friendships, or contributing to the daily chores of any household). A virtue ethicist may conclude, and you may agree, that violent gaming, at best, fails to develop any virtues, and, at worst, encourages vices, neither of which would help the gamer to flourish or lead a good life.

SK2

'Greek tragedy' is a phrase that has entered our language, and rightly so: the writers of ancient Greece created a body of work to rival any in Western literature, and their stories, characterisation, tragic and dramatic irony, and narrative structures still hold sway over our theatrical and cinematic arts.[35] Aristotle wrote extensively on theatre in his work, the *Poetics*, focusing in particular on tragedy. Aristotle's analysis of tragedy is filtered through his interest in how this dramatic form can reflect our efforts to reach the good life, and the effect that tragedy can have on the audience's emotions. The virtue ethicist can usefully employ Aristotle's theory of tragedy to understand the effects on our character of watching murderous acts in film and theatre.

The key elements for Aristotle on tragedy are the journey of the hero, who is a great man (and for Aristotle, it usually was a male protagonist), towards some sort of crisis, usually as a result of *hamartia* (an error or flaw in the hero), which then leads to the denouement, catharsis and resolution of the crisis. For Aristotle, then, theatre is a form which explores the vulnerability of a good life, even of a near-perfect life, to external factors (see page 308): errors, bad luck, other people, the gods, society – all of which mean the hero's life can go dramatically and horribly wrong, sorely testing his character. According to Martha Nussbaum's (1947–) account of Aristotle, tragedies enable playwrights to explore, in a safe way, the gap between the ideal life and the fragility of our own lives, always vulnerable to disaster.[36] As well as being a crucible in which *eudaimonia* and character can safely be tested, Aristotle argued that the theatre brought emotional benefits to the audience. In the strict narrative trajectory of a tragedy, we see the hero's life fall apart (through *hamartia*), which raises feelings of both fear and pity in the audience. As the hero approaches the denouement, or *scène à faire*, the audience's anxieties intensify until the emotion is given a cathartic release and purged as the drama is resolved, the hero dies, or defeats the beast, or finds out that his wife is his mother (page 325) and so on. So for Aristotle, theatre, and tragedy in particular, has a purifying effect on the audience – through this cathartic process – enabling them to be better able to cope with tragedy in their own life. Theatre, then, even in its most tragic form, can restore us to psychological health.

Theatre in the ancient Greek tradition contains no simulated killing, and the horrific violence of Greek tragedies only takes place off-stage, described by the chorus rather than shown to the audience. The experience of modern theatre audiences and cinema-goers, who flock to watch simulated killing in Tarantino movies or this new play (by the fictional writer Susan Kain) may still be a cathartic experience. Audiences may find relief, and release, in watching simulated violence, as Aristotle describes – after all, the negative emotions essential to catharsis (pity and fear) are triggered every day by horrific news stories from around the world. Aristotle believed that without the cathartic effect of theatre, we are liable to become 'possessed' by these emotions, damaging the balance in our souls. We are thrilled by fear, but we do not want to be afraid in real life, so watching a play like Susan Kain's enables us to indulge in the thrill of fear and to purge that desire. But the point made by McCormick above could apply here: video games are compulsive, habitual and repetitive, which is why a virtue ethicist might be worried about the dispositions being developed. Seeing a one-off play like Susan Kain's should not worry the virtue ethicist too much; but watching the play over and over again, or watching the new strand of torture-based horror movies over and over again raises the point that McCormick made, that this habitual indulgence in simulated killing creates the wrong sorts of emotions and desires.

Eating animals

When discussing the treatment of non-human animals, many moral philosophers would first want to ask the question: What is the moral status of those other animals? They would argue that once we have clarified this question, we can then determine whether or not that animal has rights and we have duties to it, or whether its interests and preferences should be included in our utility calculus. But how would a virtue ethicist approach the issue? Aristotle believed that there was a natural hierarchy of living things and, as part of his teleological view, one of the functions of things lower down the hierarchy (such as animals) was to serve the needs (for example, as food) of those beings higher up the hierarchy (such as animals). However, let us look at what a modern virtue ethicist, without Aristotle's teleological baggage, might say about the treatment of animals.

Rosalind Hursthouse has argued that the question of the moral status of animals is not a question that a virtue ethicist needs to answer.[37] This is partly because virtue ethicists have a more holistic approach (and therefore, for Hursthouse, offer a more sophisticated approach); and partly because the 'moral status' issue is highly flawed: there is no familiar set of facts that some animals share but which other animals do not share, that grants them a higher moral status. Instead, there are many different ways in which animals can be grouped (wild animals, working animals, pets, animals in laboratories, free-range animals bred for food, factory-farmed animals), each of which attracts an associated set of responsibilities, duties and other virtues that virtue ethicists would have to consider on a case-by-case basis.

EA1

The way an animal has been treated before it is eaten has a significant bearing on our decision whether or not to eat it. Factory-farmed animals, like the chickens in this example, undergo horrific suffering before they are slaughtered and arrive at our supermarkets and fast-food outlets in their millions. Broiler chickens (birds raised for meat) are bred to develop abnormally overweight bodies, which cause crippling and painful skeletal deformities. Chickens are social animals, but caged in less than a square foot of cage, they peck and attack each other, leading to the practice of debeaking of chicks after they hatch (their beak is cut off with a hot knife, without anaesthesia). Chickens live short lives of intense stress, pain and disease until they are eventually slaughtered. Not, we would agree, a life of flourishing.

Rosalind Hursthouse asks: 'Can we deny that these practices are cruel?'[38] And the straightforward answer is: 'No, we cannot deny that.' Yet it is highly likely that you eat chicken, and it is also highly likely that you do not need to eat chicken (or any factory-farmed meat) in order to survive; we eat it because it is convenient, it is cheap and we like the taste. In which case, we are failing to exhibit compassion; and we are also failing to be temperate (as Hursthouse points out, temperance requires that we do not pursue pleasure while ignoring the claims of other virtues). We can add to this the sheer quantity of factory-farmed chickens that are consumed – ten billion per year are killed in the United States alone. This suggests a further character flaw: greed (how big does a bucket of chicken wings have to be?) It is hard to identify any competing virtues which would recommend that we carry on eating factory-farmed chicken: kindness? generosity? courage? justice? Can you think of a virtue that has a genuine claim on us which competes with compassion in this situation? In which case, virtue ethics recommends that we become more compassionate, that we stop ignoring the practices of factory farming, and we change our eating habits accordingly. Are there other options available? For example, if people ate less meat, would that reduce the suffering? If farmers bred expensive organic chickens, would that be more compassionate? Would it be possible for people to become vegetarian by default around the world?

You might guess that two of the authors of this book are vegetarian (you will have to ask the other one himself why he is not!). Remember this example when you do the activity on moral blind spots (page 418).

EA2

Let us apply the CBA framework in full to this dilemma, to see how it might work in practice.

Step 1: Context

Gilbert's organic farm is a very different type of farm from the factory-farmed chickens described in the first dilemma. The term 'organic' is a term restricted to those farms which meet certain criteria, prescribed in law, and inspected and certified by an organic control body. These criteria include avoiding artificial fertilisers and pesticides, and using crop rotation to maintain soil fertility, and avoiding banned substances such as growth hormones in food (which have been frequently used in industrialised farms). There is no definition of free-range cattle or a free-range dairy farm (although there are laws governing free-range chickens), but in general this is taken to mean that Gilbert's farm tries to maximise the amount of time that his cows spend outside, grazing and moving around fields, including during winter months, where appropriate. Compared to the chickens in the factory-farms, the cattle may expect to live a fairly stress-free life, with room to move and interact with other cattle, and possibly interact with their offspring, at least for a while. But nonetheless, in the end, these cows will be shot in the head with a metal bolt (a process known as 'stunning'), then hung upside down to have their throat slit (a process known as 'sticking') at an abattoir, in readiness for the butcher. Organisations such as the RSPCA have raised concern at the sticking of animals who have not been

▶ **ACTIVITY**

Read the dilemma EA2 (page 204). Apply all three steps of the CBA framework to this dilemma: make notes about the context and options; draw up a list of V+ and V− for each option; then decide which course of action is the most appropriate.

stunned – in other words, that an animal may have its throat cut whilst it is still conscious – for example, this may be due to the stunning equipment or process not being effective. The government has strict guidance on how to minimise the pain, distress and suffering of animals when they are killed. But even when this welfare guidance is adhered to, research has shown that the behaviour of animals in abattoirs, prior to being stunned, appears to be of fear and stress. The government's Food Standards Agency noted that in the UK between 2015 and 2016, there were 4,000 serious breaches of this welfare guidance, with each breach affecting up to hundreds of animals (these included animals arriving dead at the abattoir, cattle being beaten, chicken and pigs being immersed in scalding hot water whilst still alive to soften the skin).

So, should we eat Gilbert's cows? There are three immediate options available to us: Yes, eat the cows. Yes, eat the cows but only very rarely (excuse the pun). No, do not eat the cows.

Step 2: Behaviours

The first option is that we should freely eat these organic cattle. In *Humans and Other Animals*, Hursthouse recalls some of the pleasures of having friends round for dinner, preparing and cooking the meat, so we may identify the virtue of generosity in at least this type of situation. But eating and enjoying meat in itself is not a virtuous practice. Hursthouse goes on to describe how thinking more deeply about meat-eating in relation to virtue ethics changed her:

> I began to see those [actions] as unnecessary, greedy, self-indulgent, childish, my attitude to shopping and cooking in order to produce lavish dinner parties as parochial, gross, even dissolute[39]

The context outlined above reveals that, even with an organic, 'free-range' farm, cows will still suffer, particularly in their deaths. Knowing this, and yet still eating animals, reveals the same character flaws as outlined in EA1: we are not being compassionate; we are not being kind; we are not being temperate (we do not need cattle protein to be healthy); we are ignoring or permitting cruelty.

The second option is to eat less of Gilbert's organic meat. The same arguments as in option 1 apply: no virtues are being exhibited, and all the same character flaws are being exhibited (on those occasions when meat is eaten). There is another issue that we need to consider here, namely the virtues and vices that the farmers and abattoir workers develop as part of their working life. Gail Eiznitz, chief investigator for the Humane Farming Association, interviewed large numbers of workers in slaughterhouses who recorded the chilling effects that the killing of up to 1,000 animals per day was having on abattoir workers' lives and on their personal attitudes to the animals.[40]

The third option is to eat none of the organic meat, and to avoid eating meat altogether. By recognising the unnecessary cruelty that eating animals causes, this option enables us to exhibit our compassion, our understanding, our thoughtfulness, our temperateness, whilst avoiding all the character flaws described above.

Step 3: Analysis and action

The final step in the CBA framework asks what each of the options in step 2 offers in terms of the potential for developing virtues, and avoiding the development of character flaws. But it also asks us to consider the reasons that might underpin our decision to take a particular option. You may not agree with the analysis above, you may find virtue in eating animals which have been slaughtered, but, in general, virtue ethics points towards option 3 as the right thing to do. However, we emphasised the point above (page 315) that virtue has both a behavioural and a psychological dimension: it is not enough just to act in a virtuous way, we must act from virtuous reasons. So we might decide to become a vegetarian because we have fallen in love with a vegetarian and want to demonstrate what a thoughtful person we are; or we might decide to avoid eating meat because it is too expensive; or we might become a vegetarian because eating meat is a bit disgusting (gristle, fat, bone, muscle – what is that all about?). But to a virtue ethicist, these reasons are not the right reasons (although our new habit might eventually lead to the right reasons): we should not eat meat, even from Gilbert's farm, because we are not cruel or thoughtless, but compassionate and thoughtful people.

Telling lies

The two scenarios on page 205 both focus on the failure of the subject to tell the truth. We will see below how some philosophers draw a fine distinction between lying and deception, but all forms of virtue ethics, especially its Aristotelian form, require us to develop an honest character. It is by being honest together that we, as a society, will also be able to flourish. Our success depends upon the success of our communication, which itself depends on our trust in the information exchanged, the promises made, the judgements cast and so on. It is by being honest that we as individuals will ultimately flourish, people will trust us, people will look to us for information and advice. Peter Geach argues that the virtue of honesty enables us to develop our practical wisdom; or rather that the vice of dishonesty undermines our practical wisdom.[41] Honesty, like all virtues, is developed through habituation; and dishonesty (even the telling of small lies, or white lies) is also a habit. Dishonesty is a habit that enables us to escape easily from difficult situations: when you have not done your homework, when you are being interviewed for a job, when your mum asks you awkward questions about where you have been … a lie can free us from further efforts. But the habit of lying means that we do not work hard to find alternative solutions to those tricky situations – that is, we do not use our practical wisdom, which means that we are not genuinely equipping ourselves for further tricky situations. Difficult situations do not go away in life, and lying is no permanent solution to them – you simply get a reputation as a liar. But Geach argues that there is a difference between being dishonest by lying, and avoiding being honest by deception. Geach was influenced more by the deeply Christian virtue ethics of Aquinas than those of Aristotle, and believed that lying is never permitted. But he gives the example of St Athanasius, who was escaping in a boat from his persecutors when they rowed past in the opposite direction. As they passed, the persecutors asked, 'Where is that traitor Athanasius?', to which Athanasius replied, 'Not far away.' Geach argues that Athanasius was clever enough to avoid telling the truth (to deceive) without actually lying, so no damage was done to his honest disposition.

As we have seen throughout this discussion, real moral dilemmas are messy, complex affairs, and virtue ethicists believe their theory is well-placed to deal with this complexity, as the theory offers no simple answers. It will always consider the range of motives involved, what virtues or vices are potentially being exhibited, and the impact of the action on everyone concerned, in particular the impact on people's characters (as it is this impact that will affect their choices, virtuous or vicious, in the future). Both the first and the second dilemmas bring out the importance of two particular virtues: loyalty and honesty.

TL1

In the first scenario, Shelly is married to Jacob, and generally, with any marriage, various promises and vows are made at the start of the marriage and various expectations are set up, including the expectation that they will be faithful to each other. So Shelly, even though she has been let down by her husband, still has a responsibility to him to be loyal, at least while they are married. Marriages also require a special level of trust in order to work, and dishonesty within a marriage can tear away at that trust with distressing consequences (particularly if there are children in the marriage). It is understandable why Shelly wants to act in this way – but there are special demands made on her by her marriage, demands of loyalty and honesty, that mean she should not lie to her husband (and nor should he lie to her). However, the application of practical wisdom (what ultimate outcome does Shelly want to achieve here, and how can she best achieve it?), the virtue of temperance (controlling her desire to be with her neighbour) and emotional intelligence (what would be the impact of this lie on her husband?) may mean that Shelly eventually does begin a successful relationship with her neighbour, but only after an honest conversation with, and separation from, her husband. So a virtue ethicist may conclude that she should not yet explore the new relationship at this stage, and should start telling the truth to her husband.

TL2

The case of the axe murderer also involves the virtues of honesty and loyalty, but this time they are pitted against each other. This situation differs from the first in that you are deceiving rather than lying (a bit like St Athanasius): strictly speaking, it is true that nobody with muddy boots came into your house. But that is not what the axe murderer wanted to know, and you know this yourself, so although you have not lied, you have deceived, so you are not displaying the key virtue of honesty. For other types of ethical theory, this may present a problem, but an Aristotelian virtue ethicist, one who takes things on a case-by-case basis, may argue that we need to apply the virtues that are the right thing to do in this situation. If you are someone who is generally honest, then deceiving someone in a one-off (life-or-death) situation is not going to undermine your tendency and inclination to be honest. An axe murderer at your door is just such a situation. We have seen that our relationships with other people can bring with them special demands: our partners, friends and families require loyalty that goes beyond our loyalty to strangers in our community. So you do have a special loyalty to your friend not to betray him, and to keep him safe from harm. This loyalty lays claim on you in a way that easily outweighs the claim that 'being honest to a stranger (with an axe)' has, so in this case, a virtue ethicist may conclude that although you have not told a lie, you are still being dishonest, but that dishonesty is the appropriate response here.

> ▶ **ACTIVITY**
>
> Read TL1 and TL2 on page 205. What would Aristotle say? What would a modern virtue ethicist say?

2.4 Meta-ethics

Theft in Buna [the factory], punished by civil law, is authorised and encouraged by the SS; theft in the camp, severely repressed by the SS, is considered by the civilians as a normal exchange operation; theft among prisoners is generally punished, but the punishment strikes the thief and the victim with equal gravity. We now invite the reader to contemplate the possible meaning in Auschwitz of the words 'good' and 'evil', 'just' and 'unjust'; let everyone judge ... how much of our ordinary moral world could survive on this side of the barbed wire.[1]

Primo Levi

The Italian scientist and writer Primo Levi was one of the survivors of Auschwitz, the largest slave-labour and extermination camp constructed by the Nazis, which murdered up to four million people between 1941 and 1945. In this world of 'death and phantoms', Levi describes a process of complete dehumanisation, of bestial degradation. 'It is a man who kills, who creates or suffers injustice; it is no longer a man who, having lost all his restraint, shares his bed with a corpse ... [who] waits for his neighbour to die in order to take his piece of bread'.[2] Levi describes in horrific detail the way of life which emerged among the *Häftling* (prisoners), based on desperate survival from hour to hour. He challenges us to say how our moral concepts have any meaning or application in this hell on Earth.

Levi's question demands an answer. What is the meaning of moral judgements like 'good' and 'evil', 'just' and 'unjust'? But this, in turn, prompts further questions: are the origins of moral judgements somewhere inside us, or somewhere 'out there' in the world, and are moral judgements rational or non-rational? If they are rational, then are they discoveries, like the unearthing of physical laws about the universe, or are they constructions, like the creation of civil laws and social rules? Alternatively, if moral judgements are non-rational, then are they expressions of emotions/attitudes (like 'Boo!' or 'Hooray!'), or are they the result of a special moral conscience, or moral sense, that gives us access to a mysterious realm of moral values?

These issues about the meaning and origins of ethical judgements are more abstract than the normative issues that we have looked at so far, issues around the moral principles by which we should live and the moral judgements we should make. We have already needed, on several occasions, to take a more abstract approach – for example, to ask about the meaning of words like 'good' and 'virtue' – in order to assist us in our understanding of normative ethics. Philosophers refer to this more abstract level of enquiry as meta-ethics.[3] Meta-ethics addresses fundamental questions about the meaning and origins of moral rules and terms, which many modern philosophers feel must be answered before the more practical issue of how we should live our lives can be addressed. Meta-ethical questions include:

1 Are there any moral facts?
2 What do moral concepts refer to (or mean)?
3 Does moral language make statements about reality – that is, assertions which could be true or false?
4 Can moral terms (such as 'good') be defined in natural terms (such as 'happiness')?
5 What are the origins of our moral principles?

We turn first to this final question, addressing the origins of moral judgements and principles, before turning our attention to the other questions, which focus primarily on ethical language.

The origins of moral principles: reason, emotion/ attitudes or society?

For many people, it might seem strange to ask this question, as the answer is so straightforward: it is simply that God (or gods) is the origin of our moral principles. Not our reason, not our emotions, not our society, but God. A strange question, at least for religious believers, but perhaps philosophers are strange in that they find questions where others find answers. If you go on to study the second year of the Philosophy A-level, then you will encounter a serious challenge (known as the Euthyphro dilemma) laid down by Plato against the claim that moral principles originate in God. But for now, let us explore the non-religious origins of our moral principles: do they lie in reason, or in emotion, or in our society?

The origins of moral principles in reason

Self-interest, the placement of our own interests above all others, is often set at odds against morality, which requires us to think of the interests of others in roughly equal terms to our own selfish interests. However, one straightforward account of the origins of morality is that it lies precisely *in* our self-interest, and that it is reason which brings the two clashing sides together (me on one side, you and everyone else on the other). We have already seen how Aristotelian ethics finds the origins of virtue in reason, and that being virtuous (developing the right character traits) is both good for us and good for other people (page 347). This reconciliation of self-interest and morality is a form of 'rational self-interest', as we can calculate that it is in our own best interests to be moral.

Hobbes: social contract theory

One of the most famous arguments that moral principles are based on rational self-interest was put forward by the seventeenth-century English philosopher Thomas Hobbes. In his great work *Leviathan* (1651), he develops an account of the origins of morality that became known as the social contract theory. Hobbes imagines a 'state of nature', the condition of human beings prior to any social organisation or government (the television series *The Walking Dead* gives a very good sense of what a life in a state of nature might have been like, if you substitute sabre-toothed tigers for zombies). In this natural state, of no government, each of us pursues what benefits ourselves without qualms. No one can expect anyone else to do anything other than whatever maximises their own self-interest. This state of affairs would result in what Hobbes calls a 'war of every man against every man'. There would be none of the advantages of civilisation because all of us would live in 'continual fear and danger of violent death, and the life of man, solitary, poor, nasty, brutish, and short'.[4]

Given the fact that this state of nature is bad for everyone, Hobbes reckons it is rational for everyone to want to escape it. Since the only escape consists in following rules which require co-operation between people – a kind of social contract with agreed moral principles and government – it is rational for us to agree to follow such rules so long as we can rely on others to do so too. So it is rational for self-interested people (similar to ourselves) to conform to moral behaviour and sign up to the social contract in order to avoid being harmed by other self-interested people (similar to ourselves). A social contract theory shows the practical process by which reason (driven by self-interest) brings about moral principles as a kind of compromise.

But there are other philosophers who have tried to show how morality originates in reason in a very different way: not as a construction of the social contract, but as a discovery of the moral law.

We must follow the power of reason: from the general rules determining it, right up to the point where there springs from it the concept of duty.[5]

Kant: moral rationalism

The fierce debates and disagreements between rationalists and empiricists that you encountered in the first half of this book (page 154) extended beyond epistemology; and in the eighteenth century there was controversy not just about the foundation of knowledge, but about the foundation of our very morals. For rationalist thinkers like Kant, knowledge about the world in general was acquired through the application of reason, and moral knowledge was no exception. Kant argued that morality and moral principles have their origin in reason and rational judgement, not in our emotions or our particular social upbringing. We have to determine what is right and wrong for ourselves by the application of reason, and not expect it to be determined by any higher authority (such as God or the Church). Reason tells us that a morally right act is one that proceeds from the proper motive, namely the recognition of a duty. Other motives for action (such as desire or emotion) are not moral motives. Our duties can be determined by reason, through understanding and adhering to the categorical imperative, which means universalising the maxims underpinning our actions, and valuing (unconditionally) other rational beings and never treating them as a means to an end. Because our duties are created in this rational way, they are also binding to all rational beings (page 265).

Because of its emphasis on reason, the position that Kant takes is sometimes referred to as 'moral rationalism'. It is reason which brings us an understanding of the moral law – a kind of eternal standard which our actions must comply with. Kant and his followers believed in the objective reality of this moral law. It is not a law that is constructed by humans (such as a sort of legal system), but rather is a law that is discovered (like the physical laws of gravity and motion). So for Kant, our moral principles are not only determined by reason, but they have their origins in reason, and because of this they bind all rational beings in the form of duties.

The origins of moral principles in emotion/attitudes

There has been a controversy started of late concerning the general foundations of morals; whether they be derived from reason or sentiment; whether we attain knowledge of them by chain of argument and induction, or by an immediate feeling and finer internal sense.[6]

In contrast with the rationalist approach of Kant, empiricists like David Hume identified the foundations of morality in the natural world, grounded in our human nature and psychology, with their origins in our feelings and emotions. Hume has influenced modern moral philosophy in multiple ways, most significantly in the connection he drew between our moral judgements and our emotions. But before turning to that point, let us first briefly outline the other ways that he has cast his shadow over modern ethics: Hume coined the phrase 'utility', thus inspiring the utilitarians; whilst in contrast, Hume's identification of the 'is–ought gap' helped G.E. Moore in his attacks on utilitarianism. Hume's ideas also stung Immanuel Kant from his 'dogmatic slumbers', leading Kant into a productive phase of philosophical thinking that included his writings on deontological ethics; and finally, Hume's fork led to the VERIFICATION PRINCIPLE, which influenced generations of twentieth-century linguistic philosophers. Taken together, Hume's thinking on morality provides some useful context to this whole section, and understanding Hume can enrich our understanding of the main themes within meta-ethics.

As you may recall, Hume's own moral theory was a form of virtue ethics based on our emotional responses to other people's behaviour. In Hume's discussion of virtue on page 344, a different view emerged about what 'virtue' referred to – that is, about what we were judging when we called something a virtue. Aristotle thought of virtues as referring to particular character traits: courage, self-control, practical wisdom and so on. This seems like common sense: if I say that you are virtuous, then I am talking about your behaviour, the way you are disposed to

Figure 2.29 The differences between Aristotle's and Hume's views of what a virtue such as courage means.

act. But Hume disagreed, arguing that our judgement of someone's behaviour as virtuous did not spring from their behaviour, but from *our feelings* about their behaviour. So when I say that you are virtuous, I am expressing my feelings of approval about your behaviour; I am not referring to anything intrinsic in your behaviour itself. One way of putting this might be to say that, for Aristotle, our term 'virtue' reflects something 'out there' (in people's behaviour), whereas for Hume, 'virtue' reflects something 'in here' (the feelings of sympathy provoked by people's behaviour).

So Hume would disagree with the claims of the rationalists, like Kant, that our moral principles stem from reason. Instead, he argues that our moral principles have their origins in our emotions (our response to people's actions) and our attitudes to their behaviour. If Hume is correct, and if our moral principles have their origins in our emotions (rather than 'out there' in the world), then this has profound implications for our understanding of morality in general. For example, it suggests that moral judgements cannot be 'true' or 'false'; they are simply expressions of emotions, which in turn suggests that genuine moral disagreement may not be possible (page 416). We return to Hume's claim about the primacy of emotion at various points throughout this chapter, in particular when we look at his theory of moral motivation (page 388) and when we look at the group of philosophers, known as the EMOTIVISTS, whose theory of language was influenced by Hume.

The origins of moral principles in society

When we turn to look at the meaning of moral terms in the rest of this chapter, you will encounter an argument that, whilst shocking for some people, for others is merely a statement of the obvious. This is Mackie's argument that moral judgements are always false, because although we use terms like 'good' and 'right' as if they refer to something, there is nothing actually out there in the world for them to refer to. This position lies at the more extreme end of the spectrum of 'Are moral principles discovered or constructed?' For Mackie, as for many sociologists and anthropologists, our moral principles have their origins in the society we live in. The claim is that each society has its own values, and its own ways of ensuring that its citizens come to believe in its values (through its religion, its legal and education systems, its family structures, its culture and media). We might conclude from this that morality is relative to our society: different societies have different moral principles and there is no objective way of judging between them. We have encountered this position of moral RELATIVISM when looking at virtue ethics (page 337), and we return to it again when examining Mackie's arguments (page 394).

Perhaps for a sociologist or anthropologist, it is enough to observe in a fairly neutral way that 'moral principles are constructed by society', but for one nineteenth-century thinker, Karl Marx, it was absolutely critical that we understood what lay behind this construction.

'Right' can never be higher than the economic structure of society and its cultural development which this determines.[7]

For Marx, the base of all societies is not morality, or politics or religion; these are merely the layers of justification that are added after a particular type of society has been established. The real foundations of any society lie in its economics: including the relationship between those people who have power (who own the factories, the land, the oil, and so on) and those who do not (the workers). The details of each economic system change and vary over time, but there are always the haves and the have-nots, those with power and those without. Built on top of this economic base is what Marx calls the legal and political superstructure: the laws that enforce the economic relations, and the governmental systems that sanction these laws. Again, these change over time.

Emerging from this superstructure are the intellectual justifications for this particular social set-up, and these justifications come in many forms: through the construction of a society's religion, art, literature and, of course, its moral principles. According to Marx, the features most explicitly valued by societies (ethics, religion, culture and so on) are mere side effects of its economics. Marx calls these features the ideology of a given society. A society's ideology, including its moral principles, does not bring about social change, but instead it is a cunning set of devices supported by those in power to maintain their own interests, and to make it appear that what is in the interests of the ruling class is in the interests of everyone.

So Karl Marx views morality as social construction and as an expression of the ideology of the ruling class of any society. Those in power regard certain behaviours as required by moral principles, namely those which serve their own class interest, such as the respect for private property. But the notion that this serves the interest of those required to abide by such principles is a deception. For example, the ruling class regarded theft as a great evil (and subject to execution at the time that Marx was writing), precisely because they owned the property that was at risk of being stolen. Marx wanted to alert us to the fact that the moral principles we defend are not a neutral creation emerging from the whole of a society, but a highly biased construction that primarily serves the interest of a small part of society.

However, we shall see later (page 420) the issues that arise from moral relativism, most notably that it leaves no solid ground from which we (or Marx) can judge the practices of other societies as 'right' or 'wrong' – even ones that permitted slavery or human sacrifice or the oppression of women. So let us now turn to the meaning of moral terms like right and wrong, to see if we can better understand whether they refer to something constructed by humans (as Marx argues) or something that exists independently of humans.

Two key distinctions of ethical language

An interest in the meaning of moral terms and judgements like 'right' and 'wrong' became central to moral philosophy at the turn of the last century. In the 1900s, Anglo-American philosophers started to reflect on whether, over the centuries, philosophy had actually made any progress in answering philosophical questions. It occurred to some philosophers that perhaps the answers philosophers had proposed, and even the questions they had asked, might not mean anything. So these philosophers turned their attention to refining the most important tool that they had at their disposal, namely language. This change in focus, away from substantive philosophical issues towards an investigation of language, became known as the 'linguistic turn'. The emphasis of moral philosophers was no longer on normative ethics, giving us guidance on how to act; instead, it was on meta-ethics, clarifying what ethical language meant and what moral terms like 'good' and 'right' referred to.

One of the most important issues in the philosophy of language is this: do terms refer to something 'real' and 'out there' in the world, or are they something else altogether (for example, expressions of some personal feelings)? If they are making claims about something real, then we can argue about whether those claims are true or whether they are false. But if moral language does not refer to anything real, then they are not making true or false claims about the world at all. The following activity aims to tease out some of your own intuitions about this issue, about whether a term refers to something real or not.

Experimenting with ideas

For each of issues A–E, select the option that best describes your beliefs.

Then answer the additional questions below.

A Where are **rainbows?**
  1 In raindrops in the sky
  2 In cheesy songs
  3 In the minds of people who see them
  4 Nowhere

B **Beauty** is:
  1 A perfect quality that we can all have knowledge of when we see it
  2 The name of an exclusive new perfume from Paris
  3 In the eye of the beholder
  4 An evolutionary indication of health and potential child-rearing/bearing capacity

C An **electron** is:
  1 A tiny little particle that revolves around a neutron
  2 I do not know – some kind of alien from Planet Electra?
  3 A useful theoretical concept that helps us to understand certain features of the world
  4 An invention designed to make arty students drop GCSE physics

D Are postboxes actually **red?**
  1 Of course they are
  2 Not round here, because they are all covered in graffiti
  3 No, redness is a property of the mind – a mere perception
  4 *You* might see them as red, but I see them as green

E People say that murder is **wrong** because:
  1 It really is wrong to kill
  2 They are deluded, the slaves of conventional morality
  3 They have strong feelings of disapproval that need to be expressed
  4 It is true by definition: what we mean by murder is 'wrongful killing', so of course wrongful killing is wrong

Read through your answers again. For each of the words in **bold**:

1 Do you think it refers to a property or an object that exists independently of us, out there in the world?

2 Do you think it refers to something that is not independent of us, not real, and not 'out there' in the world?

If you answered 1 for any of the questions, then you are a 'REALIST' about the word in bold. Some philosophers might say that you have an 'ontological commitment' to the existence of the property or object being talked about. In other words, you believe that it actually exists independently of you, out there in the world. If you answered 3 for any of the questions, then you are an 'ANTI-REALIST' about the word in bold. We might say that you have no ontological commitment to the existence of the property or thing. In other words, you do not believe it exists in the world, and the word refers to something else (for example, some property in our mind). If you generally answered 2 or 4, then you may need to meet with your lecturer after the next class to have a little chat about your attitude.

Question E in the activity above gets to the heart of meta-ethics, raising the issue of the status of ethical language by asking, 'What do terms (like "wrong") mean?' There are two pairs of philosophical positions that we need to clarify before we look at the specific theories which attempt to answer that question. The two pairs of positions are:

- realism and anti-realism
- cognitivism and non-cognitivism.

Moral realism and anti-realism

The first pair of positions (realism and anti-realism) are broadly concerned with the question of whether the things we are talking about refer to something real, objective or 'out there' in the world. The second pair (COGNITIVISM and NON-COGNITIVISM) are concerned with whether the sentences in which we talk about these things express beliefs that are true or false.

Let us first look at the division between realism, which you would have first encountered when studying epistemology in the first part of this book, and anti-realism. We saw above that if we believe that a term (such as 'beauty') refers to something real and 'out there' in the world, then we are realists about that term. Conversely, if we believe that a term (such as 'wrong') does not refer to something out there in the world, then we are anti-realists. To illustrate the distinction between realism and anti-realism, let us look again at some of the terms given in the activity opposite.

Contested term	Academic discipline	Realists might say this term refers to …	Anti-realists might say this term refers to …
Beauty	Aesthetics	Beautiful things out there in the world	Our response to objects that we have been socially conditioned to call 'beautiful'
Red	Epistemology	The property of redness in the world	A mental image or idea of redness
Electron	Philosophy of science	A quantum object which has a negative electrical charge	A term which has a place in a complex theoretical system that usefully explains certain phenomena witnessed in laboratories
Wrong	Moral philosophy	The extent to which an action produces pain and suffering	An expression of our disapproval at certain types of action

Figure 2.30 What realists and anti-realists might say about contested terms

In **Figure 2.30**, we sketch what a realist and an anti-realist might say about the reference of some terms contested within a particular academic discipline.

It is worth noting that realists do not necessarily agree on what the precise thing is that a term refers to. There are differences among anti-realist positions too; there might be many different anti-realist accounts of what a term such as 'beauty' refers to: cultural conventions, an indication of potential child-rearing qualities, an inner feeling of desire and so on. What realists share is their claim that terms refer to something 'out there' in the world, which exists independently of our minds. What anti-realist positions share is their rejection of realism. So how might these two positions be applied to ethical language?

Let us take the statement: *It is wrong to be dishonest.*

A moral realist would say that we are making a factual claim about the world, namely that there is a property in the world somewhere, in this case, 'wrongness' (or 'badness' or 'lack of goodness'), and dishonesty possesses that property. This claim may turn out to be false – perhaps it is not always wrong to be dishonest (see page 359) – but nonetheless, a realist believes there are facts which can help us determine the truth or falsity of this claim, so at least some of our moral statements are true. Later in the chapter, we examine two of the main moral realist positions:

- Some realists, such as the utilitarians, argue that there are 'natural' properties that our moral terms pick out, such as the pleasure or pain produced by an action. This position is known as moral NATURALISM (page 373).
- Other types of realists, such as G.E. Moore, reject naturalism and argue that there are special, non-natural features of the world which our moral terms refer to and which can be known through our moral intuitions. A position of this type is known as moral *non-naturalism* (page 379).

On the other hand, an anti-realist would not agree that this (*it is wrong to be dishonest*) is a factual claim. In this chapter, you will encounter three kinds of anti-realism, and what they all have in common is the belief that there are no mind-independent moral properties or facts:

- There are moral anti-realists who argue that when using moral terms like 'wrong', we are not making a claim about the world, because this term does not actually refer to any property or fact in the world. This version of anti-realism is known as moral non-cognitivism, and we look at two types:
  - Some anti-realists, known as the EMOTIVISTS, argue that a moral term like 'wrong' is simply an expression of a feeling of disapproval (page 405).
  - Other anti-realists, known as PRESCRIPTIVISTS, argue that a moral term like 'wrong' is a way of saying to someone, 'Do not do that!' (page 410).
- However, before we look at non-cognitivist versions of anti-realism, we also examine a third type of anti-realist position, which accepts that the moral terms like 'wrong' are part of an attempt to make claims about the world. This cognitivist form of anti-realism argues that, unfortunately, these moral claims are systematically false – in other words, they can never be true, and this is because there is no property in the world that the term 'wrong' refers to at all. This version of moral anti-realism is known as ERROR THEORY (page 402).

So in moral philosophy, realists and anti-realists disagree over whether ethical sentences are making factual claims about the world and whether ethical terms refer to mind-independent properties in the world. This debate is closely related to the disagreement between our second pair of positions (cognitivism/non-cognitivism): does ethical language express beliefs that are true or false, or does it have another function entirely?

Cognitivism and non-cognitivism

Cognitivists argue that, within a particular area of human thought and discourse, sentences used in that area are ones that express beliefs: they are statements or propositions. Moreover, one of the particular properties about statements, and about the beliefs they reflect, is that they are either true or false – they have a TRUTH-VALUE, or as some philosophers say, they are 'truth-apt'. The main task for the moral cognitivist is to articulate how ethical statements are true or false. On the other hand, moral non-cognitivists reject this view, arguing that ethical language may still be meaningful, but it certainly does not consist of statements or express beliefs capable of being true or false. The main task for the non-cognitivist is to explain what ethical language is talking about if it is not talking about the world. As you will have seen from the activity above, you can be a realist and an anti-realist about different aspects of human life and discourse, and the same is true for cognitivism and non-cognitivism. For example, you may be a cognitivist about ethical language, while also being a non-cognitivist about religious language (a topic you examine in the second year of the A-level).

Let us look at an example to illustrate the difference between cognitivism and non-cognitivism: we might ask you what your A-level teachers are like, and you might reply: 'The philosophy teacher is a brilliant woman with glasses'.[8] This statement tells us that what you believe is that the philosophy teacher is a brilliant woman with glasses. Now this statement may well be false (the teacher might be a brilliant woman with 20/20 vision), but false sentences still make claims about the world (except they are false claims).

Some philosophers (most notably the logical positivists and A.J. Ayer (1910–89)) have argued that sentences are only *meaningful* if they are connected in this way to the world – that is, they describe the world either truly or falsely. So the example above is meaningful because it tries to tell us something about the world, namely what your philosophy teacher is like. It is irrelevant for this theory of meaning whether a sentence is actually true; false sentences are still meaningful because they 'paint a picture' of the world. A theory that says that sentences are meaningful because they refer to the world (either truly or falsely) is known as a cognitivist theory of meaning. **Figure 2.31** illustrates the way this might happen.

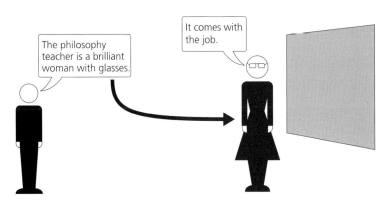

Figure 2.31 Within cognitivism, a judgement expresses our beliefs about the world (truly or falsely).

However, other philosophers have argued that there are many kinds of statements (for example, about souls, redness, beauty) which do not refer to the world at all. These types of claims are not capable of being true or false (they do not have any truth-value and are not genuine propositions). The name given to this position is 'non-cognitivism'. There are many different types of non-cognitivist theories, but what they share is a rejection of the view that certain beliefs (about souls, redness or beauty) are propositional. Taking the example above ('The philosophy teacher is a brilliant woman with glasses'), a non-cognitivist might say that the term 'brilliant' does not refer to any property in the lecturer, but may simply be an expression of approval – that this teacher is hitting all the right spots in you as a learner.

Figure 2.32 Within non-cognitivism, a statement does not express a belief about the world and is neither true nor false.

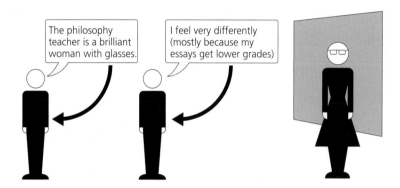

So in contrast to the cognitivists, the non-cognitivists believe that statements can be meaningful even though they do not refer to the world, and even though they cannot be shown to be true or false. The many different theories which take this approach can be thought of as 'non-cognitive', and they tend to emphasise the complexity of language, and the context within which language use takes place. You may have had disagreements with friends about whether a particular piece of music, or a film, was any good – and you may have concluded, once the shouting match had stopped, that there is no correct or incorrect answer about the aesthetic worth of the film. A non-cognitivist might resolve your dispute by saying that it is not the case that you are right and your friend is wrong, but that neither of you are making propositional claims: you are simply expressing your likes and dislikes.

Similarly, philosophers who are non-cognitivists about ethical language do not think that sentences like 'It is wrong to be dishonest' are propositions capable of being true or false. We can see how non-cognitivism can emerge from some anti-realist positions. There are moral anti-realists who argue that moral terms do not refer to any property out there in the world, but have a different function, possibly as an expression of approval or disapproval (emotivism), or perhaps as recommendations to act in a certain way (prescriptivism). Both emotivists and prescriptivists deny that ethical language refers to the world, and following from that, they both deny that ethical sentences are true or false statements, so they are both non-cognitivist positions.

Cognitivists about ethical language, however, do think that moral sentences are statements expressing true or false beliefs. It is here that we can see some overlap with moral realism, as outlined above. A moral realist believes that there are moral facts, either natural facts (like the utilitarians) or non-natural facts (as we will see with the INTUITIONISTS). Because there are these facts, a moral realist believes that ethical statements refer to these facts, and at least some of these statements are true. But there is not a straightforward overlap between moral realism and cognitivism. We saw above that there was an anti-realist position, 'error theory', that also considered moral statements in terms of their truth or falsity; and we can now see this as a cognitivist position. Error theorists claim that there are no moral facts, so although moral statements do refer to the world, they are always false (in the way that an atheist may say that claims about God are always false).

Figure 2.33 summarises the cognitivist and non-cognitivist ethical theories that we look at in the rest of this chapter, and how these theories connect to moral realism and anti-realism. The theories differ on whether there are moral facts or not; on what moral statements mean; and on what we are doing when we make moral judgements. These were the concerns of moral philosophy for much of the last century, and this chapter traces the development of meta-ethical thinking over the past 200 years.

	MORAL REALISM (Pages 372–401)		MORAL ANTI-REALISM (Pages 401–423)		
Name of the theory	Moral naturalism	Moral non-naturalism	Error theory	Emotivism	Prescriptivism
Name of philosophers associated with the theory	Bentham, Mill, Aristotle(?)	Moore	Mackie	Ayer, Stevenson	Hare
Do ethical terms refer to something mind-independent?	Yes, natural properties	Yes, non-natural properties	No (but people think they do)	No, they are expressions of emotion	No, they are commands
Is ethical language true or false?	Yes, and often true		Yes, and *always* false	No, neither true nor false	
	Cognitivism			Non-cognitivism	

Figure 2.33 Key theories of ethical language related to moral realism/anti-realism and cognitivism/non-cognitivism

---

Experimenting with ideas

Read through the following judgements and answer the questions below.

A That new ring tone on your mobile is bad.

B Lying to the police is never wrong.

C Atoms are made up of protons, neutrons and electrons.

D Your philosophy lecturer is tall.

E It was sad that her mum and dad split up.

F The creator of the universe is all-loving.

For each judgement:

1 Do you think it is either true or false – that is, it has a truth-value (you are taking a cognitivist position on this statement)?

2 Do you think it is neither true nor false – that is, it has no truth-value, but still expresses something (you are taking a non-cognitivist position on this statement)?

Moral realism

Gulliver encounters this bizarre proposal on his travels to the fictional land of Lagado, where philosophers and scientists are engaged in all sorts of madcap schemes.[10] Some philosophers in the Academy of Lagado are realists who believe that all words are names of things. Their suggestion is that it would be easier,

Figure 2.34 Realist philosophers from *Gulliver's Travels*

and would put less strain on our lungs, if we were all to carry around large bags of objects and, whenever we wanted to have a conversation with someone, we would simply take the things we needed out of our bag and then point at them in the correct sequence, so that we might be understood. So presumably these enlightened philosophers from Lagado would be able to make moral judgements by taking out of their bags the objects that the words 'good', 'bad', 'wrong' and so on referred to (whatever those objects might be!).

We have seen that realism in moral philosophy is the view that ethical facts or properties are mind-independent. For a moral realist, our ethical beliefs can be true or false, and there exist moral properties or facts which can be discovered (even if there are not actually Lagadoan moral objects that can be carried around in bags). Closely associated with realism in ethics is cognitivism, which is the idea that moral judgements can be known to be true or false because they refer to an objective moral reality. Because of this, cognivitists claim that human beings can acquire knowledge in ethics.

Realist foundations enable us to give reasons for our moral beliefs (based on the facts), and to have arguments with other people where we are genuinely disagreeing about a substantive issue (rather than simply expressing our likes and dislikes). Without these realist foundations, moral reasoning may appear empty and moral arguments become pointless (like two people arguing over which flavour of ice cream tastes the nicest – there are no objective facts that can resolve this debate (page 398)).

An important thing to note about realism is that it involves the claim that *ethical* judgements can be derived in some way from *factual* ones, be they empirical or non-empirical. And this claim involves a certain difficulty. For it is often held (as we first saw with Hume on, page 215) that it is fallacious to conclude on the basis of what *is* the case that certain things *ought* to be the case. Or, as it is sometimes put, we cannot derive an 'ought' from an 'is'. This is an important meta-ethical issue and one any realist has to deal with, and we will be returning to it again when we look again at HUME'S LAW and the naturalistic fallacy (pages 382 and 391).

But before that, we shall examine the cognitivist positions based on moral realism, which are more optimistic about ethical language, arguing that at least some of our moral statements are true. This is because the moral realist believes that ethical terms identify and pick out some feature of the world. The first realist theory we look at is naturalism, which holds that ethical concepts can be understood and defined in non-ethical terms, referring to certain objective features of the world. The second realist theory we assess is non-naturalism, which shares its realist foundations with naturalists, but disagrees with its claim that ethical terms can be reduced to non-ethical properties.

Moral naturalism

Moral naturalism looks to the world in search of moral facts and values, hoping to show that moral terms are terms which can be understood and defined by objective, natural properties in the world. The term 'naturalism' suggests a close alignment with the startling breakthroughs in the natural sciences that occurred during the eighteenth and nineteenth centuries; and just as with scientific naturalism, for the moral naturalist there can be no reference in ethics to

▶ **ACTIVITY**

Think back to the normative theories you have encountered (Divine Command theory, utilitarianism, Kantian ethics, Virtue ethics).

Which of these theories locate moral value in natural facts about the world?

non-natural properties or things; no mention of supernatural beings or spiritual/ethical realms; no reference to God, or to mysterious 'moral laws'.

So the moral naturalists try to account for, or explain, our moral concepts in terms of something in the natural world. For some critics of naturalism (most notably G.E. Moore, as we shall see below), this is problematic. These critics argue that what the naturalist is trying to do is to convert all our talk of morals into talk about something we can understand better, namely natural facts about the world and human beings. In this sense, critics say that naturalism is a reductive doctrine, in other words, that moral values can be reduced to, or explained in terms of something else. But we shall see later whether Moore is right on this matter.

In the activity on page 373, you might already have identified as naturalistic some of the moral theories we looked at in the previous chapters (such as those put forward by the utilitarians). These naturalistic theories all agree that we can analyse moral terms such as 'good' and explain them in other (naturalistic) terms – but they disagree on the precise explanation of these terms – that is, there is no consensus as to what the 'natural' properties are that moral terms refer to. In this section, we look at two forms of naturalism, both of which you are already familiar with: utilitarianism and virtue ethics.

Utilitarianism and moral naturalism

The creed which accepts as the foundation of morals the Greatest Happiness Principle holds that actions are right in proportion as they tend to promote happiness, wrong as they tend to produce the reverse of happiness. By happiness is intended pleasure, and the absence of pain.[11]

The most commonly identified naturalistic theory is utilitarianism. The hedonistic utilitarian claims that moral judgements are simply judgements about how much pleasure (a natural fact), and for how many people, an action will produce. As you may remember, Bentham begins his book *An Introduction to the Principle of Morals and Legislation* with an apparently natural fact about the psychology of human beings: namely, that we aim to secure pleasure and avoid pain. This claim is now known as psychological hedonism (hedonism comes from the Greek work *hedone*, which means 'pleasure') and this forms the naturalistic basis of Bentham's utilitarianism. From this psychological principle, Bentham goes on to draw a moral principle, which he called the utility principle, but which was later known as the greatest happiness principle. Utility, in this context, simply describes the worth of an action as is determined by the amount of pleasure and pain an action brings about. Bentham defines utility as:

… that property of an object that tends to produce benefit, advantage, pleasure, good or happiness … or … to prevent the happening of mischief, pain, evil or unhappiness.[12]

According to Bentham's reasoning, if psychological hedonism is true, and our actions are aimed at pleasure and avoiding pain, then the only reasonable moral theory is one that seeks to make such actions as consistent and effective as possible. In other words, we must follow a moral system that invokes us to maximise happiness and minimise pain (for both the individual and the sum of individuals in a community). This is the 'utility principle'. We might summarise this by saying that for Bentham, psychological hedonism implies ethical hedonism – or that a natural, descriptive fact about our psychology (that we all seek utility) implies a moral, prescriptive claim about our actions (that we ought to seek utility).

The scientific trappings of naturalism are very clear in Bentham's version of utilitarianism – his presentation of his moral theory makes it seem like another scientific success story of the nineteenth century. As you have seen, Bentham talks about a utility calculus (as if morality can be weighed up and measured by some kind of machine – see **Figure 2.35**) and he gives a detailed analysis of how the measurement of utility might be broken down. Again, Bentham uses the language of natural science in this analysis, as he talks about measuring seven different aspects of utility (that is, of the amount of pleasure or pain) in order to determine which course of action is the most utilitarian. The seven aspects we need to consider are: the intensity, duration, certainty, remoteness, fecundity, purity and extent of the pleasure or pain (see **Figure 2.4** in the utilitarianism section above).

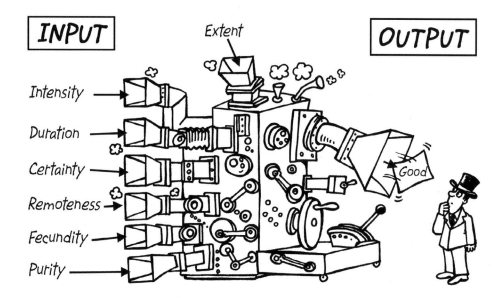

Figure 2.35 Bentham's utility calculus

There are many criticisms that can be made of Bentham's naturalistic theory and of his utility calculus (see page 211). For example, although it considers many dimensions of pleasure, the calculus ignores the quality of the pleasures and pains that are being measured. Bentham once famously wrote that pushpin (a game played in pubs at the time) was as good as poetry, and therefore that both should be treated equally in the utility calculus.[13] Mill felt that the theory needed refining, and in his book *Utilitarianism*, he defended and developed the theory. But what both Mill and Bentham have in common is their belief that moral judgements pick out natural properties in the world (the experience in sentient beings of pleasure and pain) – and this makes them firm moral realists. Moreover, because moral judgements refer to the world (to pleasures or pains), they are capable of being true or false, and this makes naturalists, like Bentham and Mill, firm cognitivists about moral language (see **Figure 2.36**).

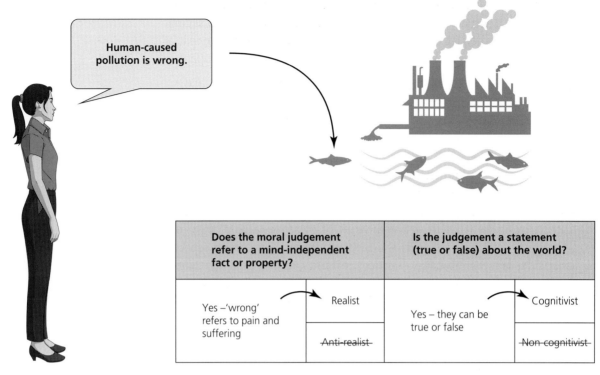

Does the moral judgement refer to a mind-independent fact or property?		Is the judgement a statement (true or false) about the world?	
Yes –'wrong' refers to pain and suffering	Realist	Yes – they can be true or false	Cognitivist
	~~Anti-realist~~		~~Non-cognitivist~~

Figure 2.36 A naturalist (utilitarian) account of moral judgements. 'Wrong' refers to a natural property of the world, i.e. pain and suffering.

We shall now turn to look at Mill's own naturalistic theory.

Mill's quote on page 374 makes it clear that he thinks that moral goodness and rightness are located in happiness, pleasure and the absence of pain. These are clearly natural terms, and in Chapter 4 of his book *Utilitarianism*, when Mill addresses the question, 'Can utilitarianism be proved?', he provides an argument that you are familiar with (page 214), which seems to build a ladder between the moral concept of 'good' and the natural facts of 'happiness' and 'pleasure'. We shall now revisit Mill's proof to see how firm the naturalistic foundations of his utilitarianism are. The examination of this proof will also neatly introduce us to one of the most damaging attacks made on naturalism (the naturalistic fallacy) and the emergence of an alternative realist approach, namely non-naturalism.

▶ ACTIVITY

Read through the extracts from Mill in anthology extract 2.2, and convert these paragraphs into a clear, stepped argument, with numbered premises and conclusions.

On the basis of this argument, why do you think utilitarianism is thought of as a form of naturalism?

What problems and weaknesses can you find in Mill's argument?

anthology 2.2

The key principle underpinning morality, according to Mill, is that 'happiness is desirable and the only thing desirable, as an end'. Mill's argument aims to show that happiness (or pleasure) is the good that we should be striving to reach, not just for us, but for everyone. In order to clarify this, it may be helpful to remind ourselves of the three important steps in Mill's proof. Step 1 attempts to show that the proof that something is desirable lies in the natural fact that it is desired and it builds on this to show that our own, individual happiness is desirable (and good) because each of us desires our own happiness. In step 2, Mill argues that because each person's (individual) happiness is good, therefore our collective happiness is the collective (moral) good. The final stage, step 3, concludes that happiness is the sole good.

Philosophers have identified problems with each step of this proof, but what concerns us here is the claim that Mill seems to be firmly grounding his ethical theory in naturalistic terms like 'desirable' and 'happiness'.

Criticism (first step)

The first step contains a fallacy, or logical error, that G.E. Moore went on to identify as the 'naturalistic fallacy'. The terms 'visible', 'audible' and 'desirable' do not all entail the same thing, so treating them as if they do is a critical mistake by Mill. The first two terms are descriptive (the first implies 'able to be seen', and the second implies 'able to be heard'), but the third term seems to smuggle in something prescriptive (it implies 'ought to be desired'). The criticism of Mill is that he has gone beyond naturalism, by conflating some natural facts about humans ('what is actually desired') with a moral concept ('what ought to be desired'). We look at Moore's naturalistic fallacy in some detail on (page 381).

The first step in the argument also gives more detail as to what is desired, and again it refers to a natural property. It is 'happiness' which Mill identifies as the object that is desired and desirable. This is the principle of psychological hedonism that Mill shares with Bentham and which is essential to utilitarianism.

Criticism (second step)

This stage in the argument is vulnerable to Hume's remarks, made a century before Mill, that moral philosophers have a tendency to glide from a discussion of what *is* the case into a discussion of what *ought* to be the case. We look at this criticism in more detail below, when we address 'the is–ought question'. The second step is attacked once again by Moore as an example of the naturalistic fallacy (page 381).

In the second step of the proof, Mill moves to the conclusion that there is a collective good which emerges from all our individual goods. It seems as if Mill is describing a mysterious 'aggregate' body – the collection of all of us – and this aggregate body desires its own good, which is the general happiness of us all. So it is not just our individual goods that refer to natural properties (our individual happiness, pleasure and pain), but it is the good in general that refers to a natural property (the sum total of our happiness, pleasure and pain).

This second step is also vulnerable to other criticisms – for example, those made by Mill's contemporary Henry Sidgwick (1838–1900),[14] and those who accuse Mill of the fallacy of composition (page 216). As you may remember, this is the fallacy of thinking that because each individual in a group shares some property in common, then the group as a whole also shares that property. So Mill is making a mistake if he concludes that the collective happiness of us all is the good, and if his reasoning behind this is that the happiness of each of us is our good. If his critics are correct, then he fails in his attempt to give firm, common-sense grounds for explaining 'good' in the natural terms of 'happiness' and 'pleasure'. In the section on the naturalistic fallacy below, we outline Moore's argument, which concludes that *any* attempt, not just the utilitarian attempts, to define good in natural terms is doomed to fail (page 382).

Virtue ethics and moral naturalism

The picture of happiness (*eudaimonia*) which is portrayed in Aristotle's *Ethics* is a much richer and deeper picture than that painted by Bentham or even Mill. Had he been alive to debate such matters, Aristotle might have despaired of the utilitarians' superficial notion of happiness, and their lack of proper beards. But Aristotle would have agreed with the utilitarians that the good we are all striving for is not derived from some mysterious realm (as perhaps his teacher Plato might have said), nor from the gods (as his contemporaries might have said), but is firmly grounded in the natural world. At first sight, both Aristotle and the twentieth-century philosophers who revived virtue ethics align closely with moral naturalism.

Hearing Aristotle described as a naturalist may not be a surprise, given the scientific approach he outlines at the start of the *Ethics*, given his interest in the natural world and given the emphasis he places on understanding what kind of beings we are, and on what we need to do in order to thrive and flourish.

We have previously emphasised (page 344) that Aristotle's concept of morality was very different to our own – for example, where we think of the moral 'good' as a value term applying to human action and judgements, and we distinguish this from the functional 'good' of can-openers and dogs (page 303). But Aristotle and the ancient Greeks would not have made that distinction. For Aristotle, there is an intimate connection, an overlapping, of the 'moral' good (that which is of highest value to us) and the functional good: if you are good at fulfilling your purpose (functional good), then that is good *for* you, not just in a self-interested sense, but in a moral sense. The moral Good is the thing that we all strive for, and we achieve it through functional goodness – that is, the virtues.

How does this relate to naturalism? Well, on the one hand, 'the good', which is the thing humans most value, is determined by looking at what, in actual fact, we all are striving for. He assesses different candidates, as any good(!) social scientist would, and having considered the claims of pleasure, wealth, honour and so on, Aristotle concludes that the good is actually *eudaimonia* – flourishing. This is simply a natural fact about human behaviour; we are all striving to live the best possible life.

On the other hand, functional goodness is determined by the type of thing that we are – in other words, by a set of very clear natural facts or properties. For Aristotle, these natural properties are determined in a teleological way. He enquires as to what our function is as human beings, and his answer lies in the biology and psychology of human beings, in our 'form' (page 307). For Aristotle, everything has its own specific form, and he determines the specific 'form' that humans have (which Aristotle calls our soul) by identifying what it is that characterises humans which makes us different from other beings, namely our capacity to reason. So here we have another natural fact about humans, that we are rational animals. If our function is to reason, then we will be good humans insofar as we reason well – and this means developing virtues (of both the intellect and character). So we can see that the key building blocks of Aristotle's ethics – virtue, *eudaimonia*, reason – are all natural properties.

However, Aristotle does not separate the normative, moral good, from the biological, functional good. Unlike utilitarianism, this is not an attempt to reduce, or interpret, moral goodness in terms of something natural (utility, pain, pleasure). Rather, Aristotle would see these two types of goodness – moral and functional – as amounting to the same thing: the good life for a human is the life of a good human (see **Figure 2.25** on page 334).

Moral non-naturalism

Intuitionism

We saw above how naturalism is the position that moral terms like 'good' and 'bad' stand for, or can be identified with, certain natural properties or facts about the world. So we can make moral judgements simply by examining, in each situation, whether those natural facts are present or absent, and thus whether the terms 'good' or 'bad' apply here. But if naturalism is wrong, and if we cannot somehow *reduce* moral terms to natural ones, then how do we come to make moral judgements? Perhaps the answer is that we just do. Moral judgements express such basic truths that we do not need to justify or explain them in terms of anything else. This rejection of a reductive position leads to the claim that moral judgements are intuitive or self-evident, and so in no need of being justified by any kind of argument. The theory that moral judgements are known intuitively is called INTUITIONISM. Like naturalism, it takes a realist position, claiming that there are moral truths to be known, and that moral judgements are capable of being true or false. Like naturalism, it is also a cognitivist theory, in that intuitionists defend the view that moral statements have meaning and express beliefs about morality that are true or false.

However, unlike moral naturalists, intuitionists think that moral predicates do not stand for natural properties, but denote special non-natural properties. These non-natural properties are seen as unique (*sui generis* is the technical philosophical term – meaning 'in its own category') and we should recognise them as such.

Intuitionism had been around for a number of centuries before the twentieth century, and in a numbers of forms, one of which was the popular 'moral sense' theory of David Hume's time. But in the early twentieth century GE. Moore's investigation into the meaning of ethical language developed into a theory that is now most commonly associated with intuitionism.

Moore's intuitionism – part 1

Beg it may be noticed that I am not an 'Intuitionist' in the ordinary sense of the term ... [W]hen I call such propositions 'Intuitions' I mean merely to assert that they are incapable of proof; I imply nothing whatever as to the manner or origin of our cognition of them.[15]

We noted above that intuitionism has had a long history, and the great debate among the moral philosophers was: 'Where do our intuitions come from?' Some, such as Francis Hutcheson (1694–1746), said our moral intuitions stemmed from an internal, God-given, moral sense (analogous to our other five senses), through which we could intuit what was right and wrong. Others, such as Samuel Clarke (1675–1729), said our intuitions stemmed from a rational faculty in our mind that had the power to grasp moral truths, in a way that is analogous to our capacity to grasp mathematical truths. G.E. Moore had no interest in this debate about the origins of our moral intuitions, which is why he said he was not an intuitionist in the ordinary sense of the term. Moore's concerns lay elsewhere.

Moore was not a great systems builder, and his influence stems from his analysis of moral concepts and language in *Principia Ethica* (1903). Not that philosophers had not analysed ethical concepts before (they had been doing that since Socrates); it is just that no moral philosopher had done it in quite the same clear and careful way that Moore did. Moore changed the face of moral philosophy, at least in Britain and America, not so much in what he said, but in the questions he asked and the way he asked them. Moore thought it was possible that moral philosophers had been trying to answer questions that simply could not be answered. So he drew the attention of Anglo-American philosophers to 'being clear about the question'.

As a consequentialist, Moore believes the moral worth of an action is determined by the good effects it brings. So we need to decide what these effects are. In other words, the question we should be asking is: 'What is Good?' The answer that Moore has reached by the end of *Principia Ethica* is that 'good' cannot be defined in natural terms (as we see on, page 381), and in fact it cannot be defined at all. Because 'good' is indefinable, it cannot be reduced to 'the greatest happiness', or to 'what people desire', or any other such non-moral good. For Moore, what is good is known intuitively, and this is why his approach is known as intuitionism.

anthology
2.15

In order to clarify what he means by indefinable, Moore likens the word 'good' to 'yellow'. If we try to say that 'yellow' means 'light travelling at a particular frequency', then we are simply wrong – 'yellow' refers to what we see when we see yellow objects, not to light-vibrations.

So, for Moore, 'yellow' is clearly comprehensible to us, yet we are not able to define it in terms of anything else. The same goes for 'good'. We know what it is when we see it, but we cannot define it in any other terms. But for Moore, it is important to note that moral properties are unlike natural properties such as 'being yellow', as we do not observe them through our ordinary senses. Moral judgements are evaluative rather than factual, so cannot be justified by purely empirical observation. Moral terms are *self-evident* and can only be known by what Moore calls 'intuition'.

Experimenting with ideas

Imagine that a series of philosophers from across history appeared on a TV quiz show and were asked the question, 'What is good?' Write down the answers that you think the following philosophers would give to that question.

Moral philosopher	Their answer to the question 'What is good?'
Aristotle	
A religious philosopher, such as Aquinas	
Kant	
Hume	
Mill	

Moore's open-question argument

The problem as Moore sees it is that all philosophers down the years have been wrong to try to define 'good' and reduce it to other terms: they have failed to see that 'good' is indefinable. In order to support this view, Moore presents us with a dilemma. When we ask the question, 'What is good?', Moore says that we are faced with three possibilities:

1 'Good' is indefinable.
2 'Good' is definable.
3 'Good' means nothing at all and 'there is no such subject as ethics'.[16]

The last option is given short shrift and rejected almost out of hand, which leaves us with only two options: either good is definable or it is not. In order to show that good cannot be defined, Moore offers an argument which has become known as the open question argument. Consider the argument as follows. Any theory which attempts to define 'good' (for example, naturalism) is saying something equivalent to:

'Good' means X (where X is some fact or set of facts).

But, says Moore, for any such definition it will always make sense to ask:

But is X really good?

So, for example, if a utilitarian says, 'Good means maximising pleasure and minimising pain for the majority', it still makes sense to ask, 'But is it really good to maximise pleasure and minimise pain for the majority?' In fact (as we saw with some of the examples against utilitarianism), not only does this question make sense, but it is a question we would want to ask when some innocent person is being punished on utilitarian grounds (for example, to placate an angry mob).

Moore goes on. If 'good' can be defined as X, then it should not make any sense to ask, 'But is X really good? We can see this by looking at another definition, such as 'A bachelor is an unmarried man'. It just does not make sense then to ask, 'But is an unmarried man really a bachelor?' because we would then be asking, 'But is a bachelor really a bachelor?' which is an absurd question.[17] However, asking a utilitarian, 'But is maximising happiness really good?' *is not* the same as asking, 'But is good really good?' Yet if the naturalist were right, then the first question would be trivial: it *would* be like asking whether good is good. So the proposed definition must be inadequate. It must mean that 'good' and 'maximising happiness' are not the same. For Moore, we can always meaningfully pose the question, 'But is X really good?' for every definition of good, including all naturalistic ones. It remains an open question whether or not it really is good. Moore believes that this open question argument shows that good is not definable, ruling out option 2 and thus undermining all meta-ethical theories that attempt to reduce "good" to a simple definition. This leaves only option 1, namely that good is indefinable.

The naturalistic fallacy

Having established that good is indefinable, Moore goes on to highlight the fallacy that he believes occurs in many arguments given by moral philosophers. The basic form of the fallacy is easy to understand: a term that is indefinable cannot be defined, and any attempt to define the indefinable is clearly fallacious. Armed with this, Moore has a field day in his attack on naturalism, as he sees this fallacy occurring all over the place in such theories. Remember that according to

Moore, the concept 'good' is indefinable, so it is a non-natural concept (it cannot be defined in terms of anything natural). But naturalists such as the utilitarian philosopher John Stuart Mill are not only attempting to define 'good' (a fallacy, because 'good' is indefinable), but they are trying to do so in naturalistic terms (a fallacy because 'good' is non-natural). What fools, thinks Moore. How could they have failed to see this? So all forms of naturalism are rejected by Moore because they are all guilty of the naturalistic fallacy. It is worth remembering that for Moore, the naturalistic fallacy is just a special case of the more general fallacy of defining the indefinable.

Moore was very clear that Mill had committed the naturalistic fallacy (on page 377). According to Moore's interpretation, Mill attempts to define 'good' as 'desired', and then he goes on to say that it is happiness that we desire. Moore says:

> the fallacy in this step is so obvious, that it is quite wonderful how Mill failed to see it.[18]

It seems clear to Moore that Mill is trying to define, in naturalistic terms, the indefinable (that is, 'good') – which is the naturalistic fallacy. This attack on Mill's theory is what Moore became most famous for, and many philosophers took this to spell the end for utilitarianism. But is Mill guilty of the naturalistic fallacy? You may remember that Mary Warnock thinks not, and let us repeat our summary of her position here. She argues that Mill is not interested in defining what 'good' is, nor is he interested in defining what 'desirable' is. He does not, Warnock says, define 'desirable' or 'good' at all.[19] According to Warnock, Mill's project is primarily an empirical one: he is describing for us what sorts of things are, as a matter of fact, considered good. Mill is trying to persuade us of the truth of utilitarianism by informing us that people already consider happiness to be good (and desirable). But that is not to say (as Moore believes) that Mill therefore considers the 'good' to mean 'happiness' or 'pleasure' and so on. If it turned out that people considered something else (say pain) to be fundamentally desirable, then it would be this thing, pain, that was the good.

According to Warnock, Mill was just pointing out that people already pursue happiness as a worthwhile goal, so they already believe it to be good (no further proof is necessary). In which case, Mill is not committing the naturalistic fallacy, and Moore's most famous argument fails to meet its mark.

Moore's argument against naturalism has parallels with Hume's law (page 391), because it is drawing a sharp distinction between the moral realm and the non-moral realm. But Hume's argument is about the logical connection between these realms (you cannot derive an 'ought' from an 'is'), whereas Moore's argument is about the linguistic or semantic connection between moral and non-moral terms. In a nutshell, Moore is saying that any attempt to give a naturalistic account of what it is to do good still leaves open the question of whether behaving in accordance with that account would be the morally good thing to do.

Moore's intuitionism – part 2

The negative part of Moore's argument is over. He believes that he has established that good cannot be defined, and that any attempt to define it will be fallacious.

He also believes that we know what is good, not through analysing it in ordinary, naturalistic terms (such as weighing up pleasure and pain), but through our discriminating intuitive faculty. So what is the positive part of Moore's argument? What does Moore think we should be striving for? In other words, what actually is good according to Moore?

Goods may all be said to consist in the love of beautiful things or of good persons.[20]

At the end of *Principia Ethica*, Moore describes those things he believes to be good (although he obviously does not define them, because to define them would be to commit the fallacy of defining the indefinable!). This final chapter, entitled 'The Ideal', is a fairly gushing account of the things that Moore believes are intrinsically valuable. Among these goods are, most importantly, the love of friendship and beauty. For Moore, we must strive to bring about these goods, and we must consider our actions in terms of their consequences: of whether they promote these goods or damage them. Alasdair MacIntyre points out that there was a large group of intellectuals, artists and writers (known as the Bloomsbury Group) who lapped up this final chapter, even calling it 'the beginning of a renaissance'.[21] Some would question, however, whether Moore was correct to say that love of friendship and beauty are 'by far the most valuable things which we know or can imagine' (*Principia Ethica*, section 113). If this is as far as our values extend then, as MacIntyre says, Moore has a somewhat impoverished view of what good is.

Experimenting with ideas

Moore identifies a) the love of beauty and b) the love of friendship as two goods that we should be striving for.

What other goods do you think need to be added to this list in order to make it more complete?

For MacIntyre, it was as if Moore had given some theoretical justification for the values that these intellectuals already held dear. But this raises the more important question of who is to judge whose intuitions of the 'good' are the correct intuitions? The hedonistic utilitarians could argue about which action promoted the most happiness, but because Moore believes the good is indefinable, we cannot really find common ground from which to resolve disagreements. At its most extreme end, we find moral intuitions that are despicable. For example, Rudolf Höss, the commandant of Auschwitz (the Nazi extermination camp where over a million Jews were murdered), wrote in his memoirs after the war that he felt what he had done was 'right'. Mill at least could give reasons against Höss's intuition by pointing to the enormous suffering of the victims of the Holocaust, but Moore could not give reasons against the Nazis beyond saying that 'their intuitions clashed with most other people's intuitions'.

So how should we categorise Moore? Is he a moral philosopher, or a philosopher of language? Does he support a utilitarian approach, or is he against it? In the final chapter of *Principia Ethica*, it becomes clear that Moore is not primarily a linguistic philosopher, although it was his attention to language that made him so influential. He had, after all, drawn the attention of moral philosophers to the precise nature of the questions they were trying to answer. But that was not all he was doing, as can be seen from that last section. Moore, like Bentham and Mill before him, is genuinely concerned with what things are good. Given that this search for what is good is so important to Moore, it is perhaps unfortunate that he is now mainly remembered as the man who accused Mill of the 'naturalistic fallacy'. Despite this rejection of naturalistic utilitarianism, Moore has sympathies with a utilitarian approach. First, he is a realist, like Bentham and Mill, because he believes that 'good' refers to something out there in the world. Second, he is a cognitivist, like Bentham and Mill, because he believes that moral judgements are propositions about the world, capable of being true or false (see **Figure 2.37**).

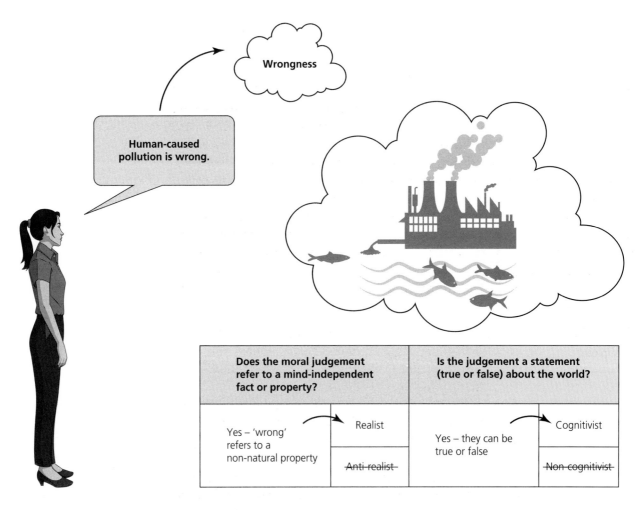

Figure 2.37 A non-naturalist (intuitionist) account of moral judgements. 'Wrong' refers to a non-natural property of the world, which we have an intuitive awareness of.

Third, Moore is a consequentialist, because he identifies moral value as lying in the outcome of actions. Fourth, some philosophers have even called Moore an 'ideal' utilitarian: ideal because he believes that goods we seek to bring about are 'ideal goods', things that are intrinsically good to a high degree. Perhaps most significantly, though, Moore is an intuitionist because he believes these values were knowable by intuition. And it was Moore's intuitionism that brought about the attack from the group of philosophers known as the 'emotivists', as we shall see below.

Issues with moral realism

The certainties that religion brought to Western moral thought – that there is a moral law, that morality is objective, that right and wrong, good and bad refer to something real and so on – have gradually unravelled over the past 300 years, since the European Enlightenment. The utilitarians appeared to have some success giving a naturalistic foundation to ethics that was objective, whilst not being religious. G.E. Moore and the intuitionists, who highlighted the problems with moral naturalism, offered a substitute that itself received widespread criticism. Moral realists have not had an easy ride over the past hundred years, and in this section we examine some further issues with the realist position that for many philosophers meant that realism had to be rejected.

Issue: Hume's fork and Ayer's verification principle

One of the strongest attacks on realism as a moral theory came from A.J. Ayer (1910–89). Ayer was a British philosopher who was very much under the influence of a group of Austrian philosophers who met in the 1920s and 1930s under the name of the Vienna Circle. These philosophers were angered by the gibberish that they thought many philosophers, particularly in the nineteenth century, had a tendency to spout. They contrasted the failure of metaphysics to progress with the success of nineteenth-century scientists, who had developed an empirical (positivist) method and had brought clarity to our understanding of the world. The Vienna Circle argued that this scientific/positivist methodology should be adopted by philosophy, and logic should be the tool to help philosophers analyse language and identify, and avoid talking about, nonsense. Their approach to philosophy became known as 'logical empiricism' or 'logical positivism', and in the first publication of the Vienna Circle in 1929, they cited Scottish enlightenment philosopher David Hume as one of their main predecessors.[22]

David Hume, writing in the mid-1700s, was a natural sceptic, who used his empiricist approach to philosophy in order to cast doubts on some fundamental metaphysical assumptions: that there is a God; that miracles are possible; that morality is founded on religion or reason; that there is a 'self' inside us; that causation exists ... the list goes on. But Hume did not simply introduce doubt and scepticism and then walk away from these issues; he sought to avoid the ungrounded and fanciful claims of metaphysics through a more analytical and careful approach to philosophy – what he terms 'mitigated scepticism'. This means accepting that although human knowledge is limited, it is still possible to gain some knowledge through the cautious application of reason and science. In his book *A Treatise of Human Nature*, Hume draws a distinction that you are familiar with as Hume's fork (page 125).

Reason is the discovery of truth or falsehood. Truth or falsehood consists in an agreement or disagreement either to the real relations of ideas, or to real existence and matter of fact. Whatever, therefore, is not susceptible of this agreement or disagreement, is incapable of being true or false, and can never be an object of our reason.[23]

So for Hume, our reasoning, which is aimed at discovering truths about the world, should be limited to these two lines of enquiry: 1) relations of ideas, meaning the way that our ideas and concepts are logically connected and follow on from one another, or as Hume says, 'abstract reasoning concerning quantity or number' – as, for example, in logic and mathematics; and 2) matters of fact, meaning those things that we directly experience in the world, which are present to our senses, which we observe, can test or measure, or as Hume says, 'experimental reasoning concerning matters of fact' – as, for example, in the sciences. If our lines of enquiry, our discussions, or our concepts drift outside of these two categories, then alarm bells should ring. Hume says (only half-jokingly) that books written about subjects falling outside of these categories should be committed to the flames of a bonfire, for they will contain nothing but sophistry and illusion (see **Figure 1.33**, page 128).

▶ **ACTIVITY**

Read the moral statements below and apply Hume's fork to them. Which would you keep (are they relations of ideas or matters of fact?), and which would you commit to the flames?

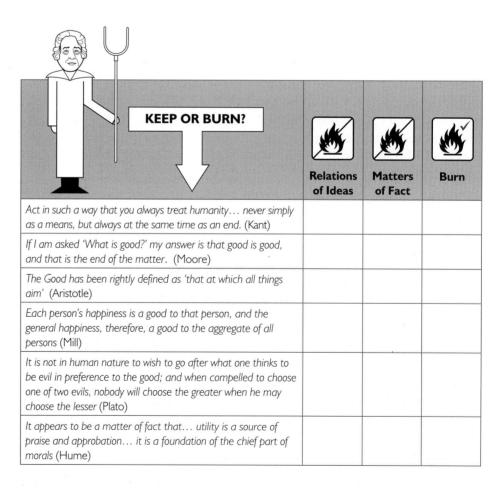

KEEP OR BURN?	Relations of Ideas	Matters of Fact	Burn
Act in such a way that you always treat humanity… never simply as a means, but always at the same time as an end. (Kant)			
If I am asked 'What is good?' my answer is that good is good, and that is the end of the matter. (Moore)			
The Good has been rightly defined as 'that at which all things aim' (Aristotle)			
Each person's happiness is a good to that person, and the general happiness, therefore, a good to the aggregate of all persons (Mill)			
It is not in human nature to wish to go after what one thinks to be evil in preference to the good; and when compelled to choose one of two evils, nobody will choose the greater when he may choose the lesser (Plato)			
It appears to be a matter of fact that… utility is a source of praise and approbation… it is a foundation of the chief part of morals (Hume)			

Like those thinkers in the Vienna Circle, Ayer was greatly affected by Hume's ideas, and in particular by Hume's fork. Having stayed in Vienna directly after university, in 1936 the (very) young Ayer wrote a book called *Language, Truth and Logic*, which popularised logical positivism in Britain and America. The theory of meaning that is now associated with Ayer is the verification principle and it is a kind of test that sentences must pass if they are to be judged genuinely meaningful. As you might guess from Ayer's empiricist roots, the verification principle emerged from the ideas behind Hume's fork, and it states that:

A sentence is meaningful if and only if:

- it is a tautology (that is, true by definition), or
- it is verifiable through sense experience.

What the principle is saying is that in order to say something meaningful, we must know what makes our statement true. Ayer believed that if a statement was not a tautology (that is, true by definition), and if there was no empirical way of discovering its truth, then it was meaningless. Like all positivists, Ayer put a lot of faith in science and in our observations of the world. He used the verification principle as a tool to sort out the good from the bad, the philosophical sheep from the metaphysical goats.

anthology
2.16

Experimenting with ideas

Read through the following sentences and decide for each whether or not it meets. Ayer's verification principle (that is, whether it is capable of being true or false).

1 Stealing money is wrong.
2 There is life after death.
3 A triangle has three sides.
4 It is good to give money to charity.
5 It is your duty to tell the truth.
6 There are tiny pixies that live in my fridge who disappear without trace as soon as I open the door.
7 The universe is expanding.
8 Bondi Beach contains more than 1 billion particles of sand.
9 It is wrong to abort a 20-week-old foetus.
10 The sunset over Victoria Falls is the most beautiful sight on earth.

Let us apply the first criterion of the verification principle to moral judgements: are statements like, 'stealing money is wrong', true by definition? You may know that to deny a genuine tautology leads to a contradiction. For example, 'a triangle has three sides' is a tautology, and 'this triangle does not have three sides' is a contradiction. But we can state, and perhaps even argue, that 'stealing money is not wrong' without contradiction. So for Ayer, moral judgements fail the first criterion of the verification principle.

What about the second criterion? For Ayer, a claim such as 'it is good to give to charity' cannot be verified by any empirical investigation. We can make any number of observations of charity giving, and we could discover, in the process, how much wealth changes hands, how much suffering is relieved as a consequence and so forth, but we would never be able to prove in the process

anthology
2.17

that the practice is good. For 'good' is not something that can be observed. Hume made a similar point about what he calls 'vice' or moral evil. If I observe a morally evil act, such as a murder, I can describe precisely what happens in terms of what my senses reveal – the kind of weapon used, the entry wound, the age of the assailant and victim and so on – just as a conscientious policeman would. But nowhere in that description would the evil be mentioned, precisely because it cannot be observed with the senses. For Hume, moral judgements do not refer to anything in the 'outside' world, but are statements referring to our inner emotions (our sympathy and the feelings of approval and disapproval that are aroused when we observe virtuous or vicious behaviour). This makes Hume a kind of subjective realist!

Adherents of logical positivism go further than Hume and they conclude that though moral judgements *appear* to be statements, they are not actually statements (they are not capable of being true or false), as they fail both criteria of the verification principle. So what does Ayer have to say about moral judgements, which include such terms as 'right' and 'good'? He agreed with those who claimed that these terms were unanalysable, but that is because he said there is nothing to analyse. 'Good' and 'right' are what Ayer calls 'pseudo-concepts': they do not refer to anything at all – and so moral realism is incorrect. It follows that if they do not refer to any property of the world, then moral judgements are not propositions and are not capable of being true or false – so cognitivism when applied to moral statements is also incorrect.

According to Ayer's verification principle, moral judgements are therefore meaningless and we need to look elsewhere to understand the role that ethical terms and statements play in our language. We examine Ayer's own theory of the meaning of moral judgements when we look at the theory of emotivism (page 405).

Issue: Hume's argument that moral judgements are not beliefs, since beliefs cannot motivate us

Hume's influence on meta-ethics, and our assessment of the strength of the realist position, does not stop with Hume's fork. Hume's first great work of philosophy was the wide-ranging and far-reaching *A Treatise of Human Nature*, which Hume seemed to think would be an eighteenth-century best-seller. Apparently, there is not much cash to be made in writing philosophy books, and the *Treatise* did not turn out to be quite the money-spinner that Hume had hoped for (as he wrote later, his book 'fell still-born from the [printing] press'). But it went on to become one of the most influential works of philosophy in the English language. The *Treatise* is an ambitious book, applying empiricism to human thought, concepts, understanding and feelings. Hume realised that his empiricist approach, and his application of 'mitigated scepticism', could also be very usefully applied to clarify our moral thinking. In the opening section of Book 3 of the *Treatise*, Hume raises two questions that have become central to meta-ethics. The first is the issue of moral motivation: what drives us towards moral actions, virtues and vices? The second is the issue of the division between descriptive statements (what *is* the case) and evaluative judgements (what *ought* to be the case). We examine this 'is–ought' question in the next section, but first let us turn to the Humean theory of moral motivation (note, this is not a misspelling of 'human').

So what is it that motivates us to action? Hume's contemporaries, the moral rationalists and religious philosophers of his day, argued that it was reason and belief, but Hume disagrees – he thinks that moral motivation lies in our feelings and emotions, and his answer had profound implications for the direction of moral philosophy. Hume provides several arguments in support of the conclusion that morality is not motivated by reason, and the conclusion is arrived at in this way:

1 A moral judgement motivates us to act: if we think of something as good, then generally we take actions to get it; if we think of something as bad, then we act to avoid it. (This is called 'internalism' – see page 400.)
2 Reason and belief, by themselves, cannot motivate us to act. (This is the Humean theory of motivation.)
3 Therefore moral judgements are not founded on reasons or belief.

Having rejected reason as a possible foundation for moral judgements, Hume concludes that moral judgements are founded on the 'passions' – in other words, our non-rational feelings, emotions and desires. Let us look at premise 2 to understand the arguments that Hume gives in his rejection of reason as a motivation for action.

The first argument turns on the clear distinction that Hume, along with many other philosophers, including Aristotle, makes between our reason and our feelings. You have already looked at Hume's analysis of reason when examining Hume's fork page 385. Our reason helps us to determine truth from falsehoods, and it uses the two prongs of Hume's fork to do this. Reason makes connections and draws conclusions through 'relations of ideas' (including logic and maths) and 'matters of fact' (including our everyday experience and scientific experiments).

The question is this: if the proposal is that moral judgements are founded on reason, then which of these categories do moral judgements come under? As you have seen, Hume's answer is that moral judgements fall into neither category, but let us have a look at this quote in full (and with the original spellings):

> *Reason is the discovery of truth or falshood. Truth or falshood consists in an agreement or disagreement either to the **real** relations of ideas, or to **real** existence and matter of fact. Whatever, therefore, is not susceptible of this agreement or disagreement, is incapable of being true or false, and can never be an object of our reason. Now 'tis evident our passions, volitions, and actions, are not susceptible of any such agreement or disagreement; being original facts and realities, compleat in themselves, and implying no reference to other passions, volitions, and actions. 'Tis impossible, therefore, they can be pronounced either true or false, and be either contrary or conformable to reason.*[24]

389

Hume's second argument against reason and belief as a motivator for *moral* action is a psychological argument – it is that, as a matter of fact, reason does not motivate us at all. And if reason does not motivate us to action at all, then it certainly cannot motivate us through moral judgements or the development of virtues and vices.

Since morals ... have an influence on the actions and affections, it follows, that they cannot be derived from reason; and that because reason alone, as we have already proved, can never have any such influence. Morals excite passions, and produce or prevent actions. Reason of itself is utterly impotent in this particular. The rules of morality, therefore, are not conclusions of our reason.[25]

We have seen that reason plays an important role in our thinking; Hume observes that it helps us to discover the truth and falsity of our beliefs. But for Hume, reason remains neutral with regard to how we should act – in other words, reason and belief do not motivate us to action. Instead it is our passions (our emotions and feelings and desires) that motivate us to act. You may remember that Aristotle shared a similar view about the role of emotions that drive us (outlined on page 332). But where Aristotle saw practical reason as an equal partner in action, Hume disagrees and sees reason as playing a more subservient role to our emotions. As Hume famously put it:

Reason is, and ought only to be, the slave of the passions, and can never pretend to any other office than to serve and obey them[26]

For example, you might believe that there is a jar of Marmite in your cupboard, and when you arrive home after a long day of A-level study, you perceive that in fact there is a jar of Marmite in your cupboard. But this matter of fact does not, in itself, motivate you to action. Instead, it is your desire (or not) to eat, and your desire (or not) to consume Marmite in particular, that motivates you to action – to reach for the Marmite and spread it onto the buttery toast. That is a fairly uncontroversial example, despite the manufacturer's claim that the sticky brown substance divides the nation in two: either you love it or you hate it. (Editor's note: other yeast-based spreads are available.) Hume gives other, more controversial examples – for example, of people who care more about their own mild discomfort than they do about the deaths of thousands of people on the other side of the world. Even though this might sicken us, Hume is arguing that it is not contrary to reason for people to have such self-oriented preferences and desires. The theory that we are moved to act by our passions, and not by reason, is known as the Humean theory of motivation. What are the implications of this theory for realism?

Hume's targets in Book 3 of the *Treatise* were rationalist and religious accounts of morality, which located the foundations of moral judgements in reason or in God, both of which Hume wished to undermine. But Hume's account of moral judgements as motivated by passion, and not belief, goes some way to undermine all moral realist positions, whether rationalist, religious, naturalist or intuitionist. For the moral realist, moral judgements refer to something 'out there' in the world, independently of our minds. A moral realist also thinks that it is possible for our moral beliefs and judgements to reflect the world in a way that is true or false – in other words, they are cognitivists about moral judgements (page 369). But Hume's theory of moral motivation points specifically towards a different conclusion. It implies that moral judgements are not true or false (they are neither relations of ideas, nor matters of fact), but instead have their source in our passions and emotions: they do not reflect any truths about the world. So Hume's theory eats away at the very foundations of moral realism.

We return to how Hume's arguments inspired philosophers in the twentieth century, who rejected moral realism and went on to embrace a new anti-realist theory called emotivism, on page 405.

Issue: Hume's is–ought gap

In Book 3 of his *Treatise*, Hume makes another observation about moral philosophy that was incisive, insightful and inspired other philosophers to explore new avenues of meta-ethical thinking. The observation became known as the is–ought gap.

You have already encountered this in one of the criticisms made above against the second step of Mill's argument (page 216), which seemed to reveal a fundamental flaw in naturalism. Many philosophers have insisted that an important distinction needs to be made between *matters of fact* and *matters of value*, between description and evaluation, between 'is' and 'ought'. Such philosophers go on to say that the distinction is such that we cannot argue from one to the other. Hume appears to have been the first philosopher to have made explicit this worry about the is–ought gap, and his idea has also become known as 'Hume's law'. There is a small paragraph buried in his *Treatise of Human Nature* that raises this point (it occurs as an afterthought to the discussion on moral motivation, outlined above), and in the twentieth century this controversy fuelled many books and articles. Hume actually wrote the following:

anthology
2.18

> In every system of morality which I have hitherto met with, ... the author proceeds for some time in the ordinary way of reasoning, and establishes the being of a God, or makes observations concerning human affairs; when of a sudden I am surprised to find, that instead of ... is and is not, I meet with ... ought, or an ought not[. It] seems altogether inconceivable, how this new relation can be a deduction from others, which are entirely different from it.[27]

What Hume says in this passage is that we cannot infer anything about what *ought* to be the case from any number of facts about what *is* the case. So, for example, the fact that humans can and do frequently eat meat does not entail therefore that they ought to eat meat. But Hume complained that too many moralists and philosophers ignore this simple principle. So this passage seems to support our intuitions about the AUTONOMY OF ETHICS, the view that moral judgements are completely different from other sorts of judgements. As we have seen, for Hume, the difference between moral judgements and other sorts of judgements lies in the motivating power of those judgements: moral judgements directly drive and influence action, whereas factual judgements do not motivate us to act in the same way. **Figure 2.38** shows the division between the moral realm and the natural realm.

In the twentieth century, many philosophers also took Hume's law to support their view that there is a fundamental distinction between facts and values, and that moral judgements are essentially different from factual propositions. So naturalism appears to be in big trouble because it *does* seem to draw evaluative conclusions (those in the moral realm) from non-moral premises (taken from the natural realm). Mill's 'proof' of utilitarianism seems to be particularly susceptible to this criticism. Mill is starting out by claiming that people happen to desire happiness; then he moves to say that therefore happiness is desirable and is a good – in other words, that people ought to desire happiness. If Hume is right, then Mill cannot so easily take the step from psychological hedonism (the factual, descriptive claim that humans seek happiness) to ethical hedonism (the moral, prescriptive claim that humans ought to seek happiness).

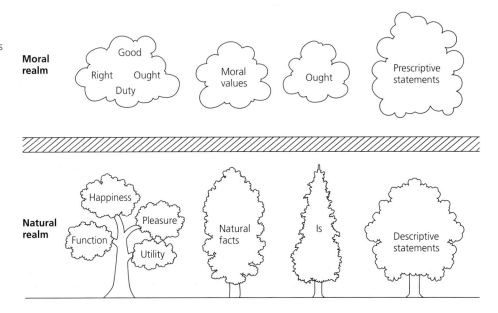

Figure 2.38 The autonomy of ethics suggests that concepts in the moral realm cannot be derived from concepts in the natural realm

Criticism

But Hume's law, at least as stated by Hume, does not support this attack on naturalism. In fact, Hume was himself a naturalist (he thought that our moral judgements were based ultimately on sympathy – a natural emotion). Hume is making a simple logical point. A deductively valid argument cannot slip into its conclusion any information that is not already in its premises. So no matter how much factual information I provide you with about some state of affairs, you cannot legitimately conclude (on factual grounds alone) anything about what *ought* to be the case. This is because the 'ought', as Hume says, 'expresses some new relation or affirmation'. So Hume's claim is a simple claim about what can and cannot legitimately be done when constructing an argument. We might restate Hume's law as this: *it is invalid to derive an evaluative conclusion (ought) from premises that are purely descriptive (is)*. It is worth noting that this goes for all valid deductive arguments, not just ones in moral philosophy: a conclusion must be based solely on what is in the premises, it cannot suddenly smuggle in new information.

Experimenting with ideas

Which of the following arguments do you think break Hume's law?

1. P Everyone desires happiness
   C Therefore happiness is desirable
2. P In order to flourish, we must fulfil our function well
   P Our function is to reason
   C Therefore we ought to reason well
3. P He is the captain
   C Therefore he ought to fulfil his duties as a captain
4. P It is wrong to cause pain
   P An abortion causes a foetus pain
   C Therefore, it is wrong to have an abortion
5. P You promised to pay back that £5
   C Therefore you ought to pay back the £5
6. P It is bedtime
   C Therefore you ought to brush your teeth

Hume is not saying that we should *never* appeal to matters of fact in order to justify our moral judgements. For example, I may want to argue that abortion is wrong (a moral judgement) by pointing out that a foetus can experience pain (a matter of fact). But according to Hume's law, if I wish to propose such an argument, I cannot rely on facts alone. If the facts are to support the moral judgement, then there must also be supporting premises which refer to some moral standards – in this case, for example, the additional premise that 'It is wrong to cause pain'.

To illustrate this idea, consider the following very simple argument, put forward night after night by tired and irritable parents up and down the country: 'Clean your teeth.' 'Why?' 'Because it is bedtime.' We can summarise this argument as follows:

P It is bedtime
C Therefore, you ought to brush your teeth

Although this is a prudential, not a moral, 'ought' (see page 264), the argument as it stands still violates Hume's law. The *fact* that it is bedtime cannot by itself give parents any reason to conclude that their children ought to brush their teeth. The premise merely states a fact, so cannot force any value judgement upon you. It may well be bedtime and yet not a good thing for you to brush your teeth (perhaps you have brushed them ten times already).

Nonetheless, the fact that it is bedtime clearly could be an important consideration in drawing a conclusion concerning what you *ought* to do (if you always go to bed without brushing your teeth, eventually they will fall out). But this, according to Hume, can only be because we are making certain assumptions in the argument which have not been made explicit. In this case, we may be assuming that it is a good thing for children to brush their teeth before sleeping (to avoid losing their teeth). So, to make the argument valid, we need to make this hidden assumption explicit:

P1 It is bedtime
(P2 At bedtime you ought to brush your teeth)
C Therefore, you ought to brush your teeth

This complete argument is now clearly valid. So Hume's point is not that facts are irrelevant to values and that we can never appeal to facts when drawing moral conclusions. Rather, his point is that we need to make our values explicit when arguing, so that we can be clear about what the argument really is.

Criticism

However, the American philosopher John Searle (1932–) has even questioned the claim that we cannot derive evaluative conclusions from descriptive premises.[28] Searle argued that there are exceptions to the claim that you cannot derive an 'ought' from an 'is'. Consider the following argument, adapted from the activity on page 391:

P You promised to pay me back my £5
C So you ought to pay up

Here the premise states a matter of fact: the fact that you made a promise to pay me back my money. And the conclusion makes a value judgement about what you ought to do. But this argument seems perfectly in order. The fact that you have made a promise seems clearly to imply that you ought to keep it, and so suggests that it is possible to bridge the is–ought gap. Searle is claiming that there are certain facts about human beings – for example, that they have instituted a practice of promise-keeping – which have implications for how they ought to act, and so perhaps some form of naturalism could be true after all.

How might Hume react to an example like this in defence of his law? One thing he might try is to find some hidden evaluative premise. Is there a hidden premise here so obvious that it seems not worth stating? In this case, the hidden premise might be, 'We ought to keep our promises'. If we were to add this, we would make the argument valid and would not have moved from an 'ought' to an 'is' (because there was an 'ought' buried in one of the premises). Another way of avoiding Searle's conclusion might be to point out that the meaning of 'promise' involves appeal to our moral obligations. So that if we fully explain the meaning of the premise becomes, 'You have made a *moral* undertaking to do something or other', and from this it seems unproblematic to conclude that you *ought* to undertake it. But here we have only moved from 'oughts' to 'oughts'. So, on this defence, the attempt to bridge the gap simply introduces values in the premises.

Issue: Mackie and the argument from relativity

Moral realism strikes a chord with many people's intuitions: our moral judgements feel like they are referring to something that actually exists: when we have an argument with someone about a moral dilemma, we think we are disagreeing about something real; when we finally see what the right thing to do is, it seems to be accompanied by a (moral) force that comes from outside of us. We could call this common-sense view 'naïve moral realism', with a nod to the naïve realism that you studied as part of the Epistemology section (page 53). Except our naïve moral realism can be turned into a more sophisticated theory and given credibility by the intellectual weight of philosophers like Kant and Mill and the spiritual traditions of religion everywhere. However, moral realism, even in its more sophisticated forms, is vulnerable to criticism under closer scrutiny, as we have seen with the three issues that we investigated above:

● Hume and A.J. Ayer seemed to be onto something when they asked, 'What are moral judgements about?' and concluded that they were not about the world, but are 'about' our emotional response to the world (page 388).

● Hume went deeper in this analysis giving strong grounds against the rationality of moral judgements – they are not beliefs about the world because beliefs cannot motivate us (and morality does motivate us).

● Hume's analysis has also been used to erode the foundations for a version of moral realism known as 'naturalism' – through identifying an unbridgeable is–ought gap that lies between the natural (descriptive) realm and the moral (prescriptive) realm.

These are complex, nuanced criticisms, which hinge on a careful conceptual analysis of moral realism and of what it is attempting to do. But there is another set of criticisms, outlined by J.L. Mackie in *Ethics: Inventing Right and Wrong*, which really go for the jugular. Mackie's title says it all, in that he thinks we are all kidding ourselves if we believe our values refer to anything 'real' that actually exists. For Mackie, our common-sense assumptions (our 'naïve' moral realism) are wrong, but most ethical thinkers ('sophisticated' moral realists from Aristotle to Kant, from Mill to Moore) are also wrong: we are all just making up morality, and we need to understand this delusion before we can move forward in our ethical thinking.

Mackie wishes to show that morality is not 'objective', it is 'subjective'. Having been forced to study grammar for several years, you will be familiar with the difference between the object of a sentence and the subject of a sentence. But in philosophy they have special meanings: a subject is a person, a conscious being who is able to think, perceive and feel, and something is 'subjective' if it is dependent on that person thinking, perceiving, feeling and so on. 'Objective' is the opposite of this. Perhaps 'objective' makes you think of something unbiased, but to a philosopher it means something that is independent of any subject (any conscious being), existing as part of the fabric of the universe. Moral realists believe that morality is objective, but Mackie thinks they are wrong.

We examine Mackie's theory (which is referred to as error theory) on page 402, and it depends on two arguments that he puts forward for rejecting moral realism: the argument from relativity and the argument from queerness. We will return to the argument from queerness on page 399, but in the remainder of this section we examine Mackie's argument from relativity.

Mackie does not present his argument from relativity in a formal way, but we could try to summarise it in the following form, as an argument to the best explanation (abduction, page xiv):

1 There are variations and some radical differences between moral codes from society to society (moral judgements appear to be made relative to each society).

2 Accompanying these radical differences are disagreements between people about moral codes.

3 Disagreements may occur between people either because:
  A there is an objective truth about the matter, but people's perceptions of it are distorted in various ways – for example, due to inadequate evidence, or
  B there is no objective truth about the matter.
4 Moral disagreements may occur between people either because:
  A there are objective moral values, but people's perceptions of these are distorted in various ways – for example, due to inadequate evidence, or
  B there are no objective moral values, they are simply reflections of different ways of living.
5 **Conclusion:** The best explanation of moral disagreements is 4B) – that is, that there are no objective moral values.

The first premise in Mackie's argument asserts that there are some radical variations between moral codes from one society to the next. The work of anthropologists and historians supports the claim that moral judgements and standards vary according to the practices and cultures that each society has. For example, in the Grand Valley in Papua New Guinea, no culture has come to dominate (partly due to its geographical features), making it an ideal place to study the differences between societies. Unlike the rest of the world, where a few cultures have come to dominate and subsume other cultures,[30] there has been no such colonisation or conquering of Papua New Guinea's Grand Valley, where there are still a thousand different languages and societies. No single language, no single culture and no single moral code: the valley is an anthropologist's dream, for here we can see, within an area the size of Texas, just how radically different moral codes can be. So, while our culture might judge all forms of cannibalism to be vile, there is clearly a more subtle distinction to be drawn in the Grand Valley, as scientist Jared Diamond discovered for himself. And which of these differing moral codes – for example, which form of cannibalism or vegetarianism – are we to say is the absolute one, the right one, the *real* one? Each set of moral codes and values in the Grand Valley has to be considered in relation to (that is, *relative to*) the society from which it emerged. The differences between moral codes that can be observed within Papua New Guinea can also be observed across the world (east and west, north and south), and across history; and it is these differences that form the basis of Mackie's argument from relativity.

As I walked between New Guinea valleys, people who themselves practised cannibalism and who were scarcely out of the stone age routinely warned me about the unspeakably primitive, vile, and cannibalistic habits of the people I would encounter in the next valley.[29]
Jared Diamond

These differences should ring alarm bells in moral philosophers, as such radical differences in moral judgements ('cannibalism is permissible' and 'cannibalism is wrong') need an explanation. However, the differences between moral codes are not enough to guarantee the conclusion that there are no objective moral values; although 'there are no objective moral values' is certainly an explanation of those differences, as Mackie puts it:

> *Radical differences between ... moral judgements make it difficult to treat those judgements as apprehensions of objective truths.*[31]

The second part of Mackie's argument from relativity looks at the disagreements that emerge from the differences between moral codes, and how these disagreements might be explained. Mackie acknowledges that disagreement in itself (even multiple disagreements, as can be found between moral codes) does not indicate that something does not exist or is not objective. After all, medieval astronomers held beliefs strongly in disagreement with modern cosmologists' beliefs about the solar system; ancient Greek thinkers held views of the elements strongly in disagreement with modern scientific views of the elements. In neither case does this mean that there is nothing objective for the scientists to investigate. But for Mackie, disagreements about ethics indicate something more problematic, as we shall see.

Experimenting with ideas

Read through the disagreements between the people in the situations below, and then answer questions that follow.

A The philosopher David Hume maintains that the universe has not been designed, and that everything in it is the result of chance processes and evolution. The theologian William Paley (1743–1805) maintains that the universe and every living thing in it has been designed – by God.

B In the eighteenth century, scientists disagreed about the nature of phlogiston. Some scientists argued that phlogiston was particles released from an object into the air when it was burned. Other scientists disagreed, arguing that phlogiston is not a particle, but an essence that permeates all substances.

C A hundred and fifty years ago, a large group of people in Denver, Colorado, believed that marriage was to one partner for life. At the same time, in Salt Lake City, in the neighbouring state of Utah, a large group people believed that marriage was to one or more partner(s) for life.

D In 2002, some weapons inspectors in Iraq argued that there was evidence that the regime was hiding weapons of mass destruction (WMDs) that posed an immediate threat to the world. Some other weapons inspectors argued that there was no evidence of WMDs in Iraq.

E On a hot summer's day in 2016, there is an ice-cream van at the local park (the music only comes on when it has run out of ice cream). One of your friends asks for bubble-gum flavour ice cream; he thinks it tastes good. None of your other friends agree – they think bubble gum ice cream tastes disgusting.

1 What is the thing that the people are disagreeing about?
2 Are they disagreeing about something that is objective, something that is 'real'?
3 How might their disagreement be resolved?

Disagreements between people and between societies, like those sketched in the activity above, need to be accounted for: why does disagreement arise? What are its causes? Mackie suggests that there may be two possible underlying causes of any kind of disagreement:

A Disagreements occur because people have different or distorted perspectives on the facts of the matter. (As may be the case with disagreements about phlogiston, and weapons of mass destruction.)

B Disagreements occur because there are no 'facts of the matter'. (As may be the case with disagreements about films, music and ice cream – bubble gum flavour … what is that all about …?! Technically, it is not even a flavour, as you can get mint bubble gum, strawberry bubble gum, banana bubble gum and so on. And why is it electric blue? Ugh, bleah, yugggh.)

Many philosophers would argue that the scientific disagreements mentioned above can be accounted for by possibility A). For example, disagreements between modern and ancient physics could be explained by noting that the ancient Greek and medieval scientists did not have access to all the evidence that is now available, and they did not have the technology, or the mathematical tools, to help them refine their observations.

Turning to moral disagreements, Mackie gives the example of monogamy, which is held up as a value in some societies (it is part of their moral code), but not held up as a value in other societies. What accounts for the differences and disagreements between these two types of society? Is it like the scientific disagreement – in other words, is it the case that some societies have access to the 'moral facts' and are right about how many people we can marry, whilst other societies are wrong (they cannot see the evidence) about these moral facts? Mackie does not think so. Instead, it is much more likely that the disagreement arises because in some societies there is a tradition of monogamy, and therefore monogamy is valued; whilst in other societies there is not a tradition of monogamy, and therefore monogamy is not valued. As Mackie says:

> *Disagreement about moral codes seems to reflect people's adherence to, and participation in, different ways of life.*[32]

So the best explanation for why there are moral disagreements is B) – that is, there are no objective facts to disagree about, and that is why there are differences from society to society. We might say that society invents the moral codes like monogamy which justify their way of life and then places these moral codes onto a pedestal (or carves them in stone or prints them in important-looking books) as if they had always been there. So the moral values that we place on things emerge from our way of life, and presumably if we lived another way of life (for example, if we had been born a thousand miles away, or a thousand years ago), then we would have different values. Unlike the scientific disagreements mentioned above, moral disagreements are not about any objective moral values – *even though it feels as if they are about that*. For Mackie, the best explanation as to why there is moral disagreement is that there are no objective moral values, and instead moral codes are invented by societies to account for their particular way of life.

Criticism

One criticism, which Mackie himself outlines and assesses, is that the argument from relativity overstates the differences in values from society to society. It may be the case that the individual moral codes are different, but these are drawn from some very basic ethical principles which are recognised in every society. For example, the 'golden rule' (or principle of universalisability); the goal of trying to promote the general happiness; and the virtues that are valued in all societies (honesty, generosity, courage, loyalty and so on, outlined on page 337).

So whilst all societies might share these deep-rooted principles, each principle is 'cashed in' slightly differently in each society, giving rise to different moral codes and hence disagreements between societies.

Mackie responds to this criticism with a further observation about what each society considers 'basic', or what is 'basic' by being shared across different societies: and this includes fanatical or radical ideals (for example, in liberal freedom, or in religious intolerance). These basic values, which include the shared principles that we approve of, as well as partially shared (fanatical/radical) ideals, could be explained in one of two ways. The first is that they express some moral objective truth (which is very worrying for people who do not share those ideals). The second is that there are no objective truths and the weight given by societies to these partially shared ideals is an emotional weight: they create a strong response in us. But, as Mackie observes, they create an equally strong and opposite response in societies with different 'basic' ideals.

Mackie may have felt that the argument from relativity was not completely watertight, and he offers another argument to sit alongside this, in support of his claim that moral values are not objective.

Issue: Mackie and the argument from queerness

Mackie's second and perhaps more important argument for his moral scepticism is the 'argument from queerness'. Moral realism raises puzzling questions to do with the kinds of things that exist in the world (ontological questions), as well as questions to do with knowledge, or how we come to know things (epistemological questions). Mackie's argument from queerness addresses both these issues, each of which are worth examining separately, and each of which teases out what Mackie calls the 'queerness' (or strangeness) of realism:

1 Metaphysical strangeness: if the universe did contain objective moral values, then these objects would be of a very strange sort, unlike anything else we have ever encountered.
2 Epistemological strangeness: if the universe did contain objective moral values, and we could become aware of them, then in order to do this we would possess some mental faculty able to perceive this, of a very strange type, utterly different from our way of knowing anything else.

Metaphysical strangeness

The moral realist posits the existence of some odd things into the world, namely objective moral facts and properties that are woven into its fabric. Intuitionists like Moore were clear about their belief in the existence of simple, indefinable properties – properties of a peculiar 'non-natural' or 'normative' sort. When reading about the intuitionists, their position may have struck you as a bit odd. Mackie points out that the intuitionists were actually being more open and honest (about these very strange properties of the world)[33] than other moral realists like Kant, Aristotle and Mill. For Mackie, all realist theories commit them to an unusual ontology, namely the existence of these queer, objective moral properties. But what makes these properties such strange ones?

Mackie argues that one of the essential, and unusual, ingredients of moral values is that they must provide a motivation to action. We noted on page 389,

anthology
2.19

when looking at Hume, that this is one of the key features that distinguishes a moral property (like goodness) from a non-moral property (like redness): it has an authority which compels us to behave in a certain way and gives us reason and motivation for doing so. These motivations that are attached to moral values are binding, categorical even. Mackie is an adherent of this view, which we have seen is known as 'moral internalism'. He believes that all moral values, not just Kantian imperatives, have at their core the assumption of a strange, magnetic quality that motivates us to act. He uses Plato's theory of forms[34] as an example of how objective moral values provide motivation, as for Plato, once we know what is good (the Form of the Good), we are compelled to pursue it. If Mackie's internalist account is correct, then this 'motivational' property of moral values is very strange indeed, as it would mean that something in the world (let's say, the moral property of 'good') would generate a motivation for action, independently of any reasons or desires that we might have. This is strange because we are used to understanding motivation in terms of our needs, desires, reasons – but how can a part of the *world* (namely, a moral property) be intrinsically motivating?

Mackie's answer is that there is no such property – there is nothing in the world that motivates us, as we would expect a moral value to motivate us. And this is a good indication that there are, in fact, no objective moral values.

Epistemological strangeness

Figure 2.39 John thinks it is wrong that humans are not doing enough to prevent global warming and save the planet.

Alongside a belief in strange moral entities, Mackie argues that the realist is committed to believing in something else strange, namely a means by which we can perceive these strange moral entities.

a) John can use his eyes to see the traffic pollution in the natural realm.
b) What strange faculty does John use to 'see' into the moral realm that this pollution is wrong?

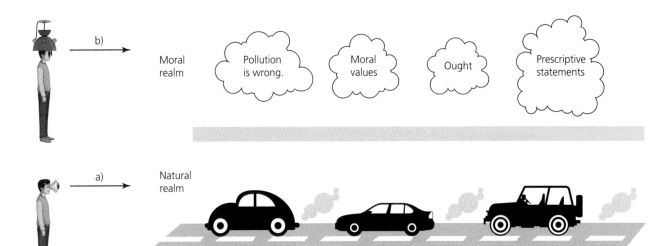

Humans possess five or so faculties (our senses) that enable us to become aware of and get to know the outside world. We see cars moving towards us, we hear the sound of traffic, we smell the exhaust fumes – all these senses combine and enable us to build up a picture of the world on our way to school or work. We make a judgement that it is wrong that our use of cars and the pollution they create is helping to destroy the planet we live in; but we cannot 'see' the wrongness. Even if we believe that this is wrong, 'wrongness' just is not something that we can see (as we try to illustrate in **Figure 2.39** on the previous page).

Mackie points out that, in order for us to detect these special moral qualities (which the realist is claiming are part of the world), we must possess some other special faculty, in addition to our five senses, that enables us to detect and gain knowledge of these moral properties. What might this be? What part of our psychological or physical make-up would enable us to become aware of our duty, or the rightness of an action, or any of the prescriptive values that people say morality consists in? Mackie argues that none of our ordinary faculties provide us with the answer: we do not sense moral values through seeing or smelling or hearing; we do not become aware of moral values through introspection, or deduction or induction. 'Moral intuition' is the simple answer given by the intuitionists, but other realists also require us to possess a similar sort of intuition, or moral sense. Mackie says this answer is inadequate ('lame' is his actual word), as it is not really an answer at all: the intuition or moral sense still needs an explanation. So moral realists are not only committed to belief in these strange moral entities, but also end up committed to a belief in a strange faculty (our moral intuition), which they cannot really describe or point to or explain, that enables us to perceive these strange moral entities. Mackie's conclusion is that the far simpler explanation is that there are no strange moral entities, objective moral values do not exist, and therefore there is no need to believe in a strange moral faculty either. Problem solved.

Having rejected any form of objective moral values, Mackie goes on to give his own account of moral judgements, which we look at on page 402.

Criticism

How might a realist respond to Mackie's point that we must possess 'strange faculty' in order to become aware of these objective moral values? Mackie acknowledges that one response is to point out that there are all sorts of other concepts that we do not perceive through the senses, but which we may argue are 'objective' properties of the world, such as our ideas of essence, number, identity, substance, and the infinite extension of time and space. If we are able to grasp those concepts through the faculty of our understanding, then the realist might argue that moral concepts are grasped in the same way – that is, through the understanding.

Moral anti-realism

Ralph leapt to his feet. 'Jack! You haven't got the conch! Let him speak.'

Jack's face swam near him. 'And you shut up! Who are you anyway? Sitting there – telling people what to do ...'

'The rules!' shouted Ralph. 'You're breaking the rules!'

'Who cares?' [...]

Ralph summoned all his wits. 'Because the rules are the only thing we've got!'[35]

William Golding, *Lord of the Flies*

Ralph and Jack are in trouble – they are 12 years old, they are rivals who hate one another, they are on a desert island, and there is nothing and no one to stop them slashing each other's throats or worse (and on this island, there is much, much worse). Ralph is right, the rules are all they have, or at least all they have to prevent their fragile little society from shattering. The question is, where do the rules come from? Ralph's rule, that you can only speak at an assembly if you are holding a conch shell, is something transported from another culture, another country, far, far away. In this new context, the rule is as fragile as the shell he holds. Jack's rule, the rule of physical power, is one that he develops as a hunter and exploits to terrifying effect as the new chief. In the end, the culture that turns the boys into a unit is a culture based on fear, on hatred of outsiders, on superstition and violent ritual. These boys are making up their moral principles as they go along, and it is not pretty.

The question we asked at the beginning of this chapter was: do we discover or invent the moral rules and principles that we feel bound by? Are Ralph, Jack and the rest simply discovering principles that other cultures have discovered, or are they inventing them? The realists of the last section believed that moral values are discovered or intuited. These realists had the corresponding (cognitivist) belief that moral judgements could be true or false, because the key terms such as 'good' and 'right' referred to certain properties or facts in the world, whether natural (in the case of utilitarians) or non-natural (in the case of intuitionists).

But in this section, we are going to look at a number of theories that reject realism. Indeed they have little in common except that they reject realism. These 'anti-realist' theories believe that moral values are *not* discovered or intuited: they are not 'out there' in the world at all. In general, anti-realists have a corresponding non-cognitivist approach to the status of moral judgements: moral judgements are not propositions about the world, and as such they are neither true nor false. According to anti-realists, moral judgements have some other meaning or purpose, or, for some cynics, they are simply nonsense.

Just as there is no single realist theory, so there is no single anti-realist theory. Anti-realism comes in various forms, and here we will be looking at three types – namely, emotivism, prescriptivism and error theory. The first two of these follow on, in historical terms, from intuitionism; the last theory, Mackie's error theory, is more recent, but perhaps reflects what cynics and sceptics have been thinking about morality for centuries.

J.L. Mackie's error theory

There are two lines of argument underpinning the theory proposed by the Australian philosopher, J.L. Mackie, in his book *Ethics: Inventing Right and Wrong*. Both lines of argument fall under the heading 'meta-ethics': the first is an ontological argument, about whether there is anything in the world that our moral judgements and values actually refer to; the second is a linguistic argument, about what we think moral judgements and values mean.

Mackie acknowledges that most of the meta-ethics of the last century involved linguistic analysis, a study of the meaning of moral language, and how our moral statements may be anchored (or not) to the world. But the question, 'What does moral language mean?' is only one question amongst many meta-ethical questions that we can investigate. Mackie thinks that this bias towards the philosophy of

► **ACTIVITY**

Look at the moral dilemmas on pages 202–205. For each dilemma:

1 Identify and write down each of the moral properties (goodness, badness, rightness, wrongness and so on) that you find in the dilemma.

2 Now compare what you found with your classmates – did they identify different moral properties?

3 Where you disagreed with your classmates, what features of the dilemmas would help you to resolve who was correct, and who was incorrect?

language (which is a charge that we ourselves are guilty of, as we look at even more linguistic analysis below when studying emotivism and prescriptivism!) is a distraction from the real task of meta-ethics. For Mackie, the key to unlocking the problems of morality (why is there so much disagreement about moral action, and so little agreement about how to solve the disagreements) is not found through linguistic or conceptual analysis. Instead, the key lies in starting with the ontological question, 'What sort of things are there in the world – and are values built into the fabric of the world?' In other words, are moral values objective?

Mackie's ontological claim: moral anti-realism

Mackie argues for the bold hypothesis: 'There are no objective moral values'. We have seen that Moore and the intuitionists certainly did believe in objective moral values, and that the property of being good, which certain actions have, is one that we know intuitively. But Mackie argues that *all* moral realists, not just intuitionists but naturalists as well, are committed to the existence of objective moral values. You can probably list them: Kant believed there exists a categorical imperative; Aristotle believed that the good lay in *eudaimonia*, which was intrinsically desirable; Mill and the utilitarians believed that the good lies in happiness, and the prevention of suffering, which is also intrinsically desirable.

As you have already seen, Mackie offers two main arguments that count both against moral realism and in support of his error theory. The first of these is his 'argument from relativity'. This is the well-known sceptical argument, put forward enthusiastically by first-year philosophy and social science undergraduates in bars all over the world, that the moral values which humans hold vary from society to society over place and time; and that your moral values are largely determined by the society in which you grew up. For Mackie, the wide variations in moral codes are more readily explained by reference to the ways of life that they reflect, rather than by reference to our perception (and, in some cases, our distorted perception) of any objective moral values.

In addition to the relativity of moral codes, we have seen how Mackie believes that the very queerness, or oddness, of moral objects and properties should make us sceptical about objective values. When you engaged in the activity on page 402, you may have found it very difficult to answer the questions, and you may not have been able to say which features of the dilemma would show that you, and not your classmate, were correct. After all, moral properties and entities are unlike any others that we know of – we cannot really point at them, or count them, or measure them, or interact with them in any way. For Mackie, they are unlike any other object or property *because they do not actually exist*! Moral values are not out there to be discovered, as the moral realists would claim, but they are invented by us.

Mackie's linguistic claim: cognitivism

It is not just philosophers who make the mistake of believing in the independent existence of moral facts and properties; even in ordinary language, we all have a tendency, when making moral judgements, to include a claim to objectivity. This ingrained claim of ethical language to objectivity is a mistake, says Mackie. But he is very clear that this mistake is not a linguistic or conceptual mistake (which is the approach that the non-cognitivists like Ayer and Hare are going to take, below). As Mackie says:

the denial of objective values will have to be put forward not as the result of an analytic approach, but as an 'error theory', a theory that although most people in making moral judgements implicitly claim ... to be pointing to something objectively prescriptive, these claims are all false.[36]

So the mistake is not an analytic mistake about misunderstanding how moral terms work. Instead, says Mackie, our moral judgements make a systematic error based on our belief in things (namely, moral properties of the world) that do not literally exist, a belief promoted by moral realism in whatever form it occurs.

A belief in objective values is built into our ordinary moral thought and language[37]

How, then, to explain the power that we feel moral values have over us? Mackie believes that we can account for the reaction that we have to moral values (many of us do feel obliged to do things that we think are morally 'good') with a psychological explanation about how we have been brought up and the social institutions within which we exist. This complex social arrangement creates a moral theory which we then project onto the world as if it were true of the world. In Mackie's terminology, we 'objectify' these social arrangements into moral codes. This, Mackie argues, is where the error arises, because we believe our projections of moral values onto the world are inherent in the world itself. And for our societies this is helpful, because objectivity gives our moral codes an authority which they would otherwise lack.

These two aspects of Mackie's theory, the linguistic and the ontological, point towards what he calls an error theory. The first aspect raised a question about our ontology: are there any objective moral values woven into the fabric of the universe? Mackie believes that the argument from relativity and argument from queerness show that this belief, in the objectivity of moral value, is false. In short, he is an *anti-realist*. The second aspect raised a question about the philosophy of language: are moral judgements statements about the world? Mackie argues that we must recognise that our moral judgements really do aim at describing the world – at the objective moral values that we believe exist in the world. In short, he is a *cognitivist* (**Figure 2.40**). The combination of these two aspects is crucial: we are genuinely describing the world with our moral judgements, except our descriptions are always false because there is nothing 'out there' to describe. This error, the permanent error that we fall into whenever we make a moral judgement, gives Mackie's theory its name: error theory. This is rather like the same criticism an atheist might make of a religious person: that believers really are describing the world when they talk about God (they are not simply expressing their feelings); it is just that there is no God, so their descriptions will always be false.

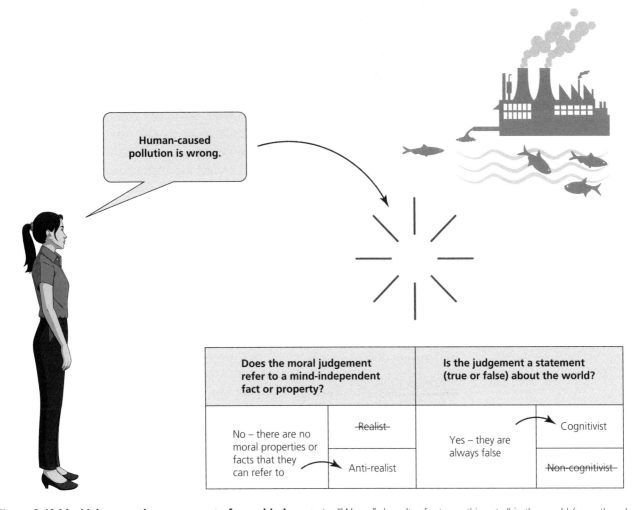

Figure 2.40 Mackie's error theory account of moral judgements. "Wrong" doesn't refer to anything at all in the world (even though we think it does).

But perhaps Mackie is wrong. Perhaps when we use moral terms we are not intending to refer to the world at all, but we are expressing something else altogether, something that picks up on the action-guiding, prescriptive aspect of ethical language. In the next two sections, we look at the emotivists and prescriptivists, who were writing before Mackie and who would agree with him that there are no moral facts, but who would reject any cognitivist account of moral language.

A.J. Ayer's emotivism theory

In every case in which one would commonly be said to be making an ethical judgement, the function of the ethical term is purely emotive. It is used to express feelings about certain objects, but not to make any assertion about them.[38]

In order to understand any philosophical movement, such as emotivism, it helps to place it in its historical context. Think back to the realist position known as intuitionism, a theory that found its footing at the beginning of the twentieth

405

century, which asserted that there existed mysterious moral facts that we could somehow intuit. Emotivism can be seen as a total rejection of the mysteries of intuitionism, and Alasdair MacIntyre thinks it is no coincidence that most of the emotivists studied under intuitionists, and were reacting against their teachers.[39] Remember that Moore thought that we knew what was 'good' through intuition – for example, the love of friendship and beauty. Now, among a certain intellectual elite, Moore's examples of 'goods' seemed obviously correct. But to everyone else, including many of Moore's pupils (such as C.L. Stevenson (1908–79)), what seemed obvious was that what Moore thought of as 'goods' were simply an expression of his own feelings and attitudes, to which he had given an objective spin that simply was not justified. So the theory of emotivism could be seen, in part, as a reaction against Moore's confident pronouncements as to what was and was not good.

One of the most prominent supporters of emotivism was the British philosopher, A.J. Ayer. Drawing inspiration both from Hume's sceptical and common-sense approach to philosophy, and from the logical positivists, Ayer developed a rigorous approach which he then applied ruthlessly to philosophical concepts and disputes. His stated goal in *Language, Truth and Logic* is to establish the purpose and method of philosophical enquiry, and in so doing ensure that philosophers would no longer waste their time on some of their traditional disputes – namely, those which have no foundation and cannot be resolved through a philosophical method. His primary target, as you may remember from page 385, was metaphysics, which Ayer describes as 'knowledge of a reality transcending the world of science and common sense'.[40] His method, as you may also remember, was the verification principle, which Ayer uses to apply to the statements that philosophers use in order to establish whether or not they are meaningful. Only those that are meaningful should be used in philosophical arguments and investigations, and these are either empirical statements that can be verified as true or false, or logical statements that are true by definition. So although Ayer's target is metaphysics and metaphysicians, he attacks his target, not by criticising their arguments, but by removing from their arguments those sentences (and hence premises) that are meaningless. Through his analysis of language, and his application of the verification principle, he concludes that all synthetic statements are empirical hypotheses (for an account of 'synthetic', see page 127) – in other words, any statement that tells us anything at all about the world is one that can be empirically verified (or empirically falsified).

But what about ethics? Given the frequency of moral judgements in our everyday lives, and their importance to us, what does Ayer think is behind moral language? This is the subject that Ayer turns to in Chapter 6 of *Language, Truth and Logic*, where he acknowledges that most people think that our knowledge of the world can be divided into two types: questions of facts and questions of values. But questions and judgements about values cannot, Ayers argues, be verified, nor can they be falsified, by looking at the world. There are no facts which can make moral judgements true or false, and in Ayer's terminology, this means that they have no factual significance: they have no literal meaning. The same holds true for judgements containing aesthetic values (like 'beautiful' and 'ugly'), which we do not discuss here. As you will have seen from the activity on page 387, moral judgements, along with all sorts of other sentences, do *look* as if they have meaning, and can be analysed and assessed. But this is a trick of our language, and Ayer argues that ethical concepts are pseudo-concepts: 'The presence of an ethical symbol in a proposition adds nothing to its factual content.'[41]

So if moral judgements, like 'Stealing money is wrong', appear to be statements, but are not actually statements, then what are they? Ayer takes his lead from Hume at this point, and gives an account of morality in terms of the feelings that moral judgements express. Hume argued that moral terms are a description of our sympathetic responses (and our approval or disapproval) to other people's behaviours (as a virtue ethicist, Hume limited his moral terms to character traits, virtues and vices). Ayer's theory is slightly different, and we shall see why shortly. Ayer concludes that moral terms are simply expressions of our feelings and emotions, like going 'Boo!' (at things we do not like) or 'Hooray!' (at things we do like). And in a nutshell, that is the theory of emotivism. Although Ayer did not use this phrase, occasionally emotivism is known, rather disparagingly, as the 'Boo/Hooray' theory. In Ayer's terms:

anthology
2.20

> [If I say] 'Stealing money is wrong' I produce a sentence with no factual meaning ... It is as if I had written 'Stealing money ! !' – where the shape and thickness of the exclamation marks show ... that a special sort of moral disapproval is the feeling which is being expressed.[42]

Now this 'emotive' account of moral terms was not new. Ogden and Richards had said almost the same thing 13 years previously, in their book *The Meaning of Meaning* (1923), writing that '"good" ... serves only as an emotive sign expressing our attitude'.[43] Ayer's emotivism also claims that moral assertions express attitudes or feelings. By arguing that all ethical statements are simply expressions of emotion, a bit like expletives, Ayer is taking a non-cognitivist stance towards moral terms. 'Good' does not refer to anything in the world, but is only an expression reflecting something in me.

It is important to note the difference between Ayer's and Hume's accounts. For Ayer, there is nothing descriptive about moral judgements. Unlike Hume's position outlined above, Ayer's emotivist theory denies that moral expressions *describe* feelings or emotions, any more than they describe other empirical facts. This is what makes Hume's theory a realist, and cognitivist, theory. But on Ayer's account, moral terms *express* a feeling, much as does a frown or an angry tone of voice. So Ayer is an anti-realist (there are no moral facts) and a non-cognitivist: moral judgements do not describe anything, they are not capable of being true or false: they are expressions not descriptions (**Figure 2.41**).

407

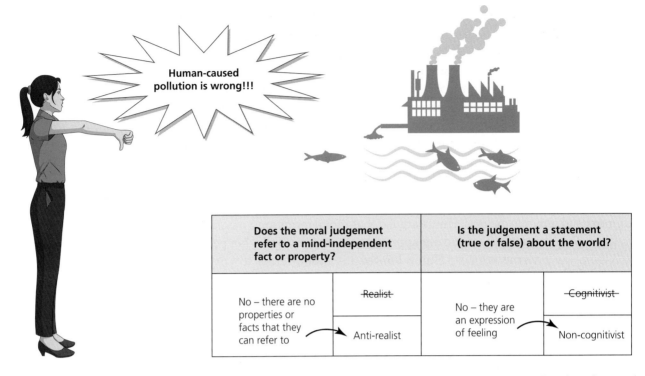

Does the moral judgement refer to a mind-independent fact or property?		Is the judgement a statement (true or false) about the world?	
No – there are no properties or facts that they can refer to	~~Realist~~	No – they are an expression of feeling	~~Cognitivist~~
	Anti-realist		Non-cognitivist

Figure 2.41 An emotivist account of moral judgements. 'Wrong' doesn't refer to anything in the world but is an expression of our disapproval.

The American philosopher C.L. Stevenson went a step further than Ayer in analysing the emotive meaning of moral judgements. He argued that moral judgements which employed terms like 'good' and 'right' were not simply expressions of a feeling, as Ayer had maintained. More importantly, Stevenson held that they were also attempts to influence other people, to persuade them to feel as we feel and to have the same attitude that we have. So Stevenson might say that when we claim, 'That's a good song', we mean, 'I like this song; you should do so as well'. Similarly, if we say, 'Abortion is wrong', we mean, 'I disapprove of abortion and so should you'. Stevenson is able to give an account of how moral terms motivate or guide action – they do so like someone shouting or urging us to do something; they motivate through the power of the emotion behind the words.

Emotivism opposes intuitionism by not regarding moral propositions as descriptive. They do not ascribe a special property to events. This means that they are not informative. They are not intended simply to indicate facts, but are designed to influence other people's behaviour by conveying approval or disapproval. So emotivism has the advantage of doing away with the mysterious 'non-natural' properties of intuitionism.

The disagreement between emotivists and intuitionists turns on their analysis of simple ethical propositions. Consider the following propositions (illustrated in **Figure 2.42**): 'Boris is big' and 'Boris is bad'.

Both these propositions have the same basic grammatical form. They both have a subject term ('Boris'), which picks out an individual in the world (Boris himself). And both statements have a predicate term ('is bad' and 'is big') saying something about Boris. The intuitionist claims that what is ascribed to Boris in both these statements is a property which we can discover in the world. Both bigness and badness are real properties of people, albeit natural

► **ACTIVITY**

Revisit sentences 1, 4, 5 and 9 on page 387, and write down the emotive meaning that Stevenson would find in them.

and non-natural ones respectively. And it is here that the emotivist takes issue with intuitionism. The emotivist claims that, although these two propositions are superficially similar, in reality they are very different. While the first does indeed ascribe a real property to Boris, the second does not. Badness is not really a property of people or actions at all. This means that the second proposition is deceptive, as it leads us to look in the world for something corresponding to the word 'bad'. And this is the error of the intuitionist who, having searched around for something corresponding to the word 'bad' and having failed to detect anything in the normal way (being unable to see, or hear, or smell Boris's badness), concludes that badness is a very peculiar or 'non-natural' property. But, in reality, says the emotivist, there is no such thing. For the real meaning of 'Boris is bad' is closer to 'Avoid Boris!' or 'Boris, yuk!' – that is to say, it expresses disapproval and does not ascribe any objective property to him at all.

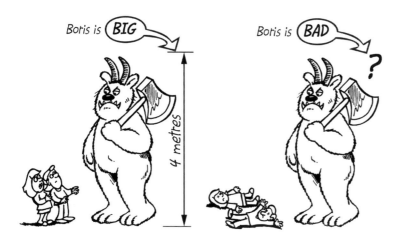

Figure 2.42 According to the emotivist, the intuitionist's mistake is to think there must be something in the world corresponding to the expression 'is bad', and so to imagine that there must be a non-natural property – badness – that Boris possesses.

Criticism

We look at further criticisms when we examine some of the issues with anti-realism (page 415), but before we address those general criticisms, here are some more immediate problems that the emotivist has to address.

We said above that emotivism explains how moral judgements motivate action. Thus ethical statements may be instruments for the control and influence of social behaviour, but so are advertisements, political speeches, bribes, blackmail, orders, etc. In order to influence someone's behaviour, in other words, I may engage in moral exhortation, but I may also threaten, plead with or bribe them. This observation raises the question of what, if anything, is distinctive about purely *moral* discourse, for according to emotivism, it would seem that it is 'ethical' to deploy any effective means to persuade someone to adopt a certain kind of behaviour. The consequence is that there can be no way of saying whether a moral argument is good or bad, but only whether or not it has the desired effect (that is, to motivate a change in other people's behaviour), and thus ethics appears to be on a par with propaganda and rhetoric.

Emotivism is also mistaken in claiming that moral discourse always involves itself in trying to change attitudes or influence action. For it is possible to condemn someone's behaviour, without holding out any hope of influencing it. Moreover, moral discourse can be meaningful without its being any expression of an emotional state. I can express a moral opinion without being emotionally excited – for example, when giving someone moral advice. Indeed, often it is regarded as important to be dispassionate in evaluating a moral dilemma, since our emotions, when they are not kept in check by reason, can cloud our ability to make moral decisions, as Aristotle pointed out (see page 321).

Kantian theorists may turn to the principle of universalisability to resist the claims of emotivism. For, following Kant, they may insist on the need for the element of *reason* in moral conduct. In other words, there is a crucial difference between saying that something is right or wrong, and expressing a liking or dislike for it. If I do something because I ought to do it, I will be prepared to act the same way if the same circumstances arise. But this is not true of feelings. If I do something because I feel like it, not because I ought to, there is no commitment to acting in a similar way in similar circumstances. Moral judgements, in other words, refer beyond the particular case in a way that feelings or emotions do not. Further, they involve not just how I ought to behave in certain circumstances, but how *anyone* ought to behave in such circumstances. What this means is that to make a moral judgement implies having principles; and while non-rational beings can have feelings and express them, only a rational being can hold universal principles of this kind.

Finally, we should return to the historical point that Alasdair MacIntyre drew to our attention at the beginning of this section (page 406). MacIntyre is not surprised that emotivism arose when it did as a successor to the intuitionist theories that came before. (For example, A.J. Ayer studied at Oxford, where the views of Prichard and Ross prevailed, while C.L. Stevenson studied under Moore at Cambridge.) This is because the intuitionists confidently proclaimed that they could intuit what was 'right' or 'good'. The emotivists then pointed out that all the intuitionists were doing was expressing their own preferences and attitudes; except the emotivists ambitiously went beyond this and claimed that *all* moral judgements, not just 'moral judgements made by intuitionist philosophers circa 1930', were expressions of feelings (which is a dramatic oversimplification of the uses of moral terms). MacIntyre maintains that the emotivists 'confused moral utterance at Cambridge after 1903 ... with moral utterance as such'.[44] If MacIntyre is right, then this undermines the emotivists' claim that their analysis applies to moral judgements everywhere and at all times.

R.M. Hare's prescriptivism theory

All the words discussed [that is, 'right', 'good' and 'ought'] have it as their distinctive function either to commend or in some other way to guide choices or actions.[45]

Richard Hare was the foremost prescriptivist of the twentieth century, developing his theory over three books and a period of 20 years, and it is his version of prescriptivism that we assess in this section. Like other moral philosophers of his time, Hare focuses almost entirely on meta-ethics and the meaning of ethical terms;[46] it is only later in his life that he turned to more normative questions. Hare's prescriptivism can be seen as a development of emotivism, insofar as it further explores the uses and purposes that moral judgements have in our dialogue with other people. But it views emotivism as too simplistic: value judgements are not expressions of feelings, they have a much more important use – namely, to tell other people how they ought to act.[47]

Like emotivism, prescriptivism is a non-cognitivist theory and denies that values are types of facts, and denies that moral discourse is informative or descriptive, or that moral judgements state moral facts. Hare uses G.E. Moore's open question argument (page 381) to show that no definition of moral terms such as 'good' can adequately account for the meaning of 'good'. For Hare, naturalists make the mistake of attempting to derive value judgements from 'statements of fact', and by doing so they miss out on one of the essential features of a value judgement – namely, that it *expresses* something. But the missing element is not a feeling (as the emotivists would assert), but something more important:

Value-terms have a special function in language, that of commending; and so they plainly cannot be defined in terms of other words which themselves do not perform this function.[48]

On Hare's analysis, making a moral judgement like 'Stealing is wrong' comes close to issuing a command, or giving advice, or offering a recommendation, or prescribing. When a doctor gives you a prescription, they are recommending a course of action, and similarly, our moral judgements are a form of prescription (hence the name, 'prescriptivism').

Experimenting with ideas

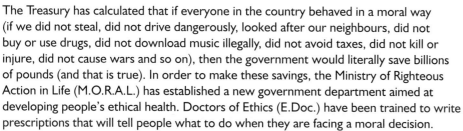

The Treasury has calculated that if everyone in the country behaved in a moral way (if we did not steal, did not drive dangerously, looked after our neighbours, did not buy or use drugs, did not download music illegally, did not avoid taxes, did not kill or injure, did not cause wars and so on), then the government would literally save billions of pounds (and that is true). In order to make these savings, the Ministry of Righteous Action in Life (M.O.R.A.L.) has established a new government department aimed at developing people's ethical health. Doctors of Ethics (E.Doc.) have been trained to write prescriptions that will tell people what to do when they are facing a moral decision. Because of your knowledge of ethics, you have been selected as one of those doctors.

1 Remind yourself of the dilemmas on pages 202–205.
2 Write out the prescriptions for the chronic conditions of the patients described in the table on page 412 – the first prescription and the last column have been completed for you.
3 Compare your prescriptions with those of your fellow E.Docs – what reasons might you give for your decision, and how do these differ from their reasons?

M.O.R.A.L. PRESCRIPTION CLINIC

Dr of Ethics: (Insert your name) .... E.Doc

Ministry of Righteous Action in Life

The condition	Your prescription	Frequency of application
Patient A wants to steal medicine from a hospital to save their partner's life.	Patient A ought not steal	Every day
Patient B has illegally downloaded 2000 music albums.		Every day
Patient C kills children and old people on a video game.		Every day
Patient D goes to watch bloody and horrific plays and films.		Every day
Patient E regularly eats factory-farmed chickens.		Every day
Patient F rears gorillas to be eaten at posh restaurants.		Every day
Patient G is married, but is having an affair.		Every day
Patient H has lied to a mad axe murderer.		Every day

So according to prescriptivism, when John Stuart Mill claimed that 'happiness was desirable', what he really meant was not that 'happiness is something we are able to desire', but that 'happiness *ought* to be desired'. In other words, by using the moral language of desirability, Mill was commending happiness as something we should strive to reach. When we tell a friend, 'It is wrong to steal medicine from that hospital', according to a prescriptivist, we are telling our friend how to act: 'Do not steal medicine from that hospital!' Thus, against the emotivist, the prescriptivist argues that ethical propositions are not expressions of the way the speaker feels, but exhortations to action. But like emotivism, prescriptivism is non-cognitivist about moral judgements insofar as it does not think they are propositions (they are not capable of being true or false), and like emotivism, it is anti-realist, in that it does not believe in any mind-independent moral properties in the world (**Figure 2.43**).

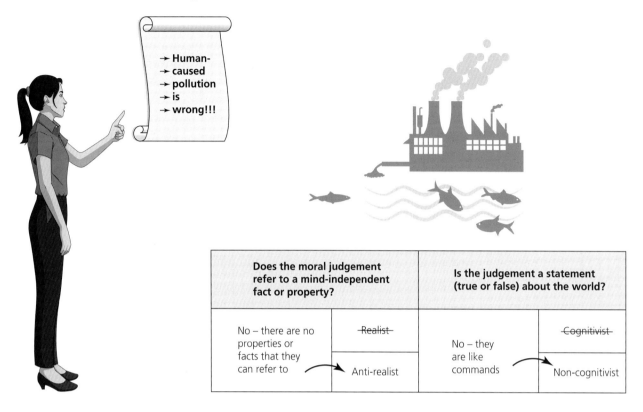

Figure 2.43 A prescriptivist account of moral judgements. "Wrong" doesn't refer to anything in the world but means "don't do that!"

However, despite their shared anti-realism and non-cognitivism, there are crucial differences between the two theories. Geoffrey Warnock highlights these differences in this way: emotivism sees moral language as an attempt to influence others, so if Theresa tells us, 'It is wrong to allow human-made pollution to destroy the environment', then she is trying to affect our attitudes and behaviour so that we do not pollute the environment.[49] But for the prescriptivist, the essence of moral language is not to influence, but to guide: by telling us it is wrong, Theresa is actually saying, 'Do not pollute the environment'. The emotivist does not think Theresa has much more to add, as for them, ethical language is non-rational. However, Hare's prescriptivism accounts for our expectation that Theresa would be able to offer reasons for her instruction, and be able to enter into a discussion and debate with us about these reasons.

A further way to understand the distinction between emotivism and prescriptivism is to distinguish between a) my telling you what to do and b) any effects or consequences of my so telling you. The prescriptivist focuses on what I am doing *in* saying, 'Pollution is wrong' – that is, recommending a certain course of action ('You ought not to pollute'). Whereas the emotivist highlights what I may hope to achieve *by* saying it (namely, for my emotive exclamations to prompt your family to rethink its decision to buy a massive, fuel-guzzling car). If naturalist theories compare value judgements to statements of fact, and emotivist theories compare them to exclamations, then the prescriptivist compares them to commands.

anthology
2.21

Viewing moral judgements primarily as commands is key to Hare's account of ethical language: all moral judgements ('It is wrong to pollute the environment') entail an imperative ('Do not cause pollution'). Hare is not saying that all imperatives are moral ones, or that moral judgements are identical to imperatives. If Descartes, in his lonely room by the fire, screams, 'Shut the door, I cannot *think* when it is so cold!' then he is issuing an imperative that applies only to that very specific context (it is a hypothetical imperative; page 264). But for Hare, moral judgements are universal imperatives, and they differ from other commands in that they do not simply speak of the obligations of a particular person in a particular situation, but imply that anyone and everyone, in a relevantly similar situation, would be likewise obliged. For the moral judgement that I make in a certain situation must be founded on certain features of that situation; and accordingly I must, in consistency, be prepared to make the same judgement in any situation which shares those features and does not differ in any other relevant respect. What is particular about the imperatives implied by our moral judgements is that these are imperatives that I am willing to apply universally. Thus Hare follows Kant in regarding *universalisability* as essential to the logic of ethical judgements, in addition to their *prescription*.

The immediate advantage of such an approach over that of emotivism is that it enables us to avoid the conclusion that moral discourse is fundamentally non-rational. The problem of getting somebody to do something, or of influencing her feelings with that end in view, is simply the problem of employing effective means to that end; and those means need not involve my putting forward reasons. For, as we saw, for a judgement to be 'emotively' effective, it is required only that it works to influence behaviour. Yet it seems to be essential to our concept of morality that we can ask for a rational response to practical questions. For Hare, prescriptive discourse is therefore concerned with answering questions about conduct, as contrasted with informative discourse, which seeks information about matters of fact. In giving moral advice, or arguing a moral point, what we are engaged in is a rational attempt to show that our position is *consistent* with the logical character of ethical discourse – namely, its being prescriptive and universalisable. Thus, for Hare, it is in virtue of the universalisability of moral propositions that rational argument in ethics is possible.

According to such an account, we are able to have moral disputes because we can advocate different moral principles. So long as there is consistency in what we prescribe, we are speaking the language of morals. In other words, the prescriptivist affirms that any imperative to action which can be universalised and consistently adhered to must count as an ethical principle.

Criticism

Prescriptivism is vulnerable to claims about the moral content of some prescriptions – if moral judgements are our personal prescriptions as to how we should behave, then what are the standards against which our personal prescriptions should be judged? Because prescriptivism is a non-cognitivist theory, it rejects the notion that there are external moral criteria (existing 'out there' in the world) which can be used as a measure of our prescriptions. For Hare, the only criterion seems to be: 'Is your judgement an imperative that you would universalise?' But there are two types of cases in which this criterion becomes inadequate when thinking about morality.

▶ **ACTIVITY**

Revisit sentences 1, 4, 5 and 9 (from the activity on page 387) and write down the meaning that Hare would find in them (bearing in mind the two elements of his theory: prescription and universalisability).

First, there are trivial prescriptions that could be universalised (such as, 'It would be good at Halloween if I started to provide sweets at my house as well as collecting them from other people's houses'). As we have already seen (page 277), although this is a prescription, and is universalisable, it does not seem to be a moral imperative. Second, and more importantly, let us take the case of prescriptions that emerge from a fanatic culture that we would want to condemn – for example, people who promoted and carried out genocides in the twentieth century (including Nazi Germany, Stalinist Russia, the Khmer Rouge in Cambodia – the list goes on[50]). Prescriptivism appears to say that, so long as people are consistent in putting forward horrific judgements, such as Höss's claim (page 383) that 'the murder of millions of Jews was right'), then their consistency makes the judgement a moral one. To be consistent, Höss would have to say, 'and if I were Jewish then I should be murdered too'; and if he accepted that, then his judgement is a universal one, and on Hare's account it must be seen as a moral judgement. But what we want to say, what our intuitions scream out to us, is that Höss is *wrong*, no matter how consistently or universally he and other murderers like him, applied their prescriptions.

Issues with moral anti-realism

The disruption caused by the 'linguistic turn' at the start of the last century has been felt throughout all areas of philosophy, and in most cases it has been seen as a positive thing: it is important that philosophers pay attention to, and take care with, the tools of their trade: words and thoughts. One consequence of the focus on language was a movement within moral philosophy towards anti-realism, because the alternative (moral realism) seemed to have lost any sure foundations. But moral anti-realism brings with it its own problems, and we look at three of these in this section:

- How is it possible for anti-realists to account for the main uses of moral language?
- Is moral progress possible within an anti-realist framework?
- Does moral anti-realism drift into moral nihilism?

Issue: can anti-realism account for how we use moral language?

In areas of practical philosophy, such as ethics, the focus on the meaning of moral judgements can divert philosophers' attention away from the practical purpose of the moral judgements. And for philosophy to remain relevant, it has to be tethered (however lightly!) to the real world: the point at which philosophy attracts most criticism is where it starts to gaze too closely at the fluff in its navel, or look too far at the world beyond the stars. If moral philosophy is to be grounded in the real world, then it must be able to account for the ways in which moral language, judgements, values and so on are used.

415

▶ **ACTIVITY**

Read through the following situations, paying close attention to the words in *italics*, and then answer the questions below.

A Your friend (whose home life has recently been in turmoil) is now months behind on her A-level homework, but she has found a website which will write her essays for her. She wants to talk to you about this, and asks you, *'Is this wrong?'* She wants a genuine response as she does not know quite what to do.

B Your two-year-old cousin has got into a habit of pinching other toddlers at nursery, which is really upsetting for them. He is a really nice kid (it is probably just a phase), but the next time you are at your aunt's house, he comes up to you, smiling, and pinches you on the forearm. Ouch! Your aunt tells him off straight away: *'That is bad! Say sorry now.'*

C You are listening to a discussion on the radio about whether government plans to introduce new grammar schools are a good thing. One person says that they would be *a good thing* as they help increase social mobility; the other person disagrees, saying that they would *bad for society overall*, as they would actually only help a small minority of children.

1 In each situation, what role does the moral language (in italics) have. How is it being used?

2 Write a list of all the other ways in which moral language could be used (giving your own situations as examples).

3 If there were no objective moral truths, what difference would this make to the conversations above?

It is easy when studying moral philosophy to forget that moral judgements are being used all the time, by everyone, everywhere, only a tiny fraction of whom have ever studied moral philosophy. The brilliant thing about moral philosophy is that, like all good philosophy, it can give us time to take stock of the world, to look up from our daily lives, to look around and reflect, to make new connections, and change our way of thinking and acting. But any moral theory worth its salt should account for the day-to-day use of moral language. From the activity above, you might have identified some of its uses as follows: moral reasoning and decision-making; commanding and telling; disagreeing and arguing; persuading and influencing.

For the moral realist, these uses are made possible because there are facts (such as objective moral laws or natural properties like pleasure and pain) about which we can reason, argue, disagree, and tell or persuade people to believe. But this is not so easy for the moral anti-realist: if there are no moral properties or facts, then what are we disagreeing or arguing or reasoning about? Below we look at how emotivism and prescriptivism address this question.

Emotivism and moral disagreement

One conclusion that can be drawn from emotivism is that value judgements are not rational, so no rational agreement is possible on ethical matters and no knowledge can be had of them. According to emotivism, different people feel differently about different things and each has an equal right to their opinion: I like strawberry ice cream, you like bubble-gum ice cream; I feel 'ugh!' when I think about capital punishment, but you feel 'hooray!' If emotivism is correct, then there is no point in having a moral discussion, since two people cannot really contradict each other when they appear to be expressing a disagreement over some moral issue.

The immediate difficulty with this conclusion is that it appears to misunderstand the true character of moral judgements. When I claim that 'The abortion of a 20-week-old foetus is wrong', I intend to contradict your claim that 'The abortion of a 20-week-old foetus is permissible'. For when we disagree on a moral issue, we argue with reasons, and it seems as if we are literally contradicting each other; we are not just expressing conflicting ethical attitudes or feelings. Emotivism appears to make such rational moral disagreement impossible. If moral judgements were purely subjective, it would be senseless for me to condemn someone who professed a different moral attitude.

Emotivism and moral reasoning

The objection above, however, need not be fatal to emotivism, and an important lesson needs to be drawn from the emotivist's defence. For emotivism can allow for rational dispute over matters of fact (for example, whether or not a 20-week-old foetus can feel pain, or can survive outside of the womb), and over the definition of terms (for example, whether a foetus is a person, or a potential person). So if we are in disagreement over some issue, it may not be irrational to argue so long as our disagreement concerns something objective, such as a factual belief about the world, or concerns the meaning of the terms we are using.

The rational approach, according to the emotivist, is to seek out any shared values that we have and use these as leverage in the argument. In the case of the argument over the abortion of a 20-week-old foetus, we may both share the view that harming innocent human beings is wrong. If I can demonstrate that the foetus is a human being (for example, by showing that a foetus has complex responses, can survive outside of the womb with special care, has all the necessary body parts in place and so on) and that it can be harmed (because it feels pain), then the other person may come to agree with me on this argument. What has happened here is that the pro-abortionist did not initially realise that their moral position was actually inconsistent, because they were unaware of certain facts.

Despite this defence of emotivism, while particular value judgements may be a matter for rational debate, ultimately, on an emotivist account, the criteria on which we base such judgements boil down to the expression of feelings. And in the final analysis, any reasons I may offer for why something is wrong can only reduce to some gut feeling for which no justification can be offered. Thus any sense that there is a rational basis for moral dispute is illusory.

Prescriptivism and commanding

Hare's prescriptivism gives a detailed account of what it is to make a moral judgement – namely, to issue commands – and his theory is more plausible than the 'Boo/Hooray' theory of emotivism. But Hare's account still seems to be a narrow one, and Warnock asks if it is really plausible to suppose that all moral discourse is primarily and essentially concerned with telling people what to do. Surely, as well as prescribing, we may deploy moral terms in order to undertake, implore, resolve, confess and so forth.[51] In other words, Hare restricts his analysis to those contexts in which one speaker addresses to another a moral judgement upon some course of action.

Prescriptivism and moral disagreement

The criticisms of prescriptivism outlined on page 414 lead to the further criticism that they undermine Hare's claim that he has shown how prescriptivism retains the rationality of moral discussion. We have seen that emotivism is unable to account for argument and discussion when it comes to ethics, and that this troubles us because we see moral discussion as having worth and purpose. Prescriptivism took us away from a simple 'Boo!' and 'Hooray!' It invited us to look at the reasons for our judgements, and it raised the question (which is a very useful one in any moral discussion), 'Would you apply that same moral judgement to yourself?' But it turns out that universalisability is not enough to save moral argument, as you might universalise a prescription that I disagree with ('Eating meat is right'), and I might universalise a judgement that you disagree with ('Eating meat is wrong'), and we want a successful moral theory to be able to show how we can have this disagreement. Realists, because they think morality describes something in the world, do give us a foundation to argue from; but anti-realists, including prescriptivists, find it difficult to give independent grounds that we can both appeal to, so we may end up 'agreeing to disagree', or drifting towards RELATIVISM or nihilism (page 420).

Issue: the problem of accounting for moral progress

> There may be humane masters, as there certainly are inhuman ones – there may be slaves well-clothed, well-fed, and happy, as there surely are those half-clad, half-starved and miserable; nevertheless, the institution that tolerates such wrong and inhumanity as I have witnessed, is a cruel, unjust, and barbarous one.[52]

Solomon Northup

In 1841, a musician from New York, Solomon Northup, was kidnapped in Washington D.C. and sold into slavery until his release 12 years later. Northup recorded this horrific ordeal, and the cruelty and brutality that he witnessed in his time as a slave on a Louisiana plantation, in his book, *12 Years A Slave*. His moral judgement of the social structures that permitted, accepted and even encouraged slavery, as 'cruel, unjust and barbarous', is a judgement that very few people would now disagree with. The judgement that once Northup, but now all of us, make about slave-owning societies are not judgements about an individual person, but about a whole society's moral codes. We might say that our ancestral societies once had a moral 'blind spot' about slavery: it was wrong, but our ancestors simply could not recognise it as such. What other 'moral blind spots' might we have had?

Experimenting with ideas

You have been tasked with looking back over our history to identify our ancestors' moral blind spots and to try to anticipate our current moral blind spots. It might help to work with one of your philosophy student colleagues on this exercise.

1 Write a list of some of the practices that our ancestors permitted, but which we now consider to be morally wrong. (You might want to consider: Roman sports; Viking methods of trial; medieval 'interrogation' techniques; Victorian forms of 'education'; ancient Britons' sacrifices; the way all previous societies have treated women, people of different ethnicities, children, people with disabilities, prisoners and so on.)
2 Why do we now consider these to be wrong? (How have our moral codes changed?)
3 Can you identify any pattern that emerges, either from the list, or from the changing moral codes? (Is there a particular direction in which our moral thinking has been heading?)

4 What practices do we currently permit (that is, we do not condemn them as morally wrong, and may even promote them as good), which, in 100 years' time, our descendants will condemn us for? (That is, what are *our* moral blind spots?)[53]

When we think about the moral codes that we now have, we are inclined to judge these as *better* than the moral codes that preceded them. In the activity above, you may have been able to give lots of examples of how our values have changed for the better over the past 2,000 years of history. The abolition of slavery that Solomon Northup campaigned for in nineteenth-century America is one such change, but others might include:

- the extension of political rights and votes to women
- the abolition of child labour (in most parts of the world)
- the application of equality laws (including civil rights, freedom of speech, property rights) to all people in society
- laws protecting people against discrimination, on the basis of sex, gender, race, age.

All of these changes have transformed human society, and in the past 200 years, these changes in our moral thinking (reflected in many of the laws introduced above) have accelerated. You would not want to live in a society where you might be sold as a slave, or hanged for stealing some food, or discriminated against because of your disability, or imprisoned without trial, or forced to work from the age of eight until your death. It is hard not to draw the conclusion that in some fundamental and significant ways, human lives have got better, that societies have progressed, and that this progress is a moral progress: the moral codes now instantiated in law (as sketched in the bullet points above), and the moral values that people hold on a personal level, have got *better*.

A moral realist might be able to explain this moral progress by arguing that where there are independent moral values and standards, it is possible for societies and individuals to move closer to these standards. They might also move further away, that is true (and sometimes societies do regress – think of Nazi Germany in the 1930s and 1940s), but nonetheless there is a yardstick we can use to measure moral codes, to see how much closer they are getting. But if there is no yardstick, no moral values or standards, then there is no possibility of moral progress – that phrase would become meaningless.

So how might a moral anti-realist account for this alleged moral progress? The issue for moral anti-realists is that they do not believe in any external or objective moral values – for them, there is no standard, and hence for them we cannot speak meaningfully about 'moral progress', because there is nothing in respect of which we can compare the two codes. On the flip side of this coin, moral anti-realism also appears to rule out the possibility of condemning the actions of other societies, ones that we think have failed to progress to a certain standard. Thus the anti-realist may have to accept that, while slavery is bad in our society, it may very well be good in other societies. This is the position known as 'moral relativism' (which has its foundations in the same premise that Mackie's argument from relativity had – see page 395).

The problem for the anti-realist, especially relativists, is that we (non-philosophers) may find it difficult to accept that condemnation of the customs of other societies is misguided, and that disagreement or argument is senseless between different cultures. In a similar vein, note that we may want to claim that the abolition of slavery, or the enfranchisement of women, represents a moral improvement to our society. So we would want to reaffirm that society today (at least in these respects) is better than it was – there has been moral progress. However, for a relativist, it is difficult to concur with this intuition. For if values are relative to the culture you are in, then as your culture develops, its values can *change*, but cannot be meaningfully said to improve. Again, to say that they have improved would appear to suppose that there is an absolute standard, a moral yardstick, against which today's and yesterday's values can be compared.

However, do we really need an absolute standard against which to compare two moral codes in order to claim that one has made greater moral progress than another? Perhaps we can compare two codes without having a standard, just as we can compare the length of two sticks without having a standard third stick. Thus to compare two codes, all that is required is that I take one code as a standard and stick to it in judging others. Certainly, from our perspective, it may not be problematic to claim that our moral system is an improvement on previous systems, precisely because from our perspective we must be, since it is us who define what is good.

Issue: whether anti-realism becomes moral nihilism

He's lying against a back wall, propped up. The face is bloated and pale and the eyes are shut, mouth open and the face belongs to some young, eighteen-, nineteen-year-old boy, dried blood, crusted, above the upper lip. 'Jesus,' Rip says. Spin's eyes are wide.

Trent just stands there and says something like 'Wild.' Rip jabs the boy in the stomach with his foot. 'Sure he's dead?' 'See him moving?' Ross giggles.[54]

Bret Easton Ellis, *Less Than Zero*

Bret Easton Ellis's characters clearly have issues. In today's politically correct language, we might call them 'ethically challenged'. They just do not have a sense of morality. It is not that they are particularly immoral, it is more as if ordinary moral feelings or a moral sense or sympathy (the kind that Hume was talking about) are simply absent from them. This makes their behaviour all the more chilling, as there is no scale of 'right' and 'wrong' against which Ellis's characters can measure their conduct. Without articulating it, these characters are what we might call nihilists.

The term 'nihilism' was coined by the Russian novelist Ivan Turgenev (1818–83), in his novel *Father and Sons*. He used it to describe a young rebel, Basarov, who rejected all moral values (*nihil* in Latin means 'nothing'). Later, it became associated with the anti-Tsarist movement, which rejected the feudal system and the moral orthodoxy of Russia in the nineteenth century. Nihilism is the rejection of a particular set of beliefs, and usually these beliefs are fundamental to our lives: for example, you might reject the possibility of knowledge ('epistemological nihilism'), or that there is any meaning to our lives ('existential nihilism'), or the existence of morality, which is the sort we are interested in here.

In philosophical terms, moral nihilism is a radical scepticism about the possibility of justification of moral principles and judgements. It is the view that there are no moral facts, no moral truths, and so no possibility of moral knowledge. In its moderate forms it may not recommend abandoning morality, since morality may express something other than facts, such as feelings or attitudes (compare this with emotivism). But radical nihilism claims that ethical discourse is fundamentally confused and should be abandoned.

Experimenting with ideas

Ministry of Righteous
Action in Life

The Ministry of Righteous Action in Life (M.O.R.A.L.) has devised a diagnostic questionnaire for teachers and young people, to determine whether or not they are nihilists. This might help the government on a wide range of law-and-order issues. Answers will remain confidential, but may be shared with the relevant police, judicial or social services in your area. Please answer yes or no to the following questions as truthfully as possible, and return this to M.O.R.A.L.:

1 When confronted with a dead body, would you prod it with your foot and giggle?
2 Do you sometimes look at the world and think, 'What is the point?'
3 Are there any objective moral truths?
4 Do you tend to wear black?
5 Do you (or would you) enjoy playing *Psycho-Tick*? (page 203)
6 Is the fact that there are no moral truths a good thing?
7 Do you agree that 'If God is dead, then everything is permitted'?
8 Is morality a human invention?
9 Are you a nihilist?
10 This questionnaire … whatever.

If you mostly answered yes, then you may be a nihilist and should inform your parents, friends and teachers of this as soon as possible, if they have not guessed already.

The connection between moral nihilism and moral anti-realism is clear. The anti-realists, like Ayer and Hare and Mackie, sought an alternative to moral realism by rejecting the realist claims that there are moral properties or facts that exist outside of our minds. The anti-realist theories, despite their differences, all agreed that there are no objective moral values and they gave alternative explanations of what we were doing when we were expressing moral judgements, since we certainly were not talking about anything 'real' in the external world. This rejection of objective, or mind-independent, moral facts by anti-realists is shared by nihilists, both of the moderate and the radical type. All nihilists are doing is taking one extra step – if there are no objective moral values, then let's stop pretending that there are any moral values at all, let's embrace the absence of moral values. So we can see how moral nihilism might emerge from moral anti-realism, as they share the same premise. But there are differences, which we can sketch out as follows:

1 Anti-realism: there are no moral facts, but with a few changes, we can still continue with our moral practices (for example, making moral judgements, having moral discussions, reasoning about morality). This is the position of the emotivists and prescriptivists.
2 Moderate nihilism: there are no moral facts, and we need to make some radical changes to our understanding of our morality in order to continue

with our moral practices. This is the position of J.L. Mackie in *Ethics: Inventing Right and Wrong*.

3 Radical nihilism: there are no moral facts, and we should abandon our moral practices as they are a sham (like continuing with religious practices without believing in God).

You have already examined in some detail the 'moderate' moral nihilism of J.L. Mackie, which he termed 'error theory'. On Mackie's account, anti-realism should make us feel somewhat uncomfortable, when it is properly thought through, as it does lead to the conclusion that we are wrong when we make moral judgements, and we are wrong all the time in this. Our error is to believe that moral judgements refer to something objective, when they do not. For Mackie, we cannot continue thinking (as the emotivists and prescriptivists did) that everything is fine with our moral practices when it simply is not: the arguments of the anti-realists are devastating for generally held views of morality, just as the arguments of atheists are devastating for generally held views about God. But Mackie is optimistic that a new system of practical morality can be constructed (just not one based on the false claims of objective morality).

Morality is not to be discovered but to be made: we have to decide what moral views to adopt, what moral stands to take.[55]

But radical nihilism is a much more worrying, and more exhilarating, theory than the anti-realist positions that we have looked at so far. While Anglo-American philosophers such as Ayer and Hare were buried in the meta-ethical analysis of meaning, on the Continent, the existentialists were engaged in a much more exciting project, and one with troubling nihilistic leanings. Just after the Second World War, the philosophy of existentialism swept through France and post-war Europe. In some forms, existentialism smacked of radical nihilism, at least as represented in the early works of Albert Camus (1913–60) and Jean-Paul Sartre.

Jean-Paul Sartre proposed a philosophy of radical freedom, in which humans are not bound by any moral obligations. For Sartre, human existence is essentially one of freedom: we are not determined to act in certain ways, as the Marxists, Freudians and Darwinists seemed to say. Moreover, we do not have a human nature, as practically every philosopher since Socrates has claimed (although these philosophers disagreed as to what our nature was – for Sartre, they were all wrong). There is no purpose to our lives, as the Aristotelians and religious philosophers have maintained. And most importantly, there are no moral laws or principles that bind us or oblige us to behave in certain ways. In one of his lectures, Sartre misquotes the Russian novelist Dostoyevsky, but this sums up his position quite nicely:

If God did not exist, everything would be permitted.[56]

Before the existentialists, the German philosopher Friedrich Nietzsche (1844–1900) dramatically proclaimed the death of God in *Thus Spake Zarathustra* (1885). This proclamation was intended to signal Western man's realisation in the nineteenth century that there is no objective basis for moral action. This recognition is, for Nietzsche, and for existentialist thinkers as such, the starting point rather than the end point for any moral philosophy. In other words, existentialism is perhaps best regarded as an attempt to produce some positive reaction to radical moral scepticism. Since values are not *given* to us by the nature of things, the existentialist demands that we take responsibility to forge our own. Søren Kierkegaard (1813–55), for example, argued that any attempt to justify one's moral position seems to involve appeal to premises which in turn must be vindicated, and that the only way to avoid an infinite regress of reasons is simply to *choose* to stand by certain premises.

According to Nietzsche, the supposed universalisable character of moral judgements that we make is not an expression of reason, as Kant argued, but represents an attempt to bind and control the exceptional individual of whom the majority is resentful. Christianity is a 'slave morality', a morality of the weak, intended to exert power over the strong. The slave morality inverts the master values of pride, courage and personal merit, replacing them with humility, meekness and equality. Nietzsche argues further that the notions of objectivity and truth generally are simply expressions of the 'will to power', the striving for freedom and strength. Because there is no absolute truth in morality or anything else, but merely a power struggle between competing value systems, what is required is a 'revaluation of all values' which will affirm life and power. Nietzsche imagines that some people, those with the strength to reject the 'slave morality' (which encourages kindness, sympathy, honesty, etc.), will be liberated by nihilism and invent a new order of values (of pride, strength and nobility). Nietzsche called these people the overmen, *Ubermensch*, a concept which was distorted and used as a philosophical foundation of Nazism.

How might an anti-realist respond to the nihilism of Sartre and Nietzsche? A nihilist who sticks to her position, and refuses to admit the validity of any moral pronouncements, would appear to be unassailable. How, then, might we persuade the committed ethical sceptic of the importance of moral beliefs? Taking our cue from certain treatments of the radical sceptic about the possibility of knowledge generally, we might ask what kind of a justification of a moral belief the nihilist is after. Clearly, she is impressed by the logical impossibility of deriving an 'ought' from an 'is', but despite this, can we really think of value terms as having no connection at all with facts? Surely some facts are so closely bound to evaluative pronouncements that to divorce them is no longer to be intelligible? For the nihilist is committed to saying that happiness is no more good than bad, even that pain could be regarded as a good thing. In other words, the nihilist can be accused of denying something so fundamental to what it is to speak meaningfully about practical decision-making and human existence that, ultimately, we cannot understand her. If, as the nihilist claims, anything goes in value judgements, we cease to think of the person as communicating at all. While there is no way the nihilist can be proved wrong, her position is, it may be claimed, futile.

Summary of meta-ethics

In the first half of the twentieth century – as part of the 'linguistic turn' – moral philosophy took a distinct step away from discussions of normative ethics and towards meta-ethics. The study of ethical language which dominated the last century forms part of meta-ethics, raising questions about the meaning and nature of moral judgements and of the evaluative terms (good, bad, right, wrong) employed in these judgements.

Some philosophers make an ontological commitment to moral properties and objects – they believe that there are things that exist 'out there' in the world to which terms like 'good' and 'right' refer. These philosophers are known as moral realists. Other philosophers do not make such an ontological commitment: they do not believe that 'good' or 'right' refer to anything out there in the world at all. These philosophers are moral anti-realists. Overlapping with the realist/anti-realist debate about the ontological status of moral terms (about whether they refer to anything that exists or not) is a semantic debate about the meaning of moral judgements. On the one hand, cognitivists believe that moral judgements refer to the world; they are propositions that correctly or incorrectly describe the world: in other words, moral judgements can be true or false. On the other hand, non-cognitivists do not believe moral judgements refer to the world, and so neither do they believe that they are capable of being true or false.

We looked at two forms of moral realism:

- Ethical naturalists, who are moral realists, argue that moral language (such as 'good') should be understood in naturalistic terms. For Aristotle, 'good' could be understood in terms of the successful fulfilment of our function. For the utilitarians, 'good' is understood in terms of the impact an action has on the pleasure, pain or happiness of the population as a whole.
- Ethical non-naturalists, who are also moral realists, argue that moral language should be understood in non-natural terms. For Moore, our intuitions reveal to us what things are good (and there are a number of goods), and he thought we should strive to bring about these good states of affairs through our actions – he was a 'consequentialist' intuitionist in that respect.

Some philosophers believe that ethics is 'autonomous' and this leads them to reject naturalism. They believe that ethics forms a unique and distinct realm which cannot be reduced to or analysed in terms of other things. Hume believed in the *logical autonomy* of ethics, claiming that it was a logical error to derive an 'ought' from an 'is' (that is, we cannot move from a discussion of facts to a conclusion that is evaluative). Non-naturalists believed that naturalism systematically makes this kind of error. Moore believed in the *semantic autonomy* of ethics, claiming that you could not define moral terms in non-moral terms. Specifically, Moore thought that moral terms were indefinable *and* non-natural, and that it was a double fallacy a) to try to define them and b) to do so in naturalistic terms. So Moore accused naturalists, and in particular the utilitarians, of committing this naturalistic fallacy. However, many philosophers doubt whether in fact the utilitarians are guilty of this fallacy.

We looked at three types of moral anti-realism, two of which (emotivism and prescriptivism) give a non-cognitivist account of moral language, and one of which (error theory) gives a cognitivist account:

- Mackie's error theory is a cognitivist theory, proposing that moral language does indeed make claims about the world, but that all these claims are false. According to Mackie, this is because moral terms like 'good' do not actually refer to anything in the world at all (he is an anti-realist), but we project our moral values onto the world and then see these values as part of the world (rather than as a projection).

- Emotivism can be seen as a reaction against the objective pronouncements of intuitionists like Moore about what was right or good. It seemed to A.J. Ayer that these pronouncements were really just expressions of personal approval or disapproval. So moral judgements expressed emotions, but had no factual content at all (they were neither true nor false).

- Prescriptivism can be seen as a reaction against emotivism. Prescriptivists such as R.M. Hare agreed with the emotivists that moral judgements were not being used to describe the world, so cannot be true or false, and instead have a non-descriptive meaning. But Hare felt that emotivism had not captured the real use of moral judgements, which was to issue recommendations, or universal imperatives, about how other people should act. So moral judgements are meant to guide action, and to urge everyone in a similar situation to behave in the same way.

3.1 How to approach the exam

You will all write an essay on 'self-indulgence'. There will be a prize of half a crown for the longest essay, irrespective of any possible merit.[1]

The task set by the harassed teacher in Waugh's novel *Decline and Fall* is designed to shut his students up, rather than to assess any worthwhile abilities they might possess. For the speed with which you can write is not in itself a particularly valuable skill. Certainly, the philosophy exam is not designed to assess how much paper you can fill in the time, and yet many students' scripts suggest they think it is. So in this section, we will be looking at what skills the exam is designed to assess and at how you can best approach it in order to demonstrate your abilities and so to maximise your marks.

The Assessment Objectives

The AQA AS- and A-level Philosophy specifications have two Assessment Objectives. These tell the examiners what they should look for in your answers when awarding marks. So if you are to succeed in the exam, it is important that you are clear both about what the different skills are that they will assess, and also which questions will assess which skills.

- **Assessment Objective 1** (AO1) concerns how well you are able to show your understanding of the topic, ideas, methods and arguments, and your ability to analyse and explain them by identifying the key ideas and showing how they fit together.
- **Assessment Objective 2** (AO2) builds on your understanding and tests your capacity to analyse philosophical positions, theories and arguments in order that you may evaluate how strong they are by exploring the quality of the reasoning, considering their implications and exploring objections and counter-arguments.

While the content of the standalone AS paper is the same as the content for Paper 1 of the full A-level, the weighting of these Assessment Objectives differ. In the AS, 80 per cent of the marks are for AO1 – Understanding – and just 20 per cent is awarded for Analysis and Evaluation, whereas in Paper 1 of the A-level there is greater emphasis on AO2, with a distribution is 60 per cent for AO1 and 40 per cent for AO2 (see **Figure 3.1** below). Both place greater weight on AO1 and this reflects the importance of being able to show good knowledge of the subject content as a grounding. So, to succeed in either exam you will need to know the material covered in this book in reasonable detail, and you will also be expected to understand and evaluate the main arguments developed in the set Anthology texts (see the specification for the list). Success will depend primarily on being able to explain these with precision and in good detail.

But philosophy is not ultimately about giving accounts of arguments and theories from the history of philosophy. Rather, philosophy is about engaging meaningfully with the arguments for yourself and so trying to support a point of view. This, however, is not an easy skill. After all, by the time you take the

AS exam, you will only have been studying philosophy for nine months, and many of the theories and positions you will be expected to evaluate were developed over many years, in complex tomes, by some of the greatest thinkers in the Western tradition. But while you should show proper respect for the great philosophers' arguments, you must not suppose that you should not question their conclusions. Be prepared to think for yourself about how plausible you find their arguments. And when you come to the exam, make sure that you are aware of some of the main difficulties that they face; you will need to explore these to access the AO2 marks.

However, exams are not really the time for *new* or *experimental* thinking. You need to do this during the year, as you learn the material and reflect on the arguments in class and in your own writing. Rather, exams are about drawing selectively on what you have learned and framing it in a way that communicates effectively in response to the precise question. So read a question carefully and make sure you are clear about its focus – that is, what precisely it is asking – before you begin to write. Make efforts to organise your material clearly and coherently so that examiners can definitely see what you are saying. In the longer questions, this means briefly planning the order you will present the ideas in and having a conclusion and an introduction (see below). In the shorter-answer questions, this means answering the questions concisely and precisely.

Here is a table showing the different weighting of marks for the AS and for Paper 1 of the A-level. (Note that the A-level Paper 1 weightings are the same as those for Paper 2, Philosophy of Mind and Philosophy of Religion, which you will be sitting in the same examination series.)

AS-level exam: (A) Epistemology and (B) Moral Philosophy			A-level Paper 1 exam: (A) Epistemology and (B) Moral Philosophy		
Questions	Marks for each question	Marks as percentage of total	Questions	Marks for each question	Marks as percentage of total
A1/B6	2	(5%)	A1/B6	3	(6%)
A2/B7	5	(12.5%)	A2/B7	5	(10%)
A3/B8	9	(22.5%)	A3/B8	5	(10%)
A4/B9	9	(22.5%)	A4/B9	12	(24%)
A5/B10	15	(37.5%)	A5/B10	25	(50%)
	Total: 40 per unit (80 for the full paper)			Total: 50 per unit (100 for full paper)	

Note that while there is more emphasis on AO2 for the full A-level, the two formats are broadly similar. Both are divided into two sections corresponding to the two units you have studied: Section A – Epistemology, and Section B – Moral Philosophy, with equal distribution of marks for both sections. The first four questions in both sections award marks for AO1 exclusively. So here you need to focus on showing how well you understand the ideas. And it is only in the final essay questions, numbers 5 and 10, that AO2 marks are awarded and so where you need to demonstrate your skills of analysis and evaluation. But, because of the greater weighting on AO2 in the A-level, the key difference between the exams is the proportion of marks awarded for the final question – at A-level it is 50 per cent, as opposed to 37.5 per cent at AS. And this means that in the A-level exam you need to devote at least half the time on this question, i.e. 45 minutes or more, while at AS you can leave yourself slightly less.

The remainder of this section focuses on the AS exam. The advice, however, applies equally well to the full A-level, with the proviso that you may want to modify the timings slightly to reflect the different mark distribution. In the A-level/Year 2 book in this series, we address the A-level exam specifically (see the exam section of the *Metaphysics of God and Metaphysics of Mind* book, ISBN 9781510400269, publishing March 2018.)

The AS exam questions

As we have seen, there is a total of 80 marks available: 40 marks on each section. So it is important that you divide your time evenly between both sections – that is, one and a half hours for each.

You should practise answering questions under timed conditions, as only then will you get a feel for the amount you can write in the time, and so of how much depth and detail can reasonably be expected of you. Notice that the exam will be written in an answer booklet which leaves a certain amount of space for each question. This provides another indication of the approximate upper limit of the amount you are expected to write. But do not feel that you ought to fill up the space allocated for each question. It is not the quantity of writing that will determine your grade, and there is a danger, when the adrenalin is pumping, that you might write far more than you should and lose focus and ramble. You need to stay in control of your material, keep a clear eye on the question and avoid including material which does not advance your answer. So it is important that you take the time to think carefully through what you want to say before you begin to write.

Questions 1–4 from Section A and 6–9 from Section B are marked only on AO1. For all these questions, therefore, you should select the relevant information and explain it with clarity and precision. Stay focused on the question so as to avoid redundancy – you will lose marks if you go off-topic. The amount of detail you need to put in will depend on the time available, but the better the relevant detail, the more marks you will collect.

Importantly in these answers, because marks are awarded for AO1 only, you will not be credited for evaluating the arguments and positions you discuss. So you should avoid suggesting problems, exploring counter-arguments or explaining why you disagree.

Here are the approximate timings for each question. Notice that these suggested timings do not correspond precisely to the division of marks. The reason for this is that the 15-mark questions are more demanding and the marks harder to access. So if you are able to do the shorter-answer questions quickly and leave yourself more time for the last question, this will help you to access the highest marks. However, you may find that you need more time to answer the shorter questions properly, in which case, it may be best for you to work through them more slowly. Remember, precision is the key to gaining marks, so care needs to be taken over framing your response and this will take time. Whatever pace you work at, be sure to leave yourself at least 30 minutes for the last question.

- 2-mark questions: 1–2 minutes
- 5-mark questions: 8–10 minutes
- 9-mark questions: 2 × 18–20 minutes
- 15-mark questions: 35–45 minutes

Two-mark questions

These questions will test your grasp of essential concepts that you have covered on the course and your ability to encapsulate them with precision. They may ask you to outline briefly a definition, theory or philosophical idea.

Practice questions

Write answers to the following two-mark questions. Give yourself two minutes for each – if you know the material, it should not take long to give a short definition.

You should try to answer in just one or two sentences. Think carefully about the wording so that you are as economical and precise as possible. Illustrations or examples are not needed, and if used they should be kept brief.

1 What is idealism?
2 What is *a priori* knowledge?
3 What is a false lemma?
4 What is moral non-cognitivism?
5 What is preference utilitarianism?
6 Give one formulation of the categorical imperative.

Then compare your answers with those below. Answers such as the following should attract full marks:

1 Idealism is the view that all that exists are minds and their ideas. Objects are no more than collections of sensations immediately appearing within minds.
2 *A priori* knowledge is knowledge which is justified independently of experience.
3 A lemma is a premise taken for granted in an argument. A false lemma is one that is not true.
4 Moral non-cognitivism is the view that moral judgements do not express beliefs and so do not admit of truth or falsehood.
5 The theory that an action is right if it maximises the satisfaction of the preferences of those affected by the action.
6 Always act according to a maxim that you can will to be a universal law.

You may want to come up with your own versions of such questions, and many will have answers in the glossary at the back of this book. Answers need to be accurate and to the point, but do not need to be developed.

Five-mark questions

The two-mark questions risk giving the impression that you can explain a difficult idea or argument in a sentence. Philosophical ideas are rarely so simple, and the five-mark questions require you to go further than just giving a pat definition. Rather, you need to give a full explanation of a philosophical issue, and this means you must try to show that you have a detailed understanding of the complexity involved. This means doing more than simply describing. A description may fail to show an understanding of *why* someone would believe the theory or position. So what you must try to do is to make sense of it in order to show how it hangs together and what considerations support it.

You need also to demonstrate that you understand and can use accurately the technical vocabulary you have learnt. This means you cannot merely gesture at an idea with a few words, but will need to analyse it – in other words, take it apart and show how it fits together. As with the two-mark questions, you will be awarded marks here for the precision with which you can explain the ideas.

It is likely that such questions will ask you to explain the reasoning of a philosopher. Your answer will not gain full marks if it does not show awareness of the way the elements of a theory or argument are structured.

So you should be clear about the distinction between the premises and conclusion of an argument or the logical interrelations between the elements of a theory.

You may include illustrative examples to support your account, which are likely be drawn from the texts, but only if these help to illuminate the ideas. Quotation, however, is not necessary.

Practice questions

Write answers to the following questions, giving yourself no more than ten minutes for each. Be sure to reflect carefully on the wording, so that your response is as clear and precise as possible.

You should try to explain the different elements of the idea and how they are connected. Examples may help to illustrate the points.

1 Outline what is meant by an innate idea.
2 Explain the time-lag argument.
3 Explain what is meant by sense data.
4 Outline the idea of the *tabula rasa*.
5 Outline and explain Hume's fork.
6 Explain the distinction that Kant draws between acting in accordance with duty and acting out of duty.
7 Explain Mackie's 'argument from queerness' against moral cognitivism.
8 Explain Mill's distinction between higher and lower pleasures.
8 Outline what Aristotle means by *eudaimonia*.
9 Explain Moore's open-question argument.
10 Explain how a utilitarian may justify lying.

Nine-mark questions (AO1)

These questions should be approached in a very similar way to the five-mark questions, and the questions are likely to use similar language ('outline', 'explain'), but the difference will be in the level of detail and in the number of points you can develop to support your explanation. Questions are likely to refer to more than one position, so you will need to compare or contrast them. Or, the arguments will have several steps, so you will need to unpack them in depth. For this reason, you will need to pay attention to the way you organise the material so that it is not just accurate, but is structured into a coherent whole.

So begin by identifying the key elements of the theory or argument and then, when giving your account of it, make sure you avoid merely describing, but show how it fits together into a logical structure which makes sense. It may be helpful to illustrate your answers with examples, either drawn from the texts or some of your own. Examples can help to show examiners that you understand an idea because you can apply it, but take care to ensure your illustrations support your answer, as, once again, if you include superfluous material you will lose marks.

Practice questions

Have a go at writing answers to these nine-mark questions. Each response should take you around 20 minutes.

In that time you will need to go into a reasonable level of detail, so if after five minutes you find you are running out of things to say, then it is likely that you need to know the topic in more depth and will need to revise further.

Make sure that you avoid merely describing, but that you explain. And be sure to pay attention to how you organise your material so that it reads as a coherent whole.

1 Outline the argument from perceptual variation.
2 Explain the difference between inductive and deductive arguments.
3 Explain how we can acquire *a priori* knowledge.
4 Explain one of Locke's arguments against innate ideas.
5 Outline and explain Descartes' trademark argument for the existence of God.
6 Explain how act utilitarianism differs from rule utilitarianism.
7 Explain Aristotle's function argument.
8 Explain the objection to Kant's ethics that it ignores the value of certain motives (such as love, friendship, kindness).
9 Explain Hume's argument that moral judgements are not beliefs.
10 Explain why anti-realism may be thought to lead to nihilism.

Fifteen-mark questions (7 AO1 + 8 AO2)

These are the only questions that test your capacity to develop an argument in defence of your own judgement. So to answer them you will need to consider arguments for and against a position, and then reach a conclusion which follows from what you have argued. These, therefore, are the most philosophically demanding of the questions, and the AO2 marks will be the hardest to pick up. So it is a good idea to try to devote more time to this question than the marking allocation would suggest. This means that if you can leave yourself 45 minutes, this is likely to be time well spent, although not if this is at the expense of precision and clarity in your other responses.

1 **Unpack the issues raised in the question ...**
   Make sure you introduce your answer by briefly outlining what the question is asking. A helpful way to approach this can be to define the key terms, to identify and briefly explain the position identified in the question and/or outline the main alternative views relevant to the issue. It can also be helpful to state briefly what you intend to conclude. This helps make it clear to the examiner where you are trying to get to, but more importantly, it makes it clear to you, and this will help you to maintain focus and avoid tangential material.

2 **Analyse some points ...**
   Then work through a series of arguments. When selecting points for discussion, make sure they are directly relevant to the question and also explain why they are relevant. When exploring the arguments, try to avoid merely juxtaposing different philosophers' views on the topic. Rather, you should examine the cogency of each view by looking at the reasons that support it and making a judgement about how strong the support is. Before moving on, say something about whether you are rejecting a position. If you are able to make each point follow from the previous point, you will help to give the essay a sense of overall development, which is something examiners will be looking for when awarding AO2 marks.

3 **Develop a coherent overall argument in support of a judgement ...**
   Having explored arguments for and against a view, avoid a conclusion which simply summarises what you have said (for example, 'I have looked at Locke's arguments and Berkeley's objections', and so on). A conclusion is not a summary, but must be a *judgement* which responds to the question. So you will need to say what the arguments you have examined show, for example, that the ontological argument fails, or that direct realism is untenable in the face of the criticisms you have looked at. And make sure your conclusion does follow from your reasoning. If you look at arguments for and against, do not just plump for a conclusion without briefly explaining why, on balance, you find one side of the case more persuasive.

Below there are some practice 15-mark questions. Notice that these use terms such as 'assess', 'critically discuss' and 'evaluate', which indicate that the examiners are awarding AO2 marks for evaluation and supporting a reasoned judgement. They may also simply present a question with no command words. But however the question is asked, the basic task, as outlined above, will be the same.

Practice questions

- Practice will be essential as preparation for answering the most demanding questions on the paper.
- For these questions give yourself 40 minutes.
- Plan the response so that it has a clear development.
- Have a clear introduction which explains the question and what your judgement will be.
- In the main body, explore in detail the arguments for and against, and make your own position clear.
- Give a clear conclusion which responds to the question. Make sure your judgement is supported by the arguments you have considered.

1 Can direct realism survive the objections made against it?
2 Assess whether we can know that the external world exists.
3 Is knowledge justified true belief?
4 Assess whether all our knowledge comes from experience.
5 Can reason alone provide substantive (synthetic) knowledge?
6 Is it possible to derive 'ought' from 'is'?
7 Assess the view that an action is morally right if it leads to the greatest happiness for the greatest number.
8 Assess the view that moral judgements do not describe reality.
9 Can a relativist theory of morals be justified?
10 Does Kant's moral theory provide an effective guide to moral conduct?

Again, you may find it helpful to look at the specification and to make up your own questions. You should also make sure you are familiar with all the terminology used in the specification, as questions are likely to be framed using this language. For other examples of the sorts of questions you might expect, look at the legacy specification past papers, which are available on the AQA website, as are specimen papers for this AS-level.

3.2 How to read philosophy

Introductory textbooks like this try to summarise and clarify some incredibly complex and significant ideas. We cannot capture the depth and richness of the original ideas, so the Anthology extracts below (page 436), and the original (well, translated) texts that are available online, give you a chance to get your intellectual teeth into the ideas of Western philosophers in their own words.

anthology
0.0

We have included in the Anthology extracts a paragraph from each of the recommended texts in the AQA specification, so that you have a quick reference, from our summary of the ideas, to the original texts themselves. When you see the Anthology extracts icon in the margin of the book, you should refer to the relevant numbered extract in the Anthology extracts.

As if you needed to be told, philosophy is hard. We would argue it is the hardest 'essay-based' subject you could do at A-level, because you are being asked to read, analyse and understand exactly the same material that a third-year undergraduate, or even a PhD student, might have to grapple with. It is hard because philosophical ideas and arguments are themselves so complex, subtle and nuanced, and they rely on a web of understanding that reaches back 2,000 years, past Kant and Hume, past Locke and Descartes, all the way to Plato, Aristotle and Socrates. It is also hard because philosophers are not the clearest of writers:

> Lord Macaulay once recorded in his diary a memorable attempt – his first and apparently his last – to read Kant's Critique: 'I received today a translation of Kant ... I tried to read it, just as if it had been written in Sanskrit'[1]

We can excuse the fact that many of the philosophers were writing before the twentieth century, when the fashion was for longer sentences, which could be hard to follow. Even if we set aside their long-winded style, philosophers are not always clear in their explanations, they often do not refer to their source material and they introduce technical jargon to try to express their new ideas.

AQA has recommended the Early Modern Texts website (www.earlymoderntexts.com) as a free online source for some of the texts in the Anthology extracts. Academics on this website have 'translated' older philosophy texts into modern language so that they are more easily understood. Some of the texts in the Anthology extracts are taken from Early Modern Texts, and so will differ from the original texts of the philosophers.

But there are things you can do to help overcome some of the difficulties of reading philosophy. First, do not try to work it all out by yourself. Philosophy is a discursive subject – in other words, it is about engaging with the thoughts and opinions and arguments of others, about debating arguments and clarifying concepts with others, and *experimenting* with these ideas to see where this takes you. So we recommend when you read and analyse these texts that you compare your analysis with other people in your class and your teacher, as well as with the summary that we ourselves have made of the texts. Second, we have also developed an interpretative framework, some philosophical 'lenses', which can help clarify what is being said, and which you can use to see beneath the surface of the text and start to understand what these philosophers are trying to say.

Philosophical lenses

Below are five lenses which will help you make sense of the extracts in the Anthology. Take each lens in turn, and apply it to the text, then move on to the next one. If you use all five lenses, and end up with a short, structured summary of what you think the main ideas are, then you are well on your way to understanding the extract.

When was this extract written, who wrote it, and why did they write it?

- Talk to your teacher to find out more about the book that this extract is from.
- Go online to get a sense of the biography and stories behind the person who wrote it.
- Go online and search for the book at the Internet Encyclopedia of Philosophy (IEP) to get a summary of its overall argument.
- Find out what is happening in the book immediately before and after the extract.

What words appear to be used in a technical way?

- Underline and make a note of those words that seem difficult to understand.
- Check in the glossary or index of this book to see if they are explained here.
- Talk to your teacher or classmates about the meaning of these words.
- Look up these words in a dictionary of philosophy (remember, ordinary dictionaries may only record the ordinary meanings of these words, not the philosophical meanings).

What are the recurring ideas in this extract?

- Once you have sorted out the vocabulary, what ideas are being examined in this extract?
- Check to see if you have encountered these ideas before (again, look in the glossary or index).
- Write a sentence summarising each idea in your own words.
- Talk to your classmates about how the ideas connect with one another in the extract.

Argument · **What indicators are there that this extract contains an argument?**

- Find signposts that a conclusion is being drawn ('therefore', 'thus', 'and so', 'it follows', 'hence').
- Look for key words indicating whether reasons are being given ('because' 'following', 'from what has been said').
- Identify the premises, evidence and assumptions on which the argument is being built.
- Check for other signs of argument ('however', 'but', 'if ... then').
- Refer back to the introduction (page x) for further questions you could ask to help tease out the argument.
- If the extract is not an argument, then what is it: an explanation, a criticism, a conceptual analysis, or something else?

Structure · **How could you break the extract down into separate, numbered 'chunks'?**

- Try numbering in the margins the main points that are being made.
- Use the signposts that you have identified to break down the extract into chunks.
- Try drawing the ideas on a page, possibly as a mind map.
- Write these chunks in your own words.
- Now try rewriting the paragraph as if you were a philosopher (which you are!), by writing down the chunks, in your own words, which flow in order: 1, 2, 3 and so on.

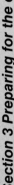

Section 4 Anthology extracts

Taken from the AQA online Anthology

Section 1 Epistemology

Is a JTB sufficient for knowledge? Gettier's original counterexample

anthology
1.1

Various attempts have been made in recent years to state necessary and sufficient conditions for someone's knowing a given proposition. The attempts have often been such that they can be stated in a form similar to the following:

a. S knows that P IFF [meaning if and only if]

P is true

S believes that P, and

S is justified in believing that P.

… I shall argue that (a) is false in that the conditions stated therein do not constitute a sufficient condition for the truth of the proposition that S knows that P.

… Case I

Suppose that Smith and Jones have applied for a certain job. And suppose that Smith has strong evidence for the following conjunctive proposition:

Jones is the man who will get the job, and Jones has ten coins in his pocket.

Smith's evidence for (d) might be that the president of the company assured him that Jones would in the end be selected, and that he, Smith, had counted the coins in Jones's pocket ten minutes ago. Proposition (d) entails:

The man who will get the job has ten coins in his pocket.

Let us suppose that Smith sees the entailment from (d) to (e), and accepts (e) on the grounds of (d), for which he has strong evidence. In this case, Smith is clearly justified in believing that (e) is true.

But imagine, further, that unknown to Smith, he himself, not Jones, will get the job. And, also, unknown to Smith, he himself has ten coins in his pocket. Proposition (e) is then true, though proposition (d), from which Smith inferred (e), is false. In our example, then, all of the following are true: (i) (e) is true, (ii) Smith believes that (e) is true, and (iii) Smith is justified in believing that (e) is true. But it is equally clear that Smith does not know that (e) is true; for (e) is true in virtue of the number of coins in Smith's pocket, while Smith does not know how many coins are in Smith's pocket, and bases his belief in (e) on a count of the coins in Jones's pocket, whom he falsely believes to be the man who will get the job.

… These two examples show that definition (a) does not state a sufficient condition for someone's knowing a given proposition

Edmund Gettier, 'Is justified, true belief knowledge?' in A. Philips Griffiths (ed.) *Knowledge and Belief*, Oxford University Press (1967)

Russell on perceptual variation

It is evident from what we have found, that there is no colour which pre-eminently appears to be *the* colour of the table, or even of any one particular part of the table – it appears to be of different colours from different points of view, and there is no reason for regarding some of these as more really its colour than others. And we know that even from a given point of view the colour will seem different by artificial light, or to a colour-blind man, or to a man wearing blue spectacles, while in the dark there will be no colour at all, though to touch and hearing the table will be unchanged. This colour is not something which is inherent in the table, but something depending upon the table and the spectator and the way the light falls on the table. When, in ordinary life, we speak of *the* colour of the table, we only mean the sort of colour which it will seem to have to a normal spectator from an ordinary point of view under usual conditions of light. But the other colours which appear under other conditions have just as good a right to be considered real; and therefore, to avoid favouritism, we are compelled to deny that, in itself, the table has any one particular colour.

Bertrand Russell, *The Problems of Philosophy*, Chapter i (online version, www.gutenberg.com)

Locke's experiment with hands in water

We are now in a position to explain how it can happen that the same water, at the same time, produces the idea of cold by one hand and of heat by the other; whereas the same water couldn't possibly be at once hot and cold if those ideas were really in it. If we imagine warmth in our hands to be nothing but a certain sort and degree of motion in the minute particles of our nerves or animal spirits, we can understand how it is possible for the same water at the same time to produce the sensations of heat in one hand and of cold in the other (which shape never does; something never feels square to one hand and spherical to the other). If the sensation of heat and cold is nothing but the increase or lessening of the motion of the minute parts of our bodies, caused by the corpuscles of some other body, we can easily understand that if motion is greater in one hand than in the other, and the two hands come into contact with a body that is intermediate between them in temperature, the particles in one hand will be slowed down while those of the other will speed up, thus causing different sensations.

John Locke, *Essay Concerning Human Understanding*, ii, viii, para. 21 (online version, www.earlymoderntexts.com)

Leibniz's response to Locke's hands experiment

Philalethes: But if the relation between the object and the sensation were a natural one how could it happen, as we see it does, that the same water can appear cold to one hand and warm to the other? That phenomenon shows that the warmth is no more in the water than pain is in the pin.

Theophilus: The most that it shows is that warmth isn't a sensible quality (i.e. a power of being sensorily detected) of an entirely absolute kind, but rather depends on the associated organs; for a movement in the hand itself can combine with that of warmth, altering its appearance. Again, light doesn't appear to malformed eyes, and when eyes are full of bright light they can't see a dimmer light. Even the 'primary qualities' (as you call them), such as unity and number, can fail to appear as they should; for, as Descartes noted, a globe appears double when it is touched with the fingers in a certain way, and an object is multiplied when seen in a mirror or through a glass into which facets have been cut. So, from the fact that something doesn't always appear the same, it doesn't follow that it isn't a quality of the object, or that its image doesn't resemble it. As for warmth: when our hand is very warm, the lesser warmth of the water doesn't make itself felt, and serves rather to moderate the warmth of the hand, so that the water appears to us to be cold; just as salt water from the Baltic, when mixed with water from the Sea of Portugal, lessens its degree of salinity even though it is itself saline. So there's a sense in which the warmth can be said to be in the water in a bath, even if the water appears cold to someone; just as we describe honey in absolute terms as sweet, and silver as white, even though to certain invalids one appears sour and the other yellow; for things are named according to what is most usual. None of this alters the fact that when the organ and the intervening medium are properly constituted, the motions inside our body and the ideas that represent them to our soul resemble the motions in the object that cause the colour, the warmth, the pain etc. In this context, resembling the object is expressing it through some rather precise relationship; though we don't get a clear view of this relation because we can't disentangle this multitude of minute impressions – in our soul, in our body, and in what lies outside us.

Gottfried Leibniz, *New Essays on Human Understanding*, ii, viii, para. 21 (online version, www.earlymoderntexts.com)

anthology 1.4

Descartes considers that he may be dreaming

Doubtful [...] As if I were not a man who sleeps at night and often has all the same experiences while asleep as madmen do when awake – indeed sometimes even more improbable ones. Often in my dreams I am convinced of just such familiar events – that I am sitting by the fire in my dressing-gown – when in fact I am lying undressed in bed!

Hopeful: Yet right now my eyes are certainly wide open when I look at this piece of paper; I shake my head and it isn't asleep; when I rub one hand against the other, I do it deliberately and know what I am doing. This wouldn't all happen with such clarity to someone asleep.

Doubtful: Indeed! As if I didn't remember other occasions when I have been tricked by exactly similar thoughts while asleep! As I think about this more carefully, I realize that there is never any reliable way of distinguishing being awake from being asleep.

René Descartes, *Meditations* (1641) Meditation 1 (online version, www.earlymoderntexts.com)

Russell on the time lag argument

The sense datum which we call hearing the thunder does not take place until the disturbance of the air has travelled as far as to where we are. Similarly, it takes about eight minutes for the sun's light to reach us; thus, when we see the sun we are seeing the sun eight minutes ago. So far as our sense-data affords evidence as to the physical sun they afford evidence to the physical sun of eight minutes ago; if the physical sun had ceased to exist within the last eight minutes, that would make no difference to the sense data which we call 'seeing the sun'.

Bertrand Russell, *The Problems of Philosophy*, Chapter iii (online version, www.gutenberg.com)

Locke argues our sensations need not resemble what causes them

Those qualities are commonly thought to be the same in those bodies as those ideas are in us, the one perfectly resembling the other; and most people would think it weird to deny this. But think about this: a fire at one distance produces in us the sensation of warmth, and when we come closer it produces in us the very different sensation of pain; what reason can you give for saying that the idea of warmth that was produced in you by the fire is actually in the fire, without also saying that the idea of pain that the same fire produced in you in the same way is in the fire? Why are whiteness and coldness in snow, and pain not, when it produces each idea in us, and can do so only through the size, shape, number, and motion of its solid parts?

John Locke, *Essay Concerning Human Understanding*, ii, viii, para. 16 (online version, www.earlymoderntexts.com)

Locke: the relation between our sensations and the objective property is arbitrary

anthology
1.8

We may conceive that the ideas of secondary qualities are also produced by the operation of insensible particles on our senses. Plainly there are plenty of bodies that are so small that we can't, by any of our senses, discover the size, shape, or motion of any one of them taken singly. The particles of the air and water are examples of this, and there are others still smaller – perhaps as much smaller than particles of air and water as the latter are smaller than peas or hail-stones. Let us suppose in the meantime that the different motions and shapes, sizes and number of such particles, affecting our various sense-organs, produce in us the different sensations that we have of the colours and smells of bodies … It is no more impossible to conceive that God should attach such ideas to motions that in no way resemble them than it is that he should attach the idea [= 'feeling'] of pain to the motion of a piece of steel dividing our flesh, which in no way resembles the pain.

John Locke, *Essay Concerning Human Understanding*, ii, viii, para. 13 (online version, www.earlymoderntexts.com)

Leibniz: the relation between our sensations and the objective property is not arbitrary

anthology
1.9

Philalethes: Now, when certain particles strike our organs in various ways, they cause in us certain sensations of colours or of tastes, or of other secondary qualities that have the power to produce those sensations. Is it conceivable that God should link the idea of heat (for instance) to motions that don't in any way resemble the idea? Yes, just as it is conceivable that he should link the idea of pain to the motion of a piece of steel dividing our flesh – a motion that in no way resembles the idea!

Theophilus: It mustn't be thought that ideas such as those of colour and pain are arbitrary, with no relation or natural connection between them and their causes; it isn't God's way to act in such an disorderly and unreasoned fashion. I hold that there is a resemblance between those ideas and the motions that cause them – a resemblance of a kind – not a perfect one that holds all the way through, but a resemblance in which one thing expresses another through some orderly relationship between them. Thus an ellipse … has some resemblance to the circle of which it is a projection on a plane, since there is a certain precise and natural relationship between what is projected and the projection that is made from it, with each point on the one corresponding through a certain relation with a point on the other. This is something that the Cartesians missed; and on this occasion you have deferred to them more than you usually do and more than you had grounds for doing.

Gottfried Leibniz, *New Essays on Human Understanding*, ii, viii, para. 13 (online version, www.earlymoderntexts.com)

Descartes on the external world

Now, I have a passive faculty of sensory perception, that is, an ability to receive and recognize ideas of perceptible objects; but I would have no use for this unless something – myself or something else – had an active faculty for producing those ideas in the first place. But this faculty can't be in me, since clearly it does not presuppose any thought on my part, and sensory ideas are produced without my cooperation and often even against my will. So sensory ideas must be produced by some substance other than me – a substance that actually has (either in a straightforward way or in a higher form) all the reality that is represented in the ideas that it produces. Either (a) this substance is a body, in which case it will straightforwardly contain everything that is represented in the ideas; or else (b) it is God, or some creature more noble than a body, in which case it will contain in a higher form whatever is to be found in the ideas. I can·reject (b), and be confident that God does not transmit sensory ideas to me either directly from himself or through some creature that does not straightforwardly contain what is represented in the ideas. God has given me no way of recognizing any such 'higher form' source for these ideas; on the contrary, he has strongly inclined me to believe that bodies produce them. So if the ideas were transmitted from a source other than corporeal things, God would be a deceiver; and he is not. So bodies exist. They may not all correspond exactly with my sensory intake of them, for much of what comes in through the senses is obscure and confused. But at least bodies have all the properties that I vividly and clearly understand, that is, all that fall within the province of pure mathematics.

René Descartes, *Meditations* (1641) Meditation 6 (online version, www.earlymoderntexts.com)

Catherine Trotter Cockburn on the coherence of the senses

[T]here is an infallible certain connexion betwixt the idea and the object; and, therefore, when an object produces an idea in one sense, we know, but from experience only, what idea it will produce in another sense. The alteration of an object may produce a different idea in one sense from what it did before, which may not be distinguished by another sense. But, where the alteration occasions different ideas in different senses, we may, from our infallible experience, argue from the idea of one sense to that of the other; so that, if a different idea arises in two senses from the alteration of an object, either in situation or distance, or any other way, when we have the idea in one sense, we know from use what idea the object so situated will produce in the other. […]

The ideas I have of distance and magnitude *by feeling* are widely different from the ideas I have of them by *seeing;* but *that something without,* which is the cause of all the variety of the ideas within in one sense, is the cause also of the variety in the other: and, as they have a necessary connexion with it, we may very justly demonstrate from our ideas of feeling of the same object what will be our ideas in seeing.

Catherine Trotter Cockburn, 'A letter from an anonymous writer to the author of The Minute Philosopher' in George Berkeley, *The Theory of Vision, or Visual Language, Shewing the Immediate Presence and Providence of a Deity, Vindicated and Explained. By the Author of Alicphron, or, The Minute Philosopher* (1732) (available online, http://Heinonline.org)

Russell: physical objects must continue to exist when unperceived by me

anthology 1.12

If the cat appears at one moment in one part of the room, and at another in another part, it is natural to suppose that it has moved from the one to the other, passing over a series of intermediate positions. But if it is merely a set of sense-data, it cannot have ever been in any place where I did not see it; thus we shall have to suppose that it did not exist at all while I was not looking, but suddenly sprang into being in a new place. If the cat exists whether I see it or not, we can understand from our own experience how it gets hungry between one meal and the next; but if it does not exist when I am not seeing it, it seems odd that appetite should grow during non-existence as fast as during existence. And if the cat consists only of sense-data, it cannot be hungry, since no hunger but my own can be a sense-datum to me. Thus the behaviour of the sense-data which represent the cat to me, though it seems quite natural when regarded as an expression of hunger, becomes utterly inexplicable when regarded as mere movements and changes of patches of colour, which are as incapable of hunger as a triangle is of playing football.

Bertrand Russell, *The Problems of Philosophy*, Chapter ii (online version, www.gutenberg.com)

Berkeley: extension is an idea in the mind

anthology 1.13

Philonous: But as we move towards or away from an object, its visible size varies, being at one distance ten or a hundred times greater than at another. Doesn't it follow from this too that size isn't really inherent in the object?

Hylas: I admit that I don't know what to think.

Philonous: You will soon be able to make up your mind, if you will venture to think as freely about this quality as you have about the others. Didn't you admit that it was legitimate to infer that neither heat nor cold was in the water from the premise that the water seemed warm to one hand and cold to the other?

Hylas: I did.

Philonous: Isn't it the very same reasoning to infer that there is no size or shape in an object from the premise that to one eye it seems little, smooth, and round, while to the other eye it appears big, uneven, and angular?

George Berkeley, *Three Dialogues between Hylas and Philonous in Opposition to Sceptics and Atheists: The First Dialogue* (1713) ed. Jonathan Bennett (2004) (online version, www.earlymoderntexts.com)

Berkeley's 'master argument'

Hylas: By that test, the point will soon be decided. What is easier than to conceive a tree or house existing by itself, independently of and unperceived by any mind whatsoever? I conceive them existing in that way right now.

Philonous: Tell me, Hylas, can you see a thing which is at the same time unseen?

Hylas: No, that would be a contradiction.

Philonous: Is it not as great a contradiction to talk of conceiving a thing which is unconceived?

Hylas: It is.

Philonous: The tree or house therefore which you think of is conceived by you.

Hylas: How could it be otherwise?

Philonous: And what is conceived is surely in the mind.

Hylas: Without question, what is conceived is in the mind.

Philonous: Then what led you to say that you conceived a house or tree existing independently and out of all minds whatsoever?

Hylas: That was an oversight, I admit; but give me a moment to think about what led me into it. It was –·I now realize, after reflection·– an amusing mistake. As I was thinking of a tree in a solitary place with nobody there to see it, I thought that was conceiving a tree as existing unperceived or unthought of, overlooking the fact I myself conceived it all the while. But now I plainly see that all I can do is to form ideas in my own mind. I can conceive in my own thoughts the idea of a tree, or a house, or a mountain, but that is all. And this is far from proving that I can conceive them existing out of the minds of all spirits.

George Berkeley, *Three Dialogues between Hylas and Philonous in Opposition to Sceptics and Atheists: The First Dialogue* (1713) ed. Jonathan Bennett (2004) (online version, www.earlymoderntexts.com)

Berkeley on hallucinations and dreams

The ideas formed by the imagination are faint and indistinct; also, they are entirely dependent on the will. But the ideas perceived by sense – that is, real things – are more vivid and clear, and they don't in that way depend on our will, because they are imprinted on our mind by a spirit other than us. So there's no danger of mixing up these real things with the foregoing ideas formed by the imagination, and equally little danger of failing to distinguish them from the visions of a dream, which are dim, irregular, and confused. And even if dreams were very lively and natural, they could easily be distinguished from realities by their not being coherently connected with the preceding and subsequent episodes of our lives, In short, whatever method you use to distinguish things from chimeras is obviously available to me too. For any such method must, I presume, be based on some perceived difference, and I don't want to deprive you of any one thing that you perceive.

George Berkeley, *Three Dialogues between Hylas and Philonous in Opposition to Sceptics and Atheists: The Third Dialogue* (1713) ed. Jonathan Bennett (2004) (online version, www.earlymoderntexts.com)

Berkeley's proof of God's existence

Philonous: [...] When I say that sensible things can't exist out of the mind, I don't mean my mind in particular, but all minds. Now, they clearly have an existence exterior to my mind, since I find by experience that they are independent of it. There is therefore some other mind in which they exist during the intervals between the times when I perceive them; as likewise they did before my birth, and would do after my supposed annihilation. And as the same is true with regard to all other finite created minds, it necessarily follows that there is an omnipresent, eternal Mind which knows and comprehends all things, and lets us experience them in a certain manner according to rules that he himself has ordained and that we call the 'laws of nature'.

George Berkeley, *Three Dialogues between Hylas and Philonous in Opposition to Sceptics and Atheists: The Third Dialogue* (1713) ed. Jonathan Bennett (2004) (online version, www.earlymoderntexts.com)

anthology 1.16

Plato on innate ideas

anthology 1.17

Meno: Yes, Socrates; but what do you mean by saying that we do not learn, and that what we call learning is only a process of recollection? Can you teach me how this is?

Socrates: I told you, Meno, just now that you were a rogue, and now you ask whether I can teach you, when I am saying that there is no teaching, but only recollection; and thus you imagine that you will involve me in a contradiction.

Meno: Indeed, Socrates, I protest that I had no such intention. I only asked the question from habit; but if you can prove to me that what you say is true, I wish that you would.

Socrates: It will be no easy matter, but I will try to please you to the utmost of my power. Suppose that you call one of your numerous attendants, that I may demonstrate on him.

Meno: Certainly. Come hither, boy.

Socrates: He is Greek, and speaks Greek, does he not?

Meno: Yes, indeed; he was born in the house.

Socrates: Attend now to the questions which I ask him, and observe whether he learns of me or only remembers.

Meno: I will.

Socrates: Tell me, boy, do you know that a figure like this is a square?

Boy: I do.

Socrates: And you know that a square figure has these four lines equal?

Boy: Certainly.

Socrates: And these lines which I have drawn through the middle of the square are also equal?

Boy: Yes.

Socrates: A square may be of any size?

Boy: Certainly.

Socrates: And if one side of the figure be of two feet, and the other side be of two feet, how much will the whole be? Let me explain: if in one direction the space was of two feet, and in other direction of one foot, the whole would be of two feet taken once?

Boy: Yes.

Socrates: But since this side is also of two feet, there are twice two feet?

Boy: There are.

Socrates: Then the square is of twice two feet?

Boy: Yes.

Socrates: And how many are twice two feet? Count and tell me.

Boy: Four, Socrates.

Socrates: And might there not be another square twice as large as this, and having like this the lines equal?

Boy: Yes.

Socrates: And of how many feet will that be?

Boy: Of eight feet. ...

Socrates:	And now try and tell me the length of the line which forms the side of that double square: this is two feet – what will that be?
Boy:	Clearly, Socrates, it will be double.
Socrates:	Do you observe, Meno, that I am not teaching the boy anything, but only asking him questions; and now he fancies that he knows how long a line is necessary in order to produce a figure of eight square feet; does he not?
Meno:	Yes.

Plato, *Meno*, trans. Benjamin Jowett (online version, www.gutenberg.org, EBook #1643) (released 2008)

Leibniz on innate ideas

I have also used the analogy of a veined block of marble as opposed to an entirely homogeneous one or to an empty page. If the soul were like an empty page, then the truths would be in us in the way that the shape of Hercules is in an uncarved piece of marble that is entirely neutral as to whether it takes shape of Hercules' shape or some other. Contrast that piece of marble with one that is veined in a way that marks out the shape of Hercules rather than other shapes. This latter block would be more inclined to take that shape than the former would and Hercules would in a way be innate in it even though it would take a lot of work to expose the veins and polish them into clarity. This is how ideas and truths are innate in us – as inclinations, dispositions, tendencies, or natural potentialities, and not as actual thinkings.

Gottfried Wilhelm von Leibniz, *New Essays on Human Understanding*, Preface (online version, www.earlymoderntexts.com)

anthology 1.18

Leibniz on how ideas can be in the mind and not perceived

Attending to something involves memory. Many of our own present perceptions slip by unconsidered and even unnoticed, but if someone alerts us to them right after they have occurred, e.g. making us take note of some noise that we've just heard, then we remember it and are aware of having had some sense of it. Thus, we weren't aware of these perceptions when they occurred, and we became aware of them only because we were alerted to them a little – perhaps a very little – later. To give a clearer idea of these tiny perceptions that we can't pick out from the crowd, I like the example of the roaring noise of the sea that acts on us when we are standing on the shore. To hear this noise as we do, we have to hear its parts, that is the noise of each wave, al- though each of these little noises makes itself known only when combined confusedly with all the others, and wouldn't be noticed if the wavelet that made it happened all by itself. We must be affected slightly by the motion of this one wavelet, and have some perception of each of these noises, however faint they may be. If each of them had no effect on us, the surf as a whole – a hundred thousand wavelets – would have no effect either, because a hundred thousand nothings can't make something!

Gottfried Wilhelm von Leibniz, *New Essays on Human Understanding*, Preface (online version, www.earlymoderntexts.com)

anthology 1.19

Locke on how our mind is like a *tabula rasa*

Everyone is conscious to himself that he thinks; and when thinking is going on, the mind is engaged with ideas that it contains. So it's past doubt that men have in their minds various ideas, such as are those expressed by the words 'whiteness', 'hardness', 'sweetness', 'thinking', 'motion', 'man', 'elephant', 'army', 'drunkenness', and others. The first question, then, is How does he acquire these ideas? It is widely believed that men have ideas stamped upon their minds in their very first being. My opposition to this in Book I will probably be received more favourably when I have shown where the understanding can get all its ideas from – an account that I contend will be supported by everyone's own observation and experience.

Let us then suppose the mind to have no ideas in it, to be like white paper with nothing written on it.

How then does it come to be written on? From where does it get that vast store which the busy and boundless imagination of man has painted on it – all the materials of reason and knowledge? To this I answer, in one word, from experience. Our understandings derive all the materials of thinking from observations that we make of external objects that can be perceived through the senses, and of the internal operations of our minds, which we perceive by looking in at ourselves. These two are the fountains of knowledge, from which arise all the ideas we have or can naturally have.

John Locke, *An Essay Concerning Human Understanding* (1690) ii, 1, paras 1 and 2 (online version, www.earlymoderntexts.com)

Locke on innate ideas

Some people regard it as settled that there are in the understanding certain innate principles. These are conceived as primary notions – letters printed on the mind of man, so to speak – which the soul receives when it first comes into existence, and that it brings into the world with it. I could show any fair-minded reader that this is wrong if I could show (as I hope to do in the present work) how men can get all the knowledge they have, and can arrive at certainty about some things, purely by using their natural faculties, without help from any innate notions or principles. Everyone will agree, presumably, that it would be absurd to suppose that

the ideas of colours are innate in a creature to whom God has given eyesight, which is a power to get those ideas through the eyes from external objects. It would be equally unreasonable to explain our knowledge of various truths in terms of innate 'imprinting' if it could just as easily be explained through our ordinary abilities to come to know things.

John Locke, *An Essay Concerning Human Understanding* (1690) i, 2, para. 1 (online version, www.earlymoderntexts.com)

Hume on concept empiricism

It may seem at first sight that human thought is utterly unbounded: it not only escapes all human power and authority, as when a poor man thinks of becoming wealthy overnight, or when an ordinary citizen thinks of being a king, but isn't even confined within the limits of nature and reality. It is as easy for the imagination to form monsters and to join incongruous shapes and appearances as it is to conceive the most natural and familiar objects. And while the body must creep laboriously over the surface of one planet, thought can instantly transport us to the most distant regions of the universe – and even further. What never was seen or

heard of may still be *conceived*; nothing is beyond the power of thought except what implies an absolute contradiction.

But although our thought seems to be so free, when we look more carefully we'll find that it is really confined within very narrow limits, and that all this creative power of the mind amounts merely to the ability to combine, transpose, enlarge, or shrink the materials that the senses and experience provide us with. When we think of a golden mountain, we only join two consistent ideas – *gold* and *mountain* – with which we were already familiar. We can conceive a virtuous horse because our own feelings enable us to conceive virtue, and we can join this with the shape of a horse, which is an animal we know. In short, all the materials of thinking are derived either from our outward senses or from our inward feelings: all that the mind and will do is to mix and combine these materials. Put in philosophical terminology: *all our ideas or more feeble perceptions are copies of our impressions or more lively ones.*

David Hume, *An Enquiry Concerning Human Understanding* (1748) Enquiry 1, section 2 (online version, www.earlymoderntexts.com)

Descartes' ontological argument

I can easily believe that in the case of God, also, existence can be separated from essence, letting us answer the essence question about God while leaving the existence question open, so that God can be thought of as not existing. But on more careful reflection it becomes quite evident that, just as having-internal-angles-equal-to-180° can't be separated from the idea or essence of a triangle, and as the idea of highlands can't be separated from the idea of lowlands, so existence can't be separated from the essence of God. Just as it is self-contradictory to think of highlands in a world where there are no lowlands, so it is self-contradictory to think of God as not existing – that is, to think of a supremely perfect being as lacking a perfection, namely the perfection of existence.

anthology 1.23

René Descartes, *Meditations* (1641) Meditation 5 (online version, www.earlymoderntexts.com)

The method of doubt

Some years ago I was struck by how many false things I had believed, and by how doubtful was the structure of beliefs that I had based on them. I realized that if I wanted to establish anything in the sciences that was stable and likely to last, I needed – just once in my life – to demolish everything completely and start again from the foundations. It looked like an enormous task, and I decided to wait until I was old enough to be sure that there was nothing to be gained from putting it off any longer. I have now delayed it for so long that I have no excuse for going on *planning* to do it rather than getting to work. So today I have set all my worries aside and arranged for myself a clear stretch of free time. I am here quite alone, and at last I will devote myself, sincerely and without holding back, to demolishing my opinions.

I can do this without showing that all my beliefs are false, which is probably more than I could ever manage. My reason tells me that as well as withholding assent from propositions that are obviously false, I should also withhold it from ones that are not completely certain and indubitable. So all I need, for the purpose of rejecting all my opinions, is to find in each of them at least *some* reason for doubt. I can do this without going through them one by one, which would take forever: once the foundations of a building have been undermined, the rest collapses of its own accord; so I will go straight for the basic principles on which all my former beliefs rested.

anthology 1.24

René Descartes, *Meditations* (1641) Meditation 1 (online version, www.earlymoderntexts.com)

The evil demon

So I shall suppose that some malicious, powerful, cunning demon has done all he can to deceive me – rather than this being done by God, who is supremely good and the source of truth. I shall think that the sky, the air, the earth, colours, shapes, sounds and all external things are merely dreams that the demon has contrived as traps for my judgment. I shall consider myself as having no hands or eyes, or flesh, or blood or senses, but as having falsely believed that I had all these things. I shall stubbornly persist in this train of thought; and even if I can't learn any truth, I shall at least do what I *can* do, which is to be on my guard against accepting any falsehoods, so that the deceiver – however powerful and cunning he may be – will be unable to affect me in the slightest.

René Descartes, *Meditations* (1641) Meditation 1 (online version, www.earlymoderntexts.com)

The *cogito*

Doubtful: This is very confusing, because I have just said that I have no senses and no body, and I am so bound up with a body and with senses that one would think that I can't exist without them. Now that I have convinced myself that there is nothing in the world – no sky, no earth, no minds, no bodies – does it follow that I don't exist either?

Hopeful: No it does not follow; for if I *convinced myself of something* then I certainly *existed*.

Doubtful: But there is a supremely powerful and cunning deceiver who deliberately deceives me all the time!

Hopeful: Even then, if he is deceiving me I undoubtedly exist: let him deceive me all he can, he will never bring it about that *I am nothing* while *I think I am something*. So after thoroughly thinking the matter through I conclude that this proposition, *I am, I exist*, must be true whenever I assert it or think it.

René Descartes, *Meditations* (1641) Meditation 2 (online version, www.earlymoderntexts.com)

Descartes' proof of material reality

I have a passive faculty of sensory perception, that is, an ability to receive and recognize ideas of perceptible objects; but I would have no use for this unless something – myself or something else – had an active faculty for producing those ideas in the first place. But this faculty can't be in me, since clearly it does not presuppose any thought on my part, and sensory ideas are produced without my cooperation and often even against my will. So sensory ideas must be produced by some substance other than me – a substance that actually has (either in a straightforward way or in a higher form) all the reality that is represented in the ideas that it produces. Either (a) this substance is a body, in which case it will straightforwardly contain everything that is represented in the ideas; or else (b) it is God, or some creature more noble than a body, in which case it will contain in a higher form whatever is to be found in the ideas. I can·reject (b), and be confident that God does not transmit sensory ideas to me either directly from himself or through some creature that does not straightforwardly contain what is represented in the ideas. God has given me no way of recognizing any such 'higher form' source for these ideas; on the contrary, he has strongly inclined me to believe that bodies produce them. So if the ideas were transmitted from a source other than corporeal things, God would be a deceiver; and he is not. So bodies exist. They may not all correspond exactly with my sensory intake of them, for much of what comes in through the senses is obscure and confused. But at least bodies have all the properties that I vividly and clearly understand, that is, all that fall within the province of pure mathematics.

René Descartes, *Meditations* (1641) Meditation 6 (online version, www.earlymoderntexts.com)

anthology 1.25

anthology 1.26

anthology 1.27

Hume's enquiry: Cartesian scepticism is self-defeating

Descartes and others have strongly recommended one kind of scepticism, to be practised in advance of philosophy or any other studies. It preserves us, they say, against error and rash judgment. It recommends that we should doubt not only all our former opinions and principles but also our very faculties. The reliability of our faculties, these philosophers say, is something we must be assured of by a chain of reasoning, deduced from some first principle that cannot possibly be fallacious or deceitful. But there is no such first principle that has an authority above others that are self-evident and convincing. And even if there were one, we couldn't advance a step beyond it except by using those very faculties that we are supposed to be calling into question. Cartesian doubt, therefore, if someone could attain to it (as plainly nobody could), would be entirely incurable, and no reasoning could ever bring us to confident beliefs about anything.

David Hume, *Enquiry Concerning Human Understanding* (1748) Enquiry 1, section 12, part 1 (online version, www.earlymoderntexts.com)

Section 2 Moral philosophy

Bentham on pleasure, pain and the principle of utility

I. Nature has placed mankind under the governance of two sovereign masters, pain and pleasure. It is for them alone to point out what we ought to do, as well as to determine what we shall do. On the one hand the standard of right and wrong, on the other the chain of causes and effects, are fastened to their throne. They govern us in all we do, in all we say, in all we think: every effort we can make to throw off our subjection, will serve but to demonstrate and confirm it. In words a man may pretend to abjure their empire: but in reality he will remain subject to it all the while. The principle of utility recognises this subjection, and assumes it for the foundation of that system, the object of which is to rear the fabric of felicity by the hands of reason and of law. Systems which attempt to question it, deal in sounds instead of sense, in caprice instead of reason, in darkness instead of light.

But enough of metaphor and declamation: it is not by such means that moral science is to be improved.

II. The principle of utility is the foundation of the present work: it will be proper therefore at the outset to give an explicit and determinate account of what is meant by it. By the principle of utility is meant that principle which approves or disapproves of every action whatsoever, according to the tendency it appears to have to augment or diminish the happiness of the party whose interest is in question: or, what is the same thing in other words, to promote or to oppose that happiness. I say of every action whatsoever, and therefore not only of every action of a private individual, but of every measure of government.

III. By utility is meant that property in any object, whereby it tends to produce benefit, advantage, pleasure, good, or happiness, (all this in the present case comes to the same thing) or (what comes again to the same thing) to prevent the happening of mischief, pain, evil, or unhappiness to the party whose interest is considered: if that party be the community in general, then the happiness of the community: if a particular individual, then the happiness of that individual.

Jeremy Bentham, *Introduction to the Principles of Morals and Legislation* (1789) Clarendon Press (2nd edn 1823, repr. 1907)

Mill's 'proof' of utilitarianism

The utilitarian doctrine is that happiness is desirable as an end, and is the only thing that is so; anything else that is desirable is only desirable as means to that end. What should be required regarding this doctrine – what conditions must it fulfil – to justify its claim to be believed? The only proof capable of being given that an object is visible is that people actually see it. The only proof that a sound is audible is that people hear it; and similarly with the other sources of our experience. In like manner, I apprehend, the sole evidence it is possible to produce that anything is desirable is that people do actually desire it. If happiness, the end that the utilitarian doctrine proposes to itself, were not acknowledged in theory and in practice to be an end, nothing could ever convince any person that it was an end. No reason can be given why the general happiness is desirable, except the fact that each person desires his own happiness, so far as he thinks it is attainable. But this is a fact; so we have not only all the proof there could be for such a proposition, and all the proof that could possibly be demanded, that happiness is a good, that each person's happiness is a good to that person, and therefore that general happiness is a good to the aggregate of all persons. Happiness has made good its claim to be one of the ends of conduct, and consequently one of the criteria of morality. But this alone doesn't prove it to be the sole criterion. To prove that in the same way, it seems, we would have to show not only that people desire happiness but that they never desire anything else.

John Stuart Mill, *Utilitarianism* (1863) (online version, Jonathan Bennett (2005), www.earlymoderntexts.com). Please note this is not the same as the original text; Bennett's version has alterations for the sake of clarity.

Mill on 'higher' pleasures

Now, it is an unquestionable fact that the way of life that employs the higher faculties is strongly preferred to the way of life that caters only to the lower ones by people who are equally acquainted with both and equally capable of appreciating and enjoying both. Few human creatures would agree to be changed into any of the lower animals in return for a promise of the fullest allowance of animal pleasures;

- no intelligent human being would consent to be a fool,
- no educated person would prefer to be an ignoramus,
- no person of feeling and conscience would rather be selfish and base,

even if they were convinced that the fool, the dunce or the rascal is better satisfied with his life than they are with theirs … If they ever think they would, it is only in cases of unhappiness so extreme that to escape from it they would exchange their situation for almost any other, however undesirable they may think the other to be. Someone with higher faculties •requires more to make him happy, •is probably capable of more acute suffering, and •is certainly vulnerable to suffering at more points, than someone of an inferior type.

John Stuart Mill, *Utilitarianism* (1863) (online version, Jonathan Bennett (2005), www.earlymoderntexts.com). Please note this is not the same as the original text; Bennett's version has alterations for the sake of clarity.

Peter Singer on killing animals

Given that an animal belongs to a species incapable of self consciousness, it follows that it is not wrong to rear and kill it for food, provided that it leads a pleasant life and, after being killed, will be replaced by another animal that will lead a similarly pleasant life and would not have existed if the first animal had not been killed. This means that vegetarianism is not obligatory for those who can obtain meat from animals that they know have been reared in this manner. In practice, I think this exemption will only apply to those who are able to rear their own animals, or have personal knowledge of the conditions under which the animals they eat were raised and killed … I am sure that some will claim that in taking this view of the killing of some non human animals I am myself guilty of 'speciesism' – that is, discrimination against beings because they are not members of our own species. My position is not speciesist, because it does not permit the killing of non human beings on the ground that they are not members of our species, but on the ground that they lack the capacity to desire to go on living. The position applies equally to members of our own species who lack the relevant capacity. This last consequence strikes many as shocking.

Peter Singer 'Killing humans and killing animals' (1979) in Peter Singer (ed. H. Kuhse) *Unsanctifying Human Life*, Blackwell (2002)

Kant on good will

Nothing can possibly be conceived in the world, or even out of it, which can be called good, without qualification, except a good will. Intelligence, wit, judgement, and the other talents of the mind, however they may be named, or courage, resolution, perseverance, as qualities of temperament, are undoubtedly good and desirable in many respects; but these gifts of nature may also become extremely bad and mischievous if the will which is to make use of them, and which, therefore, constitutes what is called character, is not good. It is the same with the gifts of fortune. Power, riches, honour, even health, and the general well-being and contentment with one's condition which is called happiness, inspire pride, and often presumption, if there is not a good will to correct the influence of these on the mind, and with this also to rectify the whole principle of acting and adapt it to its end. The sight of a being who is not adorned with a single feature of a pure and good will, enjoying unbroken prosperity, can never give pleasure to an impartial rational spectator. Thus a good will appears to constitute the indispensable condition even of being worthy of happiness.

Immanuel Kant, *Groundwork for the Metaphysics of Morals* (1785) trans. T.K. Abbott (1895) (online version, www.gutenberg.org)

Kant's example of good will and honest shopkeeping

For example, it is always a matter of duty that a dealer should not over charge an inexperienced purchaser; and wherever there is much commerce the prudent tradesman does not overcharge, but keeps a fixed price for everyone, so that a child buys of him as well as any other. Men are thus honestly served; but this is not enough to make us believe that the tradesman has so acted from duty and from principles of honesty: his own advantage required it; it is out of the question in this case to suppose that he might besides have a direct inclination in favour of the buyers, so that, as it were, from love he should give no advantage to one over another. Accordingly the action was done neither from duty nor from direct inclination, but merely with a selfish view.

Immanuel Kant, *Groundwork for the Metaphysics of Morals* (1785) trans. T.K. Abbott (1895) (online version, www.gutenberg.org)

anthology 2.6

The importance of external goods to happiness

And for this reason all men think that the happy life is pleasant and weave pleasure into their ideal of happiness and reasonably too; for no activity is perfect when it is impeded, and happiness is a perfect thing; this is why the happy man needs the goods of the body and external goods, i.e. those of fortune, so that he may not be impeded by the lack of those things. Those who maintain that, provided he is good; a man is happy on the rack or surrounded by great disasters, are talking nonsense, whether they mean to or not. Now because we need fortune as well as other things, some people think good fortune is the same thing as happiness; but it is not that, for even good fortune itself when in excess is an impediment, and perhaps should then be no longer called good fortune; since we estimate good fortune in relation to happiness.

Aristotle, *Nicomachean Ethics*, 1153b11–b22, translated by W.D. Ross, Clarendon Press (1925)

anthology 2.7

Aristotle's function argument

Presumably, however, to say that happiness is the chief good seems a platitude, and a clearer account of what it is still desired. This might perhaps be given, if we could first ascertain the function of man. For just as for a flute-player, a sculptor, or an artist, and, in general, for all things that have a function or activity, the good and the 'well' is thought to reside in the function, so would it seem to be for man, if he has a function. Have the carpenter, then, and the tanner certain functions or activities, and has man none? Is he born without a function? Or as eye, hand, foot, and in general each of the parts evidently has a function, may one lay it down that man similarly has a function apart from all these? What then can this be? Life seems to be common even to plants, but we are seeking what is peculiar to man. Let us exclude, therefore, the life of nutrition and growth. Next there would be a life of perception, but it also seems to be common even to the horse, the ox, and every animal. There remains, then, an active life of the element that has a rational principle; of this, one part has such a principle in the sense of being obedient to one, the other in the sense of possessing one and exercising thought. And, as 'life of the rational element' also has two meanings, we must state that life in the sense of activity is what we mean; for this seems to be the more proper sense of the term.

Aristotle, *Nicomachean Ethics*, 11097b22–1098a8, translated by W.D. Ross, Clarendon Press (1925)

anthology 2.8

Function, soul and *eudaimonia*

Now if the function of man is an activity of soul which follows or implies a rational principle, and if we say 'so-and-so' and 'a good so-and-so' have a function which is the same in kind, e.g. a lyre, and a good lyre-player, and so without qualification in all cases, eminence in respect of goodness being added to the name of the function (for the function of a lyre-player is to play the lyre, and that of a good lyre-player is to do so well): if this is the case, and we state the function of man to be a certain kind of life, and this to be an activity or actions of the soul implying a rational principle, and the function of a good man to be the good and noble performance of these, and if any action is well performed when it is performed in accordance with the appropriate excellence: if this is the case, human good turns out to be activity of soul in accordance with virtue, and if there are more than one virtue, in accordance with the best and most complete.

Aristotle, *Nicomachean Ethics*, 1098a9–a20, translated by W.D. Ross, Clarendon Press (1925)

The skill analogy

The development of ethical understanding, leading the agent to develop a disposition that is a virtue, is in the classical tradition standardly taken to proceed like the acquisition of a practical skill or expertise. As Aristotle says, becoming just is like becoming a builder. With a practical skill, there is something to learn, something conveyable by teaching; the expert is the person who understands through reflection what she has been taught, and thinks for herself about it. We are familiar with the notion of practical expertise in mundane contexts like that of car repair, plumbing, and so on. In the classical tradition of virtue ethics, this is an important analogy, because ethical development displays something that we can see more clearly in these more limited contexts: There is a progress from the mechanical rule- or model-following of the learner to the greater understanding of the expert, whose responses are sensitive to the particularities of situations, as well as expressing learning and general reflection.

The skill analogy brings out two important points about ethical understanding: It requires both that you learn from others and that you come to think and understand for yourself.

Julia Annas, 'Virtue ethics' in David Copp (ed.) *The Oxford Handbook of Ethical Theory*, Oxford University Press (2007)

The doctrine of the mean

In everything that is continuous and divisible it is possible to take more, less, or an equal amount, and that either in terms of the thing itself or relatively to us; and the equal is an intermediate between excess and defect. By the intermediate in the object I mean that which is equidistant from each of the extremes, which is one and the same for all men; by the intermediate relatively to us that which is neither too much nor too little – and this is not one, nor the same for all. For instance, if ten is many and two is few, six is the intermediate, taken in terms of the object; for it exceeds and is exceeded by an equal amount; this is intermediate according to arithmetical proportion. But the intermediate relatively to us is not to be taken so; if ten pounds are too much for a particular person to eat and two too little, it does not follow that the trainer will order six pounds; for this also is perhaps too much for the person who is to take it, or too little – too little for Milo, too much for the beginner in athletic exercises. The same is true of running and wrestling. Thus a master of any art avoids excess and defect, but seeks the intermediate and chooses this – the intermediate not in the object but relatively to us.

Aristotle, *Nicomachean Ethics*, 1106a25–b4, translated by W.D. Ross, Clarendon Press (1925)

Involuntary acts and the virtue of justice

A man acts unjustly or justly whenever he does such acts voluntarily; when involuntarily, he acts neither unjustly nor justly except in an incidental way; for he does things which happen to be just or unjust. Whether an act is or is not one of injustice (or of justice) is determined by its voluntariness or involuntariness; for when it is voluntary it is blamed, and at the same time is then an act of injustice; so that there will be things that are unjust but not yet acts of injustice, if voluntariness be not present as well. By the voluntary I mean, as has been said before, any of the things in a man's own power which he does with knowledge, i.e. not in ignorance either of the person acted on or of the instrument used or of the end that will be attained (e.g. whom he is striking, with what, and to what end), each such act being done not incidentally nor under compulsion (e.g. if A takes B's hand and therewith strikes C, B does not act voluntarily; for the act was not in his own power) … Therefore that which is done in ignorance, or though not done in ignorance is not in the agent's power, or is done under compulsion, is involuntary.

Aristotle, *Nicomachean Ethics*, 1135a15–b1, translated by W.D. Ross, Clarendon Press (1925)

Actions caused by desire are not involuntary actions

Since that which is done under compulsion or by reason of ignorance is involuntary, the voluntary would seem to be that of which the moving principle is in the agent himself, he being aware of the particular circumstances of the action. Presumably acts done by reason of anger or appetite are not rightly called involuntary. For in the first place, on that showing none of the other animals will act voluntarily, nor will children; and secondly, is it meant that we do not do voluntarily any of the acts that are due to appetite or anger, or that we do the noble acts voluntarily and the base acts involuntarily? Is not this absurd, when one and the same thing is the cause? But it would surely be odd to describe as involuntary the things one ought to desire; and we ought both to be angry at certain things and to have an appetite for certain things, e.g. for health and for learning.

Aristotle, *Nicomachean Ethics*, 1111a20–b1, translated by W.D. Ross, Clarendon Press (1925)

Practical wisdom and *ethica arete*

It is clear, then, from what has been said, that it is not possible to be good in the strict sense without practical wisdom, nor practically wise without moral virtue. But in this way we may also refute the dialectical argument whereby it might be contended that the virtues exist in separation from each other; the same man, it might be said, is not best equipped by nature for all the virtues, so that he will have already acquired one when he has not yet acquired another. This is possible in respect of the natural virtues, but not in respect of those in respect of which a man is called without qualification good; for with the presence of the one quality, practical wisdom, will be given all the virtues. And it is plain that, even if it were of no practical value, we should have needed it because it is the virtue of the part of us in question; plain too that the choice will not be right without practical wisdom any more than without virtue; for the one determines the end and the other makes us do the things that lead to the end.

Aristotle, *Nicomachean Ethics*, 1144b30–1145a5, translated by W.D. Ross, Clarendon Press (1925)

Moore: some concepts are incapable of definition

Consider yellow, for example. We may try to define it, by describing its physical equivalent; we may state what kind of light-vibrations must stimulate the normal eye, in order that we may perceive it. But a moment's reflection is sufficient to show that those light-vibrations are not themselves what we mean by yellow. *They* are not what we perceive. Indeed, we should never have been able to discover their existence, *unless* we had first been struck by the patent difference of quality between the different colours. The most we can be entitled to say of those vibrations is that they are what corresponds in space to the yellow which we actually perceive. Yet a mistake of this simple kind has commonly been made about good.

It may be true that all things which are good are *also* something else, just as it is true that all things which are yellow produce a certain kind of vibration in the light. And it is a fact, that Ethics aims at discovering what are those other properties belonging to all things which are good. But far too many philosophers have thought that when they named those other properties they were actually defining good; that these properties, in fact, were simply not other, but absolutely and entirely the same with goodness. This view I propose to call the naturalistic fallacy.

G.E. Moore, *Principia Ethica*, Section 10, Cambridge University Press (1993, revised edition)

Ayer's principle of verification

My own version of [the verifiability principle] ... was that 'a sentence is factually significant to any given person, if, and only if, he knows how to verify the proposition which it purports to express – that is, if he knows what observations would lead him, under certain conditions, to accept the proposition as being true, or reject it as being false'. Meaning was also accorded to sentences expressing propositions like those of logic or pure mathematics, which were true or false only in virtue of their form, but with this exception, everything of a would be indicative character which failed to satisfy the verification principle was dismissed as literally nonsensical.

A.J. Ayer, *The Central Questions of Philosophy*, Penguin (1991)

Hume: an empiricist's view of morality

Can there really be any difficulty in proving that vice and virtue are not matters of fact whose existence we can infer by reason? Take any action that is agreed to be vicious – willful murder, for instance. Examine it in all lights, and see if you can find the matter of fact or real existence that you call 'vice'. However you look at it, all you'll find are certain passions, motives, volitions, and thoughts; those are the only matters of fact in the case. The vice entirely escapes you as long as you focus on the object, i.e. the individual action, the murder. You can never find it until you turn your reflection into your own breast and find a sentiment of disapproval that arises in you towards this action. Here is a matter of fact, but it is the object of feeling, not of reason. It lies in yourself, not in the object. So when you say of some action or character that it is vicious, all you mean is that you have a feeling or sentiment of blame from contemplating it. So vice and virtue may be compared to sounds, colours, heat, and cold, which modern philosophy says are not qualities in objects but perceptions in the mind.

David Hume, *A Treatise of Human Nature* (1738) with analytical index by L.A. Selby-Bigge, Oxford University Press (1978), 3.1.1.26

Hume: the is–ought gap

I cannot forbear adding to these reasonings an observation, which may, perhaps, be found of some importance. In every system of morality, which I have hitherto met with, I have always remark'd, that the author proceeds for some time in the ordinary way of reasoning, and establishes the being of a God, or makes observations concerning human affairs; when of a sudden I am surpriz'd to find, that instead of the usual copulations of propositions, is, and is not, I meet with no proposition that is not connected with an ought, or an ought not. This change is imperceptible; but is, however, of the last consequence. For as this ought, or ought not, expresses some new relation or affirmation, 'tis necessary that it should be observ'd and explain'd; and at the same time that a reason should be given, for what seems altogether inconceivable, how this new relation can be a deduction from others, which are entirely different from it. But as authors do not commonly use this precaution, I shall presume to recommend it to the readers; and am persuaded, that this small attention wou'd subvert all the vulgar systems of morality, and let us see, that the distinction of vice and virtue is not founded merely on the relations of objects, nor is perceiv'd by reason.

David Hume, *A Treatise of Human Nature* (1738) with analytical index by
L.A. Selby-Bigge, Oxford University Press (1978), 3.1.1.27

Mackie's argument from queerness

This has two parts, one metaphysical, the other epistemological. If there were objective values, then they would be entities or qualities or relations of a very strange sort, utterly different from anything else in the universe. Correspondingly, if we were aware of them, it would have to be by some special faculty of moral perception of intuition, utterly different from our ordinary ways of knowing everything else. These points were recognised by Moore when he spoke of 'non-natural' qualities, and by the intuitionists in their talk about a 'faculty of moral intuition' … What is not so often stressed … is that the central thesis of intuitionism, is one to which any objectivist view of values is in the end committed; intuitionism merely makes unpalatably plain what other forms of objectivism wrap up.

J.L. Mackie, *Ethics: Inventing Right and Wrong*, Penguin (1977)

anthology
2.20

Ayer on the meaning of ethical statements

We begin by admitting that the fundamental ethical concepts are unanalysable, inasmuch as there is no criterion by which one can test the validity of the judgements in which they occur. So far we are in agreement with the absolutists. But, unlike the absolutists, we are able to give an explanation of this fact about ethical concepts. We say that the reason why they are unanalysable is that they are mere
pseudo-concepts. The presence of an ethical symbol in a proposition adds nothing to its factual content. Thus if I say to someone, 'You acted wrongly in stealing that money,' I am not stating anything more than if I had simply said, 'You stole that money.' In adding that this action is wrong I am not making any further statement about it. I am simply evincing my moral disapproval of it. It is as if I had said, 'You stole that money,' in a peculiar tone of horror, or written it with the addition of some special exclamation marks. The tone, or the exclamation marks, adds nothing to the literal meaning of the sentence. It merely serves to show that the expression of it is attended by certain feelings in the speaker.

A.J. Ayer, *Language, Truth and Logic*, Pelican (1980)

anthology
2.21

Hare: moral judgements entail imperatives

But to guide choices or actions, a moral judgement has to be such that if a person assents to it, he must assent to some imperative sentence derivable from it; in other words, if a person does not assent to some such imperative sentence, that is knock-down evidence that he does not assent to the moral judgement in an evaluative sense – though of course he may assent to it in some other sense (e.g. one of those I have mentioned). This is true by my definition of the word evaluative. But to say this is to say that if he professes to assent to the moral judgement, but does not assent to the imperative, he must have misunderstood the moral judgement (by taking it to be non-evaluative, though the speaker intended it to be evaluative). We are therefore clearly entitled to say that the moral judgement entails the imperative; for to say that one judgement entails another is simply to say that you cannot assent to the first and dissent from the second unless you have misunderstood one or the other; and this 'cannot' is a logical 'cannot' – if someone assents to the first and not to the second, this is in itself a sufficient criterion for saying that he has misunderstood the meaning of one or the other. Thus to say that moral judgements guide actions, and to say that they entail imperatives, comes to much the same thing.

R.M. Hare, *The Language of Morals*, Oxford University Press (1992)

Glossary

The glossary is divided into three main parts, two of which correspond to the two sections of the book: Epistemology and Moral philosophy. However, as stated in the AQA specification, in addition to the terms set out in these two sections, students must also be able to understand and use certain essential philosophical terminology, which is outlined in the first section of the glossary – in the book these are identified by the 'essential terminology' symbol. All key terms or concepts, explained here in the glossary, appear in CAPITAL LETTERS in the book the first time they are used. Those words in the glossary that are in **bold** refer to terms that you can find explained elsewhere in the glossary.

Essential terminology

A posteriori   A Latin term that describes a belief that can only be known via experience of the world: for example, that 'snow is white' or that 'the Atlantic is smaller than the Pacific'. *A posteriori* beliefs are contrasted with ***a priori*** beliefs.

A priori   A Latin term that describes knowledge that is known prior to or independently from experience. For example, that '1,000,000 + 1 = 1,000,001' can be known independently of counting a million apples, adding another one, and then recounting them. *A priori* beliefs are contrasted with ***a posteriori*** beliefs, which are ones derived from experience.

Analytic/synthetic   A term that describes the manner in which a proposition is true. An analytic truth is a proposition that is true in virtue of the meanings of the words alone. In other words, an analytic truth is one that is true by definition, for example, 'A bachelor is an unmarried man'. Analytic truths are contrasted with synthetic truths – truths that cannot be determined simply by analysing the meanings of the terms used. For example, 'All bachelors have the use of at least one kidney' is a synthetic truth.

Antecedent/consequent   A hypothetical proposition has the form, *if x then y*. For example, 'If Trump builds a wall, then Mexico will pay for it'. Part x of a hypothetical proposition – 'Trump builds a wall' – is called the antecedent, and part y – 'Mexico will pay for it' – is called the consequent.

Assertion/claim/proposition   A sentence that makes a claim about the way the world actually is; for example, 'There is a cat on my mat' or 'I am thinking about a dragon'. Like a **belief**, a proposition can be true or false. Other sentences can play different roles, for example, 'Sit down NOW' or 'What are you looking at?' Such sentences (commands, questions, exclamations) do not make specific claims about the way the world is, and hence are not propositions.

Consistent/inconsistent   Two or more beliefs or claims are said to be consistent if they can all be true at the same time (often said to be consistent *with each other*). If they cannot all be true, then they are inconsistent (with each other). A belief can also be said to be consistent with itself as long as it is possible for it to be true. An inconsistent belief is one that cannot be true because it is self-contradictory. ('Consistent' may also be used in a non-technical sense to indicate 'harmonious' or 'regular'.)

Contingent   A contingent truth is one which happens to be true, but which may not have been. In other words, it is a truth for which it is logically possible that it be false. The opposite of a contingent truth is a **necessary** one, that is, one which has to be true and could not be otherwise, or for which it is logically impossible that it be false. For example, it is a contingent truth that daffodils are yellow, since it is conceivable that they might have been blue.

Dilemma   In ethics, a moral dilemma is any situation that an **agent** faces where there is a difficulty choosing between two or more courses of action. This difficulty arises when there are moral reasons for both choosing and not choosing a course of action. It also arises when there are moral reasons against all courses of action, but where a choice has to be made.

False   A term used of beliefs and propositions. A false belief is one which is not true. One account of what makes a belief or proposition false is that it fails to correspond with the facts. So, for example, the belief that humans are descended from apes will be false if in fact they are descended from dolphins. See also **true**.

Justification   The support or grounds for holding a belief, which gives someone a reason for believing it or makes

459

them justified in believing it. The process of justifying a belief is by offering evidence. The traditional analysis of knowledge sees justification as necessary for knowledge.

Necessary/contingent truths 'Necessary' and 'contingent' are opposing terms. In the most restricted sense, a necessary truth is one which has to be true and could not be otherwise. Another way of thinking about a necessary truth is as a truth where the opposite is logically impossible; for example, that a triangle has three sides (a two-sided triangle is logically impossible and cannot be imagined). A contingent truth is one which just happens to be true, and is a truth where the opposite is logically possible, for example, it is true that Theresa May was once the prime minister of the United Kingdom (but it is entirely possible that this may never have happened).

Objective/subjective Objectivity concerns the way things really are. Subjectivity is the way they seem to a mind. A judgement or perception may be termed subjective if it is made by a particular mind (i.e. by a *subject* of experience). This usage often denotes the fact that this judgement or perception need not be accurate because it may not reflect the way things are beyond the mind. But if a judgement or perception is *objective*, this means that it does reflect the way objects really are independently of the person perceiving or making the judgement. The key problem we grapple with in the section on Perception and the Source of Knowledge can be characterised as the question of how and whether we can move from subjective experience to objective knowledge, or from sense data to knowledge of the external world. And in moral philosophy, one central meta-ethical debate concerns whether moral judgements are objective or subjective; whether they reflect some independent moral reality or whether they are dependent on (or relative to) personal attitudes, feelings or preferences.

Paradox In philosophical terms, a paradox is a contradictory, or apparently contradictory, statement. For example, 'This sentence is false' is a paradox. At first sight, we seem to have only two options: either the sentence is true or it is false. If it is true, then it appears as if the sentence must be false. But if it is false, then it appears as if the sentence must be true. Paradoxes can emerge because there is a serious issue with the concepts we are talking about, or the logical or linguistic framework that we are using.

Proof/prove The word 'proof' can be used to refer to any argument that establishes the truth of its conclusion. And to prove a conclusion is just to establish its truth by a process of reasoning. More formally, a proof is a *sound* argument – that is, a deductive argument with true premises. Because its premises are true and its reasoning valid, the conclusion of a sound argument or proof must be true. To prove in this narrower sense is to establish a conclusion by use of such a proof.

Sound argument/proof A deductive argument with true premises.

Tautology A sentence that is true by definition. For example, 'All bachelors are unmarried' or 'All squares have four sides'.

True A term used of **beliefs** and **propositions**. There are different theories of what makes a belief or proposition true. For the sake of simplicity, in this book we have been operating with the so-called correspondence theory of truth, which says that beliefs and propositions are true when they correspond with the facts, that is, when what they say about the world is the case. See also **false**.

Section 1 Epistemology

Abduction   An abductive argument (which is often described as *inference to the best explanation*), is one that proceeds from an effect to argue for the most likely cause.

Anti-realism   If you are a realist about something, then you believe that it exists independently of our minds. If you are an anti-realist about something, you think it is mind-dependent. This is closely connected to non-cognitivism. For example, in epistemology, anti-realists about perception think that material objects exist only for minds and that a mind-independent world is non-existent. (Berkeley summed up this idealist position by saying that to be is to be perceived.) An example of anti-realism in religious language is Wittgenstein's theory that religious terms need to be understood within a religious language game.

Apt belief   For Ernest Sosa, a belief is an apt one if it is a true one, and is a true one *because* of the cognitive skill of the believer.

Argument   An argument is a series of propositions intended to support a conclusion. The propositions offered in support of the conclusion are termed **premises**.

Belief   A state of mind or thought which is about the world. It is a mental representation which claims that something is the case, or that a proposition is true. For example, you may have the belief that Westminster is in London or that cod liver oil is good for your health. A belief will have some degree of evidence in support of it, but is normally regarded as weaker than knowledge, either because knowledge cannot turn out to be false, or because it requires stronger evidence.

Belief in … / Belief that …   Ordinarily when we talk about beliefs we are talking about beliefs that certain things are true (for example, you might believe that Media Studies As-level is easier than Philosophy As-level). Sometimes we talk about beliefs in certain things (for example, belief in God, or in the new England football manager). To believe in something means not only believing that it exists, but also having a certain confidence in that person or process – we adopt a positive attitude towards that person or process and are committed to it.

Clear and distinct ideas   The basic or self-justifying beliefs that Descartes hopes to use as foundations for his system of knowledge. Clear and distinct ideas, we are told, are those which can be 'intuited' by the mind by what he calls the 'light of reason'. In other words, they are truths of reason, truths that can be known with the mind alone.

Descartes' examples of clear and distinct ideas are the basic claims of logic, geometry and mathematics. Knowledge of truths of reason, it is claimed, resists any sceptical attack, since we recognise its truth immediately. Our faculty of 'intuition' permits us to recognise the truth without allowing any room for doubt or error. For example, it is in vain to ask how I know that triangles have three sides. Such knowledge is given in the very act of understanding the terms involved. There is no further evidence I need appeal to in order to justify such knowledge.

Cogito   Latin for 'I think', and shorthand for Descartes' famous argument to prove his own existence. Descartes attempted to doubt he existed, but realised that in order to doubt this, he must exist. So his own existence was **indubitable**.

Concept   Having a concept of something is what enables one to recognise it, distinguish it from other things and think about it. So if I have the concept of a hedgehog, I can think about hedgehogs, and recognise them when I encounter them, and tell the difference between them and hogs or hedges. Similarly, to have a concept of red is to be able to think about it, recognise it and distinguish it from other colours. According to traditional empiricism, all our concepts are formed as kinds of 'copy' of the original sensations.

Conclusion   A statement that comes at the end of an **argument** and that is supported by the reasons given in the argument. If an argument is sound or valid and all of the premises are true, then the conclusion will also be true.

Deductive argument (also 'deductively valid' or simply 'valid')   An argument where the truth of the conclusion is guaranteed by the truth of the premises. In other words, it is an argument in which the premises entail the conclusion. So if one accepts the truth of the premises, one must, as a matter of logical necessity, accept the conclusion. For example: either you will become a fireman or a doctor. But you can only become a doctor with a medical degree which you will never get. So you will become a fireman. A deductive argument is in contrast to an **inductive argument**.

Direct realism   The common-sense view of how perception works. Physical objects have an independent existence in space; they follow the laws of physics and possess certain properties, ranging from size and shape through to colour, smell and texture. When humans are in the presence of such objects under appropriate conditions, they are able to perceive them along with all these properties.

Empiricism   An epistemological position which holds that our beliefs and knowledge must be based on experience. David Hume was one philosopher who rigorously applied his empiricist approach to questions in the philosophy of religion.

Enlightenment   Also known as the Age of Reason. The period of European history in the eighteenth century in which thinkers and writers were optimistic about the progress that humans could make in different fields. It was characterised by critical and analytic thinking, and meant a break with the past, including a break with Christian thinking. Some of this optimism arose from the scientific discoveries of Sir Isaac Newton, which led to the belief that similar theories and laws could be developed in other areas of human thought. Famous enlightenment philosophers include Voltaire and Hume.

Epistemology   One of the three main areas of philosophical study and analysis (see also **moral philosophy** and **metaphysics**). Epistemology, or the theory of knowledge, looks at questions of what it is possible to know, what grounds our claims to knowledge are based on, what is true, what is the distinction between knowledge and belief. (The term is derived from the ancient Greek words, *episteme* meaning 'knowledge', and *logos* meaning 'account' or 'rationale'.)

Evidence   The reasons for holding a belief.

Evil demon   A device used by Descartes to generate a sceptical argument about the possibility of knowledge of the external world and of basic propositions of arithmetic and geometry. It is conceivable that there exists an extremely powerful spirit or demon bent on deceiving me. If this were the case, then all my perceptions of the world around me could be an illusion produced in my mind by the demon. Even my own body could be a part of the illusion. Moreover, the demon could cause me to make mistakes even about the most simple judgements of maths and geometry, so that I go wrong when adding 2 + 3 or counting the sides of a square.

Evolution   The process, described as natural selection by Charles Darwin, by which organisms gradually change over time according to changes in their environment and genetic mutations. Some mutations lead to traits or characteristics which make an organism better suited to an environment and more successful in having offspring that also survive and reproduce; some environmental changes mean that an organism is less suited to its environment and its offspring are less successful in surviving and reproducing. Over long periods of time, and in environmentally stable conditions, the characteristics of an organism become highly adapted to its environment and have all the appearance of being designed for that environment.

External world   All that exists outside of or independently of the mind; the physical world.

Fact   Something which is the case. For example, it is a fact that the earth revolves around the sun.

Fallacy   See the Moral philosophy glossary.

Forms (theory of)   Plato's theory of forms is a theory about types or classes of thing. The word 'form' is used to translate Plato's use of the Greek word 'idea', with which he refers to the type or class to which a thing belongs. Plato argues that over and above the realm of physical objects there is a realm of 'forms' to which individual physical things belong. So in the physical realm there are many tables, but there is also the single form of the table, the ideal or blueprint of the table, which we recognise not with our senses, but with the mind.

Foundationalism   A view about the structure of justification which claims that there are two sorts of belief: those which are basic or foundational and which require no justification (or which are self-justifying), and those which are built on top of the foundations and justified in terms of them.

Given   The given is the raw and immediate element of experience prior to any judgement. What is given to us immediately are often termed sense data, and such experience is thought to be known for certain and incorrigibly.

Hypothetical statements   'If ... then' statements which make claims about states of affairs which are not actual, but which would be if certain conditions were satisfied. Hypothetical statements are used to translate physical object language into phenomenal language in linguistic **phenomenalism**.

Idea   The uses of the word 'idea' are various within the philosophical literature, as well as in ordinary parlance. Here the word is not used in a technical or precise sense, except when in italics, where it refers to Locke's use of the word to mean anything of which the mind is conscious, including sense data, concepts and beliefs.

Idealism   Idealism as discussed here is an anti-realist theory of perception. Put forward by Berkeley, it is the view that matter does not exist independently of the mind and that all that exists are minds and their ideas. Physical objects are no more than collections of sensations appearing in minds. Objects which are not currently being perceived by any creature are sustained in existence by being perceived in the mind of God.

Incorrigible   To call a belief incorrigible is to say that it cannot be corrected or changed. Someone who honestly holds a belief which is incorrigible cannot be mistaken about it. Beliefs about our own **sense data** are often thought to be incorrigible since there appears to be no way in which I can be mistaken about my own experiences, and there appears to be no further evidence that could be brought to bear to make me change my mind about what I am experiencing. For this reason, such beliefs are often taken to be immune to sceptical attack.

Indirect realism   The view that the immediate objects of perception are **sense data** or representations and that the physical world is perceived only indirectly via these representations.

Indubitable   Not doubtable. A belief which it is not possible to doubt is indubitable.

Inductive argument   An argument where the truth of the conclusion is not fully guaranteed by the truth of the premises. For example, moving from particular examples (every raven I have seen has been black) to a generalisation (all ravens are black); or moving from our experience of the past (day has always followed night) to a prediction about the future (day will always follow night). Arguments from analogy are also inductive: they compare two things, and move from what these two things are known to have in common to draw a conclusion about other (unknown) things they are supposed to have in common.

Infallibilism   Theory of knowledge which claims that we should only count as knowledge those beliefs that it is impossible to doubt.

Inference   The move in an argument from the premises or reasons to the conclusion. For example, in the argument, 'Moriarty had blood on his hands, therefore he must be the murderer', the inference is the move made from the premise that Moriarty had blood on his hands to the conclusion that he is the murderer.

Infinite regress   A regress is a process of reasoning from effect to cause, or of going backwards in a chain of explanations. An infinite regress is one where the process never stops, where it is repeated endlessly. This is generally considered problematic in a philosophical argument, and a sign that a mistake has been made.

Innate ideas   Ideas that exist in the mind which are not acquired from experience. Plato, for example, argued that all ideas or concepts are innate and that the process of acquiring knowledge is not one of learning in the strict sense, but rather of recollecting what we already

implicitly know. So we are all born with innate knowledge of the 'forms', and it is this knowledge which enables us to recognise individual exemplars of the forms in this life. Rationalists traditionally favoured the belief that we possess such ideas. Leibniz, for example, argued that such ideas exist implicitly within the mind and that they are brought to the surface of consciousness through experience. Rationalists often use the doctrine of innate ideas to explain the possibility of *a priori* knowledge. Descartes argued that knowledge of mathematics is innate and that the discovery of mathematical truths involves the mind looking into itself to uncover them. Knowledge of the existence of God is also possible, according to Descartes, because we can look into our own mind to discover the idea and deduce his existence in an *a priori* manner, simply through careful mental scrutiny of the idea. Opposed to the doctrine of innate ideas are the empiricists, and in particular John Locke, who devoted the first book of his *Essay Concerning Human Understanding* to their repudiation. Locke argued that all the contents of the mind can be reduced to sensation variously transformed and that the mind at birth is akin to a blank paper.

Insensible/sensible   Terms often used by Locke and Berkeley to mean the same as imperceptible and perceptible. For Locke, the minute corpuscles or atoms which compose material objects are 'insensible' because they are too small for us to perceive; whereas the 'sensible' qualities of objects are those we can perceive. For Berkeley, objects consist of sensible qualities alone, for what is insensible does not exist.

Intuition   A kind of mental seeing by which rational truths can be recognised. For Descartes, the mind deploys the faculty of intuition when it sees by the 'light of reason' that 2 + 2 = 4 or that a sphere is bounded by one surface.

Knowledge   There are three sorts of knowledge: practical knowledge, knowledge by acquaintance and factual knowledge. The traditional account of factual knowledge claims that it is justified, true belief.

Lemma   A subsidiary belief or proposition used to justify or prove another belief/proposition.

Material   Made of physical matter. According to Descartes, this involved occupying physical space. In contrast, God is thought of by Christian philosophers as immaterial.

Metaphysics   One of the three main areas of philosophical study and analysis (see also **epistemology** and **moral philosophy**). Metaphysics is concerned with determining what sorts of things really exist, what is the ultimate nature of reality, where the world comes from, what is the relationship of our mind to the world. (It is said that the term 'metaphysics' came about because in ancient catalogues of Aristotle's work, his books on the nature of reality came after (in Greek, *meta*) his books on physics – hence, metaphysics.)

Method of doubt   Descartes' sceptical method used to find certainty. Descartes found that many of his beliefs had turned out to be false, and to remedy this situation he elected to cast doubt upon all his beliefs. If any beliefs showed themselves to be indubitable, and could survive the most radical scepticism, then they would have established themselves as absolutely certain. Once he had discovered such beliefs, Descartes hoped to rebuild a body of knowledge based on them which would be free from error.

Necessary/sufficient condition   A is a necessary condition for B when you have to have A in order to have B. In other words, if you do not have A, you cannot have B. By contrast, A is a sufficient condition for B when if you have A you must have B too. In other words, having A is enough or sufficient to guarantee that you have B.

Ontology   The study of being in general or of what there is. If you have an ontological commitment to something then you believe that it exists independently of you (for example, some moral realists have an ontological commitment to moral values).

Perception   The process by which we become aware of physical objects, including our own body.

Phenomenalism   An anti-realist theory of perception distinguished from idealism in that it claims that physical objects are collections not just of actual sense data, but also of potential sense data. Physical objects continue to exist unperceived since they retain the potential to be perceived.

Predicate   Many propositions can be divided into a subject and a predicate, where the subject is the thing that the sentence is about and the predicate gives us information about the subject. For example, in the sentence, 'The balloon is red', the expression 'is red' is the predicate, the term 'balloon', the subject. Some philosophers argued that in the sentence 'God exists', 'exists' is a predicate applying to 'God'. However, philosophers from Kant onwards have doubted whether existence is a genuine predicate.

Premise   Any reason given (usually in the form of a statement or claim) to support the conclusion of an argument.

Primary and secondary qualities   According to **indirect realism**, physical objects have certain primary qualities, such as size and shape, which we are able to perceive. At the same time, we also seem to perceive objects to have a set of secondary qualities, such as colours, sounds and smells. However, these qualities are not actually in the objects themselves, but rather are powers to produce these sensations in us. Such powers are a product of the arrangement of the parts of the object which are too small for us to observe.

Rationalism   The tendency in philosophy to regard reason, as opposed to sense experience, as the primary source of the important knowledge of which we are capable. Rationalists are typically impressed by the systematic nature of mathematical knowledge and the possibility of certainty that it affords. Using mathematics as the ideal of how knowledge should be, rationalists typically attempt to extend this type of knowledge into other areas of human inquiry, such as to knowledge of the physical world, or to ethics. Rationalism is traditionally contrasted with **empiricism**: the view that most of what we know is acquired through experience.

Realism   If you are a realist about something, then you believe it exists independently of our minds. If you are an anti-realist about something, you think it is mind-dependent. Examples of realist positions from epistemology are **direct realism** and **indirect realism**. What they have in common is the conviction that physical objects are real; that is, that they have an existence independently of our perception of them. See also **anti-realism**.

Reason   The capacity for rational argument and judgement. The process by which we are able to discover the truth of things by pure thought by inferring conclusions from premises. Often contrasted with instinct, emotion or imagination.

Reliabilism   A theory of knowledge which claims that the reliability of the (cognitive) process involved in generating a belief is the key factor in whether we should call it knowledge or not. Reliabilism is the claim that knowledge is a true belief that is produced by a reliable process.

Representation   In the philosophy of perception, a representation is a sense experience or collection of sense data which appears to picture some aspect of the physical world, such as an object. See also **indirect realism**.

Representative realism   A realist theory of perception which claims that physical objects impact upon our sense organs, causing us to experience sensations. These sensations are akin to pictures which represent the objects which cause them.

Scepticism   Philosophical scepticism entails raising doubts about our claims to know. Global scepticism directs its doubts at all knowledge claims and argues that we can know nothing. Scepticism can also have a more limited application to some subset of our knowledge claims; for example, concerning the possibility of knowledge of the claims of religion or of ethics. The purpose of scepticism in philosophy is first to test our knowledge claims. If they can survive the sceptic's attack, then they may vindicate themselves as genuine knowledge. Descartes used scepticism in this way so that he could isolate a few certainties which he felt could be used as a foundation to rebuild a body of knowledge free from doubt or error. Scepticism is also used as a tool for distinguishing which types of belief can be treated as known and which cannot, thereby delimiting those areas where knowledge is possible. In this way, philosophers often exclude certain regions of human enquiry as fruitless, since they cannot lead to knowledge. Empiricists, for example, often argue that knowledge of religious claims is impossible since they cannot be verified in terms of experience.

Self   What the word 'I' refers to. The essence of the person and what many philosophers, most notably Descartes, have argued we are directly aware of through introspection.

Sensation   The subjective experience we have as a consequence of perceiving physical objects, including our own bodies, such as the experience of smelling a rose, or of feeling hungry.

Sense data   What one is directly aware of in perception. The subjective elements which constitute experience. For example, when perceiving a banana, what I actually sense is a collection of sense data: the way the banana seems to me, including a distinctive smell, a crescent-shaped yellow expanse, a certain texture and taste. According to sense data theorists, we make judgements about the nature of the physical world on the basis of immediate awareness of these sense data. So, on the basis of my awareness of the sense datum of a yellow expanse, plus that of a banana smell, and so on, I judge that I am in the presence of a banana. In this way, we build up a picture of the physical world, and so all empirical knowledge can rest on the foundation of sense data.

Sense impressions   The colours, noises, tastes, sounds and smells that one is aware of when perceiving the world. Also known as **sense data**.

Sensible   See **insensible/sensible**.

Solipsism   The view that all that can be known to exist is my own mind. This is not normally a position defended by philosophers, but rather a sceptical trap into which certain ways of thinking appear to lead. For example, if it is urged that all that can be truly known is what one is directly aware of oneself, then it follows that one cannot know anything of which one is not directly aware. This might include the minds of other people (which one can only learn about via their behaviour), or, more radically, the very existence of the physical world, including one's own body (which one can only learn about via one's sense experience of it).

Statement   Indicative sentence (see **proposition**).

Subject   In grammar, the part of a **proposition** that picks out the main object which is being described or discussed: for example, in 'The red balloon popped', the subject is 'the balloon'. In the sentence, 'God is the greatest conceivable being', 'God' is the subject.

Sufficient condition   See **necessary/sufficient condition**.

Theory of forms   See **forms** and **world of forms**.

Veridical   Truthful or accurate. Perception is veridical if it is faithful to reality, and for indirect realists, this means it provides an accurate representation of the external world. Veridical perceptions contrast with hallucinations or illusions where the representation of reality is inaccurate or misleading.

Verificationism/verification principle   See the Moral philosophy glossary.

Virtue epistemology   This is a recent approach to the thinking about the concept of knowledge. It claims that we should seek to define knowledge as the true beliefs that have been brought about through sound cognitive processes (for example, epistemic virtues such as careful reasoning or clear vision) and where the beliefs are true ones *because* of the epistemic virtues that brought them about.

Section 2 Moral philosophy

Agency   The capacity of an **agent** to act in any given environment.

Agent   A being who is capable of action. **Agency** and action are typically restricted to human beings, because human beings have the capacity to reason, make a choice between two courses of action, then do what they have chosen.

Anti-realism   See **realism** and **anti-realism**.

Applied ethics   See **practical ethics**.

Argument from analogy   Arguments which compare two things and draw a conclusion about one of them on the basis of their similarities are called arguments from analogy, or analogical arguments.

Autonomy   (from the Greek *auto* – self, and *nomos* – law) An **agent** has autonomy insofar as it is rational and free. For Kant, moral autonomy was only achieved through following the categorical **imperative**.

Autonomy of ethics   See **is–ought gap**.

Categorical imperative   See **imperative**.

Cognitivism and non-cognitivism   Cognitivism in ethics is the view that moral **judgements** are **propositions** which can be known – they refer to the world and they have a **truth-value** (they are capable of being true or false). Non-cognitivism is the view that moral judgements cannot be known, because they do not say anything true or false about the world (they do not have a truth-value). There are many different forms of non-cognitivism, such as **emotivism**, **prescriptivism** and nihilism. See also **realism** and **anti-realism**.

Conclusion   See the Epistemology glossary.

Consequentialist ethics   A type of normative moral theory which views the moral value of an action as lying in its consequences. So an action is judged to be good if it brings about beneficial consequences, and bad if it brings about harmful ones. This is in contrast to **deontological ethics**. Egoism and **utilitarianism** are two examples of consequentialism.

Deontological ethics   A type of normative moral theory that views the moral value of an action as lying in its dutiful motives. Generally, deontologists (such as Kant) propose certain rules, bound by duties, which guide us as to which actions are right and which are wrong. This is in contrast to consequentialism. Kantian ethics is an example of a **deontological** theory.

Descriptive   See **prescriptive and descriptive**.

Disposition   Our tendency to behave in certain ways, our character traits. This term is used by **virtue ethicists**, who believe we ought to develop virtuous dispositions.

Divine command ethics   A type of **deontological** ethical theory, which claims that the moral value of an action is determined by the commands of God. So an action is right if it follows one of God's commands.

Duty   An action which we are required or impelled to carry out. Kant's deontological theory places duty at its centre. For Kant, duties are experienced as **imperatives**.

Emotivism/emotivist   A **non-cognitivist** theory of the meaning of moral terms and judgements. In its basic form, emotivism claims that moral judgements do not refer to anything in the world, but are expressions of feelings of approval or disapproval.

Empirical fact   A fact established by observation.

Empiricism/empiricist   See the Epistemology glossary.

Error theory   An anti-realist theory of ethical language put forward by J.L. Mackie. It proposes that our moral judgements are making objective claims about the world (so it is a **cognitivist** position), but these claims are always false (there is nothing 'out there' in the world which our moral terms actually refer to).

Ethics   See **Moral philosophy**.

Eudaimonia   According to many ancient Greek philosophers, *eudaimonia* is the goal or 'good' we are all striving for. Sometimes translated as 'happiness', it is probably closer in meaning to 'flourishing'. Aristotle's virtue ethics is centred around *eudaimonia*.

Fallacy   This refers to an **argument** which has gone wrong, either because a mistake has been made, rendering the argument invalid; or because the argument has a form, or structure, which is always invalid (see also the **naturalistic fallacy**).

Free will   Also known as metaphysical freedom. The idea of free will is that the self controls aspects of its own life, such as bodily movements like picking up a pencil. Free will can be contrasted with determinism, which is the belief that all events in the universe are the necessary consequence of physical laws, and these laws apply to human actions as well. A determinist might claim that humans are like complex pieces of biological machinery with no real freedom of will. Some philosophers believe that these two positions (free will versus determinism) are compatible with each other, and claim that humans can have free will but are also subject to deterministic laws; such a view is known as compatibilism.

Golden rule Versions of this rule have been proposed at various points within religion and moral philosophy (for example, by Confucius, Jesus, Hobbes and Kant). The basic idea is that we should be impartial, and not afford ourselves special treatment: we should treat others as we should like to be treated. See also **universalisability**.

Good Actions are good according to whether they bring about certain positive outcomes – these may be pleasure or happiness, or something more intangible (Moore believed that love of friendship and beauty were goods). **Consequentialists** believe that moral value lies in the good (or bad) consequences of an action. But 'good' also has a functional meaning, in the sense that 'good' means 'fulfilling your function well'. Aristotle believed that we had a function and hence could be good in both senses: by being good (fulfilling our function) we could reach the good (*eudaimonia*).

Good will For Kant, a good will is one that acts for the right reason (which means following rules that you could rationally will that everyone else should follow too). A good will is the only thing that is good without qualification.

Hedonism/hedonistic The claim that pleasure is the good. Many **utilitarians** are hedonists, in that they believe we ought to try to maximise pleasure (for the majority).

Hume's law See **is–ought gap**.

Hypothetical imperative See **imperative**.

Imperative In **Kantian ethics** we experience our duties as commands (imperatives) which are categorical, or absolute. These categorical imperatives are commands that we are obliged to follow no matter what, and according to Kant, only these are moral imperatives. As rational **agents** we can work out the categorical imperative by asking whether the **maxim** that lies behind our action is **universalisable**. Other imperatives, things we should do in order to achieve some goal, are conditional or hypothetical imperatives, and they are not moral according to Kant.

Intuitionism/intuitionist A **realist** theory which claims that we can determine what is right or good according to our moral intuitions. For intuitionists, the terms 'right' and 'good' do refer to something objective, but they cannot be reduced to **naturalistic** terms.

Is–ought gap Hume argued that we cannot draw a conclusion which is evaluative (containing 'ought') from **premises** which are purely factual or **descriptive**. To some philosophers this indicated the autonomy of ethics, that is, that the ethical realm was entirely distinct from other, factual or **naturalistic**, realms.

Judgement A moral judgement is a decision made (in advance or retrospectively) about the rightness or goodness of a course of action (our own or someone else's) or, for virtue theorists, of someone's character.

Kantian ethics A **deontological** ethical theory developed by or influenced by Kant. At the heart of Kantian ethics is the claim that we can determine what is right, and what our duties are, through the categorical **imperative**.

Liberty Political liberty is the freedom you have to perform acts which are not prohibited by the state. The more actions that a government prohibits through law, the less political liberty you have.

Maxim A rule underlying our actions. For example, in stealing £10 from your mum's wallet, you would (perhaps unconsciously) be acting on a rule like this: 'When I need money, I will take it from my parents without telling them.'

Meta-ethics Sometimes called 'second-order ethics', this is the study by moral philosophers of the meaning of moral **judgements**. This covers issues such as realism/anti-realism, **cognitivism/non-cognitivism**, the **is–ought gap**, the **naturalistic fallacy**, and the objectivity/subjectivity of moral judgements.

Moral dilemma See **dilemma** in the Essential terminology glossary.

Moral philosophy The philosophical study of our ideas of moral good, of how to live and of the status of moral judgements.

Moral realism and moral anti-realism Moral realists believe that in some sense moral terms refer to something real – for example, pleasure, happiness, utility, the moral law or God's command. So, from a realist position, morality is discovered. Moral anti-realists believe that moral terms do not refer to anything real, but are something else entirely – for example, expressions of feelings (**emotivism**), prescriptions to other people (**prescriptivism**) or they refer to nothing at all (**nihilism**). See also **cognitivism and non-cognitivism**.

Naturalism The view that we can explain moral concepts, such as good, in naturalistic terms, such as happiness or pleasure.

Naturalistic fallacy   G.E. Moore attacked **naturalism** because he claimed that it committed a **fallacy**, namely of trying to define the indefinable. Moore believed that moral terms such as **good** could not be defined (he held they were non-natural), and that naturalists tried to define them in naturalistic terms. He particularly singled out the **utilitarians** in his attack.

Nihilism   An extreme scepticism about the possibility of knowledge of moral values. It is the state of having no values, or the rejection of morality in its conventional form, or the belief that values are groundless or illusory.

Non-cognitivism   See **cognitivism and non-cognitivism**.

Normative ethics   Sometimes called 'first-order ethics', this term covers moral theories that offer action-guides. These are rules, principles or standards by which we make moral **judgements**, and according to which our conduct is directed. There are three general forms of normative theory: **deontological**, **consequentialist** and **virtue ethics**.

Partiality   Humans almost universally have a special interest in ourselves and in those people closest to us; we value them more highly and tend to favour them above the interests of others – this is partiality. Moral theories such as **utilitarianism** require that we take an impartial stance, and value our own interests, and the interests of those close to us, and the interests of strangers all equally. Virtue ethics does not require impartiality, and claims to be able to account for partiality within a consistent moral system.

Person   In ordinary language, this refers to human beings, but recently some philosophers have asked what is special about persons and whether a) all human beings are persons and b) some non-human beings might count as persons. The sorts of qualities that characterise persons might include **agency**, **autonomy**, rationality, self-consciousness, and so on.

Practical ethics   Like **normative ethics**, this is also a type of 'first-order' theory. It looks at the application of ethical theories to concrete situations and **moral dilemmas** that people face, such as abortion, euthanasia and the treatment of animals.

Preference utilitarianism   This is the theory which claims that an action is good according to the number of preferences it fulfils. An action is bad if it goes against the majority of (relevant) people's preferences. The strength of preferences may also be taken into account. See also **utilitarianism**.

Premise   See the Epistemology glossary.

Prescriptive and descriptive   A prescriptive statement is one that guides action; it tells us what to do. A descriptive statement, on the other hand, simply tells us the way things are.

Prescriptivism   A **non-cognitivist** view of the meaning of moral terms and judgements. Like **emotivists**, prescriptivists believe that moral language has a special use, but they believe that the purpose of moral **judgements** is to prescribe actions, in other words to urge others to act in a certain way.

Proposition   A sentence that makes a claim about the way the world actually is. **Non-cognitivists** such as the **emotivists** claim that moral **judgements** are not propositions; in other words, they are not making claims about the world and are neither true nor false.

Rationalism/rationalist   See the Epistemology glossary.

Realism/anti-realism   See moral realism/moral anti-realism.

Relativism   Moral relativism is the view that moral **judgements** vary according to (are relative to) the social context in which they are made. So, moral values or standards of conduct are different in different societies: what is right for you may not be right for me, and so on.

Right   Actions are right according to whether they ought to be done, irrespective of the particular situation, or the consequences that result from a course of action. **Deontological** theorists believe that moral value lies solely in what is right (rather than in what is **good**) and that we have obligations or duties to do what is right. However, **consequentialist** theorists are quite happy to redefine 'right' to mean 'actions that bring about the good'.

Rights   A right is an entitlement that I have to the protection of certain powers, interests or privileges. It is debatable whether we can have rights only because we make a contract within society, or whether we have 'natural rights' which exist independently of any contract. Rights may be seen as the converse of duties; thus if I have a right to X, then you have a duty to promote X or at least not interfere in my access to X.

Statement   See **proposition**.

Summum bonum   A Latin phrase meaning 'the highest good', or simply 'the Good'. For Aristotle, this was the goal of all human life, and he argued that this consisted in *eudaimonia*. Other moral philosophers, such as Plato, Mill, Kant and G.E. Moore have put forward very different views on what the Good is.

Teleological   Purpose, goal or end, deriving from the Greek word *telos*. A teleological ethical theory is one that says we should be striving to achieve certain moral goals – for Aristotelians this would be virtue; for **utilitarians** the goal would be happiness. See also **consequentialist ethics**.

Truth-value   The truth or falsity of a **proposition**. Only propositions can have truth-value. Some philosophers (**cognitivists**) claim that moral **judgements** are propositions, but other philosophers (**non-cognitivists**) claim that moral judgements are not propositions and hence do not have a truth-value.

Universalisabe   A fundamental feature of most ethical theories, and a version of the **golden rule**. A principle is universalisable if it is applied to all people equally and in the same way. Some philosophers (including **prescriptivists**) have seen this as part of the very meaning of a moral **judgement** – it applies to everyone in the same situation. **Consequentialists** (Bentham and Mill), **deontologists** (Kant) and even existentialists (Sartre) have all appealed to universalisability at some point in their theories. For Kantians, the principle of universalisability has to be a more rigorous version of the golden rule: it says that we should only act on those rules which we can will to be universal laws (that is, without contradiction or inconsistency).

Utilitarianism   A **consequentialist** moral theory, perhaps inspired by Hume (although he is closer to **virtue ethics**) and developed first by Bentham and then by Mill and Sidgwick. In most of its forms it is a **hedonistic** theory claiming that what is **good** (that is, what we ought to strive to bring about) is as much pleasure or happiness as possible for the majority of people. In its negative forms, it says we ought to strive to reduce pain or harm to the majority of people.

Utility   Welfare or use for the majority of people. For Bentham and Mill, utility came to mean 'pleasure' or 'happiness'.

Utility principle   The principle that an act or object is **good** in as much as it brings about something that is desired (for most **utilitarians**, this is pleasure or happiness). Similarly, for most utilitarians, an act or object is bad insofar as it brings about pain or unhappiness.

Verificationism   A philosophical belief about the nature of meaning. Logical positivism claims that for a proposition to be meaningful it must be (hypothetically) verifiable or true by definition – see **verification principle**. Other than truths by definition, most propositions make a specific claim about the universe – that it is this way or that; for example, that 'there is a cat on my mat' or that 'the leaves on my tree are green'. In such cases, it is easy for us to imagine how such claims could be verified or not. However, take the claim that 'Stealing is wrong'. How could we verify this claim? What could we look for in the world to see whether that claim is true or not? If it is not clear how the universe would look if the claim were true or not, then it is not clear what it is asserting, and thus logical positivists might claim that the proposition is not meaningful. See also **emotivism**.

Verification principle   The rule put forward by verificationists that a proposition is only meaningful if it can be verified either empirically (shown to be true or false by experience/observation) or by analysis of the meanings of the terms involved (through being true or false by definition). See **verificationism**.

Vice   In Aristotelian virtue ethics, a vice is a character trait or **disposition** which is to be avoided as it prevents us from flourishing (for the ancient Greeks, it is a flaw). It is the opposite of virtue. Common vices include dishonesty, lack of compassion, cowardice, selfishness, indulgence and not revising for philosophy exams.

Virtue   A character trait or **disposition** which is to be valued (for the ancient Greeks, it is a disposition which is excellent). Common virtues include wisdom, courage, self-control, honesty, generosity, compassion, kindness.

Virtue ethics   A **normative** ethical theory which locates value not in an action or its consequences, but in the **agent** performing the act. Virtue ethicists stress the need to develop virtuous **dispositions**, and to judge actions within the broader context of what someone is inclined to do. So a person may be judged to be virtuous or vicious through noting how they are disposed to act. Frustratingly, for many people, virtue ethicists fail to give us a formula (unlike **consequentialists** and **deontologists**) that guides us in what we ought to do in any particular situation.

World of forms   Plato's theory that universal concepts such as beauty and justice exist independently of human minds, in another realm. Plato called such concepts '**forms**'.

Index